The Independent States of the World

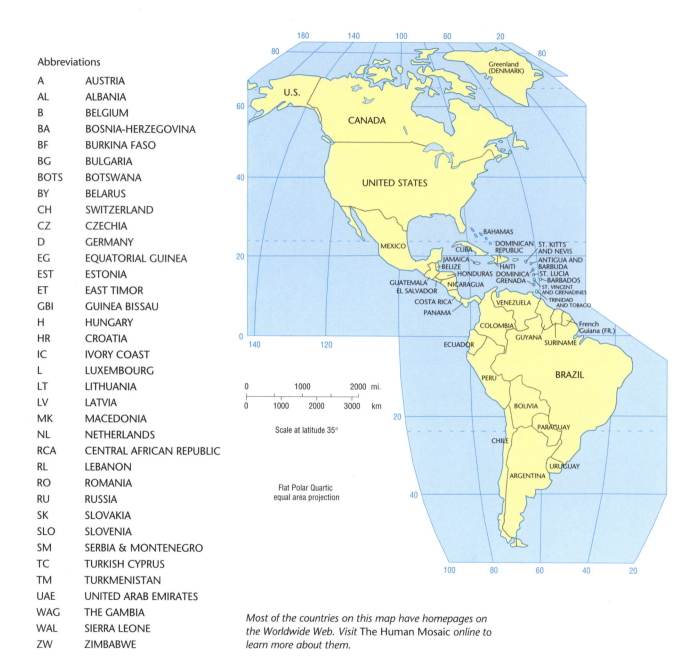

Abbreviations

A	AUSTRIA
AL	ALBANIA
B	BELGIUM
BA	BOSNIA-HERZEGOVINA
BF	BURKINA FASO
BG	BULGARIA
BOTS	BOTSWANA
BY	BELARUS
CH	SWITZERLAND
CZ	CZECHIA
D	GERMANY
EG	EQUATORIAL GUINEA
EST	ESTONIA
ET	EAST TIMOR
GBI	GUINEA BISSAU
H	HUNGARY
HR	CROATIA
IC	IVORY COAST
L	LUXEMBOURG
LT	LITHUANIA
LV	LATVIA
MK	MACEDONIA
NL	NETHERLANDS
RCA	CENTRAL AFRICAN REPUBLIC
RL	LEBANON
RO	ROMANIA
RU	RUSSIA
SK	SLOVAKIA
SLO	SLOVENIA
SM	SERBIA & MONTENEGRO
TC	TURKISH CYPRUS
TM	TURKMENISTAN
UAE	UNITED ARAB EMIRATES
WAG	THE GAMBIA
WAL	SIERRA LEONE
ZW	ZIMBABWE

Scale at latitude 35°

Flat Polar Quartic
equal area projection

Most of the countries on this map have homepages on the Worldwide Web. Visit The Human Mosaic *online to learn more about them.*

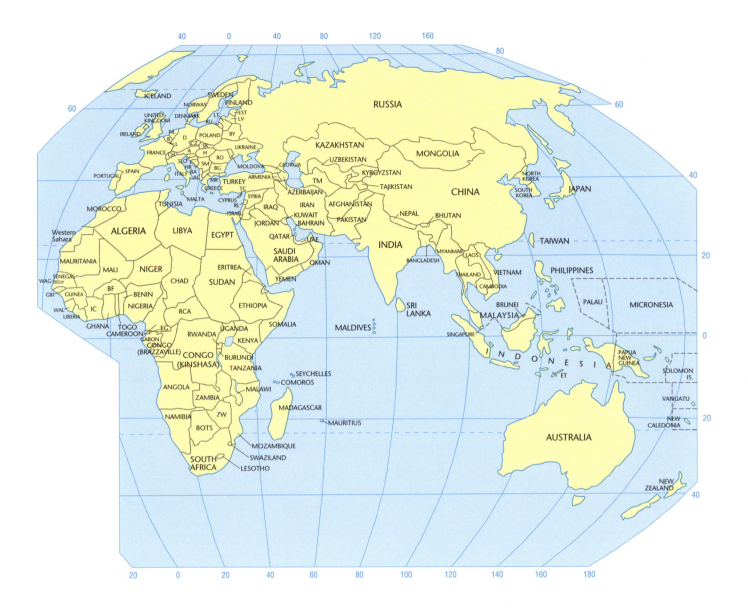

THE HUMAN MOSAIC

THE HUMAN MOSAIC

A Thematic Introduction to Cultural Geography

NINTH EDITION

TERRY G. JORDAN-BYCHKOV

University of Texas at Austin

MONA DOMOSH

Dartmouth College

W. H. Freeman and Company
New York

ACQUISITIONS EDITOR: Jason Noe

DEVELOPMENT EDITOR: Donald Gecewicz, assisted by Dan Chaskes

MARKETING MANAGER: Jeffrey Rucker

PROJECT EDITOR: Jane O'Neill

COVER AND TEXT DESIGNER: Victoria Tomaselli

ILLUSTRATION COORDINATOR: Bill Page

ILLUSTRATIONS: maps.com and Geosystems, Inc.

PHOTO EDITOR: Patricia Marx

PHOTO RESEARCHER: Laura Nash

PRODUCTION COORDINATOR: Susan Wein

MEDIA AND SUPPLEMENTS EDITOR: Joy Ohm

COMPOSITION: Sheridan Sellers, W. H. Freeman and Company Electronic Publishing Center

MANUFACTURING: RR Donnelley & Sons Company

Note: *Photographs not otherwise credited are the property of Scott, Foresman and Company.*

Library of Congress Control Number: 2002106840

Printed in the United States of America

First printing 2002

CONTENTS IN BRIEF

CONTENTS

CHAPTER 9

INDUSTRIES
A Faustian Bargain   297

CHAPTER 10

URBANIZATION
The City in Time and Space   333

SPECIAL FEATURES

MAJOR WORLD MAPS

PREFACE

Geography is a diverse academic discipline. It deals with a wide range of subjects, from spatial patterns of human occupancy to the interaction between people and their habitat. It concerns place and region and employs diverse methodologies from the social sciences, humanities, and Earth sciences. The geographer strives for a holistic view of the Earth as the home of humankind.

Because the world is in constant flux, geography is an ever-changing discipline. Geographers necessarily consider a wide range of topics and view them from several different perspectives. They continually seek new ways of looking at the inhabited Earth. For example, the rise of a feminist perspective has caused geographers to see the world anew through such concepts as "gendered space," and a "postmodernist" challenge to the tenets of science has recently led geography to a more humanistic philosophy. Every revision of an introductory text such as *The Human Mosaic* requires careful attention to such changes and innovations.

The Five Themes

The Human Mosaic has always been built around **five themes:** culture region, cultural diffusion, cultural ecology, cultural interaction, and cultural landscape. These five themes are introduced and explained in the first chapter and serve as the framework for the 11 topical chapters that follow. Each theme is applied to a variety of geographical topics: religion, language, ethnicity, politics, demography, agriculture, industry, the city, and types of culture. This thematic organization allows students to relate to the most important aspects of cultural geography at every point in the text. As instructors, we have found that beginning students learn best when provided with a precise and useful framework, and the five-themes approach provides such a framework for understanding cultural geography. A small icon accompanies each theme as a visual reminder to students when these themes recur throughout the book. They will see:

Culture Region

Cultural Diffusion

 Cultural Ecology

 Cultural Interaction

 Cultural Landscape

In our classroom experience, we have found the thematic framework to be highly successful. Our *culture region* theme appeals to students' natural curiosity about the differences among places. *Cultural diffusion* conveys the dynamic aspect of culture particularly relevant to this age of incessant and rapid change. Students acquire an appreciation for how cultural traits spread (or do not spread) from place to place. The topics employed to illustrate the concepts of diffusion include many examples to which college students can relate: for instance, reggae and rap music, computer technology and the Internet, and the impact of globalization on consumer goods around the world. *Cultural ecology,* also highly relevant in our age, addresses the complicated relationship between culture and the physical environment. *Cultural interaction* (retitled from "cultural integration" for the purpose of clarity) permits students to view culture as an interrelated whole, in which one facet acts on and is acted on by other facets—a key to understanding our complicated world. Last, the theme of *cultural landscape* heightens students' awareness of the visible character of places and regions.

Coverage and Organization

The Human Mosaic continues to provide balanced coverage between traditional geographical topics (culture, land use, political patterns, human adaptation to environment, habitat modification) and major new issues (global warming, desertification, globalization, the cybernetic age, and feminism). We feel that this balance exposes students to the breadth of cultural geography today. Adhering to a thematic organization, the book covers the following topic areas.

Chapter 1 Cultural Geography: Science or Art? introduces the student to the field and explains the five themes of culture region, cultural diffusion, cultural ecology, cultural interaction, and cultural landscape, which are used throughout the text. Globalization is now discussed in a new section in Chapter 1.

Chapter 2 Parallel Worlds: Two Types of Culture raises students' awareness very early that fundamentally differing ways of life exist. These differences are presented as a contrast between *folk* and *popular* cultures. This newly combined chapter is now presented earlier in this edition.

Chapter 3 The Geography of Religion: Spaces and Places of Faith covers the interwoven culture of religion and how it varies from place to place.

Chapter 4 Geolinguistics: A Babel of Languages introduces the student to the geographical branch of geolinguistics and the spatial groupings of languages.

Chapter 5 Ethnic Geography: Homelands and Ghettos examines the spatial and ecological aspects of ethnicity and the trend toward ethnic awareness around the world.

Chapter 6 Political Geography: A Divided World addresses the geographical aspects of human political behavior, illustrated by the breakup of empires, the drawing of international boundaries, and voting patterns.

Chapter 7 Geodemography: Peopling the Earth looks at the distribution of people across the Earth and the spatial variations of birthrates, health, population growth, and other demographic traits that exist in different regions.

Chapter 8 Agricultural Geography: Food from the Good Earth examines types of agriculture, the ecology of farming and herding, the diffusion of elements of agriculture, the interaction between agriculture and other aspects of culture, and the visible variations revealed in agricultural landscapes.

Chapter 9 Industries: A Faustian Bargain explores industry and the industrial revolution through the eyes of the cultural geographer, with particular attention to uneven spatial distribution and its ecological ramifications.

Chapter 10 Urbanization: The City in Time and Space looks at overall patterns of urbanization, how urbanization began and developed, and the differing forms of cities in developing and developed regions.

Chapter 11 Inside the City: A Cultural Mosaic complements Chapter 10 by focusing on patterns within cities such as spatial differences, regional differences, and city structures.

Chapter 12 One World or Many? The Cultural Geography of the Future addresses the question of how globalization is affecting the diversity among human cultures.

New to the Ninth Edition

With this publication, *The Human Mosaic* achieves the rare distinction of its *ninth* edition. We have revised it to speak to the young citizens of an emerging new century, in the hope that studying *The Human Mosaic* will help them adjust to and thrive in this exciting if troubled age.

In this edition, you will find diverse new features and changes:

NEW! Chapter 12, One World or Many? The Cultural Geography of the Future. This entirely new chapter examines the process of *globalization* and its impact on cultures around the world. We approach the subject by questioning current assumptions about globalization and in the process uncover many of the pros and cons associated with this international force. In addition, information on globalization has been incorporated throughout all the chapters of the text.

NEW! Chapter 2, Parallel Worlds: Two Types of Culture. Formerly two separate chapters, the topics of folk and popular culture have been merged in the ninth edition and are now introduced earlier in the book. The newly abridged treatment contrasts these fundamentally different ways of life and streamlines the presentation of their content. By placing this material earlier in the book, students are now introduced to important geographical concepts that will serve as a foundation they can apply throughout the remaining chapters.

Reorganized Table of Contents. In the ninth edition, we have chosen to reorder the 12 chapters to create a more logical flow from one topic to another. The new order of chapters will make the concepts and connections between chapters more relevant to the chapters that succeed them. In addition to the changes mentioned above, other significant organizational changes include:

Chapter 3, The Geography of Religion: Spaces and Places of Faith (formerly Chapter 6), is now introduced earlier to highlight current events surrounding religious conflict and to prepare students for the following chapters covering ethnicity and politics.

Chapter 5, Ethnic Geography: Homelands and Ghettos (formerly Chapter 9), has been moved so that it directly follows the chapters on religion and language (now Chapter 4), two topics that form much of the basis for understanding ethnicity.

Chapter 6, Political Geography: A Divided World (formerly Chapter 4), is now treated after the topics of religion, language, and ethnicity have been introduced, thus ensuring that students will be familiar with these essential contexts before taking on the complexities of geopolitics.

Chapter 7, Geodemography: Peopling the Earth (formerly Chapter 2), has been relocated just before Chapter 8, Agricultural Geography: Food from the Good Earth (formerly Chapter 3), and Chapter 9, Industries: A Faustian Bargain (formerly Chapter 12), which allows students to confront issues such as feeding the world's population and how people from different cultures sustain their livelihoods in the context of demographic concepts.

Chapter 9, Industries: A Faustian Bargain (formerly Chapter 12), has been placed earlier in the table of contents to accommodate the newly added Chapter 12 on globalization.

NEW! "Seeing Geography" Essay. Each chapter now opens with a photograph or a map selected for its ability to illustrate the five themes used throughout the text. Each thematic photo or map is revisited at the end of the chapter in an analytical essay entitled "Seeing Geography." The "Seeing Geography" essay prompts students to think about and analyze photographs in the same ways they are asked to analyze maps—through the unique geographical lenses of the five themes of *The Human Mosaic*.

Revised Map Program. To accommodate the changes of a world in flux, the authoritative map program retains its characteristic elegance and clarity while conveying the latest geographic information.

Thoroughly Updated. An updating of all statistics available to 2000–2001, reflecting censuses worldwide.

Recommended Readings. Annotated lists of 10 carefully selected books at the end of each chapter offer students the opportunity to explore topics that are of interest to them in more depth.

Retained from the Highly Acclaimed Earlier Editions

"If it ain't broke, don't fix it" is an old adage. Accordingly, we have retained the basic, classroom-tested devices that underlie *The Human Mosaic*'s earlier success:

Figure captions in most cases contain questions relevant to what is being shown. Our maps and photos are not decoration but vital parts of the learning process.

Relevant web sites are listed at the end of each chapter to lead students to related materials bearing upon the chapter's topic.

Focus On boxes appear two to three times in each chapter and present illustrative examples or highlight relevant studies that students will find interesting.

Profile boxes interspersed throughout the text present biographical sketches of famous and important contributors to cultural geography, such as Carl Ritter and Ellen Churchill Semple.

Reflecting on Geography questions scattered through each chapter are intended to help students apply what they have just learned to real world situations.

Media and Supplements

The ninth edition is accompanied by a superior media and supplements package that facilitates student learning and enhances the teaching experience. For students, we have seamlessly integrated topics from the text with the companion web site; thus the latest technology is being used to reinforce concepts from the text. For instructors, we have created a full-service ancillary package that will help in the preparation of lectures and exams, particularly in regard to electronic classroom presentations.

Aids for Student Learning

Mapping Exercises

Exploring Human Geography with Maps, Margaret Pearce, Western Michigan University, ISBN 0-7167-4917-3

This new four-color workbook uses cartographic visualization to make maps into tools for the exploration and representation of geographic ideas. It directly addresses the concepts of *The Human Mosaic*, chapter by chapter, and it includes activities accessible through *The Human Mosaic Online* at http://www.whfreeman.com/jordan. Three types of activities occur in each chapter: Exploring Geographic Information Visually; Interpreting the Language of Maps; and Other Ways of Mapping.

On the Web

The Human Mosaic Online: http://www.whfreeman.com/jordan

The companion web site serves as an online study guide. The core of the site is a range of features that encourage critical thinking and assist in study and review. Features include:

Web Activities from *Exploring Human Geography with Maps,* by Margaret Pearce, Western Michigan University

Review Tests for each chapter, by A. Steele Becker, University of Nebraska, Kearney, and Jacqueline V. Becker

Atlas

Rand McNally's Atlas of World Geography, paperback, 176 pages

Available packaged with the text (ISBN 0-7167-9817-4), or with the text and *Student Study Guide* (ISBN 0-7167-9883-2), or with the text and *Exploring Human Geography with Maps* (ISBN 0-7167-9882-4).

Study Guide

Student Study Guide, Michael Kukral, Rose-Hulman Institute of Technology, ISBN 0-7167-5617-X

The new and updated *Student Study Guide* provides a tremendous learning advantage for students using *The Human Mosaic.* This best-selling supplement contains new practice tests, chapter learning objectives, key terms, and sections on map reading and interpretation. A highly integrated manual, the *Student Study Guide* supports and enhances the material covered in *The Human Mosaic* and guides the student to a clearer understanding of cultural geography.

Aids for the Instructor

Presentation

Instructor's Resource CD-ROM and Web Site, ISBN 0-7167-4919-000

Contains *all* the text images available as Microsoft PowerPoint™ slides for use in classroom presentation. The labels on the images have been enlarged for better projection quality. It also contains the *Test Bank* as chapter-by-chapter Microsoft Word™ files that can be easily modified by the instructor.

Slide Set with Lecture Notes, ISBN 0-7167-4920-3

A set of 100 images with accompanying explanatory lecture notes for presentations.

Overhead Transparencies, ISBN 0-7167-4918-1

A handy set of 100 key maps and figures from the text for classroom presentation.

Assessment

Test Bank, Douglas Munski, University of North Dakota

The *Test Bank* is available on the *Instructor's Resource CD-ROM* and can also be accessed via the book's companion web site under the password-protected "For Instructors" section. The *Test Bank* is carefully designed to match the pedagogical intent of the text. It contains more than 1000 test questions (multiple-choice and true/false). The files are provided as chapter-by-chapter Microsoft Word files that are easy to download, edit, and print.

Acknowledgments

No textbook is ever written single-handedly or even "double-handedly." An introductory text covering a wide range of topics must draw heavily on the research and help of others. In various chapters, we have not hesitated to mention a great many geographers on whose work we have relied. We apologize for any misinterpretations or oversimplifications of their findings that may have resulted because of our own error or the limited space available.

Many geographers contributed advice, comments, ideas, and assistance as this book moved from outline through draft to publication from the first edition through the ninth. We would like to thank those colleagues who offered helpful comments during the **preparation of earlier editions:**

Christopher Airriess, Ball State University; Thomas D. Anderson, Bowling Green State University; Timothy G. Anderson, Ohio Wesleyan University; Nancy Bain, Ohio University; A. Steele Becker, University of Nebraska, Kearney; Sarah Bednarz, Texas A&M University; Craig S. Campbell, Youngstown State University; Marcelo Cruz, University of Wisconsin, Green Bay; Charles F. Gritzner, South Dakota State University; Jennifer Helzer of California State University, Stanislaus; Cecelia Hudleson, Foothill College; Gregory Jean, Samford University; Vandara Kohli, California State University, Bakersfield; Michael Kukral, Ohio Wesleyan University; William Laatsch, University of Wisconsin, Green Bay; Ann Legreid, Central Missouri State University; Ronald Lockmann, California State University, Dominiquez Hills; Jesse O. McKee, University of Southern Mississippi; Wayne McKim, Towson State University; Douglas Meyer, Eastern Illinois University; Klaus Meyer-Arendt, Mississippi State University; John Milbauer, Northeastern State University; Don Mitchell, Syracuse University; James Mulvihill, California State University, San Bernardino; Thomas Orf, Prestonburg Community College; Brian Osborne, Queen's University; Kenji Oshiro, Wright State University; Bimal K. Paul, Kansas State University; Jeffrey P. Richetto, University of Alabama; Robert Rundstrom, University of Oklahoma; Lydia Savage, University of Southern Maine; Andrew Schoolmaster III, University of North Texas;

Roger W. Stump, State University of New York at Albany; Thomas M. Tharp, Purdue University; Daniel E. Turbeville III, Eastern Washington University; Philip Wagner, Simon Fraser State University; Barbara Weightman, California State University, Fullerton; David Wilkins, University of Utah; and Douglas Wilms, East Carolina State University.

We would also like to thank those colleagues who contributed their helpful opinions during **preparation of the ninth edition:**

Jennifer Adams, Pennsylvania State University; Nigel Allan, University of California, Davis; Patrick Ashwood, Hawkeye Community College; Matthew Ebiner, El Camino College; Carolyn Gallaher, American University; Charles F. Gritzner, South Dakota State University; Sally Gros, University of Oklahoma, Norman; Debra Kreitzer, Western Kentucky University; Hsiang-te Kung, Memphis University; Cynthia A. Miller, Syracuse University; Glenn R. Miller, Bridgewater State College; Douglas Munski, University of North Dakota; Stephen Sandlin, California State University, Pomona; Ralph Triplette, Western Carolina University; Ingolf Vogeler, University of Wisconsin; and Donald Zeigler, Old Dominion University.

Our thanks also go to various staff members of W. H. Freeman and Company whose encouragement, skills, and suggestions have created a special working environment and to whom we express our deepest gratitude. In particular, we thank Melissa Wallerstein, sponsoring editor, who was among those most instrumental in bringing *The Human Mosaic* to Freeman; Jason Noe, acquisitions editor for geography; Sara Tenney, publisher, and a strong supporter of our book from the first; Donald Gecewicz, development editor, who was ably assisted by Ben Feldman and Daniel Chaskes; Jeffrey Rucker, marketing manager; Jane O'Neill, project editor; Vicki Tomaselli, designer; Sheridan Sellers, compositor and page makeup artist; Bill Page, illustration coordinator; Laura Nash, photo researcher, and Patricia Marx, photo editor; Susan Wein, production coordinator; Joy Ohm, media and supplements editor; Bridget O'Lavin, media and supplements associate editor; Diana Siemens, copy editor; Eleanor Wedge, proofreader; and Rawle Stoute, editorial assistant.

At the University of Texas, Joanne Sanders skillfully and professionally handled all word processing, occasionally serving as an in-house editor ("This just doesn't make any sense at all"—and it didn't!); and Joy Adams, serving as Webb Fellow—the research assistant to Terry Jordan-Bychkov—responded efficiently and quickly to all requests for updated statistics and other data. What a fine professional geographer she is becoming! Damon Scott, her predecessor, proved equally gifted and is also due our gratitude for his work on this edition (in which the results of some of his own research appear). The beneficial influence of all these people can be detected on every page.

ABOUT THE AUTHORS

Terry G. Jordan-Bychkov

is the Walter Prescott Webb Professor in the Department of Geography at the University of Texas at Austin. He earned his Ph.D. at the University of Wisconsin at Madison. A specialist in the cultural and historical geography of the United States, Jordan-Bychkov is particularly interested in the diffusion of Old World culture to North America that helped produce the vivid geographical mosaic evident today. He served as president of the Association of American Geographers in 1987 and 1988 and earlier received an Honors Award from that organization. He has written on a wide range of American cultural topics, including forest colonization, cattle ranching, folk architecture, and ethnicity. His scholarly books include *The European Culture Area: A Systematic Geography,* 4th edition (with Bella Bychkova Jordan, 2002), *Anglo-Celtic Australia: Colonial Immigration and Cultural Regionalism* (with Alyson L. Greiner, 2002), *Siberian Village: Land and Life in the Sakha Republic* (with Bella Bychkova Jordan, 2001), *The Mountain West: Interpreting the Folk Landscape* (with Jon Kilpinen and Charles Gritzner, 1997), *North American Cattle Ranching Frontiers* (1993), *The American Backwoods Frontier* (with Matti Kaups, 1989), *American Log Buildings* (1985), *Texas Graveyards* (1982), *Trails to Texas: Southern Roots of Western Cattle Ranching* (1981), and *German Seed in Texas Soil* (1966). Having been fascinated with maps and landscapes since childhood, Jordan-Bychkov became a geography major during his college freshman year. For him, the most rewarding aspect of geography has been field research. His only hobby is travel.

Mona Domosh

is a professor of geography at Dartmouth College. She earned her Ph.D. at Clark University. Her research has examined the links between gender ideologies and the cultural formation of large American cities in the nineteenth century, particularly in regard to such critical but vexing distinctions as consumption/production, public/private, masculine/feminine. She is currently engaged in research that takes the ideological association of women, femininity, and space in a more postcolonial direction by asking what roles nineteenth-century ideas of femininity, masculinity, consumption, and "whiteness" played in the crucial shift from American nation-building to empire-building. Domosh is the author of *Invented Cities: The Creation of Landscape in 19th-century New York and Boston* (1996) and the coauthor, with Joni Seager, of *Putting Women in Place: Feminist Geographers Make Sense of the World* (2001).

THE HUMAN MOSAIC

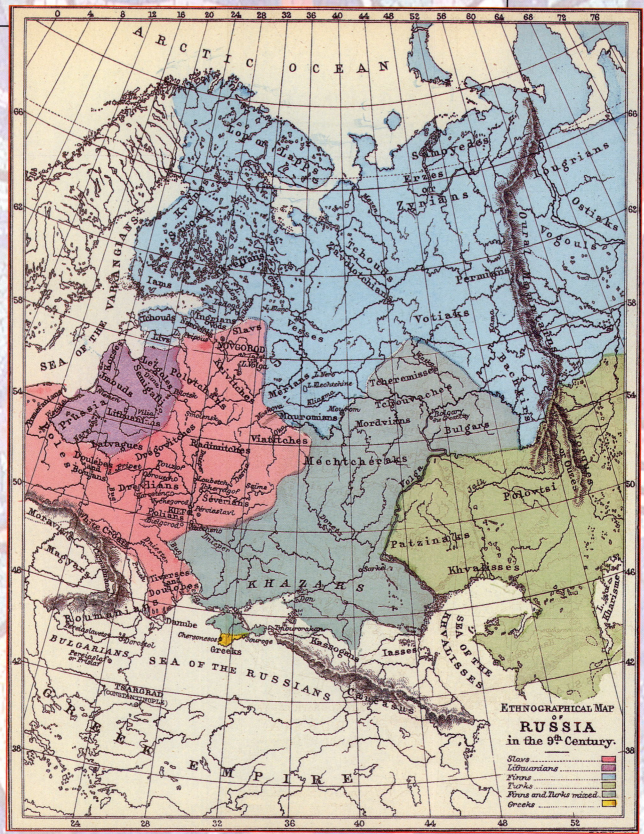

Why is Moscow, the present capital of Russia, not on the map, nor St. Petersburg, the previous capital?

ETHNOGRAPHICAL MAP
OF
RUSSIA
in the 9th Century.

Slavs ....
Lithuanians ....
Finns ....
Turks ....
Finns and Turks mixed ...
Greeks ....

Old map of the European part of Russia, published in 1898 but showing towns and ethnic areas as they were a thousand years earlier. (COURTESY OF TERRY G. JORDAN-BYCHKOV.)
Turn to Seeing Geography on page 29 for an in-depth analysis of the above question.

CHAPTER
1

CULTURAL GEOGRAPHY
Science or Art?

We shall find our planet inhabited by a weird and extraordinary
variety of fellow-boarders. Many of them, upon first acquaintance,
will appear to be possessed of . . . general characteristics we would
rather not encounter in our own children!

HENDRIK VAN LOON, 1932

Humans are, by nature, geographers, like the irreverent Mr. van
Loon (whose delightful book challenges the very xenophobia he
expresses, tongue-in-cheek, above). We are curious about the
distinctive character of places and peoples. We can think in terms of territory, or space. Our curiosity and thought processes include the essential qualities and dimensions of geography. Even nongeographers often
possess a fundamentally accurate idea of what geography involves.

If every place on Earth were identical, we would not need geography,
but in fact each is unique. Geographers define the concept of **region** to
mean a grouping of like places. The existence of regions endows the
Earth's surface with a magical quality. Beyond what we have explored
always lies the unknown, the mysterious and exotic lands that we often
populate with our fantasies and fears. Places possess an emotional significance that contributes profoundly to our identity as individual human
beings: we all must belong somewhere to be complete persons. Geography as an academic discipline is an outgrowth of both our curiosity about
lands and peoples other than our own and our need to come to grips with
the place-centered element within our souls. Because geographers deal
with these fundamentally important issues, they have, over the centuries,
generated a number of concepts that have literally changed the world (see
Focus On: Seven Cultural Geographical Ideas That Changed the World).

PROFILE

(GERMAN INFORMATION CENTER.)

Alexander von Humboldt
1769–1859

Humboldt, a world-famous German scientist, traveled widely and wrote extensively on geographical topics. In 1797, with the permission of the Spanish crown, he sailed to South America. For the next five years, he explored from Mexico to the Andes. Later, at the age of 60, he accepted an invitation from the czar of Russia to explore mineral resources. He traveled by carriage through Siberia, carefully recording and describing the landscape. His interests lay in physical geography—the study of climate, terrain, and vegetation—but Humboldt's writings reveal his belief that humans are part of ecosystems. His main contribution to geography was his attention to cause-and-effect relationships. Most geographers of earlier times merely compiled facts. When Humboldt tried to explain spatial patterns of certain physical phenomena, he found geography useful. Because he brought the prestige and methods of science to geography, he is considered one of the founders of modern geography. Humboldt never held a university position, but he was widely respected as a scholar. His most important geographical publication was *Cosmos*, a five-volume work.

For more information about Humboldt's life and achievements, see McIntyre, 1985.

Reflecting on GEOGRAPHY

Is *place,* or an attachment to place, an integral aspect of your personality?

Our natural geographical curiosity and intrinsic need for identity were long ago reinforced by pragmatism, by the practical motives of traders and empire builders who wanted information about the world for the purposes of commerce and conquest. This concern for the practical aspects of geography first arose thousands of years ago among the ancient Greeks, Romans, Mesopotamians, and Phoenicians, the greatest traders and empire builders of their time. They cataloged factual information about locations, places, and products. Indeed, **geography** is a Greek word meaning literally "to describe the Earth." Not content merely to chart and describe the world, these ancient geographers soon began to ask questions about why cultures and environments differ from place to place. By the end of the Roman era, geographers had developed theories of a spherical Earth, latitudinal climate zones, environmental influences on humans, and the role of humans in modifying the Earth. In the Dark Ages that followed the fall of the Roman Empire, Arabs became the leaders in acquiring new geographical knowledge, but with the cultural reawakening known as the Renaissance and the Age of Discovery, the center of geographical learning shifted again to Europe.

The modern academic study of geography grew from these beginnings. Under the leadership of Alexander von Humboldt and Carl Ritter (see Profiles), among others, the academic discipline of geography first appeared in Germany. Throughout *The Human Mosaic,* boxed Profiles like these appear. In them, we display our "intellectual genealogy"— the men and women who, over the centuries, helped build our proud academic discipline. Everybody has two genealogies: the ancestors who gave you life and those who gave you ideas. We should honor both.

When professional, academic geographers consider the differences and similarities among places, they want to understand what they see. They first find out exactly what variations exist among regions and places by describing them as precisely as possible. Then they try to decide

---

FOCUS ON

Seven Cultural Geographical Ideas That Changed the World

1. Maps
2. Human adaptation to habitat
3. Human transformation of the Earth
4. Sense of place

5. Spatial organization and interdependence
6. Central place theory (see Chapter 10)
7. Megalopolis (see Chapter 10)

Abridged from Hanson, 1996.

PROFILE

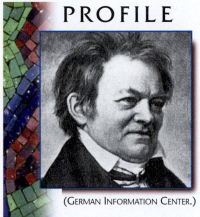

Carl Ritter
1779–1859

(GERMAN INFORMATION CENTER.)

Ritter, a long-time and close associate of Humboldt, was a professor of geography at the University of Berlin from 1820, the first such position in the world. He began his career as a tutor for a wealthy family in Frankfurt. In these comfortable surroundings, he was able to meet other intellectuals and study geography. During the long period he taught in Berlin, his work influenced the thinking of many people, including military leaders. In contrast to Humboldt, his chief concern was cultural geography, the geography of humans. He sought to bring the rigor of science to the study of human geography and believed that laws of human spatial behavior could be discovered. His first book discussed Africa, then a little-known continent, but he is best known for the massive work entitled *Die Erdkunde* [*Geography*], which appeared in 19 volumes between 1822 and his death. Ritter is widely regarded as a cofounder, with Humboldt, of the academic discipline of geography.

what forces made these areas different or alike. Geographers ask *what? where?* and *why?*

What Is Cultural Geography?

Cultural geography forms one part of the discipline, complementing physical geography (the part that deals with the natural environment). To understand the scope of cultural geography, we must first agree on the meaning of **culture.**

There are many definitions of culture, some broad and some narrow. We might define culture as learned collective human behavior, as opposed to instinctive, or inborn, behavior. These learned traits form a way of life held in common by a group of people. Learned similarities in speech, behavior, ideology, livelihood, technology, value system, and society bind people together. Culture, defined in this way, involves a communication system of acquired beliefs, memories, perceptions, traditions, and attitudes that serves to supplement and channel instinctive behavior. In short, as geographer Yi-Fu Tuan has said, culture is the "local, customary way of doing things; geographers write about ways of life." Culture, to Tuan, includes a complex of collective beliefs, habits, thoughts, behaviors, customs, values, skills, and artifacts. By this definition, then, "culture" is a categorization of individual humans into groups, on the basis of multiple criteria—in short, a classification.

A particular culture is not a static, fixed phenomenon, nor does it always govern its members. Rather, as geographers Kay Anderson and Fay Gale put it, "culture is a *process* in which people are actively engaged," a dynamic mix of symbols, beliefs, language, and practices. Individual members can and do change a culture, which means that ways of life constantly change and that tensions between opposed views are usually present. Contestation and change are part of the human condition and are reflected in culture. Cultures are never internally homogeneous because individual humans never think or behave in exactly the same manner. Within each culture are persons of different gender, creativity, intelligence, status, and rank.

Cultural geography is the study of spatial variations among cultural traits and the spatial functioning of society. It focuses on describing and analyzing the ways in which language, religion, economy, government, and other cultural phenomena vary or remain constant from one place to another, and on explaining how humans function spatially and identify with place and region (Figure 1.1 on the next page). Cultural geography is, at heart, a celebration of human diversity or, as the Russian geographer Leo Gumilev wrote, "the study of differences among peoples."

In seeking explanations for cultural diversity and place identity, geographers consider a wide array of causal factors. Some of these involve the **physical environment:** terrain, climate, natural vegetation, wildlife, variations in soil, and the pattern of land and water. Because we cannot understand culture removed from its physical setting, cultural geography offers not only a spatial perspective but also an ecological one. One of the distinctive attributes of geography is the way it bridges the social and earth sciences to study people in their habitats. For this reason, geographers tend to resist the increasing fragmentation of learning into highly specialized, segregated academic disciplines. We seek an integrative view of humankind in its physical environment, rather than a specialized, fragmented perspective. As a result, geography appears less focused than most other disciplines and is more difficult to define.

Geography offers no easy explanations for cultural phenomena, because complex causal forces are at work. Things are interconnected in very complicated ways. The complexity of the forces that affect culture can be illustrated by an example drawn from agricultural geography:

Figure 1.1

Two traditional houses of worship. Geographers seek to learn how and why cultures differ, or are similar, from one place to another. Often the differences and similarities have a visual expression. **In what ways are these two structures—one a rural Lutheran church in the treeless tundra of Iceland and the other a Greek Orthodox chapel amid the olive groves of Crete—alike and different?** (COURTESY OF TERRY G. JORDAN-BYCHKOV.)

the distribution of wheat cultivation in the world. If you look at Figure 1.2, you can see important wheat cultivation in Australia but not Africa, in the United States but not Brazil, in China but not Southeast Asia. Why does this spatial pattern exist? Partly it results from environmental factors such as climate, terrain, and soils. Some regions have always been too dry for wheat cultivation, others too steep or infertile. Indeed, there is a strong correlation between wheat cultivation and midlatitude climates, level terrain, and good soil.

Still, we should not place exclusive importance on such physical factors. People can modify the effects of climate through irrigation; the use of hothouses; or the development of new, specialized strains of wheat. They can conquer slopes through terracing, and they can make poor soils productive through fertilization. For example, farmers in mountainous parts of Greece traditionally wrested an annual harvest of wheat from tiny terraced plots where soil had been trapped behind hand-built stone retaining walls. Even in the United States, environmental factors alone cannot explain the curious fact that major wheat cultivation is concentrated in the semiarid Great Plains, some distance from states such as Ohio and Illinois, where the climate for growing wheat is better.

The cultural geographer knows that wheat has to survive in a cultural environment as well as a physical one. Agricultural patterns cannot be explained by the characteristics of the land and climate alone. Many factors com-

plicate the distribution of wheat, including people's tastes and traditions. Food preferences and taboos, often backed by religious beliefs, strongly influence the choice of crops to plant. Some cultural groups, such as the Poles, prefer dark bread made from rye flour. Other groups, particularly Native Americans, would rather eat breads made from maize, a crop given a religious role in their traditional way of life (see Focus On: "When Jesus Came, the Corn Mothers Went Away," in Chapter 3.") Obviously, wheat will not "thrive" in such cultural environments. Where wheat bread is preferred, people are willing to put great efforts into overcoming hostile physical surroundings. They have even created new strains of wheat, thereby decreasing the environment's influence on the distribution of wheat cultivation. Tariffs can also encourage or discourage wheat cultivation; for example, tariffs protect the wheat farmers of France and other European countries from competition with more efficient American and Canadian producers. In addition, wheat farming is a less profitable use of the land than dairying or fattening livestock.

This is by no means a complete list of the forces that affect the geographical distribution of wheat cultivation. It should be clear, though, that the contemporary map of wheat reflects the pushing and pulling of many factors. The distribution of all cultural elements is a result of the constant interplay of diverse causal factors. Cultural geography is the discipline that seeks such explanations.

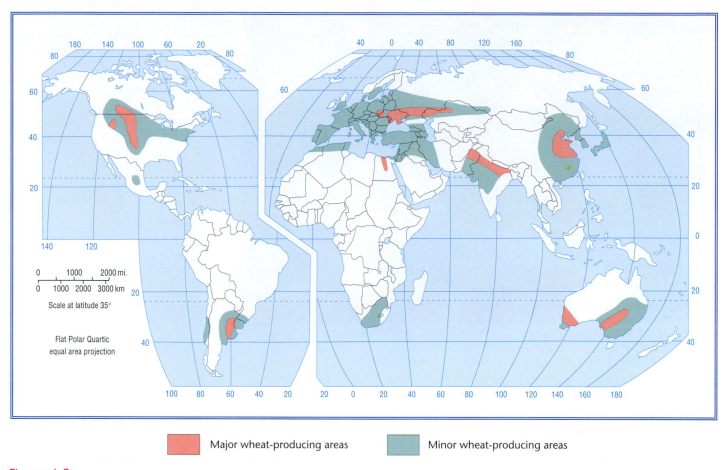

Major wheat-producing areas   Minor wheat-producing areas

Figure 1.2

Areas of wheat production in the world today. These culture regions are based on a single trait: the importance of wheat in the agricultural system. This map tells us what and where. It raises the question of why. **What causal forces might be at work to produce this geographical distribution of wheat farming?**

Themes in Cultural Geography

Our study of cultures is organized around five geographical concepts or themes: culture region, cultural diffusion, cultural ecology, cultural interaction, and cultural landscape. These themes are stressed throughout the book and give structure to each chapter.

 Culture Region

Phrased as a question, the theme of culture region could ask, "How are cultures grouped or arranged geographically?" Places and regions provide the essence of geography. How and why are places alike or different? How are they meshed together into functioning spatial networks? How do their inhabitants perceive them and identify with them? These are central geographical questions. A **culture region,** then, is a geographical unit based on characteristics and functions of culture.

Maps provide an essential tool for describing and revealing regions. If, as it is often said, one picture is worth a thousand words, then a well-prepared map is worth at least ten thousand words to the geographer. No description in words can rival a map's ability to reveal geographical patterns. Maps are valuable tools particularly because they portray spatial patterns in culture so concisely. The map has been listed as one of the geographical ideas that changed the world (refer again to Focus On: Seven Cultural Geographical Ideas That Changed the World). Three types of culture regions are recognized by geographers: formal, functional, and vernacular. We will discuss each one of these in turn, beginning with the formal type.

Figure 1.3

A traditional market on the island of New Guinea. Various facets of a multitrait formal culture region can be seen here, including the wares for sale and the people's clothing. (MUCHTAR ZAKARIA/AP PHOTO.)

Formal Culture Regions A **formal culture region** is an area inhabited by people who have one or more cultural traits in common. If cultural geography is, above all, a celebration of human diversity in the spatial dimension, then the formal culture region is a depiction of that human mosaic. Geographers use this concept to describe spatial differences in culture. For example, a German-language formal culture region can be drawn on a map of languages, and it would include the areas where German is spoken. Similarly, a wheat-farming formal culture region could describe the parts of the world where wheat is a major crop (look again at Figure 1.2).

The examples of German speech and of wheat cultivation represent the concept of formal culture region at its simplest level. Each is based on a single cultural trait. More commonly, formal culture regions depend on multiple related traits (Figure 1.3). Thus, an Inuit (Eskimo) culture region might be based on language, religion, economy, social organization, and type of dwellings. The culture region would reflect the spatial distribution of these five Inuit cultural traits. Districts in which all five of these traits are present would be part of the culture region. Similarly, Europe can be subdivided into several multitrait regions (Figure 1.4).

Formal culture regions are the geographer's somewhat arbitrary creations. No two cultural traits have the same distribution, and the territorial extent of a culture region depends on what and how many defining traits are used (Figure 1.5 on page 8). Why *five* Inuit traits and not four or six? Why not *foods* instead of (or in addition to) dwell-

ing types? Consider, for example, Greeks and Turks, who differ in language and religion. Formal culture regions defined on the basis of speech and religious faith would separate these two groups. However, Greeks and Turks hold many other cultural traits in common. Both groups are monotheistic, worshiping a single god. In both groups, male supremacy and patriarchal families are the rule. Certain folk foods, such as shish kebab, are enjoyed in common. Whether Greeks and Turks are placed in the same formal culture region or in different ones depends entirely on how the geographer chooses to define the culture region. That choice in turn depends on the specific purpose of research or teaching that the culture region is designed to serve. Thus, an infinite number of formal culture regions can be created. It is unlikely that any two geographers would use exactly the same distinguishing criteria or place cultural boundaries in the same location.

Often cultural geographers attempt to base culture regions on the *totality* of traits displayed by a culture. Because of the greater complexity of traits involved, such regions are typically even more arbitrarily delimited than are those based on fewer characteristics. These regions often spring from the geographer's intuition, derived from intimate knowledge of an area (Figure 1.6 on page 9).

The geographer who identifies a formal culture region must locate *cultural borders*. Because cultures overlap and mix, such boundaries are rarely sharp, even if only a single cultural trait is mapped. For this reason, we find cultural *border zones* rather than lines. These zones broaden with each additional cultural trait that is considered,

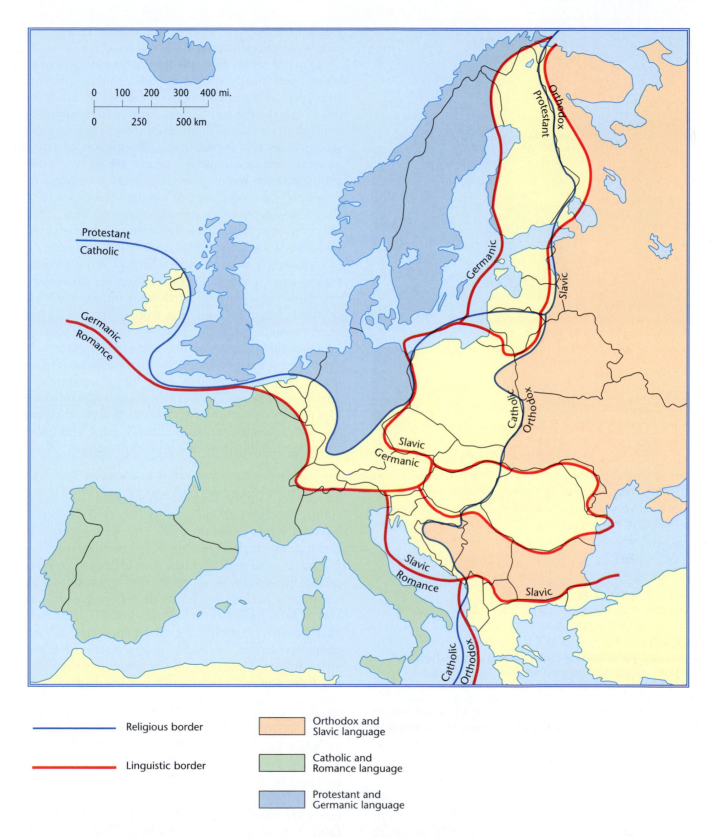

Labels on map:
Protestant
Catholic
Germanic
Romance
Germanic
Slavic
Germanic
Slavic
Catholic
Orthodox
Protestant
Orthodox
Slavic
Romance
Slavic
Catholic
Orthodox

Legend:

— Religious border

— Linguistic border

Orthodox and Slavic language

Catholic and Romance language

Protestant and Germanic language

Figure 1.4

Formal culture regions of Europe based on only two traits: language and religion. Notice how transitional areas appear between such culture regions even when only two traits are used to define them. **What does this teach us about boundaries between cultures?**

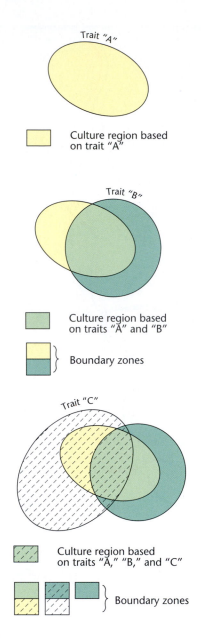

Figure 1.5
Hypothetical formal culture regions based on one, two, and three traits. Notice that no two traits have the same spatial distribution. With each additional trait, the core of the region grows smaller and the boundary zone broader. Imagine how complicated the pattern would become were 5, 10, or 100 traits included. **Do you understand now why each place on Earth is unique?**

because no two traits have the same spatial distribution. As a result, instead of having clear borders, formal culture regions reveal a center or core where the defining traits are all present. Away from the central core, the regional characteristics weaken and disappear, as is suggested in

Figures 1.4 and 1.5. Thus formal culture regions display a **core-periphery** pattern.

In a real sense, then, the human world is chaotic. No matter how closely related two elements of culture seem to be, careful investigation always shows that they do not cover exactly the same area. This is true regardless of what degree of detail is involved. Just as the map of languages does not duplicate the distribution of religions, governments, or economies, so too are no two words or pronunciations within a single dialect or language found in precisely the same area. What does this chaos mean to the cultural geographer in practical terms? First, it tells us that every feature and detail of culture is spatially unique and that the explanation for each spatial variation differs in some degree from all others. Second, it means that culture changes continually throughout an area and that every inhabited place on Earth has a unique combination of cultural features, differing from every other place in one or more respects. No place is exactly like another.

Does this cultural uniqueness of each place prevent geographers from seeking explanatory theories? Does it doom them to explaining each locale separately? The answer must be no. The fact that no two hills or rocks, no two planets or stars, no two trees or flowers are identical has not prevented geologists, astronomers, and botanists from formulating theories and explanations based on generalizations.

Functional Culture Regions The hallmark of a formal culture region is cultural homogeneity, and the formal region is abstract rather than concrete. By contrast, a **functional culture region** need not be culturally homogeneous; instead, it is an area that has been organized to function politically, socially, or economically. A city, an independent state, a precinct, a church diocese or parish, a trade area, a farm, and a Federal Reserve Bank district are all examples of functional regions. Functional culture regions have **nodes,** or central points where the functions are coordinated and directed. Examples of such nodes are city halls, national capitals, precinct voting places, parish churches, factories, and banks. In this sense, functional regions also possess a core-periphery configuration, in common with formal culture regions.

Many functional regions have clearly defined borders. A *farm* is a functional region that includes all land owned or leased by the farmer (Figure 1.7 on page 10). Its operation is directed by the farmer, who has organized the land to function as a distinct spatial unit. The node is the farmstead, which contains the home and various structures essential to farming, such as barns, implement sheds, and silos. The borders of this functional region will probably be clearly marked by fences, hedges, or walls. Simi-

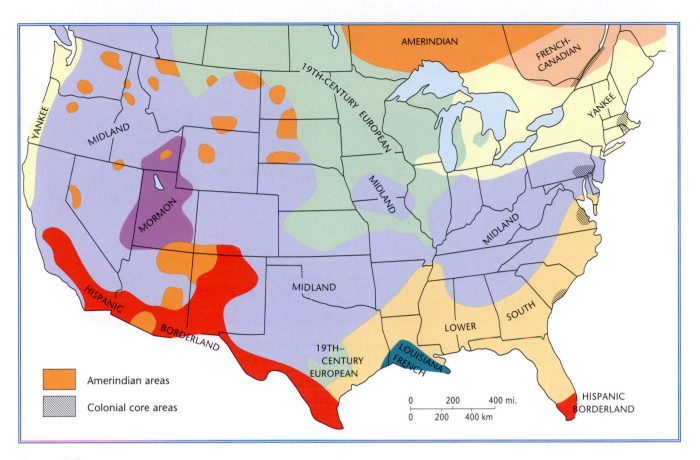

Figure 1.6

Traditional rural formal cultural regions of North America. An attempt was made to consider a totality of traits in drawing the borders of this map, making the delimitation by necessity highly subjective. Really, it is one geographer's intuitive map. The Yankee region was originally settled by colonists largely from England in the period before American independence. Marginal success in farming caused many colonists to turn to fishing, trading, manufacturing, and lumbering as occupations. In contrast, the Midland culture area embraced a great variety of ethnic groups. English, Scotch-Irish, German, Dutch, Swedish, Finnish, Welsh, and other European groups met and mingled here, importing rich and diverse agricultural heritages into a fertile land. The middle-class family farm was instituted here. The result was a farming culture that shaped the face of much of the rural United States from then on. In the Lower South, British, French, Caribbean, and African traits were combined in a plantation system of agriculture. Large estates, specializing in subtropical cash crops and depending on slave laborers, gave rise to a landed aristocracy that assumed political control of the plantation colonies. The other culture areas on the map also developed uniquely, formed by diverse cultural groups in particular environmental and temporal settings.

larly, each state in the United States and each Canadian province is a functional region, coordinated and directed from a capital and extending government control over a fixed area with clearly defined borders.

Not all functional culture regions have fixed, precise borders, however. A good example is a daily newspaper's circulation area. The node for the paper would be the plant where it is produced. Every morning, trucks move out of the plant to distribute the paper throughout the city. The newspaper may have a sales area extending into the city's suburbs, local bedroom communities, nearby towns, and rural areas. There its sales area overlaps the sales territories of competing newspapers published in other cities. It would be futile to try to define borders for such an area. How would you draw a sales area boundary for the *New York Times*? Its Sunday edition is sold in

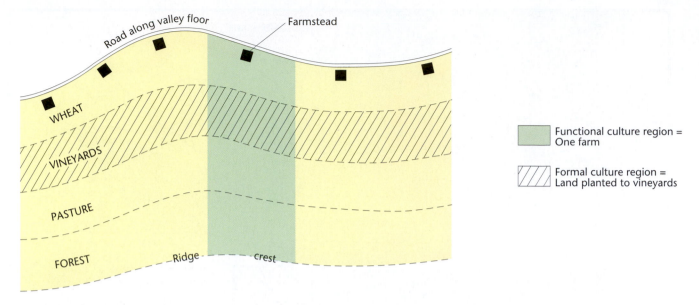

Figure 1.7

A valley filled with farms. Each farm consists of a strip of land reaching from the center of the valley up to the adjacent ridge crest. Farmsteads are at the fronts of the farms, along a road that bisects the valley. On each, the slope of the land becomes steeper as we go away from the road. On the most level land, at the front of each farm, wheat is raised, and with the steadily increasing slope toward the rear of each farm, we encounter vineyards; then pastures; and finally, on the steepest slopes at the rear of the farm, forest. Thus each farm consists of wheat fields, vineyards, pastures, and woodland with increasing distance from the road. Each of these types of land use occupies a continuous strip running lengthwise through the valley. In this situation, both formal and functional culture regions are present. Each farm constitutes a functional culture region, and the strips of wheat, vineyards, pasture, and woodland are each formal culture regions, defined by the homogeneity of land use.

some quantity even in California, thousands of miles from its node, and it is published simultaneously in different cities.

The sales areas for manufactured goods present similar problems. Every time you buy a soft drink or a beer, you are part of a functional culture region. Some beer manufacturers market their products nationwide, establishing branch breweries in various parts of the country. Schlitz, Budweiser, and Pabst are in this category. Certain others confine sales activity to selected multistate regions; and some, such as Lone Star of Texas, are marketed largely within a single state. Finally, some beers, such as Pittsburgh's Iron City brand, are sold in small local areas. Each beer has a unique market area—a functional region—and these often overlap one another. The node for each beer's functional area is the brewery.

Functional culture regions generally do not coincide spatially with formal culture regions, and this disjuncture often creates problems for the functional region. Germany provides an example (Figure 1.8). As an independent state, Germany forms a functional culture region.

Language provides a substantial basis for political unity, although the formal culture region of the German language extends beyond the political borders of Germany and includes part or all of eight other independent states. More important, numerous formal culture regions have borders cutting through German territory, and some of these have endured for millennia, causing differences among northern, southern, eastern, and western Germany. These contrasts make the functioning of the German state more difficult and help explain why Germany has been politically fragmented more often than unified.

Vernacular Culture Regions Geographers recognize a third type, the **vernacular culture region:** one that is *perceived* to exist by its inhabitants, as evidenced by the widespread acceptance and use of a special regional name. Figure 1.9 on page 12 reveals one such popular region in the United States, "Dixie." Some vernacular regions are based on physical environmental features; others find their basis in economic, political, historical, or promotional characteristics. Vernacular regions, like most

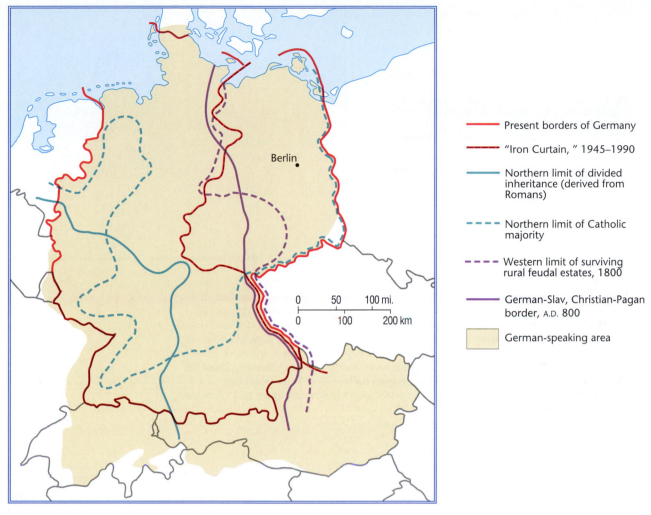

Present borders of Germany

"Iron Curtain," 1945–1990

Northern limit of divided inheritance (derived from Romans)

Northern limit of Catholic majority

Western limit of surviving rural feudal estates, 1800

German-Slav, Christian-Pagan border, A.D. 800

German-speaking area

Figure 1.8

East versus west and north versus south in Germany. As a political unit and functional culture region, Germany must overcome the disruptions caused by numerous formal culture regions that tend to make the sections of Germany culturally different. Formal and functional culture regions rarely coincide spatially. **How might these sectional contrasts cause problems for modern Germany?**

culture regions, generally lack sharp borders, and the inhabitants of any given area may claim residence in more than one such region. They vary in scale from city neighborhoods to sizable parts of continents. These perceived regions are often created by publicity campaigns, and their use in the communications media is closely linked to acceptance by the local population.

At a basic level, the vernacular region grows out of people's sense of belonging and their regional self-consciousness. By contrast, many formal or functional culture regions lack this attribute and, as a result, are far

less potent geographical entities. Self-conscious regional identity has major political and social ramifications.

Reflecting on **GEOGRAPHY**

What vernacular region(s) do you live in?

Vernacular culture regions often lack the organization necessary for functional regions, although they may be centered on a single urban node, and they frequently do

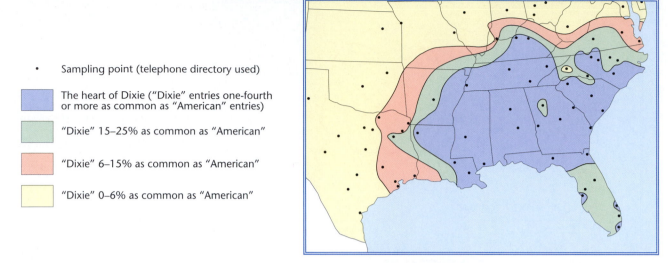

Figure 1.9

Dixie: a vernacular region. "Dixie" is loaded with historical and cultural connotations. The territorial extent of Dixie was determined by counting the number of times it appeared in telephone directories as part of the name of business establishments. The total for each city was then divided by the entries for "American," to adjust for the different population sizes of the cities, producing the percentages on the map. The higher the number, the more common the use of "Dixie." **Make a count of regional terms in your telephone directory. Does the place where you live lie within a vernacular region such as Dixie? How does the perceived "Dixie" compare to the formal region "Lower South" in Figure 1.6?** (AFTER REED, 1976: 932, WITH MODIFICATIONS FOR TEXAS.)

not display the cultural homogeneity that characterizes formal regions. They are a type unto themselves—a type rooted in culture itself.

Cultural Diffusion

How did the various elements of cultures spread to occupy the culture region where they occur today? How do ideas and technology spread geographically, or why do they not spread? These questions define our second theme, **cultural diffusion.**

Regardless of type, the culture regions of the world evolved through communication and contact among people. In other words, they are the product of the spatial spread of learned ideas, innovations, and attitudes. As Figure 1.10 shows, each element of culture originates in one or more places and then spreads. Some innovations occur only once, and geographers can sometimes trace a cultural element back to a single place of origin. In other cases, **independent invention** occurs: the same or very similar innovation is separately developed at different places by different peoples. The study of cultural diffu-

sion—the geographical origin and spread of ideas and innovations—is a very important theme. Through the study of diffusion, the cultural geographer can begin to understand how spatial patterns in culture evolved.

Any culture is the product of almost countless innovations that spread from their points of origin to cover a wider area. Some of these innovations occurred thousands of years ago, others very recently. Some spread widely (see Focus On: Cultural Diffusion: A 100 Percent American), while others remained confined to their area of origin.

Types of Diffusion Geographers, drawing heavily on the research of Torsten Hägerstrand (see Profile on page 15), recognize several different kinds of diffusion (see Figure 1.10). In **expansion diffusion,** ideas spread throughout a population, from area to area, in a snowballing process, so that the total number of knowers and the area of occurrence increase. **Relocation diffusion** occurs when individuals or groups with a particular idea or practice migrate from one location to another, spreading it to their new homeland. Religions frequently spread this way. An example is the migration of Christianity with European

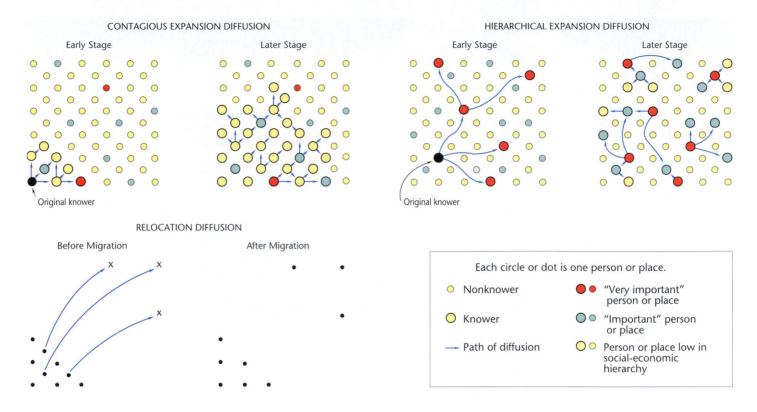

Figure 1.10

Types of cultural diffusion. These diagrams are merely suggestive; in reality, spatial diffusion is far more complex. Expansion diffusion has two subtypes: contagious and hierarchical. In hierarchical diffusion, different scales can be used, so that, for example, the category "very important person" could be replaced by "large city."

settlers who came to America. Indeed, the entire process of European overseas migration, lasting from about 1500 to 1950, constituted the most important episode of relocation diffusion in all of history.

Expansion diffusion can be further divided into three subtypes. In **hierarchical diffusion,** ideas leapfrog from one important person to another or from one urban center to another, temporarily bypassing other persons or rural territory. We can see hierarchical diffusion at work in everyday life by observing the acceptance of new modes of dress or hairstyles. By contrast, **contagious diffusion** involves the wavelike spread of ideas, without regard to hierarchies, in the manner of a contagious disease. Sometimes a specific trait is rejected, but the underlying idea is accepted, resulting in **stimulus diffusion.** For example, early Siberian peoples domesticated reindeer only after exposure to the domesticated cattle raised by cultures to their south. The Siberians had no use for cattle, but the idea of domesticated herds appealed to them, and they

began domesticating reindeer, an animal they had long hunted.

If you throw a rock into a pond and watch the spreading ripples, you can see them become gradually weaker as they move away from the point of impact. In the same way, diffusion becomes weaker as a cultural innovation moves away from its point of origin. That is, diffusion decreases with distance. An innovation will usually be accepted most thoroughly in the areas closest to where it originates. Time is also a factor, because innovations take increasing time to spread outward. Because acceptance decreases with distance, acceptance also decreases with time, producing what geographers call **time-distance decay.** Modern mass media have greatly speeded diffusion, diminishing the impact of time-distance decay.

In addition to the gradual weakening or decay of an innovation through time and distance, barriers can retard its spread. **Absorbing barriers** completely halt diffusion, allowing no further progress. For example, in

FOCUS ON

Cultural Diffusion: A 100 Percent American

Our solid American citizen awakens in a bed built on a pattern that originated in the Near East but that was modified in northern Europe before it was transmitted to America. He throws back covers made from cotton, domesticated in India; or linen, domesticated in the Near East; or silk, the use of which was discovered in China. All of these materials have been spun and woven by processes invented in the Near East. He slips into his moccasins, invented by the Indians of the Eastern woodlands, and goes to the bathroom, whose fixtures are a mixture of European and American inventions, both of recent date. He takes off his pajamas, a garment invented in India, and washes with soap, invented by the ancient Gauls. He then shaves—a masochistic rite that seems to have been derived from either Sumer or ancient Egypt. . . .

On his way to breakfast, he stops to buy a paper, paying for it with coins, an ancient Lydian invention. At the restaurant, a whole new series of borrowed elements confronts him. His plate is made of a form of pottery invented in China. His knife is of steel, an alloy first made in southern India; his fork, a medieval Italian invention; and his spoon, a derivative of a Roman original. . . .

When our friend has finished eating, . . . he reads the news of the day, imprinted in characters invented by the ancient Semites upon a material invented in China by a process invented in Germany. As he absorbs the accounts of foreign trouble, he will, if he is a good, conservative citizen, thank a Hebrew deity in an Indo-European language that he is 100 percent American.

From Linton © 1936, renewed 1964: 326–327. Adapted by permission of Prentice-Hall, Inc., Englewood Cliffs, N.J.

1998 the fundamentalist Islamic Taliban government of Afghanistan decided to abolish television. The people had 15 days to get rid of their TV sets or see them smashed by the police. Videocassette recorders and videotapes were likewise banned. They were viewed as "causes of corruption in society." As a result, the cultural diffusion of television sets was reversed, and the important role of television as a communications device that facilitated the spread of ideas was eliminated.

Even so, few absorbing barriers exist in the world. More commonly, barriers are **permeable,** allowing part of the innovation wave to diffuse through but acting to weaken and retard the continued spread. When a school board objects to long hair for boys or short skirts for girls, the principal of a high school may set limits on hair and skirt length. The hair length limit will likely be longer than the haircuts before the long-hair innovation was introduced, but shorter than the length of the new hairstyles. Likewise, the skirt length limit will likely be shorter than before, but not as short as the girls would like. In this way, the principal and school board act as a permeable barrier to cultural innovations.

Reflecting on GEOGRAPHY

What changes came to you recently by way of cultural diffusion? What specific kind of diffusion (hierarchical, contagious, stimulus) was involved?

Acceptance of innovations at any given point in space passes through three distinct stages. In the first stage, acceptance takes place at a steady, slow rate, perhaps because the innovation has not yet caught on, the benefits have not been adequately demonstrated, or a product is not readily available. During the second stage, acceptance grows rapidly and the trait spreads widely, as with a fashion style or dance fad. Often diffusion on a microscale exhibits what is called the **neighborhood effect,** which means that acceptance is usually most rapid in small clusters around an initial adopter (Figure 1.11 on page 16). Think of a fad that first appeared in your neighborhood one day; a few days later it seemed that everyone you know was doing the same thing. Direct exposure to an innovation is the best advertisement (see Focus On: Monkey See, Monkey Do on page 17). In the third stage, acceptance grows at a slower rate than in the second, perhaps because the fad is passing or because an area is already saturated with the innovation.

Although all places and communities hypothetically have equal potential for innovation, diffusion typically produces a core-periphery spatial arrangement, the same pattern observed earlier in our discussion of culture regions (see Figures 1.4 and 1.5). Hägerstrand offered an explanation of how diffusion produces such a regional configuration. The distribution of innovations can be random, but the overlap of new ideas and traits as they diffuse through area and time is greatest toward the center

PROFILE

(STIGI HÄGERSTRAND.)

Torsten Hägerstrand
1916–

A native and resident of Sweden, Hägerstrand is professor emeritus of geography at the University of Lund, where he received a doctorate in 1953. His doctoral research was on cultural diffusion, and his findings were published in 1953. His work on diffusion is significant because it is based on models and statistical techniques. As a result, it was the basis for many theories and introduced a scientific perspective into cultural geography. Sweden, and particularly Lund, became a major center of innovative work in social-scientific cultural geography. In 1968 Professor Hägerstrand received an Outstanding Achievement Award from the Association of American Geographers, and in 1985 he was awarded an honorary doctor of science degree from Ohio State University. The commendation accompanying the honorary degree noted that "his work on innovation diffusion, carried out in the 1950s and 1960s, continues to be cited as a standard against which current research is measured" and that "this distinguished individual . . . inspired a generation of scholars around the world."

and least at the peripheries (Figure 1.12 on page 17). Cores develop because innovations are more readily available in the central region.

Some other cultural geographers, most notably James Blaut and Richard Ormrod, regard the Hägerstrandian concept of diffusion as too narrow and mechanical, because it does not give enough emphasis to cultural and environmental variables and because it assumes that information automatically produces diffusion. As a result, "serious difficulties arise whenever efforts are made to apply the Hägerstrand theory in realms and epochs which are culturally distant from the modern Western world." Nondiffusion—the failure of innovations to spread—is more prevalent than diffusion, a condition Hägerstrand's system cannot accommodate.

Similarly, the Hägerstrandian system relies solely on communication and, implicitly, on the assumption that all innovations are beneficial throughout geographical space. In reality, *susceptibility* to an innovation is far more crucial, especially in a world where communication is so rapid and pervasive that it renders the friction of distance almost meaningless. In other words, we must evaluate and explain, region by region or even place by place, the differing receptiveness to innovations. The inhabitants of two regions will not respond identically to an innovation, and the geographer must seek to understand this spatial variation in receptiveness to explain diffusion or the failure to diffuse. Cultural context must not be ignored, and people often "just say no" to an innovation for good reasons. Within the context of their culture, people must perceive some advantage before they will adopt an innovation.

Globalization The modern technological age, in which improved worldwide transport and communications allow the instantaneous diffusion of ideas and innovations, has given rise to the phenomenon called **globalization.** This term refers to a world increasingly linked under the rule of capitalist economics and politics, in which international borders are diminished in importance and a worldwide marketplace is created. The implication is that globalization and an accompanying ease of diffusion will work to homogenize peoples, breaking down culture regions and eventually producing a global culture. Throughout *The Human Mosaic,* we will return to this concept, testing its validity and measuring its consequences.

Cultural Ecology

How do humans, as members of one culture or another, interact with Earth's habitat? That question defines our third theme, **cultural ecology.** Cultural geographers look on people and nature as interacting. Cultures do not exist in an environmental vacuum, for each human group and its way of life occupies a piece of the physical Earth and developed in a specific natural habitat. The cultural geographer must study the interaction between culture and environment to understand spatial variations in culture.

The word *ecology,* as used here, refers to the two-way relationship between an organism and its physical environment. It comes from two ancient Greek words: *oikos* means "house" or "habitat"; *logia* means "words" or "teachings." Thus the Greek *oikologia* could be rendered "teachings about the habitat." Cultural ecology, then, is the study of the cause-and-effect interplay between cultures and the physical environment. It is the study of (1) environmental influences on culture and (2) the impact of people, acting through their culture, on the ecosystem. An **ecosystem** is a functioning ecological system, occupying what geographer Robert Bailey calls an **ecoregion,** in which biological and cultural *Homo sapiens* lives and interacts with the physical environment.

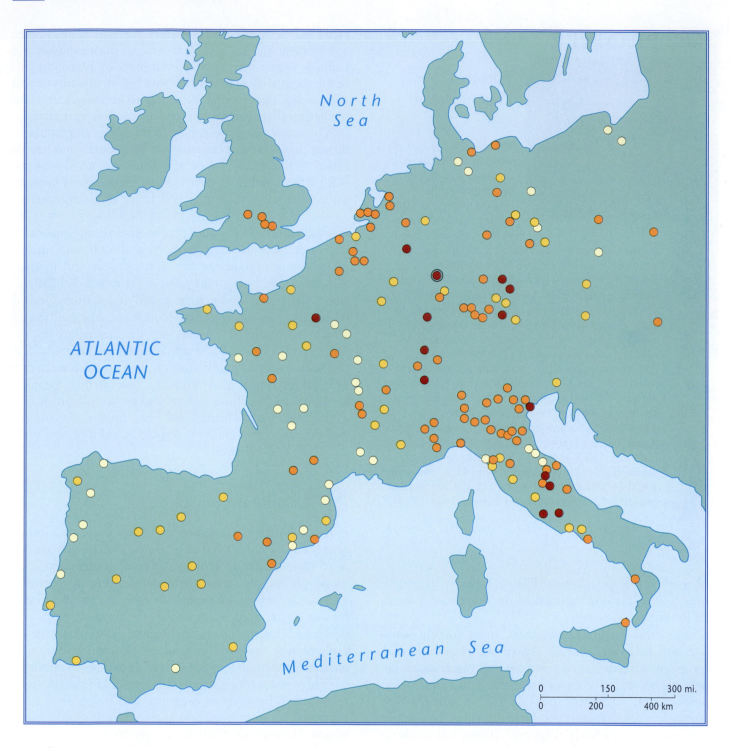

Place of innovation, 1456, Mainz

Printing shops by 1471

Printing shops by 1480

Printing shops by 1490

Printing shops by 1500

Figure 1.11

Early diffusion of the printing press in Europe. Perfected from a Chinese prototype by Johannes Gutenberg at Mainz, Germany, in the 1450s, printing presses using movable type spread rapidly through Europe. By 1500, more than 1000 print shops were operating in the 171 urban places shown. That all of the printing shops were established in cities and towns reveals hierarchical diffusion. **Does the pattern more strongly suggest expansion or relocation diffusion? (See Figure 1.10.) Is time-distance decay evident? The neighborhood effect?** The real world is always more complicated than models. (ADAPTED FROM WOLFF, 1971: 222–223.)

FOCUS ON

Monkey See, Monkey Do

Our understanding of diffusion will be enhanced if we recognize that it is natural and occurs among other animals. A story from Japan reveals this. Attendants at one seaside wildlife preserve in that country regularly put food out on the beach for an endangered native species of monkeys. The food often gets sandy, making it less appetizing. Attendants observed one monkey rinse the food with seawater before eating it. Other monkeys soon copied the practice, carefully washing off the sand, and before long food rinsing became almost universal. "Monkey see, monkey do"—that's diffusion, and we humans have no monopoly on it.

Cultural ecology implies a "two-way street," with people and the environment exerting influence on each other. Put differently, cultural ecology is based in part on the premise that culture is the human method of meeting physical environmental challenges and is thus, in some measure, an adaptive system. The term **cultural adaptation** is used in this context. This outlook borrows heavily from the biological sciences and includes the assumption that plant and animal adaptations are relevant to the study of humans. Culture serves to facilitate long-term,

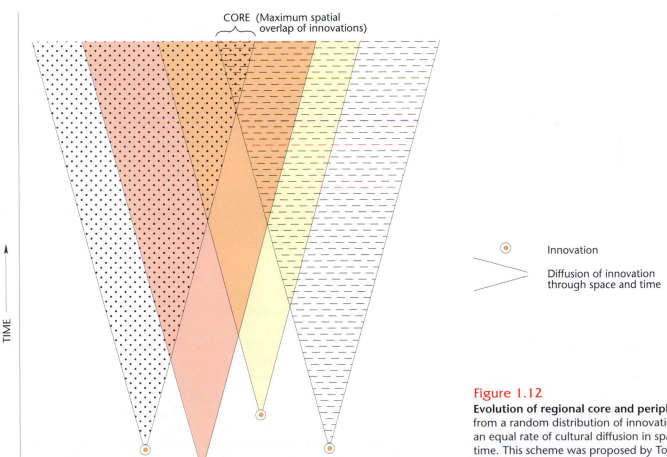

Figure 1.12
Evolution of regional core and periphery from a random distribution of innovations and an equal rate of cultural diffusion in space and time. This scheme was proposed by Torsten Hägerstrand at a symposium on diffusion held at Texas A&M University in 1984. **Can you see how time and space work together to produce core and periphery?**

successful, nongenetic human adaptation to nature and to environmental change. **Adaptive strategy** involves those aspects of culture that serve to provide the necessities of life: food, clothing, shelter, and defense. No two cultures employ the same strategy, even within the same physical environment. Such strategies involve culturally transmitted, or learned, behavior that permits a population to survive in its natural environment. Individual adaptive pathways result from the interplay between the unique character of cultures and their physical environments. Culture channels the adaptive strategy by helping to determine what is meaningful as resources in a particular setting, but the individual person exercises considerable decision-making and innovative power.

The theme of cultural ecology, the meeting ground of cultural and physical geographers, has traditionally provided a focal point for the academic discipline of geography. In fact, some geographers have proposed that geography *is* cultural ecology, that the study of the intricate relationships between people and their physical environments unites cultural and physical geography to the entire academic discipline. Although few accept this narrow definition of geography, most will agree that an appreciation of the complex people-environment relationship is necessary for concerned citizens of the twenty-first century.

Reflecting on GEOGRAPHY

Can you think of aspects of culture that have nothing to do with cultural adaptation?

Through the years, cultural geographers have developed various perspectives on the interaction between humans and the land. Four schools of thought have developed: environmental determinism, possibilism, environmental perception, and humans as modifiers of the Earth. Two of these, you will recall, are listed among the cultural geographical ideas that have changed the world (refer again to Focus On: Seven Cultural Geographical Ideas That Changed the World.)

Environmental Determinism During the first quarter of the twentieth century, many geographers adhered to the doctrine of **environmental determinism**: the belief that the physical environment is the dominant force in shaping cultures and that humankind is essentially a passive product of its physical surroundings. Humans are clay to be molded by nature. Similar physical environments produce similar cultures.

For example, environmental determinists believed that peoples of the mountains were predestined by the rugged terrain to be simple, backward, conservative, unimaginative, and freedom loving. Dwellers in the desert were likely to believe in one god but to live under the rule of tyrants. Temperate climates produced inventiveness, industriousness, and democracy. Coastlands pitted with fjords produced great navigators and fishermen.

Determinists overemphasize the role of environment in human affairs. This does not mean that environmental influences are inconsequential or that cultural geographers should not study such influences. Rather, the physical environment is only one of many forces affecting human culture and is never the sole determinant of behavior and beliefs.

Although nearly all geographers long ago abandoned environmental determinism as simplistic, the doctrine continues to resurface. For example, biologist Jared Diamond recently published an enormously popular book, *Guns, Germs, and Steel,* proposing that ecosystems rich in floral and faunal diversity were the only ones capable of producing higher civilizations. A simple answer to a complex question is always appealing—and almost always wrong.

Another very popular idea in environmental determinism is James Lovelock's **Gaia hypothesis.** He argues that there is a single planetary ecosystem, Gaia, that includes all life-forms and the land, waters, and atmosphere in which they live. Moreover, Gaia functions, almost in the manner of a single organism, as a self-regulating system that acts to control deviations in climate, to correct chemical imbalances, and to heal any other habitat damage, so as to preserve Earth as a living planet. Humans, of course, are part of Gaia, and if we become too destructive, the system will act to bring us to extinction. As with all environmental deterministic theories, the Gaia hypothesis possesses much truth and merit—but again, beware of simple answers.

Possibilism Since the 1920s, environmental determinism has fallen from favor among cultural geographers, and **possibilism** has taken its place. Possibilists do not ignore the influence of the physical environment, and they recognize that the imprint of nature exists in all cultures. However, possibilists stress that cultural heritage is at least as important as the physical environment in affecting human behavior (see Focus On: "The Facts Are Incontestable" on page 20). Each culture interacts with the habitat in different ways.

Possibilism, then, is the belief that people, rather than their environments, are the primary architects of culture (Figure 1.13). Possibilists claim that any physical environment offers a number of possible ways for a culture to develop. A culture's way of life depends on the choices people make among the possibilities that are offered by the

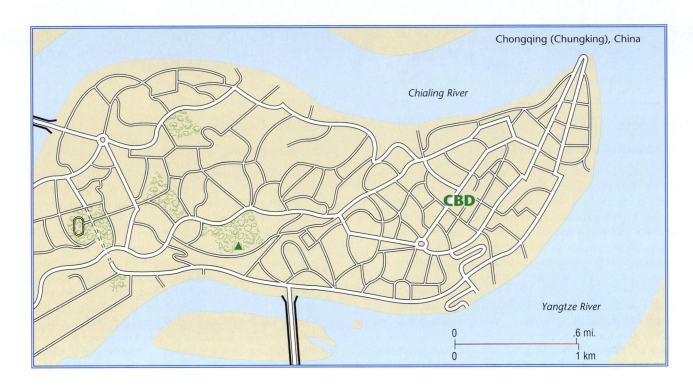

Chongqing (Chungking), China

Chialing River

CBD

▲

Yangtze River

| 0 | .6 mi. |
| 0 | 1 km |

CBD   Central business district
═══   Streets and roads
▲   Scenic overview

▱═▱   Bridge
= = =:   Tunnel
▱░▱   Park

San Francisco,
California

| 0 | 1 mi. |
| 0 | 2 km |

San Francisco Bay

CBD

▲

Pacific Ocean

▲

Figure 1.13
Chongqing (Chungking) and San Francisco. Both of these cities are among the largest in their respective countries. Both developed on elongated, hilly sites flanked on all but one side by water, and both were connected in the twentieth century by bridges leading to adjacent land across the water. In certain other respects, too—such as the use of tunnels for arterial roads—the cities are similar. Note, however, the contrast in street patterns. In Chongqing, the streets were laid out to accommodate the rugged terrain, but in San Francisco, relatively little deviation from a gridiron pattern was permitted. Note, too, that although San Francisco is much smaller in population than Chongqing, it covers a far larger area. **What do these contrasts suggest about the relative merits of environmental determinism and possibilism? About the role of culture?**

FOCUS ON

"The Facts Are Incontestable": Two Views of Creative Genius

An Environmental Determinist's View

The absence of artistic and poetic development in Switzerland and the Alpine lands [may be ascribed] to the overwhelming aspect of nature there, its majestic sublimity which paralyzes the mind. . . . This position [is reinforced] by the fact that . . . the lower mountains and hill country of Swabia, Franconia and Thuringia, where nature is gentler, stimulating, appealing, and not overpowering, have produced many poets and artists. The facts are incontestable. They reappear in France in the geographical distribution of the awards made by the Paris Salon of 1896. Judged by these awards, the [people of the] rough highlands . . . are singularly lacking in artistic instinct, while art flourishes in all the river lowlands of France. . . . French men of letters, by the distribution of their birthplaces, are essentially products of fluvial valleys and plains, rarely of upland and mountain.

From Semple, 1911. Copyright © 1939 by Carolyn W. Keene.

A Possibilist's View

All [European] patent offices report the Swiss as the foremost inventors. . . . A partial list of books published in different countries showed Switzerland to be far ahead of any other country in this sphere. . . .

The Swiss themselves attribute much importance in the growth of their industries to the religious persecutions in neighboring countries in the sixteenth and seventeenth centuries—persecutions which drove thousands of intelligent men . . . into Switzerland. The revocation of the Edict of Nantes . . . in 1685 is credited with driving sixty thousand Huguenots from France into Switzerland. They founded the silk industry of Zurich and Bern. It was a Huguenot who founded the watch business at Geneva. . . . Spanish persecution in the Low Countries and Swiss neutrality during the Thirty Years' War added to the human resources of Switzerland.

From Jefferson, 1929: 660–661.

---

environment. These choices are guided by cultural heritage. Possibilists see the physical environment as offering opportunities and limitations; people make choices among these to satisfy their needs. In short, local traits of culture and economy are the products of culturally based decisions made within the limits of possibilities offered by the environment.

Most possibilists feel that the higher the technological level of a culture, the greater the number of possibilities and the weaker the influences of the physical environment. Technologically advanced cultures, in this view, have achieved some mastery over the physical surroundings. Geographers Jim Norwine and Thomas Anderson, however, warn that even in these advanced societies "the quantity and quality of human life are still strongly influenced by the natural environment," especially climate. They argue that humankind's control of nature is anything but supreme and perhaps even illusory.

Environmental Perception Another approach to the theme of cultural ecology focuses on human perception of nature. Each person and cultural group has mental images of the physical environment, shaped by knowledge, ignorance, experience, values, and emotions. To describe such mental images, cultural geographers use the term **environmental perception.** Whereas the possibilist sees humankind as having a choice of different possibilities in a given physical setting, the environmental perceptionist declares that the choices people make will depend more on what they perceive the environment to be than on the actual character of the land. Perception, in turn, is colored by the teachings of culture. "People interact with their environment through personally and culturally apprehended behaviors," in the words of geographer Theano Terkenli.

The perceptionist maintains that people cannot perceive their environment with exact accuracy and that decisions are therefore based on distortions of reality. To understand why a cultural group developed as it did in its physical environment, geographers must know not only what the environment is like, but also what the members of the culture think it is like. An excellent example is *geomancy*, an East Asian worldview and art. **Geomancy** is a traditional system of land-use planning dictating that certain environmental settings perceived by the sages to be particularly auspicious should be chosen as the sites for houses, villages, temples, and graves. Particular configurations of terrain, compass directions, soil textures, and patterns of watercourses are perceived to be more auspicious than others. Belief in geomancy affected the location

Figure 1.14
People often settle in natural hazard areas, exposing themselves to the hazard of an earthquake and resultant landslide, as here, in the Central American country of El Salvador, where more than 1200 people died on January 13, 2001. **Why would people choose to live in such a place?** (LA PRENSA GRAFICA/AP PHOTO.)

and morphology of villages and cities in countries such as China and Korea. This particular mode of environmental perception is discussed in more detail in Chapter 3.

Some of the most productive research done by geographers in environmental perception has been on the topic of **natural hazards,** such as flooding, hurricanes, volcanic eruptions, earthquakes, insect infestations, and droughts. All cultures react to such hazards and catastrophes, but the reaction varies greatly from one cultural group to another. Some peoples reason that natural disasters and risks are unavoidable acts of the gods, perhaps even divine punishment sent down on them for their shortcomings. Often they seek to cope with the hazards by placating their gods. Others hold government responsible for taking care of them when hazards yield disasters. In Western culture, many groups regard natural hazards as problems that can be solved by technological means. If drought comes, they feel, we should find a way to manipulate the clouds and make it rain. If hurricanes kill and destroy, we should find a technology that will break up these storms.

In virtually all cultures, people knowingly inhabit hazard zones, especially floodplains, exposed coastal sites, drought-prone regions, and the environs of active volcanoes (Figure 1.14). More Americans than ever now live in areas likely to be devastated by hurricanes along the coast of the Gulf of Mexico and atop earthquake faults in California. How accurately do they perceive the hazard involved? Why have they chosen to live there? How might we minimize the eventual disasters? The cultural geographer seeks the answers to such questions and aspires, with other geographers, to mitigate the inevitable disasters through such devices as land-use planning.

Different cultures treat natural resources quite differently. What to one group is a major resource may be completely worthless or even a nuisance to another. To hunters and gatherers, the principal resources of an area may be wild berries, game animals, and flint deposits from which weapons can be fashioned. An agricultural group occupying the same environment may regard level land, fertile soils, and reliable sources of water as its most valuable resources. An industrial society may cherish the oil, coal, and other minerals buried beneath the land. We can see that people of three cultures perceive the resources of the same environment in three different ways.

Perhaps the most fundamental expression of environmental perception lies in the way different cultures see nature itself. We must understand at the outset that nature is a culturally derived concept that has different meanings to different peoples. In the **organic** view, held by many traditional groups, people are part of nature. The habitat possesses a soul, is filled with nature spirits, and must not be offended. By contrast, most Western peoples believe in the **mechanistic** view of nature. Humans are separate from and hold dominion over nature. They see the habitat as an integrated system of mechanisms governed by external forces that can be rendered into natural laws and understood by the human mind. One of the values of the Gaia hypothesis is that it at last challenges the mechanistic view of human dominion and control.

PROFILE

George Perkins Marsh

1801–1882

A few among us are gifted with the ability to perceive trends and their future consequences long before others do. George Perkins Marsh was such a person. Born to demanding Calvinist parents when America was still very young, when wilderness and open frontier were abundant and parts of his native Vermont still bore the mark of pioneering, Marsh nevertheless came to realize that people were drastically altering the physical environment, to the extent that the future of humankind was gravely endangered. At a time when the United States possessed seemingly limitless natural resources and huge expanses of fertile open land for settlement, in an era of almost unbounded optimism and belief in the steady progress of humankind toward a higher and better condition, Marsh intruded with a stern warning of future ecological disaster. His message was most effectively presented in a book, *Man and Nature; Or, Physical Geography as Modified by Human Action*, published in 1864. After Marsh's death, it made a major impact on the academic discipline of cultural geography in America. Fittingly, it was a geographer who wrote Marsh's biography.

(Source: Based on Lowenthal, 2000.)

Humans as Modifiers of the Earth Many cultural geographers, observing the environmental changes people have wrought, emphasize humans as modifiers of the habitat. This presents yet another facet of cultural ecology. In a sense, the human-as-modifier school of thought is the opposite of environmental determinism. Whereas the determinists proclaim that nature molds humankind, those cultural geographers who study the human impact on the land assert that humans mold nature (see the Profile on George Perkins Marsh).

Even in ancient times, perceptive observers realized that people influence their environment. Plato, commenting on the soil erosion in the area of Athens around 400 B.C., lamented that the once-fertile district had been stripped of its soil so that "what now remains compared to what formerly existed is like the skeleton of a sick man, all the fat and soft earth having wasted away, and only the bare framework of the land being left" (Figure 1.15). We now know that even seemingly innocuous behavior, repeated for millennia, centuries, or in some cases for mere decades, can have catastrophic effects on the environment. Plowing fields and grazing livestock can eventually denude regions, as Plato noticed. The use of air conditioners or spray cans apparently has the potential to destroy the planet's very ability to support life. Clearly, access to energy and technology is the key variable that controls the magnitude and speed of environmental alteration. Geographers seek to understand and explain the processes of environmental alteration as they vary from one culture to another and, through *applied geography*, to propose alternative, less destructive modes of behavior.

Cultural geographers began to concentrate on the human role in changing the face of the Earth long before the present level of ecological consciousness developed. They learned early on that different cultural groups have widely different outlooks on humankind's role in changing the Earth. Some, such as those rooted in the mechanistic tradition, tend to regard environmental modification as divinely approved, viewing humans as God's helpers in completing the task of creation. Humans are seen as creatures apart from, and often at war with, nature. Some other groups, organic in their view of nature, are much more cautious, taking care not to offend the forces of nature. They see humans as part of nature, meant to be in harmony with their environment (for more on this topic, see Chapter 3).

Gender differences can also play a role in the human modification of the Earth. **Ecofeminism,** a term derived from a book by Karen Warren, is a new doctrine that holds that women are inherently better ecologists and environmentalists than men. (We should not forget that the modern environmental preservation movement grew in no small part out of Rachel Carson's book *Silent Spring.*) Traditionally, women—as childbearers, gardeners, and nurturers of the family and home—dealt with life daily, whereas men—as hunters, fishers, warriors, and forest clearers—were too often associated with death and destruction. You do not have to believe that women and men are essentially different to accept the notion that women and men have a different relationship to the natural world.

Cultural Interaction

How do the many different traits within a culture influence one another? That is the central concern in our

Figure 1.15
Human modification of the Earth includes severe soil erosion. The erosion could have been caused by road building or poor farming methods. The scene is in the Amazon Basin of Brazil. **How can we adopt less destructive ways of modifying the land?** (MICHAEL NICHOLS/NATIONAL GEOGRAPHIC.)

fourth theme, **cultural interaction.** Perhaps the relationship between people and the land, the theme of cultural ecology, lies at the heart of traditional geography, but an explanation of human spatial variations also requires us to consider a whole range of cultural and economic factors. The geographer recognizes that all facets of culture are systemically and spatially intertwined. In short, cultures are complex wholes rather than conglomerations of unrelated traits. They form integrated systems in which the parts fit together causally. All aspects of culture are functionally interdependent. The theme of cultural interaction finds a place on the list of cultural geographical ideas that changed the world as "spatial organization and interdependence" (refer again to Focus On: Seven Cultural Geographical Ideas That Changed the World). Cultural interaction reflects the geographer's awareness that the immediate causes of some cultural phenomena are other cultural phenomena. A change in one element of culture requires an accommodating change in others. We cannot understand the distribution of one facet of culture without studying the variations in other facets, to see how they are interrelated and integrated causally.

For example, religious belief has the potential to influence a group's voting behavior, diet, shopping patterns, type of employment, and social standing. Traditional Hinduism, the majority religion of India, segregates people into social classes called *castes* and specifies what forms of livelihood are appropriate for each. The Mormon faith, among others, forbids the consumption of alcoholic beverages, tobacco, caffeine, and certain other products, thereby influencing both the diet and the shopping patterns of its adherents. In countless other ways, one facet of a culture influences other facets. The geographer must examine how these intracultural causal forces help determine variations in all facets of the culture.

The theme of cultural interaction, if improperly used, can lead the geographer to **cultural determinism.** Advocates of this extreme viewpoint, developed in reaction to the earlier environmental determinism, maintain that the physical environment is inconsequential as an influence on culture. Any facet of a culture, they would argue, is shaped entirely by other facets. Cultural interaction, for them, offers all the explanations for spatial variations. People and culture are the active forces; nature is passive and easily conquered. You should be wary of such claims. Julian Steward, a noted cultural ecologist, warned us long ago of "the fruitless assumption" that all culture comes from culture.

> ## Reflecting on GEOGRAPHY
> Think of examples that might support the statement that "the immediate causes of some cultural phenomena are other cultural phenomena."

The important issue of *globalization,* mentioned earlier, is as relevant to the cultural interaction theme as it is to diffusion. Globalization feeds on an intertwining of market economics, political democratization, prosperity, education, consumerism, civil tranquility, peace, industrialization, and urbanization. If globalization actually occurs in its fullest measure, it will spread through cultural diffusion and be explained by cultural interaction.

Social Science Geographers have employed two fundamentally different approaches in studying cultural interaction: the scientific and the humanistic. Those who view cultural geography as a **social science** believe that we should apply the scientific method to the study of people. Emulating physicists and chemists, they devise theories and seek regularities or universal spatial principles that cut across cultural lines to govern all of humankind. These principles ideally become the basis for laws of human spatial behavior. **Space** is the word that perhaps best connotes this scientific approach to cultural geography.

Social-scientific geographers derive much of their inspiration from the field of economics, and they tend to believe that economic causal forces are far more powerful than any others in explaining human spatial behavior. As a result, they are often accused of **economic determinism** and of pursuing a largely noncultural analysis. They

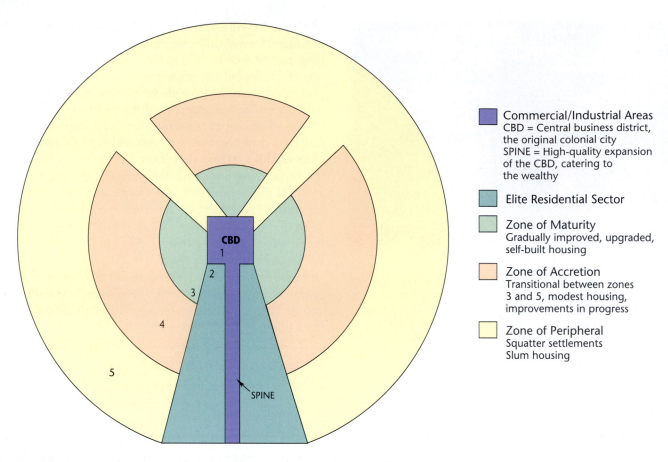

Figure 1.16

A generalized model of the Latin American city. Urban structure differs from one culture to another, and in many ways the cities of Latin America are distinctive, sharing much in common with one another. Geographers Ernst Griffin and Larry Ford developed the model diagrammed here to help describe and explain the processes at work shaping the cities of Latin America. **In what ways would this model not be applicable to cities in the United States and Canada?** (AFTER GRIFFIN AND FORD, 1980: 406.)

usually "tune out" cultural variations in their search for explanatory principles and regard networks, locations, and flows as far more important than spatial variation in culture. The social scientists also rely heavily on mathematics and geometry; they approach the task of explanation and law formulation through often-complicated multivariate statistics, equations, and diagrams.

Social scientists face a difficult problem. They have no laboratories in which to test their theories. Unlike physicists and chemists, they cannot run controlled experiments in which certain causal forces are neutralized so that others can be studied. Their solution to this problem is the technique known as **model** building. Aware that many causal forces are involved in the real world, they set up artificial model situations to focus on one or more potential factors. Hägerstrand's diagrams of different

types of diffusion and of the evolution of core-periphery patterns are examples of spatial models (see Figure 1.10). Their lack of any reference to cultural traits is a symptom of economic determinism.

Some social-scientific geographers are more sensitive to cultural variables. They devise *culture-specific* models to describe and explain certain facets of spatial behavior within specific cultures. They still seek regularities and spatial principles, but more modestly within the bounds of individual cultures. For example, several geographers proposed a model for Latin American cities, in an effort to stress similarities among them and to understand certain underlying causal forces (Figure 1.16). Obviously, no actual city in Latin America conforms precisely to their uncomplicated geometric plan. Instead, they deliberately generalized and simplified so that an urban type could be

PROFILE

Yi-fu Tuan

1930–

A native of China, and a self-described "middle-class Chinese American geographer," Yi-fu Tuan is much more than that. He is one of the best known living geographers, both within the discipline of geography and in other academic fields. In a series of more than two dozen books, he has developed a sophisticated understanding of the human experience of being in the world. His book titles range from *Landscapes of Fear* to *The Good Life* and *Topophilia*. Place, as he describes it, involves symbolism, sensation, values, and morality. It is experienced in different ways by different people, depending on their age, past experiences, and countless other personal factors. A vital aspect of human awareness is "topophilia," love people feel for certain chosen places. This humanistic view of place contrasts strongly with the simpler traditional notion of place as location. Tuan attended Oxford for undergraduate and graduate studies and received his Ph.D. in 1957 from the University of California at Berkeley. For most of his professional career, he taught at the University of Minnesota and the University of Wisconsin. He held the J. K. Wright and Vilas Chairs in Geography at the University of Wisconsin-Madison and is currently a professor emeritus in that department. You will find his wisdom quoted often in *The Human Mosaic*.

(Contributed by Prof. Paul C. Adams.)

recognized and studied. The model will look strange to a person living in a city in the United States or Canada, for it describes a very different kind of urban environment, based in another culture.

Humanistic Geography   If the social scientist seeks to minimize the differences among people in the quest for universal explanations, the **humanistic geographer** celebrates the uniqueness of each region and place. Indeed, **place** is the key word connoting the humanistic geography view, just as *space* identifies the perspective of the social-scientific geographer. The humanistic geographer

Yi-fu Tuan (see Profile) coined the word *topophilia*, literally "love of place," to describe people who exhibit a strong sense of place and the geographers who are attracted to the study of such places and peoples. Geographer Edward Relph tells us that "to be human is to have and know your place" in the geographical sense. Sense of place is among the geographical ideas that changed the world, as you will recall from earlier in this chapter. To the humanist, cultural geography is an art rather than a science. It values subjective experience over objective scientific observation. Humanistic geographers produce such works as Dan Stanislawski's *Individuality of Portugal*, in which the author describes the unique character of that country and the unpredictable forces that caused its uniqueness.

Recent decades have witnessed a resurgence of humanistic geography and the decline of the once-ascendant social-scientific approach. Daniel Gade beautifully expressed the spirit of the humanistic enterprise in geography, as well as the tension that exists between social scientists and humanists, when he declared that "economic determinism and logical positivism [or the scientific method] have failed to dispel the sense that humanistic understanding of places lies near the heart of the geographical enterprise." Anne Buttimer (see Profile), one of the leaders of the humanistic revival, declared in a similar vein that "there must be more to human geography than the *danse macabre* of materially motivated robots."

Traditional humanists in geography are as concerned about explanation as the social scientists, but they seek to explain unique phenomena—place and region—rather than seeking universal spatial laws. As the German scholar Heinrich Franke said, "The essence of place derives from a creative force at work over millennia; to comprehend and capture in prose this spirit of place is worth the sweat of the noblest among us." Indeed, most humanists doubt that laws of spatial behavior even exist. They believe in a far more chaotic world than the scientist could tolerate. Humanists reject the use of mathematics, arguing instead that the most essential human beliefs and values cannot be measured.

The debate between scientists and humanists in cultural geography is both necessary and healthy. The two groups ask different questions about place and space; not surprisingly, they obtain different answers. The scientist reduces diversity through models to seek universal causal forces, whereas the humanist exalts diversity and strives to understand the unique. Both lines of inquiry yield valuable findings. Here again we can see geography as a bridging discipline, joining the sciences and the humanities—although the resultant internal variety makes the discipline difficult to define. In *The Human Mosaic*, we

PROFILE

Anne Buttimer
1938–

(COURTESY OF ANNE BUTTIMER.)

Irish-born professor Anne Buttimer, a leader in the development of a renewed and vital humanistic perspective on geography during the past two decades, is best known for such books as *Values in Geography, Experience of Place and Space* (cowritten with David Seamon), *The Practice of Geography,* and *Geography and the Human Spirit.* She has beautifully articulated the need for a humanistic presence, a critical and cross-cultural sensitivity in the discipline, which might help us, among other things, to "rediscover wiser ways of dwelling" on the Earth. The emotional significance of place in human identity and the evolution of Western ideas about nature have been her persistent interests. Buttimer feels that humanists should not seek to divide or dominate geography, and she has consistently sought to build bridges to the sciences: "I have always been concerned about the wholeness or integrity of the geographic enterprise." In her view, the humanistic perspective, applied constructively, enhances the holistic nature of the discipline. Much honored, Professor Buttimer holds the position of Chair of Geography at the University College, Dublin. In 1986, she received an award from the Association of American Geographers, and in 1991, she received the Ellen Churchill Semple Award. In 2000, she was named president of the International Geographic Union, an organization that includes all the professional geographers of the world.

present both sides of the scientist versus humanist debate, within the theme of cultural interaction.

Cultural Landscape

What are the visible expressions of culture? What do culture regions look like? These questions provide the basis of our fifth and final theme, the **cultural landscape.** The cultural landscape is the visible, material landscape that cultural groups create in inhabiting the Earth. Cultures shape their own landscapes out of the natural habitat.

Every inhabited area has a cultural landscape, fashioned from the natural landscape, and each uniquely reflects the culture that created it (Figure 1.17). Landscape mirrors culture, and the cultural geographer can learn much about a group of people by carefully observing the landscape. Indeed, so important is this visual record of cultures that some geographers regard landscape study as geography's central interest. In fact, one of the leading journals in cultural geography is called *Landscape.*

Why is such importance attached to the cultural landscape? Perhaps part of the answer is that it visually reflects the most basic strivings of humankind: for shelter, food, and clothing. The cultural landscape reflects different attitudes about how people modify the Earth and contains valuable evidence about the origin, spread, and development of cultures, because it usually preserves various types of archaic forms. Cultures use, alter, and manipulate landscapes to express their identity. Every cultural landscape is an accumulation of human artifacts, some old and some new, some archaic and some modern.

This potential for interpretive analysis attracts many geographers to study the cultural landscape, for such visible evidence can reveal much about a past long forgotten by the present inhabitants and about the choices made and changes wrought by a people. The idea that cultural landscapes possess interpretive potential was introduced into geography by the German scholar August Meitzen (see the Profile in Chapter 8). Long ago, in observing the rural cultural landscape of central Europe, Meitzen wrote that "we walk in every village, in a sense, among the ruins of antiquity." At every step we encounter built landscape features as "readable as hieroglyphics," once we learn to decipher them, that can reveal ancient cultural diffusions, past adaptations to environment, and cultural changes through time. Echoing Meitzen, American geographer Peirce Lewis concluded that "one can read the landscape as we do a book." Taking this idea one step further, the geographer might go so far as to say that if you show us the landscape in which you live, we will tell you who you are.

Aside from containing archaic forms, landscapes also convey revealing messages about the present-day inhabitants and cultures. All humanized landscapes bear cultural meaning. Lewis further proposed that "the cultural landscape is our collective and revealing autobiography, reflecting our tastes, values, aspirations, and fears in tangible forms." Cultural landscapes offer "texts" that geographers read to discover dominant ideas and prevailing practices within a culture. For example, geographers O. F. G. Sitwell and O. S. E. Bilash proposed that "the spatial organization of settlements and the architectural form of buildings and other structures can be interpreted

Figure 1.17

Terraced cultural landscape of an irrigated rice district in Yunnan Province, China. In such areas, the artificial landscape made by people overwhelms nature and forms a human mosaic on the land. **Why is rice cultivated in such hilly areas in Asia, whereas in the United States rice farming is confined to flat plains?** (STONE.)

as the expression of values and beliefs of the people responsible for them." That is, the landscape can serve as a means to study nonmaterial aspects of culture.

Geographers now pay attention to the metaphorical and ideological qualities of landscape. Sitwell speculated about the processes that create humanized landscapes. He proposed that three figurative expressions of human worth—three cardinal virtues—are height, durability, and central location. Idioms such as "the high point of my visit," "she's at the peak of her career," "diamonds are forever," and "I love to be in the middle of things" reveal the virtues of height, durability, and centrality. If we apply these expressions of worth to architecture, then it follows that centrally located, tall structures built of steel, brick, or stone are the worthiest and most important to the particular culture in question (Figure 1.18 on the next page). In medieval Europe, cathedrals and churches best exemplified the three virtues, because they were built of stone on the central square and towered above other structures. A visitor from another land, using Sitwell's method, would correctly conclude that the church dominated and defined medieval culture. Indeed, cultural dominance, or the attempt of one group to dominate another, often appears as a major component of the landscape.

Certain other geographers, including the humanists and postmodernists, are content to study the cultural landscape for its aesthetic value, to obtain highly subjective and personal messages from the textures, colors, and forms of the built environment that help describe the essence of place. Recognizing this diversity of landscape content, Finnish geographer Tarja Keisteri distinguished the factual, concrete, physical, functioning landscape from the experiential, perceived, symbolic, aesthetic landscape, although she noted that the distinction between the two often blurs. In other words, the cultural landscape offers the possibility both for objective, scholarly analysis and for subjective, artistic interpretation. More than that, the landscape is integrally bound to the humanistic geographical concept of place and our personal sense of belonging. As geographer J. B. Jackson suggests, it provides us "with landmarks to reassure us that we are not rootless individuals without identity or place."

The physical content of the cultural landscape is both varied and complex. Most geographical studies have focused on three principal aspects of this landscape: settlement forms, land-division patterns, and architecture. In the study of *settlement forms*, cultural geographers describe and explain the spatial arrangement of buildings, roads, and other features that people construct while inhabiting an area. *Land-division patterns* reveal the way people have divided the land for economic and social uses. Such patterns vary a great deal from place to place. They range from huge corporate-owned farming complexes to small family-operated farms composed of tens or even hundreds of separate tiny parcels of land; from the fenced, privately owned home lots of American suburbs to the city's public squares. The best way to glimpse settlement and land-division patterns is through an airplane window. Looking down, you can see the multicolored abstract patterns of planted fields, as vivid as any

Figure 1.18

Folk and popular architecture both reflect culture. This log house, near Ottawa in Canada, is a folk dwelling (see Chapter 2) and stands in sharp contrast to the professional architecture of the Toronto skyline. **What conclusion might a perceptive person from another culture reach (considering the "virtues" of height, durability, and centrality) about the ideology of the culture that produced the Toronto landscape?** (LEFT: COURTESY OF TERRY G. JORDAN-BYCHKOV; RIGHT: PHOTODISC.)

modern painting, and the regular checkerboard or chaotic tangle of urban streets.

Reflecting on **GEOGRAPHY**

How does a cultural landscape differ from a natural landscape?

Perhaps no other aspect of the human landscape is as readily visible from ground level as the *architectural style* of a culture. In North American culture, different building styles catch the eye: modest white New England churches and giant urban cathedrals; hand-hewn barns and geodesic domes; wooden one-room schoolhouses and the new windowless school buildings of the urban areas. This architecture provides a vivid record of the resident culture (see Figure 1.18). For this reason, cultural geographers have traditionally devoted considerable attention to such structures.

Conclusion

The interests of cultural geographers are diverse. As geographer Daniel Gade has said, geographers investigate "the myriad components that make our planet such a complex place." It might seem to you, confronted by the various themes, subject matter, viewpoints, and methodologies described in this chapter, that cultural geographers run off in all directions, lacking unity of purpose. What does a geographer who studies architecture have in common with a colleague who studies the human role in shaping the Earth? What interests do an environmental perceptionist and a student of cultural diffusion share? Why do scholars with such apparently different interests belong in the same academic discipline? Why are they all geographers?

The answer is that regardless of the particular topic the cultural geographer studies, she or he necessarily touches on several or all of the five themes we have discussed. The themes are closely related segments of a whole. Spatial patterns in culture, as revealed by maps of culture regions, are reflected in the cultural landscape, require an ecological interpretation, imply cultural diffusion, and suggest the causal workings of cultural interaction.

As an example of how the various themes of cultural geography overlap and intertwine, let us look at one element of architecture: the traditional American log house (see Figure 1.18). Once found widely on the American frontier, many log cabins still stand in the mountains of the South and West. They are obviously part of the cultural landscape, and their spatial distribution constitutes a formal culture region that can be mapped.

Geographers who study such houses also need to employ the other themes of cultural geography to gain a complete understanding. They can use the concept of cultural diffusion to learn when and by what routes these techniques diffused and what barriers retarded their diffusion. In this particular case, the geographer would be led back to the ancient prehistory of central Europe. Further, the cultural geographer would need an ecological interpretation of the log house. How does the environment influence the log cabin? Does the use of logs for houses decline as the forests become thinned out? Do log houses differ from one climatic zone to another? Finally, the cultural geographer wants to know how the use of log houses is integrated with other facets of the culture. Did changes in the economy and standard of living lead people to reject log houses? Did changes in technology lead to more elaborate houses? Why was it once almost essential for American presidential candidates to claim birth in a log cabin? Do these humble structures possess a symbolism related to traditional American values and virtues? Why do we so often preserve log cabins as icons in our public parks and squares? Thus the geographer interested in folk housing is firmly bound by the total fabric of cultural geography, unable to segregate a particular topic such as log houses from the geographical whole. Culture region, cultural landscape, cultural interaction, cultural ecology, and cultural diffusion are interwoven.

In this manner, the cultural geographer passes from one theme to another, demonstrating the holistic nature of the discipline. In no small measure, it is this holism, this broad, multithematic approach, that distinguishes the cultural geographer from other students of culture. We believe that, by the end of the course, you will have gained a new perspective on the Earth as the home of humankind. You will agree by then, we hope, that geography is part of any good liberal arts education. Most of all, we hope you will come to treasure human cultural variety and the romance of "far-away places with strange-sounding names."

SEEING GEOGRAPHY

Why is Moscow, the present capital of Russia, not on the map, nor St. Petersburg, the previous capital?

Old map of the European part of Russia, published in 1898 but showing towns and ethnic areas as they were a thousand years earlier.

Old Map of Eastern Europe

A map is the geographer's most effective tool. It can show present or past cultural patterns. This one reveals the distribution of ethnic groups in western Russia and adjacent eastern Europe more than a thousand years ago, before Russia even existed as a country. It was compiled by some leading experts of the late nineteenth century but is still recognized as basically accurate.

What kinds of things can we learn from an old map like this? Well, for one thing, it reveals culture regions of the past. They, in turn, lead us to wonder why things changed so much in one millennium. What prompted the diffusion of ethnic Russians to dominate a much larger area by 2002? What caused the retreat or disappearance of certain other groups? (Compare with Figure 4.1.) How did Russians adapt to the new habitats they occupied, and what new cultural landscape accompanied their expansion? Why did they succeed in building a large, powerful political state while most of their neighbors failed? Why do cultural patterns change so radically? In short, how do the five themes of cultural geography—region, diffusion, ecology, interaction, and landscape—allow us to approach such questions?

Geography on the Internet

You can learn more about the discipline of geography and the subdiscipline of cultural geography on the World Wide Web. Try the following sites.

American Geographical Society

http://www.amergeog.org

America's oldest geographical organization, with a long and distinguished record; publisher of the *Geographical Review*.

Association of American Geographers

http://www.aag.org/

The leading organization of professional geographers in the United States. This site contains information about the discipline, the association, and its activities, including annual and regional meetings.

Various Definitions of Geography

www.westga.edu/~geograph/define.html

Describes geography as defined by selected famous geographers; collected at the University of West Georgia.

National Geographic Society

http://www.nationalgeographic.com/

An organization that has, for over a century, served to popularize geography with active programs of publishing and television presentations prepared for the public.

Royal Geographic Society/Institute of British Geographers

http://www.rgs.org/

Explore the activities of these allied British organizations, whose collective history goes back to the Age of Exploration and Discovery in the 1800s. . . . and don't forget to visit The Human Mosaic Online at http://www.whfreeman.com/jordan/index.htm

Sources

Bailey, Robert G. 1998. *Ecoregions: The Ecosystem Geography of the Oceans and Continents.* New York: Springer.

Blaut, James M. 1977. "Two Views of Diffusion." *Annals of the Association of American Geographers* 67: 343–349.

Carson, Rachel. 1962. *Silent Spring.* Boston: Houghton Mifflin.

Diamond, Jared. 1997. *Guns, Germs, and Steel: The Fates of Human Societies.* New York: W. W. Norton.

Franke, Heinrich. 1936. *Ostgermanische Holzbaukultur.* Breslau: W. G. Korn.

Gade, Daniel W. 1982–1983. "The French Riviera as Elitist Space." *Journal of Cultural Geography* 3: 19–28.

Griffin, Ernst, and Larry Ford. 1980. "A Model of Latin American City Structure." *Geographical Review* 70: 397–422.

Gumilev, Leo. 1990. *Ethnogenesis and the Biosphere.* Moscow: Progress Publishers.

Hägerstrand, Torsten. 1967. *Innovation Diffusion as a Spatial Process.* Translated from Swedish by Allan Pred. Chicago: University of Chicago Press.

Hanson, Susan E. (ed.). 1996. *Ten Geographic Ideas That Have Changed The World.* New Brunswick, N.J.: Rutgers University Press.

Jackson, J. B. 1994. *A Sense of Place, A Sense of Time.* New Haven, Conn.: Yale University Press.

Jefferson, Mark. 1929. "The Geographic Distribution of Inventiveness." *Geographical Review* 19: 649–661.

Keisteri, Tarja. 1990. "The Study of Changes in Cultural Landscapes." *Fennia* 168: 31–115.

Lewis, Peirce. 1983. "Learning from Looking: Geographic and Other Writing About the American Cultural Landscape." *American Quarterly* 35: 242–261.

Linton, Ralph. 1936. *The Study of Man: An Introduction.* Englewood Cliffs, N.J.: Prentice-Hall.

Lovelock, James. 1979. *Gaia: A New Look at Life on Earth.* New York: Oxford University Press.

Lowenthal, David. 2000. *George Perkins Marsh: Prophet of Conservation.* Seattle: University of Washington Press.

McIntyre, Loren. 1985. "Humboldt's Way." *National Geographic* 168: 318–351.

Meitzen, August. 1895. *Siedelung und Agrarwesen.* 3 vols. and atlas. Berlin: Wilhelm Hertz.

Norwine, Jim, and Thomas D. Anderson. 1980. *Geography as Human Ecology?* Lanham, Md.: University Press of America.

Ormrod, Richard K. 1990. "Local Context and Innovation Diffusion in a Well-Connected World." *Economic Geography* 66: 109–122.

Reed, John S. 1976. "The Heart of Dixie: An Essay in Folk Geography." *Social Forces* 54: 925–939.

Relph, Edward. 1981. *Rational Landscapes and Humanistic Geography.* New York: Barnes & Noble.

Semple, Ellen Churchill. 1911. *Influences of Geographic Environment.* New York: Henry Holt.

Sitwell, O. F. G., and Olenka S. E. Bilash. 1986. "Analyzing the Cultural Landscape as a Means of Probing the Non-Material Dimensions of Reality." *Canadian Geographer* 30: 132–145.

Stanislawski, Dan. 1959. *Individuality of Portugal.* Austin: University of Texas Press.

Steward, Julian H. 1976. *Theory of Cultural Change.* Urbana: University of Illinois Press.

Terkenli, Theano S. 1995. "Home as a Region." *Geographical Review* 85: 324–334.

van Loon, Hendrik W. 1932. *Van Loon's Geography: The Story of the World We Live In.* New York: Simon & Schuster.

Warren, Karen J. (ed.). 1997. *Ecofeminism: Women, Culture, Nature.* Bloomington: Indiana University Press.

Wolff, Philippe. 1971. *Western Languages,* A.D. *100–1500.* New York: McGraw-Hill.

Ten Recommended Books on Cultural Geography

(For additional suggested readings, see The Human Mosaic *web site:* www.whfreeman.com/jordan*)*

Anderson, Kay, and Fay Gale (eds.). 1999. *Cultural Geographies*. South Melbourne: Addison Wesley Longman Australia. The "new cultural geography" revealed in all its postmodern glory.

Buttimer, Anne. 1993. *Geography and the Human Spirit*. Baltimore: Johns Hopkins University Press. A fine and ecumenical humanistic geography that seeks an overarching unity of the discipline, by a much-honored, highly distinguished Irish geographer.

Foote, Kenneth E., Peter J. Hugill, Kent Mathewson, and Jonathan M. Smith (eds.). 1994. *Re-Reading Cultural Geography*. Austin: University of Texas Press. A beautifully compiled representative collection of some of the best works in American cultural geography at the end of the twentieth century, and a useful companion to the book edited by Wagner and Mikesell.

Goudie, Andrew. 2000. *The Earth Transformed: An Introduction to Human Impacts on the Environment*, 5th ed. Cambridge, Mass.: M.I.T. Press. A fine introduction to the theme of cultural ecology, in particular, habitat modification, as viewed by a British geographer.

Ingold, Tim. 2000. *Perception of the Environment: Essays in Livelihood, Dwelling, and Skill*. New York: Routledge. The author provides a new approach to our perception of the world around us. The core of the argument is that where we refer to cultural variation, we should instead be talking about variation in skill. Neither genetically innate nor culturally acquired, skills are incorporated into the human organism through practice and training in an environment. They are as much biological as cultural.

Johnston, R. J., Derek Gregory, and David M. Smith (eds.). 2000. *The Dictionary of Human Geography*, 4th ed. Oxford, U.K.: Basil Blackwell. A standard reference work including useful, concise definitions of all the terms you will encounter, and more.

Norton, William. 2000. *Cultural Geography: Themes, Concepts, Analyses*. London: Oxford University Press. A parallel introduction to cultural geography, from a Canadian perspective; a successful merging of traditional and "new" cultural geography by an accomplished scholar.

Thomas, William L., Jr. (ed.). 1956. *Man's Role in Changing the Face of the Earth*. Chicago: University of Chicago Press. A classic collection of mid-twentieth-century geographical writings on the human role in habitat modification. A good companion to the volume by Goudie.

Tuan, Yi-fu. 1974. *Topophilia: A Study of Environmental Perception, Attitudes, and Values*. Englewood Cliffs, N.J.: Prentice-Hall. A Chinese-born geographer's innovative and imaginative look at people's attachment to place, a central concern of cultural geography.

Wagner, Philip L., and Marvin W. Mikesell. 1962. *Readings in Cultural Geography*. Chicago: University of Chicago Press. A classic collection, edited by two distinguished Berkeley-trained cultural geographers, presenting the subdiscipline as it was at mid-twentieth century and developing the device of five themes.

Major Journals

Annals of the Association of American Geographers. Volume 1 was published in 1911. The leading scholarly journal of American geographers.

Ecumene: A Geographical Journal of Environment, Culture, Meaning. Volume I was published in 1994.

Journal of Cultural Geography. Published semiannually by the Department of Geography, Oklahoma State University, Stillwater, Okla. Volume 1 was published in 1980.

Landscape. An interdisciplinary journal devoted to the cultural landscape. Cultural geographers regularly contribute articles. Volume 1 was published in 1951.

Progress in Human Geography. A quarterly British journal providing critical appraisal of developments and trends in the discipline. Volume 1 was published in 1977.

Social and Cultural Geography. Volume 1 was published in 2000 by Routledge, Taylor, & Francis Ltd. in Great Britain.

What makes one father-daughter pair so very different from the other?

Two American father-daughter couples. (LEFT, RICHARD T. NOWITZ/CORBIS; RIGHT, ROB GAGE/FPG INTERNATIONAL.)
Turn to Seeing Geography *on page 69 for an in-depth analysis of the above question.*

CHAPTER
2

PARALLEL WORLDS
Two Types of Culture

Have you ever read the science-fiction story about the planet, a twin of Earth, that lies in our solar system but is directly on the opposite side of the Sun in the same orbit, so that we cannot see it or even know of its existence? On that planet, goes the story, live our alter egos, in a parallel world. Well, parallel worlds really do exist—but they are here on Earth itself, housed in two fundamentally different types of culture. Cultural geographers have studied both types, and this dichotomy provides an appropriate departure point for our journey through the discipline.

The first, and more ancient, is **folk culture.** The word *folk* describes a rural people who live in an old-fashioned way—a people holding to a simpler lifestyle less influenced by modern technology. A folk culture is a rural, cohesive, conservative, largely self-sufficient group that is homogeneous in custom and race, with a strong family or clan structure and highly developed rituals. Order is maintained through sanctions based in the religion or family, and interpersonal relationships are strong. Tradition is paramount, and change comes infrequently and slowly. There is relatively little division of labor into specialized duties. Rather, each person performs a variety of tasks, although duties may differ by gender. Most goods are handmade, and a subsistence economy prevails. Individualism is generally weakly developed in folk cultures, as are social classes.

In the poorer countries of the underdeveloped world, folk cultures are still common, in contrast to industrialized countries such as the United States and Canada, where unaltered folk cultures no longer exist, though

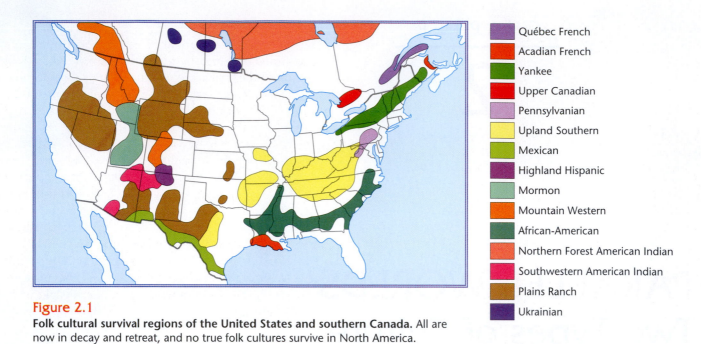

Figure 2.1

Folk cultural survival regions of the United States and southern Canada. All are now in decay and retreat, and no true folk cultures survive in North America.

Legend:
- Québec French
- Acadian French
- Yankee
- Upper Canadian
- Pennsylvanian
- Upland Southern
- Mexican
- Highland Hispanic
- Mormon
- Mountain Western
- African-American
- Northern Forest American Indian
- Southwestern American Indian
- Plains Ranch
- Ukrainian

many remnants can be found (Figure 2.1). Perhaps the nearest modern equivalent in North America is the Amish, a German-American farming sect that largely renounces the products and labor-saving devices of the industrial age, though they do practice commercial agriculture. In Amish areas, horse-drawn buggies still serve for local transportation, and the faithful own no automobiles or appliances. The Amish central religious concept of *demut,* "humility," clearly reflects the weakness of individualism and social class so typical of folk cultures, and a corresponding strength of Amish group identity is evident. The denomination, a variety of the Mennonite faith, provides the principal mechanism for maintaining order.

Folk culture includes both material and nonmaterial elements. **Material culture** includes all objects or "things" made and used by members of a cultural group: tools, utensils, food, buildings, furniture, clothing, artwork, musical instruments, vehicles, and other physical objects. The elements of material culture are visible. By contrast, **nonmaterial culture,** or *folklore,* includes the wide range of tales, songs, lore, beliefs, superstitions, and customs that passes from generation to generation as part of an oral or written tradition. Folk dialects, religions, and music all belong to nonmaterial culture. **Folk geography,** a term coined by Eugene Wilhelm, may be defined as the study of the spatial patterns and ecology of these traditional groups.

Popular culture, by contrast, occurs in large heterogeneous groups of people concentrated mainly in urban areas. Popular material goods are mass-produced by machines in factories, and a money economy prevails. Relationships among individuals are more numerous but less personal than in folk cultures, and the family structure is weaker. People are more mobile, less attached to place and environment. A distinct division of labor, reflected in myriad highly specialized professions and jobs, characterizes the earning of a livelihood, and considerable leisure time is available to most people. Secular institutions of control—such as the police, army, and courts— take the place of family and church in maintaining order. Individualism is strongly developed. If a single hallmark of popular culture exists, it is *change.* Words such as *growth, progress, fad,* and *trend* crop up often in newspapers and conversations. So pervasive is change that some people prove unable to cope with it, leading them to an insecurity expressed by the term *future shock.*

If all these characteristics seem rather commonplace and "normal" it should not be surprising (Figure 2.2). You are, after all, firmly enmeshed in the popular culture, or else you would not be attending college to seek a higher education. The large majority of people in Europe, the United States, Canada, and other "developed" countries now belong to the popular rather than the folk culture. Industrialization, urbanization, the rise of formal education, and the resultant increase in leisure time all contributed to the spread of popular culture and the consequent retreat of folklife. We and our recent ancestors abandoned the hidebound, secure, stable, traditional folk culture to embrace with enthusiasm the free, open, dynamic lifestyle offered by popular culture.

PROFILE

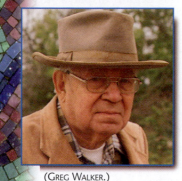

(GREG WALKER.)

Fred B. Kniffen

1900–1993

A native of Michigan, Fred Kniffen spent much of his boyhood in the transplanted New England folk culture of the upper Midwest. At the University of California at Berkeley, Kniffen studied under cultural geographer Carl Sauer and anthropologist Alfred Kroeber. This combination of geography and anthropology in his doctoral degree work provided the basis of Kniffen's interest and expertise in folk geography. He is acknowledged as the founder of American folk geography.

Beginning in 1929, Kniffen worked in the Department of Geography and Anthropology at Louisiana State University, Baton Rouge, where he was Boyd Professor Emeritus in his later years. He wrote some 125 articles and books, covering his exceptional range of interest. In his list of publications are works on folk houses, covered bridges, outdoor folk ovens, log construction, and other items of traditional material culture. Kniffen received many honors and tributes, most notably the honorary presidency of the Association of American Geographers and an Honors Award from the same group in 1978.

For more information, see Walker and Richardson, 1994.

In reality, all of culture presents a continuum, on which "folk" and "popular" represent extremes. Many gradations between the two are possible. Disadvantages, as well as the previously mentioned benefits, become apparent as one moves toward the popular end of the continuum. We forfeited much in discarding folkways. Certainly, it would not be proper to regard popular culture as somehow superior to folk culture. With popularization, we weakened both family structure and interpersonal relationships. One prominent cultural geographer, Fred Kniffen (see Profile), who lived in both folk and popular settings, felt that of all the elements of popular culture and the age of technology, "only two would I dislike to give up: inside plumbing and medical advances."

We can use our five themes of cultural geography—*region, diffusion, ecology, interaction,* and *landscape*—to study both folk and popular culture. Let's begin with culture regions.

 ## Folk and Popular Culture Regions

How do folk and popular cultures vary geographically? As a rule, elements of folk culture exhibit major variations from place to place and minor variations over time, whereas popular culture displays less difference from region to region but changes rapidly over time. For this reason, the theme of culture region is particularly well suited to the study of folk culture. *Formal* folk regions

Figure 2.2

Popular culture is reflected in every aspect of life, from the clothes we wear to the recreational activities that occupy our leisure time. (LEFT: ALEX MAJOLI/MAGNUM; RIGHT: STUART FRANKLIN/MAGNUM.)

Figure 2.3

A multilevel barn with projecting "forebay," central Pennsylvania. Every folk culture region possesses distinctive forms of traditional architecture. Of Swiss origin, the forebay barn is one of the main identifying material traits of the Pennsylvania folk culture region. This barn type crossed the Atlantic with German-speaking Swiss colonists in the 1700s. (Courtesy of Terry G. Jordan-Bychkov.)

can be delimited on the basis of both material and non-material elements.

Material Folk Culture Regions

In many parts of the world, material folk culture remains abundant. Although folk culture has largely vanished from the United States and Canada, vestiges remain in various areas of both countries. Figure 2.1 shows culture regions in which the material artifacts of 15 different North American folk cultures survive in some abundance, although they are in decline. Each region possesses many distinctive relics of material culture.

For example, the strongly Teutonic *Pennsylvanian* folk culture region features an unusual Swiss-German type of barn, distinguished by an overhanging upper-level "forebay" on one eave side (Figure 2.3). The *Yankee* folk region boasts an elaborate traditional gravestone art, featuring "winged death heads," and the attachment of barns to the rear of houses. The *Upland South* is noted in part for the abundant survival of notched-log construc-

tion, used in building a variety of distinctive house types. The *African-American* folk region displays such features as the "scraped-earth" cemetery, from which all grass is laboriously removed to expose the bare ground (Figure 2.4); the banjo, an African instrument by origin; and head kerchiefs worn by women. The *Québec French* folk region is revealed in grist windmills with sturdy stone towers and *pétanque,* a bowling game played with small metal balls, among other traits. The *Mormon* folk culture can be identified by distinctive hay derricks and clustered farm villages with a checkerboard street pattern. The Western *Plains Ranch* folk culture produced such material items as the "beef wheel," a windlass used during butchering (Figure 2.5). These examples of material artifacts are only a few of the many that survive from various folk regions.

Folklore Regions

Nonmaterial folk culture displays regional contrasts in much the same way as material folk culture does. Folk geographers consider diverse nonmaterial phenomena, such as folktales, dance, music, myths, legends, and proverbs. Nowhere has folklore been more thoroughly studied than in Europe, where some of the first research in folk geography appeared early in the nineteenth century. Even as these folk cultures were collapsing, they underwent detailed cataloging and analysis. It is ironic that today we know more about this vanished or moribund lore than we

Figure 2.4

A "scraped-earth" folk graveyard in East Texas. The laborious removal of all grass from such cemeteries is an African-derived custom. Long ago, this practice diffused from the African-American folk culture region to Caucasians in the southern coastal plain of the United States to become simply a "Southern" custom. **How might such cultural diffusion across racial lines occur?** (Courtesy of Terry G. Jordan-Bychkov.)

do about most surviving folk cultures in the world. An excellent example comes from Switzerland, where a rich folklore of German, French, Italian, and Raeto-Romanic peoples appears in perhaps the finest of all works in folk geography: the great multivolume *Atlas der Schweizerischen Volkskunde* (*Atlas of Swiss Folklore*). Figure 2.6 shows an example from that atlas, revealing the profound spatial variation of nonmaterial folk culture.

Folk music is another nonmaterial aspect of culture that reveals a highly regionalized character. Alan Lomax, an expert on the English-language folk songs of North America, recognized four folk-song culture regions in the United States: the *Northern, Southern, Western,* and *African-American* song families. The Northern folk-song tradition, characterized by unaccompanied solo singing in hard, open-voiced, clear tones with unison on the refrains, is based largely in British ballads and has not deviated greatly from the English prototype. In the Southern folk-song tradition, by contrast, unison singing is rare and the solo is high-pitched and nasal. Combining English and Scotch-Irish elements, Lomax's Southern style features ballads that are more guilt-ridden and violent than those of the North. The Western style, according to Lomax, is a blend of the Southern and Northern traditions. The African-American folk-song family contains

Figure 2.5

"Beef wheel" in the ranching country of the Harney Basin in central Oregon. This windlass device hoists the carcass of a slaughtered animal to facilitate butchering. Derived, as was much of the local ranching culture, from Hispanic Californians, the beef wheel represents the folk material culture of ranching. (COURTESY OF TERRY G. JORDAN-BYCHKOV.)

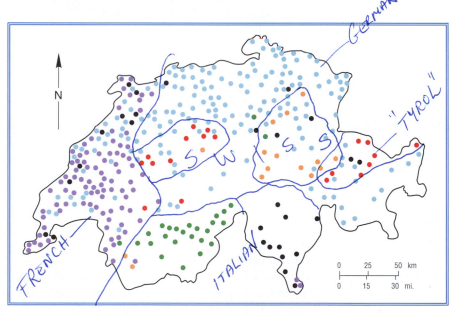

- ● Purchased at store
- ● Monks of the forest or hermits
- ● Church, chapel, or monastery
- ● Cabbage or pumpkin
- ● Hollow tree or log
- ● Stork

Figure 2.6

Switzerland: Where do newborn children come from? When you were little and asked your parents where babies come from, did you get the old runaround about storks or some other equally absurd answer? If so, don't judge them too harshly, for they were only perpetuating an old folk custom of deception. Different Swiss provinces and districts are characterized by distinctive evasive answers to this age-old question. Nonmaterial folk culture can thus provide an index to culture regions. **Where exactly would you draw the boundaries of the culture regions on this map? How many culture regions would you designate?** Cultural geographers always face the same difficult decisions in delimiting culture regions. (AFTER GEIGER, 1950, VOL. 2, PART 4: PLATES 202–205.)

Figure 2.7

Placelessness exemplified: scenes almost anywhere, developed world. Guess where these pictures were taken. The answers are provided at the end of the chapter. Compare these views to Figure 2.8. (See also Curtis, 1982. Photo at left: Donald Dietz/Stock Boston, Inc.; Top Right: David Frazier/Photo Researchers; Bottom Right: Courtesy of Terry G. Jordan-Bychkov.)

both African and British elements, featuring polyrhythmic songs of labor and worship with instrumental accompaniment; chorus group singing; clapping; swaying of the body; and a strong, surging beat. African-American and white Southern styles coexist across much of the coastal plain South, each still closely linked to its respective racial group. Both traditions display distinctive melodies, instrumentation, and motifs.

> ### Reflecting on **GEOGRAPHY**
>
> The disadvantages of living in a folk culture are evident. What advantages to such a life occur to you?

Placelessness?

Superficially, at least, popular culture varies less from place to place than does folk culture. In fact, Canadian geographer Edward Relph goes so far as to propose that popular culture produces a profound **placelessness,** a spa-

tial standardization that diminishes regional variety and demeans the human spirit, and James Kunstler speaks of the "geography of nowhere" to describe modern America. One place seems pretty much like another, robbed of its geographical essence by the pervasive influence of a continental or even worldwide popular culture (Figure 2.7). When compared with regions and places produced by folk culture, rich in their uniqueness, the geographical face of popular culture often seems expressionless (Figure 2.8). The greater mobility of people in popular culture weakens attachment to place and compounds the problem of placelessness. Geographer Richard Pillsbury laments that "so much regional identity is breaking apart today," noting also that "it is becoming more difficult to understand where America begins and the rest of the world ends." McDonald's, Levi's, CNN, and shopping malls have spread everywhere, it seems. *Globalization* looms.

But is popular culture truly regionless and placeless? The overwhelming verdict of cultural geography is no. In his book *The Clustering of America,* Michael Weiss argues that "American society has become increasingly frag-

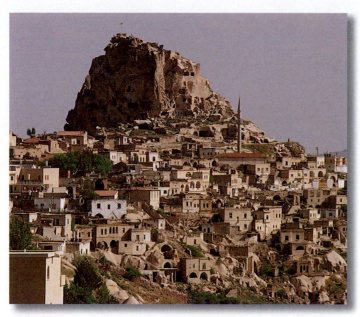

Figure 2.8
Retaining a sense of place: a hill town in Cappadocia Province, Turkey. This town, produced by a folk culture, exhibits striking individuality. **How can you tell that this is not a popular culture landscape?** (Courtesy of Terry G. Jordan-Bychkov.)

mented" and identifies 40 "lifestyle clusters" based on postal zip codes. "Those five digits can indicate the kinds of magazines you read, the meals you serve at dinner," and what political party you support. "Tell me someone's zip code and I can predict what they eat, drink, drive—even think." The lifestyle clusters, each of which is a formal culture region, bear Weiss's colorful names—such as "Gray Power" (upper-middle-class retirement areas), "Old Yankee Rows" (blue- and white-collar older ethnic neighborhoods of the Northeast), and "Norma Rae–Ville" (lower- and middle-class Southern mill towns named for the Sally Field movie about the tribulations of a union organizer in a textile manufacturing town) (Figure 2.9). For example, Old Yankee Rowers typically have a high-school education, enjoy bowling and ice hockey, and are three times as likely as the average American to live in rowhouses or duplexes. Residents of Norma Rae–Ville are mostly nonunion factory workers, have trouble making ends meet, and consume twice as much canned stew as the national average. In short, a whole panoply of popular subcultures exists in America and the world at large, each possessing its own belief system, spokespeople, dress code, and lifestyle.

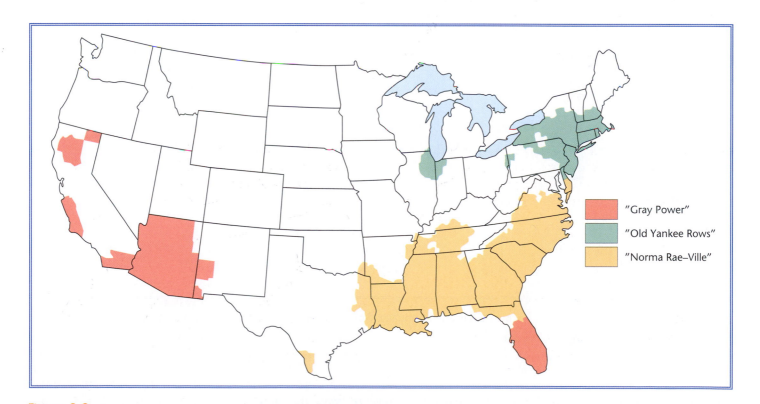

"Gray Power"

"Old Yankee Rows"

"Norma Rae–Ville"

Figure 2.9
Three examples of the 40 lifestyle clusters in U.S. popular culture. Any of the 200 television market areas that contained individual zip code areas with above-average occurrence of the lifestyle indicated are shaded in their entirety, even though only a portion of the market area was so characterized. For a description of each lifestyle, see the text. **Are these regions accurately described? What would you change?** (Adapted from Weiss, 1988: 307, 335, 362.)

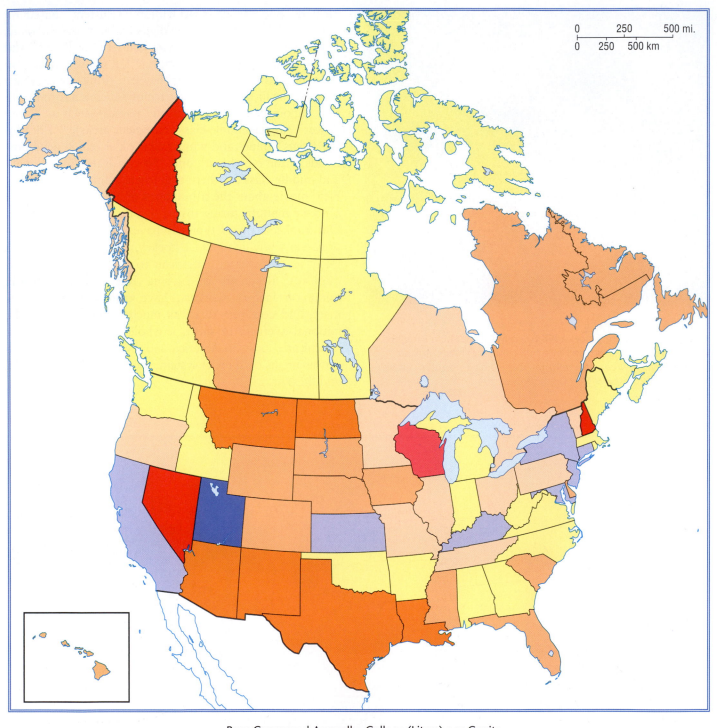

Beer Consumed Annually: Gallons (Liters) per Capita

■ Under 15 (57)	■ 20–22 (76–83)	■ 24–26 (91–98)	■ 28–30 (106–114)
■ 15–20 (57–76)	■ 22–24 (83–91)	■ 26–28 (98–106)	■ Over 30 (114)

Figure 2.10

The cultural geography of commercial beer consumption in North America. Why is the Canadian border so evident? What causal factors might be at work? New Hampshire's high values very likely reflect its relatively low tax on alcohol and its aggressive marketing of alcohol, with large stores on major interstates near the Massachusetts border. The regional pattern of wine or hard liquor consumption differs from that of beer. (SOURCES: ROONEY AND BUTT, 1978; BEER INSTITUTE, WASHINGTON, D,C,, HTTP://WWW.BEERINSTITUTE.ORG; AND THE *ANNUAL STATISTICAL BULLETIN*, BREWERS ASSOCIATION OF CANADA.)

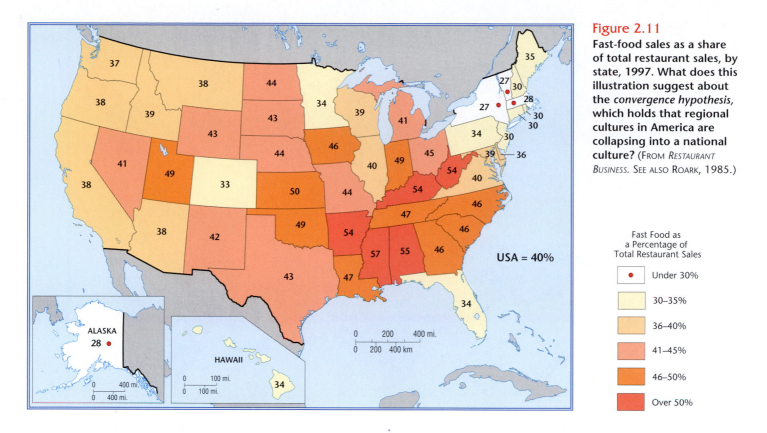

Figure 2.11
Fast-food sales as a share of total restaurant sales, by state, 1997. What does this illustration suggest about the *convergence hypothesis*, which holds that regional cultures in America are collapsing into a national culture? (FROM *RESTAURANT BUSINESS*. SEE ALSO ROARK, 1985.)

USA = 40%

Fast Food as a Percentage of Total Restaurant Sales

- • Under 30%
- 30–35%
- 36–40%
- 41–45%
- 46–50%
- Over 50%

Reflecting on GEOGRAPHY

Do you live in a "placeless" place, in "nowhere U.S.A."? If not, how is a distinctive regional form of popular culture reflected in your region?

Food and Drink

A persistent formal regionalization of popular culture is vividly revealed by what we eat and drink, which varies markedly from one part of a country to another and in different parts of the world. The highest per capita levels of U.S. beer consumption occur in the West, with the notable exception of Mormon Utah (Figure 2.10). Whiskey made from corn, manufactured both legally and illegally, has been a traditional Southern alcoholic beverage, whereas Californians place more importance on wine.

Foods consumed by members of the North American popular culture also vary from place to place. In the South, barbecued pork and beef, fried chicken, and hamburgers enjoy far greater than average popularity, whereas more pizza and submarine sandwiches are consumed in the North, the focus of Italian immigration. Indeed, pizza diffused to the southern states only in the mid-1950s.

Fast foods might seem to epitomize popular culture, yet the importance of such foods varies greatly within the United States (Figure 2.11). The stronghold of the fast-food industry is the American South; the Northeast has the fewest fast-food restaurants. The contrast is both profound and revealing. We should not expect geographical uniformity within the popular culture: placelessness has been overstated. Music provides another example.

Popular Music

The popular culture has spawned many different styles of music, all of which reveal geographical patterns in levels of acceptance. Pop musicians often receive adulation of a magnitude reserved for deities in folk culture. Elvis Presley epitomized both popular music and the associated cult of personality. Even today, a generation after his death, he retains an important place in American popular culture.

Elvis also illustrates the vivid geography of that culture. In the sale of Presley memorabilia, the nation reveals a split personality. The main hotbeds of Elvis worship lie in the eastern states, while the King of Rock and Roll is largely forgotten out West. Although it raises more questions than it answers, Figure 2.12 on the next page leaves no doubt that popular culture varies regionally.

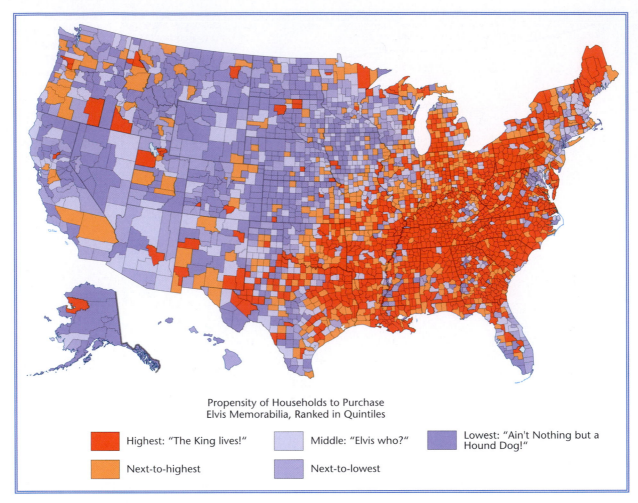

Propensity of Households to Purchase
Elvis Memorabilia, Ranked in Quintiles

Highest: "The King lives!"   Middle: "Elvis who?"   Lowest: "Ain't Nothing but a Hound Dog!"

Next-to-highest   Next-to-lowest

Figure 2.12

Purchases of Elvis Presley memorabilia, 1990s. The hotbeds of Elvis adoration lie mainly in the eastern United States, while most Westerners can take him or leave him. **What cultural factors might underlie this "fault line" in the geography of popular culture?** (Redrawn, based on data collected by Bob Lunn of DICI, Bellaire, Texas, and published by Edmonson and Jacobsen, 1993.)

Sports

Abundant leisure time is another hallmark of popular culture, and North Americans devote much of that time to watching or participating in sports. Few aspects of popular culture are as widely publicized as our games, both amateur and professional. From Little League through high school, college, Olympic, and professional contests, athletics receive almost daily attention from many of us. In fact, the rise of competitive spectator sports parallels closely the development of popular culture in North America and Europe. The further we withdrew from our folk tradition, the more important organized games became. The nineteenth century, which witnessed the industrialization and resultant popularization of our culture, also gave us football, ice hockey, baseball, soccer, and basketball—our major spectator sports. Although our folk ancestors played a variety of games, these were limited mainly to children or helped hone skills needed in everyday life. Relatively little time or attention was devoted to them. Certainly, the concept of professional athletes and admission-paying spectators is unique to the popular culture and is not to be found in folk cultures. Our folk ancestors knew nothing even remotely like our Super Bowl, World Series, Stanley Cup, or NCAA tournaments.

As commercial spectator sports diffused throughout North America, distinct regional contrasts also developed. Hotbeds of football arose in some regions, basketball became a winter mania in certain areas, baseball came to rule supreme in some states, and ice hockey ascended in still other regions. Participant sports reveal similar regionalization. Skiing, tennis, bowling, and golf vary greatly in popularity from one region to another. Some of these strong regional differences are summarized in Figure 2.13.

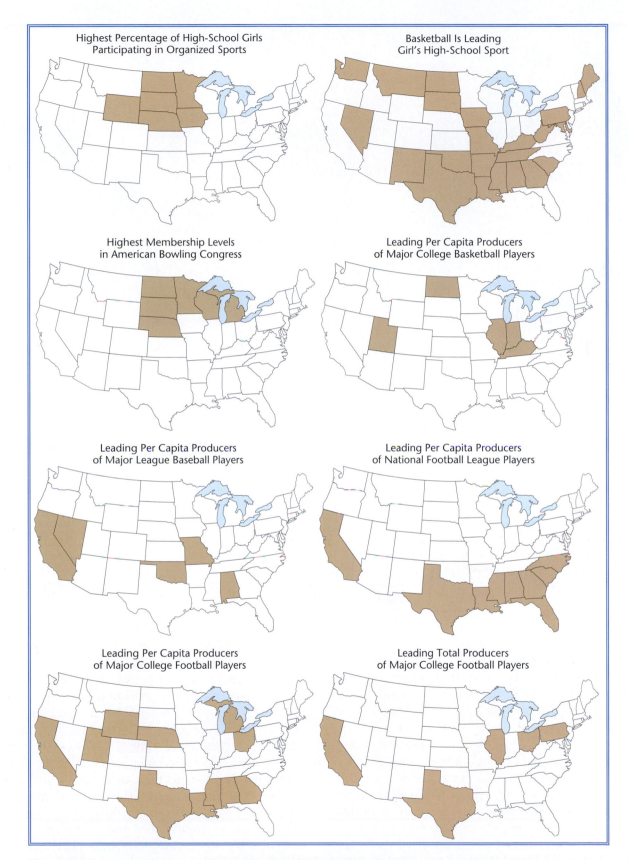

Figure 2.13
Selected geographical variations in American sports. What factors might help explain these patterns? (SOURCES: PILLSBURY, 1990A; ROONEY, 1974: 118, 152, 179; SHORTRIDGE, 1987: 70, 71; ROONEY, 1988.)

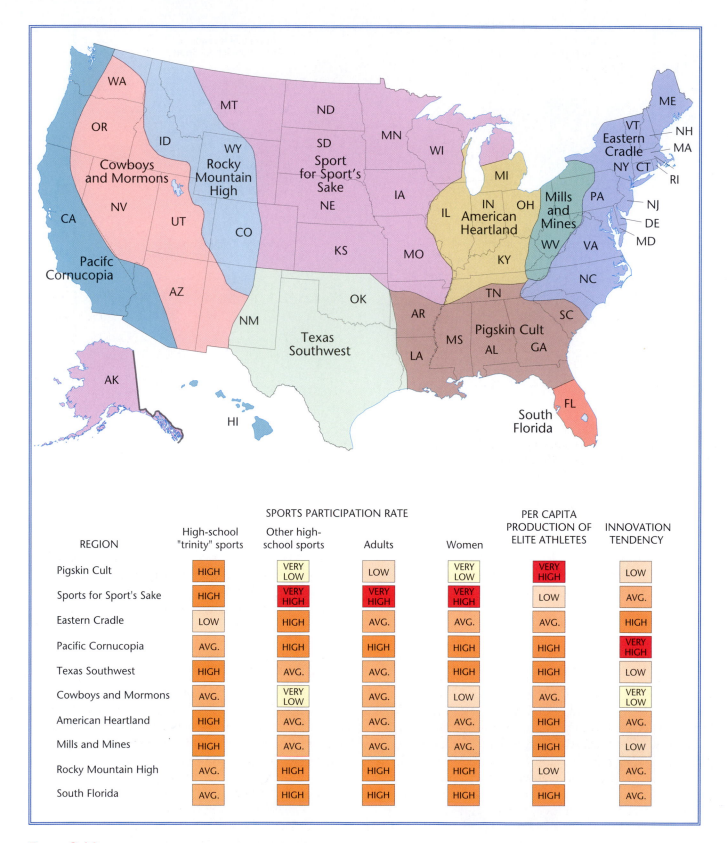

REGION	SPORTS PARTICIPATION RATE				PER CAPITA PRODUCTION OF ELITE ATHLETES	INNOVATION TENDENCY
	High-school "trinity" sports	Other high-school sports	Adults	Women		
Pigskin Cult	HIGH	VERY LOW	LOW	VERY LOW	VERY HIGH	LOW
Sports for Sport's Sake	HIGH	VERY HIGH	VERY HIGH	VERY HIGH	LOW	AVG.
Eastern Cradle	LOW	HIGH	AVG.	AVG.	AVG.	HIGH
Pacific Cornucopia	AVG.	HIGH	HIGH	HIGH	HIGH	VERY HIGH
Texas Southwest	HIGH	AVG.	AVG.	HIGH	HIGH	LOW
Cowboys and Mormons	AVG.	VERY LOW	AVG.	LOW	AVG.	VERY LOW
American Heartland	HIGH	AVG.	AVG.	AVG.	HIGH	AVG.
Mills and Mines	HIGH	AVG.	AVG.	AVG.	HIGH	LOW
Rocky Mountain High	AVG.	HIGH	HIGH	HIGH	LOW	AVG.
South Florida	AVG.	HIGH	HIGH	HIGH	HIGH	AVG.

Figure 2.14

Sports regions of the United States. "Trinity" sports are baseball, basketball, and football. "Innovations" refers to the willingness to try new, nontraditional sports. (REDRAWN FROM ROONEY AND PILLSBURY, 1992.)

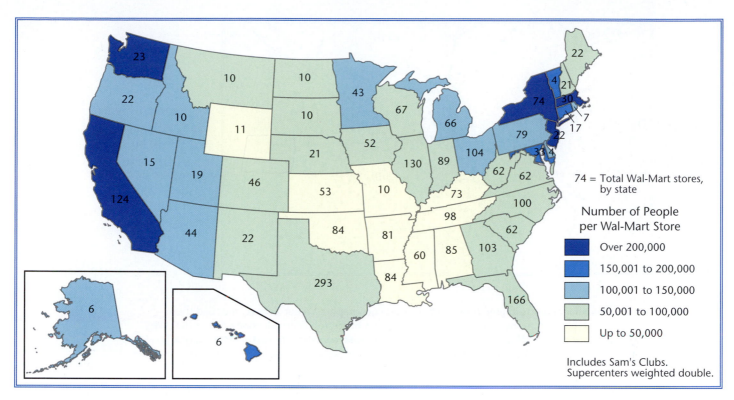

Figure 2.15

Wal-Mart in the United States, 1999. This retail chain has more than 2800 stores nationwide, but the geographical distribution is uneven, in terms of both store numbers and population per store. The company is presently expanding rapidly into the Northeast and the West Coast, reducing the regional disparities. It also has built or acquired 179 stores in Canada. (SOURCES: WAL-MART COMPANY REPORTS; U.S. CENSUS BUREAU.)

John Rooney, who initiated the geographical study of sports in popular culture back in the 1960s, and Richard Pillsbury summed up these and other regional contrasts in American athletics by designating 10 "sports regions," each with its own special character (Figure 2.14).

Shopping

Do we really all shop at the same chain stores in the popular culture? No—no more than we all listen to the same music, eat the same food, or watch the same sports. Wal-Mart provides an example. This popular chain retailer, mapped on a per capita basis, exhibits a classic core-periphery pattern (Figure 2.15). Significantly, the core area centers on the state of Arkansas, where Wal-Mart first appeared. Every other retail chain has a similar pattern of core and periphery. Popular culture has a geography.

Vernacular Culture Regions

Rather than being the intellectual creation of the professional geographer, a **vernacular culture region** is the prod-

uct of the spatial perception of the population at large. A vernacular culture region is not a formal region based on carefully chosen criteria but a composite of the mental maps of the people. Such regions vary greatly in size, from small districts covering only part of a city or town to huge, multistate areas. Like most other geographical regions, they often overlap and usually have poorly defined borders.

Almost every part of the industrialized Western world offers examples of vernacular regions based in the popular culture. Figure 2.16 on the next page shows some sizable vernacular regions in North America. Geographer Wilbur Zelinsky (see Profile on page 47) compiled these regions by determining the most common name for businesses appearing in the white pages of urban telephone directories. One curious feature of the map is the sizable, populous district—in New York, Ontario, eastern Ohio, and western Pennsylvania—where no affiliation to province is perceived. Using a different source of information, geographer Joseph Brownell sought to delimit the popular "Midwest" in 1960 (Figure 2.17 on the next page). He sent out questionnaires to postal employees in

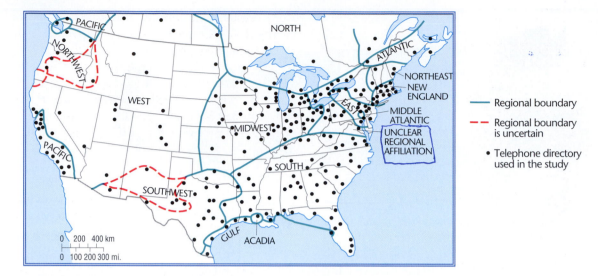

Figure 2.16

Some vernacular regions in North America. Cultural geographer Wilbur Zelinsky mapped these regions on the basis of business names in the white pages of metropolitan telephone directories. **Why are names containing "West" more widespread than those containing "East"? What might account for the areas where no region name is perceived?** (ADAPTED FROM ZELINSKY, 1980A: 14.)

the midsection of the United States, from the Appalachians to the Rockies, asking each whether, in his or her opinion, the community lay in the "Midwest." The results identified a vernacular region in which the residents considered themselves Midwesterners. A similar survey done 20 years later, using student respondents, revealed a core-periphery pattern for the Midwest (see Figure 2.17). As befits an element of popular culture, the vernacular region is often perpetuated by the mass media, especially radio and television.

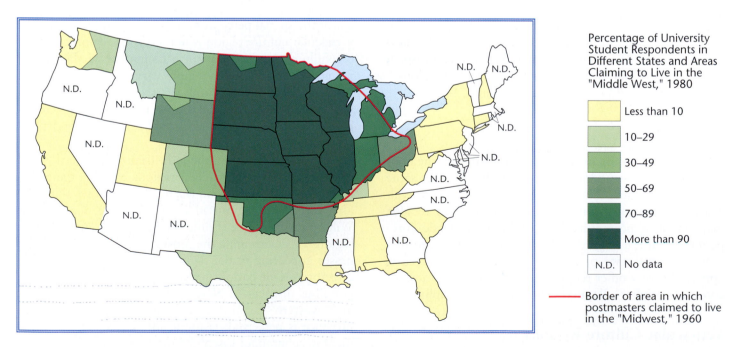

Figure 2.17

The vernacular Middle West or Midwest. Two surveys, taken a generation apart and using two different groups of respondents, yielded similar results. (SOURCE: BROWNELL, 1960: 83; SHORTRIDGE, 1989.)

PROFILE

Wilbur Zelinsky
1921–

Wilbur Zelinsky, professor emeritus at Pennsylvania State University, is one of America's most prominent cultural geographers. An Illinoisan by birth, but a "northeasterner by choice and conviction," Zelinsky received his education at the University of California at Berkeley, where he was a student of the famous geographer Carl Sauer (see Chapter 8). He received his doctorate in 1953.

As the frequent references in this chapter to his work attest, Zelinsky has made many important geographical studies of American popular culture, ranging from the diffusion of classical place names to the spatial patterns of personal given names and of religious denominations. One of his most ambitious and imaginative projects was a provocative assessment of the impact of increasingly powerful personal preference on the spatial character of American society. In 1973, Professor Zelinsky published his widely acclaimed book, *The Cultural Geography of the United States,* which went into a second edition in 1992. In addition to his research in popular culture, Zelinsky has made substantial contributions to the fields of population and folk geography.

In 1966, Zelinsky received the Award for Meritorious Contributions to the Field of Geography, presented by the Association of American Geographers. He served as president of the AAG from 1972 to 1973.

For a representative selection of Zelinsky's work, see the works listed in Sources and Ten Recommended Books on Folk and Popular Cultural Geography at the end of the chapter.

Diffusion of Folk and Popular Culture

Do elements of folk culture spread through geographical space differently from those of popular culture? Whereas folk culture spreads by the same models and processes of diffusion as popular culture (see Focus On: A Transatlantic Fish Story), diffusion operates more slowly within a folk setting. The weakly developed social stratification within folk cultures tends to retard *hierarchical diffusion,* and the inherent conservatism of such cultures produces a resistance to change. Barriers to diffusion abound. The Amish, mentioned earlier as one of the few surviving folk cultures, are distinctive today simply because they rejected innovations, believing that only things mentioned in the Bible are appropriate for use by pious people.

Agricultural Fairs

An example of the slow progress of diffusion in a folk setting can be seen in the spread of the American agricultural fair, usually held at the county level. The county fair originated in the Yankee folk region and spread west and southwest by *expansion diffusion.* According to geographer Fred Kniffen (see Profile earlier in this chapter), the first American agricultural fair was held in Pittsfield, Massachusetts, in 1810, and the idea then gained favor throughout western New England and the adjacent Hudson Valley (Figure 2.18 on the next page). From that source region it diffused westward into the American heartland, the Midwest, where it gained its widest acceptance.

Usually promoted by agricultural societies, the fairs were originally educational in purpose, and farmers could learn about improved methods and breeds. Soon an entertainment function was added, represented by a racetrack and midway, and competition for prizes for superior agricultural products became common. By the early twentieth century, the agricultural fair had diffused through most of the United States, although farmers in culture regions such as the Upland South did not accept it as readily or fully as did the Midwesterners.

Blowguns: Diffusion or Independent Invention?

Often the past diffusion of an item of folk culture is not clearly known or understood, presenting folk geographers with a problem of interpretation. An example is provided by the blowgun, a long, hollow tube through which a projectile is blown by the force of one's breath. Geographer Stephen Jett mapped the distribution of this hunting weapon and found it among folk societies in both the Eastern and Western Hemispheres, all the way from the island of Madagascar off the African east coast to the Amazonian rain forests of South America, over halfway around the world (Figure 2.19 on page 49).

Apparently the blowgun was first invented by Indonesian peoples, probably on the island of Borneo. It became the principal hunting weapon of this folk society and diffused through much of the equatorial island belt of the

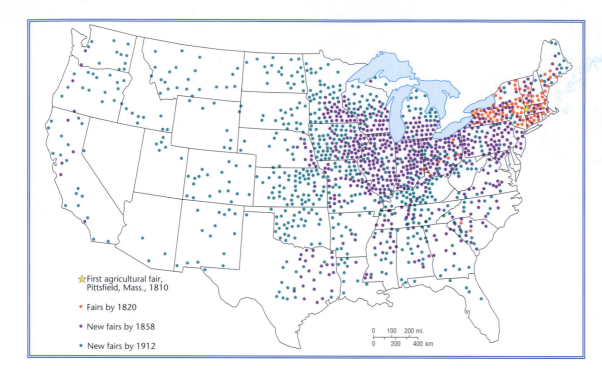

Figure 2.18
Diffusion of the American agricultural fair, 1810–1910. What type or types of cultural diffusion might have been at work here? (AFTER KNIFFEN, 1951: 45, 47, 51.)

☆ First agricultural fair, Pittsfield, Mass., 1810

• Fairs by 1820

• New fairs by 1858

• New fairs by 1912

| 0 | 100 | 200 mi. |
| 0 | 200 | 400 km |

Eastern Hemisphere. How do we account for its presence among American Indian groups in the Western Hemisphere? Was it *independently invented* by the American Indians? Was it brought to the Americas by *relocation diffusion* in pre-Columbian times? Or did it spread to the New World only after the European discovery of America? We do not know the answers to these questions, but the problem presented is one common to cultural geography—and particularly to folk geography, because the nonliterate condition of many folk cultures precludes written records that might reveal such diffusion. Certain rules of thumb can be employed in any given situation to help resolve the issue. For example, if one or more nonfunctional features of blowguns, such as a decorative motif or

FOCUS ON

A Transatlantic Fish Story

Cultural diffusion is often revealed by comparing folktales in different regions. The following tale, presented in a much-abridged form, occurs both in Celtic Wales on the island of Great Britain and among people of British extraction in the Ozark Mountains of Missouri and Arkansas. It apparently spread by relocation diffusion to America and then halfway across the continent, changing somewhat in the process. Or is independent invention the more likely explanation?

Welsh Version
    A man living on the River Towey caught a salmon from a
        small boat with a rod;
    the fish spoke Welsh and English, and turned into a naked
        girl with a fish-hook in her lip;
    she became the man's wife.

Ozark Mountain Version
    A man living up the Meramec River caught a yellow catfish
        using only his hands;
    he took it home and put it in a rain barrel;
    the fish turned into a woman;
    she became a fish again;
    he put it back into the barrel and took it back to the river.

Adapted from Miller, 1968: 59.

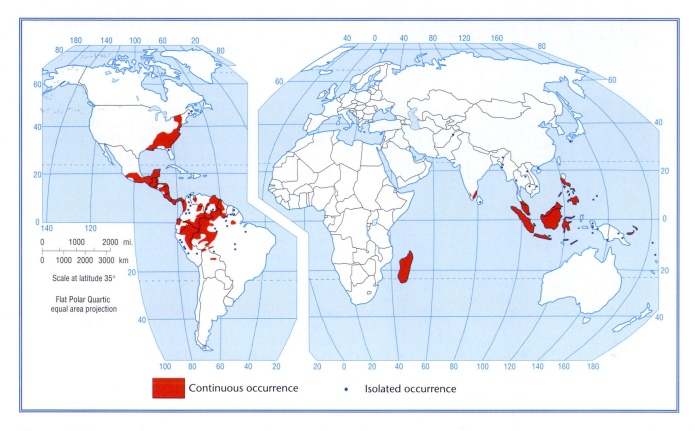

Figure 2.19

Former distribution of the blowgun among American Indians, South Asians, Africans, and Pacific Islanders. The blowgun occurred among folk cultures in two widely separated areas of the world. **Was this the result of independent invention or cultural diffusion? What kinds of data might one seek to answer this question? Compare and contrast the occurrence in the Indian and Pacific ocean lands to the distribution of the Austronesian languages (see Chapter 4).** (SOURCE: JETT, 1991: 92–93.)

specific terminology, occurred both in South America and Indonesia, then the logical conclusion would be that cultural diffusion explained the distribution of blowguns.

Reflecting on GEOGRAPHY

Should we seek to preserve intact folk cultures?

Diffusion in Popular Culture

We might expect *hierarchical diffusion* to play a greater role in popular culture, because popular society is highly stratified into classes, unlike folk culture. For example, the spread of McDonald's restaurants—beginning in 1955 in the United States and, later, internationally—occurred hierarchically for the most part, revealing a bias in favor of larger urban markets (Figure 2.20 on the next page). Also, *time-distance decay* is weaker in the diffusion of popular culture. Sometimes, however, diffusion in pop-

ular culture works differently, as a study of Wal-Mart revealed (see Figure 2.15). Geographers Thomas Graff and Dub Ashton conclude that Wal-Mart initially diffused from its Arkansas base in a largely *contagious* pattern, reaching first into other parts of Arkansas and into neighboring states. Simultaneously, as often happens in the spatial spread of culture, another pattern of diffusion was at work, one they called *reverse* hierarchical diffusion. Wal-Mart initially located its stores in smaller towns and markets, only later spreading into cities—the precise reverse of the way hierarchical diffusion normally works. This combination of contagious and reverse hierarchical diffusion led Wal-Mart within 30 years to become the nation's largest retailer. A different kind of diffusion in 1995 brought Wal-Mart into Canada, when it purchased 122 stores from rival Woolco and soon became that country's largest discount retailer in total sales.

In ancient times, innovations usually required thousands of years to complete their areal spread, and even as recently as the early nineteenth century, the time span was

Figure 2.20

Another McDonald's opens in Moscow. McDonald's, which first spread to Moscow about 1987, has always preferred hierarchical diffusion. Of all McDonald's outlets worldwide today, about 45 percent are located in foreign countries, almost always in large cities. (COURTESY OF TERRY G. JORDAN-BYCHKOV.)

still measured in decades. In the popular culture, modern transportation and communications networks now permit cultural diffusion to occur within weeks or even days. The propensity for change makes diffusion extremely important in the popular culture. The availability of devices permitting rapid diffusion enhances the chance for change in the popular culture. Wilbur Zelinsky described a personal experience with the lightning-quick expansion diffusion of a classic item of popular material culture, the hula hoop. "In August, 1958," he wrote, "I drove from Santa Monica, California, to Detroit at an average rate of about 400 miles (644 km) per day; and display windows in almost every drugstore and variety store along the way were being hastily stocked with hula hoops just off the delivery trucks from Southern California. A national television program the week before had roused instant cravings. It was an eerie sensation, surfing along a pseudoinnovation wave."

Advertising

The most effective device for diffusion in the popular culture, as Zelinsky suggests, confronts us almost every day of our lives. Commercial advertising of retail products

and services bombards our eyes and ears, with great effect. Using the techniques of social science, especially psychology, advertisers have learned to sell us products we do not need. The skill with which Madison Avenue advertising firms prepare commercials often determines the success or failure of a product. In short, the popular culture is equipped with the most potent devices and techniques of diffusion ever perfected. These devices of market advertising have speeded the diffusionary process and relegated *time-distance decay* and the *neighborhood effect* to less important positions.

At the same time, modern advertising is very place-conscious, particularly as messages became less textual and increasingly visual. As geographers Douglas Fleming and Richard Roth noted, images of place provide a vital component in many ads and are used to market products and services by linking them to popular, admired places. The "Marlboro Man" cigarette ads provide an excellent example, and even in countries as distant geographically and culturally as Egypt, the romanticized American West is used effectively to sell cigarettes. Is it not remarkable that Egyptian Muslim Arabs should respond favorably to a symbol-laden place image of a land most have never seen or ever hope to see? Such is the power of diffusion in the popular culture.

Communications Barriers

Although the communications media have the potential to allow almost instant diffusion over very large areas, spread can be greatly retarded if access to the media is denied (see Focus On: The Geography of Rock and Roll). *Billboard*, a magazine devoted largely to popular music, described such a barrier to diffusion. A record company executive complained that radio stations and disk jockeys refused to play "punk rock" records, denying the style an equal opportunity for exposure. He claimed that punk devotees were concentrated in New York City, Los Angeles, Boston, and London, where many young people had found the style reflective of their feelings and frustrations. "Rap" and "grunge" styles faced a similar problem initially. Without access to radio stations, punk rock could diffuse from these centers only through live concerts and the record sales they generated. The publishers of *Billboard* noted that "punk rock is but one of a number of musical forms which initially had problems breaking through nationally out of regional footholds," for *Pachanga*, ska, pop/gospel, "women's music," reggae, and "gangsta rap" experienced similar difficulties decades ago. Similarly, Time Warner, a major distributor of gangsta rap music, had to endure scathing criticism from the U.S. Congress in 1995, which eventually caused the company to sell the subsidiary label that recorded this form of

FOCUS ON

The Geography of Rock and Roll

Diffusion occurs rapidly in popular culture. The rock and roll musical style arose in the early 1950s, achieved its maximum diffusion within a decade, then gave way to other, often derivative, forms of music. Its chief personality, Elvis Presley, was only 42 years old at the time of his death in 1977, yet the heyday of early rock and roll had ended a decade and a half before he died.

The hearth (creative center) of rock and roll, about 1952 or 1953, was the Upper Delta country along the Mississippi River, centered on Memphis, Tennessee. Elvis, Little Richard, Fats Domino, Chuck Berry, and Jerry Lee Lewis, the chief practitioners of rock and roll, all worked in the Upper Delta. The style developed as a blending of African-American rhythm and blues and Hill Southern white rockabilly, a fast-tempo country and western style. Diffusion was achieved through the radio and from sales of inexpensive 45-rpm. records, coupled with live concerts.

The spread occurred most rapidly between 1955 and 1958; after 1963, rock and roll was in decline, although it influenced many subsequent musical styles, including the Beatles.

Barriers were encountered in the diffusion. Parental opposition to the music and lyrics as "degraded" led to the banning of rock and roll on radio stations in some cities. The barriers proved to be permeable—explicit sexual references, so common in rhythm and blues and vintage rock and roll, were softened. "Roll with me, Henry" became the less suggestive "Dance with me, Henry." Hierarchical diffusion was clearly evident. Early adopters were inquisitive, gregarious young people, trendsetters in their generation. From them acceptance spread down through lower hierarchies until the hard core of nonaccepters remained. Similar trendsetters abandoned rock and roll for other rock styles after about 1963, and the major musical phenomenon of the 1950s went into decline.

Adapted from Francaviglia, 1973.

---

rap. To control the programming of radio and television is to control much of the diffusionary apparatus in popular culture. The diffusion of innovations ultimately depends on the flow of information.

Government censorship can also provide barriers to diffusion, of varying degrees of effectiveness. In 1995 the Islamic fundamentalist regime in Iran, opposed to what it perceived as the corrupting influences of Western popular culture, outlawed television satellite dishes in an attempt to prevent citizens from watching programs broadcast in foreign countries. The Taliban government of Afghanistan went even further, banning all television sets. Control of the media can approach control of the mind in popular culture, revealing a great deal about diffusion. Even so, repressive regimes must cope with a proliferation of communication methods, including fax and the Internet. The status of inward-looking "hermit" nations is probably no longer attainable, even in totalitarian conditions, so pervasive has cultural diffusion become.

Although newspapers are potent agents of diffusion in popular culture, they also act as selective barriers, often reinforcing the effect of political boundaries. For example, between 20 and 50 percent of all news published in Canadian newspapers is of foreign origin, mainly involving the flow northward of United States news, whereas only about 12 percent of all news appearing in papers in the United States comes from foreign areas.

> ### Reflecting on GEOGRAPHY
> Because Canadian newspapers devote so much more coverage to international stories than U.S. newspapers, are Americans more provincial than Canadians as a result?

Diffusion of the Rodeo

Barriers of one kind or another always halt the diffusion of elements of popular culture before they become ubiquitous. The rodeo provides an example. Rooted in the ranching culture of the American West, it has never completely escaped that setting (Figure 2.21 on the next page). In short, a *neighborhood effect* is evident, even in popular culture.

Like so many elements of popular culture, the modern rodeo had its origins in folk tradition. Rodeos began simply as roundups of cattle in the Spanish livestock ranching system in northern Mexico and the American Southwest. In fact, the word *rodeo* is derived from the Spanish *rodear*, "to round up." Anglo-Americans adopted Mexican cowboy skills in the nineteenth century, and cowboys from adjacent ranches began to hold contests at roundup time. Eventually, some cowboy contests on the Great Plains became formalized, with prizes awarded.

The transition to commercial rodeo, with admission tickets and grandstands, came quickly as an outgrowth of

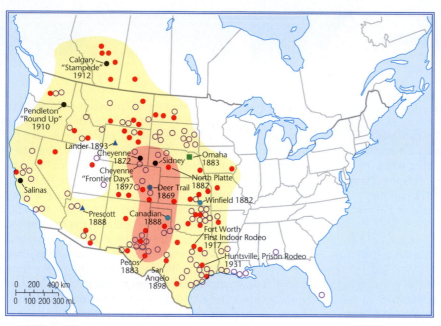

Figure 2.21

Origin and diffusion of the American commercial rodeo. Derived originally from folk culture, rodeos evolved through formal cowboy contests and Wild West shows to emerge, in the late 1880s and 1890s, in their present popular culture form. The border between the United States and Canada proved no barrier to the diffusion, although Canadian rodeo, like Canadian football, differs in some respects from the U.S. type. **What barriers might the diffusion have encountered?** (SOURCES: PILLSBURY, 1990B; AND FREDERICKSON, 1984.)

the formal cowboy contests. One such affair, at North Platte, Nebraska, in 1882, led to the inclusion of some rodeo events in a Wild West show at Omaha in 1883. These shows, which moved by railroad from town to town in the manner of circuses, were probably the most potent agent of early rodeo diffusion. Within a decade of the Omaha affair, commercial rodeos were being held independently of Wild West shows in several towns, apparently first at Prescott, Arizona, in 1888. The idea spread rapidly, as is typical of cultural diffusion in the popular culture. By the turn of the century, commercial rodeos appeared throughout much of the West. At Cheyenne, Wyoming, the famous Frontier Days rodeo was first held in 1897. By World War I, the rodeo had also become an institution in the provinces of western Canada, where the Calgary Stampede began in 1912.

Today, rodeos are held in almost every community of any size in the western United States. For example, the state of Oklahoma's annual calendar of events lists no fewer than 98 scheduled rodeos. Racial and gender lines have been crossed by the rodeo in culturally diverse Oklahoma, producing such events as the Creek Nation All Indian Rodeo at Okmulgee, the All Girls Rodeo at Duncan, and the All Black Rodeo at Wewoka. In Texas and some other states, rodeo competition has become an offi-

cial high-school sport. Professional rodeos are now held in 36 states and three Canadian provinces. The major acceptance of the rodeo in the popular culture is found west of the Mississippi and Missouri rivers (see Figure 2.21). *Absorbing* and *permeable barriers* to the diffusion of commercial rodeo were encountered at the border of Mexico, south of which bullfighting occupies a dominant position, and in the Mormon culture region centered in Utah. A uniquely Mexican form of rodeo, the *charreada*, is popular in central Mexico. Only in California did rodeo popularity penetrate the Cascade and Coastal Ranges to reach the Pacific shore.

 # Folk and Popular Cultural Ecology

What is the nature of the relationship between the habitat and the two types of culture? Do folk and popular cultures differ in their interactions with the physical environment?

Folk Ecology

Cultural ecology is an especially appropriate theme in folk geography, because folk groups possess a very close

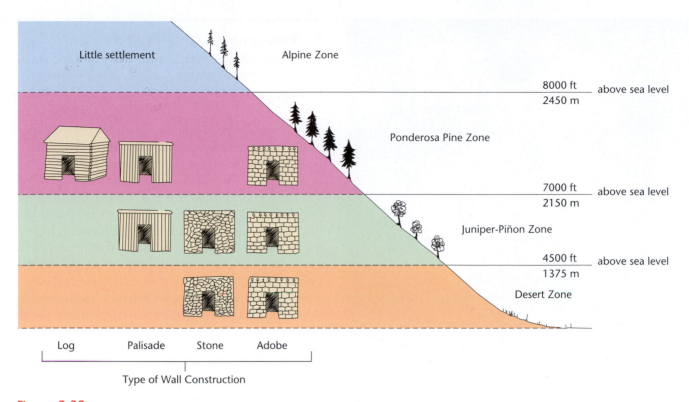

Log   Palisade   Stone   Adobe

Type of Wall Construction

Figure 2.22

The ecology of folk architecture in northern New Mexico. Buildings erected by people belonging to folk groups consist of the materials available. So it is among the Highland Hispano and southwestern American Indian folk of northern New Mexico, where the type of wall construction changes with elevation above sea level, reflecting in part the progression of microenvironments encountered at different altitudes. (ADAPTED FROM GRITZNER, 1974: 26.)

relationship with the physical environment. In most cases, their *adaptive strategies* are sustainable, unlike those of popular culture. People in folk cultures live on the land, gaining their livelihood directly through farming, herding, hunting, gathering, and fishing. A great many facets of folk culture relate at least indirectly to the local ecology and involve adaptive strategies. The languages of folk groups have the vocabularies required to exploit the habitat, their religions act to mitigate environmental hazards, their folktales honor great hunters, their proverbs offer wisdom about the weather and the proper time for planting, and their traditional architecture reflects the local building materials and climate (Figure 2.22).

Indeed, one is tempted, when dealing with folk groups, to conclude that culture is synonymous with adaptation—that folkways exist only to facilitate adjustment to the physical environment. It would be equally easy to espouse *environmental determinism*, believing that folk cultures will inevitably be guided along similar courses in similar ecological settings. Folkways, however, involve more than merely *cultural adaptation*, and a variety of folk cultures can exist in any particular *ecoregion*.

Although folk cultures may be more sensitive than popular cultures to the qualities of the soil, climate, and terrain, it does not follow that they are wholly shaped by their physical surroundings, nor is it necessarily true that folk groups live in close harmony with their environment—often soil erosion, deforestation, and overkill of wild animals can be attributed to traditional rural folk. Even so, we must always keep the cultural ecological context in mind when seeking to interpret folk culture, for otherwise we overlook a quite fundamental *possibilistic* explanatory mainspring.

The close link between culture and habitat in folk societies can be seen in *folk medicine*. People in folk societies commonly treat diseases and disorders with drugs and medicines derived from the root, bark, blossom, or fruit of plants. In the United States, folk medicine is best preserved in the Upland South, on some American Indian reservations, and in the Mexican borderland. Many folk cures have proven effectiveness.

The attitude of the Upland Southerner toward folk cures is well expressed in the comments of a root digger living in the eastern Tennessee mountains who, in an

Figure 2.23
An Appalachian root digger in Tennessee washes his harvest in a mountain stream. This activity is typical of the Upland Southern folk culture region. (MARTIN ROGERS/STOCK BOSTON, INC.)

Reflecting on GEOGRAPHY
Contrary to their popular image, folk cultures do cause environmental damage. Can you think of an example?

interview with cultural geographer Edward Price, said that "the good Lord has put these yerbs here for man to make hisself well with. They is a yerb, could we but find it, to cure every illness" (Figure 2.23). Root digging has been popularized to the extent that much of the produce of the Appalachians is now funneled to dealers, who serve a larger market outside the folk culture. However, root digging remains at heart a folk enterprise, carried on in the old ways and requiring the traditionally thorough knowledge of the plant environment.

In the Mexican folk culture region along the southern border of Texas, folk medicine is still widely practiced by *curanderos,* or "curers." More than 400 medicines are derived from both wild and domestic plants growing in the border region, perpetuating a tradition rooted in sixteenth-century Indian and Spanish sources. The local folk medicine is based on the belief that health and welfare depend on harmony between the natural and supernatural; disease and misfortune are thought to involve some disharmony. Through the use of counseling and botanical medicines, the *curandero* strives to restore harmony. In short, folk cultures tend to have an *organic* view of nature. The thriving *curandero* business along the Rio Grande is best viewed as a persistent folk element in a culture undergoing considerable change and popularization.

Their close ties to the habitat also enhance the *environmental perception* of folk groups. This becomes particularly evident when they migrate. Typically, they seek new lands similar to the one left behind. A good example can be seen in the migrations of Upland Southerners from the mountains of Appalachia between 1830 and 1930. As the Appalachians filled up, many highlanders began looking elsewhere for similar areas to settle. In their migrations, they usually moved in clan or extended-family groups. Initially, they found an environmental twin of the Appalachians in the Ozark-Ouachita Mountains of Missouri and Arkansas. Somewhat later, others sought out the hollows, coves, and gaps of the central Texas Hill Country. The final migration of Appalachian hill people brought some 15,000 members of this folk culture to the Cascade and Coastal mountain ranges of Washington State between 1880 and 1930 (Figure 2.24). The role of environmental perception and clan ties in directing these migrations can be seen in the following remarks by a Kentucky mountaineer, recorded by W. R. Clevinger in 1937: "I've been figurin' for a right smart time about leavin' fer Warshin'ton. I hear there's a good mountin country out thar where a man can still hunt, git work in mills and loggin', and git a piece of land right cheap. Some of my kin out thar have writ back, wantin' me to jine 'em."

Ecology of Popular Culture

Because popular culture is largely the product of industrialization and the rise of technology, possessing a *mechanistic* view of nature, it is less directly tied to the physical environment than folk culture. Gone is the intimate association between people and land known by our folk ancestors. Gone, too, is our direct vulnerability to many environmental forces, although our security is more apparent than real. People functioning within popular cultures have enormous potential for producing ecological disasters. Also, because popular culture encourages little intimate contact with and knowledge of the physical world, our *environmental perceptions* can become quite distorted.

Popular culture makes heavy demands on *ecosystems.* This is true even in the seemingly benign realm of recreation. Leisure time and related recreational activities have increased greatly in the United States, Canada, Europe, and other developed countries. Members of the popular

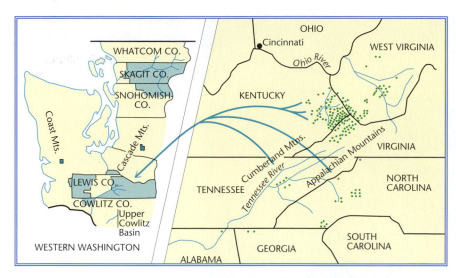

Figure 2.24

The relocation diffusion of Upland Southern hill folk from Appalachia to western Washington. Each dot represents the former home of an individual or family that migrated to the Upper Cowlitz River basin in the Cascade Mountains of Washington State between 1884 and 1937. Some 3000 descendants of these migrants lived in the Cowlitz area by 1940. **What does the high degree of clustering of the sources of the migrants and subsequent clustering in Washington suggest about the processes of folk migrations? How should we interpret their choices of familiar terrain and vegetation for a new home? Why might members of a folk society who migrate choose a new land similar to the old one?** (AFTER CLEVINGER, 1938: 120; AND CLEVINGER, 1942: 4.)

culture now spend much leisure time in some space-consuming activity in areas outside the cities. The demand for "wilderness" recreation zones has risen sharply in the last quarter-century, and no end to the increase seems at hand (Figure 2.25).

Hikers, campers, hunters, fishers, bikers, dune buggy and snowmobile enthusiasts, weekend cottagers, surfers, spelunkers, mountain climbers, boaters, sightseers, and others are making unprecedented demands on open country. Such a massive presence of people in our recreational

Figure 2.25

Popular culture impacts the environment. Our leisure activities are space consuming and make heavy demands on the physical environment. The Woodstock '99 Festival in Rome, New York, produced a prodigious volume of waste. (STEPHEN CHERNIN/AP.)

Figure 2.26
Popular culture might be better called "litter culture," even in places as remote as the Monument Valley Navajo Tribal Park, Arizona. **Why would anyone create such ugliness amid natural splendor?** (Paul A. Souders/Corbis.)

areas inevitably results in damage to the physical environment. National parks now suffer from traffic jams, residential congestion, litter, and noise pollution—very much like the urban areas (Figure 2.26). A study by geographer Jeanne Kay and her students in Utah revealed substantial environmental damage by off-road recreational vehicles, including "soil loss and long-term soil deterioration." In less congested wilderness districts, as few as several hundred hikers a month can beat down trails to the extent that vegetation is altered, erosion encouraged, and wildlife diminished. Even the best-intentioned, Green-minded visitors do some damage. One of the paradoxes of the modern age and popular culture seems to be that the more we cluster in cities and suburbs, the greater our impact on open areas. We carry our popular culture with us when we vacation in such regions.

Some countries have reacted to the recreational tourist boom by making natural areas ever more accessible, ever more crowded and damaged. Others, including the United States, have now drawn a distinction between national park tourism and wilderness areas. Access to many wild districts is now greatly restricted, in hopes that they can be saved from the damage that necessarily accompanies recreational activity. In some national parks, access by private automobile and camper pickup is restricted, and Yosemite Park in California has banned most motor vehicles. But for the greater part of the countryside, the recreational assault on the environment continues.

Added to the impact of recreational land use on the countryside is the enormous demand that cities generate for refuse dumps. Whether disposed of properly, in landfills, or merely dumped as junk, the refuse of the popular culture is altering the ecology of many rural areas, even in some remote places (Figure 2.27).

 ## Cultural Interaction in Folk and Popular Geography

In the inner workings of folk and popular cultures, do the various elements of culture interact with one another in a causal way? The answer is yes, abundantly. In folk cultures, for example, an *organic* view of nature tends to reduce practices that destroy habitats. Strong group identity tends to weaken individualism, and conservatism retards change.

But it is within our own popular culture that we can most easily see cultural interaction at work. Increased leisure time, instant communications, greater affluence for many people, heightened mobility, and weakened attachment to family and place—all attributes of the popular culture—have the potential, in interacting, to cause massive spatial restructuring. Most *social scientists* long assumed that the result of such causal forces, especially mobility and the electronic media, would be to homogenize culture, reducing the differences among places, in the

Figure 2.27

Circle Hot Springs, Alaska. At this very remote place, literally at the outermost limit of the North American highway system, the discards of popular culture pile up in a junkyard. Improbably, a hotel appears in the background! **How do you think the owner of this place perceives it?** (Courtesy of Terry G. Jordan-Bychkov.)

process of *globalization*. This assumption is called the **convergence hypothesis:** that is, we are supposedly converging in our cultural makeup, becoming more alike. In the geographical sense, this would yield *placelessness*, a concept discussed earlier in the chapter.

Impressive geographical evidence can be marshaled to support the convergence hypothesis. Wilbur Zelinsky (see Profile earlier in this chapter), for example, compared the given names of people in various parts of the United States for the years 1790 and 1968 and found that a more pronounced regionalization existed in the eighteenth century than today. The personal names that the present generation of parents bestow on children vary less from place to place than did those of our ancestors two centuries ago.

Mapping Personal Preference

Working against the convergence hypothesis is the greater personal individualism characteristic of the popular culture. Gone is the conformity of folk cultures. What is the geographical result of heightened individualism and personal preference? Geographer Ronald Abler concluded that individualism—coupled with increasingly rapid communications media, abundant leisure, and widespread wealth—had the ability to create a new regionalism in the popular culture, giving us the will and the means to diverge rather than converge. Free exercise of individual preferences could create a new spatial order. Zelinsky

concurred, asking "What things will how many persons do, and *where* will they do them?" If we decide to pursue our chosen lifestyles in geographical proximity to others who share our preferences and orientations, then a spatial restructuring will certainly occur. Hints of this trend are seen in certain segregated communities where only the elderly live, as in Sun City, Arizona, and in the residential concentration of gay people in certain districts within cities such as San Francisco (Figure 2.28 on the next page).

The media cater to and help promote such a restructuring. Special-interest media, or "narrowcasting," to use Abler's term, can help produce and nurture a spatially diverse popular culture. For example, 141 radio stations in the United States and Canada are oriented to African-Americans. Cable television stations now aim most programming at specific audiences, in a process known as target marketing. In Zelinsky's words, "The increasingly free exercise of individual preferences as to values, pleasures, self-improvement, social and physical habitat, and general lifestyle in an individualistic, affluent national community may have begun to alter the spatial attributes of society and culture."

Place Images

The same media that serve and reflect the rise of personal preference—movies, television, photography, music, advertising, art, and others—often produce *place images*,

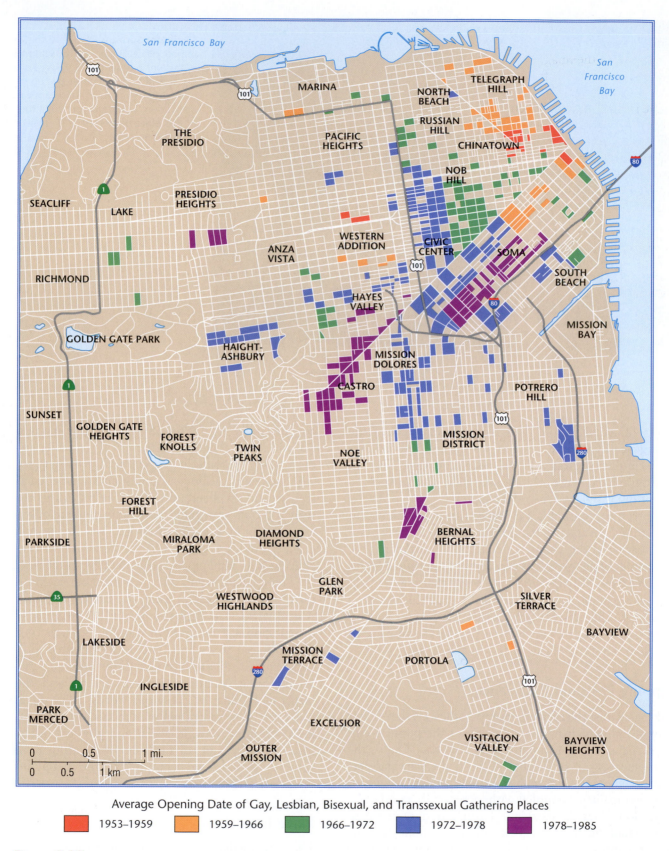

Average Opening Date of Gay, Lesbian, Bisexual, and Transsexual Gathering Places

1953–1959	1959–1966	1966–1972	1972–1978	1978–1985

Figure 2.28

Changing gay/lesbian/bisexual/transsexual residential and social space in San Francisco. Such lifestyle segregation and its rapid diffusion typify popular culture. (Source: Scott, 2003.)

a subject studied by geographers Brian Godfrey and Leo Zonn, among others. Place, portrayer, and medium interact to produce the image, which, in turn, colors our perception and cognition of places and regions we have never visited.

The images may be inaccurate or misleading, but they nevertheless create a world in our minds that has an array of unique places and place meanings. Our decisions about tourism and migration can be influenced by these images. For example, through the media, Hawaii has become in the American mind a sort of earthly paradise peopled by scantily clad, eternally happy, invariably good-looking, swarthy natives who live in a setting of unparalleled natural beauty and idyllic climate. People have always formed images of faraway places. Through the interworkings of popular culture, these images proliferate and become more vivid, if not more accurate.

Folk and Popular Cultural Landscapes

Do folk and popular cultures look different? Does each have a distinctive cultural landscape? Yes. In fact, the theme of cultural landscape allows us to grasp at once the important differences between *and among* folk and popular cultures.

Folk Architecture

Every folk culture produces a highly distinctive landscape. One of the most visible aspects of these landscapes is folk architecture, and we will use such traditional buildings to illustrate the theme of cultural landscape in folk geography.

Folk architecture springs not from the drafting tables of professional architects but from the collective memory of a traditional people (Figure 2.29). These buildings—whether dwellings, barns, churches, mills, or inns—are not based on blueprints but on mental images that change little from one generation to the next. In this sense, it is an architecture without architects. Folk buildings are extensions of a people and their region. They help provide the unique character of each district or province and offer a highly visible aspect of the human mosaic. Do not look to folk architecture for refined artistic genius or spectacular, revolutionary design. Seek in it instead the traditional, the conservative, and the functional (see Focus On: The Cultural Ecology of a Folk House). Expect from it a simple beauty, a harmony with the physical environment, a visible expression of folk culture. Material composition, floor plan, and layout are important ingredients of folk architecture, but numerous other characteristics help to classify farmsteads and dwellings. The form or shape of the roof, the placement of the chimney, and even such details as the number and location of doors and windows can be important classifying criteria. Estyn Evans (see Profile on page 61), a

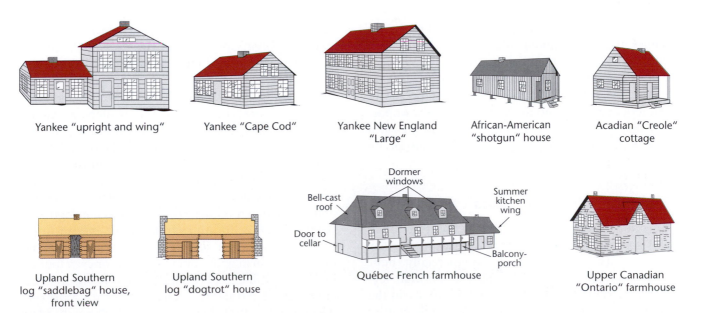

Yankee "upright and wing"   Yankee "Cape Cod"   Yankee New England "Large"   African-American "shotgun" house   Acadian "Creole" cottage

Upland Southern log "saddlebag" house, front view   Upland Southern log "dogtrot" house   Québec French farmhouse   Upper Canadian "Ontario" farmhouse

Dormer windows
Bell-cast roof
Summer kitchen wing
Door to cellar
Balcony-porch

Figure 2.29

Selected folk houses. Six of the 15 folk culture regions of North America are represented (see Figure 2.1). (After Kniffen, 1965; and Glassie, 1968.)

FOCUS ON

The Cultural Ecology of a Folk House

Folk houses, as a rule, are beautifully suited to their physical environment. Centuries of trial and error taught their builders how to construct dwellings that provide comfort and protection from the extremes and hazards of the local weather. Nowhere are these attributes of folk architecture better displayed than on Lan Yü (Orchid Island), located in the Pacific Ocean 40 miles (64 km) off the coast of Taiwan.

The inhabitants of Lan Yü, the Yami, build their folk houses mostly below ground level, in stone-lined pits, for protection from hurricanes. The sketch shows a cross section of a Yami house. A strongly reinforced, streamlined roof projects partly above ground level, exposing a section of an elongated slope to the brunt of the hurricane winds. The force of the storm wind presses down on the roof and slides by, keeping it in place. To escape the midday heat when no storms are blowing, each Yami builds a "cool tower" above ground level. These are easily replaced when hurricanes blow them away.

Adapted from Shuhua, 1977, 107.

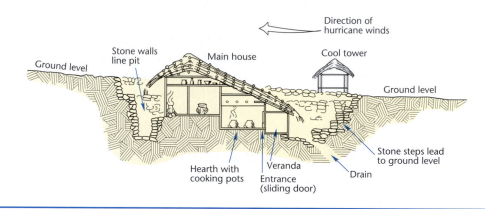

---

noted expert on Irish folk geography, considered roof form and chimney placement, among other traits, in devising an informal classification of Irish folk houses.

The house, or dwelling, is the most basic structure that people erect, regardless of culture. For most people in nearly all folk cultures, a house is the single most important thing they ever build. Folk cultures as a rule are rural and agricultural. For these reasons, it seems appropriate to focus on the folk house.

Folk Housing in North America

In the United States and Canada, folk architecture today represents a relict form in the cultural landscape. Popular culture, with its mass-produced, commercially built houses, has so overwhelmed the folk tradition that few folk houses are being built today, but many survive in the refuge regions of American and Canadian folk culture (see Figures 2.1, 2.29).

Yankee folk houses are of wooden frame construction, and shingle siding often covers the exterior walls. They appear in a variety of floor plans, including the *New England "large"* house, a huge two-and-a-half-story house built around a central chimney and two rooms deep. As the Yankee folk migrated westward, they developed the *upright-and-wing* dwelling. These Yankee houses are often massive, in part because of the cold winters, which require most work to be done indoors. By contrast, Upland Southern folk houses are smaller and built of notched logs. Many houses in this folk tradition consist of two log rooms, with either a double fireplace between, forming the *saddlebag* house, or an open, roofed breezeway separating the two rooms, a plan known as the *dogtrot* house (Figures 2.29, 2.30). An example of an African-American folk dwelling is the *shotgun* house, a narrow structure only one room in width but two, three, or even four rooms in depth. Acadiana, a French-derived folk region in Louisiana, is characterized by the half-timbered *Creole cottage*, which has a central chimney and built-in porch. Scores of other folk house types survive in the American landscape, although most such dwellings now stand abandoned and derelict.

PROFILE

E. Estyn Evans
1905–1989

Estyn Evans studied geography and anthropology under H. J. Fleure in Wales. At the young age of 23, he was invited to establish a department of geography at Queen's University in Belfast, Northern Ireland, where he remained throughout his 44-year career.

The marriage of geography and anthropology in his training led him to specialize in the field of folk geography, and he was one of the first geographers in the English-speaking world to pursue the study of material folk culture. Evans developed a deep attachment for Ireland, his adopted home. He is best known to cultural geographers for his many books and articles about the folk material culture of Ireland, in particular *Irish Heritage* (1943), *Mourne Country* (1951), *Irish Folk Ways* (1957), and *The Personality of Ireland* (1973). Evans was president of the Ulster Folk Life Society and trustee of the Ulster Folk and Transport Museum, of which he was the founder. In 1970, he was honored by being appointed a Commander of the Order of the British Empire; in 1973, he received the Victoria Medal of the Royal Geographical Society; and in 1979, he was given an Honors Award from the Association of American Geographers. He received honorary doctorates from five universities.

For more information see Glasscock, 1991.

Reflecting on **GEOGRAPHY**

The relics of folk cultural landscapes can be found in most parts of North America. Should we strive to preserve those relics, such as folk houses? Why or why not?

Canada also offers a variety of traditional folk houses (see Figure 2.29). In French-speaking Québec, one of the common types consists of a main story atop a cellar, with attic rooms beneath a curved, bell-shaped (or *bell-cast*) roof. A balcony-porch with railing extends across the front, sheltered by the overhanging eaves. Attached to one side of this French-Canadian folk house is a summer kitchen that is sealed off during the long, cold winter. Often the folk houses of Québec are built of stone. To the west, in the Upper Canadian folk region, one type of folk house occurs so frequently that it is known as the *Ontario farmhouse*. One-and-a-half stories in height, the Ontario farmhouse is usually built of brick and has a distinctive gabled front dormer window.

Now, using the sketches shown in Figure 2.29 and descriptions of eastern North American folk houses, identify the four houses illustrated in Figure 2.31 on the next page (answers are located at the end of the chapter).

The interpretation of folk architecture is by no means a simple process. Folk geographers often work for years trying to "read" such structures, seeking clues to diffusion and traditional adaptive strategies. The old problem of *independent invention* versus diffusion is raised repeatedly in the folk landscape, as Figure 2.32 on page 63 illustrates. Precisely because interpretation is often difficult, however,

Figure 2.30

A dogtrot house, typical of the Upland Southern folk region. The distinguishing feature is the open-air passageway, or dogtrot, between the two main rooms. This house is located in central Texas. (COURTESY OF TERRY G. JORDAN-BYCHKOV.)

a

b

c

d

Figure 2.31

Four folk houses in North America. Using the sketches in Figure 2.29 and the related section of the text, determine the regional affiliation and type of each. The answers are provided at the end of the chapter. (COURTESY OF TERRY G. JORDAN-BYCHKOV.)

geographers find these old structures challenging and well worth studying. Folk cultures rarely leave behind much in the way of written records, making their landscape artifacts all the more important in seeking explanations.

Landscapes of Popular Culture

Popular culture permeates the landscape of countries such as the United States, Canada, and Australia, including everything from mass-produced suburban houses to golf courses and neon-lit strips. So overwhelming is the presence of the popular culture in most American settlement

landscapes that an observer must often search diligently to find visual fragments of the older folk cultures. The popular landscape is in continual flux, for change is a hallmark of popular culture.

Perhaps no aspect of the popular landscape is more visually striking than the ubiquitous commercial malls and strips on urban arterial streets, which geographer Robert Sack calls *landscapes of consumption* (see Figure 2.7). In an Illinois college town, two other cultural geographers, John Jakle and Richard Mattson, made a study of the evolution of such a strip. During a 60-year span, the street under study changed from single-family resi-

a

b

Figure 2.32

Two polygonal folk houses. (a) A Buriat Mongol yurt in southern Siberia, near Lake Baikal. (b) A Navajo Indian hogan in New Mexico. The two dwellings, almost identical and each built of notched logs, lie on opposite sides of the world, among unrelated folk groups who never had contact with each other. Such houses do not occur anywhere in between. **Is cultural diffusion or independent invention responsible? How might a folk geographer go about finding the answer?** (PART A, COURTESY OF TERRY G. JORDAN-BYCHKOV; PART B, COURTESY OF STEPHEN C. JETT.)

dential to a commercial focus (Figure 2.33 on the next page). The researchers suggested a five-stage *model* of strip evolution, beginning with the single-family residential period. In stage 2, the introduction of gasoline stations forms the vanguard of commercialization. In stage 3, other businesses join the growing number of filling stations, multiunit housing becomes common, and absentee ownership increases. Stage 4 is clearly dominated by the commercial function; businesses catering to the drive-in trade proliferate and residential use declines sharply. Income levels of the remaining inhabitants are low.

In stage 5, the residential function of the street disappears and a totally commercial landscape prevails. Business properties expand so that off-street parking can be provided, and often a public outcry against the ugliness of the strip is raised. Such places not only represent popular aesthetic values but perhaps also reveal social and cultural problems that need redress. We must be aware, however, that the people who create the landscape perceive it differently. For example, geographer Yi-Fu Tuan suggests that a commercial strip of stores, hamburger joints, filling stations, and used-car lots may appear as visual blight to an outsider, but the owners or operators of the businesses are very proud of them and of their role in the community. Hard work and hopes color their perceptions of the popular landscape.

Perhaps no landscape of consumption is more reflective of popular culture than the indoor shopping mall, numerous examples of which now dot both urban and suburban landscapes. Of these, the largest is West Edmonton Mall in the Canadian province of Alberta, and geographer Jeffrey Hopkins published a study of this remarkable landscape. Enclosing some 5.2 million square feet (483,000 square meters) and completed in 1986, West Edmonton Mall employs 18,000 people in more than 600 stores and services, accounts for nearly one-fourth of the total retail space in greater Edmonton, earned 42 percent of the dollars spent in local shopping centers, and experienced 2800 crimes in its first nine months of operation. And there is more. West Edmonton Mall boasts a water park, a sea aquarium, an ice skating rink, a mini–golf course, a roller coaster, 19 movie theaters, and a 360-room hotel. Its "streets" feature motifs from such exotic places as New Orleans, represented by a Bourbon Street complete with fiberglass ladies of the evening. Hopkins refers to this as a "landscape of myth and elsewhereness," a "simulated landscape" that reveals the "growing intrusion of spectacle, fantasy, and escapism into the urban landscape." Geographer Jon Goss described the Mall of America, in Bloomington, Minnesota, similarly. It has 520 stores, chapels, a roller coaster, a nineteenth-century arcade, an aquarium, and even a rain forest. In this

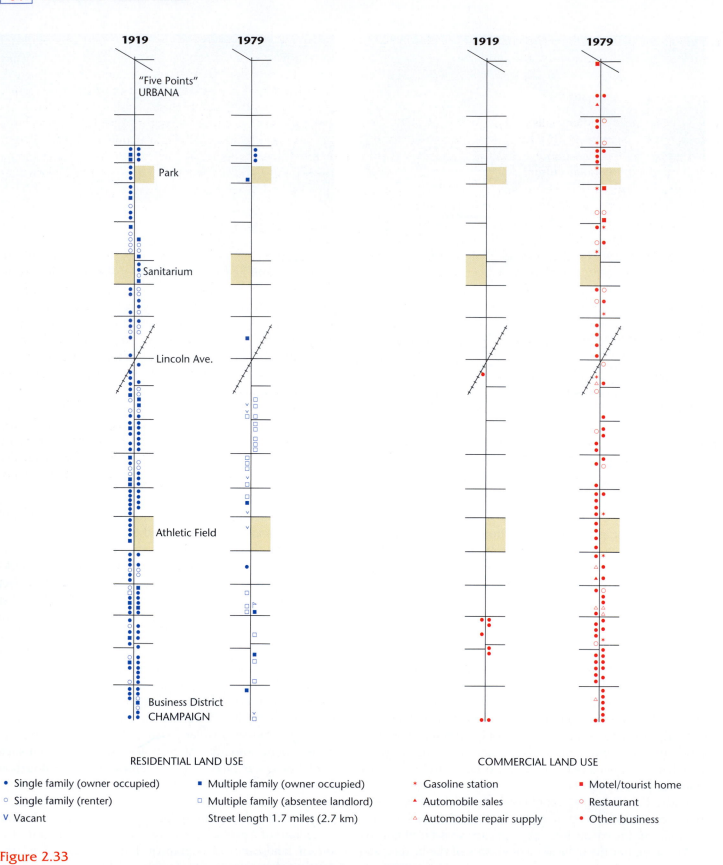

RESIDENTIAL LAND USE

COMMERCIAL LAND USE

- • Single family (owner occupied)
- ■ Multiple family (owner occupied)
- * Gasoline station
- ■ Motel/tourist home
- ○ Single family (renter)
- □ Multiple family (absentee landlord)
- ▲ Automobile sales
- ○ Restaurant
- v Vacant
- Street length 1.7 miles (2.7 km)
- △ Automobile repair supply
- • Other business

Figure 2.33

The evolution of a commercial strip in Champaign-Urbana, Illinois, 1919–1979. Popular culture reshaped a landscape. **Is the older or newer landscape "better"? Why?** (ADAPTED FROM JAKLE AND MATTSON, 1981: 14, 20.)

landscape, people could merge secular and religious needs with myth, memory, fantasy, and fun.

Leisure Landscapes

Clearly, these and other malls have leisure as one of their functions. Geographer Karl Raitz uses the term *leisure landscape* to describe a more specialized type that is also common in the popular culture.

Leisure landscapes take numerous forms, and many are related to tourism. For example, geographers Robert Mings and Kevin McHugh describe the "RV resort landscape" of greater Phoenix, where "recreational nomads" spend the winter months. Arnold Holder refers to the "golfscape" created by that popular sport, and you should know that in the United States alone golf courses occupy an area twice the size of the state of Delaware. Still another geographer, Richard Hecock, dealt with kindred *amenity landscapes,* such as in the Minnesota North Woods lake country, where, in one area he sampled, fully 40 percent of all dwellings were not permanent residences but instead weekend cottages or vacation homes. These are often rustic or even humble in appearance.

The past, reflected in relict buildings, also has been drawn into the leisure landscape. Most often, collections of old structures are relocated to "historylands," often enclosed by imposing chain-link fences and open only during certain seasons or hours. If the desired bit of visual history has perished, Americans and Canadians do not hesitate to rebuild it from scratch, undisturbed by the lack of authenticity—as, for example, at Jamestown, Virginia, or Louisbourg on Cape Breton Island, Nova Scotia. Normally the history parks are put in out-of-the-way places and sanitized to the extent that people no longer live in them. Role-playing actors sometimes prowl these parks, pretending to live in some past era, adding "elsewhenness" to "elsewhereness."

Elitist Landscapes

A distinctive aspect of popular, as opposed to folk, culture is the development of social classes. A small elite group consisting of persons of wealth, education, and refined taste occupies the top position in popular cultures. The important geographical fact about such people is that because of their wealth, desire to be around similar people, distinctive tastes, and hedonistic lifestyles, they can and do create distinctive cultural landscapes, often over fairly large areas.

Daniel Gade, a cultural geographer, coined the term *elitist space* to describe such landscapes, using the French Riviera as an example (Figure 2.34). In that district of stunning natural beauty and idyllic climate, he noted, the French elite applied "refined taste to create an aesthetically

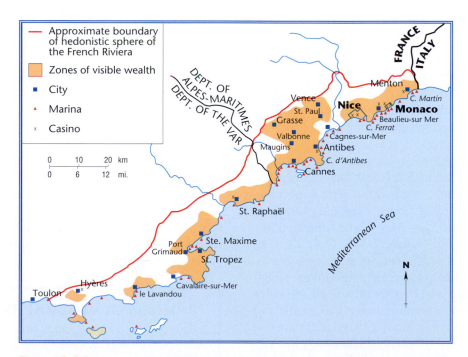

Figure 2.34

The distribution of elitist or hedonistic cultural landscape on the French Riviera. What forces in the popular culture generate such landscapes? (Adapted from Gade, 1982: 22.)

Figure 2.35
An upscale suburb of Santa Fe, New Mexico. Here architectural influences derived from the folk culture of the Pueblo Indians are required by law, producing a striking (if ironic) elitist landscape. The design, of course, is merely pseudo-Puebloan, since most of these houses are built in typical suburban frame construction and disguised with plaster and paint to look like adobe walls. A perplexing lack of genuineness, so typical of popular cultural landscapes, is the result. **Is this necessarily bad? Does it tell us anything about placelessness?** (SEE KIMMEL, 1997. PHOTO COURTESY OF TERRY G. JORDAN-BYCHKOV.)

pleasing cultural landscape" characterized by preservation of old buildings and town cores, a sense of proportion, and respect for scale. Building codes and height restrictions are rigorously enforced. Land values, in response, have risen, making the Riviera ever more elitist, far removed from the folk culture and poverty that prevailed there before 1850. Farmers and fishermen have almost disappeared from the region, though one need drive but a short distance, to Toulon, to find a "scruffy and proletarian port." It seems, then, that the different social classes generated within popular culture become geographically segregated, each producing a distinctive cultural landscape.

America, too, offers elitist landscapes. Exclusive suburbs with rigidly enforced architectural themes are common, as in Santa Fe, where the favored style is pseudo–Pueblo Indian (Figure 2.35). Another excellent example is the *gentleman farm,* an agricultural unit operated for pleasure rather than profit (Figure 2.36). Typically, gentleman farms are owned by affluent city people as an avocation, and such farms help to create or maintain a high social standing for those who own them. Some rural landscapes in America now contain many such gentleman farms; perhaps most notable among these areas are the inner Bluegrass Basin of north-central Kentucky, the Virginia Piedmont west of Washington, D.C., eastern Long Island in New York, and parts of southeastern Pennsyl-

vania. Gentleman farmers engage in such activities as breeding fine cattle, racing horses, or hunting foxes.

Geographer Karl Raitz made a study of gentleman farms in the Kentucky Bluegrass Basin, where their concentration is so great that they constitute a dominant feature of the cultural landscape. The result is an idyllic scene, a rural landscape created more for appearance than for function. Raitz provided a list of visual indicators of Kentucky gentleman farms: wooden fences, either painted white or creosoted black; an elaborate entrance gate; a fine hand-painted sign giving the name of the farm and owner; a network of surfaced, well-maintained driveways and pasture roads; and a large, elegant house, visible in the distance from the public highway through a lawnlike parkland dotted with clumps of trees and perhaps a pond or two. So attractive are these estates to the eye that tourists cruise the rural lands to view them, convinced they are seeing the "real" rural America, or at least rural America as it ought to be.

Reflecting on **GEOGRAPHY**

Can you think of other types of landscapes of popular culture to go with consumption, leisure, and elitist landscapes?

Figure 2.36
Gentleman farm in the Kentucky Bluegrass region near Lexington. Here is "real" rural America as it should be (but never was). **What is the student of popular culture to make of the contrast between Figures 2.35 and 2.36?** (Courtesy of Terry G. Jordan-Bychkov.)

Shadowed Ground

The American landscape often also has a place for tragedy and violence, for "shadowed ground," as geographer Kenneth Foote terms such places. He addresses the question of what American popular culture does with stigmatized sites, where horrible events transpired, such as disastrous floods, bloody battles, or the 2001 World Trade Center mass murder by terrorists.

Foote found that several responses were common. Many stigmatized places undergo public sanctification, with visual reminders of the tragedy. Martin Luther King's assassination site at the Lorraine Motel in Memphis falls into this category, as do the Schoolbook Depository from which President Kennedy was assassinated in Dallas and the Gettysburg Battlefield of the Civil War. Those that induce shame or revulsion are often completely obliterated from the landscape. A McDonald's restaurant in San Diego was bulldozed after a deranged man killed 21 patrons in 1984, and the fast-food chain abandoned the site. Still other stigmatized places undergo "rectification," in which they are put back into the same use, often after needed repairs, with a plaque or some other modest visual reminder of the tragedy. The level of community shame often helps to determine the fate of shadowed ground (Figure 2.37 on the next page). The

United States, for example, was very slow to commemorate the sites of concentration camps where Japanese-Americans were detained during World War II.

> ## Reflecting on **GEOGRAPHY**
> Does the place where you live contain cultural landscapes of tragedy —shadowed ground? Were stigmatized places obliterated or rectified?

These examples by no means exhaust the content of popular cultural landscapes. The very proliferation of such terms as elitist, leisure, and shadowed landscapes should remind us of how spatially varied—how geographical—popular culture is.

The American Scene

One perceptive and sensitive humanistic geographer, David Lowenthal, attempted a broader analysis, an overall evaluation of the visible impact of popular culture on the American countryside. In an article entitled "The American Scene," Lowenthal listed the main characteristics of popular landscape in the United States. Among these are the "cult of bigness"; the tolerance of present

Figure 2.37
"Shadowed ground," in this case the **Branch Davidian religious compound near Waco, Texas,** where 75 members of this sect died in 1993 in a fire during a siege by troops of the U.S. Bureau of Alcohol, Tobacco, and Firearms. The site remains highly controversial. It is a rallying point for groups that support Branch Davidian leader David Koresh's resistance to federal authorities, a target for vandals offended by his actions, and a pilgrimage site for many others. (COURTESY OF KENNETH FOOTE, AUTHOR OF *SHADOWED GROUND*.)

ugliness to achieve a supposedly glorious future; emphasis on individual features at the expense of aggregates, producing a "casual chaos"; and the preeminence of function over form.

The American fondness for massive structures is reflected in such edifices such the Empire State Building, the Pentagon, the San Francisco–Oakland Bay Bridge, and Salt Lake City's Mormon Temple. Americans have dotted their cultural landscape with the world's largest of this or that, perhaps in an effort to match the grand scale of the physical environment, which offers such superlatives as the Grand Canyon, the redwoods, and the Yellowstone geysers.

Americans, says Lowenthal, tend to regard their cultural landscape as unfinished. As a result, they are "predisposed to accept present structures that are makeshift, flimsy, and transient," resembling "throwaway stage sets." Similarly, the hardships of pioneer life perhaps preconditioned Americans to value function more highly than beauty. The state capitol grounds in Oklahoma City are adorned with little more than oil derricks, standing above busy pumps drawing wealth from the Sooner soil—an extreme but revealing view of the American landscape (Figure 2.38).

Individual landscape features, says Lowenthal, take precedence over groupings. Five buildings or houses in a

Figure 2.38
Oil derrick on the Oklahoma state capitol grounds. The landscape of American popular culture is characterized by such functionality. The public and private sectors of the economy are increasingly linked in the popular culture. **Is criticism of such a landscape elitist and snobbish?** (SEE ALSO ROBERTSON, 1996. PHOTO COURTESY OF TERRY G. JORDAN-BYCHKOV.)

SEEING GEOGRAPHY

What makes one father-daughter pair so very different from the other?

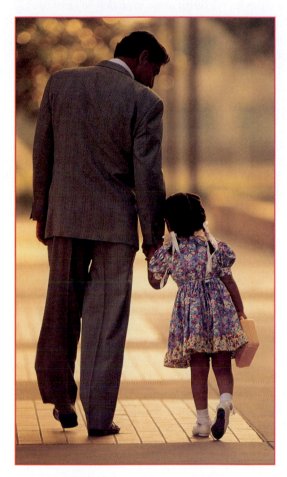

Two American father-daughter couples.

American Fathers and Daughters

Here we see two father-daughter couples, walking hand in hand down the street. They both live in the United States. But they also live in different worlds: folk and popular.

How can we tell? Well, the clothes they wear provide perhaps the main clue. The father and daughter on the left belong to the *Amish* religion, which has rejected most modern inventions and fads, retaining instead the folk lifestyle of the preindustrial age. Their clothing differs little from that of their ancestors in Pennsylvania two centuries ago. They are farmers rather than city dwellers. You can be sure that they will not get in a car and drive home, because they still prefer horse-drawn buggies.

The couple on the right is dressed very differently and clearly belongs to the popular culture. They may be going to buy a pizza or board a subway to go home. The father appears to be a businessman, and he certainly is not a farmer accustomed to working in fields with a horse-drawn plow.

And how do we know all this about their parallel, separate worlds? Mainly through the theme of cultural landscape. The clothing people wear can best be regarded as part of the visible culture—in other words, the landscape.

row may display five different architectural styles, and rarely is an attempt made to erect assemblages of structures that "belong" together. "Places are only collections of heterogeneous buildings." To be worthy, each structure must be unique and eye-catching, and architects in the popular culture vie with one another in producing attention-grabbing edifices. Each fast-food chain seems to require its own outlandish style of structure to facilitate instant visual recognition by potential customers.

Conclusion

Two fundamentally different cultures, two "parallel worlds," vie for the attention of the geographer. Popular culture possesses a vivid—if at times amusing, depressing, or simply absurd—geography. The counteracting popular trends toward placelessness and lifestyle spatial clustering are revealed through the theme of culture region. Diffusion of the popular culture occurs more rapidly than the diffusion of folk culture because of the technologies of communication and transportation, as well as the medium of advertising, a child of the popular culture. Ecologically, the influence of the physical environment on daily life has diminished, perhaps merely concealing our continued vulnerability at the very time when our ability to modify the habitat has reached unprecedented heights. The theme of cultural interaction allows us to look at the contradictory forces of individualism and convergence. Finally, an analysis of popular landscapes allows us to grasp the variety and magnitude of change being wrought by the popular culture.

Folk geographers, by contrast, study traditional, largely rural cultures. The five themes of cultural geography reveal the uniqueness of these folk regions, ecologies, diffusions, interactions, and landscapes.

Religion, a basic element of both folk and popular cultures, is vitally important in each. Chapter 3 is devoted to this major cultural trait.

Folk and Popular Culture on The Internet

You can learn more about the geography of folk and popular culture at the following web sites:

American Memory, Library of Congress
http://rs6.loc.gov

A project of the Library of Congress that presents a history of American popular culture, complete with documentation and maps.

Folk Culture from Around the World, Stillwater, Oklahoma
www.geog.okstate.edu/users/lightfoot/folk/folk.htm

This information database is located at the Department of Geography, Oklahoma State University.

Indiana University Folklore Institute
www.indiana.edu/~folklore/

The leading American academic center for folk culture studies, with international coverage of folklore.

International Folk Culture Center, San Antonio, Texas
www.ifccsa.org

This site has information on diverse aspects of folk culture, including traditional dress and the Virtual Museum of World Instruments.

Manchester Institute for Popular Culture, Manchester, U.K.
http://www.mmu.ac.uk/h-ss/mipc/

This site is dedicated to the academic study of popular culture, based at the Manchester Metropolitan University.

Pioneer America Society
http://www.uncwil.edu/people/ainsleyf/pas/pas.htm

The leading professional organization of geographers interested in both folk and popular cultural landscapes. The site describes its activities and publications, including its journal, *Material Culture*.

Popular Culture Association
http://www2.h-net.msu.edu/~pcaaca/

A multidisciplinary organization dedicated to the academic discussion of popular culture, where activities of the association are discussed.

Popular Press, Bowling Green State University
http://www.bgsu.edu/offices/press/

The leading publisher of academic studies of popular culture, including the *Journal of Popular Culture*.

Sources

Abler, Ronald F. 1973. "Monoculture or Miniculture? The Impact of Communication Media on Culture in Space," in David A. Lanegran and Risa Palm (eds.), *An Invitation to Geography*. New York: McGraw-Hill, 186–195.

Brownell, Joseph W. 1960. "The Cultural Midwest." *Journal of Geography* 59: 81–85.

Clevinger, Woodrow R. 1938. "The Appalachian Mountaineers in the Upper Cowlitz Basin." *Pacific Northwest Quarterly* 29: 115–134.

Clevinger, Woodrow R. 1942. "Southern Appalachian Highlanders in Western Washington." *Pacific Northwest Quarterly* 33: 3–25.

Curtis, James R. 1982. "McDonald's Abroad: Outposts of American Culture." *Journal of Geography* 81: 14–20.

Edmonson, Brad, and Linda Jacobsen. 1993. "Elvis Presley Memorabilia." *American Demographics* 15(8): 64.

Evans, E. Estyn. 1957. *Irish Folk Ways*. London: Routledge & Kegan Paul.

Fleming, Douglas K., and Richard Roth. 1991. "Place in Advertising." *Geographical Review* 81: 281–291.

Foote, Kenneth E. 1997. *Shadowed Ground: American's Landscape of Violence and Tragedy*. Austin: University of Texas Press.

Francaviglia, Richard V. 1973. "Diffusion and Popular Culture: Comments on the Spatial Aspects of Rock Music," in David A. Lanegran and Risa Palm (eds.), *An Invitation to Geography*. New York: McGraw-Hill, 87-96.

Frederickson, Kristine. 1984. *American Rodeo from Buffalo Bill to Big Business*. College Station: Texas A & M University Press.

Gade, Daniel W. 1982. "The French Riviera as Elitist Space." *Journal of Cultural Geography* 3: 19–28.

Geiger, Paul, et al. (eds.). 1950. *Atlas der Schweizerischen Volkskunde*. Basel: Schweizerische Gesellschaft für Volkskunde.

Glasscock, Robin E. 1991. "E. Estyn Evans, 1905–1989." *Journal of Historical Geography* 17: 87–91.

Godfrey, Brian J. 1993. "Regional Depiction in Contemporary Film." *Geographical Review* 83: 428–440.

Goss, Jon. 1999. "Once-upon-a-time in the Commodity World: An Unofficial Guide to the Mall of America." *Annals of the Association of American Geographers*, 89: 45–75.

Graff, Thomas O., and Dub Ashton. 1994. "Spatial Diffusion of Wal-Mart: Contagious and Reverse Hierarchical Elements." *Professional Geographer* 46: 19–29.

Gritzner, Charles F. 1974. "Construction Materials in a Folk Housing Tradition: Considerations Governing Their Selection in New Mexico." *Pioneer America* 6(1): 25–39.

Hecock, Richard D. 1987. "Changes in the Amenity Landscape: The Case of Some Northern Minnesota Townships." *North American Culture* 3(1): 53–66.

Holder, Arnold. 1993. "Dublin's Expanding Golfscape." *Irish Geography* 26: 151–157.

Hopkins, Jeffrey. 1990. "West Edmonton Mall: Landscape of Myths and Elsewhereness." *Canadian Geographer* 34: 2–17.

Jakle, John A., and Richard L. Mattson. 1981. "The Evolution of a Commercial Strip." *Journal of Cultural Geography* 1(2): 12-25.

Jett, Stephen C. 1991. "Further Information on the Geography of the Blowgun and Its Implications for Early Transoceanic Contacts." *Annals of the Association of American Geographers* 81: 89–102.

Kay, Jeanne, et al. 1981. "Evaluating Environmental Impacts of Off-Road Vehicles." *Journal of Geography* 80: 10–18.

Kimber, Clarissa T. 1973. "Plants in the Folk Medicine of the Texas-Mexico Borderlands." *Proceedings, Association of American Geographers* 5: 130–133.

Kimmel, James P. 1997. "Santa Fe: Thoughts on Contrivance, Commoditization, and Authencity." *Southwestern Geographer* 1: 44–61.

Kniffen, Fred B., 1951. "The American Agricultural Fair." Annals of the Association of American Geographers. 41: 43–54.

Kniffen, Fred B. 1965. "Folk-Housing: Key to Diffusion." *Annals of the Association of American Geographers* 55: 549–577.

Kunstler, James H. 1993. *The Geography of Nowhere: The Rise and Decline of America's Man-Made Landscape*. New York: Simon & Schuster.

Lowenthal, David. 1968. "The American Scene." *Geographical Review* 58: 61–88.

Miller, E. Joan Wilson. 1968. "The Ozark Culture Region as Revealed by Traditional Materials." *Annals of the Association of American Geographers* 58: 51–77.

Mings, Robert C., and Kevin E. McHugh. 1989. "The RV Resort Landscape." *Journal of Cultural Geography* 10: 35–49.

Pillsbury, Richard. 1990a. "Striking to Success." *Sport Place* 4(1): 16, 35.

Pillsbury, Richard. 1990b. "Ride 'm Cowboy." *Sport Place* 4: 26–32.

Pillsbury Richard. 1998. *No Foreign Food: The American Diet in Time and Place*. Boulder, Colo.: Westview Press.

Price, Edward T. 1960. "Root Digging in the Appalachians: The Geography of Botanical Drugs." *Geographical Review* 50: 1–20.

Raitz, Karl B. 1975. "Gentleman Farms in Kentucky's Inner Bluegrass." *Southeastern Geographer* 15: 33–46.

Raitz, Karl B. 1987. "Place, Space and Environment in America's Leisure Landscapes." *Journal of Cultural Geography* 8(1): 49–62.

Relph, Edward. 1976. *Place and Placelessness*. London: Pion.

Roark, Michael. 1985. "Fast Foods: American Food Regions." *North American Culture* 2(1): 24–36.

Robertson, David S. 1996. "Oil Derricks and Corinthian Columns: The Industrial Transformation of the Oklahoma State Capitol Grounds." *Journal of Cultural Geography* 16: 17–44.

Rooney, John F., Jr. 1969. "Up From the Mines and Out From the Prairies: Some Geographical Implications of Football in the United States." *Geographical Review* 59: 471–492.

Rooney, John F., Jr. 1988. "Where They Come From." *Sport Place* 2(3): 17.

Rooney, John F., Jr., and Paul L. Butt. 1978. "Beer, Bourbon, and Boone's Farm: A Geographical Examination of Alcoholic Drink in the United States." *Journal of Popular Culture* 11: 832–856.

Rooney, John F., Jr., and Richard Pillsbury. 1992. *Atlas of American Sport*. New York: Macmillan.

Sack, Robert D. 1992. *Place, Modernity, and the Consumer's World: A Rational Framework for Geographical Analysis*. Baltimore: Johns Hopkins University Press.

Scott, Damon. 2003 (in progress). "The Gay Geography of San Francisco." Ph.D. dissertation. University of Texas at Austin.

Shortridge, Barbara G. 1987. *Atlas of American Women.* New York: Macmillan.

Shortridge, James R. 1989. *The Middle West: Its Meaning in American Culture.* Lawrence: University Press of Kansas.

Shuhua, Chang. 1977. "The Gentle Yamis of Orchid Island." *National Geographic* 151(1): 98–109.

Tuan, Yi-fu. *Topophilia.* Englewood Cliffs, N.J.: Prentice-Hall, 1974.

Walker, H. Jesse, and Miles E. Richardson. 1994. "Fred Bowerman Kniffen, 1900–1993." *Annals of the Association of American Geographers* 84: 732–743.

Weiss, Michael J. 1988. *The Clustering of America.* New York: Harper & Row.

Wilhelm, Eugene J., Jr. 1968. "Field Work in Folklife: Meeting Ground of Geography and Folklore." *Keystone Folklore Quarterly* 13: 241–247.

Zelinsky, Wilbur. 1974. "Cultural Variation in Personal Name Patterns in the Eastern United States." *Annals of the Association of American Geographers* 60: 743–769.

Zelinsky, Wilbur. 1980a. "North America's Vernacular Regions." *Annals of the Association of American Geographers* 70: 1–16.

Zelinsky, Wilbur. 1980b. "Selfward Bound? Personal Preference Patterns and the Changing Map of American Society." *Economic Geography* 50: 144–179.

Zonn, Leo (ed.). 1990. *Place Images in Media: Portrayal, Experience, and Meaning.* Savage, Md.: Rowman & Littlefield.

Ten Recommended Books on Folk and Popular Cultural Geography

(For additional suggested readings, see The Human Mosaic *web site:* www.whfreeman.com/jordan*)*

Burgess, Jacquelin A., and John R. Gold (eds.). 1985. *Geography, the Media, and Popular Culture.* New York: St. Martin's Press. The geography of popular culture is linked in diverse ways to the communications media, and this collection of essays explores facets of that relationship.

Carney, George O. (ed.). 1998. *Baseball, Barns and Bluegrass: A Geography of American Folklife.* Boulder, Colo.: Rowman & Littlefield. A wonderful collection of readings that, contrary to the title, span the gap between folk and popular culture.

Ensminger, Robert F. 1992. *The Pennsylvania Barn: Its Origin, Evolution, and Distribution in North America.* Baltimore: Johns Hopkins University Press. A common American folk barn, part of the rural cultural landscape, provides geographer Ensminger with visual clues to its origin and diffusion; a fascinating detective story showing how geographers "read" cultural landscapes and what they learn in the process.

Foote, Kenneth E. 1997. *Shadowed Ground: America's Landscapes of Violence and Tragedy.* Austin: University of Texas Press. What happens to places in our popular culture where horrible things happen? How are they treated in the popular cultural landscape? Geographer Foote provides the answers in this fascinating study.

Glassie, Henry. 1968. *Pattern in the Material Folk Culture of the Eastern United States.* Philadelphia: University of Pennsylvania Press. Glassie, a student of folk geographer Fred Kniffen, considers the geographical distribution of a wide array of folk culture items in this classic overview.

Jordan, Terry G., Jon T. Kilpinen, and Charles F. Gritzner. 1997. *The Mountain West: Interpreting the Folk Landscape.* Baltimore: Johns Hopkins University Press. Reading the folk landscapes of the American West, three geographers reach conclusions about the regional culture and how it evolved.

Rooney, John F., Jr. 1974. *A Geography of American Sport.* Reading, Mass.: Addison-Wesley. Rooney pioneered the geographical study of sports—a vital aspect of popular culture— and discovered a rich regional variety.

Skelton, Tracey, and Gill Valentine (eds.). 1998. *Cool Places: Geographies of Youth Cultures.* London: Routledge. The engaging essays in *Cool Places* explore the dichotomy of youthful lives by addressing the issues of representation and resistance in youth culture today. Using first-person vignettes to illustrate the wide-ranging experiences of youth, the authors consider how the media have imagined young people as a particular community with shared interests and how young people resist these stereotypes, instead creating their own independent representations of their lives.

Weiss, Michael J. 1994. *Latitudes and Attitudes: An Atlas of American Tastes, Trends, Politics, and Passions.* New York: Little, Brown. Using marketing data organized by postal zip codes, Weiss reveals the geographical diversity of American popular culture.

Zelinsky, Wilbur. 1992. *The Cultural Geography of the United States,* 2nd ed. Englewood Cliffs, N.J.: Prentice-Hall. Revised edition of a sprightly, classic book, originally published in 1973, revealing the cultural sectionalism in modern America, in the era of popular culture, with attention also to folk roots.

Journals in Folk and Popular Cultural Geography

Journal of Popular Culture. Published by the Popular Culture Association from 1967 until its demise in 2002. Volume 1 appeared in 1967. See in particular Vol. 11, No. 4, 1978, a special issue on cultural geography and popular culture.

Material Culture: Journal of the Pioneer America Society. Published three times annually, this leading periodical specializes in the subject of traditional American material culture. Volume 1 was published in 1969, and prior to 1984 the journal was called *Pioneer America.*

Answers

Figure 2.7
The scenes were taken in the following unplaces: McDonald's in Tokyo, Wendy's in Idaho, and Pampas Grill in Finland.

Figure 2.31
(a) French-Canadian farmhouse, Port Joli, Québec; (b) New England "large" house, in New Hampshire; (c) Yankee upright-and-wing house, Massachusetts; (d) shotgun house, Alleyton, Texas.

Why have such different and opposed ways developed to worship one God?

Worshipers in front of a mosque in Pakistan. (COURTESY OF TERRY G. JORDAN-BYCHKOV.)
Turn to Seeing Geography *on page 110 for an in-depth analysis of the above question.*

CHAPTER
3

THE GEOGRAPHY OF RELIGION
Spaces and Places of Faith

As one of the most essential parts of culture, religion lends vivid hues to the human mosaic. It provides a good place to begin our topical study of cultural geography. **Religion** can be defined as a set of beliefs and practices through which people seek mental and physical harmony with the powers of the universe and through which they attempt to influence and accommodate the awesome forces of nature, life, and death. In literal terms, the word *religion*—derived from the Latin *religare*—means "to fasten loose parts into a coherent whole." For some cultural groups, religion is little more than a protective buffer between humans and the mysterious, potentially destructive forces of nature. Other groups have, over centuries, developed complicated systems of belief with elaborate moral codes.

Because people differ so much in their religious beliefs, geographers have long been fascinated by the subject; in fact, the Association of American Geographers includes a special interest group called the Geography of Religions and Belief Systems (Table 3.1). The link between the study of religion and cultural geography will be revealed through our five themes. Religion differs from one place to another, producing spatial variations that can be mapped as culture regions. These regions were produced by cultural diffusion and reflect a complex interplay among religion, the environment, and other aspects of culture. In turn, the spatial pattern of religion is visibly imprinted on the cultural landscape (Figure 3.1). Religion very often lies at the root of conflict between cultural groups, for

Major Religions

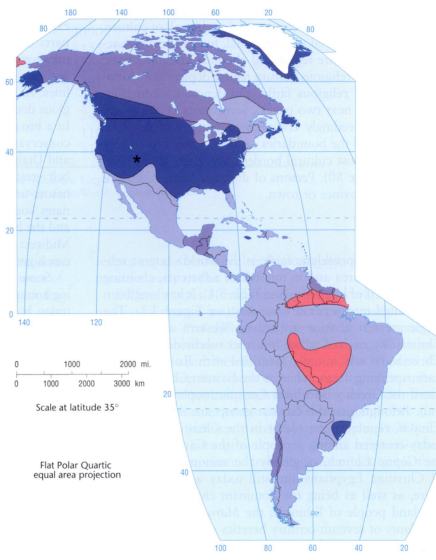

0   1000   2000 mi.

0   1000   2000   3000 km

Scale at latitude 35°

Flat Polar Quartic
equal area projection

Figure 3.2

The world distribution of major religions. Much overlap exists that cannot be shown on a map of this scale. The attempt is to show which faith is dominant. "Animism" includes a wide array of diverse tribal belief systems. "Chinese Mahayana" is the same as "Chinese composite faiths" shown in Table 3.1, and its total members figure is deleted from the Buddhist total in that table. "Mixed" Christianity means that none of the three major branches of that faith have a majority. "Protestant-derived" refers to Mormons.

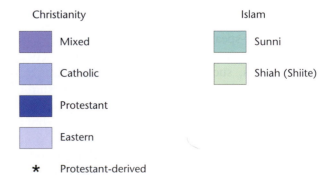

Christianity

- Mixed
- Catholic
- Protestant
- Eastern

*   Protestant-derived

Islam

- Sunni
- Shiah (Shiite)

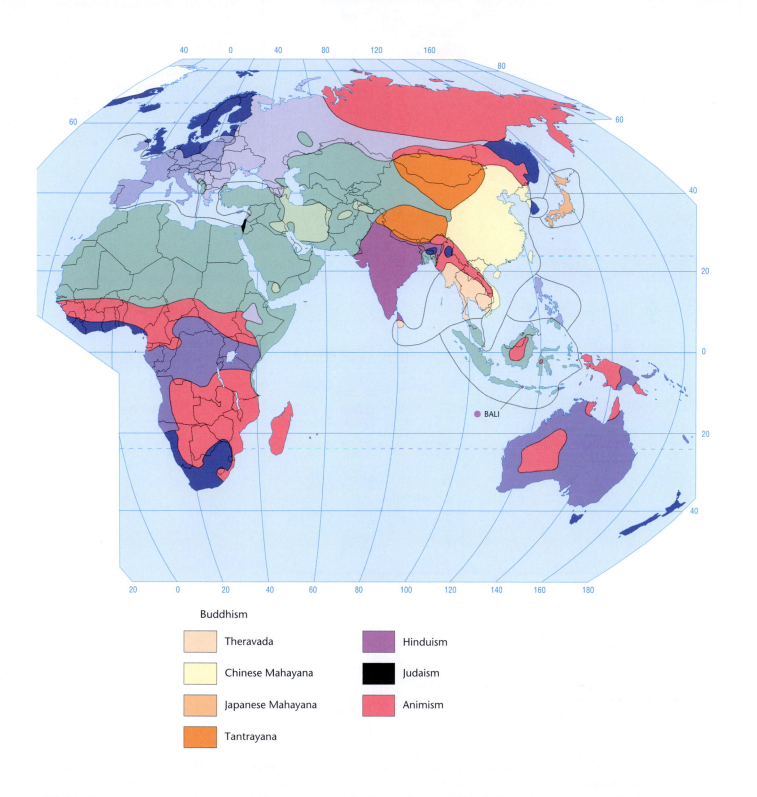

Buddhism

Theravada		Hinduism	
Chinese Mahayana		Judaism	
Japanese Mahayana		Animism	
Tantrayana			

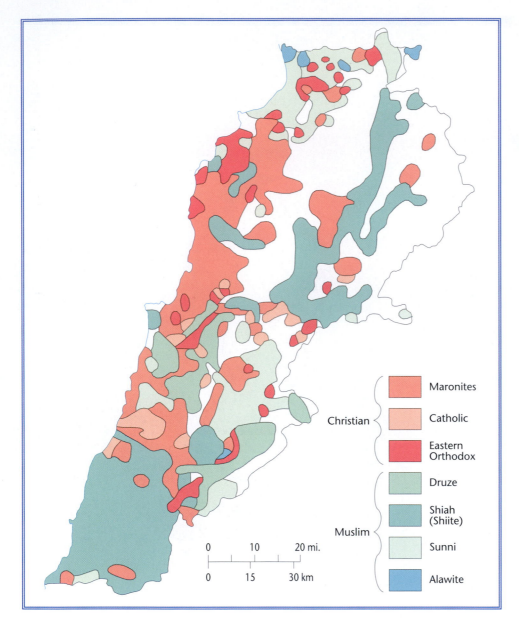

Figure 3.3
Distribution of religious groups in Lebanon. A land torn by sectarian warfare in recent times, Lebanon is one of the most religiously diverse parts of the world. Overall, Lebanon is today 37 percent Christian, 34 percent Shiite Muslim, 21 percent Sunni Muslim, and 7 percent Druze. Unshaded areas are largely unpopulated. (DERIVED, WITH CHANGES, FROM KLAER, 1966: 333; AND *THE ECONOMIST* (FEB. 24, 1996). SEE ALSO STEWART, 1996: 489–492.)

Legend:

Christian
- Maronites
- Catholic
- Eastern Orthodox

Muslim
- Druze
- Shiah (Shiite)
- Sunni
- Alawite

0 10 20 mi.
0 15 30 km

as the Five Pillars of the faith. Figure 3.5 on page 82 shows a mosque in Nigeria where the faithful pray.

Although not as severely fragmented as Christianity, Islam too has split into separate groups. Two major sects prevail. The *Shiite* Muslims, 16 percent of the Islamic total in diverse subgroups, form the majority in Iran and Iraq. *Sunni* Muslims, who represent the Islamic orthodoxy, form the large majority (see Figure 3.2). Their strength is greatest in the Arabic-speaking lands, though non-Arabic Indonesia now contains the world's largest Sunni Islamic concentration, and other large clusters live in western China and in Bangladesh and Pakistan. Islam will soon surpass Judaism to become America's second largest faith. Under Iranian and Afghan leadership, a fundamentalist revival is occurring that aims to throw off Western influences while restoring the purity of the faith.

Judaism

Judaism, a monotheistic faith, is the parent of Christianity and is closely related to Islam. Certain Hebrew prophets and leaders are recognized in all three religions. In contrast to the other monotheistic faiths, Judaism does not actively seek new converts and has remained an ethnic religion through most of its existence. It has split into a variety of subgroups, partly as a result of the forced dispersal of the Jews from Palestine in Roman times and the

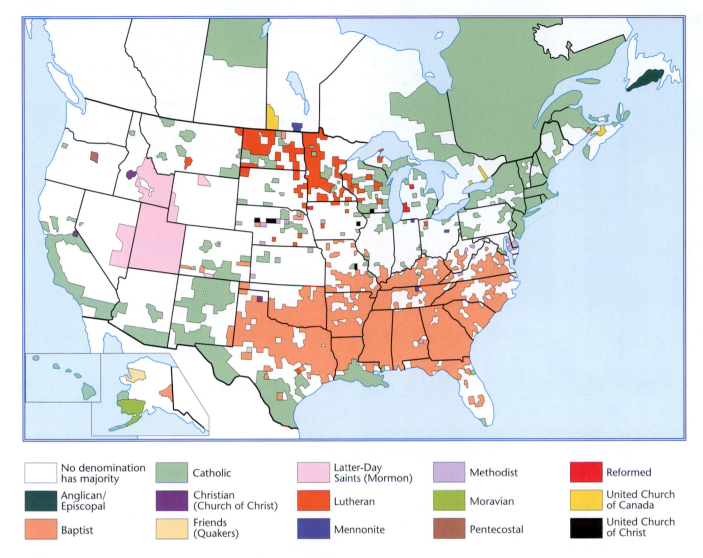

Figure 3.4
Leading Christian denominations in the United States and Canada, shown by counties for the
United States) census districts (for Canada). In the shaded areas, the church or denomination
indicated claimed 50 percent or more of the total church membership. The most striking features of
the map are the Baptist dominance through the South, a Lutheran zone in the upper Midwest,
Mormon dominance in the interior West, and the zone of mixing in the American heartland. **Why are
individual denominations less likely to dominate areas in western parts of North America?**
(SIMPLIFIED FROM BRADLEY ET AL., 1992; AND *THE NATIONAL ATLAS OF CANADA*.)

Legend:

- No denomination has majority
- Catholic
- Latter-Day Saints (Mormon)
- Methodist
- Reformed
- Anglican/Episcopal
- Christian (Church of Christ)
- Lutheran
- Moravian
- United Church of Canada
- Baptist
- Friends (Quakers)
- Mennonite
- Pentecostal
- United Church of Christ

subsequent loss of contact among the various colonies.
Jews, scattered to many parts of the Roman Empire, became a minority group wherever they were found. In later
times, they spread throughout much of Europe, North
Africa, and Arabia. Those Jews who resided in the Mediterranean lands were called the *Sephardim;* those in central
and eastern Europe were known as the *Ashkenazim.*

The late nineteenth and early twentieth centuries witnessed large-scale Ashkenazic migration from Europe to
America. The Holocaust that befell European Judaism during the Nazi years involved the systematic murder of perhaps a third of the entire Jewish population of the world,
mainly Ashkenazim. Europe ceased to be the primary
homeland of Judaism, and many of the survivors fled overseas, mainly to the newly created state of Israel and America. Judaism has about 14 million adherents throughout
the world. At present, nearly 7 million, or about half of the
world's Jewish population, live in North America.

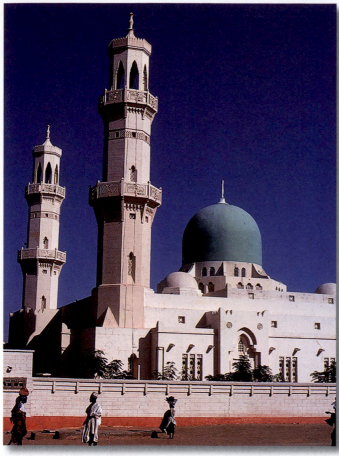

Figure 3.5

Muslim mosque, northern Nigeria. The color green is sacred in Islam and appears often on mosques and *minarets,* the tall circular towers from which the faithful are called to prayer. **Why might green be a sacred color to a desert-born religion?** (Diane Rawson/Photo Researchers.)

Hinduism

Hinduism, a religion closely tied to India and its ancient culture, claims about 800 million adherents (see Table 3.1 and Figure 3.2). A decidedly **polytheistic** religion, involving the worship of a myriad of deities, Hinduism is also linked to the *caste system,* a rigid segregation of people according to ancestry and occupation; *ahimsa,* the veneration of all forms of life, which includes the principle of noninjury to all sentient creatures; and a belief in reincarnation. No standard set of beliefs prevails, and the faith takes many local forms. Hinduism includes very diverse peoples. Once a proselytic religion, it is today a regional, national faith. An outlier of Hinduism on the distant Indonesian island of Bali suggests its former missionary activity.

Hinduism has splintered into diverse religious groups, some of which are so distinctive as to be regarded as separate religions. *Jainism* is an ancient outgrowth of Hinduism, claiming perhaps 4 million adherents, almost all in India, and tracing its roots back over 25 centuries. Although rejecting Hindu scriptures, rituals, and priesthood, the Jains share the Hindu belief in ahimsa and reincarnation. Jains adhere to a stern asceticism. *Sikhism,* by contrast, arose much later, in the 1500s, as an attempt to unify Hinduism and Islam. Centered in the Punjab state of northwestern India, where the Golden Temple at Amritsar serves as the principal shrine, Sikhism has about 23 million followers. Sikhs are monotheistic and have their own holy book, the *Adi Granth.*

Buddhism

Derived from Hinduism, Buddhism began 25 centuries ago as a reform movement based on the teachings of Prince Siddhartha, called the Buddha, or "the awakened one" (Figure 3.6). He promoted the four "noble truths": life is full of suffering; desire is the cause of this suffering; cessation of suffering comes with the quelling of desire; and an "Eight-Fold Path" of proper personal conduct and meditation permits the individual to overcome desire. The resultant state of escape and peace, achieved by very few, is known as *nirvana.*

Today, Buddhism is the most widespread religion in Asia, dominating a culture region stretching from Sri Lanka to Japan and from Mongolia to Vietnam. In the process of its proselytic spread, particularly in China and Japan, Buddhism fused with native ethnic religions such as Confucianism, Taoism, and Shintoism to form composite faiths that fall into the *Mahayana* division of Buddhism. Southern, or *Theravada,* Buddhism, dominant in Sri Lanka and mainland Southeast Asia, retains the greatest similarity to the religion's original form, whereas a special variation known as *Tantrayana,* or *Lamaism,* prevails in Tibet and Mongolia (see Figure 3.2). Buddhism's tendency to merge with native religions, particularly in China, makes it difficult to determine the number of its adherents. Estimates range from 350 million to over 500 million people (see Table 3.1). Although Buddhism in China has become enmeshed with local faiths to become part of a composite ethnic religion, elsewhere it remains one of the three great proselytic religions in the world.

Animism/Shamanism

Tribal peoples in diverse parts of the world often retain ethnic religions and are usually referred to collectively as **animists.** Currently numbering perhaps 240 million, ani-

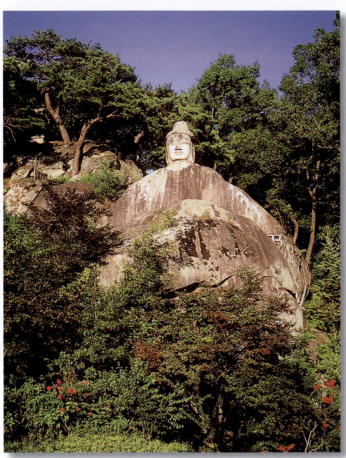

Figure 3.6
Buddhism is one of the religious faiths of South Korea. Here an image of the Buddha is carved from a rocky bluff to create sacred space and a local pilgrimage shrine. **Do such places exist in Christianity?** (Courtesy of Terry G. Jordan-Bychkov.)

mists believe that certain inanimate objects possess spirits or souls. These spirits live in rocks and rivers, on mountain peaks and heavenly bodies, in forests and swamps. Each tribe has its own characteristic form of animism and has vested a particular set of objects with spirits. A tribal religious figure, called by some a *shaman,* usually serves as an intermediary between the people and the spirits. To some other animists, the objects in question do not actually possess spirits but rather are valued because they have a particular potency to serve as a link between a person and the omnipresent god. We should not classify such systems of belief as primitive or simple, because they can be extraordinarily complex.

Sub-Saharan Africa is the greatest surviving stronghold of animism, in terms of both numbers of adherents and percentage of total population (Figure 3.7 on the next page). Along the northern edge of the animist region, Islam is rapidly winning converts, and Christian missionaries are very active throughout the area, but animism seems likely to survive in Africa. Descendants of African slaves in the Americas have kept alive such animistic faiths as *Umbanda,* which claims perhaps 30 million followers in Brazil, and *Santeria,* found mainly in Cuba. These survive beneath a facade of nominal Roman Catholicism.

Secularization

In some parts of the world, especially in much of Europe, religion has declined, giving way to *secularization* (Figure 3.8 on page 85). The number of nonreligious, agnostic, and atheistic persons in the world is reputedly about 913 million at present (see Table 3.1). The American Religious Identification Survey (see the listing under Geography of Religion on the Internet at the end of the chapter), compiled in 2001, found 30 million nonreligious adults in the United States, or about 14 percent. In the state of Hawaii, 51 percent of adults are unaffiliated with a church. Typically, secularization displays a vivid regionalization on a variety of scales. Areas of surviving religious vitality lie alongside secularized districts, in a disorderly jumble. Such patterns once again reveal the inherent spatial variety of humankind and invite analysis by the cultural geographer. In some instances, the retreat from organized religion has resulted from a government's active hostility toward a particular faith or toward religion in general. In other cases, we can attribute the decline to the failure of religions oriented to the needs of rural folk cultures to adapt to the urban scene.

Sacred Space

Geographers also recognize other types of religious culture regions. **Sacred space** provides an example. These sites consist of natural and/or human-made assemblages that possess special religious meaning, recognized as worthy of devotion, loyalty, fear, or esteem (see Figure 3.6). Sacred space can be a functional or a vernacular culture region, and in some cases both. The notion that particular places possess sacredness occurs in many different cultures, past and present, all over the world. James Griffith speaks of "supernaturally sanctioned ties between individual cultures and specific places," a link he calls *spiritual geography.* B. C. Lane says, "A sacred place is an ordinary one made extraordinary through ritual." By virtue of their sacredness, these special places might be avoided by the faithful, sought out by pilgrims, or barred to members of other religions. Often sacred space includes the site of supposed supernatural events or is viewed as

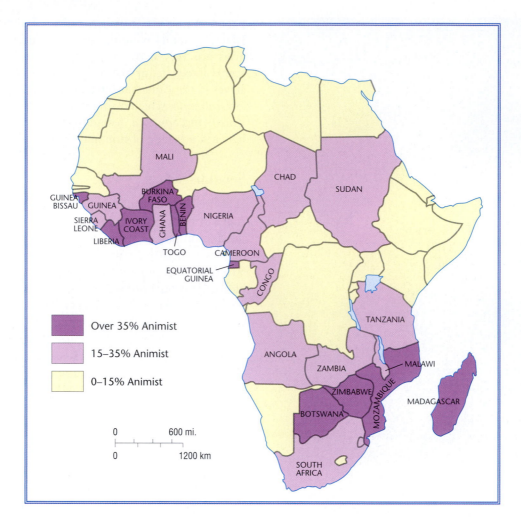

Figure 3.7

Africa is the last major stronghold of animists. Christian and Islamic missionaries are active in the remaining animist regions, but these tribal religions may survive in the long run. (DERIVED FROM JOHNSTONE, 1986: 25.)

the abode of gods. Conflict can result if two religions venerate the same space (see Focus On: Conflict over Sacred Space on page 86). In Jerusalem, for example, the Muslim Dome of the Rock, the site of Muhammad's ascent to heaven, stands above the Western Wall, the remnant of the greatest Jewish temple of antiquity (Figure 3.9 on page 86). Cemeteries are also generally regarded as a type of sacred space. So is Mount Sinai, described by geographer Joseph Hobbs as endowed "with special grace," where God instructed the faithful to "mark out the limits of the mountain and declare it sacred."

Sacred space is receiving increased attention in the world. In the middle 1990s, the internationally funded *Sacred Land Project* began to identify and protect such sites, 5000 of which have been cataloged in the United Kingdom alone. Included are such places as ancient stone circles, pilgrim routes, holy springs, and sites that convey mystery or great natural beauty. This last type falls into the category of *mystical places:* locations unconnected with established religion where, for whatever reason, some people believe that extraordinary, supernatural things can happen. The Bermuda Triangle in the western Atlantic, where airplanes and ships supposedly disappear, is a mystical place and, in effect, a vernacular culture region. Some people find the expanses of the American Great Plains to be a mystical place, and Jonathan Raban spoke of them as "a landscape ideally suited to the staging of the millennium, open to the gaze of the Almighty." Sometimes the sacred space of vanished ancient religions never loses—or later regains—the functional status of mystical place, which has happened at Stonehenge in England.

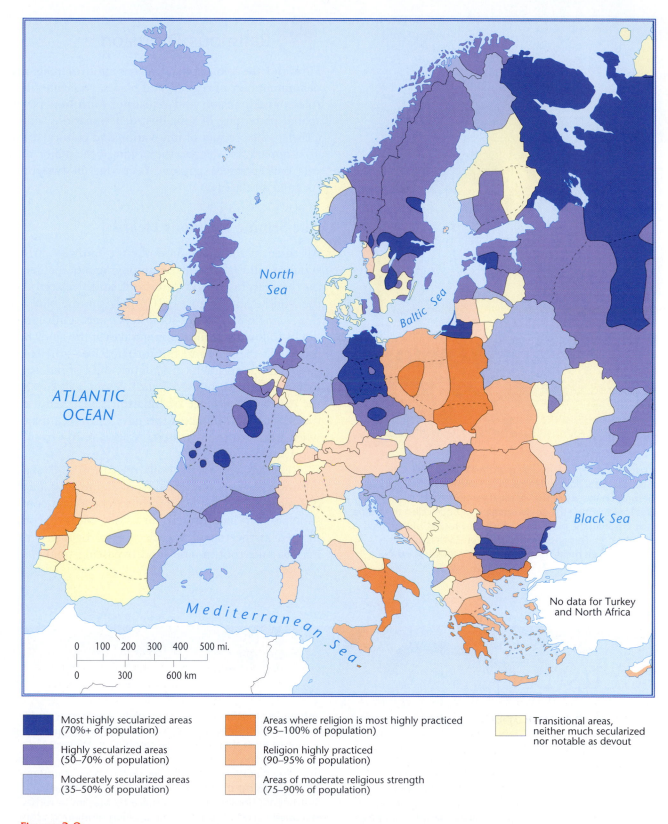

Most highly secularized areas (70%+ of population)

Highly secularized areas (50–70% of population)

Moderately secularized areas (35–50% of population)

Areas where religion is most highly practiced (95–100% of population)

Religion highly practiced (90–95% of population)

Areas of moderate religious strength (75–90% of population)

Transitional areas, neither much secularized nor notable as devout

Figure 3.8

Secularized areas in Europe. These areas, in which Christianity has ceased to be of much importance, occur in a complicated pattern. **What causal forces might have been at work?** In all of Europe, some 190 million people report no religious faith, amounting to 27 percent of the population. (SOURCE: JORDAN-BYCHKOV AND JORDAN, 2002: 104.)

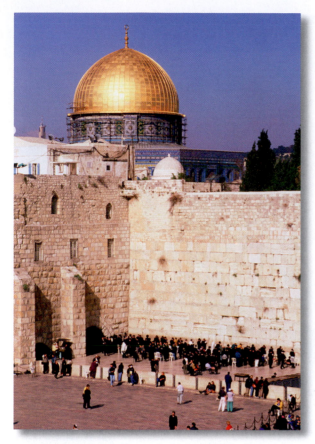

Figure 3.9

Conflict over sacred space. Jews pray at the Western Wall, the remnant of their great ancient temple in Jerusalem, in Israel. Standing above the wall, on the site of the vanished Jewish temple, is one of the holiest sites for Muslims—the golden-capped mosque called the Dome of the Rock, covering the place from which the Prophet Muhammad ascended to heaven. Perhaps no other place on Earth is so heavily charged with religious meaning and conflict. (GARY CRALLE/GETTYONE.)

 ## Religious Diffusion

How did the geographical distribution of religions and denominations, of regions and places, come about? What roles did expansion and relocation diffusion play? The spatial patterning of religions, denominations, and secularism is the product of innovation and cultural diffusion. To a remarkable degree, the origin of the major religions was concentrated spatially, occurring in two principal Asian hearth areas.

The Semitic Religious Hearth

All three of the great monotheistic faiths—Christianity, Judaism, and Islam—arose among Semitic peoples in or on the margins of the deserts of southwestern Asia, in the Middle East (Figure 3.10). Judaism, the oldest of the three, originated some 4000 years ago. Only gradually did its followers acquire dominion over the lands between the Mediterranean and the Jordan River—the territorial base of modern Israel. Christianity, child of Judaism, originated in this "Promised Land" about halfway through the temporal existence of Judaism. Seven centuries later, the Semitic hearth once again gave birth to a major faith when Islam arose in western Arabia, partly from Jewish and Christian roots.

Religions spread by both relocation and expansion diffusion. As you may recall from Figure 1.10, expansion diffusion can be divided into hierarchical and contagious subtypes. In hierarchical diffusion, ideas become implanted at the top of a society, leapfrogging across the map to take root in cities and bypassing smaller villages

FOCUS ON

Conflict over Sacred Space

When two or more religions claim the same sacred space, conflict is usually unavoidable. In 1992, at the town of Ayodhya (see Figure 3.13), in Uttar Pradesh state near the Nepal border in northern India, Hindus seized an Islamic mosque and destroyed it. They tore down the 450-year-old mosque in hopes of replacing it with a Hindu temple, claiming that the site is the precise birthplace of the pious god-king Rama, the "perfect Hindu" and protagonist of the epic tale *Ramayana.* Rama, whose very name became a synonym for the divine, is believed to have been an incarnation of the great god

Vishnu, the most important solar deity, a preserver and restorer. To Muslims, the destruction of the mosque was an affront to Allah that demanded retribution. Widespread religious rioting and violence plagued the country because of this desecration and conflict over sacred space, causing 2000 deaths. At the fifth anniversary of the mosque's destruction, bombs placed on trains by Muslim terrorists exploded in several parts of India, killing or injuring scores of people, and in December 2000, another 2000 people died in riots there. In March 2002, the Supreme Court of India forbade Hindu activists to perform ceremonies on the site and upheld a ban on building a new Hindu temple here.

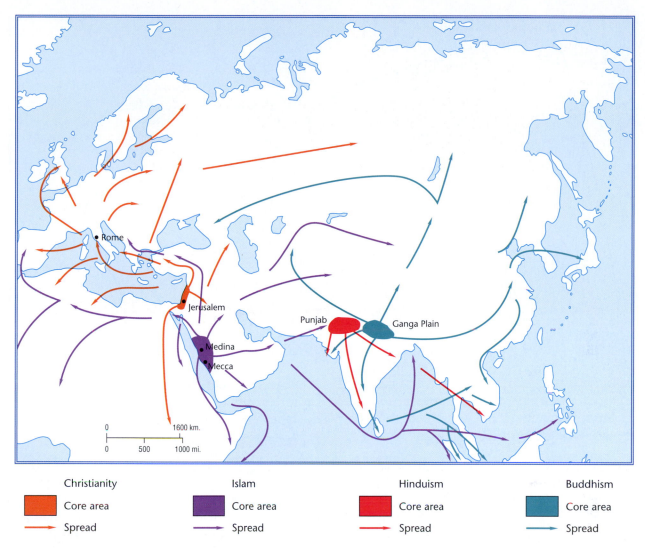

Figure 3.10

The origin and diffusion of four major religions in Eurasia. Christianity and Islam, the two great proselytic monotheistic faiths, arose in Semitic southwestern Asia and spread widely through the Old World. Hinduism and Buddhism both originated in the northern reaches of the Indian subcontinent and spread throughout southeastern Eurasia. **What special qualities might these hearth areas have had to allow them to become so important as religious source regions?**

and rural areas. Obviously, proselytic faiths are more likely to diffuse than ethnic religions, and it is not surprising that the spread of monotheism was accomplished largely by Christianity and Islam, rather than Judaism. From Semitic southwestern Asia, both of the proselytic monotheistic faiths diffused widely.

Christians, observing the admonition in the Gospel of Matthew—"Go ye therefore and teach all nations, baptizing them in the name of the Father, and of the Son, and of the Holy Ghost, teaching them to observe all things whatsoever I have commanded you"—initially spread through the Roman Empire, using the splendid system of imperial roads to extend the faith. In its early

centuries of expansion, Christianity displayed a spatial distribution that clearly reflected hierarchical diffusion (Figure 3.11 on the next page). The early congregations were established in cities and towns, temporarily producing a pattern of Christianized urban centers and pagan rural areas. Indeed, traces of this process remain in our language. The Latin word *pagus*, "countryside," is the root of both *pagan* and *peasant*, suggesting the ancient heathen connotation of rurality.

The scattered urban clusters of early Christianity were created by such missionaries as the apostle Paul, who moved from town to town bearing the news of the emerging faith. In later centuries, Christian missionaries often

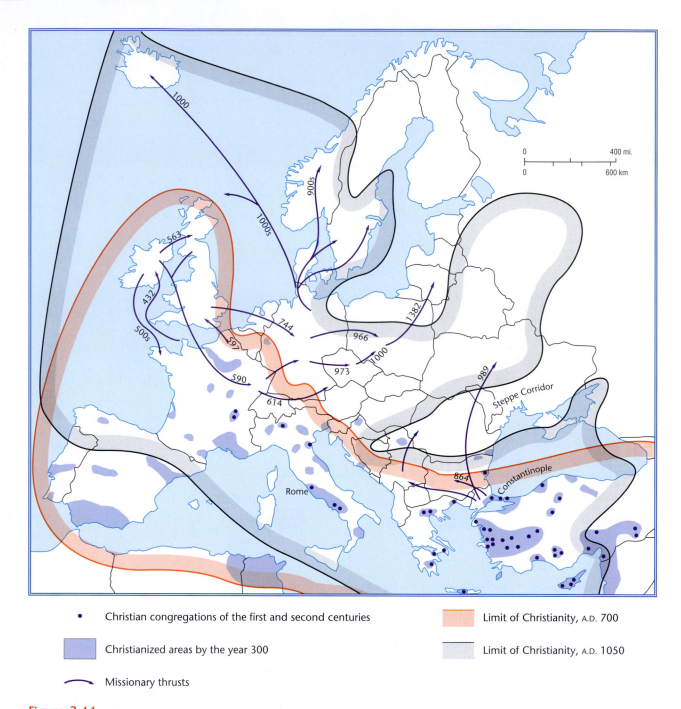

- •   Christian congregations of the first and second centuries
- ▬   Christianized areas by the year 300
- ⌒   Missionary thrusts
- ▬   Limit of Christianity, A.D. 700
- ▬   Limit of Christianity, A.D. 1050

Figure 3.11

The diffusion of Christianity in Europe, first to eleventh centuries. In what way do the patterns for the first and second centuries and for the year 300 suggest hierarchical expansion diffusion? Compare with Figure 1.10. **Who were the "knowers" (converts) and who were the laggards at this stage? What barriers to diffusion might account for the uneven advance by the year 1050? Why did retreat occur in some areas?**

used the technique of converting kings or tribal leaders, setting in motion additional hierarchical diffusion. The Russians and Poles were converted in this manner. Some Christian expansion was militaristic, as in the reconquest of Iberia and the invasion of Latin America. Once im-planted in this manner, Christianity spread farther by means by contagious diffusion. When applied to religion, this method of spread is called **contact conversion** and is the result of everyday association between believers and nonbelievers.

Figure 3.12
Nearly half of all South Koreans are Christians. Most of these are Protestants, and Presbyterianism is the leading denomination. **Why has the cultural diffusion of Christianity succeeded so impressively in Korea while failing in neighboring China and Japan?** (COURTESY OF TERRY G. JORDAN-BYCHKOV.)

Christian cultural diffusion has been so successful as to create some geographical oddities. For example, South Korea now has more Presbyterians than Scotland, where this denomination originated (Figure 3.12), and more members of the Church of England live in sub-Saharan Africa than in Great Britain.

The Islamic faith spread from its Semitic hearth area in a militaristic manner. Obeying the command in the Koran that they "do battle against them until there be no more seduction from the truth and the only worship be that of Allah," the Arabs exploded westward across North Africa in a wave of religious conquest. The Turks, once converted by the Arabs, carried out similar Islamic conquests. In a different sort of diffusion, Muslim missionaries followed trade routes eastward to implant Islam hierarchically in the Philippines, Indonesia, and the interior of China. Tropical Africa is the current major scene of Islamic expansion, an effort that has produced competi-

tion with Christians for the conversion of animists. As a result of diffusionary successes in sub-Saharan Africa and high birthrates in its older sphere of dominance, Islam has become the world's fastest growing religion in terms of the number of new adherents.

The Indus-Ganga Hearth

The second great religious hearth area lay in the plains fringing the northern edge of the Indian subcontinent. This lowland, drained by the Ganga (Ganges) and Indus rivers, gave birth to Hinduism and Buddhism. The earliest faith to derive from this hearth was Hinduism, which is at least 4000 years old. Its origin apparently lay in the Punjab, from which it diffused to dominate the subcontinent, although some historians believe that the earliest form of Hinduism was introduced from Iran with emigrating Indo-European tribes about 1500 B.C. Missionaries later carried the faith, in its proselytic phase, to overseas areas, but most of these converted regions were subsequently lost.

Buddhism began in the foothills bordering the Ganga Plain about 500 B.C., branching off from Hinduism (see Figure 3.10). For centuries it remained confined to the Indian subcontinent, but missionaries later carried the religion to China (100 B.C. to A.D. 200), Korea and Japan (A.D. 300 to 500), Southeast Asia (A.D. 400 to 600), Tibet (A.D. 700), and Mongolia (A.D. 1500). Like Christianity, Buddhism developed many regional forms and nearly died out in its area of origin, reabsorbed into Hinduism.

The diffusion of Buddhism, like that of Christianity and Islam, continues to the present day. Some 2 million Buddhists live in the United States, about the same number as Episcopalians. Mostly, their presence is the result of relocation diffusion. Immigrant Buddhists outnumber converts by three to one.

> ## Reflecting on **GEOGRAPHY**
> Why, in the entire world, did only two hearths so disproportionately produce great religious faiths?

Barriers and Time-Distance Decay

Religious ideas move in the manner of all innovation waves. They weaken with increasing distance from their places of origin and with the passage of time. Barriers often retard or halt their spread. Most commonly, barriers are of the permeable type, allowing part of the innovation wave to diffuse through it but weakening it and retarding its spread. An example is the partial acceptance of Christianity by various Indian groups in Latin America and the western United States, which serves in some instances as a camouflage behind which many aspects of the tribal ethnic religions survive. In fact, permeable barriers are *normally* present in the expansion diffusion of religious faiths (see Focus On: "When Jesus Came, the Corn Mothers Went Away"). Most religions are modified by older local beliefs as they diffuse spatially. Rarely do new ideas, whether religious or not, gain unqualified acceptance in a region.

Absorbing barriers also exist in religious diffusion. The attempt to introduce Christianity into China provides a good example. When Catholic and Protestant missionaries reached China from Europe and the United States, they expected to find fertile ground for conversion—millions of people ready to receive the Word of God. However, they had crossed the boundaries of a culture region thousands of years old, in which some basic social ideas left little opening for Christianity and its doctrine of original sin. Long before, the Chinese had settled to their own satisfaction the question of what is basic human nature. As they saw the matter, humans are inherently good. Evil desires represent merely a deviation from that natural state. People have only to shrug them off and they will return to the basic nature that they share with heaven. Consequently, the idea of original sin left the Chinese baffled. The Christian image of humankind as flawed, of a gap between creator and created, of the Fall and the impossibility of returning to godhood, was culturally incomprehensible to the Chinese.

Other aspects of Christianity added to the cultural gap. How could the fall from grace come from too much knowledge, a commodity highly prized in China? What was wrong with a giant snake in the garden of Eden to a people whose art was filled with reptilian dragons, the imperial symbol? In short, many concepts of Christianity fell on rocky soil in China. Only in the early twentieth century, as China's social structure crumbled under Western assault, did a significant, though still small, number of Chinese convert to Christianity. Many of these were "rice Christians," poor Chinese willing to become Christians in exchange for the food that missionaries gave them.

In addition, religion itself can act as a barrier to the spread of nonreligious innovations. Religious taboos can even function as absorbing barriers, preventing diffusion of foods, drinks, and practices that violate the taboo. Mormons, who are forbidden to consume products containing caffeine, have not taken part in the American fascination with coffee. Sometimes these barriers are permeable. Certain Pennsylvania Dutch churches, for example, prohibit cigarette smoking but do not object to member farmers raising tobacco for sale in the commercial market.

Religion and Globalization

What does the geographical patterning of religion and of cultural diffusion tell us about *globalization*, the idea that a world culture is being created? The missionaries of the great proselytic religions were the first people to attempt to achieve globalization, in their desire to bring all humanity into a single faith. Yet despite their many successes in winning converts, religious globalization has not occurred, nor has there been notable progress toward that goal in recent times. Christians made up one-third of the human race both in 1900 and in 2000. Instead, the world's religious map has apparently solidified, producing a small number of very different culture regions (see Figure 3.2). Several of these are at war with one another, but the battle lines never move very much.

FOCUS ON

"When Jesus Came, the Corn Mothers Went Away"

Ramón Gutiérrez has written a beautiful book, whose title is the same as the one for this box. In it, he describes the ancestral religion of the Pueblo Indians of New Mexico, which centered on the Corn Mothers, who gave life to people, plants, and animals alike. Infants received ears of maize (corn), which were kept throughout their entire lifetime. The maize ear symbolized the feminine fertility latent in seeds and the earth.

When Spanish Catholic missionaries converted the Pueblos, it seemed, superficially, as though the male deity Jesus had driven away the corn goddesses. Actually, the Virgin Mary assumed many of the roles of the Corn Mothers. After an unsuccessful rebellion, in which the Pueblos sought to evict the Spaniards and their religion, one of the Corn Mothers returned as "Our Lady of the Conquest."

In this way, two very different religions—one masculine, the other feminine—coalesced.

Adapted from Gutiérrez, 1991, 13–14, 143, 161–163.

World War III

You probably thought that the last world war ended in 1945 and that the end of the cold war between communism and democracy had prevented a third world war. Well, maybe you were wrong. The failure of religious globalization sparked the real World War III, and it has been raging for more than half a century. This world war pits Islam and its culture region against Christianity, Judaism, and Hinduism (Figure 3.13).

All around the perimeter of the Muslim realm, conflicts and wars have flared, beginning in 1947 with fighting

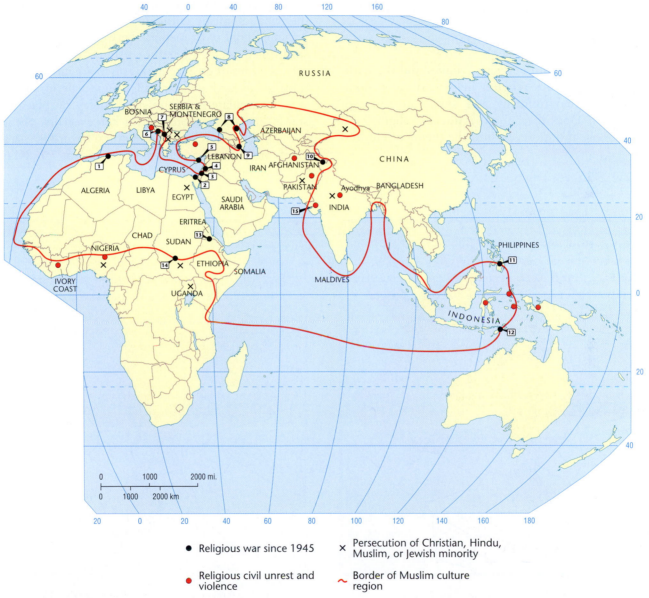

● Religious war since 1945   × Persecution of Christian, Hindu,
                                      Muslim, or Jewish minority

● Religious civil unrest and   ⌒ Border of Muslim culture
   violence   region

Figure 3.13

"World War III," a religious conflict fought on the borders of the Islamic culture region, 1947 to present. The 15 different wars that are part of this conflict are, clockwise: (1) Algerian overthrow of French rule; (2) Israel-Egypt wars of 1967 and 1972; (3) Arab-Israeli war of 1947–1948; (4) Christian-Muslim war in Lebanon, 1980s; (5) Turk-Greek war in Cyprus, 1974; (6) Bosnia, 1990s; (7) Kosovo; (8) Chechnya and Abkhazia; (9) Armenia-Azerbaijan; (10) Kashmir; (11) Muslim insurgency in Mindanao; (12) East Timor secession, 1999; (13) Ethiopia-Eritrea secession and war; (14) Muslim-Christian civil war in Sudan; (15) Muslim/Hindu mass murders in Gujarat state, India, 2002. These wars and lesser conflicts define the border of the Muslim world, like beads on a necklace or dots to connect in a picture puzzle. **What does this suggest about globalization?**

between Muslims and Jews in Palestine/Israel and between Hindus and Muslims in India/Pakistan. Those two conflicts have never really ended. Many other Muslim groups—Chechens, Azeris, Turks, Eritreans, Bosnians, Kosovars, Mindanaoans, and Algerians, among others—have risen in war against Christians, and vice versa. Nor does this world war show much sign of abating. The ultimate victim will probably be globalization.

 # Religious Ecology

What is the relationship between religion and the natural habitat? How does religion help guide our modification of the environment and shape our perception of nature? Does the habitat influence religion? All these questions, and more, fit into the theme of cultural ecology.

Appeasing the Forces of Nature

One of the main functions of many religions is the maintenance of a harmonious relationship between a people and their physical environment. That is, religion is at least perceived by its adherents to be part of the **adaptive strategy,** and for that reason physical environmental factors, particularly natural hazards and disasters, exert a powerful influence on the development of religions.

Environmental influence is most readily apparent in the tribal animistic faiths. In fact, an animistic religion's principal goal is to mediate between its people and the spirit-filled forces of nature. Animistic ceremonies and even the rites of great religions often are intended to bring rain, quiet earthquakes, end plagues, or in some other way manipulate environmental forces by placating the spirits believed responsible for these events. Sometimes the link between religion and natural hazard is visual. The great pre-Columbian temple pyramid at Cholula, near

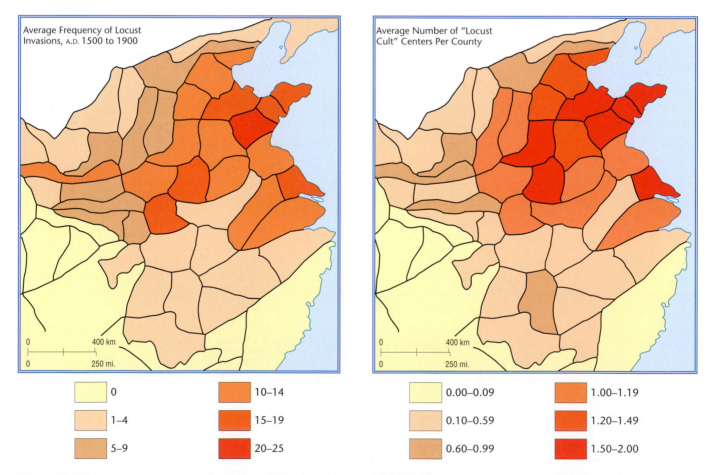

Average Frequency of Locust Invasions, A.D. 1500 to 1900

0	10–14
1–4	15–19
5–9	20–25

Average Number of "Locust Cult" Centers Per County

0.00–0.09	1.00–1.19
0.10–0.59	1.20–1.49
0.60–0.99	1.50–2.00

Figure 3.14

The frequency of locust infestations and the number of "locust cults" in China. These cults arose as an adaptive strategy in response to an environmental hazard. The worship of locusts was grafted onto the composite religion of China. (REDRAWN WITH PERMISSION FROM HSU, 1969: 734, 745.)

Figure 3.15
The model shows an ideal tomb site according to the Chinese principles of feng shui. The tall mountain range represents the spirit of the "Azure Dragon," a figure of active yang energy. The lower hills symbolize the "White Tiger," a figure of the complementary passive yin energy. The winding stream represents wealth. **Could the terrain logically have been interpreted in a different or opposite way?** (AFTER LAI, 1974.)

Puebla in central Mexico, strikingly mimics the shape of the awesome nearby volcano Popocatépetl, which towers to the menacing height of nearly 18,000 feet (5500 meters). Catholic missionaries retained the sacred status of the Cholula pyramid, although not its volcano-appeasing attribute, by erecting a church atop it.

Although the physical environment's influence on the major religions is less pronounced than it is on animistic faiths, it is still evident. Even today, environmental stress can evoke a religious response not so different from that of animistic cults. Some adherents to the Judeo-Christian tradition feel that God uses environmental disasters or degradation to punish sinners and that nature is benevolent to the devout, just as it had been in Eden. Stress can prompt attempts at mitigation. Local ministers and priests often attempt to alter unfavorable weather conditions with special services, and there are few churchgoing people in the Great Plains of the United States who have not prayed for rain in dry years. In northeastern China, repeated plagues of crop-destroying locusts gave rise over the centuries to a number of "locust cults," complete with temples. Almost 900 such temples were built, providing a place of worship for the locust and locust-gods (Figure 3.14). Suitable sacrifices and rituals were developed in an effort to avert the periodic infestations.

Animistic nature-spirits lie behind certain practices found in the great religions, such as the **geomancy,** or feng shui, of the fused Chinese and Korean Taoism/Buddhism, by which environmentally auspicious sites are chosen for houses, villages, temples, and graves. The homes of the living and the resting places of the dead must be aligned with the cosmic forces of the world. The Chinese originally invented the magnetic compass to serve such geomantic needs. For a burial site, the ideal terrain should be neither featureless and flat nor steep and rugged. The active and passive forces of Chinese cosmology, yin and yang, should correctly surround the site. As Chuen-yan David Lai, a Canadian geographer, has written: "The *yang* energy is expressed as a lofty mountain range, symbolically called the 'Azure Dragon,' and the *yin* energy as a lower ridge called the 'White Tiger.' The most auspicious model of feng shui topography is a secluded spot where these two energies converge, interact vigorously, and are kept together in harmony by surrounding mountains and streams" (Figure 3.15).

Similarly, rivers, mountains, trees, forests, and rocks often achieve the status of sacred space, even in the great religions. The river Ganga and certain lesser streams such as the Bagmati in Nepal are holy to the Hindus (Figure 3.16 on the next page), and the Jordan River has special meaning for Christians, who often transport its waters in containers to other continents for use in baptism. Most holy rivers are believed to possess soul-cleansing abilities. Hindu geographer Rana Singh speaks of the "liquid divine energy" of the Ganga, "nourishing the inhabitants and purifying them."

Mountains and other high places, likewise, often achieve sacred status both among animists and adherents

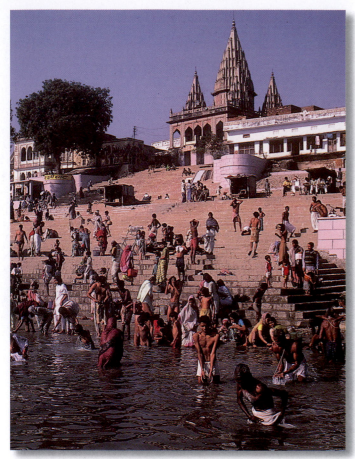

Figure 3.16
Veneration of a sacred river, the holy Ganga, at Varanasi, India. The Hindu faithful come for ritual baths on the stair-stepped banks of the river. (PORTERFIELD/CHICKERING/PHOTO RESEARCHERS.)

of the great religions (Figure 3.17). Mount Fuji is sacred in Japanese Shintoism, and many high places are venerated in Christianity, including the Mount of Olives. Some mountains tower so impressively as to inspire sects devoted to them exclusively. Mount Shasta, a massive snow-capped volcano in northern California, near the Oregon border, serves as the focus of no fewer than 30 New Age cults, the largest of which is the "I Am" religion, founded in the 1930s (see Figure 3.17, right). Geographer Claude Curran, who studied the Shasta cults, found that, although few of the adherents live near the mountain, pilgrimages and festivals held during the summer swell the population of nearby towns and contribute to the local economy. Geographer Stephen Jett, an expert on the Navajo Indians of the American Southwest, speaks of their *mythical topography*, produced when tribal legends become linked to certain topographical features, lending these special mythic places a sanctified quality.

The Environment and Monotheism

On a grander scale, some geographers seek to explain the origins of monotheism by environmental factors. The three major monotheistic faiths—Christianity, Islam, and Judaism—all have their roots among the desert dwellers of the Middle East. Lamaism, the most nearly monotheistic form of Buddhism, flourishes in the deserts of Tibet and Mongolia. In all of these cases, the people involved (Hebrews, Arabs, Tibetans, and Mongols) were once nomadic herders (refer to Chapter 8), wandering from place to place in the desert with flocks and herds of livestock. The geographer Ellen Semple (see Profile on page 97) suggested that such desert-dwelling peoples "receive from the immense monotony of their environment the impression of unity." Semple proposed that the unobstructed view of the stars and planets provided by the clear desert skies allowed the herders to see that the heavenly bodies moved across the sky in an orderly, repeated progression. This revelation supposedly suggested to the desert stargazers that a single guiding hand was responsible for the orderly system. Semple, in the classic style of environmental determinism, concluded that desert dwellers "gravitate inevitably into monotheism."

Other possibilistic rather than deterministic explanations have been proposed for the origins of monotheism. Some cultural geographers feel that we should look at the social structure of nomadic herding people for answers. Desert nomads are organized into tribes and clans ruled by a male chieftain who has dictatorial powers over the members of the group. It is possible that the all-powerful male deity of Middle Eastern monotheism is simply a theological reflection of the all-powerful, secular, male chieftain. Other geographers have noted that these monotheistic nomads lived on the edges of larger, more established culture regions. New ideas, these scholars feel, tend to develop at the borders, not at the core of regions where older structures and ideas are firmly entrenched. The fact is, however, that we do not know enough about early monotheism to say with certainty why or even where it arose. We are not even sure that the first monotheists were desert nomads, and we do know that some desert dwellers were polytheistic.

Ecotheology

Ecotheology is the name given to a rich and abundant body of literature studying the role of religion in habitat modification. More exactly, ecotheologists ask how the teachings and worldview of religion are related to our attitudes about modifying the physical environment. In the words of Lynn White, "Human ecology is deeply conditioned by beliefs about our nature and destiny—that is,

 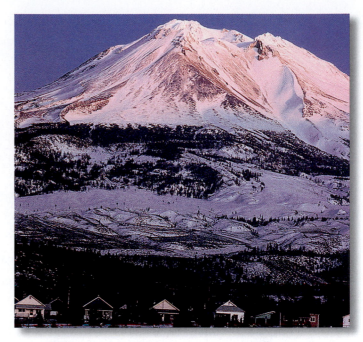

Figure 3.17

Two high places that have evolved into sacred space. The reddish sandstone Uluru, or Ayers Rock, in central Australia is sacred in Aboriginal animism and inspires awe from both near and afar. Snowy Mount Shasta in California is venerated by some 30 New Age cults, including the "I Am" religion. See Huntsinger and Fernández-Giménez, 2000: 536–558. **Why do mountains so often inspire such worship?** (Left: Michael Fogden/Bruce Coleman; Right: Joel Sartore/National Geographic.)

by religion." In some faiths, human power over natural forces is assumed. The Maori people of New Zealand, for example, believe that humans represent one of six aspects of creation, the others being forest/animals, crops, wild food, sea/fish, and winds/storms. In the Maori worldview, people rule over all of these except winds and storms.

The Judeo-Christian religious tradition also teaches that humans have dominion over nature, but it goes further to promote a teleological view. **Teleology** is the doctrine that the Earth was created especially for human beings, who are separate from and superior to the natural world (Figure 3.18 on the next page). This view is implicit in God's message to Noah after the Flood, promising that "every moving thing that lives shall be food for you, and as I gave you the green plants, I give you everything." The same theme is repeated in the Psalms, where Jews and Christians are told that "the heavens are the Lord's heavens, but the earth he has given to the sons of men." Humans are not part of nature but separate, forming one member of a God-nature-human trinity. The Judeo-Christian religious heritage, in short, has for millennia promoted a **mechanistic view of nature** that is potentially far more damaging to the habitat than an *organic* view.

Believing that the Earth was given to humans for their use, early Christian thinkers adopted the view that hu-

mans were God's helpers in finishing the task of creation, that human modifications of the environment were God's work. Small wonder, then, that the medieval period in Europe witnessed an unprecedented expansion of agricultural acreage, involving the large-scale destruction of woodlands and the drainage of marshes. Nor is it surprising that Christian monastic orders, such as the Cistercian and Benedictine monks, supervised many of these projects, directing the clearing of forests and the establishment of new agricultural colonies.

Ecofeminists have also entered this debate. They point out that the rise of the all-powerful male sky-deity of Semitic monotheism came at the expense of earth goddesses of fertility and sustainability. Because the Judeo-Christian tradition elevated a sky-god remote from the Earth, the harmonious relationship between people and the habitat was disrupted. Teleology was the inevitable result of the banishing of the Corn Mothers and all other female deities. The ancient holiness of ecosystems perished, endangering huge ecoregions. The *Gaia hypothesis* possesses an ecofeminist spirit.

Subsequently, scientific advances permitted the Judeo-Christian West to modify the environment at an unprecedented rate and on a massive scale. This marriage of technology and teleology is the root of our

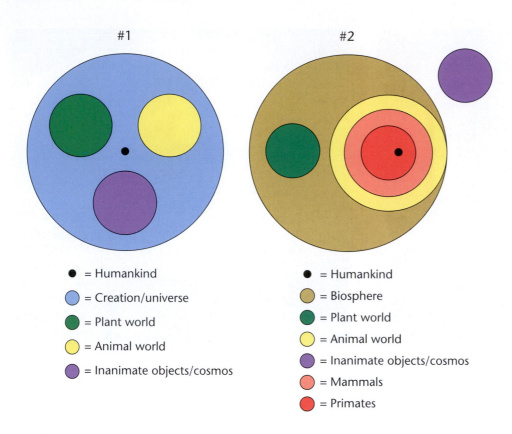

#1

#2

● = Humankind

● = Creation/universe

● = Plant world

● = Animal world

● = Inanimate objects/cosmos

● = Humankind

● = Biosphere

● = Plant world

● = Animal world

● = Inanimate objects/cosmos

● = Mammals

● = Primates

Figure 3.18
Models of the universe. Model 1 represents the traditional, Judeo-Christian, Biblical/scriptural, teleological view, in which humankind is central to creation and autonomous from the natural world. Model 2 describes the modern scientific/elitist view, which rests on the findings of Darwin and others. Proponents of these two views will likely develop unique outlooks on environmental modification. **Are other models conceivable?**

modern ecological crisis. By contrast, the great religions of Asia and many animistic tribal faiths contain teachings and beliefs that protect nature (see Focus On: The Yanoama World View). In Hinduism, for example, geographer Deryck Lodrick found that the doctrine of ahimsa had resulted in the establishment of many animal homes, refuges, and hospitals, particularly in the northwestern part of India. The hospitals, or *pinjrapoles*, are also closely linked to the Jains. In this view of the world, people are part of and at harmony with

FOCUS ON

The Yanoama World View

Persons of Judeo-Christian religious heritage need to be reminded that most other cultures do not perceive humans, God, and nature as a trinity of distinct entities. The world view of the Yanoama, an animistic Indian tribe of the Brazilian-Venezuelan borderland, is instructive.

> Religion impinges on all aspects of life, without the conceptual distinction between man, nature, and the divine that characterizes Judeo-Christianity. No omnipotent God exists. There is no material world surrounding the Yanoama and existing independently of them, no world that they view as capable of being dominated and turned to satisfy their own needs. . . . Mysteriously, man can share a common life

with an animal, or even with some natural phenomenon, such as the wind or thunder. People not only live now in intimate association with the monkeys, tapirs, deer, and birds of the forest, but also have been—or might be—these very creatures. There is an easy transmutability among the Yanoama between what [we] commonly define as different realms: the human, natural, and divine. . . . Thus, adult males share spirits, or souls, with other creatures. Among these, the harpy eagle and the jaguar are particularly prevalent. The alter egos of females are associated spiritually with totally different creatures, such as butterflies.

PROFILE

Ellen Churchill Semple

1863–1932

(COURTESY OF GEOFFREY J. MARTIN.)

Born in Louisville, Kentucky, of a well-to-do family, Semple received a master's degree from Vassar and then went to Germany to study. At that time, few women attended universities in Germany, and it is claimed she had to listen to geography lectures from outside the classroom door. When she returned to America, she brought with her some of the ideas of German geography and subsequently developed many of her own theories. She wrote eloquently and voluminously. Best known, perhaps, is her book *Influences of Geographical Environment,* published in 1911 and still very readable today, almost a century later. Among the almost countless intriguing ideas presented in her works is the theory that religions are largely the product of the physical environment. Her books gained a very wide readership, among both professional geographers and educated laypersons. She served on the geography faculties at the University of Chicago and Clark University for many years and was a well-known personality in geography. In selecting Semple as president in 1921, the Association of American Geographers became the first national professional academic organization in the United States to place a woman in its highest position.

nature. Such religions would presumably not threaten the ecological balance.

Geographer Yi-fu Tuan disagrees. He points to a discrepancy between the stated ideals of religions and reality. Even though China enjoys an "old tradition of forest care" based on its composite religion, the Chinese woodlands have been systematically destroyed through the millennia. Nor are the Asian and tribal religions consistently protective of the environment. Buddhism, like Hinduism, protects temple trees but demands huge quantities of wood for cremations (Figure 3.19 on the next page). Animistic shifting cultivators (see Chapter 8) sometimes make offerings to appease the woodland spirits before destroying huge acreages of forest with machete and fire. The ancient earth goddesses demanded that fields be cleared from the forest for the land to be fruitful, and habitat destruction remains habitat destruction. Civilization itself, argues Tuan, is the exercise of human power over nature. Religion can resist but not overcome that exercise. Also, if people are assumed to be part of nature, then one might conclude that no stewardship of the land by humankind seems logical, since we and all our works are "natural."

Godliness and Greenness

We should consider, too, that the Judeo-Christian tradition is not lacking in concern for environmental protection. In the Book of Leviticus, for example, farmers are instructed by God to let the land lie fallow one year in seven and not to gather food from wild plants in that "sabbath of the land." Robin Doughty, a humanistic cultural geographer, suggests that "Western Christian thought is too rich and complex to be characterized as hostile toward nature," although he feels that Protestantism, "in which worldly success symbolizes individual predestination," may be more conducive to "ecological intemperance." Moreover, some fundamentalist Protestant sects view ecological crisis and environmental deterioration as a gauge to predict Christ's return and the end of the present age, according to geographer Janel Curry-Roper. Thus they welcome ecological collapse and, obviously, are unlikely to be of much help in solving the related problems.

Some conservative, fundamentalist Protestants, however, have adopted conservationist views, citing Biblical admonitions. The Flood story from the Old Testament, in which Noah saves diverse animals by bringing them onto the ark, is now viewed by many fundamentalists as a call to protect endangered species. An ecotheological focus underlies the multidenominational National Religious Partnership for the Environment, which includes many evangelical Protestant members. The hope is to mobilize the Christian Right against wanton environmental destruction in the same way that they oppose abortion.

This link between godliness and Greenness has now gone worldwide. In the years following a conference in Italy in the middle 1980s—which brought together Greens and religious leaders representing Christianity, Islam, Judaism, Hinduism, and Buddhism—some 130,000 projects linking the Green teachings inherent in these faiths to the ecology movement have arisen. For example, in Russia, the Orthodox Church is working to create wildlife preserves on monastery lands. The Patriarch of Constantinople, leader of Eastern Orthodox Christianity, has made the fight against pollution a church policy, and the Church of England has declared that abuse of nature is blasphemous. In Asia, a Buddhist Protection

Figure 3.19
Wood gathered for Hindu cremations at Pashupatinath, on the sacred river Bagmati, in Nepal. These cremations contribute significantly to the ongoing deforestation of Nepal and reveal the underlying internal contradiction in Hinduism between conservation as reflected in the doctrine of ahimsa and sanctioned ecologically destructive practices. **Do such contradictions exist in your own religious faith?** (Courtesy of Terry G. Jordan-Bychkov.)

of Nature project emphasizes the teachings of that faith about nature. Leaders of nine major religions met in 1995 to discuss environmental concerns, and in that same year the Eastern Orthodox Church announced that damaging the natural habitat constituted a sin against God. The Green teachings of long-dead saints such as Christianity's St. Francis of Assisi, who treasured birds and other wildlife, now receive heightened attention.

Religion and Environmental Perception

Religion can also influence the way people perceive their physical environment. Nowhere is this more evident than in the perception of environmental hazards such as floods, storms, and droughts. Hinduism and Buddhism teach followers to accept such hazards without struggle, to regard them as natural and unavoidable. This attitude, once again, represents an **organic view of nature.** Christians are more likely to view storm, flood, or drought *mechanistically,* as unusual and preventable. As a result, they will generally take steps to overcome the hazard. Sometimes, however, Christians see natural disasters as divine punishment for their sins, in which case worshipers feel they can prevent future disasters by repenting.

Within a single major religion, people's relationship with the land can vary from one sect to another (see Focus On: Russians Love Dandelions). A study conducted in several adjacent southwestern settlements in the United States by Florence Kluckhohn suggests that individual religious groups see this trinity of people, God, and nature differently. The large majority (72 percent) of Latin-American Catholics interviewed felt that humans are subject to nature. Most Mormons (55 percent) saw humans in harmony with nature, a relationship preserved by proper living and hard work. The most common response from Protestant Anglo-Texans (48 percent) held that humans control nature and can overcome environmental hazards.

Similarly, a study by John Sims and Duane Baumann revealed that residents of Alabama—where intense, conservative Protestantism prevails—were more likely to react to a tornado threat fatalistically, relying on God to see them through; whereas Illinoisans—as adherents of a liberal, low-intensity Protestantism—felt in control of their own destinies and took more measures to protect themselves. Perhaps partly as a result, the mortality rate per tornado is markedly lower in the Midwest than in the South.

Reflecting on **GEOGRAPHY**

Does your religious faith influence your views about how people should treat the physical environment?

FOCUS ON

Russians Love Dandelions

Americans, Russians, and Europeans share, nominally at least, the Christian faith. And yet the Russians have a very different view of nature:

Even a common wild flower can tell us something about a culture. We have all seen dandelions — those hardy little yellow flowers that sprout as weeds in lawns and produce a fluff-ball of seeds.

In America and Europe, gardeners wage eternal war on dandelions, working hard to dig them up or poison them with herbicide. To the western eye, dandelions spoil the uniform grassy expanse of a lawn or park. They intrude unpleasantly in a garden of vegetables or domestic, planted flowers. Except to children, who delight in blowing the seed puffs on each other, dandelions are enemies to western peoples.

Not so in Russia. In city parks and around rural vacation homes, dandelions grow in profusion in May and June. Instead of tidy, neatly mowed lawns and carefully planted flower gardens, Russians prefer a *natural* look. To the western eye, everything in Russia seems neglected and weedy.

But to the Russian eye, this ragged expanse of dandelions and other weeds is beautiful and desirable. An American or German strolling through a city park in Russia will be seized by a desire to run a power lawnmower over the whole area. Not the Russian. It is not that they are lazy or slovenly. Rather, they simply prefer more natural, less artificial surroundings.

Perhaps we westerners *fear* nature and seek, even in trivial ways, to tame and overwhelm it. To announce our victory over the natural physical environment. Maybe that is why we hate dandelions.

Perhaps Russians, at the end of their long, severe winter, rejoice when nature revives, green growth renews,

(COURTESY OF TERRY G. JORDAN-BYCHKOV.)

and little yellow flowers bloom. Maybe that's why they love dandelions.

And perhaps dandelions can teach us something worth knowing about a foreign culture . . . and about our own.

From travel journal of Terry G. Jordan-Bychkov, composed on a park bench in Yaroslavl, Russia, June 2000.

Cultural Interaction in Religion

How does religion impact other aspects of culture? Can nonreligious elements within a culture help shape a faith? Just as the interaction between religious belief and the environment can shape both religions and the land, religious faith is similarly intertwined with other aspects of culture. Spatial variations in religious belief influence and are influenced by social, economic, demographic, and political patterns in countless ways.

Religion and Economy

In the economic sphere, religion can guide commerce, determine which crops and livestock are raised by farmers and what foods and beverages people consume, and even help decide the type of employment a person has and in what neighborhood they reside (see Focus On: Religion and Economy: The Cargo Cults of Melanesia). Every known religion expresses itself in food choices, to one degree or another. Within some faiths, certain plants and livestock, as well as the products derived from them, are

FOCUS ON

Religion and Economy: The Cargo Cults of Melanesia

Cultural interaction is perhaps nowhere more startlingly revealed than in the so-called cargo cults of the western Pacific tropical islands, the area known as Melanesia. There, a religion has arisen based on the hoped-for arrival of Western material goods delivered in American cargo-laden ships and airplanes. Saviorlike Americans will bring the cargo to the islands. Kal Muller tells of one such cult on the New Hebridean island of Tanna:

> On the volcano's rim looms a blood-red cross. Nearby, men with "U.S.A." daubed on their bodies shoulder make-believe rifles of bamboo. Soldiers of Christ? Hardly. On the New Hebridean island of Tanna, both cross and marchers herald a hoped-for messiah of material riches—a savior cryptically called John Frum. Some followers of the mythical

Frum consider him a beneficent spirit; others see him as a god come to earth, or as the "king of America." All believe he will someday usher in a prosperous, work-free millennium of unlimited "cargo"—pidgin English for Western material goods. . . .

> In 1942, World War II reached Tanna's shores. U.S. troops landed on nearby islands, bringing food, arms, prefabricated houses, jobs, and legions of jeeps. . . . But with the war's end, the cargo disappeared, and islanders . . . turned to mock military drills in the hope of luring GIs—and cargo-laden Liberty ships—back to Tanna. . . .

> Although Frum fails to materialize—as has been the case for [over a half-century]—his followers remain devout, often attributing his absence to their own shortcomings or to governmental intervention.

From Muller, 1974.

in great demand because of their roles in religious ceremonies and traditions. When this is the case, the plants or animals tend to spread with the faith.

For example, in some Christian sects in Europe and the United States, celebrants drink from a cup of wine that symbolizes the blood of Christ during the sacrament of Holy Communion. The demand for wine created by this ritual aided the diffusion of grape growing from the sunny lands of the Mediterranean to newly Christianized districts beyond the Alps in late Roman and early medieval times. The vineyards of the German Rhine were the creation of monks who arrived from the south between the sixth and ninth centuries. For the same reason, Catholic missionaries introduced the cultivated grape to California. In fact, wine was associated with religious worship even before Christianity arose. Vineyard keeping and wine making spread westward across the Mediterranean lands in prehistoric times in association with worship of the god Dionysus.

Religion also can often explain the absence of individual crops or domestic animals in an area. The environmentally similar lands of Spain and Morocco, separated only by the Strait of Gibraltar, show the agricultural impact of food taboos. On the Spanish, Roman Catholic side of the strait, pigs are common and pork a delicacy, but in Muslim Morocco on the African side. only about 12,000 swine can be found throughout the entire country. The Islamic avoidance of pork underlies this contrast. Fig-

ure 3.20 maps the pork taboo. Judaism also imposes restrictions against pork and other meats, as is stated in the following passage from the Book of Leviticus:

> These shall ye not eat, of them that chew the cud, or of them that divide the hoof: as the camel, because he cheweth the cud, but divideth not the hoof; he is unclean unto you. And the coney, because he cheweth the cud, but divideth not the hoof; he is unclean unto you. And the hare, because he cheweth the cud, but divideth not the hoof; he is unclean unto you. And the swine, though he divide the hoof, and be cloven-footed, yet he cheweth not the cud; he is unclean unto you.

Scholars explain the Islamic and Judaic pork taboos in various ways. Some suggest that these two cultures were primarily concerned with the danger of parasites (trichinosis) or that they considered pigs unclean. Other scholars have suggested a theory based on economy and ecology, after observing that pork avoidance is characteristic of the monotheistic faiths that arose among desert nomads. The proponents of this view believe that nomadic herding originated on the borders of the great farming areas of the ancient Middle East, near the Tigris, Euphrates, Nile, and other rivers. Population pressures forced people to settle farther and farther from the riverbanks, so that eventually some groups lost access to irri-

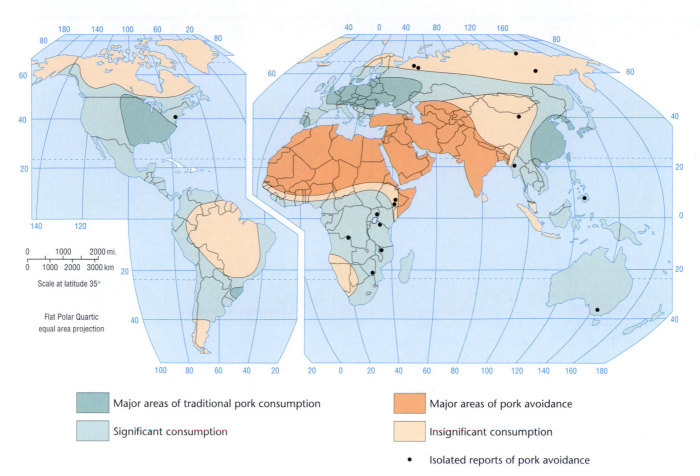

Major areas of traditional pork consumption

Significant consumption

Major areas of pork avoidance

Insignificant consumption

•   Isolated reports of pork avoidance

Figure 3.20

Consumption and avoidance of pork are influenced by religion. Some religions and churches—such as Islam, Judaism, and Seventh-Day Adventism—prohibit the eating of pork. Cultural groups with a traditional fondness for pork include central Europeans, Chinese, and Polynesians. **Can you explain the pattern in North America?** (BASED IN PART ON SIMOONS, 1994.)

gation waters and were forced to abandon most crop farming and turn to animal husbandry. The poor quality of the range required them to wander from place to place in the desert as nomads, seeking forage for their livestock. Pigs, valuable animals to the sedentary farmers of the river valleys, require shade, are poor travelers, and found little to eat in the desert. As a result, the nomads relied instead on sheep, goats, horses, camels, and, in some areas, cattle. Because environmental conditions prevented the nomads from owning pigs, they declared pork undesirable in a "sour grapes" reaction. In time, this declaration found religious expression as a taboo. Ages later, as a final "revenge," Muslim nomads imposed their religion, complete with the pork taboo, on the farming people of the river valleys.

Muslims are also not permitted any alcoholic beverages. The Koran states: "O ye who have believed, wine,

games of chance, idols, and divining arrows are nothing but an infamy of Satan's handiwork. Avoid them so that ye may succeed." Christians failed to reach a consensus on this taboo. Some Christian denominations prohibit all consumption of alcohol, in the belief that it is detrimental to health, welfare, and behavior, whereas others, as described above, even use wine in religious ceremonies. In the United States, such groups as the Baptists, Mormons, and Seventh-Day Adventists support prohibition; Roman Catholics, Lutherans, and several other denominations tolerate alcohol. The economic imprint of these different attitudes can be seen in a map of "wet" and "dry" areas in the United States. Texas provides an excellent example because it is religiously diverse and by law allows each community to decide in local-option elections whether alcohol may be sold or served (Figure 3.21 on the next page). Almost without exception, Catholic and Lutheran

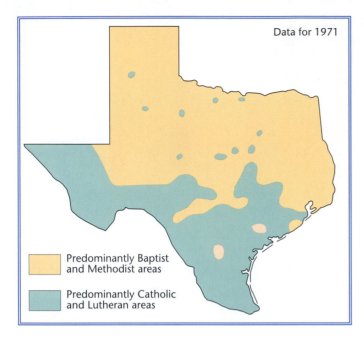

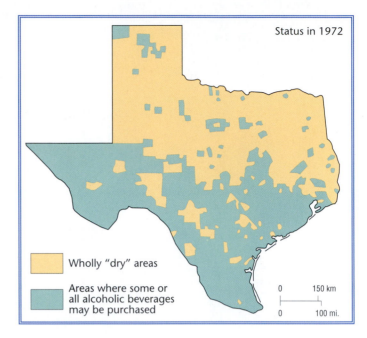

Figure 3.21

The distribution of religion and alcohol sales in Texas. Catholics and Lutherans generally choose to be "wet," whereas Baptists and Methodists favor prohibition. **How is it possible that denominations that are all Christians could disagree on such a basic issue?** (SOURCE: JORDAN ET AL., 1984: 116, 148.)

areas in Texas are "wet," whereas Baptist and Methodist counties vote "dry."

Most Hindus will not eat fish. India regularly suffers food shortages and dietary deficiencies even though the nearby oceans teem with protein-rich fish. Among Christians, Seventh-Day Adventists have a finless-fish taboo and also will not eat pork. When missionaries of this church converted the population of Pitcairn Island in the South Pacific to their faith, the island's economic self-sufficiency collapsed, because the people had previously depended heavily on pork and finless fish in their diet.

You will note that nearly all of these examples directly refute *economic determinism*. In fact, they seem to suggest that cultural determinism is the more valid concept. Avoid that simplistic doctrine, too. Easy answers to complex issues are almost invariably wrong.

Religious Pilgrimage

For many religious groups, journeys to sacred places, or **pilgrimages,** play an important role in the faith (Figure 3.22). Pilgrimages are typical of both ethnic and proselytic religions. They are particularly significant to followers of Islam, Hinduism, Shintoism, and Roman Catholicism.

The sacred places vary in character. Some have been the setting for miracles; a few are the source regions of religions or areas where the founders of the faith lived and worked; others contain holy physical features such as rivers, caves, springs, and mountain peaks; and still others are believed to house gods or are religious administrative centers where leaders of the church reside. Examples include the Arabian cities of Mecca and Medina in Islam; Rome and the French town of Lourdes in Roman Catholicism; the Indian city of Varanasi on the holy Ganga River, a destination of Hindu pilgrims; and Ise, the hearth of Shintoism in Japan. Places of pilgrimage might be regarded as the *nodes* of functional culture regions.

Religion provides the stimulus for pilgrimage by offering those who participate the reward of soul purification or the attainment of some desired objective in their lives. Pilgrims often journey great distances to see major shrines. Other sites, of lesser significance, draw pilgrims only from local districts or provinces. Pilgrimages can have tremendous economic impact, because the movement of pilgrims amounts to a form of tourism.

In some favored localities, the pilgrim trade provides the only significant source of revenue for the community. Lourdes, a town of 16,300, attracts between 4 and 5 million pilgrims each year, many seeking miraculous cures at the famous grotto where the Virgin Mary supposedly appeared. Not surprisingly, among French cities, Lourdes ranks second only to Paris in number of hotels, although

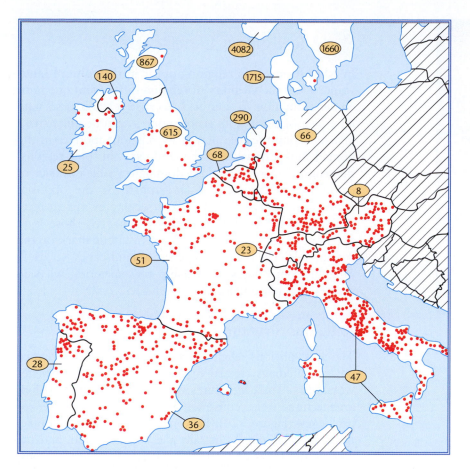

• One major pilgrimage shrine, 1990

Each circled number represents thousands of inhabitants per religious pilgrimage shrine (major and minor).
For example: 1660 equals 1,660,000 inhabitants.

No data

Figure 3.22

Distribution of major religious pilgrimage shrines in western Europe. These sites are most numerous in Roman Catholic areas and in regions of surviving religious vitality (compare with Figure 3.8). Nineteen of these shrines attract more than a million pilgrims each year, massively affecting the local economies. The numbers indicate resident population per site by country. **Do pilgrimage sites exist in your home region?** (ADAPTED FROM NOLAN AND NOLAN, 1989: 31.)

most of these are small. Mecca, a small city, annually attracts hundreds of thousands of Muslim pilgrims from every corner of the Islamic culture region. By land, by sea, and (mainly) by air, the faithful come to this hearth of Islam, a city closed to all non-Muslims. Such mass pilgrimages obviously have a major impact on the development of transportation routes and carriers.

Religion and Political Geography

Americans, accustomed by their heritage to the doctrine of separation of church and state, are usually unaware of how closely religion and politics are intertwined in much of the world. A **theocracy** is a government in which religious leaders run the country. Afghanistan, for example, was formerly ruled by the Islamic organization called *Tal-*

iban. Vatican City, a fully independent state, is ruled by the pope. Religious practices and traits often change abruptly at political boundaries, such as along parts of the Franco-Belgian border in western Europe (Figure 3.23 on the next page).

In cases where religion provides a basis for nationalism, a **state church** is often created. Such a church is recognized by law as the only one in the state, and the government controls both church and state. In Norway, for example, the constitution until recently had established the Lutheran faith as the state church, and pastors and officials were appointed government employees.

In some nations, political parties are linked to particular church groups. As a result, voting returns often duplicate the religious map. Such ties are particularly common in Europe, where political parties have such names

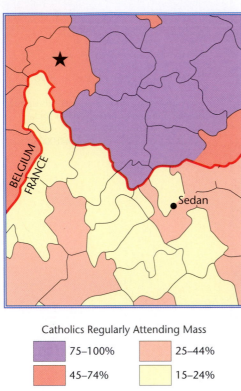

Catholics Regularly Attending Mass

75–100%	25–44%
45–74%	15–24%

—— Franco–Belgian border

★ Beauraing

Figure 3.23

Attendance at mass along the Franco-Belgian border, about 1950. The people on both sides of the boundary speak French and share many other cultural traits, yet Catholicism remains a vital force only on the Belgian side. The political border has become a religious border. Beauraing is a major Catholic pilgrimage site lying on the Belgian side of the border. **What developments in the respective countries might help explain this striking pattern?** (ADAPTED FROM BOULARD, 1960.)

as Catholic People's Party or Christian Democrats. It is common in these countries for churchgoers to be advised from the pulpit about how they should vote. Even in countries like the United States, where legal separation of church and state is maintained, voting patterns often reflect denominational patterns.

Reflecting on GEOGRAPHY

Does your religious faith influence the economic, social, dietary, and political decisions you make?

 # Religious Landscapes

In what forms does religion appear in the cultural landscape? Does the visibility of religion differ from one faith or denomination to another? Because religion is so vital an aspect of culture, its visible impress can be quite striking, reflecting the role played by religious motives in the human transformation of the landscape. In some regions, the religious aspect offers the dominant visible evidence of culture, producing *sacred landscapes*. At the opposite extreme are areas almost purely secular in appearance. Religions differ greatly in visibility, but even those least apparent to the eye usually leave some subtle mark on the countryside. The content of religious landscapes is varied, ranging from houses of worship to cemeteries, wayside shrines, and place-names.

Religious Structures

The most obvious religious contributions to the landscape are the buildings erected to house divinities or to shelter worshipers. These structures vary greatly in size, function, architectural style, construction material, and degree of ornateness (Figure 3.24). To Roman Catholics, for example, the church building is literally the house of God, and the altar is the focus of vital ritual. Partly for these reasons, Catholic churches are typically large, elaborately decorated, and visually imposing. In many towns and villages, the Catholic house of worship is the focal point of the settlement, exceeding all other structures in size and grandeur.

To many Protestants—particularly the traditional Calvinistic chapel-goers of British background, including Methodists and Baptists—the church building is, by contrast, simply a place to assemble for worship. The result is an unsanctified, smaller, less ornate structure. The simpler church buildings of these Protestants appeal less to the senses and more to the personal faith. For this reason, their traditional structures are typically not designed for comfort, beauty, or high visibility, but instead appear deliberately humble (see Figure 3.24, bottom left). Similarly, the religious landscape of the Amish and Mennonites in rural North America, the "plain folk," is very subdued, because they reject ostentation in any form. Some of their adherents meet in houses or barns, and the churches that do exist are very modest in appearance, like those of the southern Calvinists.

In Islam, mosques are usually the most imposing items in the landscape, whereas the visibility of Jewish synagogues varies greatly. Hinduism has produced large numbers of visually striking temples for its multiplicity of gods, but much worship is practiced in private house-

Figure 3.24

Traditional religious architecture takes varied forms. St. Basil's Church on Red Square in Moscow reflects a highly ornate Russian landscape presence, whereas the plain board chapel in the American South demonstrates an opposite tendency favoring visual simplicity by British-derived Protestants. The ornate Hindu temple in Varanasi, India, offers still another sacred landscape. **What meanings might the faithful see in such landscapes?** (COURTESY OF TERRY G. JORDAN-BYCHKOV.)

holds. Houses of worship can also reveal a subtler content and message. In Polynesian Maori communities of New Zealand, for example, the *marae*, a structure linked to the pagan gods of the past, generally stands alongside the Christian chapel, which reflects the Maoris' conversion (Figure 3.25 on the next page). The landscape thus reflects the blending of two faiths.

Nature religions such as *animism* generally place only a subtle mark on the landscape. Nature itself is sacred, and few shrines are needed. Still, animistic shrines can still be found, often as survivals and relics. In Korea, for example, where animism merged with Buddhism and the Chinese composite religion, animistic shrines survive in the landscape (Figure 3.26 on the next page).

Paralleling this contrast in church styles are attitudes toward wayside shrines and similar manifestations of faith. Catholic culture regions typically abound with shrines, crucifixes, crosses, and assorted visual reminders of religion, as do some Eastern Orthodox Christian areas. One of the authors of this textbook vividly recalls driving along a mountain road in Bavaria on a summer night many years ago, when suddenly the headlights illuminated a realistic, life-sized crucifix in a shrine bordering the pavement. Instinctively, his foot went to the brake, and it was several seconds before he could adjust to the reality of this Catholic sacred landscape. Protestant areas, by contrast, are bare of such symbols and do not startle the night driver. Their landscapes, instead, display such

Figure 3.25

In the Maori community of Tikitiki, on North Island, New Zealand, a traditional Polynesian *marae,* or shrine (on the left) stands beside a Christian chapel (on the right). The religious landscape, in this odd juxtaposition, tells us much about the composite faith held by the modern Maori. (COURTESY OF TERRY G. JORDAN-BYCHKOV.)

features as signboards advising the traveler to "Get Right with God," a common sight in the southern United States.

The distinction between sacred and profane in the cultural landscape is not always easy for the outsider to discern. Along the Ganga River in Varanasi, India, steps—or *ghats*—lead down to the stream at many places (see Figure 3.16). To the uninitiated, these may seem intended for the convenience of fishers, swimmers, and people doing laundry. The more important role of the ghats, however, is to facilitate ritual bathing in the holy Ganga—the main goal of pilgrims coming to the city. Also, the ghats provide a place for funeral pyres in the cremation of the dead.

Most tribal ethnic religions do not stand out in the cultural landscape. Animistic groups regard many objects as sacred, but these items are commonplace and would not reveal their religious significance to the eyes of an outsider. Tribal religions often do not have separate houses of worship.

Landscapes of the Dead

Religions differ greatly in the type of tribute they award to the dead. This variation appears in the cultural landscape. Hindus cremate their dead. Having no cemeteries, their dead leave no obvious mark on the land. In the same way, the few remaining Zoroastrians, called Parsees, who preserve a once-widespread Middle Eastern faith now confined to parts of India, have traditionally left their dead exposed to be devoured by vultures.

Figure 3.26

Stacked stones at a pilgrimage site in South Korea, perpetuating an ancient animistic/shamanistic practice. These stones had meaning in ancient times, a meaning since lost. **What might it have been?** (COURTESY OF TERRY G. JORDAN-BYCHKOV.)

Figure 3.27
Landscape of the dead, landscape of the living. The Beni Hassan Islamic necropolis in central Egypt lies in the desert, just beyond the irrigable land, while the living make intensive use of every parcel watered by the Nile River. The mud brick structures are all tombs. Thus, the doubly dead landscape is sacred, whereas the realm of living plants and people is profane. (Courtesy of Terry G. Jordan-Bychkov.)

In Egypt, on the other hand, spectacular pyramids and other tombs were built to house dead leaders. These monuments, as well as the modern graves and tombs of the rural Islamic folk of Egypt, lie on desert land not suitable for farming (Figure 3.27). Muslim cemeteries are usually modest in appearance, but spectacular tombs are sometimes erected for aristocratic persons, giving us such sacred structures as the Taj Mahal in India (Figure 3.28), one of the architectural wonders of the world.

Chinese who practice their composite religion typically bury their dead, setting aside land for that purpose and erecting monuments to their deceased kin. In parts of pre-Communist China, as much as 10 percent of the land in some districts was covered by cemeteries and ancestral shrines, greatly reducing the acreage available for agriculture.

Christians also typically bury their dead in sacred places set aside for that purpose. These vary significantly from one Christian denomination to another. Some graveyards, particularly those of southern Calvinists and Mennonites, are very modest in appearance, reflecting the reluctance of these groups to use any symbolism that might be construed as idolatrous. Among certain other Christian groups, cemeteries are places of color and elaborate decoration (Figure 3.29 on the next page).

Cemeteries often preserve truly ancient cultural traits, for people as a rule are reluctant to change their practices relating to the dead. The traditional rural cemetery of the southern United States provides a case in point. Freshwater mussel shells are placed atop many of the elongated grave mounds, and rose bushes and cedars are planted

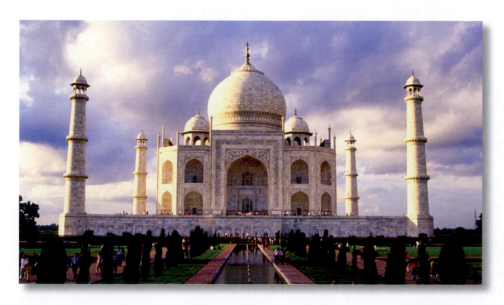

Figure 3.28
The Taj Mahal in Agra, India. Built as a Muslim tomb, it is perhaps the most impressive religious structure in the world. (Pallava Bagla/Corbis.)

Figure 3.29
Two different Christian landscapes of the dead. In the Yucatán Peninsula of Mexico, the dead rest in colorful, aboveground crypts, whereas in Amana, Iowa, communalistic Germans prefer tidiness, order, and equality. (LEFT: MACDUFF EVERTON/CORBIS; RIGHT: COURTESY OF TERRY G. JORDAN-BYCHKOV.)

throughout the cemetery. Recent research suggests that the use of roses may derive from the worship of an ancient, pre-Christian mother goddess of the Mediterranean lands. The rose was a symbol of this great goddess, who could restore life to the dead. Similarly, the cedar evergreen is an age-old pagan symbol of death and eternal life, and the use of shell decoration derives from an animistic custom in West Africa, the geographic origin of slaves in the American South. Although the present Christian population of the South is unaware of the origins of their cemetery symbolism, it seems likely that their landscape of the dead contains animistic elements thousands of years old, revealing truly ancient beliefs and cultural diffusions.

Religious Names on the Land

"St.-Jean," "St.-Aubert," "St.-Damase-des-Aulnaies," "Ste. Perpétue de L'Islet," "St.-Pamphile," "St.-Adalbert"—so read the placards of town names as one drives from the St. Lawrence River south in Québec, paralleling the Maine border. All this saintliness is merely a part of the French-Canadian religious landscape, as Figure 3.30 shows. The point is that religion often inspires the names that people place on the land. Within Christianity, the use of saints' names for settlements is very common in Roman Catholic and Greek Orthodox areas, especially in overseas colonial lands settled by Catholics, such as Latin America and French Canada. In areas of the Old World that were settled long before the advent of Christianity,

saints' names were often grafted onto pre-Christian names, as in Alcazar de San Juan, in Spain, which combines Arabic and Christian elements.

> ### Reflecting on **GEOGRAPHY**
> What is the most visible element of the religious landscape where you live?

Toponyms in Protestant regions display less religious influence, but some imprint can usually be found. In the southern United States, for example, the word *chapel* as a prefix or suffix, as in Chapel Hill and Ward's Chapel, is very common in the names of rural hamlets. Such names accurately convey the image of the humble, rural Protestant churches that are so common in the South.

Conclusion

Religion is firmly interwoven in the fabric of culture, a bright hue in the human mosaic, for religions vary greatly from one area to another, a regional diversity so profound as to give special significance to James Griffith's admonition that we should all "learn, respect, and walk softly." This religious spatial variation leads us to ask how these distributions came to be, a question best answered through the methods of cultural diffusion. Some religions, proselytic denominations, actively en-

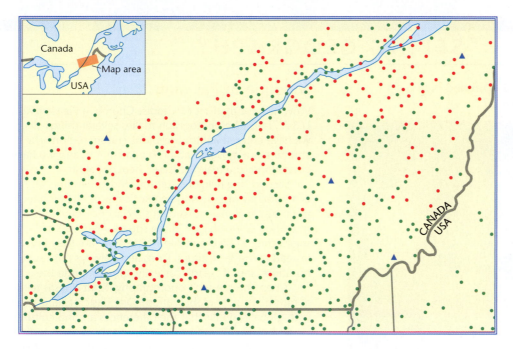

Figure 3.30

Religious place-names dot the map of French Canada. In the French-Canadian province of Québec, the dominant Roman Catholic religion finds an expression in the names given to towns and villages. Saints' names are dominant in the areas of purest French settlement. Nearer the U.S.-Canadian border, in townships settled by English-speaking people, religious place-names are rare. **On this basis, where exactly would you draw the French Catholic–English Protestant border at the time of initial settlement? Is that border still in the same location today?**

▲ Names beginning with Notre Dame

• Names beginning with Saint or Sainte

• Other names

courage their own diffusion. Other religions erect barriers to expansion diffusion by restricting membership to one particular ethnic group.

The theme of cultural ecology reveals some fundamental ties between religion and the physical environment. One major function of many religious systems, particularly the animistic faiths, is to appease and placate the forces of nature and to achieve harmony between the people and the physical environment. Religions differ in their outlook on environmental modification by humans. Religion is systemically related to economy and politics, among other things. Everything from tourism to nationalism can have a religious component, validating the theme of cultural interaction.

The cultural landscape abounds with expressions of religious belief. Places of worship—temples, churches, and shrines—differ in appearance, distinctiveness, prominence, and frequency of occurrence from one religious culture region to another. These buildings provide a visual index to the various faiths. Cemeteries and religious place-names also add a special effect to the landscape that tells us about the religious character of the population. In all these ways, and more, the five themes of cultural geography prove relevant to the study of the world's religions.

Geography of Religion on the Internet

You can learn more about the geography of religion on the Internet at the following web sites:

American Religious Identification Survey 2001
http://www.gc.cuny.edu/studies/studies_index.htm

This work by Barry A. Kosmin, Egon Mayer, and Ariela Keysar of the Graduate Center of the City University of New York contains the latest data on religious affiliations in the United States.

Global Mapping International
http://www.adherents.com/

This web site contains statistics on religious adherence worldwide.

Glenmary Research Center
www.glenmary.org

Among other activities, the center conducts a census of religious denominations in the United States every 10 years; the 2000 census, listing membership by county, appeared late in 2001.

SEEING GEOGRAPHY

Why have such different and opposed ways developed to worship one God?

Worshipers in front of a mosque in Pakistan.

Mosque in Pakistan

Wow! It's not the First Methodist Church in Pleasantville, U.S.A., is it? The photograph makes several things clear. First, we have entered another religious culture region. The structure is a mosque rather than a church, and we have crossed into the realm of Islam, here in Pakistan.

Second, the religious cultural landscape offers abundant clues that we are viewing an exotic place. The architecture of the mosque alone has its own special character. And the multitude of worshipers in the square—what a sight! Why might they all be dressed in white? Why are they outside instead of inside? Cultural landscapes always raise such questions and, if "read" correctly, often provide the answers.

When you see such photography, what does it tell you about the issue of globalization? One basic belief associated with globalization is that the differences among cultures are weakening, as Western ways overwhelm non-Western cultures. Can you see *any* evidence of globalization? Would we find such evidence if we could enter the picture and walk the streets?

Material History of American Religion Project, New York, N.Y.

www.materialreligion.org

Based at Columbia University, this site has information about religious material objects, including religious landscapes, in the United States.

World Council of Churches

www.wcc-coe.org

An interdenominational group, headquartered in Geneva, Switzerland, the World Council of Churches works for greater cooperation and understanding among different faiths.

Sources

Boulard, Fernand. 1960. *An Introduction to Religious Sociology.* M. J. Jackson (trans.). London: Darton, Longman and Todd.

Bradley, Martin B., et al. 1992. *Churches and Church Membership in the United States.* Atlanta: Glenmary Research Center.

Curran, Claude W. 1991. "Mt. Shasta, California, and the I Am Religion," in *Abstracts, The Association of American Geographers 1991 Annual Meeting, April 13–17, Miami, Florida.* Washington, D.C.: Association of American Geographers, 42.

Curry-Roper, Janel M. 1990. "Contemporary Christian Eschatologies and their Relation to Environmental Stewardship." *Professional Geographer* 42: 157–169.

Doughty, Robin W. 1981. "Environmental Theology: Trends and Prospects in Christian Thought." *Progress in Human Geography* 5: 234–248.

The Economist (February 24, 1996).

Government of Canada. 1974. *The National Atlas of Canada,* 4th ed. Ottawa: Government of Canada, Surveys and Mapping Branch.

Griffith, James S. 1992. *Beliefs and Holy Places: A Spiritual Geography of the Pimería Alta.* Tucson: University of Arizona Press.

Gutiérrez, Ramón A. 1991. *When Jesus Came, the Corn Mothers Went Away.* Stanford, Calif.: Stanford University Press.

Hobbs, Joseph J. 1995. *Mount Sinai.* Austin: University of Texas Press.

Hsu, Shin-Yi. 1969. "The Cultural Ecology of the Locust Cult in Traditional China." *Annals of the Association of American Geographers* 59: 734, 745.

Huntsinger, Lynn, and María Fernández-Giménez. 2000. "Spiritual Pilgrims at Mount Shasta, California." *Geographical Review* 90: 536–558.

Jett, Stephen C. 1997. "Place-Naming, Environment, and Perception Among the Canyon de Chelly Navajo of Arizona." *Professional Geographer* 49: 481–493.

Johnstone, Patrick. 1986. *Operation World*, 4th ed. N.p.: S. T. L. Books.

Jordan, Terry G., et al. 1984. *Texas: A Geography.* Boulder, Colo.: Westview Press.

Jordan-Bychkov, Terry G., and Bella Bychkova Jordan. 2002. *The European Culture Area: A Systematic Geography*, 4th ed. Lanham, Md.: Rowman & Littlefield.

Klaer, Wendelin. 1966. *Heidelberger Geographische Arbeiten* 15: 333.

Kluckhohn, Florence R., et al. 1961. *Variations in Value Orientations.* Evanston, Ill.: Row, Peterson.

Lai, Chuen-yan David. 1974. "A Feng Shui Model as a Location Index." *Annals of the Association of American Geographers* 64: 506–513.

Lane, B. C. 1988. *Landscapes of the Sacred.* New York: Paulist Press.

Lodrick, Deryck O. 1981. *Sacred Cows, Sacred Places: Origins and Survivals of Animal Homes in India.* Berkeley: University of California Press.

Muller, Kal. 1974. "Tanna Awaits the Coming of John Frum." *National Geographic* 145: 707, 714.

Nolan, Mary Lee, and Sidney Nolan. 1989. *Christian Pilgrimage in Modern Western Europe.* Chapel Hill: University of North Carolina Press.

Raban, Jonathan. 1996. *Bad Land: An American Romance.* New York: Pantheon Books.

Semple, Ellen Churchill. 1911. *Influences of Geographical Environment.* New York: Henry Holt.

Simoons, Frederick J. 1994. *Eat Not This Flesh: Food Avoidances in the Old World,* 2nd ed. Madison: University of Wisconsin Press.

Sims, John H., and Duane D. Baumann. 1972. "The Tornado Threat: Coping Styles of the North and South." *Science* 176: 1386–1392.

Singh, Rana P. B. 1994. "Water Symbolism and Sacred Landscape in Hinduism." *Erdkunde* 48: 210–227.

Smole, William J. 1976. *The Yanoama Indians: A Cultural Geography.* Austin: University of Texas Press, 23.

Stewart, Dona J. 1996. "Economic Recovery and Reconstruction in Postwar Beirut." *Geographical Review* 86: 489–492.

Stump, Roger W. (ed.). 1986. "The Geography of Religion." Special issue, *Journal of Cultural Geography* 7: 1–140.

Tuan, Yi-fu. 1968. "Discrepancies Between Environmental Attitude and Behavior: Examples from Europe and China." *Canadian Geographer* 12: 176–191.

White, Lynn, Jr. 1967. "The Historical Roots of our Ecologic Crisis." *Science* 155: 1203–1207.

Ten Recommended Books on the Geography of Religion

(*For additional suggested readings, see* The Human Mosaic *web site:* www.whfreeman.com/jordan)

Al-Faruqi, Isma'il R., and David E. Sopher. 1974. *Historical Atlas of the Religions of the World.* New York: Macmillan. Pretty much what its title promises, this informative atlas allows you to see cultural diffusion in action over the centuries and millennia.

Gottlieb, Roger S. (ed.). 1995. *This Sacred Earth: Religion, Nature and Environment.* London: Routledge. A good introduction to ecotheology.

Halvorson, Peter L., and William M. Newman. 1994. *Atlas of Religious Change in America, 1952–1990.* Atlanta: Glenmary Research Center. The changing pattern of denominational membership in the United States in the last half of the twentieth century, revealing the strengthening of some regions and the weakening of others.

Harpur, James. 1994. *The Atlas of Sacred Places.* New York: Henry Holt. A useful depiction of the location of sacred places, or "sacred space," as we labeled it; you will be amazed by their number and diversity.

Jordan, Terry G. 1982. *Texas Graveyards: A Cultural Legacy.* Austin: University of Texas Press. The only book by a geographer on this aspect of the religious landscape, very revealing in a state possessing a wide array of ethnic groups.

Park, Chris. 1994. *Sacred Worlds: An Introduction to Geography and Religion.* London: Routledge. An introductory text on the geography of religion.

Pui-lan, Kwok (ed.). 1994. *Ecotheology: Voices from South and North.* New York: World Council of Churches Publications. A very readable sampling of recent ecotheological thought.

Sopher, David E. 1967. *The Geography of Religions.* Englewood Cliffs, N.J.: Prentice-Hall. The first introduction to the geography of religion to appear in English, it remains a classic.

Stoddard, Robert H., and Alan Morinis (eds.). 1997. *Sacred Places, Sacred Spaces: The Geography of Pilgrimages.* Baton Rouge: Geoscience Publications. Published by the Department of Geography and Anthropology at Louisiana State University, these 14 essays, each by a different author, draw attention to Christian, Muslim, Hindu, and lesser Asian pilgrimage traditions, as seen from the perspective of cultural geography.

Stump, Roger W. 2000. *Boundaries of Faith: Geographical Perspectives on Religious Fundamentalism.* Lanham, Md.: Rowman & Littlefield. After describing the background of fundamentalist movements within various world religions occurring in several countries, the author explains commonalities and clarifies political implications. One of the first examinations of the spatial strategies inherent in fundamentalism.

How does it feel to be illiterate?

Street scene in Hong Kong. (Its modern name, since annexation to China in 1997, is Xianggang.) (NIK WHEELER/BLACK STAR/PICTUREQUEST.)
Turn to Seeing Geography *on page 140 for an in-depth analysis of the above question.*

CHAPTER
4

GEOLINGUISTICS
A Babel of Languages

Language contains the very essence of culture and provides the single most common variable by which different cultural groups are identified. A mutually agreed-upon system of symbolic communication, language offers the main means by which learned customs and skills pass from one generation to the next. Because languages vary spatially and tend to form spatial groupings, they reinforce the sense of region and place. Geographer Yi-fu Tuan wrote of "the role of human speech in the creation of place."

Language also facilitates the cultural diffusion of innovations and even helps to shape the way we think and how we perceive and name our environment. For all these reasons and more, cultural geographers study language, employing the five themes of region, diffusion, ecology, interaction, and landscape. The term **geolinguistics** describes this branch of the discipline.

Most cultural groups have their own distinctive form of speech, either a separate language or a dialect (Figure 4.1). **Languages** can be defined as tongues that cannot be mutually understood. A speaker of one language cannot comprehend the speaker of another. **Dialects,** by comparison, are variant forms of a language that have not lost mutual comprehension. A speaker of English can generally understand the various dialects of that language, regardless of whether the speaker comes from Australia, Scotland, or Mississippi. Nevertheless, the dialect is distinctive enough in vocabulary and pronunciation to label its speaker. About 6000 languages and many more dialects are spoken today.

Languages

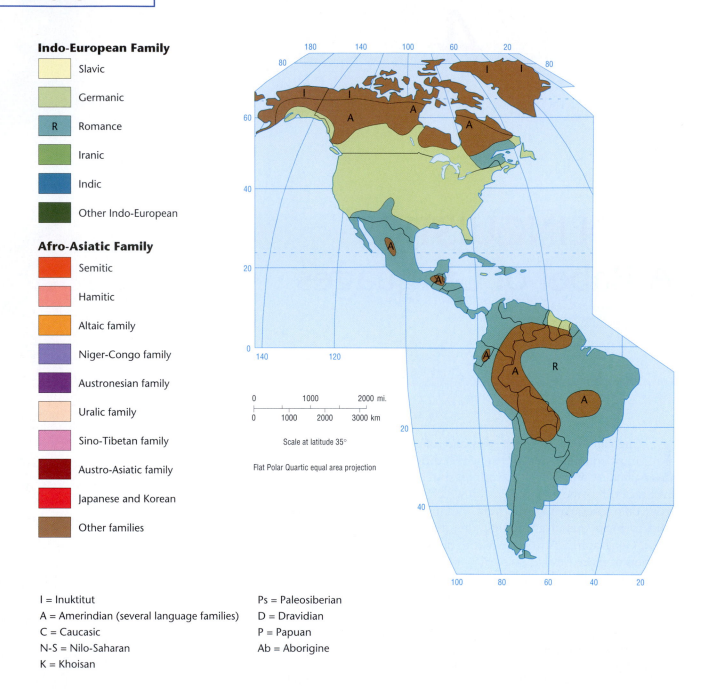

Indo-European Family

- Slavic
- Germanic
- R Romance
- Iranic
- Indic
- Other Indo-European

Afro-Asiatic Family

- Semitic
- Hamitic
- Altaic family
- Niger-Congo family
- Austronesian family
- Uralic family
- Sino-Tibetan family
- Austro-Asiatic family
- Japanese and Korean
- Other families

I = Inuktitut
A = Amerindian (several language families)
C = Caucasic
N-S = Nilo-Saharan
K = Khoisan

Ps = Paleosiberian
D = Dravidian
P = Papuan
Ab = Aborigine

0   1000   2000 mi.
0   1000   2000   3000 km

Scale at latitude 35°

Flat Polar Quartic equal area projection

When different linguistic groups come into contact, a **pidgin** language often results, characterized by a very small vocabulary derived from the languages of the groups in contact. Pidgins primarily serve the purposes of trade and commerce. An example is Tok Pisin, the largely English-derived pidgin spoken in Papua New Guinea, where it has become the official national language in a country where many native Papuan tongues

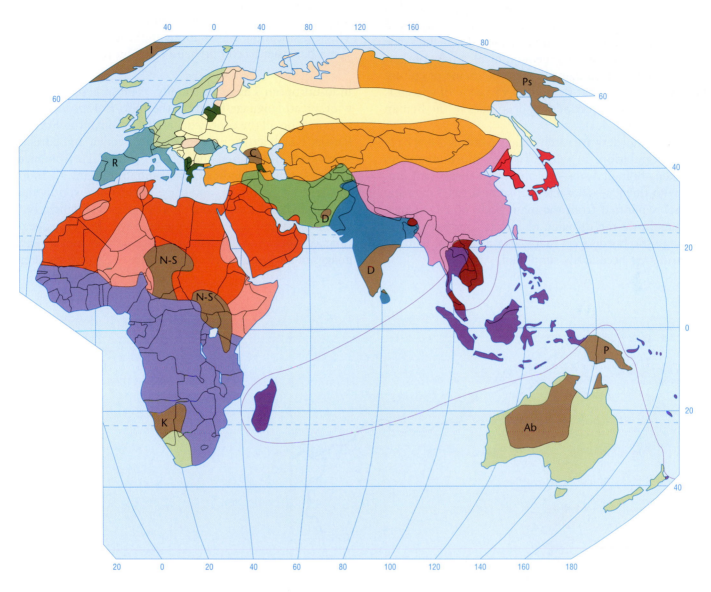

Figure 4.1

The major linguistic formal culture regions of the world. Although there are thousands of languages and dialects in the world, they can be grouped into a few linguistic families. Note the broad geographical extent of the Indo-European language family.

are spoken. The New Guinea pidgin also includes Spanish, German, and Papuan words and is not readily intelligible to a speaker of English. In other situations, one existing language may be elevated to the status of a **lingua franca,** or a language of communication and commerce, over a wide area where it is not a mother tongue. The Swahili language enjoys lingua franca status in much of East Africa.

Linguistic Culture Regions

What is the geographical patterning of languages? Do the various languages provide the basis for formal and functional culture regions? Indeed they do. In fact, the logical place to begin our geographical study of languages, dialects, and pidgins is with the theme of culture region. We will find that the spatial variation of speech is remarkably complicated, adding deep hues to the human mosaic (see Figure 4.1).

Language borders are rarely sharp. Many regions have a mixed population, in which two or more languages are spoken. Bilingualism—the ability to speak two languages with fluency—characterizes some areas. Linguistic "islands," separated from the main body of a language, often complicate the drawing of borders further (Figure 4.2). Linguistic borders on maps, like all formal cultural boundaries, are necessarily simplified.

Language Families

One way that geolinguists often simplify the mapping of languages is by grouping them into **language families:** tongues that are related and share a common ancestor. This classification makes the complicated linguistic mosaic a bit easier to comprehend (see Figure 4.1).

Indo-European Language Family   The largest and most widespread language family is the *Indo-European,* which is spoken on all the continents and is dominant in Europe, Russia, North and South America, Australia, and parts of southwestern Asia and India (see Figure 4.1). Romance, Slavic, Germanic, Indic, Celtic, and Iranic are all Indo-European subfamilies, and they, in turn, are subdivided into individual languages. For example, English is a Germanic Indo-European language. Seven Indo-European tongues, including English, are among the top 10 languages in the world, ranked by number of native speakers

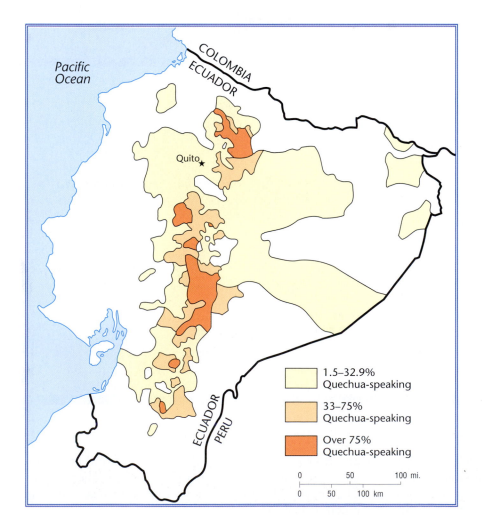

Figure 4.2

The formal culture region of Quechua, the main Indian language of Ecuador, South America, 1950. The core-periphery configuration typical of formal regions is evident. Urban populations are excluded. **Does the distribution of Quechua, mapped in this manner, suggest whether the language is advancing or retreating?** (SOURCE: KNAPP, 1987: 53–57.)

TABLE 4.1   The Ten Leading Languages in Numbers of Native Speakers*

Language	Family	Speakers (in millions)	Main Areas Where Spoken
Han Chinese (Mandarin)	Sino-Tibetan	885	China, Taiwan, Singapore
Hindi/Urdu	Indo-European	426	Northern India, Pakistan
Spanish	Indo-European	358	Spain, Latin America, southwestern United States
English	Indo-European	343	British Isles, Anglo-America, Australia, New Zealand, South Africa, Philippines, former British colonies in tropical Asia and Africa
Arabic	Afro-Asiatic	235	Middle East, North Africa
Bengali	Indo-European	207	Bangladesh, eastern India
Portuguese	Indo-European	176	Portugal, Brazil, southern Africa
Russian	Indo-European	167	Russia, Kazakhstan, parts of Ukraine and other former Soviet republics
Japanese	Nipponese	125	Japan
German	Indo-European	100	Germany, Austria, Switzerland, Luxembourg, eastern France, northern Italy

* "Native speakers" means mother tongue.

(Sources: Encyclopaedia Britannica, 2000; and World Almanac Books, 2001.)

(Table 4.1), and roughly half of the world's population can speak one or another of these far-flung kindred languages.

If we compare the vocabularies of various Indo-European tongues, we can readily see their kinship. For example, the English word *mother* is similar to the Polish *matka*, the Greek *meter*, the Spanish *madre*, the Farsi *madar* in Iran, and the Sinhalese *mava* in Sri Lanka. Such similarities in vocabulary reveal that these languages long ago had a common ancestral tongue.

Afro-Asiatic Family   A second language family is the *Afro-Asiatic*, consisting of two major divisions, Semitic and Hamitic. The Semitic languages cover the area from the Arabian Peninsula and the Tigris-Euphrates river valley in the Fertile Crescent of Iraq westward through Syria and North Africa to the Atlantic Ocean. Despite the considerable size of this domain, there are fewer speakers of the Semitic languages than you might expect, because most of the areas that Semites inhabit are sparsely populated deserts. Arabic is by far the most widespread Semitic language and has the greatest number of native speakers, about 235 million. Although many different dialects of Arabic are spoken, the written form is standard.

Hebrew also is a Semitic tongue, closely related to Arabic. For many centuries, Hebrew was a "dead" language, used only in religious ceremonies by millions of Jews scattered around the world. With the creation of the state of Israel in 1948, a common language was needed to unite the immigrant Jews, who spoke the languages of many different countries. Hebrew was revived and made the official national language of what otherwise would have been a **polyglot,** or multilanguage, state. Amharic, a third major Semitic tongue, today claims 18 million speakers in the mountains of East Africa.

Smaller numbers of linguistically related people who speak Hamitic languages share North and East Africa with the Semites. These tongues originated in Asia but today are spoken almost exclusively in Africa, by the Berbers of Morocco and Algeria, the Tuaregs of the Sahara, and the Cushites of East Africa.

Other Major Language Families Most of the rest of the world's population speaks languages belonging to one or another of six remaining major families. Africa south of the Sahara Desert is dominated by the *Niger-Congo* language family, also called *Niger-Kordofanian,* spoken by about 325 million people. The greater part of the Niger-Congo culture region belongs to the Bantu subgroup, which includes Swahili, the lingua franca of East Africa. Both Niger-Congo and its Bantu constituent are fragmented into a great many different languages and dialects.

Flanking the Slavic Indo-Europeans on the north and south in Asia are the speakers of the *Altaic* language family, including Turkic, Mongolic, and several other subgroups. The Altaic homeland lies largely in the inhospitable deserts, tundra, and coniferous forests of northern and central Asia. Also occupying tundra and grassland areas adjacent to the Slavs is the *Uralic* family. Finnish and Hungarian are the two most important Uralic tongues, and both enjoy the status of official legal languages in their respective countries.

One of the most remarkable language families in terms of distribution is the *Austronesian.* Representatives of this group live mainly on tropical islands stretching from Madagascar, off the east coast of Africa, through Indonesia and the Pacific Islands, to Hawaii and Easter Island. This longitudinal span is more than half the distance around the world. The language area also covers a north-south, or latitudinal, range from Hawaii and Taiwan in the north to New Zealand in the south. The largest single language in this family is Malay-Indonesian, with 58 million native speakers, but the most widespread is Polynesian.

Dominated numerically and spatially by Chinese, *Sino-Tibetan* is one of the major language families of the world. The Sino-Tibetan speech area extends throughout most of China and Southeast Asia. Han Chinese (Mandarin) is spoken in a variety of dialects as a mother tongue by 885 million people and serves as the official form of speech in China. Among the other Sino-Tibetan languages are Burmese and Tibetan, which border the Chinese speech region on the south and west. Another major Asian family probably joins *Japanese* and *Korean,* with about 200 million speakers. Japanese and Korean perhaps have some link to the Altaic family, but even their kinship to each other remains controversial and unproven.

In Southeast Asia, the Vietnamese, Cambodians, Thais, and some tribal peoples of Malaya and parts of India speak languages that constitute the *Austro-Asiatic* family. They occupy a remnant peripheral domain and have been encroached on by Sino-Tibetan, Indo-European, and Austronesian.

Other Language Families Occupying refuge areas after retreat before rival groups are remnant language families such as *Khoisan,* found in the Kalahari desert of south-

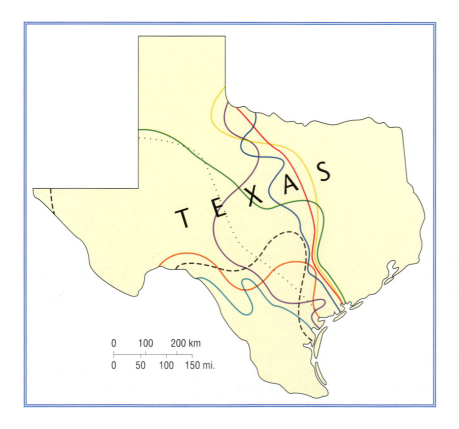

Eastern and Northern Borders of

——— Remuda (group of saddle horses)

——— Resaca (channel)

——— Vaquero (cowboy)

——— Arroyo (dry creek)

——— Pilón (something extra)

——— Mesa (flat-topped hill)

——— Frijoles (pinto beans)

········ Toro (bull)

– – – Acequia (irrigation ditch)

Figure 4.3
Isoglosses cluster into "bundles." Many words have been adopted from Spanish into English in the western and southern parts of Texas. Note that the isogloss for each of these representative "loanwords" is slightly different from every other one but that the result is a "bundle" of isoglosses, dividing Texas into two dialect regions. **Where would you draw a dialect border based on these isoglosses?** (SOURCE: Atwood, 1962.)

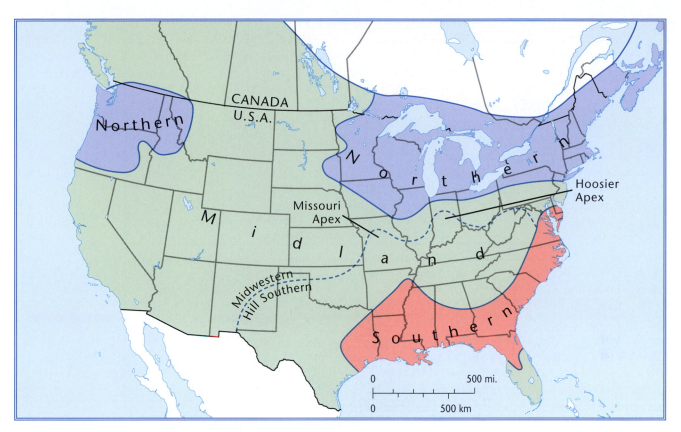

Figure 4.4

Major dialects of North American English, with a few selected subdialects. Compare these with the Anglo-American subcultures shown in Figure 1.6. **Why does no distinctively Canadian dialect of English exist? What type of cultural diffusion might have produced the outlier of the Northern dialect in the Pacific Northwest?** (AFTER CARVER, 1986; AND KURATH, 1949.)

western Africa and characterized by distinctive clicking sounds; *Dravidian,* spoken by hundreds of millions of people in southern India, adjacent northern Sri Lanka, and a part of Pakistan; Australian *Aborigine; Papuan; Caucasic; Nilo-Saharan; Paleosiberian; Inuktitut;* and a variety of *American Indian* families. In a few cases, individual minor languages represent the last sole survivors of former families. *Basque,* spoken in the borderland between Spain and France, is such a survivor, unrelated to any other language in the world.

Reflecting on GEOGRAPHY

Would the world be a better place if everyone spoke the same language? Why or why not?

English Dialects in the United States

At the opposite end of the linguistic continuum from language families are *dialects,* and they, too, reveal a vivid geography. Geolinguists map dialects by using **isoglosses:** the borders of individual words or pronunciations. No two isoglosses are identical. Figure 4.3 provides an example of how isoglosses crisscross one another. In most cases, however, multiple isoglosses parallel one another, in "bundles," and these serve as dialect boundaries. Even so, geolinguists often disagree about how many dialects are present in an area or exactly where isoglosses should be drawn.

The dialects of American English provide examples. At least three major dialects, corresponding to major culture regions, developed in the eastern United States by the time of the American Revolution: the Northern, Midland, and Southern dialects (Figure 4.4) (see Profile, Hans Kurath, on page 121). As the three subcultures expanded westward, their dialects spread and fragmented. Nevertheless, the dialects retained much of their basic character even beyond the Mississippi River. The three dialects have distinctive vocabularies and pronunciations. Drawing the dialect boundaries is often tricky, and disagreements can occur

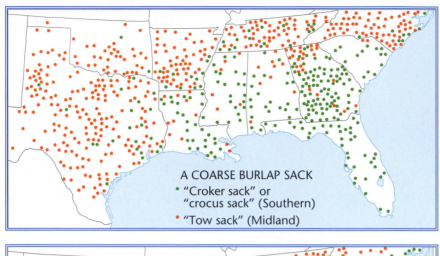

A COARSE BURLAP SACK
- "Croker sack" or
  "crocus sack" (Southern)
- "Tow sack" (Midland)

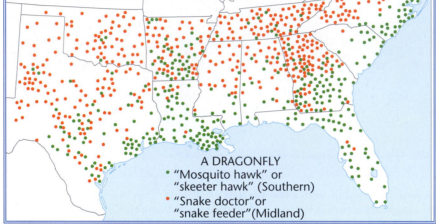

A DRAGONFLY
- "Mosquito hawk" or
  "skeeter hawk" (Southern)
- "Snake doctor"or
  "snake feeder"(Midland)

Figure 4.5

Some Midland and Southern words in the American South. Each dot represents one person interviewed who gave the response indicated. **If you were drawing the isoglosses for these words, where exactly would you place them? If these two maps were your only evidence, where would you draw the Midland-Southern dialect border?** These are common problems for the linguistic geographer, and they illustrate the artificiality of dialect maps and all formal culture regions. (Sources: Wood, 1971: 325, 337–339; Kurath, 1949; and Atwood, 1962: 196, 199.)

(Figure 4.5). One scholar detects two major dialects in the American South, whereas another expert, equally well qualified, finds five or six. Viewing the chaotic pattern of isoglosses, yet another geolinguist asks, in all seriousness, "Do dialect borders exist?"

Today, many of the regional words in American English dialects are becoming old-fashioned, but new words displaying regional variations are still being coined. For instance, the following terms are all used to describe a controlled-access divided highway: *freeway, turnpike, parkway, thruway, expressway,* and *interstate.* Of these, *parkway* and *turnpike* seem to be used mainly in the Northeast and Midwest, whereas *freeway* is used in California.

Many African-Americans speak their own distinctive form of English. Black English, or *Ebonics,* is a variety of the Southern dialect bearing considerable African influence in pitch, rhythm, and tone. It grew out of a pidgin that developed on the early slave plantations and is today spoken by about 80 percent of African-Americans.

Although we are sometimes led to believe that Americans are becoming more alike, as a national culture overwhelms regional ones, the current status of American English dialects suggests otherwise. Linguistic divergence is still under way, and dialects continue to mutate on a regional level, just as they always have. Local variations in grammar and pronunciation proliferate, confounding the proponents of standardized speech and defying the homogenizing influence of radio, television, and other mass media.

PROFILE

(UNIVERSITY OF MICHIGAN.)

Hans Kurath

1891–1992

Although a native of Austria, Professor Kurath was best known for his pioneer studies of the linguistic geography of the eastern United States, one of which is listed among the readings at the end of this chapter. He immigrated to America in 1907 and was educated at the University of Texas and the University of Chicago. Most of his academic career was spent at Brown University, where he served as professor of Germanics and linguistics, and at the University of Michigan, where he was professor of English until retiring in 1961. Cultural geographers have profited greatly from Kurath's seminal works on American English dialects, works rich in maps of vocabulary and pronunciation usages. His research provided part of the basis for Figure 4.4. Much honored and widely respected, Kurath held honorary doctorates from the universities of Chicago and Wisconsin.

See Schneider, 1992.

Linguistic Diffusion

How did the mosaic of languages and dialects come to exist? This question has puzzled us for thousands of years, as the Tower of Babel story in the Bible suggests. Our theme of *cultural diffusion* allows us to begin to find answers.

Languages have diffused spatially since time immemorial. The process has seen a relatively small number of tongues expand at the expense of most others. Ten thousand years ago, the human race consisted of only one million people, speaking an estimated 15,000 languages. Today, a population 6000 times larger speaks only 40 percent as many tongues. Fewer than a hundred modern languages enjoy official national status in independent countries, and another hundred have some lesser legal recognition. Only 1 percent of all languages have as many as 500,000 speakers. Some experts feel that all but 300 languages will be extinct or dying by the year 2100. Clearly, cultural diffusion has worked to favor some languages and eliminate others. Each passing decade witnesses the extinction of more minor languages.

Reflecting on GEOGRAPHY

Can you think of reasons why the number of languages has declined so profoundly in the last 10,000 years?

Different types of cultural diffusion have helped shape the linguistic map. *Relocation diffusion* has been extremely important, for languages spread when groups, in whole or part, migrated from one area to another. Some individual tongues or entire language families are no longer spoken in the regions where they originated, and in certain other cases the linguistic hearth is peripheral to the present distribution (compare Figures 4.1 and 4.6, which is on the next page).

Indo-European Diffusion

The earliest speakers of Indo-European, according to a widely accepted new theory, lived in southern and southeastern Turkey, a region known as Anatolia, about 9000 years ago (see Figure 4.6). They possessed a new invention—agriculture—and their ancient diffusion to the west and north, bringing them into Europe, represented the expansion of a farming people at the expense of hunters and gatherers. The initial prehistoric advance of the Indo-Europeans, then, apparently hinged on a major innovation—plant and animal domestication—and probably proceeded gradually and peacefully. As these people dispersed and lost contact with one another, different Indo-European groups gradually developed variant forms of the language, causing fragmentation of the language family.

In later millennia, the diffusion of certain Indo-European languages—in particular Latin, English, and Russian—occurred in conjunction with the territorial spread of great political empires. In such cases of imperial conquest, relocation and *expansion diffusion* were not mutually exclusive. Relocation diffusion often involved a relatively small number of speakers, a conquering elite who came to rule an alien people. The language of the conqueror, implanted by relocation diffusion, often gained wider acceptance through expansion diffusion. Typically, the conqueror's language spread hierarchically—adopted first by the more important and influential persons and by city dwellers. The diffusion of Latin with Roman conquests often occurred in this manner, as did Spanish in Latin America.

Austronesian Diffusion

One of the most impressive examples of linguistic diffusion is revealed by the Austronesian languages. From a presumed hearth 5000 years ago in the interior of Southeast Asia, completely outside the present Austronesian

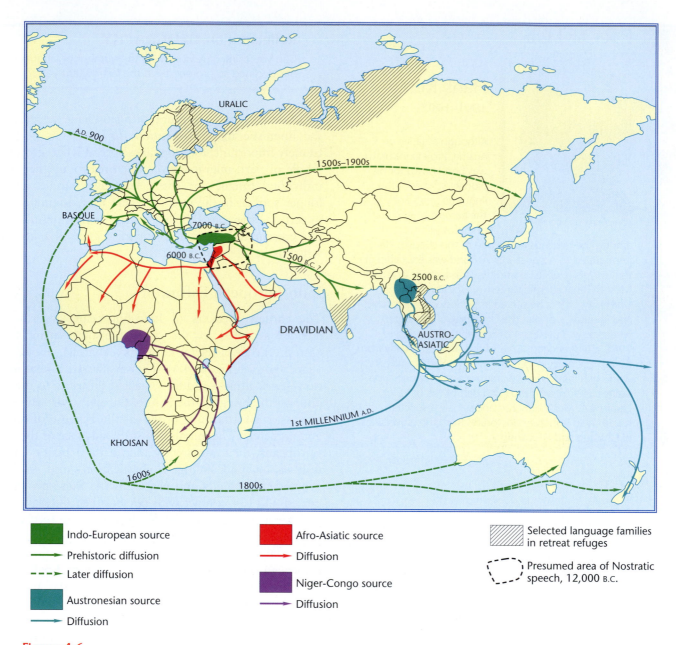

Figure 4.6

Origin and diffusion of four major language families in the Eastern Hemisphere. The prehistoric diffusion of Indo-European speech to the west and north probably occurred in conjunction with the diffusion of agriculture from the Middle Eastern center, as did the early spread of the Afro-Asiatic family. All such origins, lost in time, are speculative. As these and other groups advanced, certain linguistic families retreated to refuges in remote places, where they hold out to the present day. Sources, dates, and routes are mostly speculative. **What processes allow one language to replace another?** (SOURCES: KRANTZ, 1988; AND RENFREW, 1989.)

culture region, speakers of this language family initially spread southward into the Malay Peninsula (see Figure 4.6). Then, in a process lasting perhaps several thousand years and requiring remarkable navigational skills, they migrated through the islands of Indonesia and sailed in tiny boats across vast, uncharted expanses of ocean to New Zealand, Easter Island, Hawaii, and Madagascar. If

agriculture was the technology permitting Indo-European diffusion, sailing and navigation provided the key to the spread of the Austronesians, bringing them to many islands never before inhabited.

Most remarkable of all was the diffusionary achievement of the Polynesian people, who form the eastern part of the Austronesian culture region. Polynesians occupy a

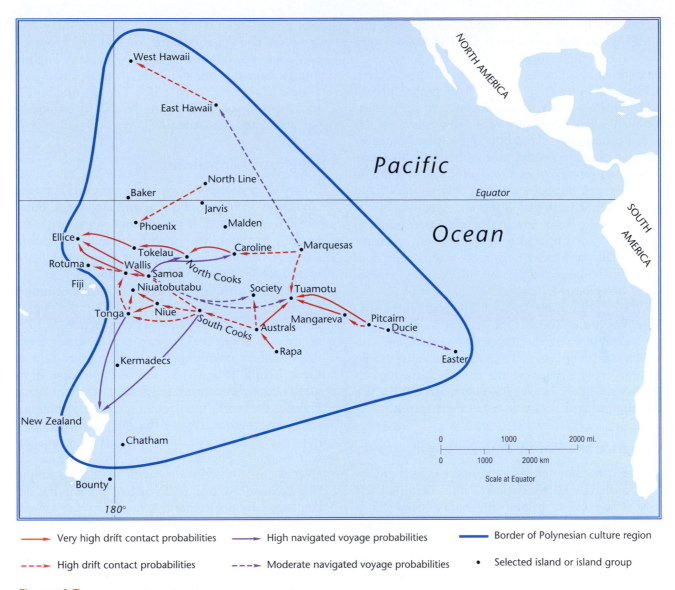

Figure 4.7
Probabilities of selected Polynesian drift and navigation voyages in the Pacific Ocean.
According to a computer model, the outer arc of Polynesia, represented by Hawaii, Easter
Island, and New Zealand, could have been reached only by navigated voyages. The earliest
known Polynesian pottery shards have recently been found in Tonga by archaeologists David
Burley and William Dickinson, suggesting that the first distinctively Polynesian culture
originated there. (ADAPTED FROM LEVISON, WARD, AND WEBB, 1973: 5, 33, 35, 43, 61.)

triangular-shaped realm consisting of hundreds of Pacific
islands, with New Zealand, Easter Island, and Hawaii
at the three apexes (Figure 4.7). The Polynesians' watery
leap of 2500 miles (4000 kilometers) from the South
Pacific to Hawaii, a migration in outrigger canoes against
prevailing winds into a new hemisphere with different
navigational stars, must rank as one of the greatest
achievements of seafaring. No humans had previously
found the isolated Hawaiian Islands, and the Polynesian
sailors had no way of knowing ahead of time that land
existed in that quarter of the Pacific.

The relocation diffusion that produced the remarkable
present distribution of the Polynesian languages has long
been the subject of controversy. How, when, and by what
means could a traditional people have achieved the diffusion? What skills were required? Geolinguists Michael
Levison, Gerard Ward, and John Webb studied this prehistoric diffusion. Their method, both unusual and rewarding, involved the development of a computer *model*,
into which was incorporated data on winds, ocean currents, vessel traits and capabilities, island visibility, duration of voyage, and the like. Both *drift* voyages, in which

the boat simply floats with the winds and currents, and *navigated* voyages were considered. Over 100,000 voyage simulations were run through the computer.

The authors concluded, on the basis of these experiments, that the Polynesian triangle had probably been entered from the west, from the direction of the ancient Austronesian hearth area, by way of western insular chains in a process of "island hopping"—that is, migrating from one island to another one visible in the distance. The core of eastern Polynesia was probably reached in navigated voyages, but once attained, drift voyages could easily explain much internal diffusion. A peripheral region, an "outer arc from Hawaii through Easter Island to New Zealand," was apparently attainable only by means of "intentionally navigated" voyages—daring feats that must be ranked among the greatest human achievements of all time (see Figure 4.7).

Note that in this application of the geographer's spatial skills, Webb and Ward employed the themes of culture region (present distribution of Polynesians) and cultural ecology (currents, winds, visibility of islands) to help describe and explain the workings of a third theme, cultural diffusion. Again, as suggested in Chapter 1, the five themes unite rather than divide cultural geography.

Searching for the Primordial Tongue

Using techniques that remain controversial, certain linguists are probing even more deeply into the origin and diffusion of languages, seeking still more elusive prehistoric tongues. Evidence is building that an ancestral speech called *Nostratic,* spoken in the Middle East 12,000 to 20,000 years ago, was ancestral to six modern language families: Indo-European, Uralic, Altaic, Afro-Asiatic, Caucasic, and Dravidian (see Figure 4.6). A speculative 500-word Nostratic dictionary has been compiled, containing words such as *kuni* ("wife," "woman"), which became, for example, the ancient Indo-European *gwen* (and modern English *queen*); the archaic Altaic *küni*; and the old Afro-Asiatic *KwVn*. Contemporary with Nostratic, apparently, were several other ancient tongues, including *Dene-Caucasian,* which reputedly gave rise to Sino-Tibetan, and one American Indian family called *Na-Dene.*

These pioneering scholars are now attempting to establish a kinship among Nostratic, Dene-Caucasian, and other ancient languages in order to find the primordial tongue, the single original speech from which they presume all languages are ultimately derived. They seek nothing less than the original linguistic hearth area, almost certainly in Africa, where complex speech first arose and from which it diffused. Here again, the evidence comes from comparative vocabularies. For example, there

was a primordial word, *tik* (or *dik*), meaning "one" or "to point one finger or arm," or "finger." From it reputedly come the Nostratic *deik* (to point) (and English *digit*, finger); Niger-Kordofanian *dike*, "one"; Afro-Asiatic *tak*, "one"; Uralic *otik*, "one"; Sino-Tibetan *tik*, "one"; Austric (Austronesian plus Austro-Asiatic) *tik* or *ting*, "hand" or "arm"; and Na-Dene *tikhi*, "one."

Linguistic Globalization

It may seem a large leap from the primordial tongue to a consideration of *globalization* and languages, but in fact the two are related. If we humans began with one language, why should we not return to that condition? If one language became 15,000 and now 6000 and will dwindle to 300 within a century, then why not one?

Put differently, are the forces of modernization working to produce, through cultural diffusion, a single world language? And if so, what will that language be? English? Worldwide about 343 million people speak English as their mother tongue and perhaps another 350 million speak it well as a second, learned language. If we add other reasonably competent speakers who can "get by" in English, the world total reaches about 1.5 billion, more than any other language. Also, the Internet is one of the most potent agents of diffusion, and its language, overwhelmingly, is English (see Focus On: Cyberspeech). English earlier diffused widely with the British Empire and U.S. colonialism, and today it has become the de facto language of globalization. A minor rival, *Esperanto*—a synthetic language with words borrowed from many

FOCUS ON

Cyberspeech

English may be the mother tongue of less than 6 percent of the world's population, but it completely dominates the Internet. Here is the percentage of home pages, by the top 10 languages:

English	82.3%	Italian	0.8%
German	4.0%	Portuguese	0.7%
Japanese	1.6%	Swedish	0.6%
French	1.5%	Dutch	0.4%
Spanish	1.1%	Norwegian	0.3%

Sources: Alis Technology; and Internet Society.

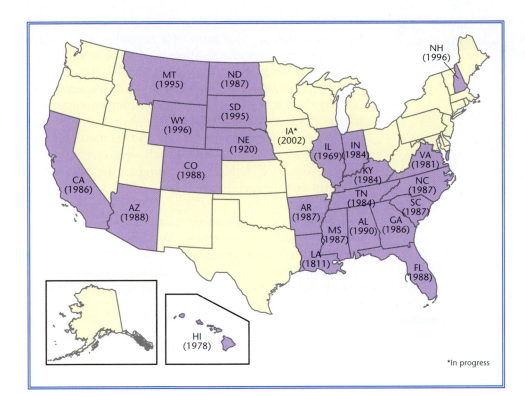

Figure 4.8
States of the United States that have some form of official English-only laws. Dates show the year enacted. **Why would we need English-only laws? What happened in the 1980s to prompt so many such laws in that decade?**

*In progress

existing tongues—never attained much acceptance, and English now appears to be the only viable candidate.

But is the diffusion of English to the entire world population likely? Even in the United States, fully 23 states have felt that the position of English was sufficiently insecure to require passage of English-only laws (Figure 4.8).

Consider, too, the case of India, where the English language imposed by British rulers was retained after independence as the country's language of business, government, and education. It provided some linguistic unity for India, which had 800 indigenous languages and dialects. Even so, many people resent its use and "will not rest until English is driven out of the country," ridding India of a hated legacy of colonialism. Moreover, the spoken English of India has drifted away from standard British English and is difficult to understand. So has that of Singapore, a separate language now called Singlish. Many other regional, English-based languages have developed, languages that could not be understood in London or Chicago.

Reflecting on GEOGRAPHY

Compare the levels of globalization of religion and language. Is globalization most likely to occur in religious faith or in speech? Why do you think so?

So, will globalization and cultural diffusion produce one world language? Probably not. More likely, a situation similar to the one we found in religion will occur—the world divided among 5 or 10 languages. And that will occur only if globalization itself endures.

Linguistic Ecology

Do languages have any connection to the physical habitat, to *ecoregions*? Is there a cultural ecology of languages? Yes. None of our five themes ever fail us in the study of cultural geography. In fact, the theme of cultural ecology contributes greatly to the geographical study of languages. The specific physical habitats in which languages evolve help shape their vocabularies, and the environment can guide the migrations of linguistic groups or provide refuges for languages in retreat. The following section, from the viewpoint of the *possibilist*, suggests some ways in which the physical environment influences vocabulary and the distribution of language.

Habitat and Vocabulary

Humankind's relationship to the land played a strong role in the development of linguistic differences (see Focus On:

FOCUS ON

An English Speaker Walks in the Desert

Our individual languages evolve in particular physical environmental surroundings. When speakers of these languages try to cope with a very different ecological setting, they find the vocabulary inadequate. The remarks of an American humanist, describing his walk across the desert of Sonora and Arizona, are very revealing:

> I know no desert language.
> I struggle with a tongue forged on another continent, with words spawned in green forests under gray, soggy skies.

Quote from Bowden, 1984.

An English Speaker Walks in the Desert). The environment even influences vocabulary. For example, the Spanish language—which originated in Castile, a land rimmed by hills and high mountains—is especially rich in words describing rough terrain, allowing speakers of this tongue to distinguish even subtle differences in the shape and configuration of mountains, as Table 4.2 reveals. Similarly, Scottish Gaelic possesses a rich vocabulary to describe types of rough terrain—a common attribute of

the Celtic languages, spoken by hill peoples. In the Romanian tongue, also born of a rugged terrain, words relating to mountainous features tend to be keyed to use of that terrain for livestock herding. English, by contrast, developed in wet coastal plains, and consequently our language is very poor in words describing mountainous terrain (Figure 4.9). By contrast, English abounds with words describing flowing streams and wetlands. In the rural American South alone, one finds *river, creek, branch, fork, prong, run, bayou,* and *slough*. This vocabulary indicates that the area is a well-watered land with a dense network of streams.

Clearly, then, language serves an *adaptive strategy,* at least in traditional societies. Vocabularies are highly developed for those features of the environment that involve livelihood. Without such detailed vocabularies, it would be difficult to communicate sophisticated information relevant to the adaptive strategy.

The Habitat Provides Refuge

Another environmental influence on language is the protection and isolation offered by inhospitable environments. Such areas often provide hard-pressed, outnumbered linguistic groups refuge from aggressive neighbors and are, accordingly, referred to as **linguistic refuge areas.** Rugged hill and mountain areas, excessively cold or dry climates, dense forests, remote islands, and extensive marshes and swamps can all offer protection to minority language groups. For one thing, unpleasant

Figure 4.9

A scene in the desert of the western United States. Our English language fails us in our attempt to describe this scene. **"Mountains," yes, but what kind of mountains? (See Table 4.2.) "Desert" and "cacti," yes, but can we be more specific?** Our English language cannot describe such a place adequately, because it is the product of a very different cultural ecology. As a result, our environmental perception will be less precise in such places. **Does this inadequacy of English mean that it would be a less-than-satisfactory world language?** (DAVID MUENCH/CORBIS.)

TABLE 4.2   Some Spanish Words Describing Mountains and Hills

Spanish Word	English Meaning
candelas	Literally "candles"; a collection of *peñas*
ceja	Steep-sided breaks or escarpment separating two plains of different elevation
cejita	A low escarpment
cerrillo or *cerrito*	A small *cerro*; a hill
cerro	A single eminence, intermediate in size between English *hill* and *mountain*
chiquito	Literally "small," describing minor secondary fringing elevations at the base of and parallel to a *sierra* or *cordillera*
cordillera	A mass of mountains, as distinguished from a single mountain summit
cuchilla	Literally "knife"; the comblike secondary crests that project at right angles from the sides of a *sierra*
cumbre	The highest elevation or peak within a *sierra* or *cordillera*; a summit
eminencia	A mountainous or hilly protuberance
loma	A hill in the midst of a plain
lomita	A small hill in the midst of a plain
mesa	Literally "table"; a flat-topped eminence
montaña	Equivalent to English *mountain*
pelado	A barren, treeless mountain
pelon	A bare conical eminence
peloncilla	A small *pelon*
peña	A needlelike eminence
picacho	A peaked or pointed eminence
pico	A summit point, English *peak*
sandia	Literally "watermelon"; an oblong, rounded eminence
sierra	An elongated mountain mass with a serrated crest
teta	A solitary, conical mountain in the shape of a woman's breast
tinaja	A solitary, hemispheric mountain shaped like an inverted bowl

(Source: Hill, 1896.)

environments rarely attract conquerors. Also, mountains tend to isolate the inhabitants of one valley from those in adjacent ones, retarding the contacts that might lead to linguistic diffusion.

Examples of these linguistic refuge areas are numerous. The rugged Caucasus Mountains and nearby ranges in central Eurasia are populated by a large variety of peoples (Figure 4.10 on the next page). Similarly, the Alps, the Himalayas, and the highlands of Mexico are linguistic shatter belts—areas where diverse languages are spoken. Mountains provide isolation and are natural shatter belts. The Indian tongue Quechua clings to a refuge in the Andes Mountains of South America (see Figure 4.2); and in the Rocky Mountains of northern New Mexico, an archaic form of Spanish survives, largely as a result of an isolation that ended only in the early 1900s. The Dhofar, a mountain tribe in the back country of Oman in Arabia, preserves Hamitic speech, a family otherwise vanished from

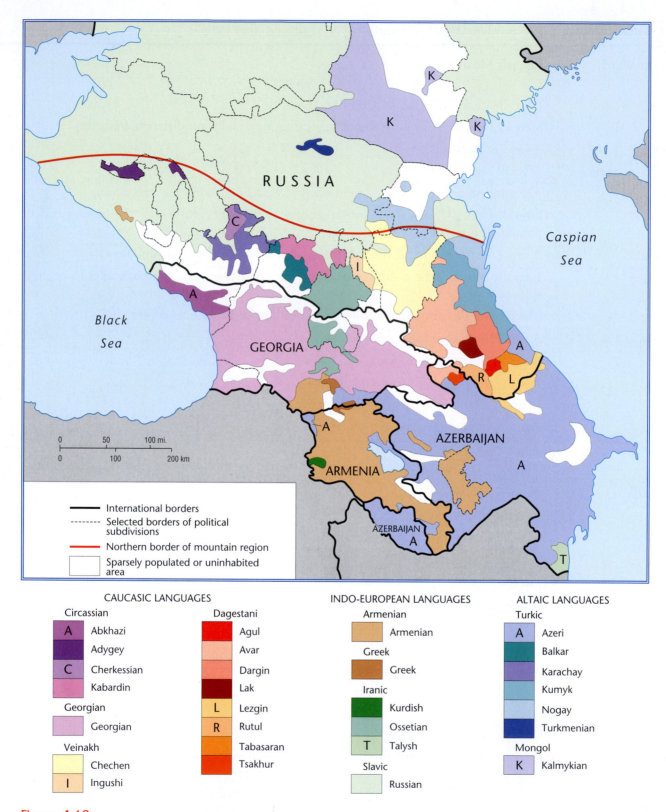

CAUCASIC LANGUAGES				INDO-EUROPEAN LANGUAGES		ALTAIC LANGUAGES	
Circassian		**Dagestani**		**Armenian**		**Turkic**	
A	Abkhazi		Agul		Armenian	A	Azeri
	Adygey		Avar	**Greek**			Balkar
C	Cherkessian		Dargin		Greek		Karachay
	Kabardin		Lak	**Iranic**			Kumyk
Georgian		L	Lezgin		Kurdish		Nogay
	Georgian	R	Rutul		Ossetian		Turkmenian
Veinakh			Tabasaran	T	Talysh	**Mongol**	
	Chechen		Tsakhur	**Slavic**		K	Kalmykian
I	Ingushi				Russian		

Figure 4.10

The environment is a linguistic refuge in the Caucasus Mountains. The rugged mountainous region between the Black and Caspian seas—including parts of Armenia, Russia, Georgia, and Azerbaijan—is peopled by a great variety of linguistic groups, representing three major language families. Mountain areas are often linguistic shatter belts because the rough terrain provides refuge and isolation. For more information about this fascinating and diverse region, see Wixman, 1980.

all of Asia. Bitterly cold tundra climates of the far north have sheltered Uralic and Inuktitut speakers, and a desert has shielded Khoisan speakers from Bantu invaders. On the Sea Islands, off the coast of South Carolina and Georgia, some remnants of an African language, Gullah, can still be heard, protected for centuries by insularity. In short, hostile and isolated environments protect linguistic groups that are willing to endure the hardships they present.

Still, environmental isolation can no longer be the vital linguistic force it once was. It becomes harder and harder to discover spots on the Earth so isolated that they remain little touched by outside influences. Today, inhospitable lands may offer linguistic refuge, but it is no longer certain that they will in the future. Even an island situated in the middle of the vast Pacific Ocean can offer no reliable refuge in an age of airplanes and satellite-transmitted communications. Similarly, marshes and forests provide refuge only if they are not drained and cleared by farmers who want new farmlands. The reality of the world is no longer isolation but contact.

The Habitat Guides Migration

Migrating people often were attracted to new lands that seemed environmentally similar to their homelands, where they could pursue adaptive strategies already known to them. Germanic Indo-Europeans sought familiar temperate zones in America, New Zealand, and Australia. Semitic peoples rarely spread outside arid and semiarid climates. Ancestors of the modern Hungarians, a Uralic linguistic stock, left the grasslands of inner Eurasia in the tenth century and found a new home in the grassy Alföld, one of the few prairie areas of Europe.

Environmental barriers and natural routeways have often guided linguistic groups into certain paths. The wide distribution of the Austronesian language group, as we have seen, cannot be fully understood without studying prevailing winds and water currents in the Pacific and Indian oceans. Migrating Indo-Europeans entering the Indian subcontinent through low mountain passes in the northwest were deflected by the Himalayas and the barren Deccan Plateau into the rich Ganga-Indus river plain. Even today in parts of India, according to Charles Bennett, the Indo-European/Dravidian "language boundary seems to approximate an ecological boundary" between the water-retentive black soils of the plains and the thinner, reddish Deccan soils.

Because such physical barriers as mountain ridges can retard groups from migrating from one area to another, they often serve as linguistic borders. In parts of the Alps, speakers of German and Italian live on opposite sides of a major ridge. Portions of the mountain rim along the northern edge of the Fertile Crescent in the Middle East form the border between Semitic and Indo-European tongues. Linguistic borders that follow such physical features generally tend to be stable, and they often endure for thousands of years. Language borders that cross plains and major routes of communication are often unstable, as, for example, the Germanic-Slavic boundary on the North European Plain (Figure 4.11).

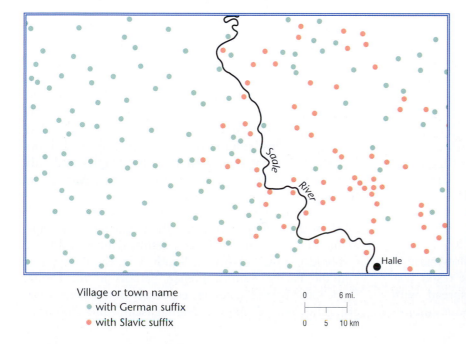

Village or town name
● with German suffix
● with Slavic suffix

0   5   10 km

0   6 mi.

Figure 4.11

Long ago—1200 years ago to be exact—the German-Slavic language border on the plains of northern Europe paralleled the Saale River. This fact is revealed by the names of villages and towns. Many Slavic place-names survive east of the river, but the modern language border lies much farther east, and no Slavic speakers remain here. **Why do language borders often shift in plains areas?** (SOURCE: JORDAN-BYCHKOV AND JORDAN, 2002.)

Culturo-Linguistic Interaction

How do languages and dialects interact causally with other facets of culture? Language is intertwined with all aspects of culture. The theme of cultural interaction permits us to probe some of these complex links between speech and other cultural phenomena. The complicated linguistic map cannot be understood without reference to the social, demographic, political, and technological characteristics of the groups in question. At root, linguistic cultural interaction often reflects the dominance of one group over another—a dominance based in culture.

Technology and Linguistic Dominance

One language group can achieve cultural dominance over neighboring groups in a variety of ways, often with profound results for the linguistic map of the world. Technological superiority is usually involved. Earlier, we saw how plant and animal domestication—the technology of the "agricultural revolution"—aided the early diffusion of the Indo-European language family.

An even more basic technology was the invention of writing. This invention apparently arose about 5300 years ago in Egypt, and shortly after that, by *independent invention,* among the Sumerians in what is today Iraq. Much later, the Indians in Central America and the Chinese independently developed writing systems. Writing helped civilization advance, giving written languages a big advantage over those that remained spoken only, an advantage that still operates today.

Transportation technology also profoundly affects the geography of languages. Ships, railroads, and highways usually spread the languages of the cultural groups who build them, sometimes spelling doom for the speech of less technologically advanced peoples whose lands are suddenly opened to outside contacts. The Trans-Siberian Railroad, built about a century ago, spread the Russian language eastward to the Pacific Ocean, and the Alaska Highway through Canada carried English into American Indian refuges. At present, the construction of highways into Brazil's remote Amazonian interior threatens the Indian languages of that region.

Language and Empire

Alphabets also facilitated record keeping, allowing governments and bureaucracies to develop. The result was empire building, and languages tend to spread with imperial expansion. Highly organized, literate empires

Figure 4.12

The mesh of language and empire in South America. The Treaty of Tordesillas, signed by Spain and Portugal in 1494, established the political basis for the present linguistic pattern in South America. Portugal was awarded the eastern part of the continent and Spain the rest. The Portuguese language was implanted in Portuguese territory, and today it has diffused westward from its source. In this way, languages spread with empires.

represent simply another technological advantage for the languages of the empires. The imperial expansion of European and U.S. power across the globe altered the linguistic patterns among millions of people. The United Kingdom, France, the Netherlands, Belgium, Portugal, Spain, and the United States ruled overseas empires (Figure 4.12). This empire building superimposed Indo-European tongues on the map of the tropics and subtropics. The areas most affected were Asia, Africa, and the Austronesian island world.

Even though the imperial nations have given up part or all of their colonial empires, the languages they transplanted overseas survived. As a result, English still has a foothold in much of Africa, South Asia, the Philippines, and the Pacific islands. French persists in the former French and Belgian colonies, especially in northern, western, and central Africa; Madagascar; and Polynesia

(Figure 4.13). In most of these areas, English and French function as the languages of the educated elite and enjoy a role as languages of government, commerce, and higher education. In fact, they often enjoy official legal status. The colonial tongues also function in such settings as a lingua franca, helping hold together states in which the native languages are multiple and divisive.

The Social Morale Model

Once a language diffuses spatially as a result of technological advantage or imperial conquest, the replacement of the indigenous languages can begin. Geographer Charles Withers proposed a *social morale model* to explain the process by which, over time, the conquered group is placed in a lower social class, loses pride in its

Figure 4.13

French, the colonial language of the empire, shares this sign on the isle of Bora Bora in French Polynesia with the native variant of the Polynesian tongue. Until recently, French rulers allowed no public display of the Polynesian language and tried to make the natives adopt French. **Why would France have pursued such a policy?** (Courtesy of Terry G. Jordan-Bychkov.)

language and culture, and eventually abandons both. An educational system based solely on the socially dominant language produces bilingualism, and the number of *monoglots,* or persons able to speak only one tongue, declines (Figure 4.14 on the next page). If the conquered group had been literate, they usually lapse at this stage into illiteracy in their traditional language. Often, no legal or religious status is accorded to the conquered language, conveying the message of social inferiority—the old way of speech is primitive and its use is socially degrading. One of the first acts of the new republican government of France in 1793 was to mandate the elimination of regional languages and dialects, using the apparatus of government to achieve that goal. In the modern world, where communications media are so pervasive, denying the oppressed language groups access to broadcast facilities can hasten the process of decline.

The linguistic geography of the United States reveals the profound decline of languages other than English, illustrating the social morale model. Almost up to the present day, American Indians in both the United States and Canada have been subjected to linguistic assaults from the dominant culture (see Focus On: Conquering the Indian with Words on page 133). Large numbers of Indian children have been taken from their families and placed in special boarding schools, often hundreds of miles from their homes. In these schools, run by the white-controlled Bureau of Indian Affairs, the Indian children were long forbidden on pain of punishment to speak their own languages. These and other assaults reduced the number of Indian languages in the territory of the United States from about 300 in the year 1500 to 175 today, only 20 of which are being passed on to the next generation. Fifty-five of these languages are spoken by fewer than 10 persons. The Navajo tongue, which had 148,000 speakers in 1990, is known to only one in three Navajo first-graders today. Even in remote Labrador in Canada, the percentage of Inuits who speak Inuktitut at home has declined to 88 percent.

A similar process led to the abandonment of most immigrant minority languages in the United States. As late as 1910, one out of every four Americans could speak some language other than English with the skill of a native (as compared to 14 percent in 1990). This was a result of the mass immigrations from Germany, Poland, Italy, Russia, China, and many other foreign areas. Much of this linguistic diversity has given way to English, partly because these imported languages lacked legal status. Only the Spanish-speaking population experienced any long-term success in preserving its speech in the United States. Spanish speakers achieved this, however, at the price of discrimination and lower socioeconomic status.

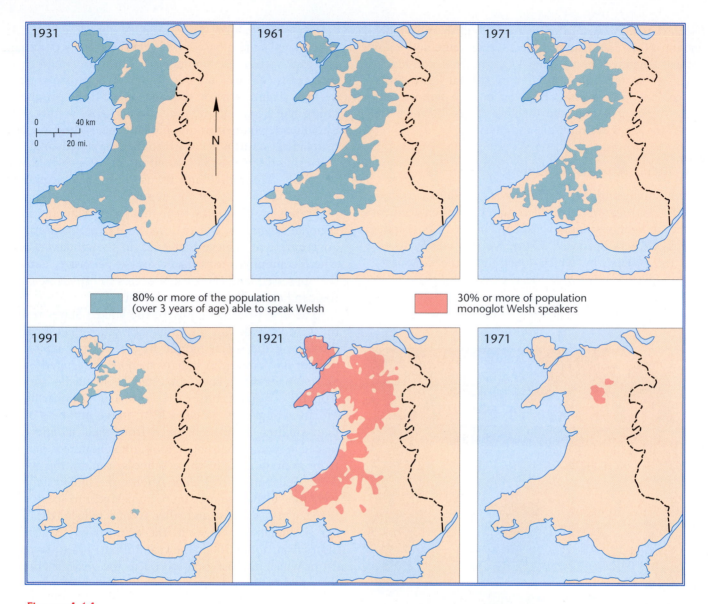

Figure 4.14
Retreat of the Welsh language in the twentieth century. For centuries, the Welsh have been dominated by English-speaking people in the United Kingdom. As a result, the language has declined. Between 1931 and 1991, the number of Welsh speakers fell from 909,000 to 497,000. Meanwhile, the district known as the *Bro Gymraeg,* where Welsh is spoken, shrank and began to fragment. **Is survival less likely once territorial fragmentation has occurred?** English penetrated along the coast and valleys, causing Welsh to retreat into the hilliest terrain. Monoglots are people who are able to speak only one language, in this case Welsh. Note how their retreat has been far more profound than that of the bilingual Welsh speakers. Bilingualism is often a transitional phase in the extinction of minority languages. (AFTER WILLIAMS, 1937; JONES AND GRIFFITHS, 1963; BOWEN AND CARTER, 1975; AND AITCHINSON AND CARTER, 1994.)

Morale is not always broken by conquest and subsequent discrimination. The Greeks endured lengthy periods of rule by Romans and Turks without succumbing linguistically to either conqueror, and they remained convinced that their culture was superior to those of their conquerors. The Chinese absorbed Mongol invaders and made Chinese out of them. Sometimes the languages of conquered and conqueror blend, as happened after the Norman-French conquest of England over nine centuries ago.

FOCUS ON

Conquering the Indian with Words

An Odawa Indian, born on Manitoulin Island, Ontario, Canada, remembers the problems language caused him when, as a child, he first left the Indian reservation and entered the English-speaking world that surrounded and dominated it:

Many of us as children were not even permitted to speak our own language. Of course, we still tried to speak our own language, but we were punished for it. Four or five years ago they were still stripping the kids of their clothes up around Kenora and beating them for speaking their own language. I was punished several times for speaking Indian not only on the school grounds but off the school grounds and on the street, and I lived across from the school. Almost in front of my own door my first language was forbidden me, and yet when I went into the house my parents spoke Indian.

Our language is so important to us as a people. Our language and our language structure related to our whole way of life. How beautiful that picture language is where they only tell you the beginning and the end, and you fill in everything, and they allow you to feel how you want to feel. Here we manipulate and twist things around and get you to hate a guy. The Indian doesn't do that. He'll just say that some guy got into an accident, and he won't give you any details. From there on you just explore as far as you want to. You'll say: "What happened?" and he'll tell you a little more. He only answers questions. All of the in-between you fill in for yourself as you see it. We are losing that feeling when we lose our language at school. And that changes our relationship with our parents. All of a sudden we begin saying to our parents "you're stupid." We have begun to equate literacy [in English] with learning, and this is the first step down. The parents know that, but they are unable to do anything about it. And we take on the values, and the history of somebody else.

From Pelletier, 1969: 23–24. Copyright © 1969 by Pantheon Books, a Division of Random House, Inc. With permission.

> ### Reflecting on GEOGRAPHY
> Should English be made the official language of the United States? Why or why not?

The Economic Development Model

Withers, who developed the social morale model, also proposed an *economic development model*. New technologies and adaptive strategies, particularly industrialization accompanied by urbanization, can break up the social structure needed to perpetuate an indigenous language. The transition from subsistence farming to factory laboring, which accompanies industrialization, is generally destructive to minority tongues, particularly when the language of the factory is not that of the farm. Urban-industrial areas then become the "holes in the Swiss cheese" of minority speech, depriving the minority language of the cultural centers that might allow its survival. Moreover, industrialization tends to draw populations out of the rural linguistic refuge areas, leaving far fewer people behind to perpetuate the language. Withers called this process the *clearance model*. By contrast, if the indus-

trial development occurs in the refuge area, it draws in speakers of the dominant language, producing a *change-over model*, in which the native speakers are over-whelmed by an intrusion of foreigners.

In Great Britain, the plight of the Welsh language (a Celtic Indo-European tongue), one of the most thoroughly studied cases of linguistic decline, illustrates Withers's social morale, economic development, clearance, and changeover models (see Figure 4.14). The retreat of Welsh before English in the twentieth century was nearly catastrophic. Its speakers were long denigrated, and the British educational system promoted English. Urbanization and industrialization knocked "holes" in the spatial fabric of Welsh, and massive rural emigration followed, directed to the English-speaking towns and factories. Geographer Keith Buchanan referred to the decline of Welsh and other Celtic languages as a "liquidation" carried out by the ruling English to produce a loyal, obedient workforce for the mines and factories. The day seemed near when the inhabitants of Wales would not know what the names of the towns, rivers, and mountains of their native land meant or even be able to understand their very family names. Then, in a policy reversal, the British government extended educational and media rights

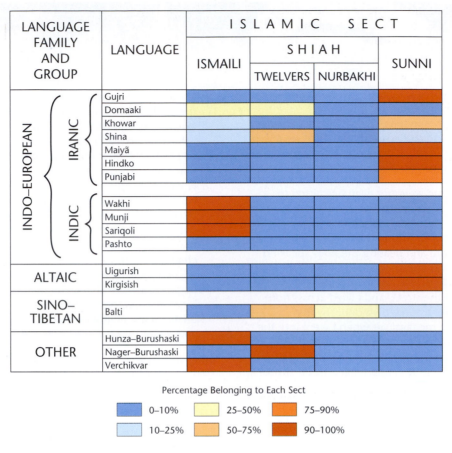

LANGUAGE FAMILY AND GROUP			LANGUAGE	ISLAMIC SECT			
					SHIAH		
				ISMAILI	TWELVERS	NURBAKHI	SUNNI
INDO–EUROPEAN	IRANIC		Gujri				
			Domaaki				
			Khowar				
			Shina				
			Maiyã				
			Hindko				
			Punjabi				
	INDIC		Wakhi				
			Munji				
			Sariqoli				
			Pashto				
ALTAIC			Uigurish				
			Kirgisish				
SINO–TIBETAN			Balti				
OTHER			Hunza–Burushaski				
			Nager–Burushaski				
			Verchikvar				

Percentage Belonging to Each Sect

- 0–10%
- 10–25%
- 25–50%
- 50–75%
- 75–90%
- 90–100%

Figure 4.15

The correlation between language and religion in the Hindu Kush and Himalayan mountains of northern Pakistan. How might such a correlation develop? You should know that correlations do not prove cause-and-effect relationships, so the evidence of linkages between religion and language is circumstantial. For more information about the Muslim sects shown, look back to Chapter 3. (Source: Kreutzmann, 1995: 109, 117.)

to Welsh, and Wales attained political autonomy within the United Kingdom. As a result, a modest revival of the Welsh language is under way today, based among an elite.

Language and Religion

Cultural integration yields situations in which a language group is linked to a particular religious faith or denomination, a linkage that greatly heightens cultural identity. Perhaps Arabic provides the best example of this cultural link. It spread from a core area on the Arabian Peninsula with the Islamic faith. Had it not been for the evangelical fervor of the Muslims, Arabic would not have diffused so widely. The other Semitic languages also correspond to particular religious groups. Hebrew-speaking people are of the Jewish faith, and the Amharic speakers in Ethiopia

are Coptic, or Eastern, Christians. Indeed, we can attribute the preservation and revival of Hebrew to the remarkable tenacity of the Jewish faith.

This link between speech and faith can often be seen even within very small areas. German geographer Hermann Kreutzmann, who studied the cultures of isolated mountain valleys in northernmost Pakistan, found that over 90 percent of the speakers of 12 of the 17 languages he studied in that region belonged to one or another of the four local Muslim sects (Figure 4.15). In other words, the language spoken by mountain people usually helps to determine their religious denomination.

Certain languages even acquired a religious status. Latin survived mainly as the ceremonial language of the Roman Catholic Church and Vatican City. In non-Arabic Muslim lands, such as Iran, Arabic is still used in religious ceremonies. Great religious books can shape languages by providing them with a standard form. Martin Luther's translation of the Bible led to the standardization of the German language, and the Koran is the model for written Arabic. The early appearance of a hymnal and the Bible in the Welsh language aided the survival of that Celtic tongue, and Christian missionaries in diverse Third World countries have translated the Bible into local languages, with similar results. In Fiji, the appearance of the Bible in one of the 15 local dialects elevated it to the dominant native language of the islands.

Sometimes the influence of religion on language is far more subtle. For example, as Indo-European-speaking farmers spread northward into the boreal forests of Europe thousands of years ago, they mixed with peoples who worshiped bears, as part of the so-called *bear cults.* These natives would not even utter the word *bear,* for fear of offending the sacred animal. The invading Indo-Europeans implanted their language but adopted the bear-worship cult of the forest peoples. No longer wanting to use their ancient Indo-European word for bear, *arksos,* for fear of offending the bear-god, they created new words—cautious euphemisms—such as the English "bear" ("the brown one") or the Russian "medved" ("he who knows how to find honey")!

Figure 4.16

Samoan, a Polynesian language belonging to the Austronesian family, becomes part of the linguistic landscape of Apia, the capital of independent Western Samoa in the Pacific Ocean. When this area was still a British colony, such a visual display of the native language would not have been permitted. **Can political independence preserve Samoan in the face of globalization?** (COURTESY OF TERRY G. JORDAN-BYCHKOV.)

 ## Linguistic Landscapes

In what ways are languages visible and, as a result, part of the cultural landscape? Road signs, billboards, graffiti, placards, and other publicly displayed writings not only reveal the locally dominant language but also can be a visual index to bilingualism, linguistic oppression of minorities, and other facets of linguistic geography (Figure 4.16). Furthermore, geographer Johanna Drucker points out, "As we observe words in the landscape, they charge and activate the environment, sometimes undermining, sometimes reinforcing our perceptions." Differences in alphabets render many foreign linguistic landscapes vividly alien (Figure 4.17 on the next page).

Messages

Linguistic landscapes send messages, both friendly and hostile. Often these messages have a political content and deal with power, domination, subjugation, or freedom. In Turkey, for example, minorities speaking Kurdish or Arabic are not allowed any visual display of their languages or alphabets. Traveling across Turkey, you might conclude, on the basis of the linguistic landscape, that everybody speaks only Turkish. That is exactly what the gov-

ernment of Turkey wants, and its linguistic minorities are visually reminded daily of their inferior position. The Canadian province of Québec, similarly, has tried to eliminate English-language signs.

Toponyms

Also revealing in the cultural sense are the names that people place on the land, the names given to settlements, terrain features, streams, and various other aspects of their surroundings. These place-names, or **toponyms,** often directly reflect the spatial patterns of language, dialect, and ethnicity (see Figure 4.11). Toponyms become part of the cultural landscape when they appear on signs and placards. Look again at our example of religious toponyms (see Figure 3.30). These names can be very revealing. Toponyms, as geographer Stephen Jett said, can often provide insights into "linguistic origins, diffusion, habitat, and environmental perception." As you drive through English-speaking portions of North America, you read highway signs such as "Huntsville City Limits," "Harrisburg 25," "Ohio River," "Newfound Gap, Elevation 5,048," or "Entering Cape Hatteras National Seashore." Many place-names consist of two parts—the *generic* and the *specific.* For example, in the American place-names we listed above—Huntsville, Harrisburg,

Figure 4.17
Linguistic landscapes can be vividly alien. For those people, like Americans, who are visually accustomed to the Latin alphabet, the linguistic landscape of countries such as Korea appears exotic, and we lapse suddenly into illiteracy. Some visitors experience an emotion akin to fright or panic when confronted with alien linguistic landscapes. (COURTESY OF TERRY G. JORDAN-BYCHKOV.)

Ohio River, Newfound Gap, and Cape Hatteras—the specific segments are *Hunts, Harris, Ohio, Newfound,* and *Hatteras.* The generic parts, which tell what *kind* of place is being described, are *ville, burg, river, gap,* and *cape.*

Generic toponyms are of greater potential value to the cultural geographer than specific names because they appear again and again throughout a culture region. There are literally thousands of generic place-names, and every culture or subculture has its own distinctive set of them. They can be particularly valuable in tracing the spread of a culture, and they often aid in the reconstruction of culture regions of the past. Sometimes they provide information about changes people wrought long ago in their physical surroundings. We will look at each of these ways that cultural geographers use generic toponyms.

Generic Toponyms of the United States

The three previously mentioned dialects of the eastern United States (see Figure 4.4)—Northern, Midland, and Southern—illustrate the value of generic toponyms in cultural geographical detective work. For example, New Englanders, speakers of the Northern dialect, often used the terms *center* and *corners* in the names of the towns or hamlets. Outlying settlements frequently bear the prefix *east, west, north,* or *south* with the specific name of the township as the suffix. Thus, in Randolph Township, Orange County, Vermont, we find settlements named Randolph Center, South Randolph, East Randolph, and North Randolph. A few miles away, across the Windsor County line, lies Hewetts Corners.

These generic usages and duplications are peculiar to New England, and we can locate areas settled by New Englanders as they migrated westward by looking for such place-names in other parts of the country. Westward from New England—through upstate New York and Ontario and into the upper Midwest—we can observe a trail of "Centers" and name duplications that clearly indicate their path of migration and settlement (Figure 4.18). Thus we can see the toponymic evidence of New England in areas as far afield as Walworth County, Wisconsin, where Troy, Troy Center, East Troy, and Abels Corners are clustered; in Dufferin County, Ontario, where one finds places such as Mono Centre; and even in distant Alberta, near Edmonton, where the toponym Michigan Centre doubly suggests a particular cultural diffusion. The trace of New England even reaches the Pacific shore, where "Center" and "Corners" suffixes abound in the Seattle area. Similarly, we can identify Midland American areas by such terms as *gap, cove, hollow, knob* (a low, rounded hill), and *burgh,* as in Stone Gap, Cades Cove, Stillhouse Hollow, Bald Knob, and Pittsburgh. We can recognize Southern speech by such names as *bayou, gully,* and *store* (for rural hamlets), as in Cypress Bayou, Gum Gully, and Halls Store.

Toponyms and Cultures of the Past

Place-names often survive long after the culture that produced them vanishes from an area. Such archaic toponyms preserve traces of the past. Australia abounds in Aborigine toponyms, even in areas from which the native peoples disappeared long ago (Figure 4.19 on page 138). No toponyms are more permanently established than those identifying physical geographical features, such as rivers and mountains. Even the most absolute conquest, exterminating an aboriginal people, usually does not entirely destroy such names. Quite the contrary, in fact.

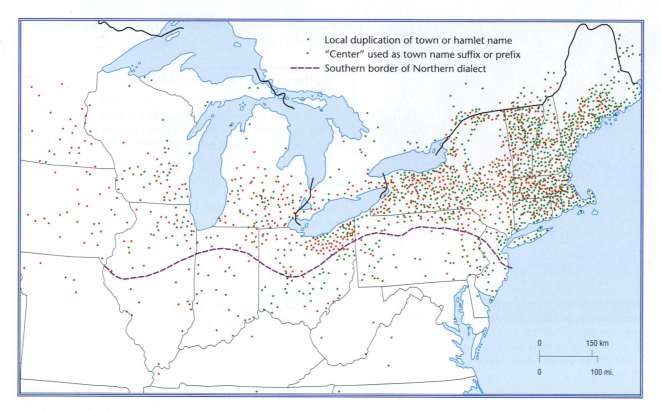

Local duplication of town or hamlet name
"Center" used as town name suffix or prefix
Southern border of Northern dialect

0 150 km

0 100 mi.

Figure 4.18
Generic place-names reveal the migration of Yankee New Englanders and the spread of the Northern dialect. Two of the most typical place-name characteristics in New England are the use of *Center* in the names of the principal settlements in a political subdivision and the tendency to duplicate the names of local towns and villages by adding the prefixes *East, West, North,* and *South* to the subdivision's name. As the concentration of such place-names suggests, these two Yankee traits originated in Massachusetts, the first New England colony. Note how these toponyms moved westward with New England settlers but thinned out rapidly to the south, in areas not colonized by New Englanders. Compare this illustration with Figures 1.6 and 4.4.

Geographer R. D. K. Herman speaks of *anticonquest,* in which the defeated people finds its toponyms venerated and perpetuated by the conqueror, who at the same time denies the people any real power or cultural influence. The superabundance of American Indian toponyms in the United States provides an example (see Focus On: American Indian Names on the Land on page 139).

In Spain and Portugal, seven centuries of Moorish rule left behind a great many Arabic place-names, as Figure 4.20 on the next page shows. An example is the prefix *guada* on river names (as in Guadalquivir and Guadalupejo), a corruption of the Arabic *wadi,* meaning "river" or "stream." Thus Guadalquivir, corrupted from Wadi-al-Kabir, means "the great river." The frequent occurrence of Arabic names in any particular region or province of Spain reveals a survival of Moorish cultural influence in that area, rather than anticonquest.

New Zealand, too, offers some intriguing examples of the subtle messages that can be conveyed by archaic toponyms. The native Polynesian people of New Zealand are the Maori. Cultural geographer Hong-key Yoon has observed that the survival rate of Maori names for towns varies according to size. The four largest New Zealand cities all have European names. Next lowest in the urban hierarchy are 20 regional centers, with populations of 10,000 to 100,000, and 40 percent of these have Maori names. Almost 60 percent of the small towns, with fewer than 10,000 inhabitants, bear Maori toponyms. Similarly, only 20 percent of New Zealand's provinces have Maori names, but 56 percent of the counties do. Nearly all streams, hills, and mountains retain Maori names. The implication is that British settlement of New Zealand remains largely an urban phenomenon.

Figure 4.19
An Australian Aborigine specific toponym joined to an English generic name, near Omeo in Victoria state, Australia. Such signs give a special, distinctive look to the linguistic landscape and speak of a now-vanished culture region. **Why would the conquerors adopt the toponyms of the defeated enemy?** (COURTESY OF TERRY G. JORDAN-BYCHKOV.)

Do these Maori toponyms, which are heard and seen as one drives across New Zealand, help make the country a unique place? What is the mental impact of such names, visually displayed on signs, on New Zealanders of European origin? Linguistic landscapes not only bear

meaningful messages but also help shape the very character of places.

Toponyms and Environmental Modification

Generic place-names also inform us about humankind's alteration of the environment in past times. From about A.D. 800 to 1300, Germanic peoples cleared forests in lands from England eastward into present-day Poland, an activity well commemorated in toponyms. Sometimes these names even indicate how the clearing was accomplished. In Germany, the generic suffixes *roth* and *reuth*, as in *Neuroth* and *Bayreuth*, mean "rooted out" or "grubbed out" and refer to the Teutonic practice of digging out roots after cutting down the trees.

In the eastern woodlands of the United States, agricultural American Indians cleared considerable forest areas before the coming of Columbus. Their abandoned grass-covered fields survived, and white settlers preserved a record of the aboriginal deforestation by placing such generic names on the land as *prairie*, which refers to grassy areas. More than 200 of these generic terms appear in wooded eastern Texas alone, suggesting the wide extent of American Indian forest-clearing activities.

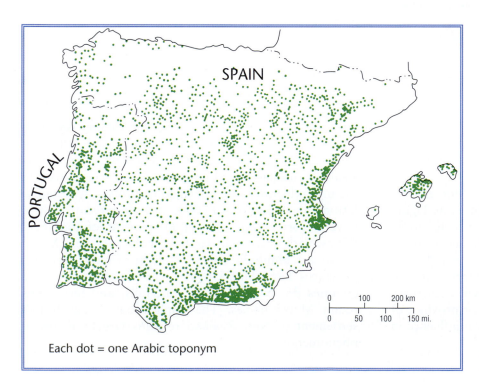

Each dot = one Arabic toponym

Figure 4.20
Arabic toponyms in Iberia. Arabic, a Semitic language, spread into Spain and Portugal with the Moors over a thousand years ago. A reconquest by Romance Indo-European speakers subsequently rooted out Arabic in Iberia, but a reminder of the Semitic language survives in toponyms. **Using this map, speculate about the direction of the Moorish invasion and retreat, the duration of Moorish rule in different parts of Iberia, and the main centers of former Moorish power.** (SOURCE: HOUSTON, 1967.)

FOCUS ON

American Indian Names on the Land

From one part of the country to another, from Walla Walla to Waxahachie, from Kalamazoo to Saskatchewan, North America's map is dotted with all kinds of Indian names. They are on our lips every day. They constitute an integral part of the flavor of modern life and culture. The names of 27 of the 50 states and 4 of the 10 Canadian provinces are Indian in origin.

These place-names represent various types of linguistic treatment. Often the English-speaking settlers merely took over, more or less accurately, the name given to a place by the Indians themselves. Frequently, such names were descriptive of the landscape or of the life about it. Mackinac Island is a shortening of *Michilimackinac,* "great turtle." Mississippi is simply "big river." The name *Chicago* has several

interpretations, the most likely being "garlic field," the final *-o* serving really as a locative suffix.

Many times in the course of our name giving, the Indian name was translated into its English equivalent. As the survey of place names in South Dakota puts it, "When a creek is called White Thunder, Blue Dog, or American Horse, the Indian influence is obvious, since these adjectives are not those which a white man would use with these nouns. Four Horns, Greasy Horn, and Dog Ear are other examples." The survey neglected to mention Stinking Water and Stinking Bear creeks, both of which are further convincing and delightful illustrations of this same process.

From Marckwardt, and Dillard, 1980. Copyright © 1958, 1980, by Oxford University Press, Inc. Reprinted by permission.

Conclusion

Language, then, is an essential part of culture that can be studied using the five themes of cultural geography. Its families, dialects, vocabulary, pronunciation, and toponyms display distinct spatial variations that can be shown on maps of linguistic culture regions. Languages ebb and flow across geographical areas through the processes of diffusion. Relocation and expansion diffusion, both hierarchical and contagious, are apparent in the movement of language, and all the concepts of cultural diffusion can be applied to language.

Language and physical environment interact in a linguistic ecology. The Austronesian people rode the prevailing winds and ocean currents to carry their speech and toponyms across the vast Pacific and Indian oceans. Environment helps shape vocabulary, and the secrets of ancient environmental alteration are sometimes revealed in toponyms.

The study of cultural interaction shows that language is causally related to other elements of culture. In fact, language is the basis for the expression of all elements of culture, so the geography of languages is closely bound to the geographies of religion, politics, technology, and economy. Certain tongues advanced with empire-building armies; others shared the evangelical diffusion of religious faiths; still others served the purposes of commerce and trade. Language is firmly enmeshed in the cultural whole. We can see language in the landscapes created by literate societies. The visible alphabet, public signs, and generic toponyms create a linguistic landscape that can accentu-

ate the alien appearance of lands where we cannot understand the speech, comprehend the alphabet, or decipher the toponyms.

Language and religion, the subjects of this chapter and chapter 3, both provide potent bases for *ethnicity.* Chapter 5 will be devoted to ethnic geography.

Linguistic Geography on the Internet

Dictionary of American Regional English
http://polyglot.lss.wisc.edu/dare/dare.html

Discover a reference web site that describes regional vocabulary contrasts of the English language in the United States and includes numerous maps.

GeoNative
http://www.geocities.com/Athens/9479/welcome.html

This site provides information about endangered minority tongues.

Mother Tongue
http://www.people.fas.harvard.edu/~witzel/index.html

Visit the newsletter of the Association for the Study of Language in Prehistory, which features an ongoing discussion of the roots of and links among various languages and language families, including Nostratic.

Atlas of North American English
http://www.ling.upenn.edu/phono_atlas/home.html

SEEING GEOGRAPHY

How does it feel to be illiterate?

Street in Hong Kong, China

You stand in the streets of Hong Kong, China, viewing this scene. You are all by yourself. What feelings and emotions might enter your mind?

If you are not Chinese and have no knowledge of the language, you have suddenly become illiterate. How does that restrict you? What can you accomplish in this alien linguistic landscape? As you seek a meal or a pharmacy or a bus to a particular destination or a place to spend the night, you will probably begin to ignore the written signs and start looking in shop windows and seeking people who can speak English. (Fortunately, there are many English speakers in Hong Kong, because it was a British colony until very recently.)

Why, you may ask, don't they put the signs in multiple languages? For one thing, look how little open space is left for signs. Also, why should the Chinese do that, when we in America generally fail to extend such courtesy to foreigners?

Does this landscape make you feel uncomfortable? Unwelcome? Ill at ease? Homesick? Such is the power of many cultural landscapes and other aspects of foreign cultures. Wandering through the human mosaic will often put you in such a position.

Street scene in Hong Kong. (Its modern name, since annexation to China in 1999, is Xianggang.)

Explore the TELSUR project web site from the University of Pennsylvania, which provides updates on a major ongoing study designed to produce a phonological atlas of North America.

Sources

Aitchison, John, and Harold Carter. 1994. *A Geography of the Welsh Language, 1961–1991.* Cardiff, U.K.: University of Wales Press.

Atwood, Elmer B. 1962. *The Regional Vocabulary of Texas.* Austin: University of Texas Press.

Bennett, Charles J. 1980. "The Morphology of Language Boundaries: Indo-Aryan and Dravidian in Peninsular India," in David E. Sopher (ed.), *An Exploration of India: Geographical Perspectives on Society and Culture.* Ithaca, N.Y.: Cornell University Press, 234–251.

Bomhard, Allan R., and John C. Kerns. 1994. *The Nostratic Macrofamily.* Berlin: Mouton de Gruyter.

Bowden, Charles. 1984. "A Desert Tale: Cherishing the Hidden Waters." *Texas Humanist* 6(July-August): 6.

Bowen, E. G., and Harold Carter. 1975. "The Distribution of the Welsh Language in 1971." *Geography* 60: 1–5.

Buchanan, Keith. 1977. "Economic Growth and Cultural Liquidation: The Case of the Celtic Nations," in Richard Peet (ed.), *Radical Geography: Alternative Viewpoints on Contemporary Social Issues.* Chicago: Maaroufa Press, 125–143.

Drucker, Johanna. 1984. "Language in the Landscape." *Landscape* 28(1): 7–13.

Encyclopaedia Britannica. 2000. *2000 Britannica Book of the Year.* Chicago: Encyclopaedia Britannica.

Herman, R. D. K. 1999. "The Aloha State: Place Names and

the Anti-Conquest of Hawaii." *Annals of the Association of American Geographers* 89: 76–102.

Hill, Robert T. 1896. "Descriptive Topographic Terms of Spanish America." *National Geographic* 7: 292–297.

Houston, James M. 1967. *The Western Mediterranean World.* New York: Praeger.

Jett, Stephen C. 1997. "Place-Naming, Environment, and Perception Among the Canyon de Chelly Navajo of Arizona." *Professional Geographer* 49: 481–493.

Jones, Emrys, and Ieuan Griffiths. 1963. "A Linguistic Map of Wales, 1961." *Geographical Journal* 129: 192–196.

Jordan-Bychkov, Terry G., and Bella Bychkova Jordan. 2002. *The European Culture Area: A Systematic Geography.* Lanham, Md.: Rowman & Littlefield, Chapter 4.

Knapp, Gregory. 1987. *Geografía Quichua de la Sierra del Ecuador.* Quito: Abya Yala.

Kreutzmann, Hermann. 1995. "Linguistic Diversity and Regional Differentiation of Denominational Groups in the Hindukush-Karakoram." *Erdkunde* 49: 109–117.

Levison, Michael, R. Gerard Ward, and John W. Webb. 1973. *The Settlement of Polynesia: A Computer Simulation.* Minneapolis: University of Minnesota Press.

Marckwardt, Albert H., and J. L. Dillard. 1980. *American English,* 2nd ed. New York: Oxford University Press.

Pelletier, Wilfred. 1969. "Childhood in an Indian Village," in Satu Repo (ed.), *This Book is About Schools.* New York: Pantheon Books.

Renfrew, Colin. 1989. "The Origins of Indo-European Languages." *Scientific American* 261(4): 106–114.

Schneider, Edgar W. 1992. "In Memoriam, Hans Kurath." *English World-Wide* 13: 111–113.

Tuan, Yi-fu. 1991. "Language and the Making of Place." *Annals of the Association of American Geographers* 81: 684–696.

Williams, Trevor. 1937. "A Linguistic Map of Wales." *Geographical Journal* 89: 146–151.

Wood, Gordon R. 1971. *Vocabulary Change: A Study of Variation in Eight of the Southern States.* Carbondale: Southern Illinois University Press.

World Almanac Books. 2001. *World Almanac and Book of Facts 2001.* New York: World Almanac Books.

Yoon, Hong-key. 1986. "Maori and Pakeha Place Names for Cultural Features in New Zealand," in *Maori Mind, Maori Land: Essays on the Cultural Geography of the Maori People from an Outsider's Perspective.* Bern, Switzerland: Peter Lang, 98–122.

of the best overall presentations of American English dialects from the standpoint of vocabulary.

Cassidy, Frederic C. (ed.). 1985–1996. *Dictionary of American Regional English.* 3 vols. Cambridge, Mass.: Harvard University Press. (Volume 4 expected 2002.) A massive compilation of words used only regionally within the United States, with maps showing distributions.

Desforges, Luke, and Rhys Jones (eds.). 2001. "Geographies of Languages/Languages of Geography." Special issue of *Social and Cultural Geography* 2(3): 261–346. The manifold ways in which geographers have examined the spaces and places of various languages.

Krantz, Grover S. 1988. *Geographical Development of European Languages.* New York: Peter Lang. Presents a new theory and model of how the Indo-European languages fragmented as linguistic diffusion occurred in prehistoric Europe.

Kurath, Hans. 1949. *Word Geography of the Eastern United States.* Ann Arbor: University of Michigan Press. The classic seminal study that gave rise to the geographical study of American English dialects.

Laponce, J. A. 1987. *Languages and Their Territories.* Anthony Martin-Sperry (trans.). Toronto: University of Toronto Press. Treats the themes that (1) languages protect themselves by territoriality and (2) the modern political state typically acts overtly to destroy minority languages.

Moseley, Christopher, and R. E. Asher (eds.). 1994. *Atlas of the World's Languages.* London: Routledge. A wonderfully detailed color map portrait of the world's complex linguistic mosaic; thumb through it at your library and you will come to appreciate how complicated the patterns and spatial distributions of languages remain, even in the age of globalization.

Williams, Colin H. (ed.). 1988. *Language in Geographical Context.* Clevedon, U.K., and Philadelphia: Multilingual Matters. Eight geolinguists provide an introduction to the field, with examples drawn mainly from Europe, especially the British Isles.

Withers, Charles W. J. 1988. *Gaelic Scotland: The Transformation of a Culture Region.* London: Routledge. A geographer analyzes one of the dying Celtic languages within the framework of the models presented earlier in this chapter.

Wixman, Ronald. 1980. *Language Aspects of Ethnic Patterns and Processes in the North Caucasus.* Research Paper No. 191. University of Chicago, Dept. of Geography. A cultural geographer surveys a part of the most complex linguistic maze in the entire world—the Caucasus Mountains.

Ten Recommended Books and Special Issues on Geolinguistics

(*For additional suggested readings, see* The Human Mosaic *web site:* www.whfreeman.com/jordan)

Carver, Craig M. 1986. *American Regional Dialects: Word Geography.* Ann Arbor: University of Michigan Press. One

A Journal in Geolinguistics

World Englishes. Published by the International Association for World Englishes, the journal documents the fragmentation of English into separate languages around the world. Edited by Larry E. Smith.

When does cuisine cease to be ethnic and become simply "American"? What role does cultural diffusion play in the process?

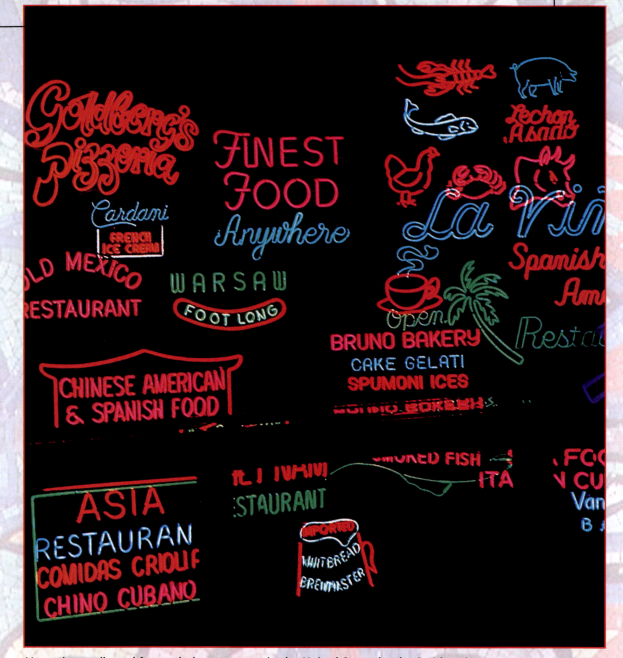

Neon signs collected from ethnic restaurants in the United States by the Smithsonian Institution in Washington, D.C. (COURTESY OF TERRY G. JORDAN-BYCHKOV.)
Turn to Seeing Geography on page 174 for an in-depth analysis of the above question.

ETHNIC GEOGRAPHY
Homelands and Ghettos

A statue of the American national hero Paul Revere, mounted on his horse, towers over a pedestrian mall near the Old North Church in Boston. Close by is the Revere home, lovingly preserved. As American as apple pie, you may say, a shrine to national independence. But what language are the elderly women speaking as they sit on benches near the statue and go about their knitting? Certainly it is not good Yankee English, by the sound of it. Closer inspection reveals Italian family names, such as Giuffre's Fish Market, on almost every business establishment in Revere's neighborhood; Italian pizzerias; an Italian-dominated outdoor vegetable market; a Sons of Italy lodge hall; and Italian-American women leaning out of upper-story windows on opposite sides of the street to converse, Naples-style. Revere, himself of French ethnic extraction, would be astounded. Boston's North End is Italian! A pilgrimage to the site where the American Revolution began has become a trip to Little Italy.

A half-continent away, the Midwestern town of Wilber, settled by Bohemian immigrants beginning about 1865, bills itself as "The Czech Capital of Nebraska" and annually invites visitors to attend a "National Czech Festival." Celebrants are promised Czech foods such as *koláce*, *jaternice*, poppyseed cake, and *jelita*; Czech folk dancing; "colored Czech postcards and souvenirs" imported from Europe; and handicraft items made by Nebraska Czechs (bearing an official seal and trademark to prove authenticity). "Czech Foods, Czech Refreshments, Czech Bands," proclaim the festival leaflets, offering "breathtaking pageants of old world history" as well. "Many shops are decorated in the Czech motif and ethnic music can be heard on the streets during most hours of the day. Many items of Czech heritage . . . are sold. Czech baking and meat items are offered daily by local merchants who use authentic recipes." Thousands

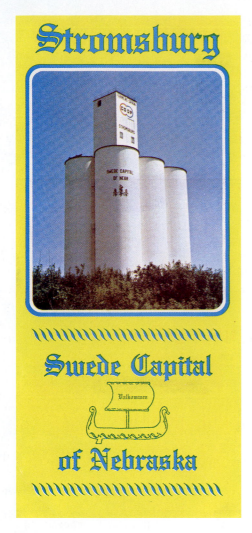

Figure 5.1
The town of Stromsburg, Nebraska. Proud of its Swedish heritage, Stromsburg holds a "Swedish Festival" each year in June.

persons in its population, about one in every 10 persons. Many other countries, as well, present an ethnic crazy-quilt pattern.

What exactly is an ethnic group? Controversy has surrounded attempts to formulate a definition. The word *ethnic* is derived from the Greek word *ethnos,* meaning a "people" or "nation," but that definition is too broad. For our purposes, an **ethnic group** consists of people of common ancestry and cultural tradition, living as a minority in a larger society, or host culture. A strong feeling of group identity, of belonging, characterizes ethnicity. Membership in an ethnic group is involuntary, in the sense that a person cannot simply decide to join; instead, he or she must be born into the group. Wsevolod Isajiw, accordingly, referred to the members of an ethnic community as an "involuntary group." Often, however, individuals choose to discard their ethnicity. In some cases, outsiders can join an ethnic group by marriage. Russian geographer Leo Gumilev (see Profile) suggested that ethnicity rests centrally on group self-awareness, an identity based partly on belief in a real or imagined common ancestor and partly on the existence of "the other"—the alien host culture that daily reminds the ethnic group that it is different.

Perhaps the main difficulty encountered in defining *ethnic* is that different groups base their identities on different traits. For some, such as the Jews, ethnicity primarily means religion; for the Amish, it is both folk culture and religion; for Swiss-Americans, it is national origin; for German-Americans, it is ancestral language; for Cuban-Americans, it is perhaps mainly anti-Castro, anti-Marxist sentiment. Race, religion, language, folk culture, place of origin, and politics can all help provide the basis of the we-they dichotomy that underlies ethnicity. This still leaves some issues unresolved. How, for example, are we to classify the 2 million people who, in the 2000 U.S. Census, claimed to be both African-American and some other ethnicity?

Making a definition of *ethnic* still more difficult is the distinction between *immigrant* and *indigenous* groups. Many if not most ethnic groups around the world originated when they migrated from their native lands and settled in a new country. In their old home, they often belonged to the host culture and were not ethnic; but, transplanted by relocation diffusion to a foreign land, they simultaneously became a minority and ethnic. Chinese are not ethnic in China, but if they come to America they are. Indigenous ethnic groups continue to live in their ancient homes and become ethnic when absorbed into larger political states. The Navajo Indians, for example, reside on their traditional and ancient lands and became ethnic only when the United States annexed their territory.

of visitors attend the festival each year. Without leaving Nebraska, these tourists can move on to "Norwegian Days" at Newman Grove, the "Greek Festival" at Bridgeport, the Danish "Grundlovs Fest" in Dannebrog, "German Heritage Days" at McCook, the "Swedish Festival" at Stromsburg, the "St. Patrick's Day Celebration" at O'Neill, several Indian tribal "powwows," and assorted other ethnic celebrations (Figure 5.1).

Now, much of this is fake, designed to create a local tourist industry. Geographer Steven Hoelscher speaks of "the invention of ethnic place" by people no longer ethnic but desiring to cash in on their ancestors' ethnicity. Even so, ethnicity persists in most countries, forming one of the brightest hues in the human mosaic. In the year 2000, the United States had over 28 million foreign-born

PROFILE

Leo Nikolayevich Gumilev

1912–1992

Leo Gumilev, born in St. Petersburg, Russia, to parents venerated as poets, earned doctorates in both geography and history. A highly innovative thinker, he focused on how ethnic and cultural groups originate and evolve—a process called *ethnogenesis*. He proposed that *cultural ecology* played the largest role in the process, an idea he fully developed in his most famous book *Ethnogenesis and the Biosphere* (1975), which was later translated into English and also made available to the Russian public in a popular edition.

Gumilev's ideas were highly unpopular among Soviet Communist authorities, who as Marxists believed in *economic determinism* and regarded ethnicity as a legacy of capitalist exploitation that would disappear in the classless communist society. Gumilev was persecuted and served in penal labor camps for some years in the Stalinist era because of his views. Later he was released and named professor at the university in his native Leningrad (now St. Petersburg). Gumilev became a symbol of the struggle for intellectual freedom in Russia.

Prepared by Bella Bychkova Jordan.

Ethnic groups are the keepers of distinctive cultural traditions and the focal points of various kinds of social interaction. They can provide not only group identity but also friendships, marriage partners, recreational outlets, business success, and a political power base. These groups offer the cultural security and reinforcement so essential for minorities, but they can also give rise to suspicion, friction, distrust, clannishness, and even violence.

This is not to say that ethnic minorities remain unchanged by their host culture. **Acculturation** often occurs, meaning that the ethnic group adopts enough of the ways of the host society to be able to function economically and socially. On the other hand, **assimilation** implies a complete blending with the host culture and involves the loss of all distinctive ethnic traits. For example, the American host culture now includes many descendants of Germans, Scots, Irish, French, Swedes, and Welsh. Intermarriage is perhaps the most effective assimilatory device. Many students of American culture have long assumed that all ethnic groups would be assimilated in the American "melting pot," but relatively few have been, instead using acculturation as their way of survival. The past three decades, in fact, have witnessed a resurgence of ethnic identity in the United States, Canada, Europe, and elsewhere. Indeed, ethnicity easily made the transition from folk to popular culture, confounding many social scientists who predicted assimilation. As a result, popular culture reveals a vivid ethnic component.

Ethnic geography is the study of the spatial and ecological aspects of ethnicity. Ethnic groups often practice unique adaptive strategies and usually occupy clearly defined areas, whether rural or urban. In other words, the study of ethnicity has built-in geographical dimensions, and ethnic geography is the result. Not surprisingly, then, an Ethnic Geography Specialty Group exists within the major professional organization, the Association of American Geographers.

 # Ethnic Regions

How are ethnic groups distributed geographically? Do ethnic culture regions have a special spatial character? The theme of culture region allows us to answer these questions.

Formal ethnic culture regions exist in most countries, from Brazil to China (Figure 5.2 on the next page). To map these regions, geographers rely on data as diverse as surnames in telephone directories and census totals for national origin. Each method produces a slightly different map, given the cultural complexity of the real world (Figure 5.3 on page 147). Regardless of the mapping method, ethnic culture regions reveal a vivid mosaic of minorities in most countries of the world.

Ethnic Homelands and Islands

Ethnic culture regions fall into several categories. The first two of these are ethnic homelands and ethnic islands. The difference is size, in terms of both area and population. Ethnic homelands cover large areas, often overlapping state and provincial borders, and have sizable populations. The residents of homelands typically seek or enjoy some measure of political autonomy or self-rule. By contrast, ethnic islands are small dots in the rural countryside, usually occupying an area smaller than a county and serving as home to several hundred to several thousand people (at

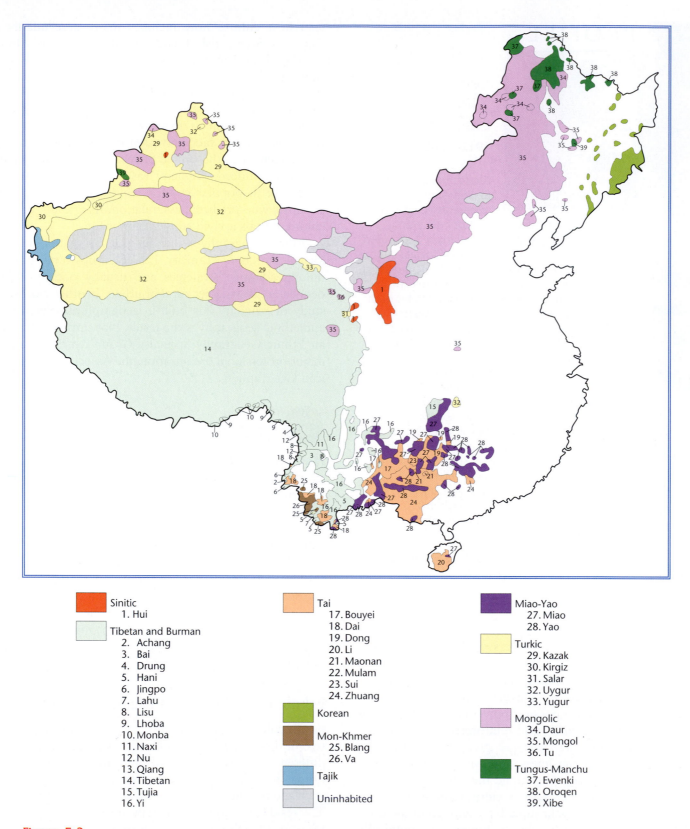

Sinitic
1. Hui

Tibetan and Burman
2. Achang
3. Bai
4. Drung
5. Hani
6. Jingpo
7. Lahu
8. Lisu
9. Lhoba
10. Monba
11. Naxi
12. Nu
13. Qiang
14. Tibetan
15. Tujia
16. Yi

Tai
17. Bouyei
18. Dai
19. Dong
20. Li
21. Maonan
22. Mulam
23. Sui
24. Zhuang

Korean

Mon-Khmer
25. Blang
26. Va

Tajik

Uninhabited

Miao-Yao
27. Miao
28. Yao

Turkic
29. Kazak
30. Kirgiz
31. Salar
32. Uygur
33. Yugur

Mongolic
34. Daur
35. Mongol
36. Tu

Tungus-Manchu
37. Ewenki
38. Oroqen
39. Xibe

Figure 5.2

Ethnic minorities in China. Most ethnic groups are Turkic, Mongolic, Tai, Tibetan, or Burman in speech, but the rich diversity extends even to the Tajiks of the Indo-European language family. Unshaded areas are Han (Mandarin) Chinese, the host culture. **Which of these ethnic regions are homelands and which islands? Why are China's ethnic groups concentrated in sparsely populated peripheries of the country?** (SOURCE: ADAPTED AND SIMPLIFIED FROM CARTER, 1980.)

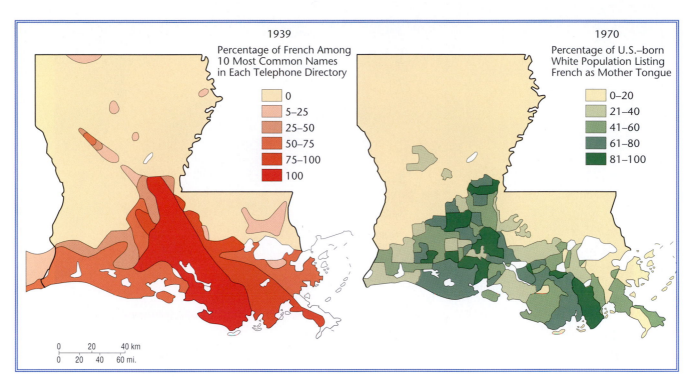

1939
Percentage of French Among
10 Most Common Names
in Each Telephone Directory

- 0
- 5–25
- 25–50
- 50–75
- 75–100
- 100

1970
Percentage of U.S.–born
White Population Listing
French as Mother Tongue

- 0–20
- 21–40
- 41–60
- 61–80
- 81–100

0   20   40 km
0   20   40   60 mi.

Figure 5.3

Acadiana, the Louisiana French homeland, as mapped by two different methods. The 1939 map was compiled by sampling the surnames in telephone directories. The 10 most common names in each directory were determined, and the percentage of these 10 that was of French origin was recorded. When no telephone directories were available, surnames on mailboxes were used. Look through the telephone directory for your hometown. **What are the 10 most common family names? What ethnic backgrounds do the names reveal? What distortions or inaccuracies might result from using only telephone directories to enumerate ethnic groups?** The 1970 map is based on U.S. census data for the Caucasian population's "mother tongue," defined by the Bureau of the Census as the language spoken in the home during the respondent's childhood. (AFTER MEIGS, 1941: 245; AND ALLEN, 1978.)

most). Homeland populations usually exhibit a strong sense of attachment to the region. Most homelands belong to indigenous ethnic groups and include special, venerated places that serve to symbolize and celebrate the region—shrines to the special identity of the ethnic group. In its fully developed form, the homeland represents that most powerful of geographical entities, one combining the attributes of both *formal* and *functional* culture regions.

Homelands, because of their size, age, and geographical segregation, tend to strengthen ethnicity. As Gumilev said, "When a people have occupied a homeland for a long time, they develop modes of life, behavior, tastes, and relationships that they regard as the *correct* ones." Indeed, ethnicity could scarcely exist devoid of culture regions. Geography helps create ethnicity.

North America houses a number of viable ethnic homelands (Figure 5.4 on the next page), including *Acadiana*, the Louisiana French homeland now increasingly identi-

fied with the Cajun people and also recognized as a vernacular region; the *Hispano* or Spanish-American homeland of highland New Mexico and Colorado; the *Tejano* homeland of South Texas; the Navajo Reservation homeland in Arizona and New Mexico; and the French-Canadian homeland centered on the valley of the lower St. Lawrence River in Québec. Some geographers would also include *Deseret*, a Mormon homeland in the Great Basin of the intermontane West. Certain other ethnic homelands have experienced decline and decay. These include the Pennsylvania "Dutch" homeland, weakened to the point of extinction by assimilation, and the southern *Black Belt*, diminished by the collapse of the plantation-sharecrop system and the resulting African-American outmigration to urban areas. Mormon absorption into the American cultural mainstream has largely negated Mormon ethnic status, whereas nonethnic immigration has damaged the Hispano homeland. At present, the most

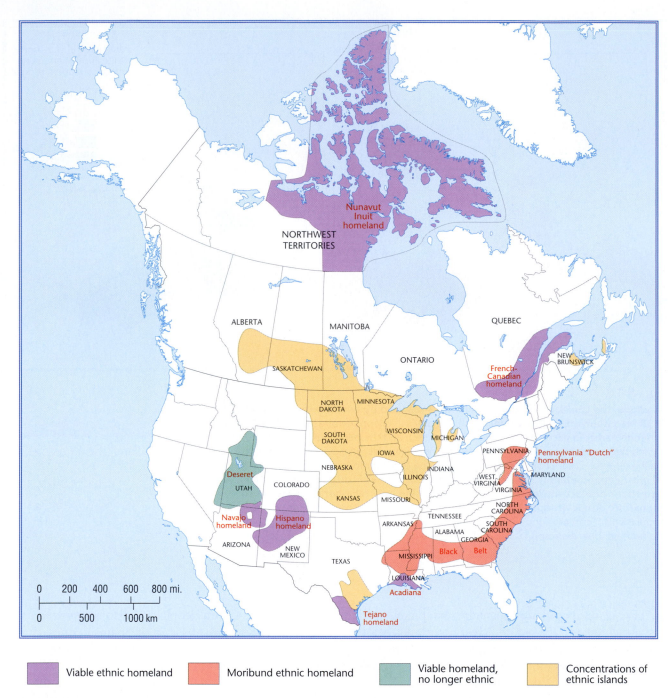

■ Viable ethnic homeland	■ Moribund ethnic homeland	■ Viable homeland, no longer ethnic	■ Concentrations of ethnic islands

Figure 5.4

Selected ethnic homelands in North America, past and present, and concentrations of rural ethnic islands. The Hispano homeland is also referred to as the Spanish-American homeland. **What might cause a homeland to become moribund?** Nunavut became a functioning political unit within Canada in 1999. (SOURCES: ARREOLA, 1993; CARLSON, 1990; MEINIG, 1965; AND NOSTRAND AND ESTAVILLE, 2001.)

vigorous ethnic homelands are those of the French Canadians and South Texas Mexican-Americans.

If ethnic homelands succumb to assimilation, their people absorbed into the host culture, then a geographi-

cal residue, or **ethnic substrate,** remains. The resulting culture region, though no longer ethnic, nevertheless retains some distinctiveness. It differs from surrounding regions in a variety of ways. In seeking to explain its dis-

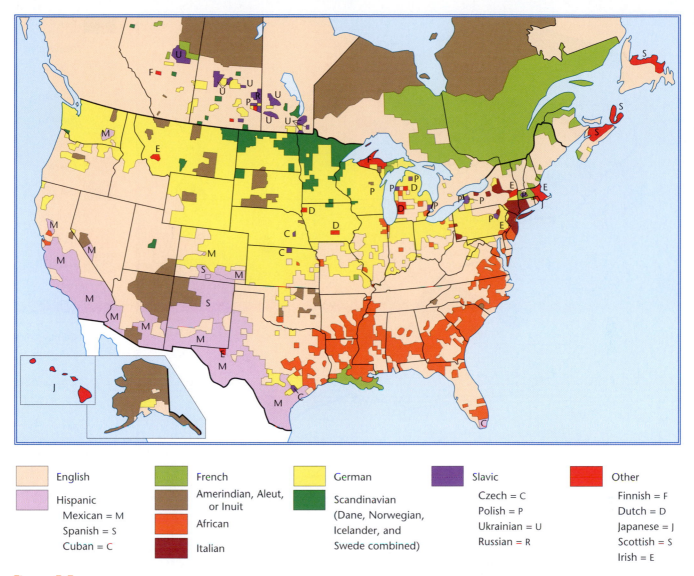

Figure 5.5

Ethnic and national-origin groups in North America. Notice how the border between Canada and the United States generally also forms a cultural boundary. **What might have caused this striking correlation?** Several ethnic homelands appear, as do many ethnic islands. Areas shown as "Scandinavian" are those where the total of all Scandinavian origins combined exceeds the origins of any other group. (SOURCES: U.S. CENSUS, 1990; ALLEN AND TURNER, 1987: 210; CENSUS OF CANADA, 1991; AND DAWSON, 1936: IV.)

tinctiveness, geographers often discover an ancient, vanished ethnicity. For example, the Italian province of Tuscany owes both its name and some of its uniqueness to the Etruscan people, who ceased to be an ethnic group 2000 years ago, when they were absorbed into the Latin-speaking Roman Empire. More recently, the massive German presence in the American heartland (Figure 5.5), now largely nonethnic, helped shape the cultural character of the Midwest, which can be said to have a German ethnic substrate.

Ethnic islands are much more numerous than homelands or substrates. Large areas of rural North America have many ethnic islands, as Figure 5.4 suggests. Figure 5.6 on the next page provides some Midwestern examples of ethnic islands, revealing the crazy-quilt pattern typical of much of the American heartland. Germans, the largest single group in American ethnic islands, are clustered principally in southeastern Pennsylvania and in Wisconsin; whereas Scandinavians, primarily Swedes and Norwegians, came mainly to Minnesota, North Dakota, and western

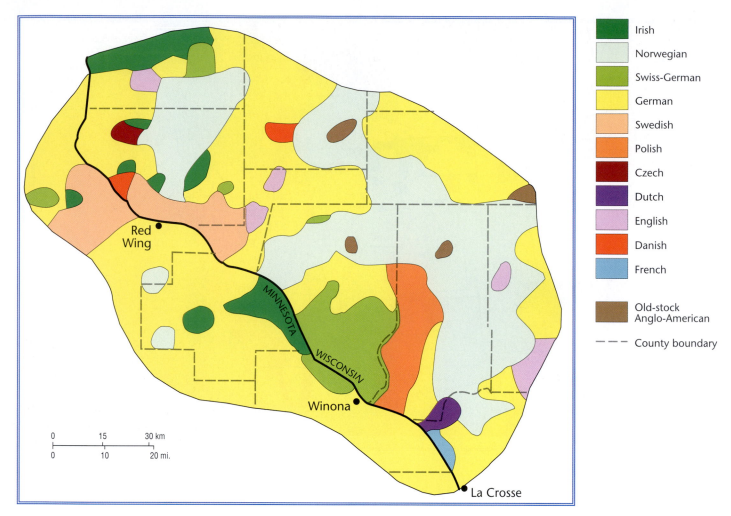

Irish
Norwegian
Swiss-German
German
Swedish
Polish
Czech
Dutch
English
Danish
French

Old-stock
Anglo-American
– – – County boundary

Figure 5.6
Ethnic islands in the rural American heartland. Illustrated is the distribution of ethnic groups in a small portion of western Wisconsin and southeastern Minnesota. **Why are such ethnic islands more common in the American Midwest than in Canadian Prairie Provinces?** (AFTER HILL, 1942; AND MARSHALL, 1949.)

Wisconsin. Ukrainians settled mainly in the Canadian Prairie Provinces (Figure 5.7). Other Slavic groups established scattered colonies in the Midwest and Texas.

Ethnic islands develop because, in the words of geographer Alice Rechlin, "a minority group will tend to utilize space in such a way as to minimize the interaction distance between group members," facilitating contacts within the ethnic community and minimizing exposure to the outside world. The ideal shape of such an ethnic island is circular or hexagonal, and many do approximate that configuration (Figure 5.8). People are drawn to rural places where others of the same ethnic background are found. Ethnic islands survive from one generation to the next because most land is inherited. In addition, land is typically sold within the ethnic group, which helps to pre-

serve the identity of the island. A social stigma is often attached to the sale of land to outsiders. Even so, the smaller size of ethnic islands makes their populations more susceptible to acculturation and assimilation.

Ethnic Neighborhoods and Ghettos

Formal ethnic culture regions also occur in cities throughout the world. Minority people tend to create ethnic residential quarters (Figure 5.9 on page 152). Here, also, two types exist. An **ethnic neighborhood** is a voluntary community where people of like origin reside by choice. Such neighborhoods are, in the words of Peter Matwijiw, an Australian geographer, "the results of preferences shown by different ethnic groups . . . toward maintaining

Figure 5.7

In a Ukrainian ethnic island near Edmonton, Alberta, an ethnic church shines in the sunlight as a storm approaches. Ukrainians settled particularly in the transition zone between prairie and woodland in western Canada, an ecological setting similar to their European homeland. (COURTESY OF TERRY G. JORDAN-BYCHKOV.)

group cohesiveness." An ethnic neighborhood has many benefits: common use of language, nearby kin, stores and services specially tailored to a certain group's tastes, the presence of factories that rely on an ethnically based division of labor, and institutions important to the group—such as churches and lodges—that remain viable only when a number of people live close enough to participate in their activities often.

The second type of urban ethnic quarter is a **ghetto.** The term has traditionally been used to describe an area within the city where a certain ethnic group is *forced* to live. Use of the word *ghetto* should be reserved for areas of residential segregation where an ethnic group lives because it has very little choice in the matter—options are limited or don't exist. In other words, a ghetto is an involuntary community and is as much a functional culture

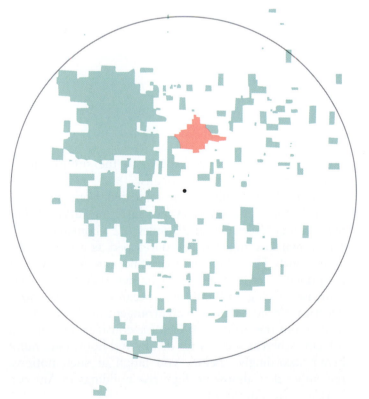

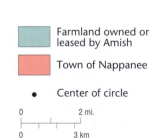

Farmland owned or leased by Amish

Town of Nappanee

• Center of circle

0   2 mi.

0   3 km

Figure 5.8

The Amish ethnic island at Nappanee, Indiana. A roughly circular configuration is evident, suggesting the ideal shape of such ethnic enclaves. **What factors might have acted to prevent the island from attaining a perfectly circular shape? Does this appear to be a pattern reflecting areal growth, stagnation, or retreat?** (DERIVED FROM RECHLIN, 1976: 40.)

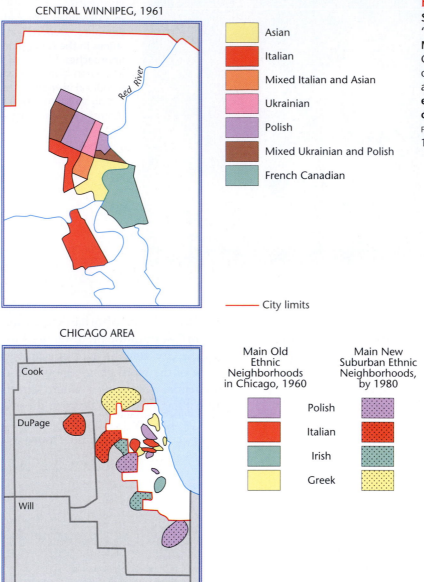

CENTRAL WINNIPEG, 1961

Asian

Italian

Mixed Italian and Asian

Ukrainian

Polish

Mixed Ukrainian and Polish

French Canadian

Red River

——— City limits

CHICAGO AREA

Cook

DuPage

Will

Main Old Ethnic Neighborhoods in Chicago, 1960

Main New Suburban Ethnic Neighborhoods, by 1980

Polish

Italian

Irish

Greek

Figure 5.9

Selected ethnic neighborhoods and "ethnoburbs" in Winnipeg, Manitoba, and in the Chicago area. Central city ethnic neighborhoods are often relocated to the suburbs as acculturation progresses. **What ethnic neighborhoods exist in the city where you live?** (SOURCES: ADAPTED FROM MATWIJIW, 1979: 50; AND WINSBERG, 1986: 142–143.)

region as a formal one. The node could be a concentration of gathering places for members of the group, such as clubs, dance halls, or shops.

Whether an ethnic group lives in a ghetto or voluntarily forms its own neighborhood usually depends on the extent of discrimination by the host culture. For example, because American society discriminates more against black people and Asians than it does against Italians, an African-American ghetto or a Chinatown is more likely to exist than an Italian ghetto. In Cleveland, for example, African-Americans are confined to a ghetto by discriminatory housing practices and are much more highly segregated residentially than are Caucasian ethnic groups. Italians, Poles, Jews, Appalachian folk, and other Caucasian ethnic groups in Cleveland occupy neighborhoods rather than ghettos and disperse to the suburbs more readily than do African-Americans.

Even when ethnic groups relocated from neighborhoods to the suburbs, residential clustering survived. The San Gabriel Valley, about 20 miles (32 kilometers) from downtown Los Angeles, has developed as a major Chinese suburb. Housebuilders there take care not to violate the principles of feng shui (see Chapter 3) and never have staircases facing the entrance, because many Chinese-Americans believe that such an arrangement allows wealth to flow out the front door. Chinese consider the numeral 8 lucky, whereas 4 connotes death, and houses are numbered accordingly. (Before you laugh at such notions, remember that almost no high-rise buildings in America have a thirteenth floor.)

Ethnic residential quarters have long been a part of urban cultural geography. In ancient times, conquerors often forced the vanquished native people to live in ghettos. Religious minorities usually received similar treatment. Sometimes walls built around such ghettos set them off from the rest of the city. Islamic cities had Christian districts, and medieval European cities had Jewish ghettos.

Ethnic neighborhoods became typical in the northern United States and in Canada after about 1840, coinciding with the urbanization and industrialization of North America. Instead of dispersing through the residential areas of the city, immigrant groups clustered together. To some degree, ethnic groups that migrated to cities came from different parts of Europe from those that went to rural areas. Whereas Germany and Scandinavia supplied most of the rural settlers, the cities drew much more heavily on Ireland and eastern and southern Europe. Catholic Irish, Italians, Poles, and Jews from eastern Europe became the main urban ethnic groups, although lesser numbers of virtually every nationality in Europe came to the cities of North America (see Figure 5.9). These groups were later joined by French Canadians, Southern blacks, Puerto Ricans, Appalachian whites, American Indians, Asians, and other groups not of European birth. Ethnic neighborhoods will receive additional attention in Chapter 11.

Recent Ethnic Migrants

In recent decades, as immigration laws have changed, the ethnic variety in North American cities has grown even greater, and the sources of immigration have changed fundamentally. Asia, rather than Europe, is now the principal source of immigrants for both Canada and the United States, with Chinese, Koreans, and Vietnamese constituting the most numerous immigrant groups. Asia supplied 37 percent of all legal immigrants to the United States in the mid–1990s. People of Japanese ancestry form the largest national-origin group in Hawaii, and Washington State elected the first Chinese-American governor in the country's history in 1996. Many West Coast cities, from Vancouver to San Diego, have acquired very sizable Asian populations. Vancouver, already 11 percent Asian by 1981, has since absorbed many more Asian immigrants, particularly from Hong Kong, which became part of China in 1997.

Latin America, including the Caribbean countries, has also surpassed Europe as a source of immigrants coming to North America. East Coast cities have absorbed large numbers of immigrants from the West Indies. In many important cultural respects, Miami has become a West Indies–Caribbean city (Figure 5.10), and the two largest national-origin groups coming to New York City as early

Figure 5.10

Little Havana, or Pequeña Habana, the original Cuban ethnic neighborhood in Miami, Florida. Cubans have become so numerous in Miami that they now dominate the city culturally, socially, and economically. Little Havana, however, has since become dominated by Central Americans. (Courtesy of Terry G. Jordan-Bychkov.)

as the 1970s were from the Dominican Republic and Jamaica, displacing Italy as the leading source of immigrants. As a result, the image of both Canada and the United States as predominantly "European" in population is changing.

Perhaps too often, we think of immigrant ethnic groups only in a North American context. We need to remember that 28 million ethnic Chinese reside outside China and Taiwan. Most of these overseas Chinese do not live in North America but in Southeast Asian countries and even Polynesia (Figure 5.11 on the next page). Indonesia has over 7 million, Thailand nearly 6 million, and Malaysia more than 5 million. Pacific Islanders exhibit a similar pattern. Auckland, New Zealand, has the largest Polynesian population of any city in the world. Australia, Argentina, and Brazil also house large ethnic populations. Even European countries such as Germany, the United Kingdom, Italy, and Spain—long known as sources rather than destinations of migrants—today are home to millions of Africans, Turks, and Asians. Immigration-based ethnicity is far from being a phenomenon limited to North America.

Figure 5.11
Store owned by a prosperous ethnic Chinese retailer on the isle of Bora Bora in French Polynesia. The population of the island is overwhelmingly Polynesian. Only 0.8 percent of the people are Europeans, 6.6 percent are "Demis"—a mixture of white and Polynesian—and less than 0.5 percent are Asian. Yet this store and many others in the archipelagoes of the Pacific are owned by persons of Chinese extraction. Why don't Polynesians own such stores? Because (1) they have no tradition of retailing and (2) theirs is a communal society that shares wealth. If a Polynesian were to open a store, all of his or her relatives would have the right to come and take merchandise for free, sharing the wealth. The store would fail within a month. And so the way was left open for the Chinese, who have a very different culture. (COURTESY OF TERRY G. JORDAN-BYCHKOV.)

Regardless of the source of urban immigrants, the neighborhoods they create tend to be transitory. As a rule, urban ethnic groups remain in neighborhoods while undergoing acculturation. As a result, their central-city ethnic neighborhoods experience a life cycle (Figure 5.12) in which one group is replaced by another, later-arriving one. We can see this process in action in the succession of groups that dominated certain neighborhoods and then moved on to more desirable areas. Boston's West End was mainly an Irish area in the nineteenth century. As the twentieth century began, Irish were replaced in this deteriorating neighborhood by Jews, who in turn were replaced in the late

TABLE 5.1 The Ten Largest National Origin/Ethnic Groups in Three Multinational Countries

United States		Canada		Russia	
Ancestry Group	Percentage of Total Population	Ancestry Group	Percentage of Total Population	Ethno-linguistic Group	Percentage of Total Population
German	13.8	French	33.8	Russian	80.8
Hispanic	12.6	English	26.3	Tatar	3.9
African	12.6	German	5.0	Ukrainian	2.3
Irish	8.6	Asian	4.8	Chuvash	1.2
English/British	8.3	Scottish	4.8	Bashkir	1.0
U.S./American	8.2	Italian	3.9	Belarussian	0.7
Italian	5.3	Irish	3.9	Mordva	0.6
Asian	4.0	Ukrainian	2.3	Chechen	0.6
French	3.1	Native American	2.1	Udmurt	0.5
Scottish	3.0	Jewish	1.4	Armenian	0.5

The U.S. figures are for the first-reported ancestry of all respondents, though many of these people also reported another ancestry, which is not reflected in the figures. Seven million people, or 3 percent of the total, reported their first ancestry as mixed racial.

(Sources: Demographic Yearbook of Russia, 2000; U.S. Census of 2000; and Government of Canada. U.S. and Russia data are for 2000, Canada for 1991.)

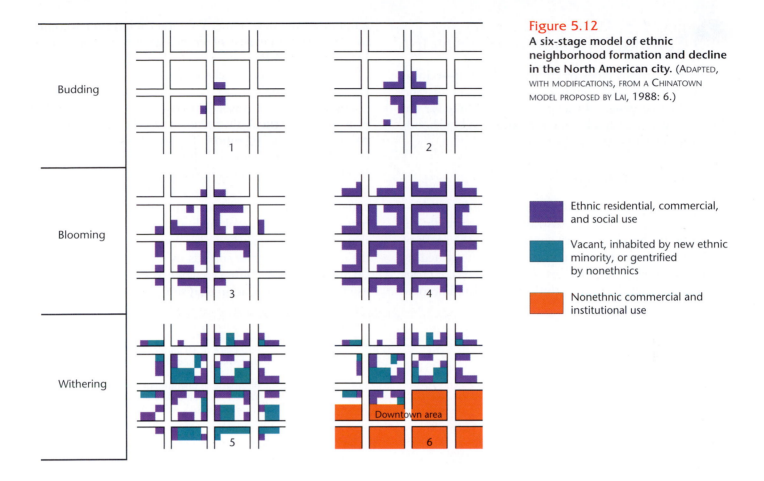

Figure 5.12

A six-stage model of ethnic neighborhood formation and decline in the North American city. (Adapted, with modifications, from a Chinatown model proposed by Lai, 1988: 6.)

Ethnic residential, commercial, and social use

Vacant, inhabited by new ethnic minority, or gentrified by nonethnics

Nonethnic commercial and institutional use

1930s by Poles and Italians. In Miami's Little Havana neighborhood, Central Americans replaced Cubans (see Figure 5.10). The list of groups that passed through one Chicago neighborhood from the nineteenth century to the present provides an almost complete history of American migratory patterns. First came the Germans and Irish, who were succeeded by the Greeks, Poles, French Canadians, Czechs, and Russian Jews, who were soon hard-pressed by the Italians. The Italians, in turn, were challenged by Chicanos and a small group of Puerto Ricans. As this succession occurred, the older groups often established new ethnic neighborhoods in suburban areas.

Ethnic Mix and National Character

Now we turn to a brief comparison of ethnic culture regions in several of the larger multiethnic countries of the world. Any country is the sum of its cultural parts. Each country has its own unique mix of national-origin and ethnic groups, revealed in a mosaic of homelands, islands, neighborhoods, and ghettos that help shape its national character. Russia, for example, has less diversity than the United States and a different array of minorities (Table 5.1). Canada, too, displays striking differences from the

United States, most notably in its far higher proportions of English, French, Scots, and Ukrainians. Germans, Africans, and Hispanics are poorly represented in Canada, adding to the contrast.

These differences are vividly revealed in the mosaic of national-origin groups (see Figure 5.5). In turn, varied ethnic mixes produce different national characters in different countries, even if ethnic assimilation occurs. National origin need not imply ethnicity, and it often does not. Most people in the United States who claim German origin, for example, are not German-Americans. Rather, they have been much acculturated and often assimilated, becoming part of the host culture. The massive absorption of Germans into the mainstream culture of the United States has been a major factor in shaping a national character distinct from that of Canada, as have the other striking differences in the ethnic makeup of the two countries.

Reflecting on **GEOGRAPHY**

Why does the French-Canadian homeland endanger the continued existence of a unified Canada, whereas other North American homelands present no such threat?

Cultural Diffusion and Ethnicity

How do the various types of cultural diffusion—relocation, hierarchical, and contagious—help us understand the complicated geographical patterns of ethnicity? Do ethnic homelands, islands, ghettos, and neighborhoods result from different types of diffusion?

Migration and Ethnicity

Much of the ethnic pattern in many parts of the world—including North America, Australia, and virtually all urban neighborhoods on every continent—is the result of *relocation diffusion*. In fact, ethnicity is often created by the migration process itself, as people leave countries where they belonged to a nonethnic majority and become a minority in a new home. Voluntary migration accounts for the great majority of ethnic groups in the United States and Canada.

In most such cases, **chain migration** is involved. An individual or small group decides to migrate to a foreign country. These "innovators" are natural leaders who influence others, particularly friends and relatives, to accompany them in the migration. The word spreads to nearby communities, and soon a sizable migration is under way from a fairly small district in the source country to a comparably small area or neighborhood in the destination country (Figures 5.13 and 5.14). In village after village, the first emigrants often rank high in the local social order, so that *hierarchical diffusion* also comes into play. That is, the *decision* to migrate spreads by a mixture of hierarchical and contagious diffusion, whereas the actual migration itself represents relocation diffusion.

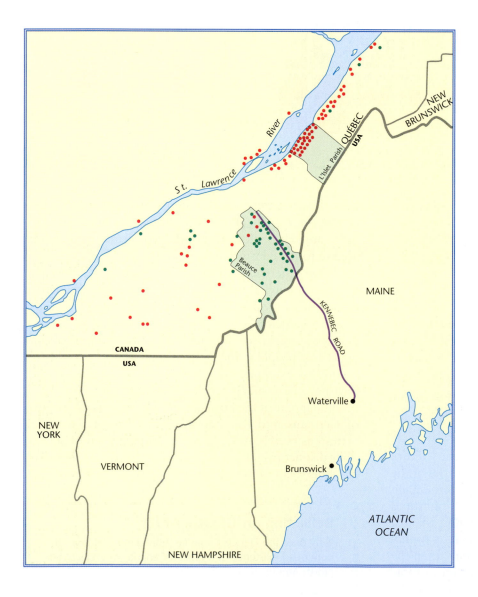

- Birthplace of 10 immigrants to Brunswick, Maine, 1880–1900

- Birthplace of one immigrant to Waterville, Maine, 1890–1925

Figure 5.13

Ethnic chain migration from French Canada to the United States. Ethnic islands and urban neighborhoods typically result from chain migration. One of the more significant ethnic migrations of the late nineteenth and early twentieth centuries was the movement of French Canadians to the factory towns of New England, a migration accomplished by many small clusters of people. This map shows the clustered sources of French Canadians who migrated to the towns of Brunswick and Waterville in Maine between 1880 and 1925. The parish of Beauce supplied most of the Waterville French, whereas L'Islet Parish was the leading source of Brunswick French. **What sequence of events might have led to this clustering of migration source and destination?** (AFTER ALLEN, 1972: 377; SEE ALSO ALLEN, 1974.)

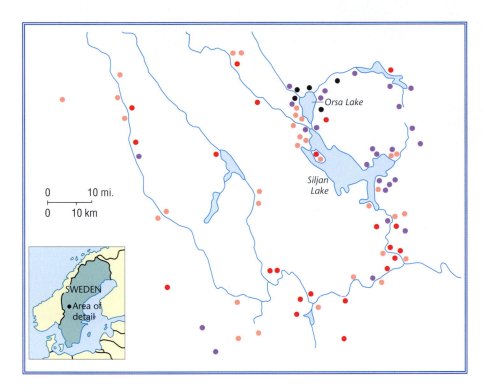

Figure 5.14

Contagious diffusion of the decision to emigrate in a portion of Dalarna Province, Sweden, 1860–1875. Many Swedes left for the American Midwest in the latter half of the nineteenth century, and the decision to emigrate spread through the countryside, passing from one settlement to the next. This particular emigration peaked during a famine from 1868 to 1870. **Draw on the map the most likely paths of diffusion. How might the decision to emigrate have begun? How did it leap so far south, to the two 1864–1867 communities at the bottom of the map?** (ADAPTED AND SIMPLIFIED FROM OSTERGREN, 1988: 116.)

The process of chain migration continues even after the first emigrants have departed. From their new home, they write letters back to their native place, extolling the virtues of the new life and imploring others to join them. Such letters written from the United States became known as *America letters* (see Focus On: An America Letter on page 159).

Chain migration caused the movement of people to become *channelized*, a process in which a specific source region becomes linked to a particular destination, so that neighbors in the old country became neighbors in the new country as well. This process was at work three centuries ago and still operates today. The recent mass migration of Latin Americans to Anglo-America provides an example. Research by geographer Richard Jones revealed that different parts of the southwestern United States draw upon different source regions in Mexico (Figure 5.15 on the next page).

Involuntary migration also contributes to ethnic diffusion and the formation of ethnic culture regions. Refugees

from Cambodia and Vietnam created ethnic minorities in North America, as did Guatemalans and Salvadorans fleeing political repression in Central America. Often, such forced migrations may result from policies of *ethnic cleansing*, in which countries expel minorities to produce cultural homogeneity in their populations. In Europe, the newly independent country of Croatia has systematically expelled its Serb minority in a campaign of ethnic cleansing. Following forced migration, the relocated group often engages in voluntary migration to concentrate in some new locality. Cuban political refugees, scattered widely throughout the United States in the 1960s, reassembled in south Florida, and Vietnamese continue to gather in Southern California and Texas.

Return migration represents another type of ethnic diffusion and involves the voluntary movement of a group back to its ancestral or native country or homeland. One of the most notable such movements now under way is the large-scale return since 1975 of African-Americans from the cities of the northern and western United States

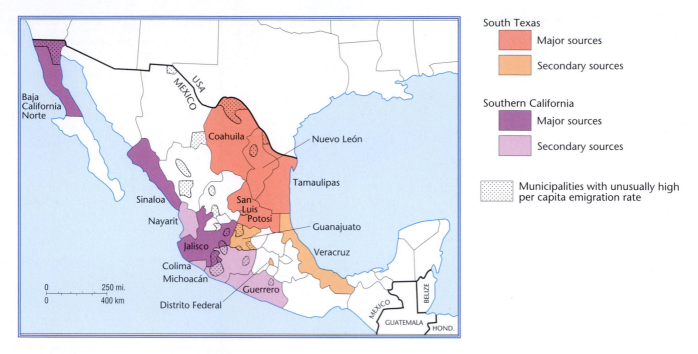

Figure 5.15

Sources by state and county of undocumented Mexican nationals apprehended by the Immigration and Naturalization Service in South Texas and Southern California. A weighted index was employed to assign values to the different Mexican states. **Why are certain areas greater contributors than others? How might such clustered or channelized migration sources influence the ethnic cultures in the two extremities of the Hispanic borderland? Might it help explain Hispanic cultural contrasts between Southern California and South Texas?** For answers, see the sources listed here. (DERIVED FROM JONES, 1982: 165–166; AND JONES, 1988: 17.)

to the Black Belt ethnic homeland in the South. This type of ethnic migration is also channelized, for—as geographers John Cromartie and Carol Stack discovered—over two-thirds of the migrants "follow well-worn paths back to homeplaces or other locations where relatives have settled." For example, geographer James Johnson found that 7 percent of African-Americans in Los Angeles County, California, moved away between 1985 and 1990, including many who went to the American South. By the year 2000, the once dominantly African-American South Central district of Los Angeles had become largely Hispanic in population. Indeed, the decade of the 1990s witnessed the largest return migration of blacks to the American South ever, from all parts of the United States.

Similarly, many of the 200,000 or so expatriate Estonians, Latvians, and Lithuanians left Russia and other former Soviet republics to return to their newly independent Baltic home countries in the 1990s, losing their ethnic status in the process. Clearly, migration of all kinds turns the ethnic mosaic into an ever-changing kaleidoscope.

> **Reflecting on GEOGRAPHY**
>
> Why might African-Americans have begun return migration to the South after 1975, and why did this movement accelerate in the 1990s?

Simplification and Isolation

When groups migrate and become ethnic in a new land, they have, in theory at least, the potential to introduce the totality of their culture by relocation diffusion. Conceivably, they could reestablish every facet of their traditional way of life in the new country. If they were to do so, then a visit to an ethnic homeland, island, or neighborhood in, say, North America would be akin to a visit to Europe, Asia, Africa, or Latin America.

However, ethnic immigrants never successfully introduce their culture in totality overseas. A profound cultural **simplification** occurs. As geographer Cole Harris noted, "Europeans established overseas drastically simplified ver-

FOCUS ON

An America Letter

The following excerpts are from a letter written in 1832 by the first German settler in Texas to a friend back in Germany. This *America letter* was eventually published in a German newspaper and prompted a large chain migration from northwestern Germany to Texas.

Each married immigrant who wishes to engage in farming receives 4,440 acres of land, including hills and valleys, woods and meadows with creeks flowing through. That is virtually a count's estate, and within a short time the land will be worth $700 to $800. Farmers who own 700 head of cattle are common hereabouts. Europeans are especially welcome in the colony, and I was given excellent land, upon which I built my home.

The land here is hilly, covered partly with forest and partly with natural prairies. There are various types of trees. The climate is similar to that of Sicily. There is no real winter, and the coldest months are almost like March in Germany. Bees, birds, and butterflies stay all through the winter season. The soil requires no fertilizer. The main crops are tobacco, rice, indigo, sweet potatoes, melons of special goodness, wheat, rye, and vegetables of all kinds. Peaches are found in abundance growing wild in the forest, as are mulberries, walnuts, plums, persimmons as sweet as honey, and wine grapes in great quantity. There is much wild game, and hunting and fishing are free. The prairies are filled with the most lovely flowers. The more children you have, the better, for you will need them as field laborers. Mosquitoes and gnats are common only near the coast. Formerly there were no taxes at all, and now we have only community taxes. Each year you need work barely three months to make a living.

There is freedom of religion here and English is the prevailing language. Up the river there is much silver to be found, but Indians still live there.

All Germans who come to the colony will be given land at once. When you arrive at San Felipe, ask for Friedrich Ernst of Mill Creek. It is thirty miles from there to my place, and you will find me without any difficulty. For my friends and former countrymen, I have built a shelter on my estate where they can stay while selecting their land.

Your friend,

Fritz Ernst

Translated, adapted, and rearranged from Hermann Achenbach, 1835: 132–135; and Detlef Dunt, 1834: 4–16.

---

sions of European society." This happens, in part, because of chain migration: Only spatial fragments of a culture diffuse overseas, borne by groups from particular places migrating in particular eras. In other words, some simplification occurs at the point of departure. Still, more cultural diversity is implanted in the new home than survives. Only selected traits are successfully introduced, and others undergo considerable modification before becoming established in the new homeland. In other words, *absorbing barriers* prevent the diffusion of many traits, and *permeable barriers* cause changes in many other traits, greatly simplifying the migrant cultures. In addition, choices that did not exist in the old home become available to immigrant ethnic groups. They can borrow alien ways from groups they encounter in the new land, invent new techniques better suited to the adopted place, or modify traditional or alien ways as they see fit. Most immigrant ethnic groups resort to all these devices, in varying degrees.

The displacement of a group and its relocation in a new homeland can have widely differing results. Perhaps most commonly, the relocation weakens tradition and upsets an age-old balance, causing a rapid discarding of traditional traits and accelerated borrowing, invention, and modification—in short, *acculturation*. The degree of isolation of an ethnic group in the new home helps determine if traditional traits will be retained, modified, or abandoned. If the new settlement area is remote and contacts with outsiders are few, diffusion of traits from the Old World is more likely. Because contacts with alien groups are rare, little borrowing of traits can occur. Isolated ethnic groups often preserve in archaic form cultural elements that disappear from their ancestral country. That is, they may, in some respects, change less than their kinfolk back in the mother country. Language and dialects offer some good examples of this preservation of the archaic. Germans living in ethnic islands in the Balkan region of southeastern Europe preserve archaic South German dialects better than do Germans living in Germany itself, and some medieval elements survive in the Spanish spoken in the Hispano homeland of New

Mexico. Irish Catholic settlers in Newfoundland, whose communities remained rather isolated, retained far more of their traditional Celtic culture than did fellow Irish who colonized Ontario, where contacts with non-Irish occurred frequently.

Ethnic Ecology

How do ethnic groups interact with their habitat? Is there a special bond between ethnic groups and the land they inhabit that helps to form their self-identity? Truly, ethnicity is very closely linked to cultural ecology. The *possibilistic* interplay between people and physical environment is often evident in the pattern of ethnic culture regions, in ethnic migration, and in ethnic persistence or survival.

Ethnogenesis

In fact, the very process by which indigenous ethnic groups originate, **ethnogenesis,** often has an ecological base. As Leo Gumilev (see earlier Profile) said, such groups "originate on the earth's surface in particular physical geographical conditions." He drew particular attention to **ecotones**—the sharp borders between *ecoregions,* for example, the border between forest and prairie or mountains and plains. Ecotones, said Gumilev, encourage the development of new cultural groups, because a new *adaptive strategy* is needed to use the environmentally diverse dual habitat available along ecotones. In short, *cultural adaptation* can play a role in ethnogenesis.

For example, why are Russians different from other Slavic peoples? At what point in history, and *where,* did Russians diverge from the parent Slavic culture to become a separate people? Gumilev proposes that the Russians developed on the forest-grassland ecotone north of the Black Sea in Eurasia.

Cultural Preadaptation

For those ethnic groups created by migration, or relocation diffusion, a different but related cultural ecological concept, cultural preadaptation, must be considered. **Preadaptation** involves a complex of adaptive traits possessed by a group in advance of migration that gives them the ability to survive and a competitive advantage in colonizing the new environment. Most often, preadaptation occurs in groups migrating to a place environmentally similar to the one they left behind. The adaptive strategy they had pursued before migration works reasonably well in the new home.

> **Reflecting on GEOGRAPHY**
>
> Using the concept of preadaptation, speculate about why North America became primarily a zone of overseas settlement by people from northwestern Europe (the British Isles, France, the Netherlands, Germany, and Scandinavia).

The preadaptation may be accidental, but in most cases the immigrant ethnic group deliberately chooses a colonization area that physically resembles its former home. The state of Wisconsin, dotted with scores of ethnic islands, provides some fine examples of preadapted immigrant groups that sought environments resembling their homelands. Particularly revealing are the choices of settlement sites made by Finns, Icelanders, English, and Cornish who came to Wisconsin (Figure 5.16). The Finns—coming from a cold, thin-soiled, glaciated, lake-studded, coniferous forest zone in Europe—settled the North Woods of Wisconsin, a land very similar in almost every respect to the one from which they migrated. Icelanders, from a bleak, remote island in the North Atlantic, located their only Wisconsin colony on Washington Island, an isolated outpost surrounded by the waters of Lake Michigan. The English, accustomed to good farmland, generally founded ethnic islands in the better agricultural districts of southern and southwestern Wisconsin. Cornish miners from the Celtic highlands of the County of Cornwall in southwestern England sought out the lead-mining communities of southwestern Wisconsin, where they continued their traditional occupation.

Elsewhere in the American heartland, thousands of ethnic Germans from wheat-growing communities on the open steppe grasslands of southern Russia, the so-called Russian-Germans, settled the prairies of the Great Plains. There they established thriving wheat farms like those of their eastern European source area, using varieties of grain brought from their semiarid homeland. Ukrainians in Canada chose the *aspen belt*—an ecotone mixture of prairie, marsh, and scrub forest—as their settlement zone in Manitoba, Saskatchewan, and Alberta, because it resembled their former European home.

Such ethnic niche-filling has continued to the present day. Cubans have clustered in southernmost Florida, the only part of the United States mainland to have a *tropical savanna* climate identical to that in Cuba; and many Vietnamese settled as fishers on the Gulf of Mexico, especially in Texas, where they could continue their traditional livelihood.

Ethnic Environmental Perception

This deliberate site selection by ethnic immigrants represents rather accurate environmental perceptions of the

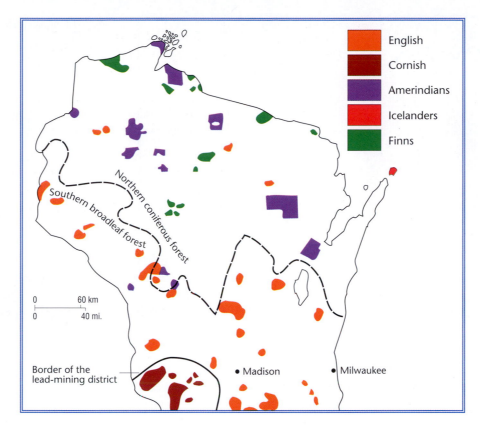

Figure 5.16

The ecology of selected ethnic islands in Wisconsin. Notice that Finnish settlements are concentrated in the infertile North Woods section, as are the American Indian reservations. The Finns went there by choice, and the Indians survived there because few white people were interested in such land. The English, by contrast, are found more often in the better farmland south of the border of the North Woods. Some of the English were miners from Cornwall, and they were drawn to the lead-mining country of southwestern Wisconsin, where they could practice the profession already known to them. Icelanders, an island people, chose an island as their settlement site in Wisconsin. **On a national scale (see Figure 5.5), can you detect similar correlations between ethnic groups and habitats?** (AFTER HILL, 1942.)

new land. As a rule, however, immigrants perceive the *ecosystem* of their new home to be more like that of their abandoned native land than is actually the case. Their perceptions of the new country emphasize the similarities and minimize the differences. Perhaps the search for similarity results from homesickness or an unwillingness to admit that migration has brought them to a largely alien land. Perhaps growing to adulthood in a particular kind of physical environment retards one's ability to perceive a different ecosystem accurately. Whatever the reason, the distorted perception occasionally caused problems for ethnic farming groups. Sometimes crops that thrived in the old homeland proved poorly suited to the particular American setting. A period of trial and error was often necessary to come to terms with the New World environ-

ment. In a few instances, the misperception was of such magnitude that economic disaster resulted and the ethnic island had to be abandoned. In such cases, cultural **maladaptation** is said to occur.

Even if the colonization area differed in some important respect from the mother country, ethnic immigrants often used their skills as farmers to choose a settlement site wisely, thereby aiding their economic success and cultural survival. In the colonization of rural North America, for example, Germans and Czechs consistently chose the best farmland, a choice that helped them to become prosperous and superior farmers. Geographer Russel Gerlach, researching the German communities of the Ozarks, found that whereas Appalachian southern settlers in that region chose easy-to-work sandy and bottomland soils, Germans

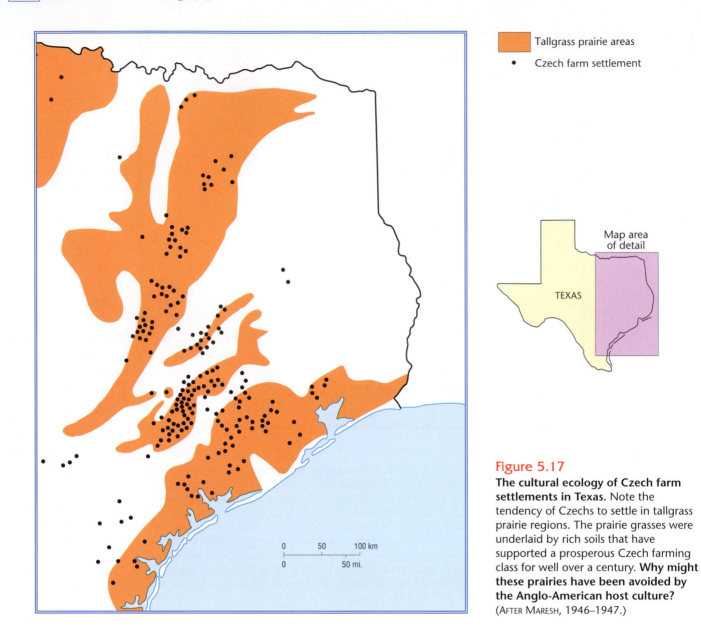

Tallgrass prairie areas

• Czech farm settlement

Map area of detail

TEXAS

0   50   100 km

0   50 mi.

Figure 5.17

The cultural ecology of Czech farm settlements in Texas. Note the tendency of Czechs to settle in tallgrass prairie regions. The prairie grasses were underlaid by rich soils that have supported a prosperous Czech farming class for well over a century. **Why might these prairies have been avoided by the Anglo-American host culture?** (AFTER MARESH, 1946–1947.)

often chose superior soils that were harder to work. In Lawrence County, Missouri, for example, the Germans were relative latecomers but still obtained some of the best land when they selected dark-soiled prairie lands that earlier Anglo-American settlers had avoided. In Gerlach's words, "A map showing the distribution of Germans in the Ozarks can also be a map of the better soils in the region." A similar ability to select choice soils can be detected among the Czechs in Texas, the state containing the largest rural population of that ethnic group in the United States. Figure 5.17 reveals the remarkable degree to which the Czech farming communities in Texas are concentrated in tallgrass prairie regions underlaid by dark,

fertile soils. By contrast, Anglo-Texans tended to avoid open prairies as farming sites, and no other group was as drawn to this ecological niche as the Czechs.

 ## Ethnic Cultural Interaction

How is ethnic identity linked to other aspects of culture? To *place*? If ethnicity possesses a vital link to ecology, it is also firmly integrated into the fabric of culture. The very concept of ethnicity can find a basis in the theme of cultural interaction. The particular combination of traits that fuses to form an ethnic identity becomes, in a sense,

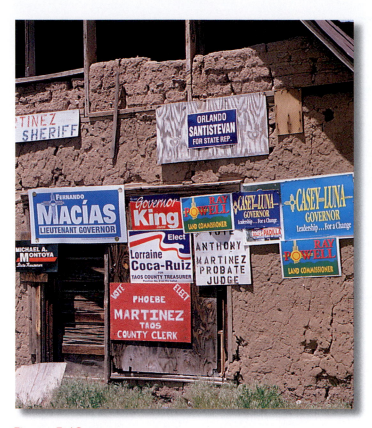

Figure 5.18
Political posters at election time, in the Hispano ethnic homeland of northern New Mexico. Ethnicity influences the voter's selection of a candidate to support. **What evidence of acculturation can you discern?** (Courtesy of Terry G. Jordan-Bychkov.)

portance to *ecotones* in the birth of ethnic groups. But Gumilev realized that too strong a reliance on such influences can lead to *environmental determinism*. Meeting and interacting with other cultural groups can also foster ethnogenesis, he said.

Let us return to his example of Russian ethnogenesis. The forest-prairie ecotone where the Russians, originally a forest folk, emerged as a people was also precisely where they met and mixed with Mongols and Turks, people of the grasslands, adopting many aspects of their ways of life. Russians, then, are as much a result of interactions between Slavs and non-Slavs as they are a people of the ecotone. If we wanted to create some new jargon—and we really do not desire that—we might call these contact zones "culturotones."

Ethnicity and Business Activity

To illustrate how ethnicity both influences and feeds upon the integration of culture, we present three examples from America. Geographer Hansgeorg Schlichtmann speaks of economic *performance*, meaning the level of success "in making a living and accumulating wealth," noting that interethnic differences in performance have often been observed. He adds that ethnic groups exhibit contrasts in economic orientation, ranging from those seeking self-sufficiency through a diversified agricultural economy to those seeking economic success by specializing in particular products for market. We have chosen both rural and urban examples, involving contrasts in types of business activity, choices of employment, and farming practices to illustrate the integration of ethnicity and economy.

Differential ethnic preferences give rise to distinct patterns of purchasing goods and services. These patterns, in turn, are reflected in the types of businesses and services available in different ethnic neighborhoods in a city. Geographer Keith Harries made a detailed study of businesses in the Los Angeles urban area, comparing Anglo-American, African-American, and Mexican-American neighborhoods (Figure 5.20 on page 165). He found that East Los Angeles Chicano neighborhoods have unusually large numbers of food stores, eating and drinking places, personal services, and repair shops. These Hispanic areas have, in fact, three times as many food stores as Anglo neighborhoods. In large part, this pattern reflects the dominance of small corner grocery stores and the fragmentation of food sales among several kinds of stores, such as *tortillerias*. The large number of eating and drinking places is related to the Mexican custom of gathering in *cantinas* (bars), where much of the social life is centered. Abundant small barbershops provide one reason that personal service establishments rank so high.

something greater than the sum of its parts. The secret to this magic lies in the fact that one aspect of culture acts on and is acted on by all other aspects. This interaction never happens exactly the same way in any two groups, and the resulting uniqueness underlies ethnic distinctiveness.

For example, ethnicity plays a role in determining what members of an ethnic group eat, what religious faith they practice, how they vote (Figure 5.18), whom they marry, how they earn a living, and in what ways they spend their leisure time. In the process, an identity emerges. The complicated pattern of ethnic homelands, ghettos, and neighborhoods influences the spatial distribution of diverse cultural phenomena (Figure 5.19 on the next page).

The Cultural Role in Ethnogenesis

At an even more basic level, cultural interaction also influences *ethnogenesis*—the emergence of indigenous groups. As we saw earlier, Gumilev attributed much im-

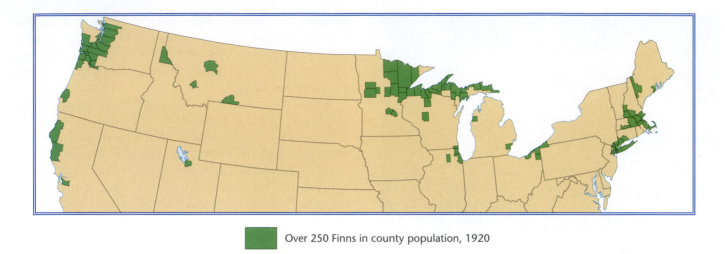

Over 250 Finns in county population, 1920

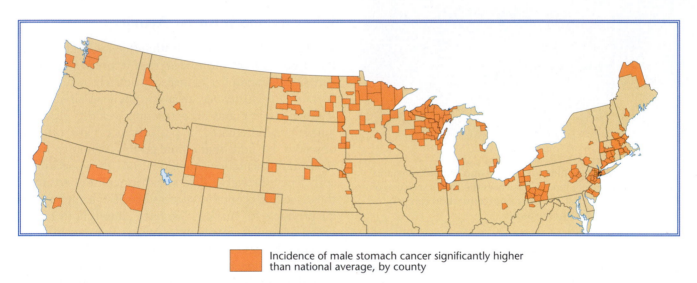

Incidence of male stomach cancer significantly higher
than national average, by county

Figure 5.19

**Finnish ethnic areas and the incidence of stomach cancer in the northern United
States. What ethnic behavior on the part of Finnish-Americans might explain this
striking spatial correlation?** For a possible explanation, see the Answer section at the end
of the chapter. (SOURCES: ALLEN AND TURNER, 1987; AND SHANNON AND PYLE, 1992.)

African-American South Los Angeles ranks highest in
personal service businesses, and vacant stores rank second. Eating and drinking places are the third most numerous there. In contrast to the Chicano eastern part of town,
the south has relatively few bars but a large number of
liquor stores and liquor departments in grocery stores
and drugstores. Secondhand shops are very common, but
there are no antique or jewelry stores and only one book-
stationery shop. A distinctive African-American personal
service enterprise, the shoeshine parlor, is found only in
South Los Angeles.

Anglo neighborhoods rank high in professional and
financial service establishments, such as doctors' and lawyers' offices and banks. These services are much less common in the non-Anglo neighborhoods. Furniture, jewelry,
antique, and apparel stores are also more numerous
among the Anglos, as are full-scale restaurants.

Contrasts similar to those observed by Harries in the
urban scene can also be found in rural areas and small
towns. An example can be taken from a study by geographer Elaine Bjorklund of an ethnic island in southwestern
Michigan settled in the mid-nineteenth century by Dutch

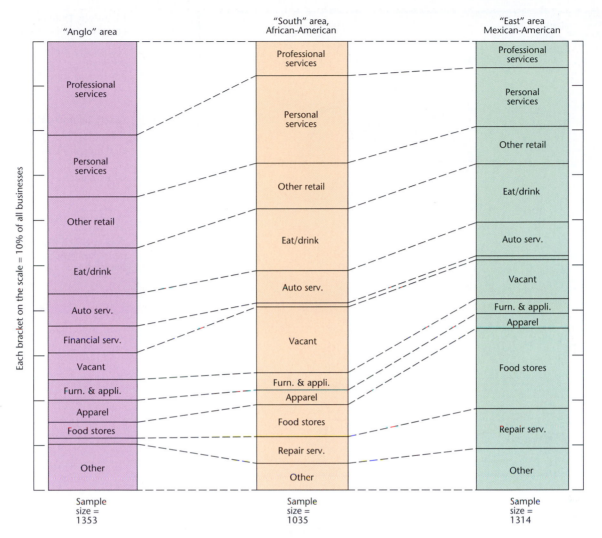

Figure 5.20

Types of businesses found in Anglo-American, African-American, and Mexican-American neighborhoods of Los Angeles, California. "Professional services" include medical and legal services and the like, whereas "personal services" are represented by businesses such as barbershops and shoeshine parlors. **Do such differences exist among ethnic neighborhoods in your city?** (After Harries, 1971: 739.)

Calvinists (Figure 5.21 on the next page). Their descendants adhered to a strict moral code and tended to regard the non–Dutch Reformed world outside their ethnic island as sinful and inferior. This adherence to the precepts of the Calvinist Reformed Church was clearly the main manifestation of their ethnicity, because the Dutch language had died out in the area. The impact of the Calvinist code of behavior on business activity in this Dutch ethnic island was apparent in various ways. As recently as 1960, no taverns, dance halls, or movie theaters existed there except in the city of Holland, and no business activity was permitted on Sunday. Because traditional Calvinists believe that leisure and idleness are evil, most present-day farmers work at second jobs during slack seasons in the agricultural year.

Ethnicity and Type of Employment

Closely related to type of business is type of employment. In many urban ethnic neighborhoods, specific groups gravitated early to particular kinds of jobs. These job identities, never rigid, were stronger in the decades

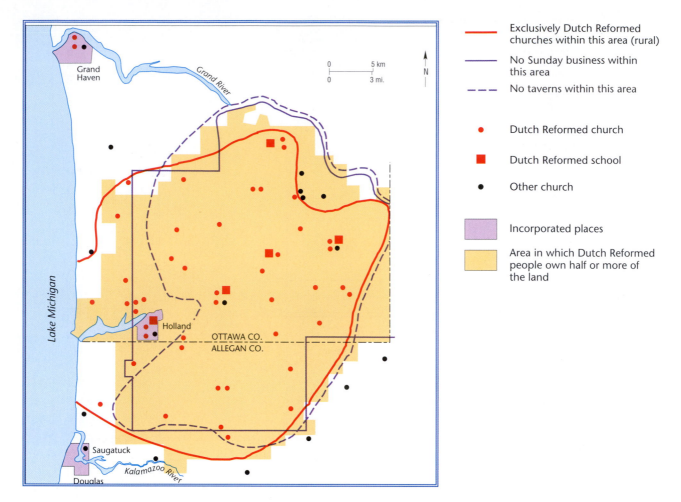

Figure 5.21

The impact of ethnicity in southwestern Michigan, about 1960. An ethnic island of Dutch Reformed (Calvinist) immigrants was established here in the 1840s and has survived to the present. The Calvinists kept taverns, movie theaters, non-Calvinist churches, and Sunday business activity out of their area. Note, too, that these several traits, though causally related, do not have exactly the same geographical distribution. **Why?** Look again at Figure 1.5 (AFTER BJORKLUND, 1964: 235.)

immediately following immigration than they are today because of advancing acculturation, but some notable examples can still be found. In some cases, the identification of ethnic groups and job types is strong enough to produce stereotyped images in the American popular mind, such as Irish police, Chinese launderers, Korean grocers, Italian restaurant owners, and Jewish retailers.

The contrast in ethnic activity in the restaurant trade is striking. Certain groups proved highly successful in marketing versions of their traditional cuisines to the population at large. In particular, the Chinese, Mexicans, and Italians succeeded in this venture (Figure 5.22). Each dominates a restaurant region in North America far larger than its ethnic homeland, island, or neighborhood.

In Boston, Irish once provided most of the laborers in the warehouse and terminal facilities near the central business district, Italians dominated the distribution and marketing of fresh foods, Germans gravitated to the sewing machine and port supply trades, and Jews found employment in merchandising and the manufacture of ready-made clothing. Italians in the northeastern United States still control the terrazzo and ceramic tile unions, and Czechs dominate the pearl button industry. In many cases, these ethnic job identities were related to occupational skills developed in the European homeland. A more recent example is the immigration of Basques from Spain to serve as professional jai alai players in the cities of southern Florida, where their ancient ethnic ball game has

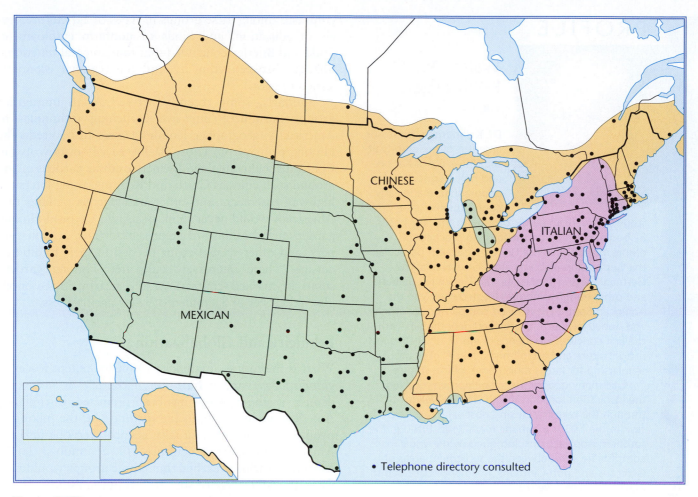

Figure 5.22

Dominant ethnic restaurant cuisine in North America. In each region, the cuisine indicated is that of the leading type of ethnic restaurant. **Why do Mexican foodways balloon northward faster than the main diffusion of Mexican-Americans? Why does Italian cuisine prevail so far south of the major concentration of Italian-Americans?** All ethnic cuisines were considered in compiling the map, based on telephone yellow page listings. (AFTER ZELINSKY, 1985: 66.)

become a major medium of legal gambling. In the United States as a whole today, one Hindu extended clan/caste, the Patels, owns close to half of all motels. An older example, also provided by Basques, involved their concentration in sheep ranching areas of the American West, where they found employment as herders, a skill well developed in their European homeland.

Reflecting on GEOGRAPHY

Can you think of other examples in which ethnic minorities are associated with particular types of employment or professions?

Ethnicity and Farming Practices

Even within the same occupation, different ethnic groups often retain distinctiveness. For example, a popular belief in the United States holds that farmers of German ethnic origin are superior to British-Americans as tillers of the soil. As early as 1789, Benjamin Rush, describing the Pennsylvania Germans, enumerated 16 ways "in which they differ from most of the other farmers" of that state.

Germans in the South still retained their agricultural superiority in the 1930s, according to a study by Walter Kollmorgen, a pioneer in the field of ethnic geography (see Profile). His research on a German ethnic island in Alabama revealed that German-Americans practiced a

PROFILE

Walter M. Kollmorgen

1907–

Dr. Kollmorgen, professor emeritus of geography at the University of Kansas and noted agricultural geographer, made early contributions to the study of American ethnic groups. In the late 1930s, he began research on the farming practices of ethnic minorities in the United States—in particular, the Germans in Alabama and Pennsylvania, the German Swiss in Tennessee, the French in Louisiana, and other ethnic minorities located mainly in the American South. His detailed comparisons of ethnic and nonethnic farmers provided geographers with the first conclusive evidence of ethnic distinctiveness in agriculture and established a model of rigorous scholarship for later ethnic geographical studies.

Like many geographers, Kollmorgen received the inspiration for his research while traveling through the countryside and observing what he saw. In the 1930s, he made many tours through the southern Appalachians. Intrigued by the visual contrasts he saw between the settlement areas of Germans and non-Germans, Kollmorgen decided to make a comparative study.

Kollmorgen was honored for meritorious contributions by the Association of American Geographers in 1953 and 1962, and he served as honorary president of that organization in 1968.

contrasts among these groups in types of agriculture, levels of education, and kinds of nonfarm employment, Todd and Brierley concluded that fundamental functional linkages between ethnicity and the regional economic structure exist.

Similarly, some recently arrived Asian immigrant groups introduced intensive gardening techniques to America, as geographer Jennifer Helzer discovered. The Hmong people from Laos, 50,000 of whom now live in California, cultivate their distinctive ethnic gardens in and around such cities as Chico and Redding, using interstate highway easements and other odd parcels of land that Americans would never think of using. A typical Hmong garden includes mustard greens, bitter melon, chili peppers, and other special crops needed in their traditional cuisine. These intensively cultivated Hmong gardens stand in marked contrast to the nearby monotonous almond groves of Sacramento Valley agribusiness.

Ethnicity and Globalization

What is the future of ethnicity? Will the potent forces of *globalization* wipe it out? For a century or more, the demise of ethnic groups has been predicted. In capitalist America, we heard about the *melting pot,* the mixing of peoples that would eventually absorb everyone into the American mainstream culture. In communist lands, Marxist doctrine preached that ethnic groups would vanish in the golden age of socialist egalitarianism.

Well, it did not happen, under either capitalism or communism. Michael Novak was among the first to note the remarkable persistence of ethnicity, writing of "the rise of the unmeltable ethnics." Then, late in the twentieth century, an *ethnic resurgence,* especially among indigenous groups, became evident in many countries around the world. In a very real way, many ethnic groups and their geographical territories have become bulwarks of resistance to globalization.

 ## Ethnic Landscapes

What is the *visible* aspect of ethnicity? Ethnicity is often, or even usually, visible, and we can properly speak of ethnic landscapes. Ethnic landscapes often differ from mainstream landscapes in styles of traditional architecture, in the patterns of surveying the land, in the distribution of houses and other buildings, and in the degree to which they "humanize" the land. In particular, many rural areas bear an ethnic imprint on the cultural landscape (Figure 5.23). Often the imprint is subtle, discernible only to those who pause and look closely. Sometimes

more diversified agriculture, had higher incomes, and owned land more often than did Anglos. "Agricultural practices," he concluded, "represent to a considerable extent a projection of patterns introduced by the Germans and the non-Germans." A more recent study by Russel Gerlach revealed that in the 1970s, farmers of German descent living in the Missouri Ozarks remained distinct in many respects from non-Germans. They owned larger farms, had more acreage under cultivation, and were less likely to be tenant farmers.

Similar differences along ethnic lines can be detected in present-day Canada. In a study of southern Manitoba, geographers D. Todd and J. S. Brierley compared the rural economies in German Mennonite, Slavic, British, French, and Dutch communities there. After detecting

Figure 5.23

Oldenburg, a German Catholic town in Indiana, announces its ethnic landscape to the arriving visitor. (Courtesy of Terry G. Jordan-Bychkov.)

it is quite striking, flaunted as an "ethnic flag" and immediately visible, even to the untrained eye (Figure 5.24). Persistence, change, and degree of subtlety in the ethnic landscape can provide valuable evidence of acculturation and the level of group pride (see Focus On: "The Face of the Fox": Indian and Non-Indian Landscapes in Iowa on page 171).

Finnish Landscapes in America

A good example of ethnicity in the cultural landscape of rural America is provided by the *sauna*. In Finland, these small steam bathhouses, usually built of logs, are seen at almost every farmstead. The Finns find it refreshing in cold weather to take a steam bath in the superheated sauna, often followed by a naked romp in the snow. The sauna is an important element in the cultural landscape of Finland. When Finns came to America, they brought the sauna with them. Geographers Cotton Mather and Matti Kaups made a study of this Finnish landscape feature in Minnesota and Michigan. They found the sauna to be an excellent visual indicator of Finnish-American ethnic islands. In one sample area, an almost purely Finnish rural district in the Upper Peninsula of Michigan, 88 percent of all Finnish-American residences had a sauna out back. In an area of greater ethnic mixture in northern Minnesota, 77 percent of Finnish houses had adjacent saunas, as contrasted with only 6 percent of non-Finnish residences in the same district.

Cultural landscapes, though, can lie, or at least distort reality. "White" Finns—those on the conservative side of the political spectrum—fostered and promoted the image of upper Midwestern Finns as a colorful rural folk living in log cabins and bathing in saunas. Professor Kaups examined this Finnish-American ethnic landscape more deeply and discovered something rather startling. A sizable element, the so-called "Red" Finns—those with leftist political affiliations—were essentially invisible. Although very numerous in the mining and logging towns of upper Michigan, Wisconsin, and Minnesota, these socialist Finns left almost no landscape trace. Kaups had to look in

Figure 5.24

An "ethnic flag" in the cultural landscape. This maize granary, called a *cuezcomatl,* is unique to the Indian population of Tlaxcala state, Mexico. The structure holds shelled maize. In Mexico, even the cultivation of maize long remained an Indian trait, as the Spaniards preferred wheat. (Courtesy of Terry G. Jordan-Bychkov.)

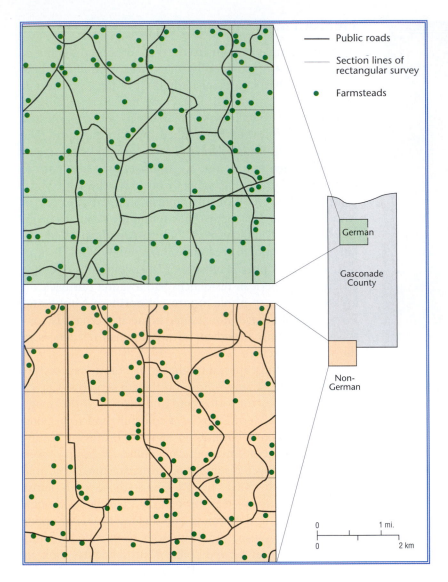

Public roads

Section lines of
rectangular survey

● Farmsteads

German

Gasconade
County

Non-
German

Figure 5.25
Distribution of farmsteads in German and non-German rural parts of Gasconade County, Missouri, 1970. Both areas have identical survey systems and similar road patterns, yet the German farmers generally situate their houses farther from the public roads than do non-Germans. **Can you think of any reasons why the German-Americans are distinctive in this way?** (AFTER GERLACH, 1976: 71.)

cemeteries to find such evidence as the communist hammer and sickle carved on gravestones. The quaint cultural landscape of saunas and log cabins will greatly mislead the casual observer. You should always look for the subtle as well as the overt in cultural landscapes.

Ethnic Settlement Patterns

Even within the constraints of a governmentally imposed land-survey system, some ethnic groups created their own distinctive settlement patterns. Often this was accomplished even where a rigid checkerboard survey was present.

In the Missouri Ozarks, for example, Germans and non-Germans alike settled a region of rectangular survey. In a close look at present-day settlement maps, we can see that rather different patterns developed. German-American farmsteads lie on public roads much less often than do non-German houses (Figure 5.25). In many instances, the Germans built their farmhouses well away from the nearest public road.

Similarly, some Russian-German Mennonite colonists in the Prairie Provinces of Canada created clustered street villages in a rectangular survey area, in marked contrast to their non-Mennonite neighbors (Figure 5.26). Mennonites duplicated the villages they had known in Russia, whereas other farmers in the area lived out on their land in dispersed farmsteads. Apparently, the cohesive bond of ethnicity encouraged these immigrants to live in clustered communities, where they enjoyed close daily contact with people of their own ethnic group.

The Mescalero Apache Indians of New Mexico also make an ethnic statement in their settlement pattern, as geographer Martha Henderson discovered. Despite a

FOCUS ON

"The Face of the Fox": Indian and Non-Indian Landscapes in Iowa

America's Indian reservations have distinctive cultural landscapes. Below is one non-Indian visitor's reaction to the Fox Indian countryside, surrounded by Anglo-American farmland in central Iowa:

> One fall day I chanced to drive through the Iowa countryside, the landscape wrought by white Iowa farmers: rolling hills stretched out, and impressed upon the hills were rectangular shapes, sharp and precise, each shape its own color. An Iowa farmer looking out upon his handiwork must have sensed, it seemed to me, his enormous power and must have felt great pride. Here and there, along a river or on some steep slope, nature was allowed to hold forth—trees and grass and brush—but not to encroach. Then I drove onto the roads of the Fox community. Immediately nature leapt up: the terrain was formed of hills and bluffs and streams; trees were seen in any direction in small and large clusters and covering whole hills, and some reached high. In the spaces that remained, grass and weeds and brush threatened to reach as high. Growth was beneath me, around me on all sides, and overhead.
>
> There, I recognized, was the difference. Passing through the countryside of white Iowa, one senses, as the Iowa farmer must sense, that he stands on top of what he sees, and a relationship is compellingly conveyed: man and his works. Entering the Fox community, one senses, as a Fox must sense, that he is enveloped.

If a Fox Indian were to provide a similar impression of a nearby Anglo cultural landscape, how might he or she express it? Would the Indian likely have a high opinion of massive transformation of the natural landscape?

Quoted from Gearing, 1970: 47.132–135.

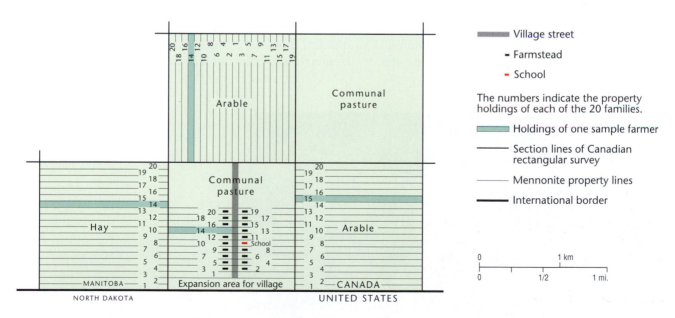

Village street
Farmstead
School

The numbers indicate the property holdings of each of the 20 families.

Holdings of one sample farmer
Section lines of Canadian rectangular survey
Mennonite property lines
International border

0 — 1 km
0 — 1/2 — 1 mi.

Figure 5.26

A Mennonite street village in Manitoba, Canada. The Mennonites, a German-speaking religious sect from Russia, settled this area in 1875. Accustomed to living in such farm villages in Russia, the Mennonites created similar settlements in Canada. The fragmentation of landholdings and communal pasture are also Old World customs. The Mennonites created this village, named Neuhorst, in spite of the Canadian rectangular survey system, which encouraged scattered farmsteads and unit-block holdings. Although many such villages later disappeared, some survive as part of the Mennonite ethnic landscape. From a distance, these surviving villages are revealed by long rows of cottonwood trees, which line the central street. **What advantages would clustered village settlement offer to an ethnic group? What disadvantages?** (AFTER WARKENTIN, 1959: 359.)

century of efforts by the federal government to disperse these eastern Apaches through their reservation, in the Anglo-American manner, they persist in clustering in villages *matrilocally* (that is, near the maternal clan home). In the process, the Apaches "continue to display vestiges of the precontact heritage" in the landscape.

Urban Ethnic Landscapes

Ethnic cultural landscapes also appear in the urban setting, in both neighborhoods and ghettos. A fine example is the brightly colored exterior mural typically found in Mexican-American ethnic neighborhoods in the southwestern United States (Figure 5.27). These began to appear in the 1960s in Southern California, and they exhibit influences rooted in both Spain and the Indian cultures of Mexico, according to geographer Dan Arreola. A wide variety of wall surfaces offer the opportunity for this ethnic expression, from apartment house and store exteriors to bridge abutments. The subjects also cover a wide range, from religious motifs to political ideology, from statements about historical wrongs to urban zoning disputes. Often they are specific to the site, incorporating well-known elements of the local landscape and thus heightening the sense of place and ethnic "turf." Inscriptions can be in either Spanish or English, but many Mexican murals do not contain a written message, relying instead on the sharpness of image and vividness of color to make an impression.

Usually the visual ethnic expression is more subtle. Color alone can connote and reveal ethnicity to the trained eye. Red, for example, is a venerated and auspicious color to the Chinese, and when they established Chinatowns in Canadian and American cities, red paint proliferated (Figure 5.28). Light blue is a Greek ethnic color, derived from the flag of their ancestral country, and Greeks avoid red, perceived as the color of their ancient enemy, the Turks. Green, an Irish Catholic color, also finds favor in Muslim ethnic neighborhoods in countries as far-flung as France and China, because it is the sacred color of Islam.

> ### Reflecting on GEOGRAPHY
> Can you give additional examples of urban ethnic landscapes from the town or city where you live?

Conclusion

The five themes of cultural geography have provided new perspectives on ethnicity. By now, we hope, you are beginning to think and see as geographers do. The world is compartmentalized regionally in terms of culture, and this complicated division takes many forms and has diverse causes. Explanations never turn out to be simple. Everything is interconnected and intertwined.

Next we will apply the five themes to the study of political geography. Much that we learned about religion, language, and ethnicity will be important in Chapter 6.

Figure 5.27
Mexican-American exterior mural, Barrio Logan, San Diego, California. This mural bears an obvious ideological-political message and helps create a special sense of place in the Mexican barrio of the city. **Can you identify the persons and events depicted in the mural?** See also Arreola, 1984. (COURTESY OF TERRY G. JORDAN-BYCHKOV.)

Figure 5.28
Two urban ethnic landscapes. Houses painted red reveal the addition of a Toronto residential block to the local Chinatown. The use of light blue trim, the Greek color, coupled with the planting of a grape arbor at the front door of a dwelling in the Astoria district of Queens, New York City, marks the neighborhood as Greek. (COURTESY OF TERRY G. JORDAN-BYCHKOV.)

Ethnic Geography on the Internet

You can learn more about ethnic geography on the Internet at the following web sites:

Ethnic Geography Specialty Group, Washington, D.C.
http://everest.hunter.cuny.edu/aegsg

This web site provides information about a specialty group within the Association of American Geographers, whose membership includes nearly all U.S. specialists in the study of ethnic geography.

Digital Atlas of New York City
http://130.166.124.2/Nypage1.html

Produced by the California Geographical Survey and the Department of Geography at California State University, Northridge, this site offers color maps of race and ancestry for North America's most ethnically diverse city, with data by census tract.

Sources

Achenbach, Hermann, 1835. *Tagebuch meiner Reise nach den Nordamerikanischen Freistaaten* [Diary of my trip to the North American free states]. Düsseldorf: Beyer and Wolf.

Allen, James P. 1972. "Migration Fields of French Canadian Immigrants to Southern Maine." *Geographical Review* 62: 366–383.

Allen, James P. 1974. "Franco-Americans in Maine: A Geographical Perspective." *Acadiensis* 4: 32–66.

Allen, James P. 1978. Map of Louisiana French, based on the U.S. Census of 1970, distributed at the annual meeting of the Association of American Geographers, New Orleans.

Arreola, Daniel D. 1984. "Mexican American Exterior Murals." *Geographical Review* 74: 409–424.

Arreola, Daniel D. 1993. "The Texas-Mexican Homeland." *Journal of Cultural Geography* 13(2): 61–74.

Bjorklund, Elaine M. 1964. "Ideology and Culture Exemplified in Southwestern Michigan." *Annals of the Association of American Geographers* 54: 227–241.

Carlson, Alvar W. 1990. *The Spanish American Homeland: Four Centuries in New Mexico's Río Arriba.* Baltimore: Johns Hopkins University Press.

Carter, Timothy J., et al. 1980. "The Peoples of China." Map supplement, *National Geographic* (July): 158.

Cromartie, John, and Carol B. Stack. 1989. "Reinterpretation of Black Return and Nonreturn Migration to the South, 1975–1980." *Geographical Review* 79: 297–310.

Dawson, C. A. 1936. *Group Settlement: Ethnic Communities in Western Canada.* Toronto: Macmillan.

Demographic Yearbook of Russia. 2000. Moscow: Goskomstat Rossii.

Dunt, Detlef, 1834. *Reise nach Texas, nebst Nachrichten von diesem Lande; für Deutsche, welche nach Amerika zu gehen beabsichtigen* [A trip to Texas, together with news of that country, for Germans who plan to come to America]. Bremen: Wiehe.

Gearing, Frederick O. 1970. *The Face of the Fox.* Chicago: Aldine.

SEEING GEOGRAPHY

When does cuisine cease to be ethnic and become simply "American"? What role does cultural diffusion play in the process?

Neon signs collected from ethnic restaurants in the United States by the Smithsonian Institution in Washington, D.C.

American Restaurant Neon Signs

This remarkable image comes not from a cultural landscape but from a montage of neon signs collected for an exhibit some years ago at the Smithsonian Institution in Washington, D.C. The exhibit represented a small sampling of the kinds of ethnic foods available commercially in the United States. It showed how ethnically diverse America had become.

What, more precisely, can these diverse, artificially assembled fragments from many cultural landscapes tell us? That we are a multiethnic society? Of course. As cultural geographer Richard Pillsbury recently said, America has "no foreign food" because we have accepted every possible foreign cuisine and made it our own.

Cultural interaction is also revealed here. Massive changes in U.S. immigration laws in the 1960s had the effect of greatly diversifying the immigrant stream, allowing such a food diversity to become established.

Implicit in the photo, too, are culture regions—in the form of ethnic neighborhoods. Each of these signs comes from an ethnic neighborhood, and the further regional implication is that such neighborhoods are proliferating.

Cultural diffusion is also obvious. How else could these different cuisines have reached our shores than by relocation diffusion?

So, in this manner, landscape images demand cultural interactive explanations, imply cultural regions, and require cultural diffusion. The various themes of cultural geography work together, are inseparable, and constitute a functioning whole.

Gerlach, Russel L. 1976. *Immigrants in the Ozarks: A Study in Ethnic Geography*. Columbia: University of Missouri Press.

Harries, Keith D. 1971. "Ethnic Variation in Los Angeles Business Patterns." *Annals of the Association of American Geographers* 61: 736–743.

Harris, R. Colebrook. 1977. "The Simplification of Europe Overseas." *Annals of the Association of American Geographers* 67: 469–483.

Helzer, Jennifer J. 1994. "Continuity and Change: Hmong Settlement in California's Sacramento Valley." *Journal of Cultural Geography* 14(2): 51–64.

Henderson, Martha L. 1990. "Settlement Patterns on the Mescalero Apache Reservation Since 1883." *Geographical Review* 80: 226–238.

Hill, G. W. 1942. "The People of Wisconsin According to Ethnic Stocks, 1940." *Wisconsin's Changing Population*. Bulletin, Serial 2642. Madison: University of Wisconsin.

Hoelscher, Steven D. 1998. *Heritage on Stage: The Invention of Ethnic Place in America's Little Switzerland*. Madison: University of Wisconsin Press.

Isajiw, Wsevolod W. 1994. "Definitions of Ethnicity: New Approaches." *Ethnic Forum* 14(1): 9–16.

Jett, Stephen C., and Virginia E. Spencer. 1981. *Navajo Architecture: Forms, History, Distributions*. Tucson: University of Arizona Press.

Johnson, James H., Jr., and Curtis C. Roseman. 1990. "Recent Black Outmigration from Los Angeles: The Role of Household Dynamics and Kinship Systems." *Annals of the Association of American Geographers* 80: 205–222.

Jones, Richard C. 1982. "Channelization of Undocumented Mexican Migrants to the U.S." *Economic Geography* 58: 156–176.

Jones, Richard C. 1988. "Micro Source Regions of Mexican Undocumented Migration." *National Geographic Research* 4: 11–22.

Kaups, Matti E. 1995. "Cultural Landscape—Log Structures as Symbols of Ethnic Identity." *Material Culture* 27(2): 1–19.

Kollmorgen, Walter M. 1941–1943. "A Reconnaissance of Some Cultural-Agricultural Islands in the South." *Economic Geography* 17: 409–430; 19: 109–117.

Lai, David C. 1988. *Chinatowns: Towns within Cities in Canada*. Vancouver: University of British Columbia Press.

Mannion, John J. 1974. *Irish Settlement in Eastern Canada: A Study of Cultural Transfer and Adaptation*. Toronto: University of Toronto Press.

Maresh, Henry R. 1946–1947. "The Czechs in Texas." *Southwestern Historical Quarterly* 50: 236–240.

Marshall, Douglas. 1949. "Minnesota's People." *Minneapolis Tribune* (August 28): section 4, p. 1.

Mather, Cotton, and Matti E. Kaups. 1963. "The Finnish Sauna: A Cultural Index to Settlement." *Annals of the Association of American Geographers* 53: 494–504.

Matwijiw, Peter. 1979. "Ethnicity and Urban Residence: Winnipeg, 1941–71." *Canadian Geographer* 23: 45–61.

Meigs, Peveril, III. 1941. "An Ethno-Telephonic Survey of French Louisiana." *Annals of the Association of American Geographers* 31: 243–250.

Meinig, Donald W. 1965. "The Mormon Culture Region." *Annals of the Association of American Geographers* 55: 191–220.

Novak, Michael. 1972. *The Rise of the Unmeltable Ethnics.* New York: Macmillan.

Pillsbury, Richard. 1998. *No Foreign Food: American Diet in Time and Place.* Boulder, Colo.: Westview.

Rechlin, Alice. 1976. *Spatial Behavior of the Old Order Amish of Nappanee, Indiana.* Geographical Publication No. 18. Ann Arbor: University of Michigan.

Rush, Benjamin. 1875. *An Account of the Manners of the German Inhabitants of Pennsylvania.* Philadelphia: Samuel P. Town.

Schlichtmann, Hansgeorg. 1977. "Ethnic Themes in Geographical Research on Western Canada." *Canadian Ethnic Studies* 9: 9–41.

Shannon, Gary W., and Gerald F. Pyle. 1992. *Disease and Medical Care in the United States: A Medical Atlas of the Twentieth Century.* New York: Macmillan.

Todd, D., and J. S. Brierley. 1977. "Ethnicity and the Rural Economy: Illustrations from Southern Manitoba." *Canadian Geographer* 21: 237–249.

Warkentin, John. 1959. "Mennonite Agricultural Settlements of Southern Manitoba." *Geographical Review* 49: 342–368.

Winsberg, Morton D. 1986. "Ethnic Segregation and Concentration in Chicago Suburbs." *Urban Geography* 7: 135–145.

Zelinsky, Wilbur. 1985. "The Roving Palate: North America's Ethnic Restaurant Cuisines." *Geoforum* 16: 51–72.

Ten Recommended Books on Ethnic Geography

(*For additional suggested readings, see* The Human Mosaic *web site:* www.whfreeman.com/jordan)

Allen, James P., and Eugene J. Turner. 1987. *We the People: An Atlas of America's Ethnic Diversity.* New York: Macmillan. A superb, award-winning atlas of color maps showing each national origin and ethnic group in the United States, by county, and accompanied by a highly informative text.

Berry, Kate A., and Martha Henderson (eds.). 2002. *Geographical identities of Ethnic America: Race, Space, and Place.* Reno: University of Nevada Press. Eighteen different experts on American ethnic geography explain how place shapes ethnic/racial identities, and in turn how these groups create distinctive spatial patterns and ethnic landscapes.

Gumilev, Leo. 1990. *Ethnogenesis and the Biosphere.* Moscow: Progress Publishers. The classic study of the relationship between ethnogenesis and the habitat, or ethnic ecology, by a distinguished Russian geographer who was persecuted by communist authorities for his beliefs.

Jordan, Terry G., and Matti E. Kaups. 1989. *The American Backwoods Frontier: An Ethnic and Ecological Interpretation.* Baltimore: Johns Hopkins University Press. The authors use the concepts of cultural preadaptation and ethnic substrate to reveal how the forest colonization culture of the American eastern woodlands developed and helped shape half a continent.

Louder, Dean R., and Eric Waddell (eds.). 1993. *French America: Mobility, Identity, and Minority Experience Across the Continent.* Baton Rouge: Louisiana State University Press. A comprehensive geographical study of the Franco-American and French-Canadian peoples in their North American diaspora.

McKee, Jesse O. (ed.). 2000. *Ethnicity in Contemporary America: A Geographical Appraisal,* 2nd ed. Lanham, Md.: Rowman & Littlefield. This clear and thoughtful text offers a geographical analysis of U.S. immigration patterns and the development of selected ethnic minority groups, focusing especially on their origin, diffusion, socioeconomic characteristics, and settlement patterns within the United States; many well-known geographers contributed chapters.

Noble, Allen G. (ed.). 1992. *To Build in a New Land: Ethnic Landscapes in North America.* Baltimore: Johns Hopkins University Press. A superb study of widely differing traditional ethnic cultural landscapes in the United States and Canada, revealing what diverse countries we inhabit.

Nostrand, Richard L., and Lawrence E. Estaville, Jr. (eds.). 2001. *Homelands: A Geography of Culture and Place Across America.* Baltimore: Johns Hopkins University Press. A collection of essays on an array of North American ethnic homelands, together with in-depth treatment of the geographical concept of homeland.

Ostergren, Robert. 1988. *A Community Transplanted: The Trans-Atlantic Experience of a Swedish Immigrant Settlement in the Upper Middle West, 1835–1915.* Madison: University of Wisconsin Press. This excellent case study is particularly revealing of the processes of cultural diffusion at work in the decision to emigrate, of chain migration, and of the clustering in ethnic islands in America.

Yoon, Hong-key. 1986. *Maori Mind, Maori Land: Essays on the Cultural Geography of the Maori People.* Bern, Switzerland: Peter Lang. A highly readable study of the indigenous Polynesian ethnic group in New Zealand; also useful as a comparison to the situation in North America.

Answer

Figure 5.19

It has been suggested that the Finns' fondness for smoked fish may help explain their high cancer rate.

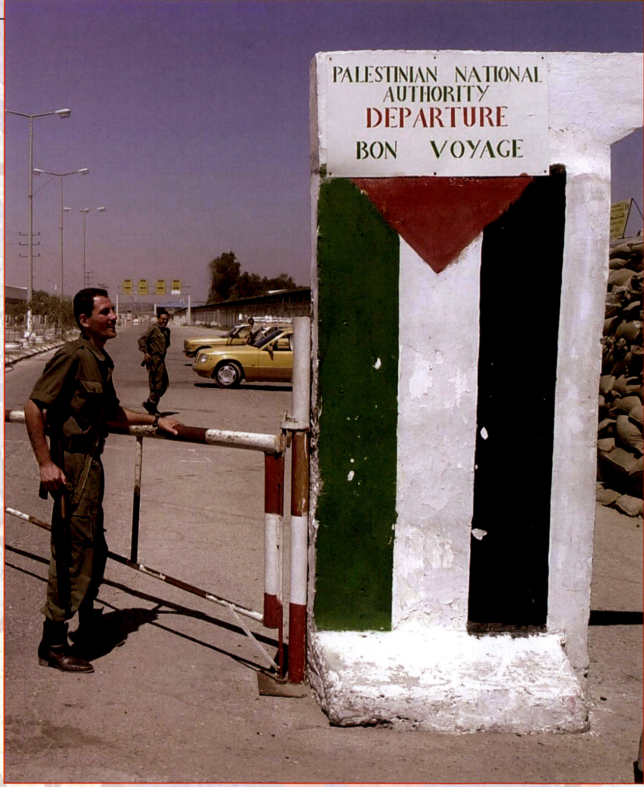

The border between Israel and the Gaza Strip, part of the Palestinian Arab homeland. (AGENCE FRANCE PRESSE/CORBIS.)
Turn to Seeing Geography *on page 213 for an in-depth analysis of the above question.*

6

POLITICAL GEOGRAPHY
A Divided World

From the breakup of empires to regional differences in voting patterns, from the drawing of international boundaries to congressional redistricting in the American democracy, from territorial disputes to separatist violence, human political behavior possesses a geographical aspect. National policies about environmental protection, guerrillas seeking a secure base for their operations, and the natural defense provided for an independent country by a surrounding sea all reveal an intertwining of ecology and politics. These spatial and environmental connections provide the basis of the subdiscipline of **political geography.** Many geographers pursue such interests, as is suggested by the presence of a designated political geography specialty group within the Association of American Geographers and the publication in the United Kingdom of a scholarly journal bearing the name *Political Geography.* As Gearóid Ó Tuathail has said, political geography "is about power, an ever-changing map revealing the struggle over borders, space, and authority."

 ## Political Culture Regions

How is political geography revealed in culture regions? The theme of culture region is essential to the study of political geography, because an array of both formal and functional political regions exists. Among these, the most important and influential is the *independent country.*

Independent Countries

The most outstanding political geographical fact is that the Earth is divided into nearly 200 independent countries, producing a vivid mosaic

Independent Countries

Abbreviations

A	AUSTRIA
AL	ALBANIA
B	BELGIUM
BA	BOSNIA-HERZEGOVINA
BF	BURKINA FASO
BG	BULGARIA
BOTS	BOTSWANA
BY	BELARUS
CH	SWITZERLAND
CZ	CZECHIA
D	GERMANY
EG	EQUATORIAL GUINEA
EST	ESTONIA
ET	EAST TIMOR
GBI	GUINEA BISSAU
H	HUNGARY
HR	CROATIA
IC	IVORY COAST
L	LUXEMBOURG
LT	LITHUANIA
LV	LATVIA
MK	MACEDONIA
NL	NETHERLANDS
RCA	CENTRAL AFRICAN REPUBLIC
RL	LEBANON
RO	ROMANIA
RU	RUSSIA
SK	SLOVAKIA
SLO	SLOVENIA
SM	SERBIA & MONTENEGRO
TC	TURKISH CYPRUS
TM	TURKMENISTAN
UAE	UNITED ARAB EMIRATES
WAG	THE GAMBIA
WAL	SIERRA LEONE
ZW	ZIMBABWE

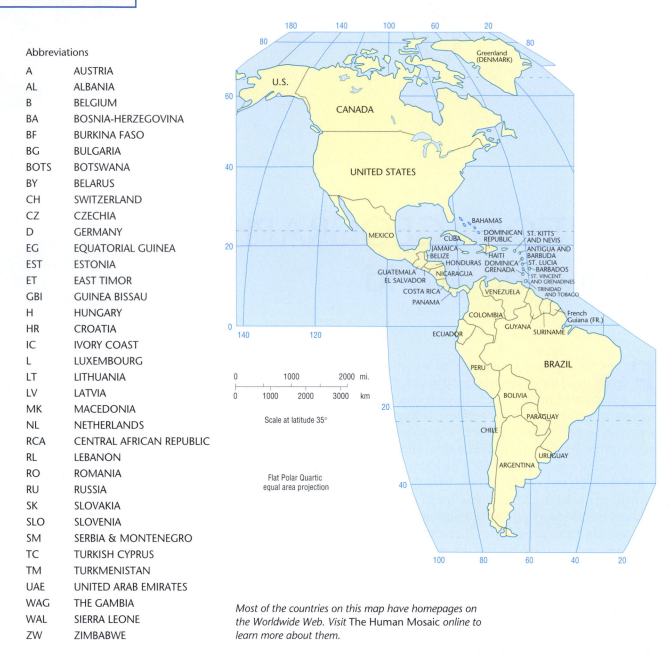

Most of the countries on this map have homepages on the Worldwide Web. Visit The Human Mosaic online to learn more about them.

of *functional culture regions* (Figure 6.1). Add to those countries the hundreds of other provinces and districts that enjoy some level of autonomy, without being fully independent, and the pattern becomes even more complex. Closer inspection reveals that some parts of the world are fragmented into many different countries, whereas others exhibit much greater unity. The United States occupies about the same amount of territory as Europe, which is partitioned among 46 independent countries. Imagine the complexity if every state in the United States were independent. The continent of Australia is politically united, whereas South America

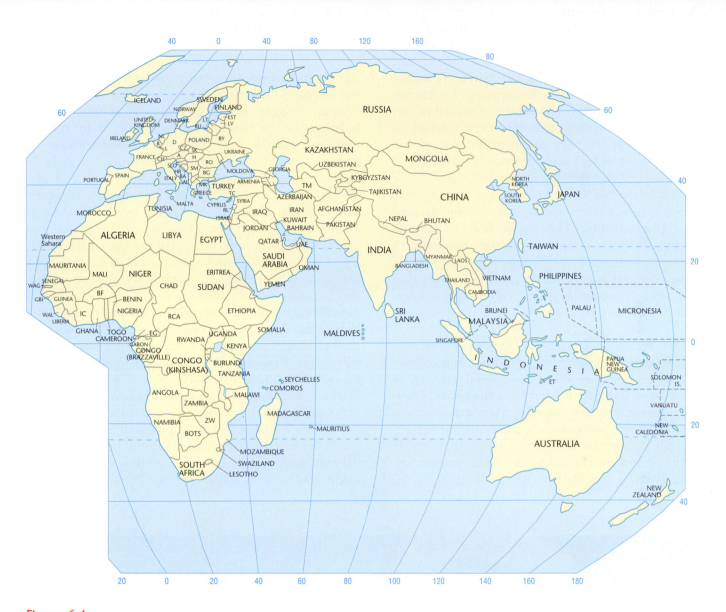

Figure 6.1

The independent countries of the world. In the twentieth century, the map was in rapid flux, with a proliferation of countries. This process began after World War I with the breakup of such empires as Austria-Hungary and Turkey, then intensified after World War II when the overseas empires of the British, French, Italians, Dutch, Americans, and Belgians collapsed. More recently, the Russian-Soviet empire disintegrated.

has 12 independent entities and the African mainland has 47.

The independent country gives tangible geographical expression to one of the most common human characteristics: the need to belong to a larger group that controls its own piece of the Earth, its own territory. So universal is this trait that scholars coined the term **territoriality** to describe it. Some geographers believe that territoriality is instinctual in humans, as zoologists have demonstrated in the case of certain animal species. They claim that the spatial fragmentation of humankind into independent countries is natural and unavoidable, a product of the animal part of our brain, as are feelings of nationalism (see Focus On: The Territorial Imperative).

Some geographers disagree. To them, territoriality is *learned*. Robert Sack, for example, regards territoriality as a cultural strategy that uses power to control area and communicate that control, thereby subjugating the inhabitants and acquiring resources. He warns against uncritical borrowing of concepts from students of animal behavior and argues, for example, that the precise marking of borders is a concept originally unique to Western culture. Certain other geographers suggest a rather recent origin for nationalism, within the past 150 to 500 years.

Whether learned or instinctual (or some combination of the two), human territoriality is a thoroughly geographical phenomenon. The implication we should derive from this fact is that nationalism, the sense of "we," springs in no small part from attachment to region and place. Geography and national identity cannot be separated, and it is no accident that territoriality is a spatial word.

Distribution of National Territory One of the most fundamental geographical aspects of an independent country is the shape and configuration of the national territory. As a rule, the more compact the territory, the better. Theoretically, the most desirable shape for a country is circular or hexagonal. These two geometric forms maximize compactness, allow short communication lines, and minimize the amount of border to be defended. Of course, no countries actually enjoy this ideal degree of compactness, al-

though some—such as France, Poland, Congo (Kinshasa), and Brazil—come close (Figure 6.2).

Any one of several unfavorable territorial distributions can inhibit national cohesiveness. Potentially most damaging to a country's stability are enclaves and exclaves. An **enclave** is a district surrounded by a country but not ruled by it. Enclaves can be either self-governing (Lesotho in Figure 6.2) or an exclave of another country. In either case, its presence can be a problem for the surrounding country. Potentially just as disruptive is the *pene-enclave,* an intrusive piece of territory with only the smallest of outlets (The Gambia in Figure 6.2).

Exclaves are pieces of national territory separated from the main body of a country by the territory of another (Kaliningrad District in Figure 6.2; Figure 6.3 on page 182). Alaska is an exclave of the United States. Exclaves are particularly undesirable if a hostile power holds the intervening territory, for defense of such an isolated area is always difficult and may stretch national resources to the breaking point. Moreover, an exclave's inhabitants, isolated from their fellow countrymen, may develop separatist feelings, causing additional problems. Pakistan provides a good example of the national instability created by exclaves. Pakistan was created in 1947 as two main bodies of territory separated from each other by almost 1000 miles (1600 kilometers) of territory in northern India. West Pakistan had the capital and most of the territory, but East Pakistan housed most of the people. West Pakistan hoarded the country's wealth, exploiting East Pakistan's resources and giving little in return. Ethnic dif-

FOCUS ON

The Territorial Imperative

For some time, zoologists have recognized that animal behavior in many species is partly motivated by a territorial instinct—a need to possess and defend a home area as individuals or as members of a group. Territory provides these animals a sense of identity and satisfies a basic need for belonging. Such an instinct is found in animals as diverse as the mockingbird, lemur, crab, and prairie dog. For these animals and others, the attachment to territory is genetic, a need perhaps even stronger than the sex drive.

Robert Ardrey, in his book *The Territorial Imperative,* says that humans are territorial animals, motivated by the same instinct that affects mockingbirds and prairie dogs. In other words, the political organization of territory into provinces and countries is the product of animal instinct—as are nationalism,

patriotism, and the desire to defend territory against invaders. On the smallest scale, the territorial imperative finds human expression in the homestead and family. Then it ranges upward from clan and tribe, through neighborhood, district, and province, to reach humankind's ultimate territorial creation—the independent country. The territory involved may be a family's suburban yard, the domain of a street gang in the ghettos of New York City, the hilly refuge of a Stone Age tribe in New Guinea, or the expanses of an empire. In Ardrey's words, "The dog barking at you from behind his master's fence acts for a motive indistinguishable from that of his master when the fence was built." Is human territorialism learned or instinctual? Ardrey argues for instinct, but many social scientists do not agree. The question is still being debated.

Based on Ardrey, 1966.

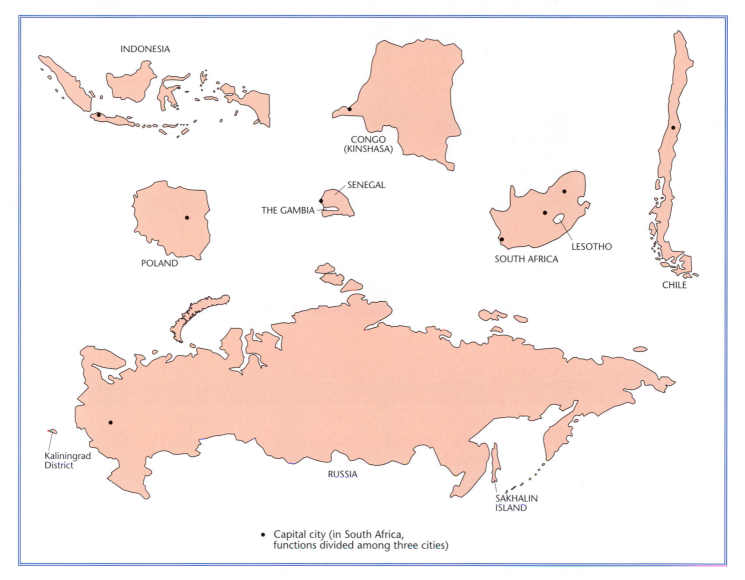

Figure 6.2

Differences in the distribution of national territory. The map, drawn from Eurasia, Africa, and South America, shows wide contrasts in territorial shape. Poland and, to a lesser extent, Congo (Kinshasa) approach the ideal hexagonal shape, but Russia is elongated and has an exclave in the Kaliningrad District, whereas Indonesia is fragmented into a myriad of islands. The Gambia intrudes as a pene-enclave into the heart of Senegal, and South Africa has a foreign enclave, Lesotho. Chile must overcome extreme elongation. **What problems can arise from elongation, enclaves, fragmentation, and exclaves?**

ferences between the peoples of the two sectors further complicated matters. In 1971, a quarter of a century after its founding, Pakistan disintegrated. The distant exclave seceded to become the independent country of Bangladesh (see Figure 6.1).

Even when a national territory is in one piece, instability can develop if the shape of the state is awkward. Narrow "shoestring" countries, such as Chile, The Gambia, and Norway, can be difficult to administer, as can nations consisting of separate islands (see Figures 6.1 and 6.2). In these situations, transportation and communications become difficult, causing administrative problems. The multi-island country of Indonesia is threatened by several major secession movements, and one of these—in East Timor—recently succeeded (see Figure 6.1). Similarly, the three-island country of Comoros, in the Indian Ocean, is today troubled by the separatist movement on Anjouan Island (see Figure 6.1).

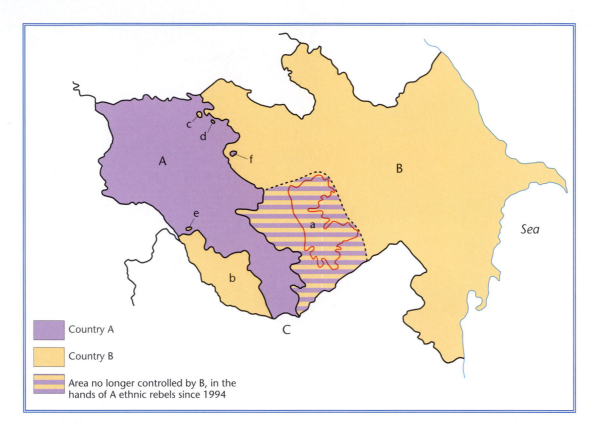

Country A

Country B

Area no longer controlled by B, in the hands of A ethnic rebels since 1994

Figure 6.3

Two independent countries, *A* and *B*. *A* seeks to liberate region *a*, where a population speaking the same language and adhering to the same religion as the people of *A* live. In a war lasting from 1990 to 1994, the people of *a* seceded from *B*, and a tenuous ceasefire was arranged. *B*, meanwhile, has an exclave, *b*, on the opposite, western side of *A*, and the people of *b* form another ethnic minority, unrelated to *B*. Country *B* also possesses several much smaller enclaves—*c*, *d*, and *e*, the last of which is regarded as part of *b* (an exclave of an exclave!). *A* also has a tiny exclave, *f*. In other words, the distribution of national territories is troublesome to both *A* and *B*, particularly given the hostile relations between them. These are real countries. Using an atlas, try to identify them. If you fail, the answer appears at the end of this chapter. **Have any recent events occurred here?** (Sources: Office of the Geographer, U.S. Department of State, personal communication,1997; and Smith et al., 1997: 37.)

Boundaries Political territories have different types of boundaries. Until fairly recent times, many boundaries were not sharp, clearly defined lines, but instead zones called **marchlands.** Today, the nearest equivalent to the marchland is the **buffer state,** an independent but small and weak country lying between two powerful, potentially belligerent countries. Mongolia, for example, is a buffer state between Russia and China; Nepal occupies a similar position between India and China (see Figure 6.1). If the buffer state falls under the domination of one or the other powerful neighbor, it becomes a **satellite state** and loses much of its independence.

Most modern boundaries are lines rather than zones, and we can distinguish several types. **Natural boundaries** follow some feature of the natural landscape, such as a river or mountain ridge. **Ethnographic boundaries** find

their basis in some cultural trait, usually in a particular language or religion; and **geometric boundaries** are regular, often perfectly straight lines drawn without regard for physical or cultural features. The United States–Canada boundary west of the Lake of the Woods is a geometric border. So are most county and state (or province) borders in the central and western United States and Canada. Some boundaries are of mixed type, composites of two or more of the types listed.

Relic boundaries no longer exist as international borders, but they often leave behind a trace in the local cultures. With the reunification of Germany in the autumn of 1990, the old Iron Curtain border between the former German Democratic Republic in the east and the Federal Republic of Germany in the west was quickly dismantled (Figure 6.4). In a remarkably short time span, measured

Figure 6.4

A boundary disappears. In Berlin, the view toward the Brandenburg Gate changed radically between 1989 and 1991,when the Berlin Wall was destroyed and Germany reunited. (Courtesy of Terry G. Jordan-Bychkov.)

in weeks, the Germans reopened severed transport lines and created new ones, knitting the enlarged country together. Even so, remnants and reminders of the old border remained. Most of the border continued to function as provincial boundaries within Germany and to separate two parts of the country with strikingly different levels of prosperity. The most outstanding geographical aspect of international borders is their divisive character. As Germans knit back together a country long cut in two by an international boundary, other recently independent countries in Europe, such as Estonia and Latvia, enforced their new borders by severing some existing roads.

Have political boundaries been weakened by the computer age? (See Focus On: Political Borders in Cyberspace.) How is this weakening relevant to the process of globalization and the declining role of the independent state that some experts feel accompanies the process?

Spatial Organization of Territory Independent countries differ greatly in the way their territory is organized for purposes of administration. Political geographers recognize two basic types of spatial organization: unitary and federal. Unitary countries are characterized by power being concentrated centrally, with little or no provincial authority. All major decisions come from the central government, and policies are applied uniformly throughout the national territory. France and China are unitary in structure, even though one is democratic and the other totalitarian. A federal government, by contrast, is a more

geographically expressive political system. It acknowledges the existence of regional cultural differences and provides the mechanism by which the various regions can perpetuate their individual characters. Power is diffused, and the central government surrenders much authority to the individual provinces. The United States, Canada, Germany, Australia, and Switzerland provide examples, though exhibiting varying degrees of federalism. The trend in the United States, particularly since the defeat of the Confederacy in the Civil War, has been toward a more unitary, less federal government, with fewer states' rights. In Canada, on the other hand, federalism remains vital, representing an effort to counteract French-Canadian demands for Québec's independence.

Whether federal or unitary, a country functions through some system of political subdivisions, usually on several different levels. In federal systems, these subdivisions sometimes overlap in authority, with confusing results. For example, the Indian reservation in the United States occupies a unique and ambiguous place in the federal system of political subdivisions. These semiautonomous enclaves are legally sanctioned political territories that only indigenous Americans can possess. Although not sovereign, they do have certain self-government rights that conflict with other local authority. Reservations do not fit neatly into the American political system of states, counties, townships, precincts, and incorporated municipalities. They add to the confusion that so often typifies federal systems.

FOCUS ON

Political Borders in Cyberspace

What happens to political boundaries in cyberspace? E-mail, the Internet, and the World Wide Web can cross borders in ways not previously possible, although radio, telephone, and fax machines possess some of the same border-defying qualities. In Germany, for example, Nazi and neo-Nazi propaganda is prohibited, yet the dissemination of this material is protected in the United States by the First Amendment as freedom of speech. What happens when this propaganda originates in the United States and is posted electronically to online bulletin boards worldwide? Can the German government prosecute the originator of the message—an American—for violating a German law?

How can countries impose their laws and boundaries on the computer age? Only by restricting access to computers and phone lines, both of which require a totalitarian regime. The computer age is eroding political boundaries by allowing information and ideas to diffuse more rapidly and completely. As a result, political barriers to cultural diffusion have become very fragile.

Centrifugal and Centripetal Forces The spatial organization of territory, degree of compactness, and type of boundaries can influence an independent country's stability. However, other forces are also at work, and cultural factors often make or break a country. The most viable independent countries, least troubled by internal discord, have a strong feeling of group solidarity among their population. Group identity is the key.

Geographers refer to factors that promote national unity and solidarity as **centripetal forces.** By contrast, anything that disrupts internal order and encourages destruction of the country is called a **centrifugal force.** Many nations have one principal centripetal force that, more than any other single factor, provides fuel for nationalistic sentiment. Such a unifying force is referred to as the **raison d'être**—the "reason for being." For example, the Jewish faith is the raison d'être for Israel. We consider an array of centripetal and centrifugal forces later, in the sections on political ecology and politico-cultural interaction.

Supranational Political Bodies

The third major type of political functional culture region, in addition to independent countries and their governmental subdivisions, is the **supranational organization** (Figure 6.5).

Self-governing countries form international associations of one kind or another for purposes of trade, military assistance, or mutual security. In the twentieth century, supranational organizations grew in number and importance, coincident with and counterbalancing the proliferation of independent countries. Some represent the vestiges of collapsed empires, such as the British Commonwealth, French Community, and Commonwealth of Independent States (CIS)—the latter a shadow of the former Soviet Union. Most supranationals, such as the Arab League or the Association of Southeast Asian Nations (ASEAN), possess little cohesion. Atop the pyramid of supranationals is the *United Nations,* headquartered in New York City, which maintains peacekeeping and charitable functions, while at the same time invoking sanctions against "rogue" countries.

The *European Union,* or EU, is by far the most powerful and successful supranational organization in the world (see Figure 6.5). In common with many independent countries, it grew from a central core area of six countries in the 1950s to a present membership of 15. At first the EU was merely a customs union whose purpose was to lower or remove tariffs that hindered trade, but it gradually took on more and more of a political role. Perhaps its main purpose was to weaken the power of its member countries to the point that they could never again wage war against one another—a response to the devastation of Europe in two world wars. The member countries have all sacrificed some of their sovereign powers to the EU administration. A single monetary currency, the *euro,* has been adopted by most EU members. Most international borders within the EU are now completely open, requiring no passport checks. The EU may eventually create a unified Europe.

Reflecting on GEOGRAPHY

Should the various member countries of the European Union continue to sacrifice aspects of their independence to create a stronger union?

Political Globalization

Do supranational organizations—in particular, the United Nations—represent the movement we described earlier as *globalization?* The answer seems to be negative. The number of independent countries may diminish in the twenty-

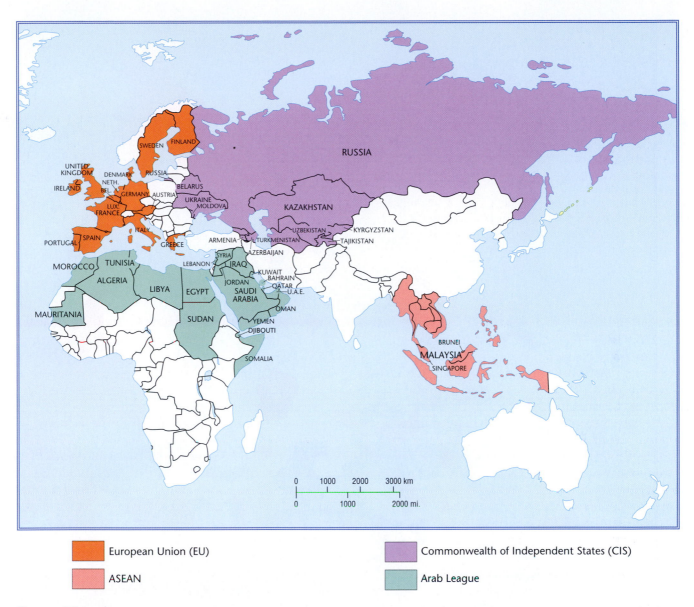

Figure 6.5
Some supranational political organizations in the Eastern Hemisphere. These organizations vary greatly in purpose and cohesion. ASEAN stands for the Association of Southeast Asian Nations, and its purposes are both economic and political. **What might this map indicate about globalization?**

first century—reversing an opposite trend in the 1900s—but a world-state does not seem possible.

Perhaps the most ambitious attempt to achieve political globalization was the *British Empire,* which spread on all continents and oceans. "The sun never sets on the British Empire," it was once said. But it did. This proud empire collapsed.

Electoral Geographical Regions

When people vote in elections, another vivid mosaic of political culture regions is created. A free vote of the people on some controversial issue provides one of the purest expressions of culture. Revealed in the process are attitudes reflecting religion, ethnicity, and ideology. Geographers can devise *formal culture regions* based on voting patterns, giving rise to the subspecialty known as **electoral geography.**

Voting tendencies over many decades can be mapped, revealing deep-rooted, formal electoral behavior regions. Europe provides a vivid example (Figure 6.6 on the next page). Some districts and provinces there have a long record of rightist sentiment, and many of these lie toward the center of Europe. Peripheral areas, especially in the east, are often leftist strongholds. Every country where free elections are permitted has a similarly varied electoral

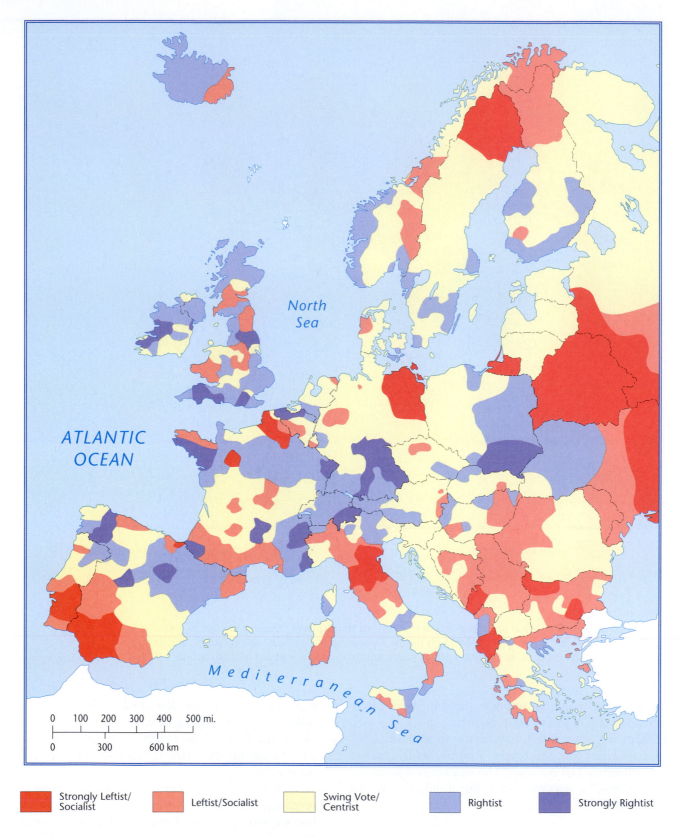

North
Sea

ATLANTIC
OCEAN

Mediterranean Sea

| 0 | 100 | 200 | 300 | 400 | 500 mi. |

| 0 | 300 | 600 km |

Strongly Leftist/
Socialist

Leftist/Socialist

Swing Vote/
Centrist

Rightist

Strongly Rightist

Figure 6.6

The electoral geography of Europe. A conservative-rightist core contrasts with a socialist-leftist periphery. Data are based on elections held in the period 1950 to 1995. In the formerly communist countries, the record of free elections began only in 1990. (SOURCE: JORDAN-BYCHKOV AND JORDAN, 2002: 226.)

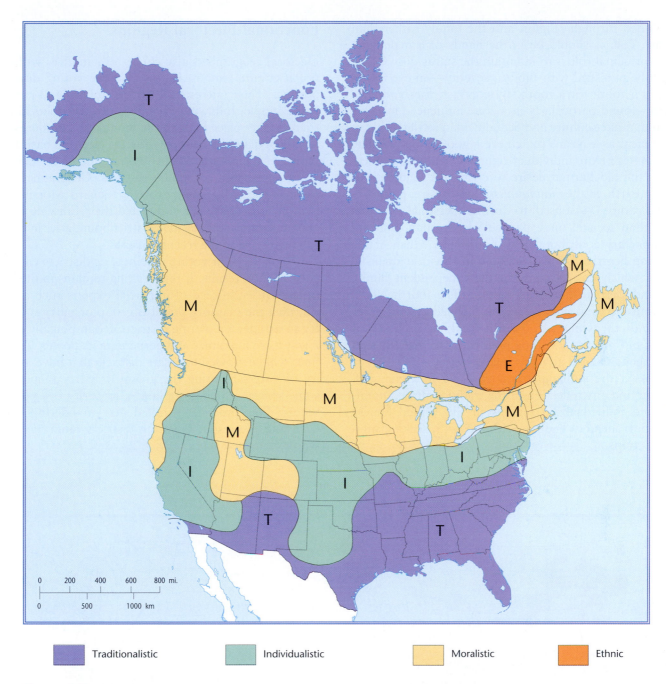

Figure 6.7
Political subcultures in North America. The four types are described in the text. Compare these regions with those shown in Figure 1.6 and also with Figures 6.8, 6.12, and 6.13. (Sources: Elazar, 1994: 230–243; and O'Reilly and Webster, 1998: 506.)

geography. In other words, cumulative voting patterns typically reveal sharp and pronounced sectional contrasts. Electoral geographers refer to these borders as *cleavages*.

Such electoral culture regions also exist in the United States and Canada, based in "traditionalistic," "moralistic," "individualistic," and "ethnic" political ideologies,

according to Daniel Elazar (Figure 6.7). In the *traditionalistic* subculture—which includes the Lower South, the Hispanic borderland, and diverse American Indian groups—family and social class are more important than the state or the individual. For this subculture, the "best government is the least government," and order is best maintained through religion and the family rather than the law. Politics should be in the hands of a male elite, whose principal role is to maintain the status quo. Crime should be punished with Biblical severity—an eye for an eye and a tooth for a tooth. By contrast, the *moralistic* system—found particularly in a zone influenced by New England Yankee culture and Scandinavian settlers—views government as a means to achieve a good society. Public good comes before individual rights or benefits, a reflection of the old Puritan desire to create the Kingdom of God on Earth. In the *individualistic* subculture, politics—seen as "dirty"—is used to further personal interests rather than societal ones, particularly through lobbying and monetary contributions to politicians. Much of the American heartland is a stronghold of the individualistic system, which has its roots in the independent family farm and German-American culture. The fourth North American electoral culture region, labeled *ethnic,* coincides with the separatist, French-speaking province of Québec in Canada. A leading political party there has an ethnic agenda aimed at achieving secession.

Look at the voting patterns revealed in Figure 6.8. Can you find any reflection of the traditionalistic, moralistic, and individualistic regions in the United States? Now, look ahead to Figures 6.12 and 6.13, seeking similar reflections.

Functional Electoral Regions

Electoral geographers also concern themselves with *functional* culture regions, in this case the voting district or precinct. Their interests are both scholarly and practical. For example, following each U.S. census, political redistricting takes place to establish voting areas of more or less equal population, and these form the electoral basis for the House of Representatives in Washington, D.C. State legislatures are based on similar districts. Geographers often assist in the redistricting process. Richard Morrill of the University of Washington directed the redrawing of both congressional and legislative district boundaries in his state following one of the recent censuses.

The pattern of voting precincts or districts can influence election results. If redistricting remains in the hands of legislators, instead of impartial experts such as Morrill, then the majority political group or party will often try to arrange the voting districts geographically in such a way as to maximize and perpetuate its power. Cleavage lines will be crossed to create districts that have a majority of voters favoring the group or party in power or some special ethnic group and a minority of opposition voters. This practice is called **gerrymandering** (Figure 6.9), and the resultant voting districts often have awkward, elongated shapes.

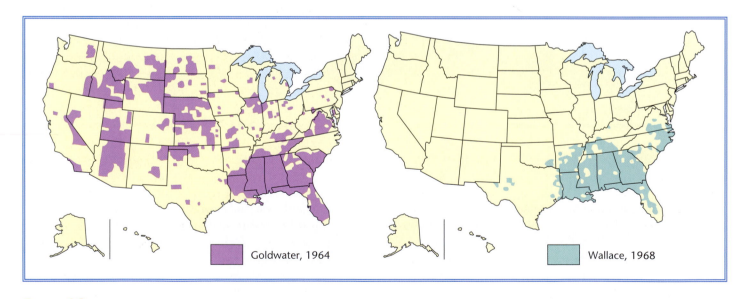

Goldwater, 1964

Wallace, 1968

Figure 6.8

The Lower South (see Figure 1.6) forms part of the traditionalistic political subculture (see Figure 6.7). Two elections for the presidency of the United States, in 1964 and 1968, revealed the Lower South to be different from the rest of the country. **How might Barry Goldwater—a conservative Republican—and George Wallace—an Independent populist in favor of racial segregation—have appealed to a traditionalistic subculture?** (Brunn, 1974: 279, 281.)

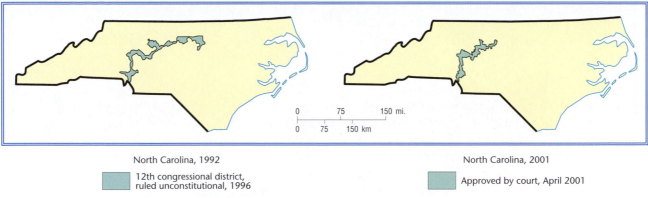

North Carolina, 1992

12th congressional district, ruled unconstitutional, 1996

North Carolina, 2001

Approved by court, April 2001

Figure 6.9
Gerrymandering of a congressional district in North Carolina. The North Carolina Twelfth District was created in 1992 to ensure an African-American majority, so that an additional minority candidate could be elected to Congress. Note the awkward shape of these districts, often a sign of gerrymandering. In 1996, the North Carolina district and others gerrymandered for racial purposes were declared unconstitutional. The lines were redrawn, but although the district still looks very much gerrymandered, the courts approved the revised version. (SOURCE: *NEW YORK TIMES*.)

 # Political Diffusion

Do political ideas, institutions, and countries expand and spread by means of cultural diffusion? Yes. Moreover, political boundaries can act as barriers to the spread of ideas or knowledge, thereby retarding diffusion (see Focus On: Political Boundaries as Barriers to Cultural Diffusion). Also, political events and developments can trigger that most basic type of diffusion—human migration, or *relocation* diffusion. Clearly, the diffusionary concepts outlined in Chapter 1 can profitably be applied to political geography.

Country Building as Diffusion

Some independent countries sprang full-grown into the world, but most diffused outward from a small nucleus called a **core area,** annexing adjacent lands, often over many centuries. Generally, core areas possess a particularly attractive set of resources for human life and culture. Larger numbers of people cluster there than in surrounding districts, particularly if the area has some measure of natural defense against aggressive neighboring political entities. This denser population, in turn, may produce enough wealth to support a large army, which then provides the base for further expansion and relocation diffusion from the core area.

During this expansion, the core area typically remains the country's single most important district, housing the capital city and the cultural and economic heart of the nation. The core area functions as the *node* of a func-

tional culture region. France expanded to its present size from a small core area around the capital city of Paris. China diffused from a nucleus in the northeast, and Russia originated in the small principality of Moscow, as Figure 6.10 on the next page shows. The United States grew westward from a core between Massachusetts and Virginia on the Atlantic coastal plain, an area that still has the national capital and the densest population.

Clearly, the diffusion of independent countries in this manner produces the *core-periphery* configuration, described in Chapter 1 as being typical of both functional and formal culture regions. The core dominates the periphery, and a certain amount of friction exists between the two. Peripheral areas generally display pronounced, self-conscious regionality and occasionally provide the settings for secession movements. Even so, countries that diffused from core areas are, as a rule, more stable than those created all at once to fill a political void. The absence of a core area, to which citizens can look as the national node, can leave a country's national identity blurred and makes it easier for various provinces to develop strong local or even foreign allegiances. Belgium and Congo (Kinshasa) offer examples of countries without political core areas.

Potentially, countries with multiple, competing core areas are the least stable of all. This situation often develops when two or more independent countries are united. The main threat is that one of the competing cores will form the center of a separatist movement and dissolve the country. In Spain, Castile and Aragon united in 1479, but the union remains shaky more than five centuries later—in part because the old core areas of the two former

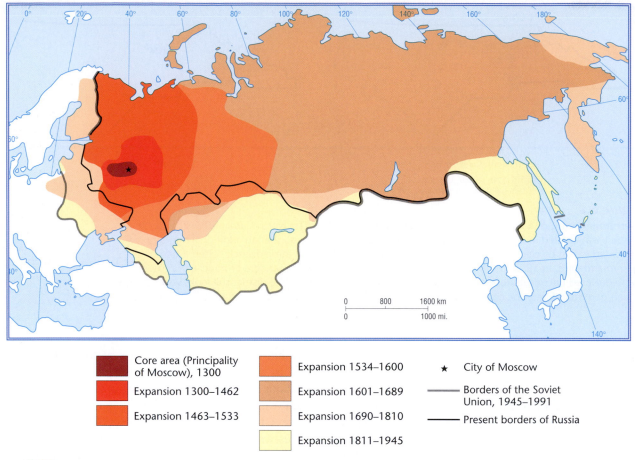

Figure 6.10
Russia developed from a core area. Can you think of reasons why expansion to the east was greater than expansion to the west? What environmental goals might have motivated Russian expansion?

Core area (Principality of Moscow), 1300

Expansion 1300–1462

Expansion 1463–1533

Expansion 1534–1600

Expansion 1601–1689

Expansion 1690–1810

Expansion 1811–1945

★ City of Moscow

Borders of the Soviet Union, 1945–1991

Present borders of Russia

countries, represented by the cities of Madrid and Barcelona, continue to compete for political control and to symbolize two language-based cultures, Castilian and Catalan.

Diffusion of Independence and Innovations

The principles of cultural diffusion can also be applied to a great variety of other political phenomena. Contagious expansion diffusion often operates in the political sphere. It can be seen in the spread of political independence in Africa. In 1914, only two African countries—Liberia and Ethiopia—were fully independent of European colonial or white minority rule. Ethiopia later fell temporarily under Italian control. Influenced by developments in India and Pakistan, the Arabs of North Africa began a movement for independence. Their movement began to gain momentum in the 1950s and swept southward across most of the continent between 1960 and 1965. By 1994, independence had spread into

all remaining parts of the continent, even including the Republic of South Africa, formerly under white minority rule (Figure 6.11).

The diffusion of African self-rule occasionally encountered barriers. Independence spread rapidly in the 1950s and 1960s because most European powers had grown disenchanted with colonialism and viewed their African colonies more as burdens than as assets. Portugal, by contrast, clung tenaciously to its African colonies until a change in government in Lisbon reversed a 500-year-old policy and the colonies were quickly freed. Similarly, France sought to hold onto Algeria, because many European colonists had settled there, but the country nonetheless achieved independence in 1962.

On a quite different scale, political innovations also spread within independent countries. American politics abound with examples of cultural diffusion. A classic case is the spread of suffrage for women, a movement that culminated in 1920 with the ratification of a constitutional

FOCUS ON

Political Boundaries as Barriers to Cultural Diffusion

Political boundaries can strongly affect how we look at the world. For instance, geographers have shown that a political boundary can be a strong barrier against cultural diffusion, against the flow of information from one area to another. A study of schoolchildren in Dals Ed, in Sweden, and Halden, just across the border in Norway, shows that the children can easily recall place-names in their own country but not those of the neighboring country. Although language differences between Sweden and Norway are slight, the border puts a powerful barrier between schoolchildren only miles apart.

When the children of Dals Ed and Halden drew mental maps of both countries, each group showed a marked preference for its own national locations. On the Swedish maps, areas of desirability sloped gently away from Swedish places that the children knew. The nearby Norwegian border looked like a geological fault line. Preference suddenly dropped away.

A partial explanation for this phenomenon is that the children on each side of the border are open to quite different sources of information. The Swedish geographer T. Lundén has analyzed textbooks on both sides of the border and has demonstrated clearly how the geographical content in them differs, always offering the readers more information about us than about them.

Adapted from Gould and White, 1974: 143–146.

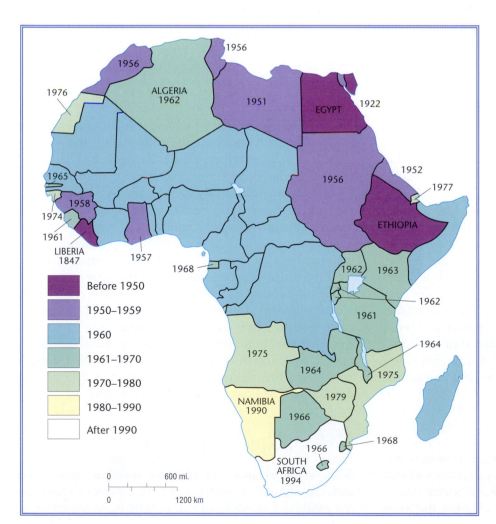

Figure 6.11

Independence from European colonial or white minority rule diffused through Africa. Independence for Africans was an idea first implanted in the northeastern and western reaches of the continent. Between 1959 and 1994, self-rule and independence spread all the way south. **What barriers might have slowed this diffusion, so that 35 years were required for it to run its course?**

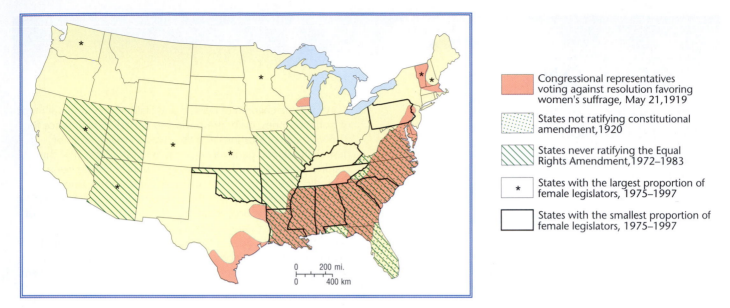

Figure 6.12

The diffusion of suffrage for women in the United States and of the Equal Rights Amendment. The suffrage movement gained national acceptance through a constitutional amendment in 1920. Both the suffrage movement and the campaign for an Equal Rights Amendment (ERA) for women failed to gain approval in the Lower South, an area that also lags behind most of the remainder of the country in the election of women to public office. Compare this map to Figure 1.6. **What might be the barriers to diffusion in the Lower South?** The states failing to ratify the ERA lay mostly in the same area. The ERA movement did not succeed, in contrast to the earlier suffrage movement. (ADAPTED IN PART FROM PAULIN AND WRIGHT, 1932.)

amendment (Figure 6.12). Opposition to women's suffrage was strongest in the Deep South, a region that later exhibited the greatest resistance to ratification of the Equal Rights Amendment and the most reluctance to elect women to public office.

Federal statutes permit, to some degree, laws to be adopted in the individual functional subdivisions. In the United States and Canada, for example, each state and province enjoys broad law-making powers, vested in the legislative bodies of these subdivisions. The result is often a patchwork legal pattern that reveals the processes of cultural diffusion at work. A good example is provided by the movement in the United States to reduce littering by requiring beverage manufacturers to market their products in reusable or deposit containers (Figure 6.13). This innovation encountered barriers and failed to diffuse through the entire country.

Politics and Migration

Very often political events provide the motivation for migration, both voluntary and forced. An excellent example is provided by the breakup of the Soviet Union into 15 independent countries in 1991. During the long

period of Soviet unity, the various national groups within that country had begun to migrate into one another's territories in large numbers. Ethnic Russians had settled in all parts of the Soviet Union, even though only one of the 15 constituent republics was Russian by identity. Likewise, many members of the other 14 major ethnic groups had relocated outside their republics.

When the Soviet Union dissolved, a profound reverse migration set in almost immediately. Ethnic Russians returned to Russia, Estonians to Estonia, Azeris to Azerbaijan, and so on. By 1995, about 2 million ethnic Russians had migrated to Russia. Fully a half-million of these came from recently independent Kazakhstan in Central Asia. In that same period, 150,000 ethnic Kazakhs returned to Kazakhstan from Russia and other former Soviet republics. This process continues to the present day, though the flow of migrants has slowed.

 ## Political Ecology

What is the relationship between political phenomena and the natural habitat? Political culture regions do not exist, nor do political ideas diffuse, in an environ-

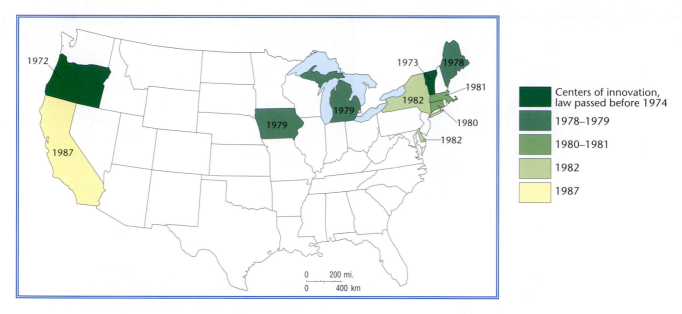

Figure 6.13

The diffusion of state laws requiring deposit or return beverage containers. Two states, one on the Pacific and the other far away in New England, served as the innovation centers. The movement met barriers to further diffusion. The California law of 1987 was far weaker than earlier ones, suggesting a permeable barrier. Beyond these two centers lay absorbing barriers, because no additional states passed such laws. **What were these barriers in the path of diffusion?**

mental vacuum. Spatial variations and the spread of political phenomena often can be linked to terrain, soils, climate, natural resources, and other facets of the physical environment. The term **geopolitics** is often used to describe this influence of the habitat on political entities (although many people now use geopolitics as a synonym for political geography). Conversely, established political authority can be a powerful instrument of environmental modification, providing the framework for organized alteration of the landscape and for environmental protection. In these ways, political entities influence and are influenced by the physical surroundings.

Folk Fortresses

Before modern air and missile warfare, a country's survival was enhanced by some sort of natural protection, such as surrounding mountain ranges, deserts, or seas; bordering marshes or dense forests; or outward-facing escarpments. **Folk fortress** is the name given to such natural strongholds by political geographers. The folk fortress might shield an entire country or only its core area. In either case, a folk fortress was a valuable asset. Surrounding seas have helped shelter the British Isles from invasion for the last 900 years. In Egypt, desert wastelands on east and west insulated the fertile, well-watered Nile Valley core. In the same way, Russia's core area lay

shielded by dense forests, expansive marshes, bitter winters, and vast distances.

> ### Reflecting on **GEOGRAPHY**
>
> The term "Fortress America" has been used by some people to describe the political ecology of the United States. Does the United States have a folk fortress?

Countries without natural defense have often been hard-pressed to maintain their independence. Korea, a land bridge leading from China to Japan, has repeatedly attracted invaders from both directions. Only rarely has Korea achieved unity and full independence. Poland, on the open plains of northern Europe, has been overrun and partitioned many times by hostile neighbors.

Closely related to the concept of the folk fortress is the distribution of terrain. Ideally, a country should have mountains and hills around its edges and plains in the interior (see Focus On: Terrain and Political Geography). Such a pattern not only facilitates defense but also provides a natural unit of enclosed plains as the basis for a cohesive country. Few countries enjoy entirely satisfactory landform patterns, although France—centered on the plains of the Paris Basin and flanked by bordering mountains and hills such as the Alps, Pyrenees, Ardennes, and Jura—

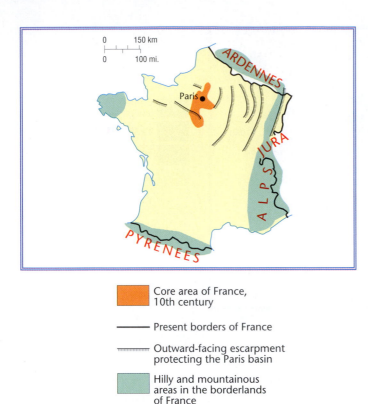

Core area of France, 10th century

Present borders of France

Outward-facing escarpment protecting the Paris basin

Hilly and mountainous areas in the borderlands of France

Figure 6.14

The distribution of landforms in France. Terrain features such as ridges, hills, and mountains offer protection. Outward-facing escarpments formed a folk fortress protecting the core area and capital of France until as recently as World War I. Hill districts and mountain ranges lent stability to French boundaries in the south and southeast.

comes very close to the ideal (Figure 6.14). Mountain-ridge borders are also desirable, because they stand out on the landscape and cross thinly populated country. Rivers, by contrast, prove much less suitable as borders. They often change course and frequently flow through densely settled valleys, creating all sorts of potentially provocative situations for the countries on either bank.

An undesirable arrangement of physical features may disrupt a country's internal unity. A rugged mountain range, a desert, or some other barrier cutting through the middle of the territory forms perhaps the least desirable pattern from the perspective of internal unity. Such barriers disrupt communications and often isolate one part of a country from another. Separatist sentiments grow more easily when shielded by environmental barriers. In addition, internal mountain ranges provide excellent potential guerrilla bases where insurgents can live in relative safety. Peru, which straddles the Andes with fringes of territory in the Amazon Basin and the Pacific coastal lowlands,

faces such a problem. So does Spain, which consists of many plains areas separated by hills and mountains. Both Peru and Spain have problems of internal unity, partly because of their unfavorable physical settings.

Perhaps the best borders of all for independent countries are those marked by seacoasts. Islands and the small continent that hosts Australia provide excellent natural barriers to expansive or acquisitive neighbors. Among others, Iceland, Sri Lanka, and Madagascar have benefited from their island locations. However, island nations are not necessarily free from attacks by neighbors, as the histories of Hawaii, Cuba, and the Philippines show. In addition, disputes still arise among independent countries about the placement of borders in adjacent ocean areas. Peninsular location provides some of the same advantages as islands for such countries as Italy, India, and Turkey, although peninsulas usually prove harder to defend.

Expanding countries often regard coastlines as the logical limits to their territorial growth, even if they belong to other countries. This was true of the United States's drive to the Pacific Ocean in the first half of the nineteenth century, an expansion justified by the doctrine of *manifest destiny.* This doctrine was based on the belief that the Pacific shoreline offered the logical and predestined western border for the United States. A similar doctrine long led Russia to seek expansion in the directions of the Mediterranean and Baltic seas and Pacific and Indian oceans.

The Heartland Theory

Discussions of environmental influence, manifest destiny, and the outward probings of Russia lead naturally to the **heartland theory** of Halford Mackinder (see Profile on page 197). As early as 1904, Mackinder became concerned with the balance of power in the world and in particular with the possibility of world conquest based upon natural habitat advantage. His heartland theory, heavily tinged with *environmental determinism,* held that the continent of Eurasia would be the most likely base from which a successful campaign for world conquest could be launched. Eurasia dwarfs all other continents in size and natural resources and is home to three-fourths of the human race. In examining this huge landmass, Mackinder discerned two environmental regions. The **heartland,** or interior, of Eurasia lies remote from the sea, except for the frozen ocean of the polar north, which functions more as a continuation of the Eurasian landmass (Figure 6.15 on page 196).

The densely populated coastal fringes of Eurasia in the east, south, and west (see Chapter 7), called the **rimland,** form the second great physical-strategic region of Eurasia.

FOCUS ON

Terrain and Political Geography

Berchtesgaden, situated in the Bavarian Alps, lies amid a wreath of high mountains. In the era before modern transportation and communication, these mountains isolated and sheltered the valley, shielding it from both cold winter winds and invading armies.

In this setting, Berchtesgaden developed as an independent principality ruled by a religious order. For six and a half centuries, from 1156 to 1803, Berchtesgaden maintained its independence—three times as long as the United States has existed. The borders of the principality, which followed the surrounding mountain ridges, scarcely changed at all during this long period. Even after Berchtesgaden lost its independence and was annexed by Bavaria and later Germany, most of its mountain-marked border survived as part of the international boundary between Germany and Austria. In this way, terrain and the political pattern are often linked.

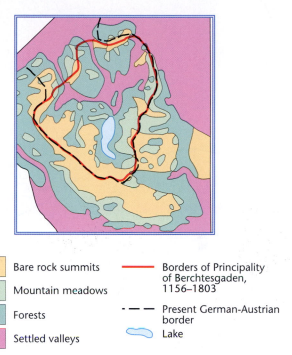

▨ Bare rock summits	⬛ Borders of Principality of Berchtesgaden, 1156–1803
▨ Mountain meadows	
▨ Forests	- - - Present German-Austrian border
▨ Settled valleys	⬯ Lake

Remote from the sea, the heartland was invulnerable to the naval power of the former great rimland empires such as Britain and Japan, but the cavalry and infantry of the heartland could spill out through diverse natural gateways and invade the rimland region. In fact, mounted nomadic warriors had done just that from time immemorial, surging outward to conquer and pillage. The Mongol conquest of China and Tatar depredations in Europe provide historical examples. For this reason, in Mackinder's view, a unified heartland power could probe into the coastlands with impunity, eventually conquering the maritime countries and annexing their navies. This sea power could then be turned against the outlying continents and islands until the entire world was subject to the heartland.

Mackinder believed that the unification of the heartland could best be achieved from the East European Plain, the most densely populated and economically productive part of the heartland. Russia had already achieved that unification at the time he proposed the theory. Mackinder, in effect, predicted Russian conquest of the world, a prospect that became more alarming after the commu-

nist revolution there in 1917. The leaders of rimland empires and the United States employed a policy of containment by fortifying the rimland and fighting numerous wars against outward probes by heartland-based communism. This policy, in no small measure, found its origin in Mackinder's theory.

In this way, a geographer's theory entered the halls of government and influenced strategic decisions for a half-century or more. Overlooked all the while were the fallacies of the heartland theory. Mackinder had overestimated the power potential of the thinly settled Eurasian interior, which consists largely of frozen tundra, parched desert, and expansive forests with sterile soils. He failed to anticipate the role of airborne warfare and ballistic missiles, as well as the inherent economic weakness of the Marxist system. Russia proved unable to hold together its own heartland empire, much less conquer the rimland and world. In the end, Mackinder's heartland theory, influential as it was, belongs to the discredited doctrine of environmental determinism and serves as yet another warning against such simplistic reasoning.

Heartland		Gateways connecting heartland and rimland		Maximum extent of Russian/ Soviet/communist dominance
Rimland		Maximum territorial extent of Russia/Soviet Union, 1945–1990		United States military conflict involvement, 1941–1991
East European Plain		Outer edge of Rimland		

Figure 6.15

Heartland versus rimland in Eurasia. For most of the twentieth century, the heartland, epitomized by the Soviet Union and communism, was seen as a threat to America and the rest of the world, a notion based originally on the environmental deterministic theory of the political geographer Halford Mackinder. Control of the East European Plain would permit rule of the entire heartland, which, in turn, would be the territorial base for world conquest. In the cold war, 1945 to 1990, the United States and its rimland allies sought to counter this perceived menace by a policy of containment—resisting every expansionist attempt by the heartland powers. (AFTER MACKINDER, 1904; AND SPYKMAN, 1944.)

Heartland versus Rimland Today

The heartland-rimland contest today has a far less consequential impact. It has become, as geographer Graham Smith explains, a contest for the political soul of Russia, the world's largest country. Russians today are torn between wanting to join the West—the prosperous, democratic, capitalistic rimland—and a desire to stand apart as a distinctive, hybrid Eurasian people, inward-looking and secure in their heartland folk fortress, which they must defend against Western culture, the Islamic world, and China.

Warfare and Environmental Destruction

Many political actions and decisions have an ecological impact, but perhaps none is as devastating as warfare. "Scorched earth," the systematic destruction of resources, has been a favored practice of retreating armies for millennia. Even military exercises and tests can be devastating. Certain islands in the Pacific were rendered uninhabitable, perhaps forever, by American hydrogen bomb testing in the 1950s. The Persian Gulf War of 1991 included an oil spill of 294 million gallons (1.1 billion liters) covering 400 square miles (1000 square kilometers) in

PROFILE

Halford J. Mackinder

1861–1947

Mackinder developed a fascination for spatial patterns and maps at a young age. At school in England, he was caned by a teacher for drawing maps instead of writing Latin exercises. His interest in geography persisted, and in 1887 he became one of Oxford University's first lecturers in geography.

Much influenced by the scientific geography found in nineteenth-century German universities, Mackinder introduced many of the German concepts into England. Previously, the Royal Geographical Society of London had been interested mainly in exploration rather than in analytical studies and theories. Mackinder's famous heartland theory was first proposed in a scholarly address to the society in 1904 and was later enlarged to book form. He served as a member of Parliament for 12 years, and after World War I he helped redraw the boundaries of Europe. In 1945, he received the Royal Geographical Society's highest honor, the Patron's Medal. His influence on analytical political geography and on the foreign policy decisions of the great powers was very great indeed.

For more information about Mackinder and his work, see Blouet, 1987.

the Gulf waters, with attendant loss of flora and fauna; the burning of oil fields; the mass bulldozing of sand by the Iraqis to make defensive berms, with consequent wind erosion and loss of vegetation; and the solid-waste pollution produced by 500,000 coalition forces in the Arabian desert, including 6 million plastic bags discarded weekly by American forces alone (Figure 6.16).

Clearly, warfare—and especially modern "high-tech" warfare—is environmentally catastrophic. From an ecological standpoint, it does not matter who started or won a war. Everyone loses when such destruction occurs, given the worldwide interconnectedness of the life-supporting ecosystem.

Political Ecology Narrowly Defined

We have used "political ecology" in a very broad context. Increasingly today, in the world at large, the term has a far more restricted meaning. It refers to a form of political activism dealing with the issue of who controls natural resources and who makes the political decisions that impact the habitat. The new political ecology is about power and the environmental consequences of the struggle between haves and have-nots. Activists oppose the mindless destruction of habitats and the displacement of indigenous peoples by those who wield political economic power.

Many countries, including the United States, now have a *Green Party* that pursues a political-ecological agenda. Those less enchanted with politics practice **ecoterrorism,** a violent sabotaging of the activities of the lumber industry, commercial fishing, the development of open lands, and other enterprises seen as ecologically destructive.

Figure 6.16
A Kuwaiti oil field ablaze during the Persian Gulf War, 1991, giving a new meaning to "scorched earth." Severe ecological damage almost invariably accompanies warfare. **Could modern war be waged without such damage?** (NOEL QUIDU/GAMMA LIAISON.)

Politico-Cultural Interaction

How are politics intertwined with the diverse other aspects of culture? Although we learn a great deal from studying how the physical environment and political phenomena interact, we gain an even broader perspective by examining the ties between politics and culture. The growth of independent countries, voting patterns, and other topics that interest political geographers are largely explained in cultural terms. In addition, political decisions often have far-reaching effects on the distribution of such cultural elements as economy, land use, and migration. Indeed, the political organization of territory, both past and present, is revealed to some degree in almost every facet of culture.

The Nation-State

The link between political pattern and culture finds its epitome in the **nation-state,** created when a *nation*—a people of common heritage, memories, myths, homeland, and culture, speaking the same language and/or sharing a particular religious faith—achieve independence as a separate country. Nationality is *culturally* based in the nation-state, and the country's raison d'être lies in that cultural identity. The more the people have in common culturally, the more stable and potent is the resultant

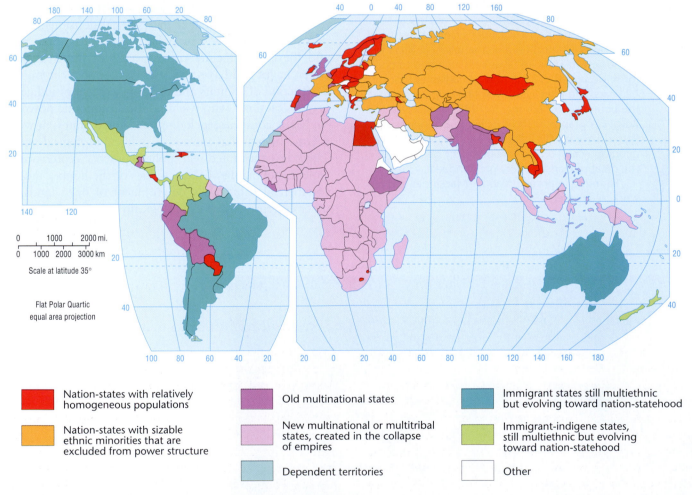

■ Nation-states with relatively homogeneous populations	■ Old multinational states	■ Immigrant states still multiethnic but evolving toward nation-statehood
■ Nation-states with sizable ethnic minorities that are excluded from power structure	■ New multinational or multitribal states, created in the collapse of empires	■ Immigrant-indigene states, still multiethnic but evolving toward nation-statehood
	■ Dependent territories	□ Other

Figure 6.17

Nation-states, multinational countries, and other types. This classification, as is true of all classifications, is arbitrary and debatable. **How would you change it, and why?**

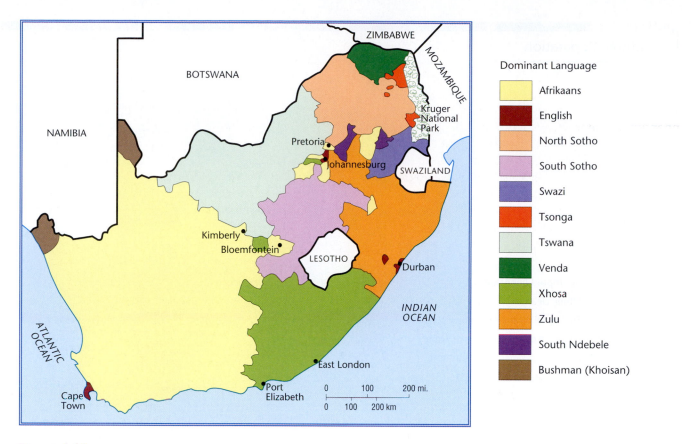

Figure 6.18
Languages of the Republic of South Africa, a multinational state. The mixture includes 10 native tribal tongues and 2 languages introduced by settlers from Europe.

nationalism. Although some experts regard the nation-state as a modern aberration, largely a product of the nineteenth and twentieth centuries, such entities, at least on the tribal level, have characterized much of human history and may be linked to instinctual territoriality.

Examples of modern nation-states include Germany, Sweden, Japan, Greece, Korea, Armenia, and Finland (Figure 6.17). Each of these countries has a culturally homogeneous population, with only small minority groups. Their homogeneity represents a *centripetal force*. Many other independent countries also function as nation-states because power rests in the hands of a dominant, nationalistic cultural group, but sizable ethnic minorities reside in the national territory as second-class citizens. They present a *centrifugal force* disrupting the country's unity. Israel is such a nation-state, a Jewish country by definition trying to cope with a sizable, restive, underprivileged Arab minority. Similarly, many of the new nation-states carved out of the defunct Soviet Union and Yugoslavia, such as Estonia, Georgia, and Serbia, contain large, territorially compact ethnic minorities, as do some much older nation-states, including France and China. In sum, we can define a nation-state as an independent country that exists as the result of the efforts and desires of a culturally homogeneous and powerful majority.

The Multinational Country

Many independent countries—the large majority, in fact—are not nation-states. Instead, they possess some other raison d'être and usually have federal rather than strong central governments. Switzerland, Canada, the United Kingdom, South Africa (Figure 6.18), and Belgium provide examples of older multinational countries. A much larger number have arisen in recent decades, as a result of the collapse of European-based colonialism, mainly in Africa. Political boundaries drawn in colonial times without regard to the integrity of cultural or tribal groups passed down, unaltered, to the newly independent countries. As a result, their populations are often quite diverse.

Ethnic Separation

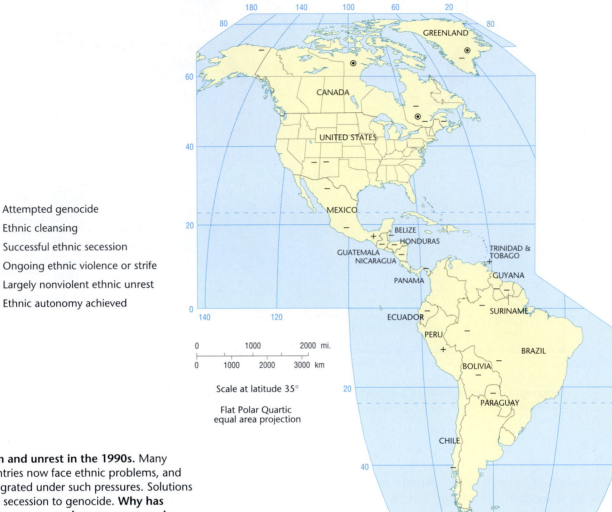

- • Attempted genocide
- × Ethnic cleansing
- ○ Successful ethnic secession
- + Ongoing ethnic violence or strife
- − Largely nonviolent ethnic unrest
- ◉ Ethnic autonomy achieved

Figure 6.19

Ethnic separatism and unrest in the 1990s. Many independent countries now face ethnic problems, and some have disintegrated under such pressures. Solutions have ranged from secession to genocide. **Why has ethnic conflict become so much more common in recent times?** (SOURCES: SMITH, 1992: 140–142; OLDALE, 1990; AND LEAN, 1990: 50–51.)

Ethnic Separatism

Ethnic groups are cultural minorities living in multinational countries. Those that inhabit ethnic *homelands* (see Chapter 5) often seek greater autonomy or even full independence as nation-states (Figure 6.19). This separatist mood has touched multinational countries and nation-states alike. Even some old and traditionally stable multinational countries have felt the effects of this movement, including Canada and the United Kingdom. Some multi-

national countries collapsed under the pressure, splintering into multiple nation-states. The Soviet Union, Yugoslavia, and Czechoslovakia provide examples. Certain other countries discarded the *unitary* form of government and adopted an ethnic-based *federalism,* in hopes of preserving unity. The impact of ethnic nationalism ranges from simple unrest to insurgencies, forced deportations, attempted genocides, and successful secessions.

Francophones in Canada represent a cultural-linguistic minority group seeking secession. Approximately 7 million

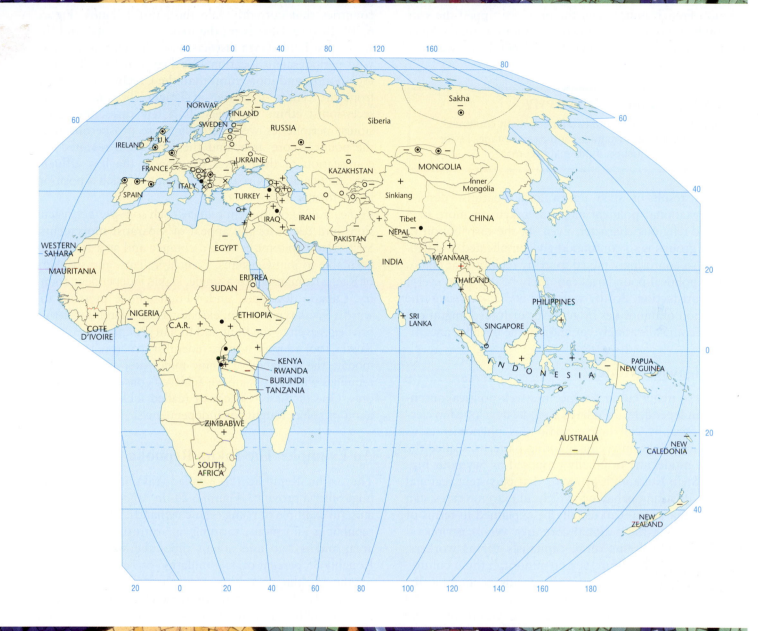

French Canadians form a large part of that country's population, concentrated in the province of Québec. Descended from French colonists who immigrated in the 1600s and 1700s, these *Canadiens* lived under English or Anglo-Canadian rule and domination from 1760 until well into the twentieth century. Even the provincial government of Québec long remained in the hands of the English. A political awakening eventually allowed the French to gain control of their own homeland province, and as a result Québec differs in many respects from the rest of Canada. The laws of Québec retain a predominantly French influence, whereas the remainder of Canada adheres to English common law. The provincial flag, adopted in 1948, preserves the old fleur-de-lis symbol of the French monarchy. French is the sole legal language of Québec, and visible use of English was largely expunged. In several elections, a sizable minority among the French-speaking population favored independence for Québec, and many Anglo-Canadians emigrated from the province. The issue remains unresolved. In 1995, over half of the

French-speaking electorate voted for independence but the non-French minority in the province tipped the vote narrowly in favor of continued union with Canada. Since then, however, the campaign for independence seems to have weakened.

> ### Reflecting on **GEOGRAPHY**
> Should Canada split into two independent countries? What would the advantages and disadvantages be for independent Québec, if this split occurred?

As a result of such unrest and separatist desires, the international political map has taken on more of a linguistic-religious character. Even so, the distribution of cultural groups is so confoundingly complicated and peoples are so confusingly mixed in many regions that ethnographic political boundaries can rarely be drawn to everybody's satisfaction. Border wars and *ethnic cleansing* (the elimination of minorities by genocide or forced migration) could become alarmingly common in the decades ahead.

The Cleavage Model

Why do so many cultural minorities seek political autonomy or independence? Perhaps a *model* developed in electoral geography can help explain this phenomenon as well as shed light on regional voting patterns. Called the **cleavage model** and originally proposed by Seymour Lipset and Stein Rokkan, it proposes that persistent regional patterns in voting behavior (which, in extreme cases, can presage separatism) can usually be explained in terms of tensions pitting the national core area versus peripheral districts, urban versus rural, capitalists versus workers, and power-group culture versus minority ethnic culture. Not infrequently, these tensions coincide geographically, with the result that the core area monopolizes power and wealth, is more urbanized, and links government to the ruling elite culture. Ethnic minorities, then, often live in peripheral, largely rural, and less affluent areas, excluded from the power structure.

The great majority of ethnic separatist movements shown in Figure 6.19, and particularly those that have moved beyond unrest to violence or secession, involve groups living in national peripheries, away from the core area of the country. Every republic that seceded from the defunct, Russian-dominated Soviet Union lay on the borders of that former country. Similarly, the Slovenes and Croats, who withdrew from the former Yugoslavia, occupied border territories peripheral to Serbia and the national capital at Belgrade. Northern Ireland lies on the periphery of the United Kingdom, as does rebellious Kur-

distan in relation to Iraq, Iran, Syria, and Turkey—the countries that currently rule the Kurdish lands (Figure 6.20). Restive Tibet is on the margins of China, and the Arab West Bank–Gaza districts under Israeli rule are likewise peripheral in location (see Figure 6.19). Slovakia, long poorer and more rural than the Czechia and remote from the center of power at Prague, became another secessionist ethnic periphery. In a few cases, the secessionist peripheries were actually more prosperous than the political core area, and the separatists resented the confiscation of their taxes to support the less affluent core. Slovenia and Croatia both occupied such a position in the former Yugoslavia.

Federalist government reduces such *core-periphery* tensions and decreases the appeal of separatist movements. Switzerland epitomizes such a country and as a result has been able to join Germans, French, Italians, and speakers of Raeto-Romansh into a single, stable independent country. Canada developed under Francophone pressure toward a Swiss-type system, extending considerable self-rule privileges even to the Inuit and Indian groups of the north. Russia, too, adopted a more federalist structure to accommodate the demands of ethnic minorities, and 31 ethnic republics within Russia have achieved considerable autonomy. One of these, Chechnya (called Ichkeria by its inhabitants) has fought for independence.

An Example: The Sakha Republic

The Sakha Republic (also called Yakutia), in Russia's huge Siberia province (Figure 6.21 on page 204), provides a useful example of rising ethnic demands. The peripheral republic is enormous, forming one-fifth of Russia's land area, and is two and a half times the size of Alaska. Roughly 35 percent of its population of 1 million consists of ethnic Sakha, or Yakuts, a people of Turkic origin (see Chapter 4). Russians, who outnumber the Sakha people in the republic, are concentrated in 10 urban areas, while the Sakha are dominant in the rural/small-town core of the republic.

The demands of the Sakha led to a declaration of "state sovereignty" in 1990. The republic now has its own elected president and parliament, a flag and coat-of-arms (Figure 6.22 on page 205), and a constitution. It has attained some measure of economic independence, especially authority over mineral rights, and the republic can prohibit nuclear testing on its territory. A survey in 1995 revealed that 72 percent of all ethnic Yakuts felt more loyalty to Sakha than to Russia. Surprisingly, a third of all Russians living in the republic expressed this same loyalty.

The Sakha Republic does not seek independence from Russia. Still, its autonomy represents the embryo of a

Figure 6.20

Kurdistan. This mountainous homeland of the Kurds now lies divided among several countries. The Kurds, numbering 25 million, have lived in this region for millennia. They seek independence and have waged guerrilla war against Iran, Iraq, and Turkey, but so far, independence has eluded them. **What might cause so large and populous a nation to fail to achieve independence?** (SOURCE: OFFICE OF THE GEOGRAPHER, U.S. DEPARTMENT OF STATE.)

Main roads

Borders of Sakha

Russian-dominated towns and cities

Other settlements

Ethnic Sakha heartland

Figure 6.21

The Republic of Sakha, a part of Russia, has achieved considerable autonomy, as a result of ethnic considerations. For its location in Russia, see Figure 6.19. **What would hinder the republic if it sought full independence?** (SOURCE: JORDAN AND JORDAN-BYCHKOV, 2001: 4.)

Figure 6.22

Coat of arms of the ethnic Republic of Sakha in Russia. The inscription is bilingual—Sakhan and Russian—and the picture of the horse rider is taken from ancient primitive rock art. **Why might this ancient image have been used in the coat of arms of a republic seeking increased autonomy?** (SOURCE: COURTESY OF THE GOVERNMENT OF THE REPUBLIC OF SAKHA.)

country. Ongoing Russian emigration from Sakha further complicates the matter. It is increasingly difficult, here as elsewhere in the modern world, to determine exactly what an independent country is. Words such as *sovereignty* have become blurred in meaning.

Political Imprint on Economic Geography

The *core-periphery* economic contrasts implicit in the *cleavage model* clearly reveal that the internal spatial arrangement of the independent country influences economic patterns, presenting a cultural interaction of politics and economy. In addition, laws differ from one country to another, and these laws often have an impact on economic land use. As a result, political boundaries can take on an economic character as well.

For example, the U.S.-Canadian border in the Great Plains crosses an area of environmental and cultural sameness. The land and people on both sides of the boundary are similar. Yet the presence of the border, representing two different bodies of law and regulations, fostered differences in agricultural practices. In the United States, an act passed in the 1950s encouraged sheep raising by guaranteeing an incentive price for wool. No such law was passed in Canada. As a result, sheep became far more numerous on the American side of the border, while Canadian farmers devoted more attention to hogs. Figure 6.23 illustrates the difference.

The Corruption Index

Culture and politics interact in diverse other ways. In some countries, for example, corruption is rampant among governmental officials, and bribe taking is common. Often, these countries possess a *traditionalistic* political ideology, described earlier. In certain other countries, corruption is rare, and these often have a *moralistic* ideology. Different cultures tolerate different levels of government corruption.

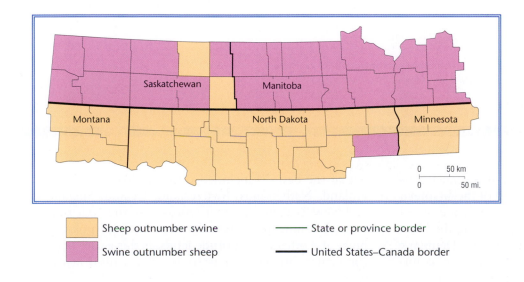

Sheep outnumber swine
Swine outnumber sheep
State or province border
United States–Canada border

Figure 6.23

The political impact on economy. Government intervention can be seen in the choice of livestock in the border area between the United States and Canada. Sheep are more numerous than swine on the U.S. side of the boundary, partly because of government-backed price incentives for wool. The map reflects conditions in the 1960s. Since then, the contrast has essentially disappeared. **Why might that have happened?** (SOURCE: REITSMA, 1971: 220–221. SEE ALSO REITSMA, 1988.)

Government Corruption

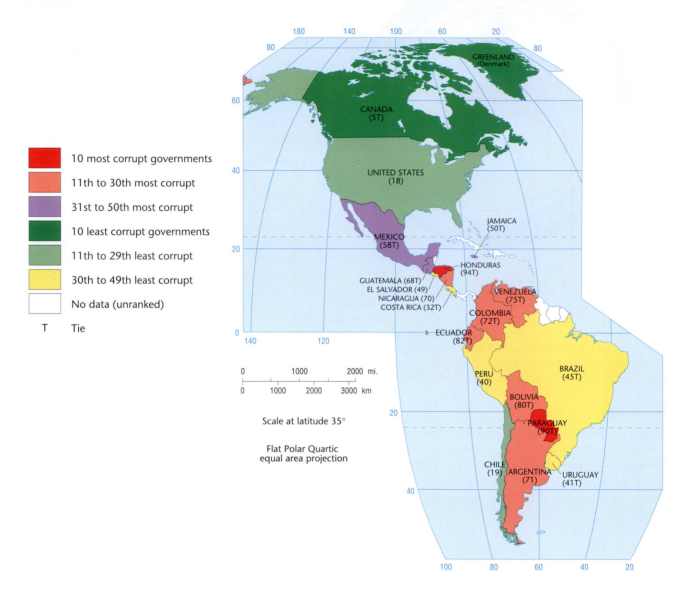

Figure 6.24

The "perceived corruption index," a measure of governmental corruption in 99 countries. What might explain this pattern? (SOURCE: TRANSPARENCY INTERNATIONAL, BERLIN WEB SITE.)

Transparency International (see the listing in Political Geography on the Internet at the end of the chapter), an independent agency based in Berlin, has measured corruption in 99 different countries, providing the basis for a highly interesting map (Figure 6.24). Denmark (including Greenland), ranked as the least corrupt country, and Cameroon, in Africa, as the worst. The remainder of the best 10 included Canada, Norway, Sweden, Finland, Netherlands, Switzerland, Iceland, Singapore, and New Zealand. In other words, 7 of the 10 least corrupt governments lay wholly or partially in polar, subpolar and other high-latitude lands. Is this a case of environmental influence, or is some other causal factor at work?

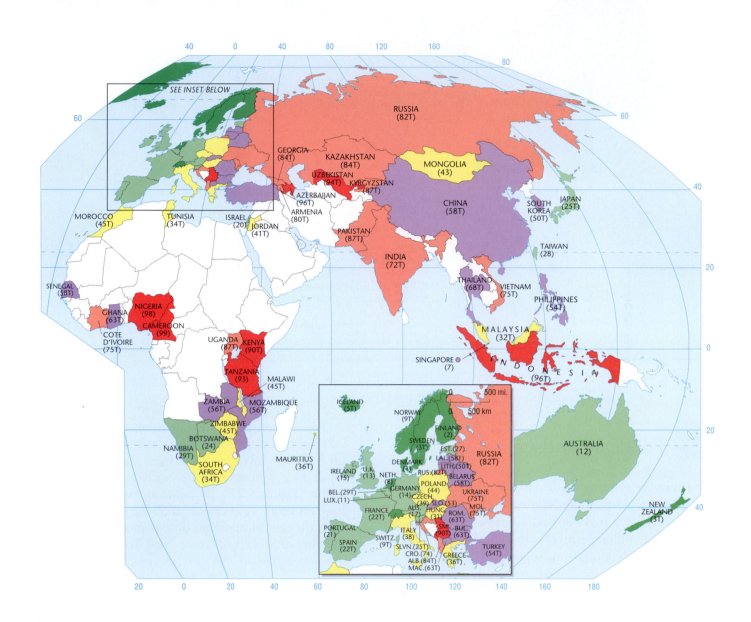

Islamic Law

As we saw in Chapter 3, politics is often intertwined with religion. Some countries function as *theocracies*. In many others, internal religious divisions acquire a political expression. Perhaps the best example is Nigeria, divided between a Muslim north and a Christian/animist south (Figure 6.25 on the next page). In the past few years, all of the states of northern Nigeria have come under the legal code of Islam, as printed in the Koran—to the delight of most Muslim inhabitants but the displeasure of local Christian minorities. The country might fragment along this new politico-religious border. At the very least, this movement strengthens the centripetal forces already at work in this troubled country.

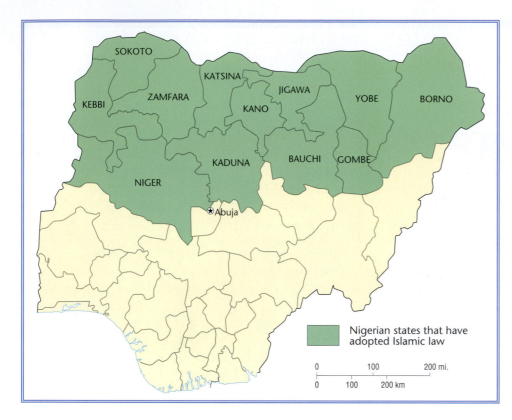

Nigerian states that have adopted Islamic law

Political Landscapes

What are the visible manifestations of political geography? Does a political landscape exist? Various types of political decision making find a visible expression, and the cultural landscape reveals the imprint of politics in diverse ways. Nationalism, separatism, the legal code, and central authority can all be highly visible, as can the boundaries separating independent countries. All of these, collectively, constitute the political landscape.

Imprint of the Legal Code

Many laws find their way into the cultural landscape. Among the most noticeable are those that regulate the land-surveying system, because the law often requires that land be divided in specific geometric patterns. As a result, political boundaries can become highly visible (Figure 6.26). In Canada, the laws of the French-speaking province of Québec encourage land survey in long, narrow parcels, but most English-speaking provinces, such as Ontario, adopted a rectangular system. Thus, the political border between Québec and Ontario can be spotted easily from the air.

Legal imprint can also be seen in the cultural landscape of urban areas. In Rio de Janeiro, height restrictions on buildings have been enforced for a long time. The result is a waterfront lined with buildings of uniform height (Figure 6.27). By contrast, most American cities have no height restrictions, allowing skyscrapers to dominate the central city. The consequence is a jagged skyline, like that of San Francisco or New York City.

Physical Properties of Boundaries

Perhaps no more purely human creation exists than a demarcated political boundary, and these can be strikingly visible. Geographers Dennis Rumley and Julian Minghi speak of *border landscapes* and have edited a book with that name. As a general rule, political borders are most visible where tight restrictions limit the movement of people between neighboring countries. Sometimes such boundaries are even lined with cleared strips, barriers, pillboxes, tank traps, and other obvious defensive installations. At the opposite end of the spectrum are international borders, such as that between the United States and Canada, that are unfortified, thinly policed, and in many places very nearly invisible. Even so, undefended borders of this type are usually marked by regularly spaced boundary pillars or cairns and by customs

Figure 6.26
Can you find the United States–Mexico border in this picture? Why does the cultural landscape so vividly reveal the political border? The scene is near Mexicali, the capital of Baja California Norte. (Courtesy of Terry G. Jordan-Bychkov.)

houses and colorfully striped guardhouses at crossing points (Figure 6.28 on the next page).

The visible aspect of international borders is surprisingly durable, sometimes persisting centuries or even millennia after the boundary becomes a relic. Ruins of boundary defenses, some dating from ancient times, are common in certain areas. Hadrian's Wall in England marks the northern border during one stage of Roman occupation and parallels the modern border between England and Scotland. The Great Wall of China provides another reminder of past boundaries (Figure 6.29 on the next page).

A quite different type of boundary, marking the territorial limits of urban street gangs, is evident in the central areas of many American cities. The principal device used by these teenage gangs to mark their turf is spray-paint graffiti. Geographers David Ley and Roman Cybriwsky studied this phenomenon in Philadelphia. They found borders marked by externally directed, aggressive epithets, taunts, and obscenities, placed there for the benefit of neighboring gangs. A street gang of white youths, for example, plastered its border with a black gang's neighborhood with slogans such as "White Power," "Do Not Enter [District] 21-W, —," and similar graffiti painted on walls. The gang's "core area," its "home corner," contains internally supportive graffiti, such as "Fairmount

Figure 6.27
Legal height restrictions, or their absence, can greatly influence urban landscapes. Kuala Lumpur, a city in Malaysia, lacks such controls, and its skyline is punctuated by spectacular skyscrapers, the tallest in the world. In Rio de Janeiro, by contrast, height restrictions allow the natural environment to provide the "high-rises." (Left: S. Thinakaran/AP Photo; Right: Martin Wendler/ Peter Arnold, Inc.)

Figure 6.28
Even peaceful, unpoliced international borders often appear vividly in the landscape. Sweden and Norway insist on cutting a swath through the forest to mark their common boundary. **Why would they do this?** (COURTESY OF TERRY G. JORDAN-BYCHKOV.)

Rules" or a roster of gang members. Thus a perceptive (and courageous) observer can map the gang territories on the basis of these political landscape features.

The Impress of Central Authority

The attempt to impose centralized government appears in many facets of the landscape (see Focus On: Politics, Religion, and Cultural Landscape). Railroad and highway patterns focused on the national core area, and radiating like the spokes of a wheel to reach the hinterlands of the country, provide good indicators of central authority. In Germany, the rail network developed largely before unification of the country in 1871. As a result, no focal point stands out. On the other hand, the superhighway system of autobahns, encouraged by Hitler as a symbol of national unity and power, tied the various parts of the Reich to such focal points as Berlin and the Ruhr industrial district.

"Military landscapes" also abound, directly linked to central authority's defense of the country and often concentrated in border districts. The military presence can

Figure 6.29
The Great Wall of China is probably the most spectacular political landscape feature ever created and one of the few made by humans that is visible from outer space. The wall, which is 1500 miles (2400 kilometers) long, was constructed over many centuries by the Chinese in an ultimately unsuccessful attempt to protect their northern boundary from adjacent tribes of nomadic herders. **Can you think of comparable modern structures?** (COURTESY OF TERRY G. JORDAN-BYCHKOV.)

FOCUS ON

Politics, Religion, and Cultural Landscape

Political reshaping of the cultural landscape can take many forms. Consider a remarkable event in Afghanistan in the year 2001, before the collapse of the ruling Taliban government. A fundamentalist Islamic theocracy, the Taliban declared that several ancient Buddhist images, carved into cliffs and dating from the era before Islam originated, were sacrilegious idols. Said the mullah Muhammad Omar, a Taliban official, "These false idols have been gods of the infidels."

The Taliban decided to destroy these huge statues, which were as much as 2000 years old, represented the world's most significant Buddhist statuary heritage, and dominated the cultural landscape in one valley of Bamiyan Province. Despite worldwide protests, the demolition was carried out as planned, bringing the cultural landscape into visual compliance with extremist Muslim fundamentalism but destroying one of the world's great art treasures. Photo below on the left shows the statuary before the destruction; photo on the right, after.

(LEFT: PAUL ALMASY/CORBIS; RIGHT: REUTERS/CORBIS.)

result in fairly sizable areas being cleared of their permanent inhabitants to provide space for defensive installations and maneuvers.

The visibility of provincial borders within a country can reflect the central government's strength and stability. Stable, secure countries, such as the United States, often permit considerable display of provincial borders. Most state boundaries within the United States are marked with signboards or other features announcing the crossing. By contrast, unstable countries, where separatism threatens national unity, often suppress such visible signs of provincial borders.

Reflecting on **GEOGRAPHY**

What visible imprints of the Washington, D.C.–based central government can be seen in the political landscape of the United States?

National Iconography on the Landscape

The cultural landscape is rich in symbolism and visual metaphor, and political messages are often conveyed through such means with an intensity that varies greatly from one country to another. In the United States, flags

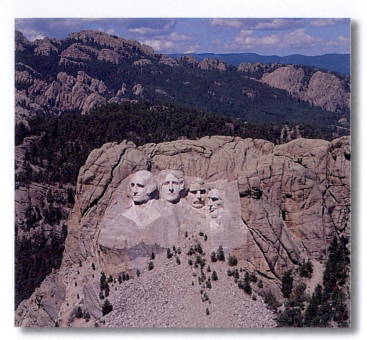

Figure 6.30

Mount Rushmore, in the Black Hills of South Dakota, presents a highly visible expression of American nationalism, an element of the political landscape. **If political landscapes are created by an elite, in an effort to legitimize and justify their control over territory, then who might disapprove of this monument?** (BROWNIE HARRIS/THE STOCK MARKET.)

and eagles convey clear messages to citizen and visitor alike. Statues of national heroes or heroines and of symbolic figures such as the goddess Liberty or Mother Russia form important parts of the political landscape, as do assorted monuments (Figure 6.30). The elaborate use of national colors can be very powerful visually. Landscape symbols such as the Rising Sun flag of Japan, the Statue of Liberty in New York harbor, and the Latvian independence pillar in Riga (which stood unmolested throughout half a century of Russian-Soviet rule) evoke deep patriotic emotions. The sites of heroic (if often futile) resistance against invaders, as at Masada fortress in Israel and the Alamo in Texas, prompt similar feelings of nationalism.

Some geographers feel that political iconography on the landscape derives from an elite, dominant group within a country's population and that the purpose is to legitimize or justify its power and control over an area. The dominant group seeks both to rally emotional support and to arouse fear in potential or real enemies. As a result, the iconographic political landscape is often controversial or contested, representing only one side of an issue. Look again at Figure 6.30. The area in which Mount Rushmore stands, the Black Hills, is sacred to

local American Indian tribes, but whites seized it long ago. How might these Indians, the Sioux, perceive this monument? Are any other political biases contained in it? Cultural landscapes are always complicated and subject to differing interpretations and meanings, and political landscapes are no exception.

Conclusion

Political spatial variations—from local voting patterns to the spatial arrangement of international power blocs—add yet another dimension to the complex human mosaic. In particular, independent countries function as vital functional culture regions. They help shape many other facets of culture. Political culture regions constantly change as political innovations ebb and flow across their surfaces. Political phenomena as varied as the nation-state, separatist movements, women's suffrage, and the territorial expansion of countries move along the paths of diffusion.

Cultural ecology helps us understand the links between systems of power and the physical environment. Countries do not exist in an environmental vacuum. The spatial patterns of landforms often find reflection in boundaries, core areas, folk fortresses, and global strategies. Cultural interaction underscores the relationships between politics and other facets of culture. Harmony and stability within countries often depend on relative cultural homogeneity of the population. The interaction of politics and culture is also revealed in the economy, and politics leaves diverse imprints on the cultural landscape.

 Political Geography on the Internet

European Union
http://www.europa.eu.int

Information about the 15-member supranational organization that is, increasingly, reshaping the internal political geography of Europe.

Political Geography Specialty Group, Association of American Geographers
http://garnet.acns.fsu.edu/~dpurcell/pgsg1.html

This site provides details about the activities and meetings of specialists in political geography.

United Nations
http://www.un.org

Search the worldwide organization with a membership that includes the large majority of independent countries.

SEEING GEOGRAPHY

Why are some parts of the world fragmented into many small states and homelands?

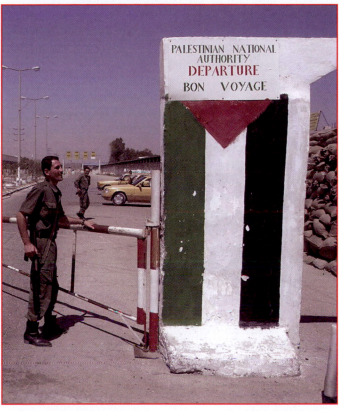

The border between Israel and the Gaza Strip, part of the Palestinian Arab homeland.

Israel–Gaza Strip Border

Are you a "border junkie"? Do approaching and crossing a political border—particularly one that divides countries hostile or unfriendly to each other—raise your pulse level and get your adrenalin flowing? Does the sight of gun-toting border guards, the prospect of a search of your vehicle, and the presence of barriers at once alarm and fascinate you? Then you are a border junkie. Hope you enjoy your "high."

Here you stand at the border crossing of Erez between Israel and the Palestinian Arab–controlled Gaza Strip in the year 2001. It is a dangerous place. The guards are tense and ready for anything. So, in this manner, landscape images demand cultural interactive explanations, imply culture regions, and require cultural diffusion. The various themes of cultural geography work together, are inseparable, and constitute a functioning whole.

Various geographically based emotions cause your border junkie status. You are about to enter a different functional culture region. The people on the other side are different religiously, linguistically, and in standard of living. The cultural interactions that produced this border are numerous, complex, and in some measure ancient. The political landscape leaves no doubt of the existence of the border or culture region. It is a very special place, indeed, where two nations claim the same land.

The site contains politically diverse information about such ventures as peacekeeping and conflict resolution.

Transparency International, Berlin
http://www.transparency.org/

Check the latest government corruption index (CPI) and bribe-payers index (BPI), which rank the governments of most independent countries—a sobering eye-opener.

Sources

Ardrey, Robert. 1966. *The Territorial Imperative: A Personal Inquiry into the Animal Origins of Property and Nations.* New York: Atheneum.

Blouet, Brian W. 1987. *Halford Mackinder: A Biography.* College Station: Texas A & M University Press.

Brunn, Stanley D. 1974. *Geography and Politics in America.* New York: Harper & Row.

Elazar, Daniel J. 1994. *The American Mosaic: The Impact of Space, Time, and Culture on American Politics.* Boulder, Colo.: Westview Press.

Gould, Peter, and Rodney White. 1974. *Mental Maps.* Baltimore: Penguin.

Jordan, Bella Bychkova, and Terry G. Jordan-Bychkov. 2001. *Siberian Village: Land and Life in the Sakha Republic.* Minneapolis: University of Minnesota Press.

Jordan-Bychkov, Terry G., and Bella Bychkova Jordan. 2002. *The European Culture Area: A Systematic Geography,* 4th ed., Lanham, Md.: Rowman & Littlefield, Chapter 7.

Lean, Geoffrey, et al. 1990. *Atlas of the Environment.* New York: Prentice-Hall.

Ley, David, and Roman Cybriwsky. 1974. "Urban Graffiti as Territorial Markers." *Annals of the Association of American Geographers* 64: 491–505.

Lipset, Seymour M., and Stein Rokkan (eds.). 1967. *Party Systems and Voter Alignments: Cross-National Perspectives.* New York: Free Press.

Mackinder, Halford J. 1904. "The Geographical Pivot of History." *Geographical Journal* 23: 421–437.

Morrill, Richard L. 1981. *Political Redistricting and Geographic Theory.* Washington, D.C.: Association of American Geographers, Resource Publications.

Oldale, John. 1990. "Government-Sanctioned Murder." *Geographical Magazine* 62: 20–21.

O'Reilly, Kathleen, and Gerald R. Webster. 1998. "A Sociodemographic and Partisan Analysis of Voting in Three Anti–Gay Rights Referenda in Oregon." *Professional Geographer* 50: 498–515.

Ó Tuathail, Gearóid. 1996. *Critical Geopolitics.* Minneapolis: University of Minnesota Press.

Paulin, C., and John K. Wright. 1932. *Atlas of the Historical Geography of the United States.* New York: American Geographical Society and the Carnegie Institute.

Reitsma, Hendrik J. 1971. "Crop and Livestock Production in the Vicinity of the United States–Canada Border." *Professional Geographer* 23: 216–223.

Reitsma, Hendrik J. 1988. "Agricultural Changes in the American-Canadian Border Zone, 1954–1978." *Political Geography Quarterly* 7: 23–38.

Rumley, Dennis, and Julian V. Minghi (eds.). 1991. *The Geography of Border Landscapes.* London: Routledge.

Sack, Robert D. 1986. *Human Territoriality: Its Theory and History.* Studies in Historical Geography, No. 7. Cambridge: Cambridge University Press.

Smith, Dan. 1992. "The Sixth Boomerang: Conflict and War," in Susan George (ed.), *The Debt Boomerang.* London: Pluto Press.

Smith, Dan, et al. 1997. *The State of War and Peace Atlas,* 3rd ed. New York: Penguin.

Smith, Graham. 1999. "Russia, Geopolitical Shifts and the New Eurasianism." *Transactions of the Institute of British Geographers* 24: 481–500.

Spykman, Nicholas J. 1944. *The Geography of the Peace.* New York: Harcourt Brace.

Ten Recommended Books on Political Geography

(For additional suggested readings, see The Human Mosaic *web site:* www.whfreeman.com/jordan*)*

Dalby, Simon, and Gearóid Ó Tuathail (eds.). 1998. *Rethinking Geopolitics.* London: Routledge. Fifteen contributors to this postmodernist collection address questions of political identity and popular culture, state violence and genocide, militarism, gender and resistance, cyberwar and mass media. They suggest that political geography needs to be reconceptualized for the twenty-first century.

Demko, George J., and William B. Wood (eds.). 1994. *Reordering the World: Geopolitical Perspectives on the Twenty-First Century.* Boulder, Colo.: Westview Press. A collection of essays dealing with post–cold war political geography—the "new world order" in which the power dominance of the United States seems unchallenged.

Herb, Guntram H., and David H. Kaplan (eds.). 1999. *Nested Identities: Nationalism, Territory, and Scale.* Lanham, Md.: Rowman & Littlefield. A collection of essays by 14 leading political geographers focusing on the geographical issue of territoriality, through the device of case studies of troubled countries and regions at different scales.

Hooson, David (ed.). 1994. *Geography and National Identity.* Oxford: Blackwell. Essays examine the connection between identity and homeland in a wide variety of settings and argue that the globalization of culture has strengthened the bonds between place and identity.

Martis, Kenneth C. 1989. *The Historical Atlas of Political Parties in the United States Congress, 1789–1989.* New York: Macmillan. An electoral atlas that reveals shifting and enduring cleavages in the voting by members of the U.S. Senate and House of Representatives.

O'Loughlin, John (ed.). 1994. *Dictionary of Geopolitics.* Westport, Conn.: Greenwood Press. A basic reference book on political geography.

Shelley, Fred M., J. Clark Archer, Fiona M. Davidson, and Stanley D. Brunn. 1996. *Political Geography of the United States.* New York: Guilford Press. A historical survey of the role of U.S. regionalism in shaping the American political system.

Wallerstein, Immanuel. 1991. *Geopolitics and Geoculture: Essays on the Changing World-System.* Cambridge: Cambridge University Press. A collection of Wallerstein's essays that link the collapse of the Soviet Union to the end of U.S. hegemony around the world.

Williams, Colin H. (ed.). 1993. *The Political Geography of the New World Order.* London: Belhaven. A collection of essays that explore the geopolitical consequences of the collapse of the Soviet Union and the rising importance of Europe and Japan.

Zelinsky, Wilbur. 1988. *Nation into State: The Shifting Symbolic Foundations of American Nationalism.* Chapel Hill: University of North Carolina Press. The United States as a political presence in the cultural landscape.

A Political-Geographical Journal

Political Geography (formerly *Political Geography Quarterly*, name changed in 1992). The only English-language journal devoted exclusively to political geography. Published by Butterworth Scientific Ltd., Sevenoaks, Kent, England. Volume 1 appeared in 1982.

Answers

Figure 6.3

A, Armenia; *B*, Azerbaijan; *C*, Iran; *a*, Nagorno-Karabakh; *b*, the Nakhichevan Autonomous Republic; *c*, the Okhair Eskipara enclave; *d*, Sofulu enclave; *e*, Kyarki enclave; and *f*, Bashkend enclave.

A street scene in the large city of Kolkata, India. (JAYANTA SHAW/REUTERS.)
Turn to Seeing Geography *on page 257 for an in-depth analysis of the above question.*

GEODEMOGRAPHY
Peopling the Earth

Population geography, or **geodemography**, includes the spatial and ecological aspects of population, including density, distribution, fertility, gender, living standard, health, age, nutrition, mortality, and mobility. All of these demographic characteristics vary from one region or country to another, helping shape the mosaiclike pattern of the world. We deal here with some of the most basic attributes of the human condition, and some cultural geographers, such as David Hooson, regard geodemography as "the most essential geographical expression."

The most essential demographic fact is that well over 6 billion people inhabit the Earth today. In the Bible, God instructed humans to "be fruitful and multiply," and that we have certainly done. In the process, we have become very different from one another in a great variety of demographic ways. These differences provide the subject matter of geodemography. As always, we will approach our study using the five themes of cultural geography.

 ## Demographic Regions

In what ways do demographic traits vary regionally? How is the theme of culture region expressed in terms of population characteristics?

Population Distribution and Density

If the 6,250,000,000 inhabitants of the Earth were evenly distributed across the land area, the **population density** would be about 108 persons per square mile (42 per square kilometer). However, people are very unevenly distributed, creating huge disparities in density. Greenland, for example, has 0.1 person per square mile (0.04 per square kilometer),

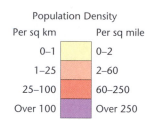

Population Density

Per sq km   Per sq mile

0–1   0–2

1–25   2–60

25–100   60–250

Over 100   Over 250

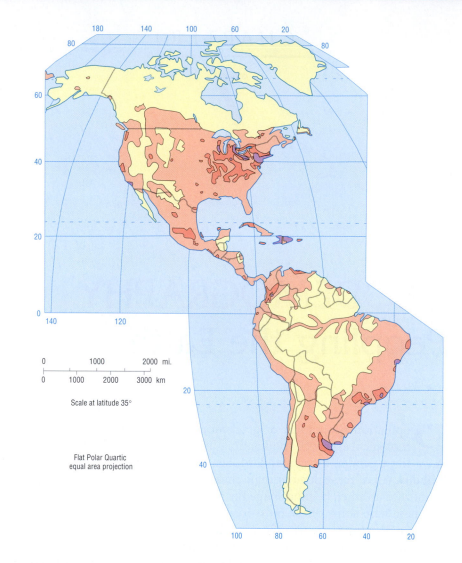

Scale at latitude 35°

Flat Polar Quartic
equal area projection

Figure 7.1

Population density in the world. Try to imagine the diverse causal forces—physical, environmental, and cultural—that have been at work over the centuries to produce this complicated spatial pattern. It represents the most basic cultural geographical distribution of all. (SOURCES: POPULATION REFERENCE BUREAU; STATISTICAL ABSTRACT OF THE UNITED STATES; UNITED NATIONS POPULATION INFORMATION NETWORK; AND WORLD POPULATION DATA SHEET.)

whereas Bangladesh has 2300 per square mile (890 per square kilometer) (Figure 7.1).

If we consider the distribution of people by *continents,* we find that 72.7 percent of the human race lives in Eurasia—Europe and Asia. The continent of North America is home to only 7.9 percent of all people; Africa to 13.2 percent; South America to 5.7 percent; and Australia and the Pacific islands to 0.5 percent. If we consider population distribution by political units, we find that 21 percent of all humans reside in China; 17 percent in India; and only 4.6 percent in the United States (Table 7.1). In fact, one out of every 50 humans lives in just one valley of one province of China: the Red Basin of Sichuan.

We can divide population density into categories such as *thickly settled* areas, which have 250 or more persons per square mile (100 or more per square kilometer); *moderately settled* areas, with 60 to 250 persons per square mile (25 to 100 per square kilometer); *thinly settled* areas,

inhabited by 2 to 60 persons per square mile (1 to 25 per square kilometer); and *largely unpopulated* areas, with fewer than 2 persons per square mile (fewer than 1 per square kilometer). These categories represent formal demographic regions based on the single trait of population density. As Figure 7.1 shows, a fragmented crescent of dense settlement stretches along the western, southern, and eastern edges of the huge Eurasian continent. Two-thirds of the human race is concentrated in this crescent, which contains three main population clusters: eastern Asia, the Indian subcontinent, and Europe. Outside of Eurasia, only scattered districts are densely settled. Despite our image of a crowded world, thinly settled regions are much more extensive than thickly settled ones and appear on every continent. Thin settlement characterizes the northern sections of Eurasia and North America, the interior of South America, most of Australia, and a desert belt through North Africa and Arabia into the heart of Eurasia.

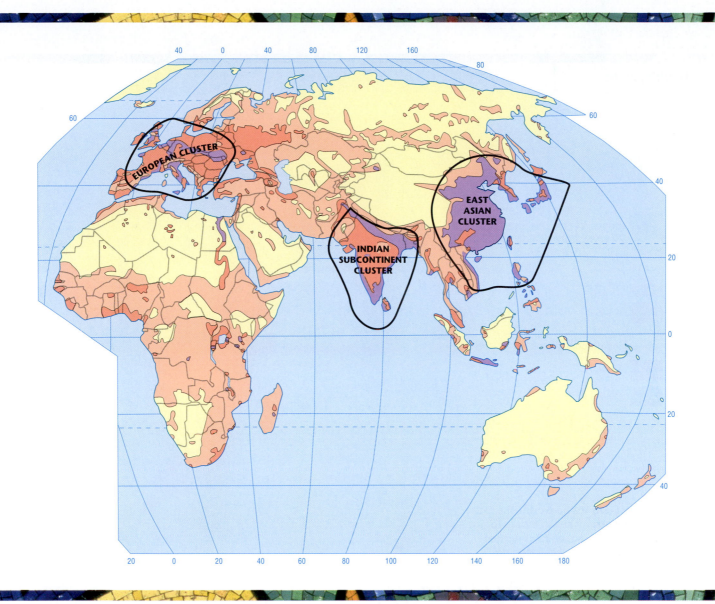

TABLE 7.1   The Ten Most Populous Countries, 2000–2001

Country	Population	As Percentage of World Total	People per square mile	People per square kilometer
China	1,295,000,000	21.2	350	135
India	1,030,000,000	16.8	811	313
United States*	281,422,000	4.6	76	29
Indonesia	212,200,000	3.5	289	116
Brazil	170,100,000	2.8	52	20
Pakistan	150,600,000	2.5	490	189
Russia	144,000,000	2.3	22	9
Bangladesh	129,000,000	2.1	2305	890
Japan	126,900,000	2.1	870	336
Nigeria	123,300,000	2.0	346	134

*The U.S. population by mid-2002 had risen to an estimated 286 million.

(*Source:* World Population Data Sheet, 2001 and 2002; selected national censuses, 2000, 2001.)

Fertility Rate

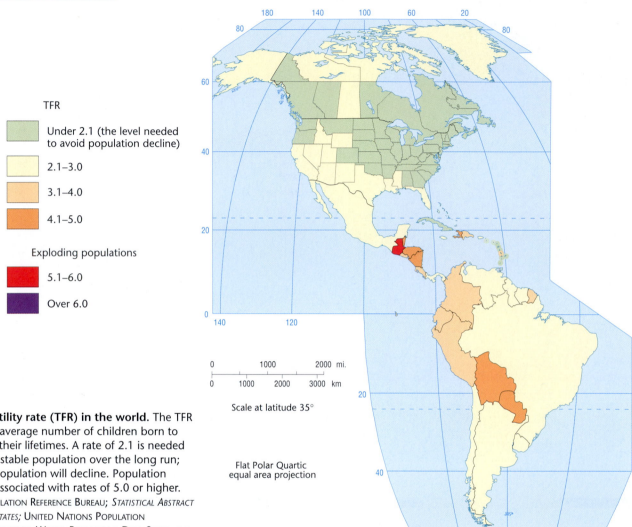

TFR

- Under 2.1 (the level needed to avoid population decline)
- 2.1–3.0
- 3.1–4.0
- 4.1–5.0

Exploding populations

- 5.1–6.0
- Over 6.0

Scale at latitude 35°

Flat Polar Quartic equal area projection

Figure 7.2

The total fertility rate (TFR) in the world. The TFR indicates the average number of children born to women over their lifetimes. A rate of 2.1 is needed to produce a stable population over the long run; below that, population will decline. Population explosion is associated with rates of 5.0 or higher. (SOURCES: POPULATION REFERENCE BUREAU; *STATISTICAL ABSTRACT OF THE UNITED STATES;* UNITED NATIONS POPULATION INFORMATION NETWORK; WORLD POPULATION DATA SHEET; AND UNITED NATIONS POPULATION DIVISION.)

Although population density allows us to view the distribution of people, it does not tell us anything about standard of living, overpopulation, or underpopulation. Some of the most densely populated areas in the world have the highest standards of living—and even suffer from labor shortages (for example, the major industrial areas of western Europe). In certain other cases, regions designated as thinly settled may actually be severely overpopulated, marginal agricultural lands. Although 1000 persons per square mile (400 per square kilometer) is a "dense" population for a farming area, it is "sparse" for an industrial district. For this reason, *physiological density*—the density beyond which people cease to be

nutritionally self-sufficient using their particular *adaptive strategy*—would be far more useful as an index of overpopulation, although it is almost impossible to measure. Americans, for example, consume far more food and other resources than do most other people in the world. Our physiological density would be at the breaking point if we did not annex the resources of much of the rest of the world.

Density, whether absolute or physiological, is a static concept. It conceals the changes that occur constantly, in particular, pronounced regional differences in population growth or decline. To gain a dynamic perspective, we need to consider the geography of demographic change.

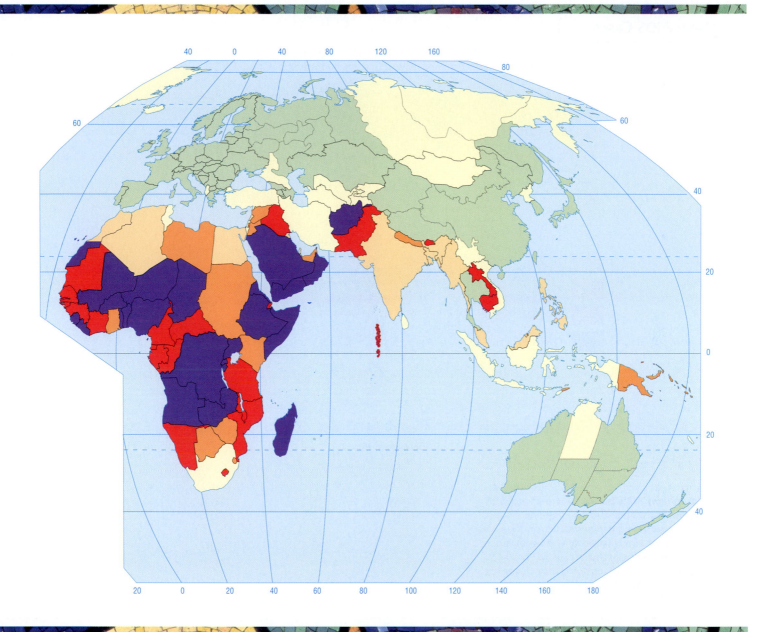

Patterns of Natality

Births can be measured by several geodemographic methods. The older way was simply to calculate the **birthrate:** the number of births per year per thousand population.

More revealing is the **total fertility rate,** or **TFR,** measured as the average number of children born per woman during all her reproductive years. The TFR is better because it focuses on the female segment of the population, reveals family size, and gives an indication of future developments. A TFR of 2.1 is needed to produce a stabilized population eventually, one that does not increase or decrease. Once achieved, this condition is called **zero population growth.**

The TFR varies markedly from one part of the world to another, revealing a vivid geography (Figure 7.2). In Europe, the fertility rate now stands at 1.4, and many countries are experiencing population decline. The lowest TFR is 1.1 in Bulgaria and Czechia, followed by 1.2 in eight other European countries plus Russia. Every country

New AIDS Cases

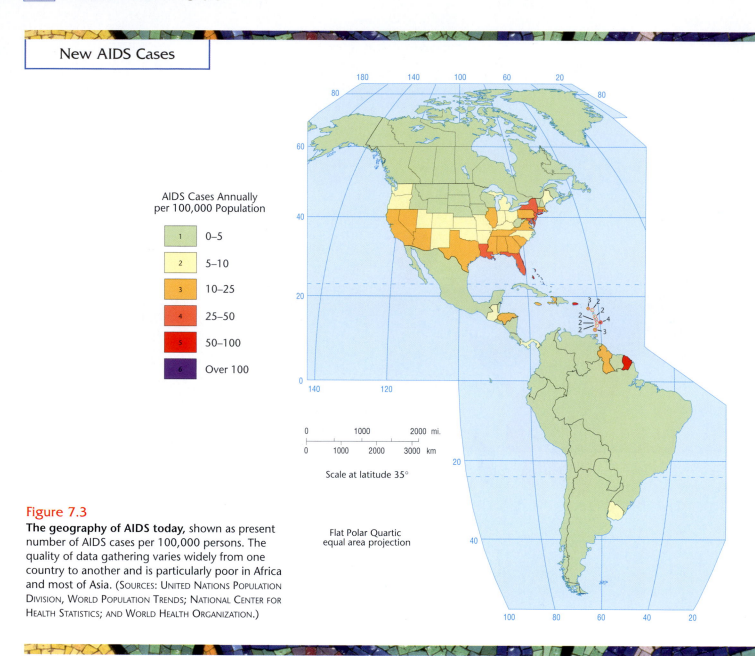

AIDS Cases Annually
per 100,000 Population

1	0–5
2	5–10
3	10–25
4	25–50
5	50–100
6	Over 100

Scale at latitude 35°

Flat Polar Quartic
equal area projection

Figure 7.3

The geography of AIDS today, shown as present number of AIDS cases per 100,000 persons. The quality of data gathering varies widely from one country to another and is particularly poor in Africa and most of Asia. (SOURCES: UNITED NATIONS POPULATION DIVISION, WORLD POPULATION TRENDS; NATIONAL CENTER FOR HEALTH STATISTICS; AND WORLD HEALTH ORGANIZATION.)

with a rate of 2.0 or lower will eventually experience population decline, unless the TFR increases abruptly.

By contrast, sub-Saharan Africa has the highest TFR (5.8) of any sizable part of the world, led by Niger with 7.5, Somalia with 7.0, and Burkina Faso with 6.8. Elsewhere in the world, only Oman, on the Arabian Peninsula, can rival the African rate.

The Geography of Mortality

Another way to assess demographic change is to analyze **death rates:** the number of deaths in a year per 1000 population. Such a study reveals both similarities to and differences from the map of TFR. The highest death rates occur in sub-Saharan Africa, the worst area in the world for life-threatening diseases. By contrast, the American tropics generally have rather low death rates, as is also true of the desert belt across North Africa, the Middle East, and central Asia. In these regions, the preponderantly young population depresses the death rate. Because of its much older population, most of Europe—including Russia—displays a somewhat higher death rate. Australia, Canada, and the United States, which continue to attract mostly young immigrants, have low death rates.

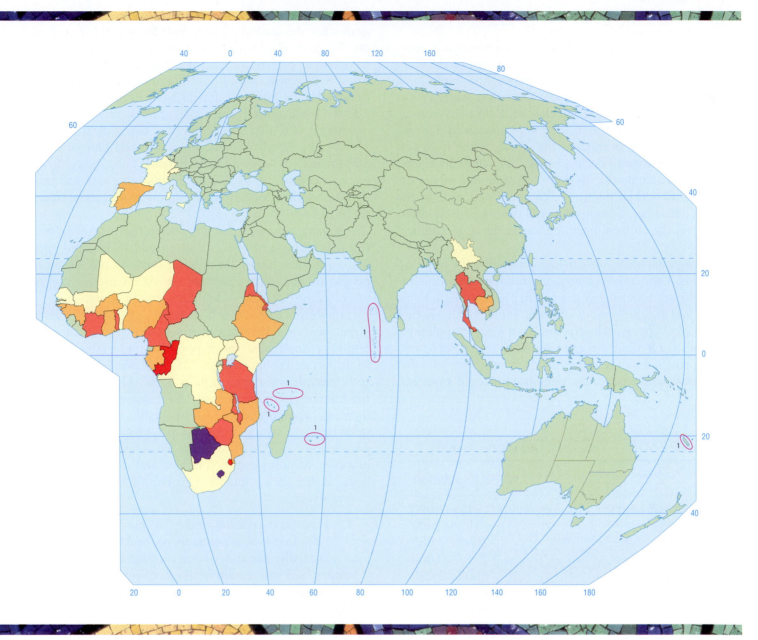

Perhaps the tropical African zone of high mortality is linked to the fact that primates, including human beings, evolved as biological species there. Nature, ever seeking a balance, developed effective diseases to control human population in the region where our species originated. Human migration out of Africa occurred so relatively recently and rapidly, about 60,000 years ago, that on other continents we temporarily escaped many of the disease and predator controls of our original homeland. Also, shifting climatic patterns imposed a great desert belt between the outward-diffusing human race and our African source, blocking the spread of diseases of the humid tropics. The latest great epidemic to threaten humankind, AIDS, apparently also developed in tropical Africa and shows the highest incidence there (Figure 7.3). Unlike many other fatal diseases of the African tropics, AIDS has a proven ability to take root in temperate lands. Even so, 70 percent of the 36 million HIV+ persons in the world live in sub-Saharan Africa.

Death comes in different forms geographically. In the developed world, most people die of age-induced degenerative conditions, such as heart disease, or from maladies caused by industrial pollution of the environment. Many types of cancer fall in the latter category. By contrast, contagious diseases are the leading cause of death in poorer countries.

Population Explosion

When considered together, the spatial contrasts in population density, TFR, and mortality reveal one of the epic problems of the modern age: the **population explosion**, the dramatic increase in world population since 1900. The crucial element triggering this explosion has been a dramatic decrease in the death rate, particularly for infants and children, in most of the world, without an accompanying universal decline in the TFR. In many traditional cultures, only two or three offspring in a family of six to eight children might live to adulthood, and when improved health conditions allowed more of the children to survive, the cultural norm encouraging large families persisted.

On a global scale, we can easily describe the population crisis. Until very recently, the number of people in the world has been increasing geometrically, doubling in shorter and shorter periods of time. Table 7.2 shows the progression. The overall effect of even a few population doublings is startling. An example of geometric progression is provided by the legend of the king who was willing to grant any wish to the person who could supply a

TABLE 7.2	World Population Growth
Year	**World Population**
40,000 B.C.	1,500,000
8000 B.C.	10,000,000
Birth of Christ	200,000,000
1000	275,000,000
1300	380,000,000
1500	450,000,000
1650	500,000,000
1750	700,000,000
1800	910,000,000
1850	1,200,000,000
1900	1,600,000,000
1950	2,600,000,000
1960	3,000,000,000
1965	3,200,000,000
1970	3,610,000,000
1975	4,000,000,000
1980	4,400,000,000
1985	4,850,000,000
1990	5,300,000,000
2000	6,067,000,000
2002	6,250,000,000
2112 (estimated)	7,000,000,000

grain of wheat for the first square of his chessboard, two grains for the second square, four for the third, and so on. To cover all 64 squares and win, the candidate would have had to present a cache of wheat larger than today's worldwide wheat crop. Looked at another way, it is estimated that 61 billion humans have lived in the entire 200,000-year period since the species *Homo sapiens* originated. Of these, 6.25 billion (or almost exactly 10 percent) are alive today. Think of that! One of every 10 humans who ever lived on Earth is alive today! If we were to consider only those humans who survived into adulthood, the proportion alive today would come closer to 20 percent!

Humans reproduced at an extraordinarily modest rate throughout most of history, but around 1700 rapid population growth began. At present, some 83 million more people are born each year than die. At the present rate of increase, the population doubles every 51 years.

Some scholars foresaw long ago that an ever-increasing population would eventually present difficulties. The most famous pioneer observer of population growth, Thomas Malthus (see Profile on page 226) published *An Essay on the Principles of Population* in 1798. He believed that the human ability to multiply far exceeds our ability to increase food production. Consequently, Malthus maintained that "a strong and constantly operating check on population" will necessarily act as a natural control on numbers. Malthus regarded famine and war as inevitable because they curb population growth (Figure 7.4).

He wrote:

I think I may fairly make two postulata.
First, that food is necessary to the existence of man.
Secondly, that the passion between the sexes is necessary, and will remain nearly in its present state. . . .
Assuming, then, my postulata as granted, I say, that the power of population is indefinitely greater than the power in the earth to produce subsistence for man.
Population, when unchecked, increases in a geometrical ratio. Subsistence only increases in an arithmetical ratio. A slight acquaintance with numbers will show the immensity of the first power in comparison of the second.

The adjective *Malthusian* entered the English language to describe the dismal future Malthus foresaw.

Or Population Implosion?

But was Malthus right? From the very first, his ideas were controversial. The founders of communism, Karl Marx and Friedrich Engels, blamed poverty and starvation on

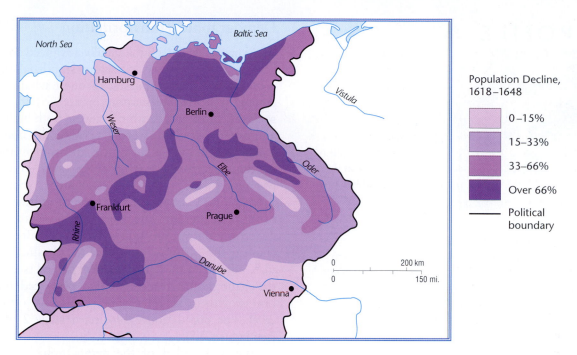

Figure 7.4

War as a device for population control in central Europe, 1618–1648. Thomas Malthus regarded war as inevitable to help control population growth. He would understand this map, which reveals how effective war can be in destroying people. The Thirty Years' War, with its attendant killing, starvation, and disease, drastically reduced the population in some central European provinces. Population density was greatly altered. **What might be the impact on society of such horrendous population loss?** (AFTER *WESTERMANNS GROSSER ATLAS*, 1956: 107.)

the evils of society, further suggesting that when times were especially hard, the poor found ways to achieve birth control.

Others question whether the world, even today, is overpopulated (see Focus On: Is the World Really Overcrowded?). And, as we noted earlier, some countries today experience population decline. The European Baltic coun-

tries of Estonia and Latvia lost 13 percent and 11 percent, respectively, of their populations between 1989 and 2001.

Many other countries with growing populations have achieved significant decreases in the growth rate. Vietnam, for example, reduced its TFR from 4.0 in 1987 to 2.7 a decade later, and southeastern Vietnam had a TFR of 1.9 in 1997. India hopes to achieve a TFR of 2.1—the

FOCUS ON

Is the World Really Overcrowded?

Those who fear overpopulation often conjure up the specter of a world in which people are elbow to elbow, with no open space left. How crowded is the present world, really? If all of humanity stood in such a crowd, how much area would be covered?

Allowing 4 square feet (0.37 square meter) for each human, the present world population of 6.25 billion would

require about 25 billion square feet, or roughly 900 square miles (2330 square kilometers). This is the size of one typical county in the American Midwest. Amazingly, even at that size, the world population is taxing natural resources to the utmost.

Adapted from Bunge, 1973: 288.

PROFILE

Thomas R. Malthus

1766–1834

Born in the shire of Surrey, England, Malthus studied theology at Cambridge and became an ordained clergyman. While still a curate, he began to write his essay on population. Gradually, writing and lecturing became his major interests. In 1805, he was appointed a professor of modern history and political economy at Haileybury College in England, a position he held until his death. Long before most scholars were concerned with overpopulation, Malthus warned of it. His famous treatise, *An Essay on the Principle of Population,* was published in 1798. Karl Marx, Charles Darwin, and many others read and commented on his work. Malthus rejected most artificial birth-control techniques as theologically unacceptable, approving only delayed marriage and moral restraint. He believed warfare, famine, and disease would solve the problem if people failed to seek a more humane solution. In recent decades, his ideas have received renewed attention as the world experiences a population crisis.

For more information about Malthus and his influence, see the books coedited by Dupâquier and Fauve-Chamoux (in the Sources section) and by Coleman and Schofield (in Ten Recommended Books on Population Geography).

replacement level—by 2010 and zero population growth by 2045.

As we enter the new millennium, the fact is that the world's population is growing more slowly than before. The world's TFR has fallen to 2.9. Although many of Malthus's concerns remain valid, and although Malthusianists still predict famine, pestilence, and doom, things are just not playing out the way he expected. One demographer even declared that "the population explosion is over." Others toss around such terms as *demographic collapse* and *population implosion.* All this leads us to the phenomenon known as the demographic transformation.

Reflecting on GEOGRAPHY

Was Thomas Malthus correct? If so, why? If not, why not?

Demographic Transformation

All industrialized, technologically advanced countries have achieved low fertility rates and stabilized or declining populations, having passed through what is called the **demographic transformation** (Figure 7.5). In *preindustrial societies*, birth and death rates were both high, leading to almost no population growth. With the coming of the *industrial era*, medical advances and improvements in diet set the stage for a drop in death rates. Human life expectancy in the industrialized countries soared from an average of 35 years in the eighteenth century to 75 years or more at present. The result was population explosion as fertility outran mortality. Eventually, after a lag, a decline in the birthrate followed the decline in the death rate. Finally, in the *postindustrial period* (see Chapter 9), the demographic transformation produced zero population growth or actual decline (Figure 7.6 on pages 228–229). The population explosion is stage 2 of the model (see Figure 7.5).

Stages 3 and 4 of the demographic transformation require effective methods of birth control. Traditionally, in some cultures, *infanticide*—the killing of newborns—served as the principal method of birth control. *Abortion*, almost as controversial a technique, is still used in some parts of the world. Far more common today are various contraceptive devices (Figure 7.7 on page 230).

Age Distributions

Some countries have overwhelmingly young populations, with close to half of their people under 15 years of age. Benin is such a country, with 49 percent in that age category, as are some nations in Latin America, Africa, and tropical Asia (Figure 7.8 on pages 232–233). The proportion for all of sub-Saharan Africa is 44 percent. Others, generally the countries that industrialized early, have a great preponderance of people in the over 15–under 65 age bracket. A growing number of affluent countries have remarkably aged populations. In Sweden, for example, fully 17 percent of the people have now passed the traditional retirement age of 65, and many other European countries are not far behind. What a contrast emerges when we compare Europe with Africa, Latin America, or parts of Asia, where the average person never even lives to age 65. In Mauritania, Niger, Afghanistan, Guatemala, and many other countries, only 2 to 3 percent of the people have reached that age. Very different cultures result in populations that have disproportionate numbers of young or aged people, adding another component to the human mosaic. Geographers Tracey Skelton and Gill Valentine have edited a book called *Cool Places*, a first attempt to study public places and other locales disproportionately shaped by the presence of young people.

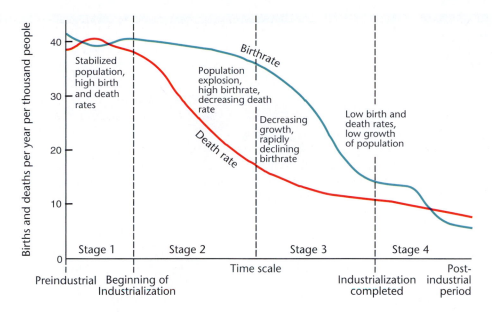

Figure 7.5

The demographic transformation as a graph. The "transformation" occurs in several steps, as the industrialization of a country progresses. Initially, in stage 2, the death rate declines rapidly, causing a population explosion as the gap between the number of births and deaths widens. Then, in stage 3, the birthrate begins a sharp decline. The transformation ends when, in stage 4, both birth and death rates have reached low levels, by which time the total population is many times greater than at the beginning of the transformation. In the postindustrial phase, population decline eventually begins. **Why does the gap between birth and death rates occur during industrialization?**

Age structure also differs spatially within individual countries. For example, rural populations in the United States and many other countries are usually older than those in urban areas. The flight of young people to the cities has left some rural counties in the rural midsection of the United States with populations 45 years or older in median age. Some warm areas of the United States have become retirement havens for the elderly; parts of Arizona and Florida, for example, have populations far above average in age. Communities such as Sun City near Phoenix, Arizona, legally restrict residence to the elderly. In Great Britain, coastal districts have a much higher proportion of elderly than does the interior, causing the map to resemble a hollow shell and suggesting that the aged often migrate to seaside locations when they retire. These, then, would be the age antipodes of Skelton and Valentine's *Cool Places.*

A very useful graphic device for comparing age characteristics is the **population pyramid** (Figure 7.9 on page 234). Careful study of such pyramids not only reveals the past progress of birth control but also allows geographers to predict future population trends. Youth-weighted pyramids, broad at the base, suggest the rapid growth typical of the population explosion. Those excessively narrow at the base represent countries approaching population stability or in demographic decline.

Geography of Gender

Although the human race is divided almost evenly between females and males, geographical differences do occur in the **sex ratio:** the numerical ratio between men and women. Recently settled areas typically have more males than females, as is evident in parts of Alaska, northern Canada, and tropical Australia (Figure 7.10 on pages 236–237). At the latest census, males constituted 53 percent of Alaska's inhabitants. By contrast, Mississippi's population was 52 percent female, reflecting in part the emigration of young males seeking better economic opportunity elsewhere. Some poverty-stricken parts of South Africa are as much as 59 percent female. The population pyramid is also useful in showing gender ratios (see Figure 7.9).

Daphne Spain refers to these as *gendered spaces,* which she finds in homes, in schools, at work, and sometimes regionally. In other words, males and females are

Annual Population Change

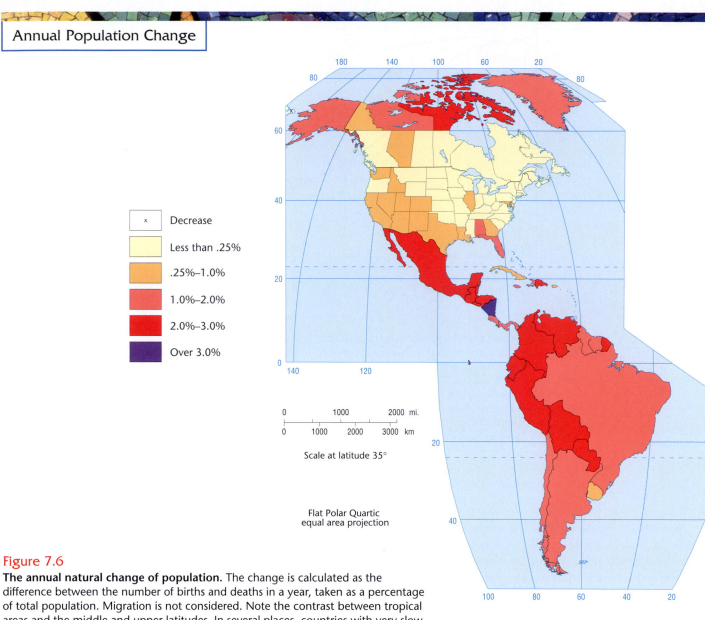

Decrease

Less than .25%

.25%–1.0%

1.0%–2.0%

2.0%–3.0%

Over 3.0%

0   1000   2000 mi.

0   1000   2000   3000   km

Scale at latitude 35°

Flat Polar Quartic
equal area projection

Figure 7.6

The annual natural change of population. The change is calculated as the difference between the number of births and deaths in a year, taken as a percentage of total population. Migration is not considered. Note the contrast between tropical areas and the middle and upper latitudes. In several places, countries with very slow increase border areas with extremely high growth. **How could Africa, a continent so afflicted with epidemic diseases, still have a high rate of natural increase?** (SOURCES: POPULATION REFERENCE BUREAU; *STATISTICAL ABSTRACT OF THE UNITED STATES;* UNITED NATIONS POPULATION INFORMATION NETWORK; AND WORLD POPULATION DATA SHEET.)

often spatially segregated, with attendant inequality of status, access to knowledge, and well-being. Some cultures impose gendered space more vigorously than others; in Muslim countries, for example, women face many restrictions on where they may go. Gender-specific place taboos occur in most cultures, as on the Mount Athos Peninsula in Greece, where Orthodox Christian monastic orders bar entry to all women and, indeed, to females of any mammal species.

Other causal forces also influence the geography of gender. Prolonged wars reduce the male population. A disturbing tendency exists in certain countries, most notoriously China and India, to engage in female-specific infanticide or abortion, which results from a culturally

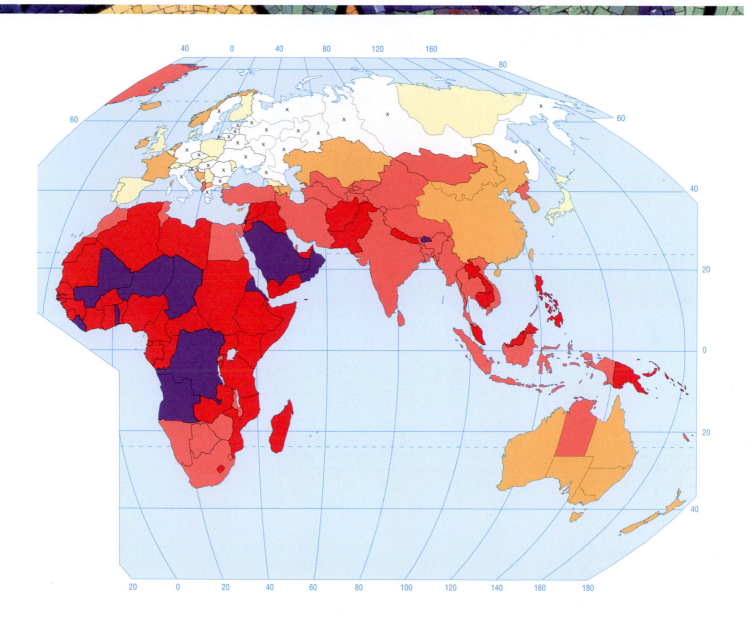

based preference for male offspring. Ultrasound devices are now available even to rural peasants in China that allow gender identification of fetuses. About 100,000 such devices were in use as early as 1990 in China; and by the middle of that decade there were 121 males for every 100 females among children two years of age or younger. The sex ratio in China is being radically changed, and a profound gender imbalance already exists there. In India, too, there were only 927 girls for each 1000 boys in 2001. That ratio had earlier dropped from 962 in 1981 to 945 in 1991, a trend that is obviously continuing. Gender-specific abortion is most prevalent in northern India—where, for example, the 2001 census found only 793 girls for each 1000 boys in Punjab state.

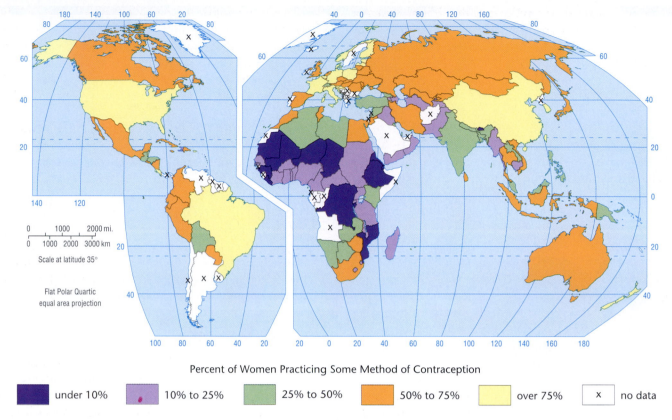

Percent of Women Practicing Some Method of Contraception

| under 10% | 10% to 25% | 25% to 50% | 50% to 75% | over 75% | x no data |

Figure 7.7

The geography of contraception in the modern world, as measured by the percentage of women using devices of any sort. Contraception is much more widely practiced than abortion, but cultures differ greatly in their level of acceptance. Several different devices are included. (Source: World Population Data Sheet.)

Standard of Living

We can use various demographic traits to assess *standard of living* and look at it geographically. Figure 7.11 on pages 238–239 represents one simple attempt to map living standards, using the **infant mortality rate:** a measure of how many children per 1000 die before reaching one year of age. Many experts believe that the infant mortality rate is the best single index of living standards, because it reveals many different factors: health, nutrition, sanitation, access to doctors, availability of clinics, education, ability to obtain medicines, and adequacy of housing. A vivid geographical pattern is revealed by the infant mortality rate. Nowadays, we often hear of "north versus south" in terms of prosperous, developed, midlatitude countries versus poor, underdeveloped, tropical nations.

An even better measure of living standards, or quality of life, is the United Nations *Human Development Index,* which combines literacy, life expectancy, education, and wealth (Figure 7.12 on pages 240–241). The highest possible score is 1.000, and the two top-ranked countries are Canada and Norway. All 25 of the lowest ranked countries lie in Africa.

Diffusion in Population Geography

How does demography relate to the theme of cultural diffusion? Two examples will show the connection. Epidemic diseases, which of course influence morality rates, represent *contagious diffusion* in its most basic form. The migration of people from one place to another, altering population densities, offers the purest type of *relocation diffusion.*

Migration

Humankind is not tied to one locale. Our species apparently evolved in Africa, and ever since we have proved remarkably able to adapt culturally to new and different physical environments. We have made ourselves at home in all but the most inhospitable climates, shunning only such places as ice-sheathed Antarctica and the shifting sands of Arabia's "Empty Quarter." Our permanent habitat extends from the edge of the ice sheets to the seashores, from desert valleys below sea level to high mountain slopes. This far-flung distribution is the product of migration.

For those people who migrate, the process generally ranks as one of the greatest events of their lives. Even prehistoric migrations often remain embedded in folklore for centuries or millennia (Figure 7.13 on page 242). Recognizing the fundamental importance of migration, geographers have long devoted much attention to it. Geographer Yi-fu Tuan (see the Profile in Chapter 1) regards migration as a form of escapism, of flight to a place believed to be better.

Migration takes place when people decide that moving is preferable to staying, when the difficulties of moving seem more than offset by the expected rewards. Although migration is relocation diffusion, the decision to migrate can spread by means of expansion diffusion. Every migration, from the ancient dispersal of our species out of Africa to the present-day movement toward urban areas, is governed by a host of **push-and-pull factors** that act to make the old home unattractive or unlivable and the new land attractive. Generally, the push factors are the key ones, because a basic dissatisfaction with the homeland is prerequisite to voluntary migration. The most important factor prompting migration throughout the thousands of years of human existence is economic. More often than not, migrating people seek greater prosperity through better access to resources, especially land.

Some cultural ecologists see migration in a different light, as a biological species seeking to fill every possible environmental niche. Ecologically, migration is a trial-and-error process that, more often than not, leads to grief rather than success. In other words, certain individuals among us may be preconditioned genetically to strike out into new lands and places, a compulsion not grounded in any rational consideration of push-and-pull factors.

In the nineteenth century, more than 50 million European emigrants, seeking better lives outside their native lands, changed the racial and ethnic character of much of the Earth. By 1970, about one-half of all Caucasians did not live in the European homelands of their ancestors. International migration often occurs because a country has a negative image in the minds of some of its people. Foreign lands seem more attractive to them.

Reflecting on GEOGRAPHY

Should the citizens of overpopulated countries have, as a basic human right, the opportunity to migrate to less densely settled countries?

Today, migration patterns are very different (Figure 7.14 on page 242). Europe, for example, now receives immigrants rather than sending out emigrants. International migration stands at an all-time high, much of it labor migration associated with the process of *globalization*. About 160 million people today live outside the country of their birth.

Forced migration also often occurs. The westward displacement of the American Indian population of the United States, the dispersal of the Jews from Palestine in Roman times, the export of African slaves to the Americas, and the "clearances" of Scottish farmers by landlords to make way for large-scale sheep raising provide depressing examples. Today, refugee movements are all too common, prompted mainly by despotism, war, ethnic hatreds, and famine. Recent decades have witnessed a flood of refugees. Perhaps as many as one-tenth of those people who today live outside their native country are refugees.

Disease Diffusion

A new depth of meaning is given to the term *contagious diffusion* when we consider the spread of diseases. The previously mentioned AIDS epidemic provides an example (see Figure 7.3). Those cultural geographers who study diseases and their diffusion work in the subdiscipline called *medical geography*. (See the book by Melinda Meade and Robert Earickson in the Ten Recommended Books section at the end of the chapter.)

The origin and early diffusion of AIDS remains controversial and incompletely understood, but several recent studies are interesting. It now seems probable that the virus labeled HIV-1, which has caused most of the epidemic, originated among a chimpanzee subspecies found in Gabon and surrounding countries (Figure 7.15 on page 243). This subspecies is now near extinction as a result of the destruction of the local rain forest. Somehow the virus was transmitted from chimpanzees to people, and the earliest documented case, in 1959, was contracted by a man living in Kinshasa on the Congo River. Although he may not have been the first victim, researchers are now almost certain that only a single transmission of the disease from chimpanzee to human is at the root of the entire epidemic.

Several theories exist to explain this diffusion. The first, and simplest, is based on the fact that the people of this part of Africa eat chimpanzees as part of their normal diet. This was especially true of workers cutting logging roads through the Gabon rain forest. The infected meat also could have been ingested by farmers making new fields in the forest. More intriguing, if less plausible, is Edward Hooper's theory. He claims that an experimental polio vaccine was made using chimpanzee tissue and widely administered by health officials between 1957 and

Youth and Old Age Populations

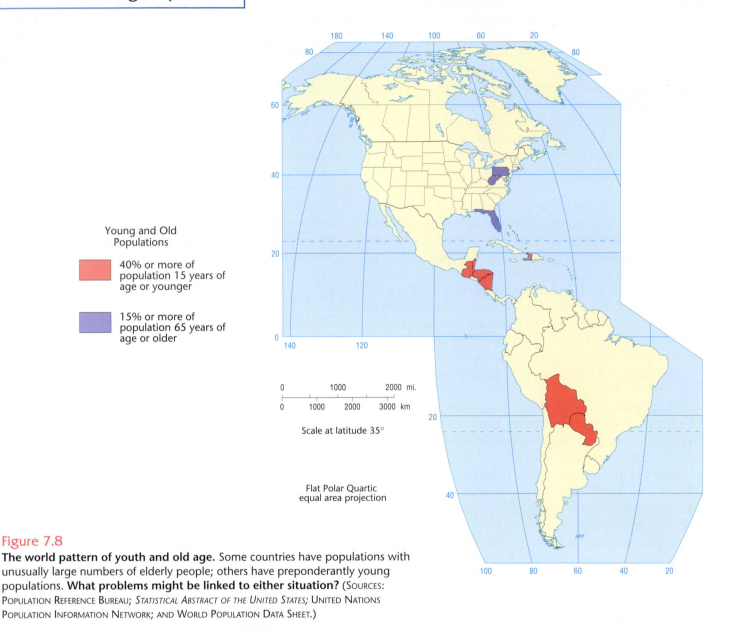

Young and Old Populations

40% or more of population 15 years of age or younger

15% or more of population 65 years of age or older

0   1000   2000 mi.

0   1000   2000   3000 km

Scale at latitude 35°

Flat Polar Quartic equal area projection

Figure 7.8

The world pattern of youth and old age. Some countries have populations with unusually large numbers of elderly people; others have preponderantly young populations. **What problems might be linked to either situation?** (Sources: Population Reference Bureau; *Statistical Abstract of the United States*; United Nations Population Information Network; and World Population Data Sheet.)

1960 in what was then the Belgian-ruled part of tropical Africa—today Congo (Kinshasa), Burundi, and Rwanda. The earliest recorded cases of AIDS all occurred in or near places where the vaccine had been given (see Figure 7.15). Most experts reject Hooper's idea, believing instead that the transferal of HIV-1 from chimpanzees occurred as early as 1930 and simply because of the regional dietary practice.

The disease then apparently moved throughout central and western Africa, following transport routes and greatly benefiting from rapid urbanization of the region. Among those infected, it seems, were Haitians who came from the West Indies to the newly independent Republic of Congo (Kinshasa) to fill civil service posts in the early 1960s. They probably took AIDS back to their Caribbean nation, and Europeans visiting central Africa also diffused

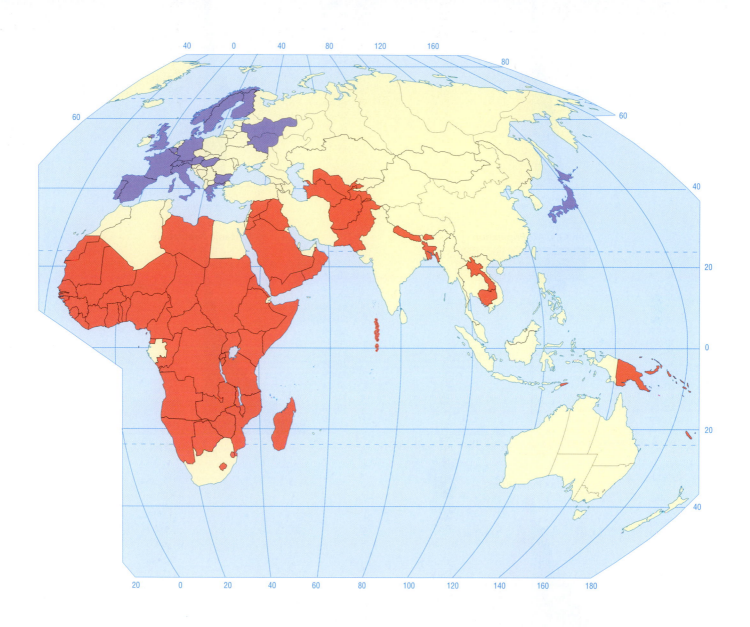

the disease to their homelands. American male homosexuals vacationing in Haiti likely contracted the virus and spread it through the gay community in the United States, leading many Americans to conclude, falsely, that AIDS is a disease linked exclusively to homosexual behavior. Similarly, western Europe became a secondary diffusion area.

Although one might expect all diseases to spread exclusively by contagious diffusion, in fact they spread through all types of diffusion. Relocation diffusion—in the forms of tourism, long-distance truck transportation in Africa, and the temporary migration of Haitian civil servants to the Congo—apparently played a role in the spread of AIDS. Hierarchical diffusion is implicit in the tendency of AIDS to gain footholds in urban areas and to be spread by people affluent enough to participate in international tourism.

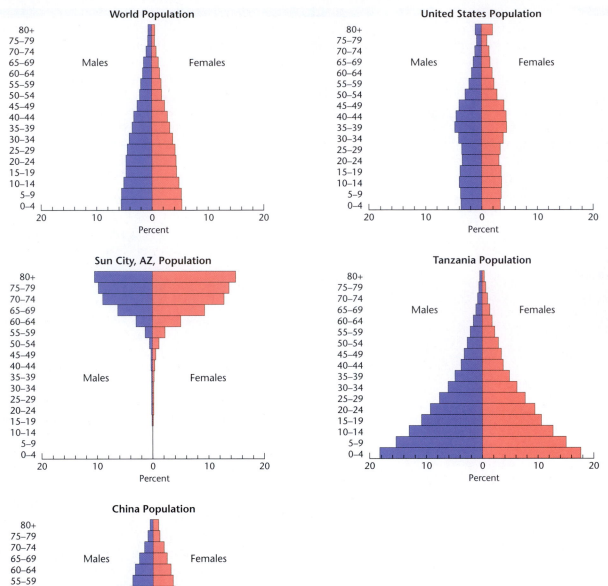

Figure 7.9

Population pyramids for the world and selected countries and communities. Tanzania displays the classic stepped pyramid of an exploding population, whereas the U.S. "pyramid" looks more like a precariously balanced pillar. **How do these pyramids help predict future population growth?** (SOURCE: POPULATION REFERENCE BUREAU.)

Diffusion of Fertility Control

Cultural diffusion in population geography isn't just about migration and contagious diseases. For example, the final two stages of the demographic transformation depend on the successful cultural diffusion of effective methods of birth control and, in addition, acceptance of the notion that small families are preferable to large ones. Sustained fertility decline arose as an innovation in Europe in the first half of the 1800s. France was the place of origin (Figure 7.16 on page 244). The idea spread slowly at first, but eventually diffused through most of Europe. As a rule, fertility decline became accepted as countries industrialized, largely because children were no longer needed to help with farm work.

In some largely rural countries, resistance to fertility control persisted, causing the population explosion. Faced with the unwillingness of people to reduce the birthrate voluntarily, a few countries—most notably China—adopted a policy of enforced fertility control. Chinese authorities sought not merely to halt population growth but, ultimately, to decrease the number of people. All over China today, one sees billboards and posters admonishing the citizens that "one couple, one child" is the ideal family (Figure 7.17 on page 245). Violators face huge monetary fines, cannot request new housing, lose the rather generous old-age benefits provided by the government, forfeit their children's access to higher education, and may even lose their jobs. Late marriages are encouraged. In response, between 1970 and 1980, the TFR in China plummeted from 5.9 births per woman to only 2.7, then to 2.2 by 1990, 2.0 by 1994, and 1.8 in 2000. China achieved one of the greatest short-term reductions of birthrates ever recorded, and stringent enforcement of the policy continues. Cultural diffusion, then, can be coerced. In recent years, the Chinese population control program has been less rigidly enforced, as economic growth eroded the government's control over the people. This relaxation has allowed more couples to have two children instead of one; however, the rise of economic opportunity and migration to cities has led other couples voluntarily to have smaller families. China, through a combination of coercive policies and economic growth, has completed the demographic transformation.

> ### Reflecting on GEOGRAPHY
> Are the governments of overpopulated countries justified in legally requiring small families? In requiring involuntary sterilization?

Population Ecology

How is the theme of cultural ecology relevant to the study of population geography? At the most basic level, a successful *adaptive strategy* permits a people to exist and reproduce in a given ecosystem. Cultural ecologists believe that population size and growth offer an index to successful adaptation. Maladaptive strategies can lead to a dwindling of a people's numbers or even to its extinc-

tion. Similarly, when groups migrate to new places as settlers, their success or failure will depend in part on *preadaptation:* the extent to which a group's ways of life, their adaptive strategies in the old home, preconditioned them for success in the new land. Preadaptation is often a matter of chance, particularly when prior knowledge of the new land is sketchy or when migrants have little control over their destinations.

Environmental Influence

Regardless of adaptive strategy, population is often influenced in a possibilistic manner by the local availability of resources. In the middle latitudes, population densities tend to be greatest where the terrain is level, the climate is mild and humid, the soil is fertile, mineral resources are abundant, and the sea is accessible. Conversely, population tends to thin out with excessive elevation, aridity, coldness, ruggedness of terrain, and distance from the coast (Figure 7.18 on page 246).

Climatic factors influence where people settle. Most of the sparsely populated zones in the world have, in some respect, "defective" climates from the human viewpoint (see Figure 7.1). The thinly populated northern edges of Eurasia and North America are excessively cold, and the belt from North Africa into the heart of Eurasia matches the major desert zones of the Eastern Hemisphere. Humans remain creatures of the humid and subhumid tropics, subtropics, or midlatitudes and have not fared well in excessively cold or dry areas. Small populations of Inuit (Eskimo), Sami (Lapps), and other peoples live in some of the less desirable areas of the Earth, but these regions do not support large populations. Humans have proved remarkably adaptable in the biological sense, and our cultures contain adaptive strategies that allow us to live in many different physical environments; but perhaps, as a species, we never fully forgot the climatic features of sub-Saharan Africa, where we began. In avoiding cold places, we may reveal even today the tropical origin of our species.

Humankind's preference for lower elevations holds especially true for the middle and higher latitudes. Indeed, most mountain ranges in those latitudes stand out as regions of sparse population. By contrast, inhabitants of the tropics often prefer to live at higher elevations, concentrating in dense clusters in mountain valleys and basins (see Figure 7.1). By doing so, they escape the humid, hot climate of the tropic lowlands. For example, in tropical portions of South America, more people live in the Andes Mountains than in the nearby Amazon lowlands. The capital cities of many tropical and subtropical nations lie in mountain areas above about 3000 feet (900 meters) in elevation.

Gender Ratio

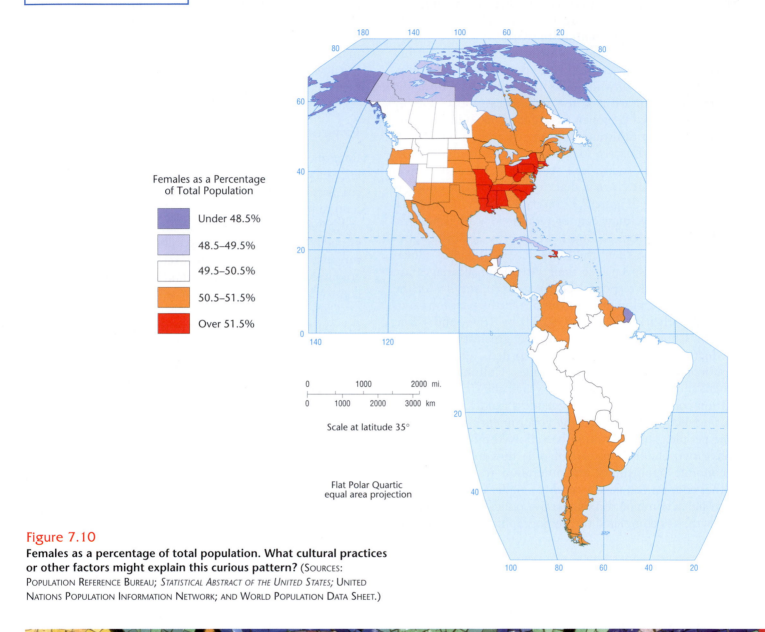

Females as a Percentage
of Total Population

- Under 48.5%
- 48.5–49.5%
- 49.5–50.5%
- 50.5–51.5%
- Over 51.5%

Scale at latitude 35°

Flat Polar Quartic
equal area projection

Figure 7.10

**Females as a percentage of total population. What cultural practices
or other factors might explain this curious pattern?** (SOURCES:
POPULATION REFERENCE BUREAU; *STATISTICAL ABSTRACT OF THE UNITED STATES;* UNITED
NATIONS POPULATION INFORMATION NETWORK; AND WORLD POPULATION DATA SHEET.)

Our tendency is also to live on or near the seacoast, for a variety of reasons. The continents of Eurasia, Australia, and South America resemble hollow shells, with the majority of the population clustered around the rim of each continent (see Figure 7.1). In Australia, half the total population lives in just five port cities, and most of the remainder is spread out over nearby coastal areas. This preference for living by the sea stems partly from the trade and fishing opportunities the sea offers. At the same time, continental interiors tend to be regions of climatic ex-

tremes. For example, Australians speak of the "dead heart" of their continent, an interior land of excessive dryness and heat. People also seek places where fresh water is available. In desert regions, population clusters reflect the locations of scattered oases and occasional rivers, such as the Nile, that rise from sources outside the desert (Figure 7.19 on page 247).

Still another environmental factor that affects population distribution is disease. Some diseases attack valuable domestic animals, depriving people of food and clothing

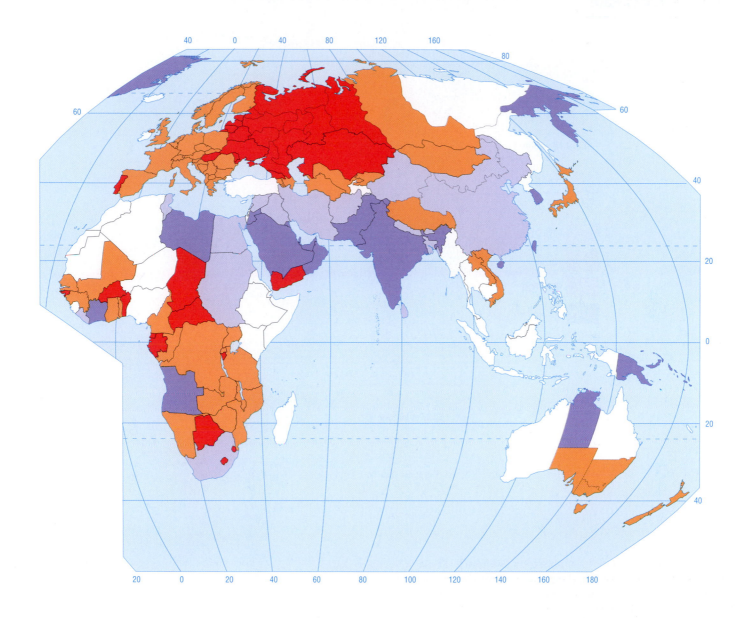

resources. Such diseases have an indirect effect on population density. For example, in parts of East Africa, livestock is attacked by a form of sleeping sickness. This particular disease is almost invariably fatal to cattle but not to humans. The people in this part of East Africa depend heavily on cattle, which provide food, represent wealth, and serve a religious function in some tribes. The spread of a disease fatal to cattle has caused entire tribes to migrate away from infested areas, leaving them unpopulated (Figure 7.20 on page 248).

Environmental Perception and Population Distribution

Perception of the physical environment plays a major role when a group of people chooses where to settle and live. Different cultural groups often "see" the same physical environment in different ways. These varied responses to a single environment influence the distribution of people. A good example appears in a part of the European Alps shared by German- and Italian-speaking people. The

Infant Mortality Rate

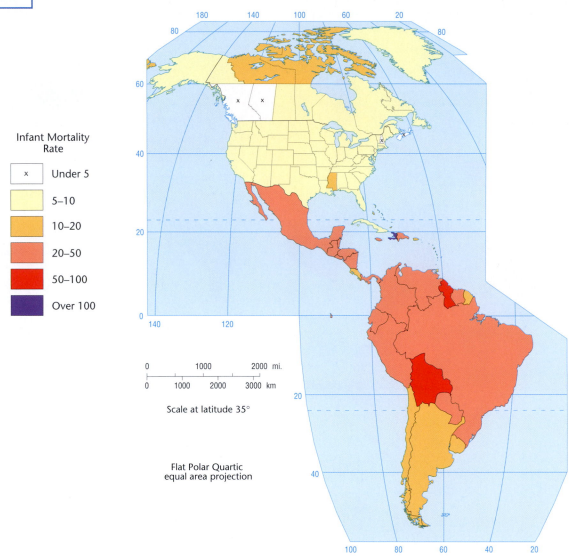

Figure 7.11

The present world pattern of infant mortality rate. The numbers indicate the number of children, per 1000 born, who die before reaching one year of age. The world's infant mortality rate is 57. Experts believe that this rate is the best single measure of living standards. **What would it not reveal about standard of living?** (SOURCES: POPULATION REFERENCE BUREAU; *STATISTICAL ABSTRACT OF THE UNITED STATES;* UNITED NATIONS POPULATION INFORMATION NETWORK; AND WORLD POPULATION DATA SHEET.)

mountain ridges in that area—near the point where Switzerland, Italy, and Austria join—run in an east-west direction, so that each ridge has a sunny, south-facing slope and a shady, north-facing one. German-speaking people, who rely on dairy farming, long ago established permanent settlements some 650 feet (200 meters) higher on the *shady* slopes than the settlements of Italians, who are culturally tied to warmth-loving crops, on the *sunny*

slopes. This example demonstrates contrasting cultural attitudes toward land use and different perceptions of the best use for one type of physical environment.

Sometimes, the same cultural group changes its perception of an environment over time, with a resulting redistribution of its population. The coal fields of western Europe provide a good case in point. Before the industrial age, many coal-rich areas—such as southern Wales, the

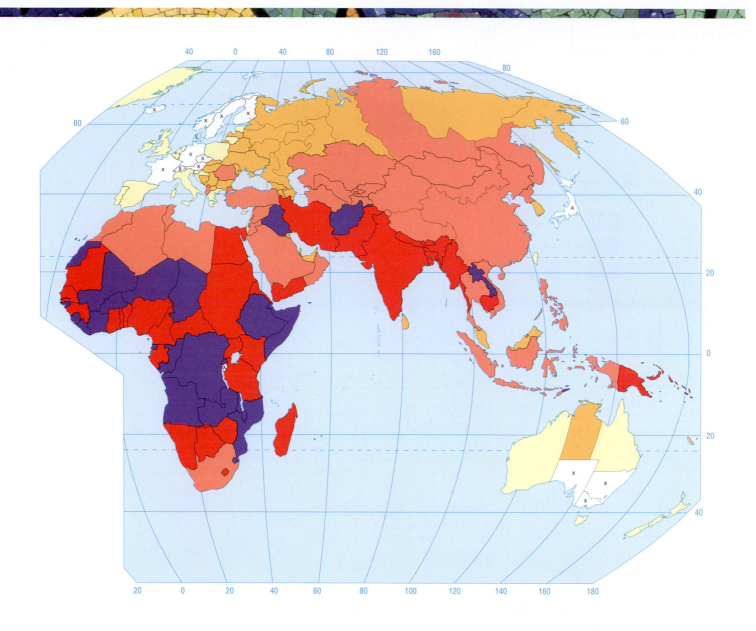

lands between the headwaters of the Odra and Vistula rivers in Poland, and the Midlands of England—were only sparsely or moderately settled. Then the development of steam-powered engines and the increased use of coal in the iron-smelting process created a tremendous demand. Industries grew up near the European coal fields, and people flocked to these areas to take advantage of the new jobs. In other words, once a technological development gave a new cultural value to coal, many sparsely populated areas containing that resource acquired large concentrations of people.

Recent studies indicate that much of the interregional migration in the United States today is prompted by a desire for a pleasant climate and other desirable physical environmental traits, such as beautiful scenery. Surveys of immigrants to Arizona revealed that its sunny, warm

Human Development

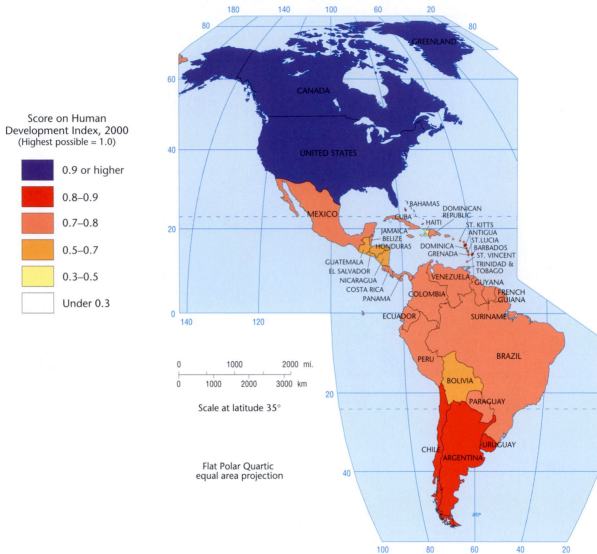

Score on Human
Development Index, 2000
(Highest possible = 1.0)

■ (dark blue)	0.9 or higher
■ (red)	0.8–0.9
■ (light red/salmon)	0.7–0.8
■ (orange)	0.5–0.7
■ (yellow)	0.3–0.5
□ (white)	Under 0.3

0   1000   2000 mi.

0   1000   2000   3000 km

Scale at latitude 35°

Flat Polar Quartic
equal area projection

Figure 7.12

Rankings of the Human Development Index, which uses multiple criteria to measure standard of living or quality of life. **Why does Russia rank so relatively low?** (SOURCE: *HUMAN DEVELOPMENT REPORT 2000.*)

climate is a major reason for migration. Attractive environment provided the dominant factor in the growth of the population and economy of Florida. The most desirable environmental traits that serve as stimulants for American migration include (1) mild winter climate and mountainous terrain, (2) a diverse natural vegetation that includes forests and a mild summer climate with low humidity, (3) the presence of lakes and rivers, and (4) nearness to the seacoast. Different age and cultural groups often express different preferences, but all are influenced by

their perceptions of the physical environment in making decisions about migration. Misinformation is at least as important as accurate impressions, because a person will often form strong images of an area without ever visiting it.

Reflecting on **GEOGRAPHY**

What is your ideal climate? Do you now live in a place with such a climate? If not, do you intend to migrate for this reason?

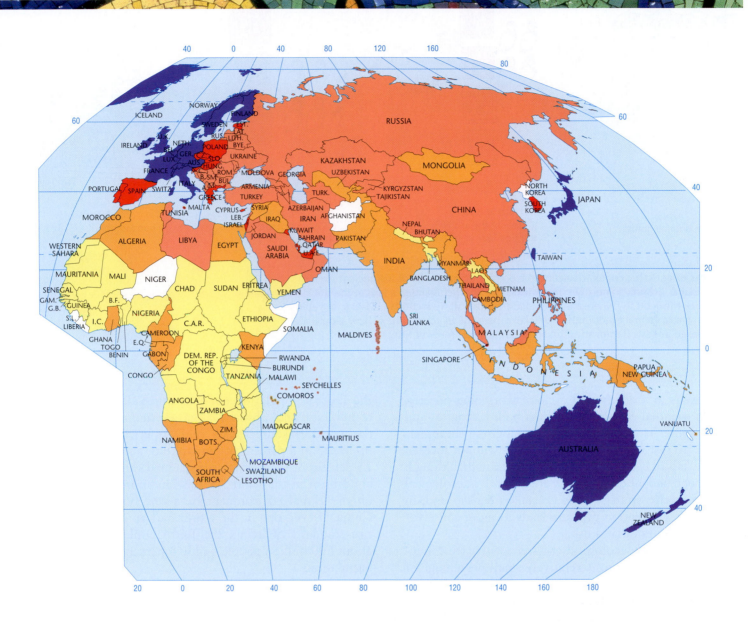

Population Density and Environmental Alteration

People modify their habitats through their *adaptive strategies*. Particularly in areas where population density is high, radical alterations often occur. This can happen in fragile environments even at relatively low population densities, because the carrying capacity of the Earth varies greatly from one place to another and from one culture to another.

We face a worldwide ecological crisis in part because, at present densities, many of our adaptive strategies are not sustainable. The population explosion and the ecological crisis are closely related. For example, in Haiti, where rural population pressures have become particularly severe, most available biomass is now being collected into small, intensively cultivated kitchen gardens, leaving the surrounding fields and pastures increasingly denuded and humus-deficient. In short, overpopulation can precipitate environmental destruction—which, in

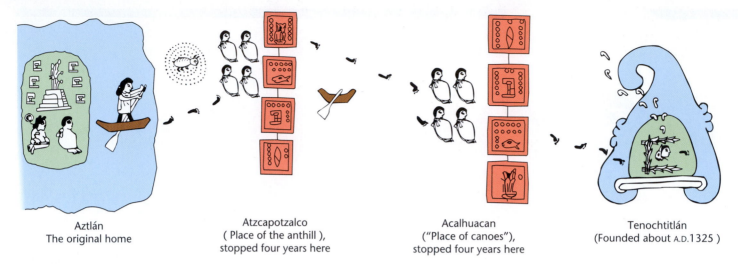

Aztlán
The original home

Atzcapotzalco
(Place of the anthill),
stopped four years here

Acalhuacan
("Place of canoes"),
stopped four years here

Tenochtitlán
(Founded about A.D.1325)

Figure 7.13

Segments of an Aztec codex, depicting the prehistoric migration of the ancient Aztecs from an island, possibly in northwestern Mexico, to another island in a lake at the site of present-day Mexico City, where they founded their capital, Tenochtitlán. Clearly, the epic migration was a central event in their collective memory. **In your culture, how would a remembered ancestral migration be commemorated?** (AFTER DE MACGREGOR, 1984: 217.)

turn, results in a downward cycle of worsening poverty, with an eventual catastrophe that is both ecological and demographic. Thus many cultural ecologists believe that attempts to restore the balance of nature will not succeed until we halt or even reverse population growth, although they recognize that other causes are at work in ecological crises. Adaptive strategy is as crucial as density and, in some cases, population pressure leads to more conservational techniques of land use.

The worldwide ecological crisis is not strictly a function of overpopulation. A relatively small percentage of the Earth's population controls much of the industrial technology and absorbs a gargantuan percentage of the world's resources each year. Americans, who make up less than 5 percent of humankind, account for about 25 percent of the resources consumed each year. Thus, a child born in the United States has more of an impact on the global environment than one born in India or China. If everyone in the world had an average American standard of living, the Earth could support only about 500 million people—only 8 percent of the present population.

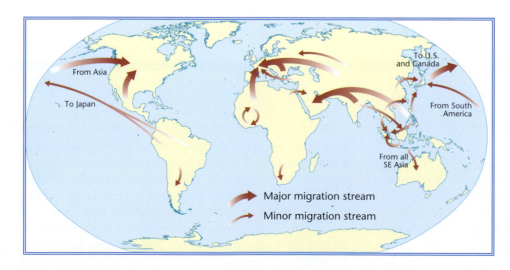

Major migration stream

Minor migration stream

Figure 7.14

Major and minor migration flows today. Why have these flows changed so profoundly in the past hundred years? (SOURCE: POPULATION REFERENCE BUREAU.)

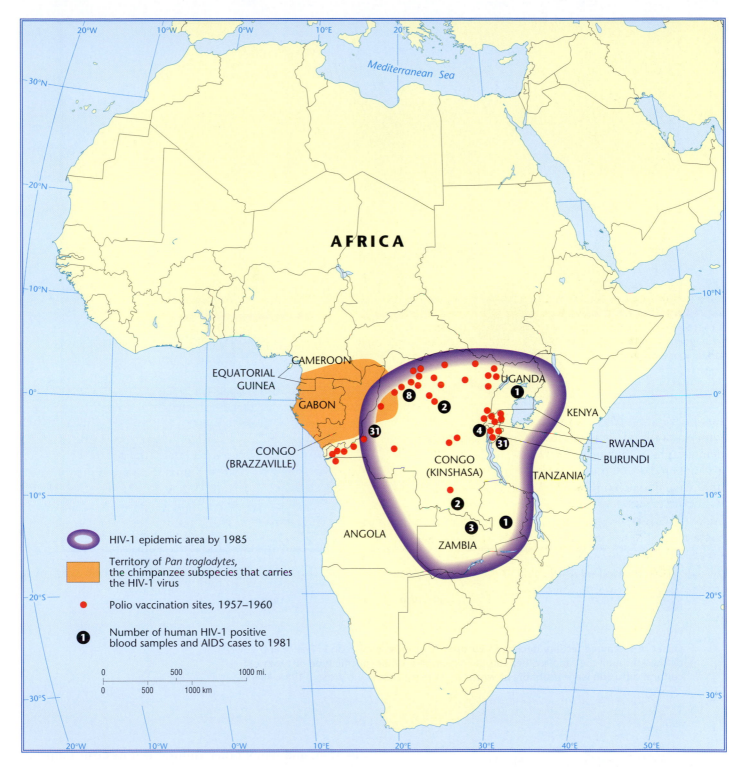

Figure 7.15

Early diffusion of the HIV-1 virus that causes AIDS, involving an infected chimpanzee subspecies. (Sources: Shannon et al., 1991: 49, 68, 73; Gould, 1993; Paul, 1994; and Hooper, 1999.)

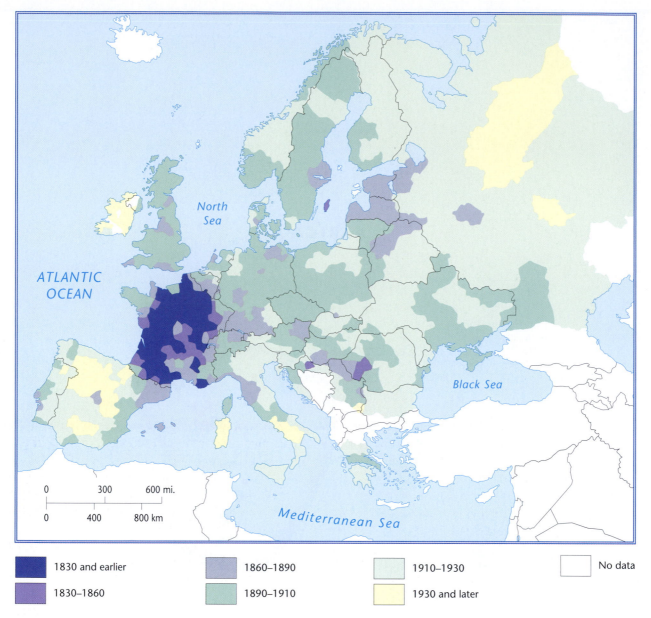

Figure 7.16
Onset of sustained fertility decline in Europe. The movement began in France and slowly diffused through the various other European countries. **What specific type or types of cultural diffusion were probably at work?** (ADAPTED FROM COALE AND WATKINS, 1986: 484FF.)

Legend:
- 1830 and earlier
- 1830–1860
- 1860–1890
- 1890–1910
- 1910–1930
- 1930 and later
- No data

Culturo-Demographic Interaction

Can we gain additional understanding of demographic patterns by using the theme of cultural interaction? Are culture and demography intertwined? Yes, in diverse and causal ways. Culture influences population density, migration, and population growth. Inheritance laws, food preferences, politics, differing attitudes toward mi-

gration, and many other cultural features can influence demography.

Cultural Factors

Many of the forces that influence the distribution of people are basic characteristics of a group's culture (see Focus On: Culture and Population on page 247). For example, we must understand the rice preference of people living in Southeast Asia before we can try to interpret the dense

concentrations of people in rural areas there. The population in the humid lands of tropical and subtropical Asia expanded as this highly prolific grain was domesticated and widely adopted. Environmentally similar rural zones elsewhere in the world, where rice is not the staple of the inhabitants' diet, never developed such great population densities. Similarly, the introduction of the potato into Ireland in the 1700s allowed a great increase in rural population, because it yielded much more food per acre than did traditional Irish crops. Failure of the potato harvests in the 1840s greatly reduced the Irish population, through both starvation and emigration.

Geographers have found major cultural contrasts in attitudes toward population growth. France—where, as we have seen, sustained fertility decline first took root in the world—suffered demographically as a result. When the birthrate in nineteenth-century France declined rapidly, neighboring countries, such as Germany, Italy, and the United Kingdom, did not experience the same decline. Consequently, the French population did not keep pace numerically with that in nearby lands (Table 7.3 on page 248; Figure 7.21 on page 249). France, the most populous of these four countries in 1800, became the least populous shortly after 1930. During this same period, millions of Germans, British, and Italians emigrated overseas, whereas relatively few French left their homeland. At the same time, the French Canadians of the province of Québec, whose ancestors had left France long before, still favored large families. Consequently, the

10,000 people who settled in Québec between 1608 and 1750 multiplied into today's population of about 7 million (Table 7.3). This number does not include many French Canadians who migrated from Canada to New England and other areas. Clearly, some factor in the culture of France worked to produce their demographic decline. What might the reason be?

Cultural groups also differ in their tendency to migrate. Religious ties bind some groups to their traditional homelands. Sometimes travel outside the sanctified bounds of the motherland is considered immoral, and religious duties—in particular the responsibilities to tend ancestral graves and perform rites at parental death—kept many Chinese in their native land. The Navajo Indians of the American Southwest practice the custom of burying the umbilical cord in the floor of the hogan (house) at birth. Psychologically, this seems to strengthen the Navajo attachment to the home and retard migration. Other religious cultures place no stigma on emigration. In fact, some groups consider migration a way of life. The Irish, unwilling to accept the poverty of their native land, proved so prone to migration that the population of Ireland today is only about half what it was in 1840.

Culture can also condition a people to accept or reject crowding. **Personal space**—the amount of space that individuals feel "belongs" to them as they move about their everyday business—varies from one cultural group to another. When Americans talk with one another, they typically stand farther apart than, say, Italians do. The large

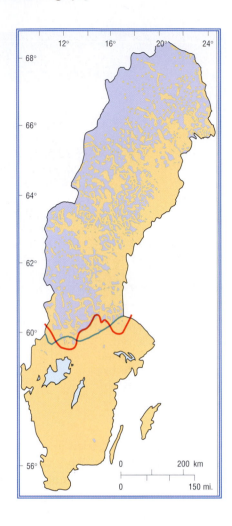

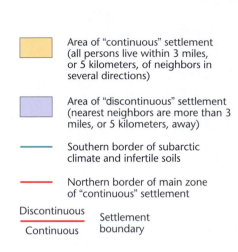

Area of "continuous" settlement (all persons live within 3 miles, or 5 kilometers, of neighbors in several directions)

Area of "discontinuous" settlement (nearest neighbors are more than 3 miles, or 5 kilometers, away)

Southern border of subarctic climate and infertile soils

Northern border of main zone of "continuous" settlement

Discontinuous
_____ Settlement
Continuous   boundary

Figure 7.18

Environment and population distribution in Sweden. The northern boundary of the thickly settled area corresponds closely to the southern limit of the bitterly cold subarctic climate and the infertile, acidic soils of the coniferous forests. **Does a similar boundary exist in North America?** (ADAPTED FROM STONE, 1962: 379.)

personal space demanded by the American may well come from a heritage of sparse settlement. Early pioneers felt uncomfortable when they first saw smoke from the chimneys of neighboring cabins. As a result, American cities sprawl across large areas, with huge suburbs dominated by separate houses surrounded by private yards. Most European cities are compact, and their residential areas consist largely of row houses or apartments.

Reflecting on **GEOGRAPHY**

How much "personal space" do you need? How does this affect the way you live?

Political Factors

The political mosaic of the world is linked to population geography in many ways. Governmental policies often influence the fertility rate, as we have seen in China, and forced migration is usually the result of political forces.

Governments can also restrict voluntary migration. Two independent countries, Haiti and the Dominican Republic, share the tropical Caribbean island of Hispaniola in the West Indies. Haiti, which supports 638 persons per square mile (246 per square kilometer), is far more densely settled than the Dominican Republic, which has only 450 persons per square mile (174 per square kilometer) (Figure 7.22 on page 250). Government restrictions make migration from Haiti to the Dominican Republic difficult and help maintain the different population densities. If Hispaniola were one country, its population would be more evenly distributed over the island.

Governments also set in motion most *involuntary* migrations. These have become particularly common in the past century or so, usually to achieve *ethnic cleansing*—the removal of unwanted minorities in *nation-states*. Ethnic cleansing happened most recently in the Balkans, in southeastern Europe, but it is an age-old practice. In Europe alone, between 1920 and 1950, about 33 million people were ethnically cleansed, leaving some territories almost completely depopulated for a time.

FOCUS ON

Culture and Population

A study of the Tenetehara and the Tapirapé, two Indian tribes of central Brazil, shows the range of population choices available to different cultures within the same physical and material environment. Before European contact, both tribes inhabited similar tropical forest areas, had the same level of technology, and were horticulturists who depended on hunting, fishing, and wild fruits to supplement their diets. Yet the Tapirapé population was, by choice, relatively small and stable, whereas the Tenetehara population of perhaps 2000 was at least twice as large and probably expanding.

Among the Tenetehara, there was little effort to limit family size. Men took pride in the number of children they fathered. Women, eager to bear children, would leave a husband whom they considered sterile. There seem to have been few cultural values in the tribe that would discourage large families.

The Tapirapé, however, had an explicit idea of maximum family size. When asked why their families were no larger, they would say, "The children would be hungry." In Tapirapé society, this meant "hungry for meat," which was sometimes scarce—but no scarcer than for the more numerous Teneteharas. In other words, Tapirapé population controls were based not on possible starvation levels but on a specific desire for a larger quantity of meat in their diets. Other cultural factors also played a role in the Tapirapé decision. As a result, the tribe set limits on how many children a woman should have (no more than three living and no more than two of the same sex). To keep their society within its desired limits, they practiced infanticide.

Adapted from Wagley, 1973: 145–156.

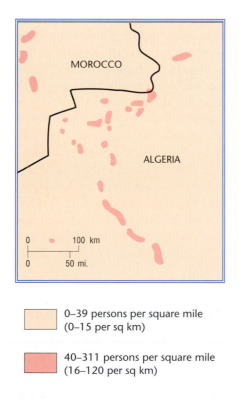

0–39 persons per square mile
(0–15 per sq km)

40–311 persons per square mile
(16–120 per sq km)

Figure 7.19

Population distribution reveals the availability of water in a desert. These scattered clusters of people lie in the Sahara Desert of North Africa, and the pattern is typical of many arid regions. Dot clusters indicate the presence of oases; lines reveal stream courses. (After Mattingly and Schmidt, 1971.)

Economic Factors

Economic conditions often influence population density in profound ways. The process of industrialization over the past 200 years has caused the greatest voluntary relocation of people in world history. Within industrial nations, people moved from rural areas to cluster in manufacturing regions. Agricultural changes can also influence population density. For example, the complete mechanization of cotton and wheat cultivation in twentieth-century America allowed those crops to be raised by a much smaller labor force. As a result, profound depopulation occurred, to the extent that many small towns serving these rural inhabitants ceased to exist.

When geographers apply the theme of cultural interaction in their demographic research, they often obtain negative results that are as enlightening as positive correlations. For example, many experts had long assumed that vegetarianism in India, based in Hindu religious belief, led to protein deficiency, malnutrition, and resultant health problems in many rural areas of that country. A study by Aninda Chakravarti, a cultural geographer, revealed no spatial correlation between vegetarians and the consumption of animal protein (Figure 7.23 on page 251). That is, nonvegetarians also eat little or no meat. Instead, the greatest protein deficiency occurs in areas where rice, rather than wheat bread, accounts for the greater part of the cereal consumption. Chakravarti found that meat was too expensive even for those who had no taboo against it

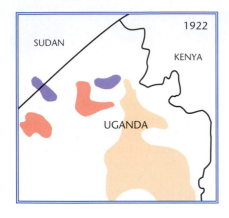
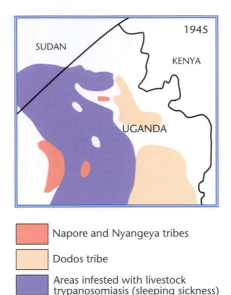
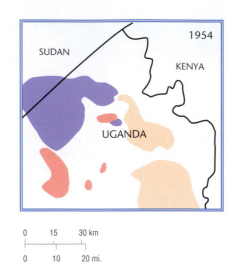

Napore and Nyangeya tribes

Dodos tribe

Areas infested with livestock trypanosomiasis (sleeping sickness)

Figure 7.20

Disease can influence settlement. The effect is apparent in this example in northeastern Uganda, East Africa. Note in particular the changing distribution of the Napore and Nyangeya groups based on the spread and eradication of sleeping sickness. (ADAPTED FROM DESHLER, 1960: 549.)

and that the custom of "polishing" rice, to make it pure white in color, removed most of its nutritive value.

Gender and Geodemography

Gender often interacts with other factors to influence geodemographic patterns and migrations. Together, gender, race, and nationality can create situations in which women from specific countries are viewed as desirable immigrants. In nineteenth-century America, Irish female immigrants often found work as domestic servants. Another more recent and sinister example is provided by geographer James Tyner, who studied migration from the Philippines to Japan. Incredibly, 93 percent of this migration consists of female "entertainers." In part, poverty in the Philippines

provided the push factor in this movement, but Tyner also points to more complex pull factors, such as the male Japanese stereotyped view of Filipinas as highly desirable, exotic sex objects, culturally inferior to themselves and "willing victims" who gladly become prostitutes.

Migration for the purpose of marriage also often differs along gender lines. In some parts of rural India, particularly the northwest, marriage typically takes place between individuals from different villages. Because it is traditional in those parts of India for the woman to move into the household of her husband, females are much more likely to migrate than are males. A fifth or fewer of all married women in northern and western India live in the village of their birth; and in many districts their marriage migration has taken them 18 miles (29 kilometers) or

TABLE 7.3	Population of France, Québec, Germany, Italy, and the United Kingdom (in Millions), 1720–1930					
Country	1720	1800	1850	1900	1930	Increase from 1720 to 1930
France	19	27	36	38	42	2.2 times
Québec	0.02	0.2	0.9	1.7	2.8	140 times
Germany	14	25	35	56	64	4.6 times
Italy	13	18	23	32	41	3.2 times
United Kingdom	7	11	27	37	46	6.8 times

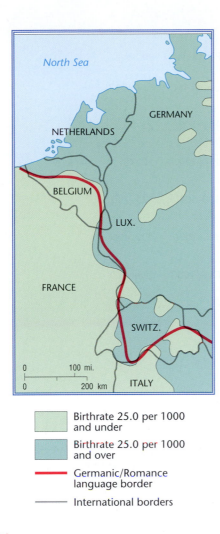

Figure 7.21

Birthrate pattern in western Europe, 1910. Notice how the birthrate border paralleled the linguistic rather than the political boundary. French-speaking people in France, southern Belgium, western Switzerland, and northwestern Italy—together with their Romance-language kinsmen, the Romansh-speaking people of eastern Switzerland—were reproducing at a lower rate than their German-speaking neighbors. **What cultural factors might have helped produce this contrast?** In later decades, this contrast disappeared altogether. (ADAPTED FROM JORDAN, 1973: 73).

more from their original home (Figure 7.24 on page 251). By contrast, in southern India and in Kashmir in the far north, females are much less likely to marry outside their village. Cultural differences lie at the root of these contrasts. In some parts of southern India, for example, matrilineal societies—those that trace lineage through the mother—encourage females to remain close to their place of birth. Even in patrilineal southern Indian communities, a preference for marriage within the village prevails, so marriage migration is uncommon.

The Settlement Landscape

How is the distribution of people reflected in the cultural landscape? Differing densities and arrangements of population are revealed, at the largest scale, by maps showing the distribution of dwellings. We can illustrate these cultural landscape contrasts by using the example of *rural* settlement types. Farm people differ from one culture to another, one place to another, in how they situate their dwellings, producing greatly contrasting rural cultural landscapes. They range from tightly *clustered* villages on the one extreme to fully *dispersed* farmsteads on the other, as shown in Figure 7.25 on page 252.

Farm Villages

In many parts of the world, farming people group themselves together in clustered settlements called **farm villages.** These tightly bunched settlements vary in size from a few dozen inhabitants to several thousand. Contained in the village **farmstead** are the house, barn, sheds, pens, and garden. The fields, pastures, and meadows lie out in the country beyond the limits of the village, and farmers must journey out from the village each day to work the land.

Farm villages are the most common form of settlement in much of Europe, in many parts of Latin America, in the densely settled farming regions of Asia (including much of India, China, and Japan), and among the sedentary farming peoples of Africa and the Middle East (see Focus On: Overlooking a Village in India on page 253). These compact villages come in many forms. Most are irregular clusterings—a maze of winding, narrow streets and a jumble of farmsteads (Figures 7.25a and 7.26 on page 253). Such *irregular clustered* farm villages developed spontaneously over the centuries, without any orderly plan to direct their growth. Other types of farm villages are very regular in their layout and reveal the imprint of planned design. The *street village,* the simplest of these planned types, consists of farmsteads grouped along both sides of a single, central street, producing an elongated settlement (Figures 7.25b and 7.27 on page 254). Street villages are particularly common in eastern Europe, including much of Russia. Another type, the *green village,* consists of farmsteads grouped around a central open place, or green, which forms a commons (Figure 7.25c). Green villages occur throughout most of the plains areas of northern and northwestern Europe, and English immigrants laid out some such settlements in colonial New England. Also regular in layout is the *checkerboard village,* based on a gridiron pattern of streets meeting at right angles (Figure 7.25g). Mormon farm villages in Utah are of this

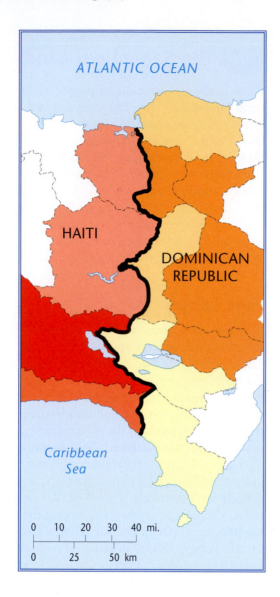

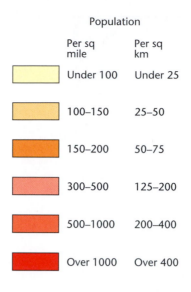

Population

	Per sq mile	Per sq km
	Under 100	Under 25
	100–150	25–50
	150–200	50–75
	300–500	125–200
	500–1000	200–400
	Over 1000	Over 400

Figure 7.22

Population density contrast along the Haiti–Dominican Republic boundary. Migration across this political frontier on the island of Hispaniola in the Caribbean has been restricted, causing the boundary to become a demographic border as well. **What other factors might have helped create this pattern?** (SOURCE: UNITED NATIONS POPULATION INFORMATION NETWORK.)

type, and checkerboard villages also dominate most of rural Latin America and northeastern China.

Why do so many farm people huddle together in villages? Traditionally, the countryside was unsafe, threatened by roving bands of outlaws and raiders. Farmers could better defend themselves against such dangers by grouping together in villages. In many parts of the world, the populations of villages have grown larger during periods of insecurity and shrunk again when peace returned. Many farm villages occupy the most easily defended sites in their vicinity, and geographers call these *strong-point* settlements.

In addition to defense, the quality of the environment helps determine whether people settle in villages. In deserts and in limestone areas where the ground absorbs moisture quickly, farmsteads huddle together at the few sources of water. Such *wet-point* villages cluster around oases or deep wells. Conversely, a superabundance of

water—in marshes, swamps, and areas subject to floods—prompts people to settle in villages on available *dry points* of higher elevation.

Various communal ties strongly bind villagers together. Groups of farmers linked to one another by blood relationships, religious customs, communal landownership, or other similar bonds usually form clustered villages. Mormon farm villages in the United States provide an excellent example of the clustering force of religion. Communal or state ownership of the land—as in China and parts of Israel—encourages the formation of farm villages.

Isolated Farmsteads

In many other parts of the world, the rural population lives in dispersed, isolated farmsteads, often some distance from their nearest neighbors (see Figure 7.25d). These dispersed rural settlements grew up mainly in

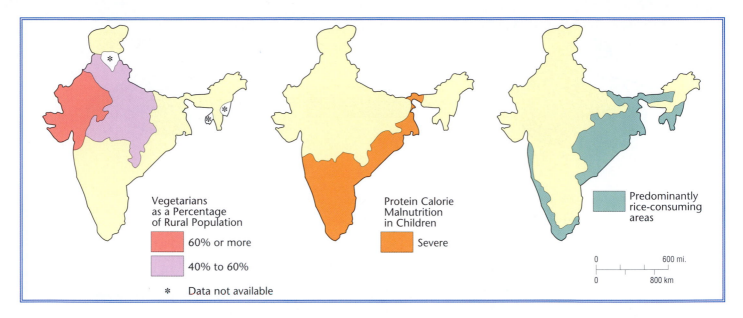

Figure 7.23

Protein malnutrition, vegetarianism, and rice consumption in India. In studying cultural integration, the geographer sometimes finds that the obvious answers are wrong. The disease and death that can result from protein deficiency are apparently unrelated to vegetarianism; instead, a link to rice consumption is suggested. (AFTER CHAKRAVARTI, 1982.)

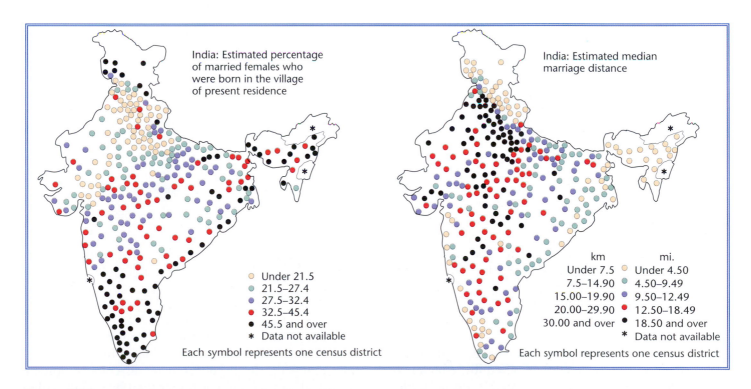

Figure 7.24

Female marriage migration in rural India. Major differences in the tendency of women to migrate for the purpose of marriage and in the distance of migration can be seen from one part of India to another. **What might be some of the cultural causes of this spatial pattern?** (SOURCE: ADAPTED FROM LIBBEE AND SOPHER, 1970: 352, 354.)

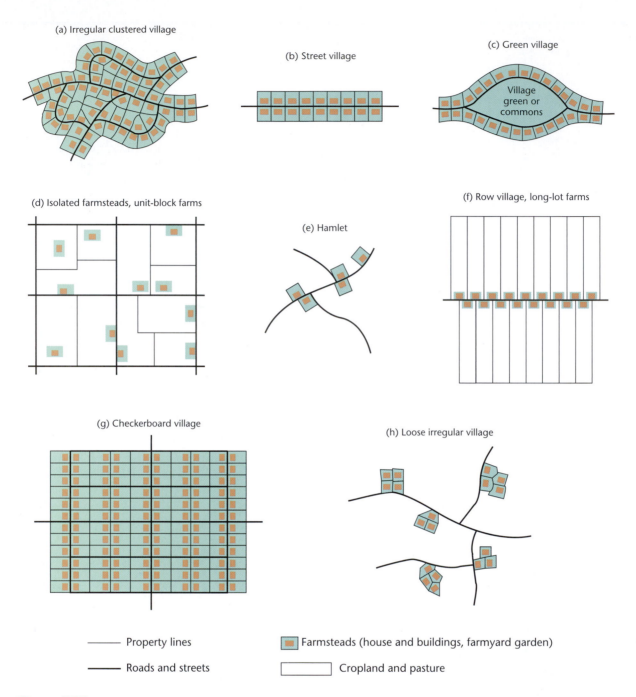

Figure 7.25
Rural settlement landscapes. The way individual farmers choose to locate their farmsteads leads to a general settlement pattern on the land. In some areas, farmsteads are scattered and isolated. In areas where farmsteads are grouped, there are several possible patterns of clustering.

Anglo-America, Australia, New Zealand, and South Africa—that is, in the lands colonized by emigrating Europeans. But even in areas dominated by village settlements—such as Japan, Europe, and parts of India—some isolated farmsteads appear (Figure 7.28 on page 254).

The conditions encouraging dispersed settlement are precisely the opposite of those favoring village develop-

ment. These include peace and security in the country-side, removing the need for defense; colonization by individual pioneer families rather than by socially cohesive groups; agricultural private enterprise, as opposed to some form of communalism; and well-drained land where water is readily available. Most dispersed farmsteads originated rather recently and date primarily

FOCUS ON

Overlooking a Village in India

On the steep ascent of the first range of hills bordering the southern edge of the great Ganges [Ganga] Valley in the Indian state of Madhya Pradesh, I ask my hired driver to stop the car, overlooking a tightly clustered farm village in the plain below. The village, tucked up against the foot of the hill, is open to my view from above. I look down on a disorderly jumble of tile-roofed, mud-walled farmsteads, each consisting of single-story buildings grouped protectively around a central courtyard. So compact is the settlement that it is difficult to tell where one farmstead leaves off and the neighboring ones begin. Rounded

mounds of threshed rice straw rise from many courtyards, and an occasional shade tree conceals parts of the village from my view. From the narrow dusty lanes and tiny courtyards, a rich variety of village noises drifts up to me on my godlike perch—the noises of animals and people going about their daily routines, noises unchanged for thousands of years. Off into the hazy distance stretch tan fields, another reminder that it is December, a month of gathering. Near the village are bright green rectangles of vegetables, irrigated and lush in the subtropical winter sun. Here is simplicity, continuity, attachment to place.

From the travel journal of Terry G. Jordan-Bychkov, 1975.

---

from the colonization of new farmland in the last two or three centuries.

Reflecting on **GEOGRAPHY**

What disadvantages might a settlement pattern of isolated farmsteads present for the people who live there?

Semiclustered Rural Settlement

Some forms of rural settlement share characteristics of both clustered and dispersed types and may best be referred to as *semiclustered*. The most common type of semiclustered settlement, the *hamlet*, consists of a small number of farmsteads grouped loosely together (see Figure 7.25e). As in villages, the hamlet farmsteads lie in a

Figure 7.26

Two irregular clustered villages. The village on the left with adjacent irrigated grain fields is near Gonggar in southeastern Tibet. The village nestles against a hill, and much of it is built on land unfit for cultivation. The village shown on the right is in northern Switzerland. Although halfway around the world from the village in Tibet, it also shows the irregular plan. (COURTESY OF TERRY G. JORDAN-BYCHKOV.)

Figure 7.27
Street village beside the great Siberian river Lena in the Sakha Republic (Yakutia), part of Russia. Farmsteads lie along a single street, creating an elongated settlement. One can distinguish Russian ethnic villages in Sakha by this form, whereas the native Yakut villages have a checkerboard pattern. In this way, the cultural landscape reveals the ethnicity of the inhabitants. (COURTESY OF TERRY G. JORDAN-BYCHKOV.)

settlement nucleus separate from the cropland, but the hamlet is smaller and less compact, containing as few as three or four houses (Figure 7.29). Hamlets appear most often in poorer hill districts, especially in parts of western Europe, China, India, the Philippines, and Vietnam.

Occasionally, several hamlets lie close to one another, sharing a common name. These constitute a *loose irregular village* (see Figure 7.25h). The individual clusters in such a group are often linked to various clans or religious groups. These loose villages occur most commonly in southeastern Europe, Malaya, Bangladesh, southern Japan, and India. Loose irregular villages involve a deliberate segregation of inhabitants, either voluntary or involuntary. In India, farmers of the "untouchable" caste—the lowest ranking group in the caste system—are occasionally segregated from other people in this manner.

The *row village*, a third common type of semiclustered settlement, consists of a loose chain of farmsteads spaced at intervals along a road, river, or canal, often extending for many miles (see Figure 7.25f). The individual farmsteads lie farther apart than those in a street village and do not abut one another. Row villages appear in the hills and marshlands of central and northwestern Europe; along the waterways in French-settled portions of North America, especially Québec and Louisiana; and in southern Brazil and adjacent parts of Argentina. In the extensive French Cajun row villages along Bayou Lafourche in Louisiana, dwellings lie sufficiently close to one another

Figure 7.28
A truly isolated farmstead, in the Vestfjörds district of northwestern Iceland. This type of rural settlement dominates almost all lands colonized by Europeans migrating overseas. Iceland was settled by Norse Vikings a thousand years ago. (COURTESY OF TERRY G. JORDAN-BYCHKOV.)

Figure 7.29
A seaside hamlet on the Olafsfjörd in northern Iceland. The inhabitants pursue both dairying and fishing. **Why might a hamlet have developed here instead of a village?** (Courtesy of Terry G. Jordan-Bychkov.)

that a baseball could be thrown from house to house for more than a hundred miles.

Reading the Cultural Landscape

The rural settlement forms described above provide a chance to "read" the cultural landscape. In doing so, we must always be cautious, looking for the subtle as well as the overt and not jumping to conclusions too quickly.

For example, the Maya Indians of the Yucatán Peninsula in Mexico reside in checkerboard villages, a rural settlement landscape that is both revealing and potentially misleading (Figure 7.30 on page 256). Before the Spanish conquest, Mayas lived in wet-point villages of the irregular clustered type, situated alongside *cenotes*, natural sinkholes that provided water in a land with no surface streams. The Spaniards destroyed these settlements, replacing them with checkerboard villages. Wide, straight streets accommodated the wheeled vehicles of the European conquerors.

Superficially, the checkerboard landscape suggests a cultural victory by the Spaniards. If you look more closely, though, you will see that, in fact, Mayan culture prevailed. Even today, many Mayas make little use of wheeled vehicles in village life, and many of the Spaniards' "streets" serve merely as rights-of-way for Indian footpaths that wind among boulders and outcroppings of bedrock. Irregularities in the checkerboard, coupled with a casual distribution of dwellings, suggest Mayan resistance to the new geometry. Spanish-influenced architecture—flat-roofed houses of stone, the town hall, a church, and a hacienda mansion—remain confined to the area near the central plaza, with newer examples along highway entrances to the village. The Catholic church stands on the very place where an ancient Maya temple had been. A block away,

the traditional Maya pole huts with thatched, hipped roofs prevail, echoed by cook houses of the same design. Indian influence increases markedly with distance from the plaza.

The dooryard gardens surrounding each hut are full of traditional Indian plants—such as papayas, bananas, chili peppers, nuts, yucca, and maize—with only a few citrus trees to reveal Spanish influence. In the same yards, each carefully ringed with dry rock walls, as in pre-Columbian times, pigs descended from those introduced by the conquerors share the ground with the traditional turkeys of the Maya and apiaries for indigenous stingless bees. Occasionally, the Mayan language is heard drifting from hammocks in the pole huts, although Spanish prevails. So does Catholicism, but the absence of huts around the once-sacred cenote suggests a lingering pagan influence.

Sometimes, then, the overt aspects of cultural landscape are merely a facade. We should always look deeper and become sensitive to subtle visual clues.

Conclusion

In our study of population geography, we have seen that humankind is unevenly distributed over the Earth. Spatial variations in fertility, death rates, rates of population change, age groups, gender ratios, and standards of living also exist, and we depicted these patterns as culture regions. The principles of cultural diffusion proved useful in analyzing human migration and also helped explain the spread of birth control and diseases.

By adopting the viewpoint of cultural ecology, we saw how the environment and people's perception of it influence the distribution of people and sometimes help

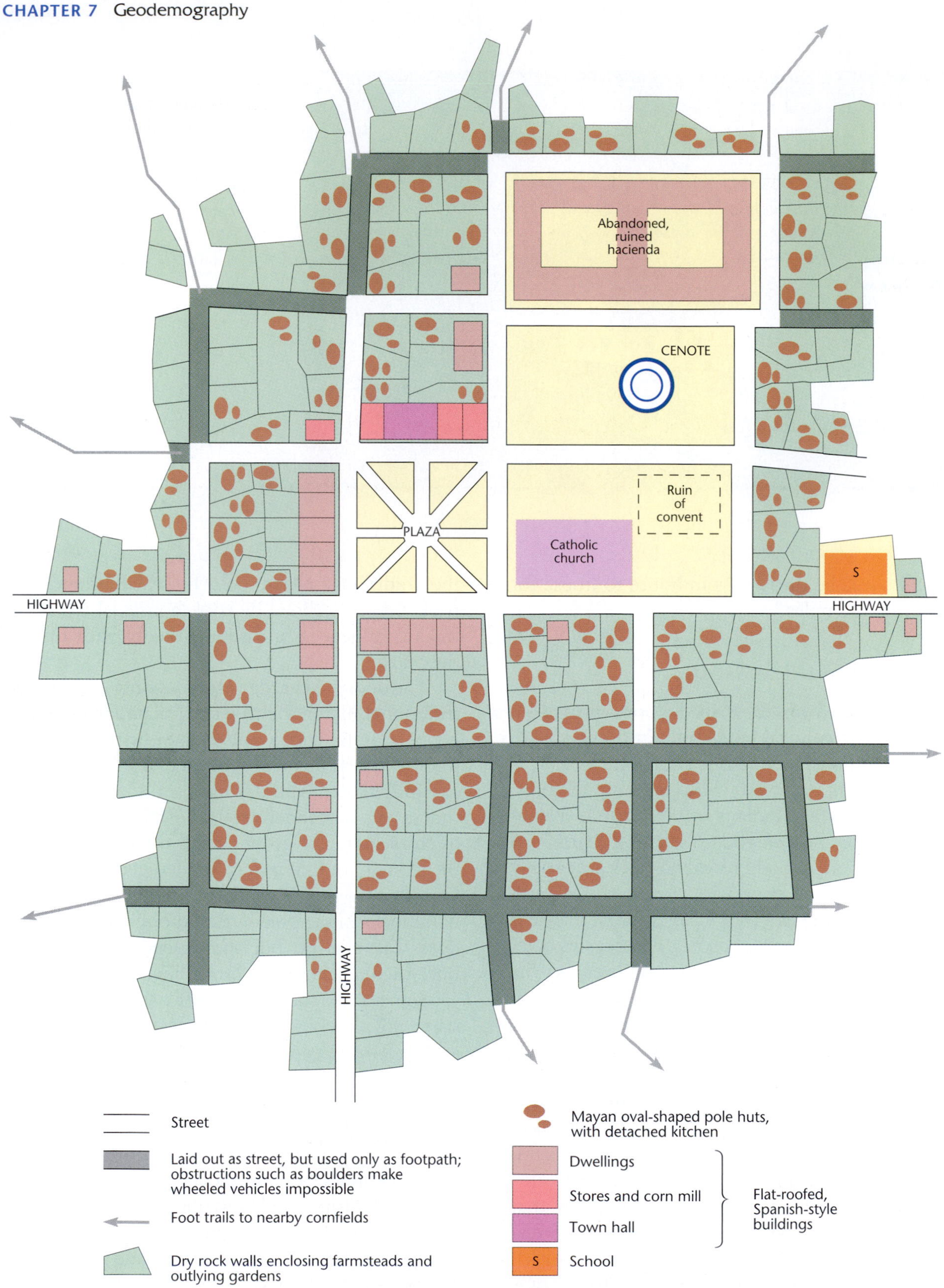

Figure 7.30

A hypothetical modern Mayan checkerboard farm village in Yucatán Province, Mexico. Spanish influence—seen in the grid pattern, plaza, church, hacienda, and flat-roofed buildings—weakens with distance from the center, and the rigid checkerboard masks a certain irregularity of farmstead layout. A cenote is a large, deep sinkhole filled with water, and these natural pools served a major religious function among the Mayas before Christianity came. (Source: Composite of 1987 field observations by Terry G. Jordan-Bychkov in some 15 villages east and southeast of Mérida.)

guide migrations. We also found that population density is linked to the level of environmental alteration and that overpopulation can have a destructive impact on the environment.

Cultural interaction suggests how demography and mobility are linked to such elements of culture as food preferences, migration taboos, politics, and economic opportunity. Cultural attitudes can encourage people to be mobile or to stay in one place and can lead them to accept crowding or to feel uncomfortable without plenty of personal space. In many ways, then, spatial variations in demographic traits are enmeshed in the fabric of culture.

How people distribute themselves over the Earth's surface finds a vivid expression in the cultural landscape. Using the example of the rural landscape, we have seen how different cultures developed distinctive settlement forms, each of which reflects a unique distribution of population on the local level.

SEEING GEOGRAPHY

Street in Kolkata, India

Do you need your "personal space"? Most Americans and Canadians do. If so, Kolkata (formerly Calcutta), India, is a place you might want to avoid. The photo was taken in March 2001, on precisely the day the Indian government announced that the country's population had well exceeded 1 billion and that 181 million had been added to India's population between the censuses of 1991 and 2001. West Bengal state, where Kolkata is located, has the highest population density in the country.

Why do people form such unpleasant clusters—regions of extremely dense population? The theme of cultural interaction would tell us of *push factors* that encourage people to leave their farms and move to the city. Some can no longer make a living or feed their families from the tiny plots of land they work. Others are forced off the land by landlords who want to convert to mechanized western methods of agriculture that use far less labor (see Chapter 8). But cultural interaction also tells us of *pull factors* exerted by cities such as Kolkata—the hope or promise of better-paying jobs, the encouragement of friends and relatives who had come to the city earlier, or the greater availability of government services.

And so, pushed and pulled, they come to the teeming, overcrowded city, to jostle and elbow their way through the streets.

Would you feel comfortable walking here? If not, why not?

A street scene in the large city of Kolkata, India.

Population Geography on the Internet

Learn more about the world's population at the following web sites:

Population Association of America
http://www.popassoc.org/
An interdisciplinary society of professionals working on the study of population.

Demography and Population Studies, Canberra, Australia
http://demography.anu.edu.au/VirtualLibrary/
An Internet guide to the subject, based at the Australian National University.

National Center for Health Statistics (NCHS)
http://www.cdc.gov/nchswww/products/pubs/pubd/netpubs.htm
Most NCHS reports can be viewed here using Adobe Acrobat Reader software. The reports include U.S. data on births, deaths, divorces, and marriages subdivided by age, fertility rate, life expectancy, and race.

Population Index, Office of Population Research, Princeton University
http://popindex.princeton.edu
This database provides bibliographic information and abstracts of articles from 400 journals in related fields.

Center for Demography and Ecology
http://www.ssc.wisc.edu/cde/
A multidisciplinary faculty research center based at the University of Wisconsin–Madison.

Population Reference Bureau, Inc., Washington, DC
http://www.prb.org/
An organization concerned principally with the issues of overpopulation and standard of living. The bureau has various publications.

Statistical Abstract of the United States
http://www.census.gov/prod/www/statistical-abstract-us.html
The *Statistical Abstract* from the U.S. Census Bureau can be viewed using Adobe Acrobat Reader software. This annual publication features data on education, health and nutrition, labor, income, and population.

United Nations High Commissioner for Refugees
http://www.unhcr.ch/
A United Nations web site that provides basic information about refugee situations worldwide, including those of western Africa, Bosnia, and Asia. The site includes regularly updated maps showing refugee locations and populations and photos of refugee life.

U.S. Centers for Disease Control and Prevention, Atlanta, Georgia
http://www.cdc.gov/
A clearinghouse for the latest information on health and epidemics in the United States.

World Health Organization, Geneva, Switzerland
http://www.who.int/home-page/
Learn about the group that distributes information on health, mortality, and epidemics, as it seeks to improve health conditions around the globe.

World Population Data Sheet, Washington, D.C.
http://www.prb.org/content/navigationmenu/other_reports/2000-2002/2001_world_population_data_sheet.htm
This site gives updated demographic information for every country in the world, from the Population Reference Bureau.

Worldwatch Institute, Washington, DC
http://www.worldwatch.org
This organization is concerned with the ecological consequences of overpopulation and the wasteful use of resources. It seeks sustainable ways to support the world's population and brings attention to ecological crises.

Sources

Bunge, William W. 1973. "The Geography of Human Survival." *Annals of the Association of American Geographers* 63: 275–295.

Chakravarti, Aninda K. 1982. "Diet and Disease: Some Cultural Aspects of Food Use in India," in Allen G. Noble and Ashok K. Dutt (eds.), *India: Cultural Patterns and Processes*. Boulder, Colo.: Westview Press, 301–323.

Coale, Ansley J., and Susan C. Watkins. 1986. *The Decline of Fertility in Europe*. Princeton, N.J.: Princeton University Press.

de Macgregor, María T. de Gutiérrez. 1984. "Population Geography in Mexico," in John J. Clarke (ed.), *Geography and Population*. Oxford: Pergamon.

Deshler, Walter. 1960. "Livestock Trypanosomiasis and Human Settlement in Northeastern Uganda." *Geographical Review* 50: 541–554.

Dupâquier, J., and A. Fauve-Chamoux (eds.). 1983. *Malthus Past and Present*. New York: Academic Press.

Garnett, Alice. 1935. "Insolation, Topography, and Settlement in the Alps." *Geographical Review* 25: 601–617.

Gelbard, Alene, Carl Haub, and Mary M. Kent. 1999. "World Population Beyond Six Billion." *Population Bulletin* 54(1): 3–44.

Gober, Patricia. 1985. "The Retirement Community as a Geographical Phenomenon: The Case of Sun City, Arizona." *Journal of Geography* 84: 189–198.

Gould, Peter. 1993. *The Slow Plague: A Geography of the AIDS Pandemic*. Oxford: Blackwell.

Hooper, Edward. 1999. *The River: A Journey to the Source of HIV and AIDS*. Boston: Little, Brown.

Hooson, David J. M. 1960. "The Distribution of Population as the Essential Geographical Expression." *Canadian Geographer* 4: 10–20.

Human Development Report 2000. 2000. New York: United Nations Publications.

Johnston, R. J. 1976. "Population Distributions and the Essentials of Human Geography." *South African Geographical Journal* 58: 93–106.

Jordan, Terry G. 1973. *The European Culture Area: A Systematic Geography.* New York: Harper & Row.

Libbee, Michael J., and David E. Sopher. 1970. "Marriage Migration in Rural India," in L. A. Kosinski and R. M. Prothero (eds.), *People on the Move.* Harlow, England: Longman.

Malthus, Thomas R. 1989 (original work published 1798). *An Essay on the Principle of Population.* Patricia James (ed.). Cambridge: Cambridge University Press.

Mattingly, Paul F., and Elsa Schmidt. 1971. "The Maghreb: Population Density." *Annals of the Association of American Geographers* 61 (Map Supplement No. 15).

Paul, Bimal K. 1994. "AIDS in Asia." *Geographical Review* 84: 367–379.

Shannon, Gary W., Gerald F. Pyle, and Rashid L. Bashshur. 1991. *The Geography of AIDS: Origins and Course of an Epidemic.* New York: Guilford.

Skelton, Tracey, and Gill Valentine (eds.). 1998. *Cool Places: Geographies of Youth Cultures.* London: Routledge.

Spain, Daphne. 1992. *Gendered Spaces.* Chapel Hill: University of North Carolina Press.

Stone, Kirk H. 1962. "Swedish Fringes of Settlement." *Annals of the Association of American Geographers* 52: 373–393.

Tuan, Yi-fu. 1998. *Escapism.* Baltimore: Johns Hopkins University Press.

Tyner, James A. 1996. "Filipina Migrant Entertainers." *Gender, Place and Culture* 3: 77–93.

Wagley, Charles. 1973. "Cultural Influences on Population: A Comparison of Two Tupi Tribes," in Daniel R. Gross (ed.), *Peoples and Cultures of Native South America.* Garden City, N.Y.: Doubleday.

Westermanns Grosser Atlas zur Weltgeschichte. 1956. Braunschweig, Germany: Georg Westermann.

World Population Data Sheet. 2002. Washington, D.C.: Population Reference Bureau.

Ten Recommended Books on Population Geography

(For additional suggested readings, see The Human Mosaic *web site:* www.whfreeman.com/jordan*)*

Castles, Stephen, and Mark J. Miller. 1998. *The Age of Migration: International Population Movements in the Modern World,* 2nd ed. New York: Guilford. A global perspective on migrations, why they occur, and the effects they have on different countries, in an age of unprecedented volume of migration. Explores how migration has led to the formation of ethnic minorities in numerous countries as well as its impact on domestic politics and economics.

Coleman, David, and Roger Schofield (eds.). 1986. *The State of Population Theory: Forward from Malthus.* New York: Basil Blackwell. A collection of essays aimed at improving existing population theory originating from a 1984 demography symposium. Topics range from hunter-gatherer populations to sub-Saharan systems of reproduction to religion and reproduction in contemporary Europe.

Currey, Bruce, and Graeme Hugo (eds.). 1984. *Famine as a Geographical Phenomenon.* Dordrecht, Netherlands: D. Reidel. A collection of papers on the geography of famine and rural development aimed at researchers, policy makers, and aid workers. Argues that geographers have an important role to play in preventing famines and developing advance warning systems in areas of potential food shortages.

Gesler, Wilbert M. 1991. *The Cultural Geography of Health Care.* Pittsburgh: University of Pittsburgh Press. Examines health and disease in their cultural context with examples from the Appalachians, India, and China. Attention is given to the role culture plays in the development of different health care delivery systems.

Jones, Huw. 1990. *Population Geography,* 2nd ed. New York: Guilford. An undergraduate text devoted to population dynamics and presented in a spatial and temporal context. Case studies are drawn widely from developed and less developed countries.

Mackay, Judith. 1993. *The State of Health Atlas.* New York: Simon & Schuster. A collection of 35 color maps of current health conditions around the world, including population control, fertility, and life expectancy.

Massey, Doreen. 1994. *Space, Place, and Gender.* Minneapolis: University of Minnesota Press. A collection of Massey's essays that theorize about the social structure of space and place with special attention to their intersection with gender. Included are discussions of uneven regional development and the social construction of gender relations.

Meade, Melinda S., and Robert J. Earickson. 1999. *Medical Geography,* 2nd ed. New York: Guilford. Surveys the perspectives, theories, and methodologies that geographers use in studying human health; a primary text that undergraduates can readily understand.

Newman, James L. 1995. *The Peopling of Africa: A Geographic Interpretation.* New Haven, Conn.: Yale University Press. Explores the role of genetic background, language, occupation, and religion as well as differing natural and human environmental circumstances in the peopling of Africa before the arrival of European colonialists.

Roberts, Brian K. 1996. *Landscapes of Settlement.* London: Routledge. Discusses the role and significance of rural settlements drawing from global case studies. Outlines the formation of different spatial arrangements at the farmstead, hamlet, and village scales.

Journals in Population Geography

Gender, Place and Culture: A Journal of Feminist Geography. Published by the Carfax Publishing Co., P.O. Box 2025, Dunnellon, FL 34430. Volume 1 appeared in 1994.

Population Bulletin. Published quarterly by the Population Reference Bureau, 1875 Connecticut Ave. NW, Suite 520, Washington, DC 20009.

Population and Environment: A Journal of Interdisciplinary Studies. Volume 1 was published in 1996.

Why does the "human mosaic" in this scene have curved lines?

A rural scene in southern Brazil. (S. Maze/Woodfin Camp/PictureQuest.)
Turn to Seeing Geography *on page 294 for an in-depth analysis of the above question.*

AGRICULTURAL GEOGRAPHY
Food from the Good Earth

The world's huge population seeks its livelihood in various ways, but all of us depend, either directly or indirectly, on agriculture for the daily food that permits our survival. We can too easily forget that the entire urban-industrial society rests, none too securely, on the base of the food surplus generated by farmers and herders, and that without agriculture there could be no cities or universities, no factories or offices.

Agriculture, the tilling of crops and rearing of domesticated animals to produce food, feed, drink, and fiber, has been the principal enterprise of humankind through all of recorded history. Even today, agriculture remains by far the most important economic activity in the world, occupying the greater part of the land area and employing about 40 percent of the working population. In some parts of Asia and Africa, over three-quarters of the labor force is devoted to agriculture. North Americans, on the other hand, live in an urban society in which less than 2 percent of the population work as agriculturists. As recently as 1880, 44 percent of all Americans were farmers, but since then we have relied on an ever smaller segment of our population to produce the food and fiber we need. Europe's population is as thoroughly nonagricultural as North America's. Most of the rest of the world, however, remains a land of farm villages, like those described at the end of Chapter 7.

 ## Agro-Regions

How is the theme of culture region relevant to agriculture? Over the course of thousands of years, farmers adapted to different habitats, creating an array of different types of agriculture, each of which occupies a formal **agro-region** (Figure 8.1). Each type has a name.

Agricultural Regions

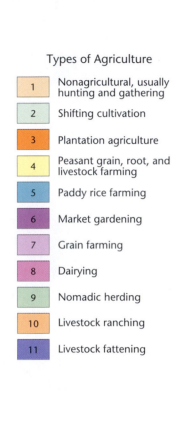

Types of Agriculture

1	Nonagricultural, usually hunting and gathering
2	Shifting cultivation
3	Plantation agriculture
4	Peasant grain, root, and livestock farming
5	Paddy rice farming
6	Market gardening
7	Grain farming
8	Dairying
9	Nomadic herding
10	Livestock ranching
11	Livestock fattening

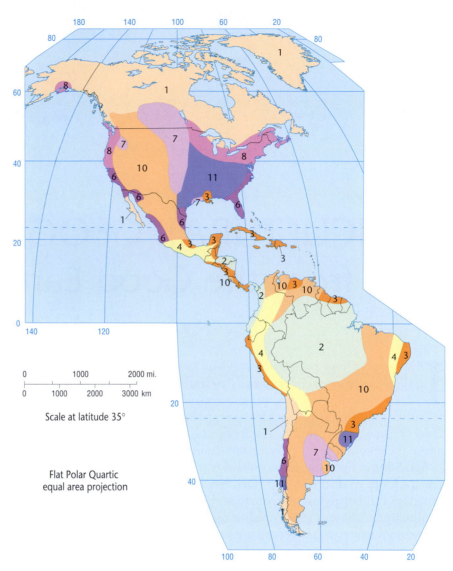

0   1000   2000 mi.

0   1000   2000   3000 km

Scale at latitude 35°

Flat Polar Quartic
equal area projection

Figure 8.1

Agricultural regions of the world today. (BASED ON GRIGG, 1969; AND WHITTLESEY, 1936, WITH MODIFICATIONS.)

Shifting Cultivation

The native peoples of tropical lowlands and hills in the Americas, Africa, Southeast Asia, and Indonesia practice a land-rotation agricultural system known as **shifting cultivation.** Using machetes or other bladed instruments, shifting cultivators chop away the undergrowth from small patches of land and kill the trees by removing a strip of bark completely around the trunk. After the dead vegetation dries out, the farmers set it on fire to clear the land. Because of these clearing techniques, shifting culti-

vation is also called *slash-and-burn* agriculture. Working with digging sticks or hoes, the farmers then plant a variety of crops in the ash-covered clearings, varying from the maize (corn), beans, bananas, and manioc of American Indians to the yams and nonirrigated rice grown by hill tribes in Southeast Asia (Figure 8.2 on page 264). Different crops typically share the same clearing, a practice called **intertillage.** This technique allows taller, stronger crops to shelter lower, more fragile ones from the tropical downpours and reveals the rich lore and learning acquired by shifting cultivators over many centuries. Rela-

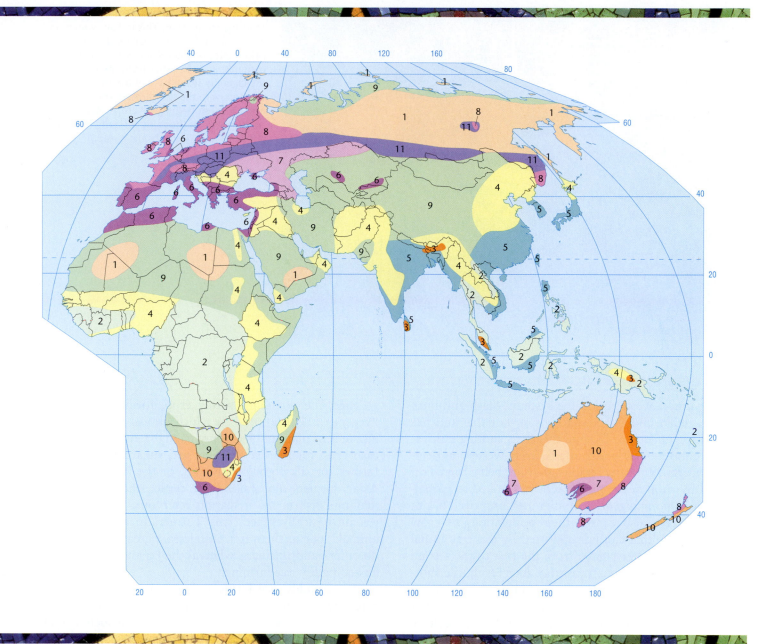

tively little tending of the plants is necessary until harvest time, and no fertilizer is applied to the fields, because the ashes from the fire are sufficient to feed the crops.

Farmers repeat the planting and harvesting cycle in the same clearings for perhaps four or five years, until the soil loses much of its fertility. Then these fields are abandoned, and the farmers prepare new clearings to replace them. The abandoned cropland lies unused and recuperates for 10 to 20 years before farmers clear and cultivate it again. Shifting cultivation represents one form of **subsistence agriculture:** food production mainly for the fam-

ily and local community rather than for market. Farm animals play only a small role in shifting cultivation. Farmers keep few if any livestock, often relying on hunting and fishing for much of their food supply.

The technology of shifting cultivation may seem crude and poorly developed, but it has proved to be an efficient adaptive strategy for the people who practice this system. Slash-and-burn farming returns more calories of food for the calories spent on cultivation than does modern mechanized agriculture. We should never assume that modern Western agricultural methods are superior to those of

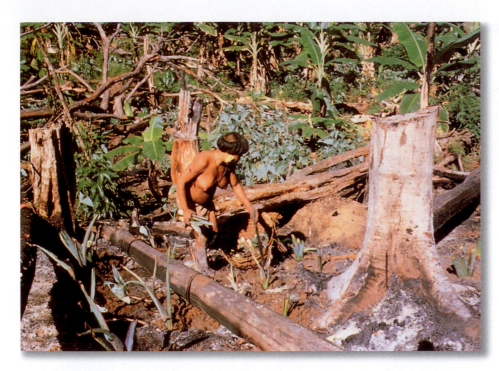

Figure 8.2

Shifting cultivation. This Indian woman in the Amazon Basin of Brazil tends a typical field. Note the intertillage, which includes bananas, and the ashes from the burning of the clearing at the base of the tree stump. Women were the first farmers and domesticated perhaps all crops. **Are "primitive" methods necessarily inferior?** (HELEN TREMBLY/FAMILIES OF THE WORLD.)

traditional non-Western farming systems. Slash-and-burn farming, unlike modern systems, is sustainable and has endured for millennia. Despite this fact, shifting cultivators are continuously under attack from Western agricultural "experts." In many regions, they are being forced off the land by rural development schemes linked to globalization or by nonindigenous immigrants. Improved health conditions have also caused their populations to grow beyond the size that can be supported by this traditional farming system. They passed from the first to the second stage of the demographic transition. As a result, the shifting cultivators must shorten the period when the land is recuperating, causing environmental deterioration. For these reasons, an ecologically benign type of agriculture has declined.

Paddy Rice Farming

Peasant farmers in the humid tropical and subtropical parts of Asia practice a highly distinctive type of subsistence agriculture called **paddy rice farming.** From the monsoon coasts of India through the hills of southeastern China and on to the warmer parts of Korea and Japan stretches a broad region of diked, flooded rice fields, or paddies, many of which perch on terraced hillsides (Figure 8.3). The paddy must be drained and repaired each year. The terraced paddy fields form a striking cultural landscape, the hallmark of this type of agriculture (see Figure 1.17).

Rice, the dominant paddy crop, forms the basis of "vegetable civilizations" in which almost all the caloric intake is of plant origin. Many paddy farmers also raise a cash crop for market, such as tea, sugarcane, mulberry bushes for silkworm production, or the fiber crop jute. Asian farmers also raise pigs, cattle, and poultry and maintain fish in the irrigation reservoirs, although they remain basically vegetarians. Farmers in India use draft animals such as the water buffalo to a greater extent than do other paddy farmers, whereas the Japanese have mechanized paddy rice farming.

Most paddy rice farms are tiny. A landholding of 3 acres (about 1 hectare) is considered adequate to support a farm family. Asian farmers can survive on such a small scale of operation partly because irrigated rice provides a very large output of food per unit of land. Still, the paddy farmers must till their small patches most intensively to harvest enough food. They must carefully transplant the small rice sprouts from seed beds to the paddy. People from Western cultures can scarcely imagine the magnitude of tedious hand labor involved. Often, paddy farmers also plant and harvest the same parcel of land two times each year—a practice known as **double-cropping**—while applying large amounts of organic fertilizer to the land. So productive is this system that per-acre yields exceed those of American agriculture.

The modern era has witnessed a restructuring of paddy rice farming in the more developed countries such as Japan, Korea, and Taiwan. In some cases, the entire terrace

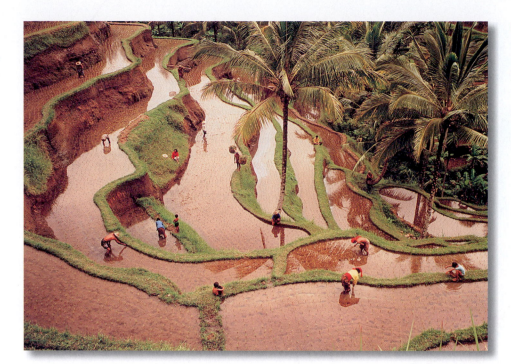

Figure 8.3
Cultivation of rice on the island of Bali, Indonesia. Paddy rice farming traditionally entails enormous amounts of human labor and yields very high productivity per unit of land. **What are the disadvantages of such a system?** (DENIS WAUGH/TONY STONE IMAGES.)

structure has been reengineered to produce larger fields that can be worked with machines. In addition, dams, electric pumps, and reservoirs now provide a more reliable water supply, and high-yielding seeds, pesticides, and chemical fertilizers boost production further. Most paddy rice farmers now produce mainly for urban markets.

Peasant Grain, Root, and Livestock Farming

In colder, drier Asian farming regions that are climatically unsuited to paddy rice farming—as well as in the river valleys of the Middle East, in parts of Europe, in Africa, and in the mountain highlands of Latin America and New Guinea—farmers practice a diverse system of agriculture based on bread grains, root crops, and herd livestock (Figures 8.4 on the next page and 8.5 on page 267). Because they still adhere to *folk cultures,* these farmers are called **peasants.** The dominant grain crops in these regions are, variously, wheat, barley, sorghum, millet, oats, and maize. Many farmers in these areas also raise a cash crop, such as cotton, flax, hemp, coffee, or tobacco.

These farmers also raise herds of cattle, pigs, sheep, and, in South America, llamas and alpacas. The livestock pull the plow; provide milk, meat, and wool; serve as beasts of burden; and produce manure for the fields. They also consume a portion of the grain harvest. In some areas, such as the Middle Eastern river valleys, the use of irrigation helps support this peasant system. Modernization has made few inroads.

Plantation Agriculture

In certain tropical and subtropical areas, Europeans and Americans imposed a commercial agricultural system on the native types of subsistence agriculture. This system is called **plantation agriculture.** A plantation is a huge landholding devoted to the efficient, large-scale, specialized production of one tropical or subtropical crop for market. Plantation agriculture long relied on large amounts of hand labor. The plantation system originated in the 1400s on Portuguese-owned sugarcane-producing islands off the coast of tropical West Africa—São Tomé and Principe—but the greatest concentration is now in the American tropics. Most plantations lie near the seacoast, close to the shipping lanes that carry their produce to nontropical lands such as Europe, the United States, and Japan.

Most workers live right on the plantation, where a rigid social and economic segregation of labor and management produces a two-class society of the wealthy and the poor. Traditionally, as in the antebellum southern United States, many plantation owners relied on slaves to provide the needed labor. Today, because of the capital investment required, corporations or governments are usually the owners of plantations. Tension between labor and management is not uncommon, and the societal ills of the plantation system remain far from cured (Figure 8.6 on page 267).

The plantation provided the base for European and American economic expansion into tropical Asia, Africa,

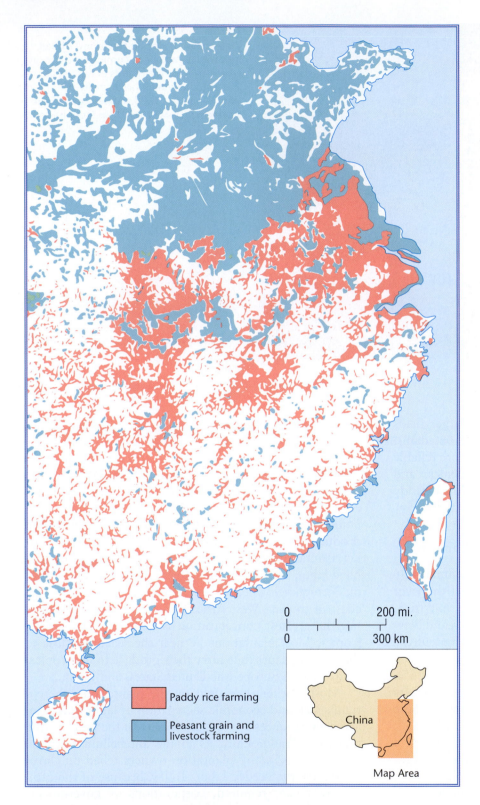

0   200 mi.

0   300 km

Paddy rice farming

Peasant grain and
livestock farming

China

Map Area

and Latin America. It maximizes the production of luxury crops for Europeans and Americans: sugarcane, bananas, coffee, coconuts, spices, tea, cacao, and tobacco (Figure 8.7). Similarly, Western textile factories require cotton, sisal, jute, hemp, and other fiber crops from the planta-

tion areas. Much of the profit from these plantations is exported, along with the crops themselves, to Europe and North America.

Each plantation district in the tropical and subtropical zones tends to specialize in one crop. Coffee and tea, for

Figure 8.5
Peasant grain, root, and livestock agriculture in highland New Guinea. Distinctive "raised fields" with sweet potato mounds are found here among the farmers of highland New Guinea. These people raise diverse crops but give the greatest importance to sweet potatoes, together with pigs. **Why might they go to the trouble of creating these small mounds?** (Courtesy of Terry G. Jordan-Bychkov.)

Figure 8.6
Plantation agriculture. This sign was erected by the management at the entrance to a banana plantation in Costa Rica. "Welcome to Freehold Plantation, a workplace where labor harmony reigns; in mutual respect and understanding, we united workers produce and export quality goods in peace and harmony." **How does this message suggest that, in fact, not all is harmonious here and that the tension of the two-class plantation system might simmer below the surface?** (Courtesy of Terry G. Jordan-Bychkov.)

instance, grow in the tropical highlands, with coffee dominating the upland plantations of tropical America and tea confined mainly to the hill slopes of India and Sri Lanka. Today, coffee remains the economic lifeblood of many less developed countries, whereas sugarcane and bananas are the major lowland plantation crops of tropical America. In most cases, plantation workers process the crop at least partially before sending it to the distant market. For example, sugar is generally milled and cotton ginned on the plantation. This combination of raising and partially

Figure 8.7
Tea plantation in the highlands of Papua New Guinea. Although profitable for the owners and providing employment for a small labor force, the plantation recently displaced a much larger population of peasant grain, root, and livestock farmers. This is one result of globalization. **Should the government have prevented such a displacement?** (Courtesy of Terry G. Jordan-Bychkov.)

processing the crop is a major distinguishing trait of the plantation system.

Globalization has brought major changes to plantation agriculture. Increasingly, machines have replaced hand labor, and the former workers, unemployed, flock to the cities of the Third World countries. The mechanized, modernized system is called a *neoplantation*.

Market Gardening

The growth of urban markets in the last few centuries also gave rise to other commercial forms of agriculture, including **market gardening,** also known as truck farming. Unlike plantations, truck farms are located in developed countries and specialize in intensively cultivated nontropical fruits, vegetables, and vines. They raise no livestock. Many districts concentrate on a single product such as wine, table grapes, raisins, olives, oranges, apples, lettuce, or potatoes, and the entire farm output is raised for sale rather than for consumption on the farm. Many truck farmers participate in cooperative marketing arrangements and depend on migratory seasonal farm laborers to harvest their crops. Market garden districts appear in most industrialized countries. In the United States, a broken belt of market gardens extends from California eastward through the Gulf and Atlantic coast states, with scattered districts in other parts of the country. The lands around the Mediterranean Sea are dominated by market gardens.

Livestock Fattening

In **livestock fattening,** farmers raise and fatten cattle and hogs for slaughter. One of the most highly developed fattening areas is the famous Corn Belt of the midwestern United States, where farmers raise maize and soybeans to feed cattle and hogs. A similar system prevails over much of western and central Europe, though the feed crops there are more commonly oats and potatoes. Smaller zones of commercial livestock fattening appear in overseas European settlement zones such as southern Brazil and South Africa.

One of the main traditional characteristics of livestock fattening is the combination of crop and animal raising. Farmers breed many of the animals they fatten, especially hogs. In the last half of the twentieth century, under the impetus of globalization, livestock fatteners began to specialize their activities; some concentrated on breeding animals, others on preparing them for market. In the factorylike **feedlot,** farmers raise imported cattle and hogs on purchased feed (Figure 8.8). Such feedlots are most common in the western and southern United States, partly because winters are less severe there.

Although commercial livestock fattening is often organized with assembly-line precision and has proved profitable, the specter of famine in recent years has brought its nutritional efficiency into question. In the 1900s, world grain production rose significantly faster than world population growth, and cereals provide most of

Figure 8.8
Cattle feedlot for beef production. This feedlot, in Colorado, is reputedly the world's largest. **What ecological problems might such an enterprise cause?** (WILLIAM STRODE/WOODFIN CAMP.)

Figure 8.9

A "wheat landscape" in the Palouse Country, a grain farming region on the borders of Washington and Oregon. Grain elevators are a typical part of such agricultural landscapes. The raising of one crop such as wheat over entire regions is called *monoculture*. **What problems might be linked to monoculture?** (COURTESY OF TERRY G. JORDAN-BYCHKOV.)

the protein intake of the world's people. But in the same century, meat eating soared in the Western world, particularly in the United States, wiping out most of these gains. At least one-half of America's harvested agricultural land is planted with feed crops for livestock, and over 70 percent of the grain raised in the United States goes for livestock fattening. Livestock are not an efficient method of protein production. A cow, for instance, must eat 21 pounds (9.5 kilograms) of protein to produce 1 pound (0.5 kilogram) of edible protein. Plants are far more efficient protein converters. The protein lost through conversion from plant to meat could make up almost all of the world's present protein deficiencies. The food that today feeds Americans alone would feed 1.5 billion at the consumption level of China. This basic inefficiency has spread to some poorer nations, such as Costa Rica and Brazil, where rain forest is being destroyed and shifting cultivators displaced to make way for cattle pasture to fatten beef for America's fast-food restaurants.

Grain Farming

Grain farming is a type of specialized agriculture in which farmers grow wheat or, less often, rice or corn for commercial markets. Wheat belts stretch through Australia, the Great Plains of interior North America, the steppes of Russia and Ukraine, and the pampas of Argentina. Together, the United States, Canada, Argentina, Russia, and Ukraine produce 27 percent of the world's wheat. Farms

in these areas are generally very large. They range from family-run wheat farms to giant corporation or collective farms (Figure 8.9). Extensive rice farms, operated under the same commercial system, occupy small areas of the Texas-Louisiana coastal plain and lowlands in Arkansas and California.

Widespread use of machinery, chemical fertilizers, pesticides, and improved seed varieties enables grain farmers to operate on this large scale. The planting and harvesting of grain is more completely mechanized than any other form of agriculture. Commercial rice farmers employ such techniques as sowing grain from airplanes. Harvesting is usually done by hired migratory crews using corporation-owned machines (Figure 8.10 on the next page). Perhaps the ultimate development is the *suitcase farm* in the Wheat Belt of the northern Great Plains of the United States. The people who own and operate these farms do not live on the land. Most of them own several suitcase farms, lined up in a south-to-north row through the Plains states. They keep fleets of farm machinery, which they send north with crews of laborers along the string of suitcase farms to plant, fertilize, and harvest the wheat. The progressively later ripening of the grain as one moves north allows these farmers to maintain crops on all their farms with the same crew and the same machinery. Except for visits by migratory crews, the suitcase farms are uninhabited.

Such highly mechanized, absentee-owned, large-scale operations, or **agribusinesses,** are rapidly replacing the traditional American family farm, an important part of

Figure 8.10
Mechanized wheat harvest on the Great Plains of the United States. North American grain farmers operate in a capital-intensive manner, investing in machines, chemical fertilizers, and pesticides. **What long-term problems might such methods cause? What benefits are realized in such a system?** (ROGER DU BUISSON/THE STOCK MARKET.)

our rural heritage. Geographer Ingolf Vogeler documented the decline of family farms in the American countryside and argued that U.S. governmental policies, prompted by the forces of globalization, have consistently favored agribusiness interests, hastening the decline. We have now reached the point where the American family farm, though perpetuated as a myth and icon, is no longer of much consequence in the grain lands.

Dairying

In many ways, the specialized production of dairy goods closely resembles livestock fattening (see Focus On: Thomas Hardy on the Geography of Dairying). In the large dairy belts of the northern United States from New England to the upper Midwest, western and northern Europe, southeastern Australia, and northern New Zealand, the keeping of dairy cows depends on the large-scale use of pastures. In colder areas, some acreage must be devoted to winter feed crops, especially hay. Dairy products vary from region to region, depending in part on how close the farmers are to their markets. Dairy belts near large urban centers usually produce fluid milk, which is more perishable, whereas those farther away specialize in butter, cheese, or processed milk. New Zealanders, remote from world markets, produce much butter, which can be exported more easily than milk.

> ### Reflecting on **GEOGRAPHY**
> Why is *dairying* confined to northern Europe and the overseas lands settled by northern Europeans? (See Figure 8.1.)

As with livestock fattening, in recent decades a rapidly increasing number of dairy farmers have adopted the feedlot system and now raise their cattle on feed purchased from other sources. Feedlots are especially common in the southern United States. Often situated on the suburban fringes of large cities for quick access to market, the dairy feedlots are factory farms. Farmers buy feed and livestock replacements, instead of breeding and raising them on the farm. In these large-scale, automated operations, the number of cows is far greater than on family-operated dairy farms. Like industrial factory owners, feedlot dairy owners rely on hired laborers to help maintain their herds. Although less pleasing to the eye and nose than traditional dairy farms, the feedlots represent another stage in the rise of globalization-induced agribusiness and the decline of the family farm.

Nomadic Herding

In the dry or cold lands of the Eastern Hemisphere, particularly in the deserts, prairies, and *savannas*—tropical grasslands lightly strewn with trees —of Africa, Arabia, and the interior of Eurasia, **nomadic livestock herders** graze cattle, sheep, goats, and camels (Figure 8.11) (see Focus On: The Wandering Life of the Tatars on page 272). North of the tree line in Eurasia, the cold *tundra*— a region covered with mosses, sedges, grass, and lichens— forms another zone of nomadic herders, who raise reindeer. The main characteristic of nomadic herding is the continued movement of people with their livestock in search of forage for the animals. Some nomads migrate from lowlands in winter to mountains in summer; others shift from desert areas in winter to adjacent semiarid

FOCUS ON

Thomas Hardy on the Geography of Dairying

Farming culture regions are readily observable, and you need not be a professional geographer to observe them. Some of the finest "geography" has been written by regional novelists. Among these writers, none surpasses Thomas Hardy, who penned beautiful descriptions of the countryside of his native southern England. Here is his word picture of a late nineteenth-century commercial dairy region, the Vale of Frome:

> She found herself on a summit commanding the . . . Valley of the Great Dairies, the valley in which milk and butter grew to rankness. . . . It was intrinsically different from the Vale of Little Dairies, Blackmoor Vale, which . . . she had exclusively known till now. The world was drawn to a larger pattern here. The enclosures numbered fifty acres instead of ten, the farmsteads were more extended, the groups of cattle formed tribes hereabout; there only families. These myriads of cows stretching under her eyes from the far east to the far west outnumbered any she had ever seen at one glance before.

The green lea was speckled as thickly with them as a canvas by Van Alsloot or Sallaert with burghers. . . .

> Suddenly there arose from all parts of the lowland a prolonged and repeated call—Waow waow waow. It was . . . the ordinary announcement of milking-time—half-past four o-clock, when the dairymen set about getting in the cows. The red and white herd nearest at hand, which had been phlegmatically waiting for the call, now trooped towards the steading in the background, their great bags of milk swinging under them as they walked. . . .

> Long thatched sheds stretched round the enclosure, . . . their eaves supported by wooden posts rubbed to a glossy smoothness by the flanks of infinite cows and calves of bygone years. . . . Between the posts were ranged the milchers. . . . The dairy-maids and men had flocked down from their cottages and out of the dairyhouse with the arrival of the cows from the meads. . . . Each girl sat down on her three-legged stool, her face sideways, her right cheek resting against the cow. . . .

From Hardy, 1891.

---

plains in summer, or from tundra in summer to nearby forests in winter. Many nomads place a high value on the horse, which has traditionally been kept for use in warfare, or the camel. Nomads in sub-Saharan Africa are the only ones who depend mainly on cattle.

Necessity dictates that the few material possessions the nomads have be portable, including the tents they use for housing. Usually, the nomads obtain nearly all of life's necessities from livestock products or by bartering with the sedentary farmers of adjacent river valleys and oases. For centuries, nomads presented a periodic military threat to even the greatest farming civilizations—for example, the Mongols, who attacked China, could not be held back even by the Great Wall.

Figure 8.11
Kurdish nomadic herders in Kurdistan, in far eastern Turkey, have brought these livestock, mainly sheep, to the high mountain pastures in mid-May, even before the snows have completely melted. The scene is near Lake Van. **What might prompt the Kurds to make this difficult seasonal migration?** (Courtesy of Terry G. Jordan-Bychkov.)

FOCUS ON

The Wandering Life of the Tatars

The great explorer Marco Polo saw many wondrous things on his journey across Asia, and he possessed a geographer's eye. Here is his description of nomadic herders, people previously unknown to Europeans:

> The Tatars never remain fixed, but as the winter approaches remove to the plains of a warmer region, in order to find sufficient pasture for their cattle; and in summer they frequent cold situations in the mountains, where there is water and verdure, and their cattle are free from the annoyance of horseflies and other biting insects.

During two or three months they progressively ascend higher ground, and seek fresh pasture, the grass not being adequate in any one place to feed the multitudes of which their herds and flocks consist. Their huts or tents, formed of rods covered with felt, exactly round, and nicely put together, can be gathered into one bundle, and made up as packages. . . . They eat flesh of every description, horses, camels, and even dogs, provided they are fat. They drink mare's milk, which they prepare in such a manner that it has the qualities and flavor of white wine.

From Walsh, 1948.

Today, nomadic herding is in decline almost everywhere. A number of national governments have established policies encouraging nomads to practice **sedentary cultivation** of the land. A practice begun in the nineteenth century by British and French colonial administrators in North Africa, the settling of nomadic tribes allows greater control by the central governments. Moreover, many nomads are voluntarily abandoning their traditional life to seek jobs in urban areas or in the Middle Eastern oil fields. Further impetus to abandon nomadic life recently came from severe drought in sub-Saharan Africa's *Sahel* region, which decimated livestock herds. Nomadism survives mainly in remote areas, and this traditional way of life may soon vanish altogether.

Livestock Ranching

Superficially, **ranching** might seem similar to nomadic herding, but in reality it is a fundamentally different livestock-raising system. Although both nomadic herders and livestock ranchers specialize in animal husbandry to the exclusion of crop raising and both live in arid or semiarid regions, livestock ranchers have fixed places of residence and operate as individuals rather than within a tribal organization. In addition, ranchers raise livestock for market on a large scale, not for their own subsistence, and they are typically of European ancestry rather than being an indigenous people.

Livestock ranchers, faced with the advance of farmers, long ago retreated into areas with climates too harsh for crop production. There they raise only two kinds of animals in large numbers: cattle and sheep. Ranchers in the United States and Canada, tropical and subtropical Latin America, and the warmer parts of Australia specialize in cattle raising. Midlatitude ranchers in the Southern Hemisphere specialize in sheep, to the extent that Australia, New Zealand, and Argentina produce 65 percent of the world's export wool. Sheep outnumber people 6 to 1 in Australia, and 13 to 1 in New Zealand.

Urban Agriculture

In recent decades, yet another type of agriculture has arisen, as people have migrated to cities. We might best call this **urban agriculture.** Millions of city dwellers, especially in Third World countries, now produce enough vegetables, fruit, meat, and milk from tiny plots within the cities and suburbs to provide most of their food, often with a surplus to sell. In China, urban agriculture now provides 90 percent or more of all vegetables consumed, and in African metropolises such as Nairobi and Kampala, 20 percent of all food comes from city lands. Even a developed country such as Russia derives nearly half of its food from such operations, and neighborhood gardens can also be found in inner-city areas of North America.

Nonagricultural Areas

Some lands do not support any form of agriculture. They typically lie in areas of extreme climate, particularly deserts and subarctic forests, as are found in much of Canada, Australia, and Siberia. Often these areas are inhabited by **hunting and gathering** groups of native peoples, such as the Inuit and Australian Aborigines, who gain a livelihood by hunting game, fishing where possible, and gathering edible and medicinal wild plants. At one time, before agriculture began, all humans lived as hunters and gatherers. Today, fewer than 1 percent of humans are so employed, preserving the ancient ways. Even fewer depend entirely on hunting and gathering, given the various inroads of the modern world. In most hunting and gathering societies, a division of labor by gender occurs. Males perform most of the hunting and fishing, whereas females carry out the equally important task of gathering harvests from wild plants. Hunters and gatherers can be specialized, depending on only a few sources for their food. Much more commonly, they are unspecialized, relying on a great variety of animals and plants.

> ### Reflecting on GEOGRAPHY
>
> What types of agriculture occur in the three main densely populated areas of the world? (Compare Figures 7.1 and 8.1.) Are these two characteristics—type of agriculture and population density—causally linked?

Agricultural Diffusion

Can the theme of cultural diffusion help us understand the map of agro-regions? Yes, in several ways. The various agro-regions we've discussed result from *cultural diffusion*. Agriculture and its many components are inventions; they arose as innovations in certain source areas and diffused to other parts of the world.

Origin and Diffusion of Plant Domestication

Agriculture apparently began with plant rather than animal domestication. A **domesticated plant** is one deliberately planted, protected, cared for, and used by humans. Such plants are also genetically distinct from their wild ancestors because of deliberate improvement through selective breeding by agriculturists, and they tend to be bigger than wild species, bearing larger, more abundant fruit or grain. For example, the original wild Indian maize grew on a cob only 0.75 inch (2 centimeters) long—that is, one-tenth to one-twentieth the size of the cobs of domesticated maize.

Plant domestication and improvement constituted a process, not an event. It began as the gradual culmination of hundreds, or even thousands, of years of close association between humans and the natural vegetation. The first step in domestication was the perception that a certain plant was useful, which led initially to protection of the wild plant and eventually to deliberate planting.

Cultural geographer Carl Johannessen suggests that the domestication process can still be observed today. He believes that by studying current techniques used by native subsistence farmers in places such as Central America, we can gain insight into the methods of the first farmers of prehistoric antiquity. Johannessen points out that two steps are typically required to develop and improve plant varieties: (1) selection of seeds or shoots only from superior plants; and (2) genetic isolation from other, inferior plants to prevent cross-pollination. Johannessen's study of the present-day cultivation of the *pejibaye* palm tree in Costa Rica revealed that native cultivators actively engage in seed selection. All choose the seed of fresh fruit from superior trees, ones that bear particularly desirable fruit, as determined by size, flavor, texture, and color. Such trees are often given personal names, an indication of the value placed on them. Superior seed stocks are built up gradually over the years, with the result that elderly farmers generally have the best selections. Seeds are shared freely within family and clan groups, allowing speedy diffusion of desirable traits.

Johannessen also reported that some American Indian groups clearly knew of the need for genetic isolation to reduce contamination from cross-pollination in maize plants. In Panama, for example, one Indian tribe of shifting cultivators raised 14 varieties of maize, each in a field separated from all the others by intervening forest.

When, where, and how did these processes of plant domestication develop? Cultural geographers, among others, have done research on this problem. One early leader was the famous American cultural geographer Carl Sauer (see Profile on page 276). Most experts now believe that the process of domestication occurred at many different times and locations, involving repeated *independent invention*.

Sauer believed that domestication did not develop in response to hunger. He maintained that necessity was not the mother of agricultural invention, because starving people must spend every waking hour searching for food and have no time to devote to the centuries of leisurely experimentation required to domesticate plants. Instead, this invention was accomplished by peoples who had enough food to remain settled in one place and devote considerable time to plant care. The first farmers were probably sedentary folk, rather than migratory hunters and gatherers. He reasoned that domestication did not occur in grasslands or large river floodplains because primitive cultures would have had difficulty coping with the thick sod and periodic floodwaters. Sauer also believed that the hearth areas of domestication must have

Diffusion of Agriculture

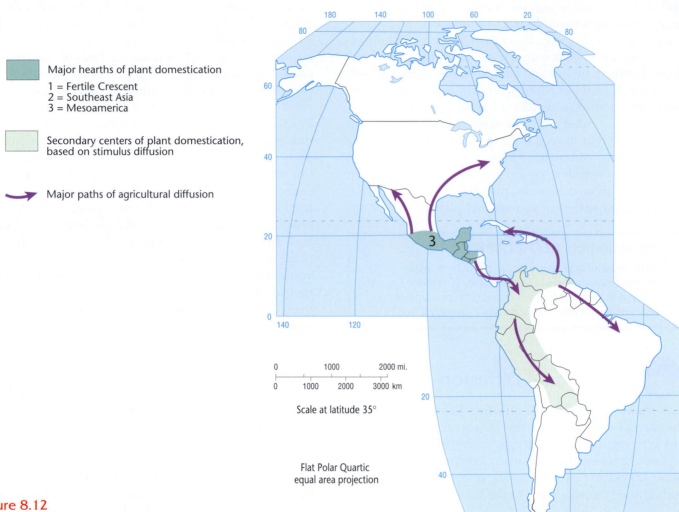

Major hearths of plant domestication
1 = Fertile Crescent
2 = Southeast Asia
3 = Mesoamerica

Secondary centers of plant domestication, based on stimulus diffusion

Major paths of agricultural diffusion

0   1000   2000 mi.
0   1000   2000   3000 km

Scale at latitude 35°

Flat Polar Quartic
equal area projection

Figure 8.12

The origin and diffusion of agriculture. Because of the antiquity of this cultural diffusion and the paucity of evidence, the map must be regarded as speculative. (SOURCES: COWAN AND WATSON, 1992; C. SAUER, 1952; AND J. SAUER, 1993, WITH MODIFICATIONS.)

been in regions of *biodiversity* where many different kinds of wild plants grew, providing abundant vegetative raw material for experimentation and crossbreeding. Such areas typically occur in hilly districts, where climates change with differing sun exposure and elevation above sea level.

Many geographers believe that agriculture arose in at least three such regions of biodiversity (Figure 8.12). Per-

haps the oldest among these primary centers is the Fertile Crescent in the Middle East, which gave us the great bread grains—wheat, barley, rye, and oats—as well as grapes, apples, olives, and many other crops. The oldest archaeological evidence of crop domestication comes from that region, suggesting an origin about 10,000 years ago. When diffusion from the Fertile Crescent brought agriculture to northern and eastern Africa, a secondary

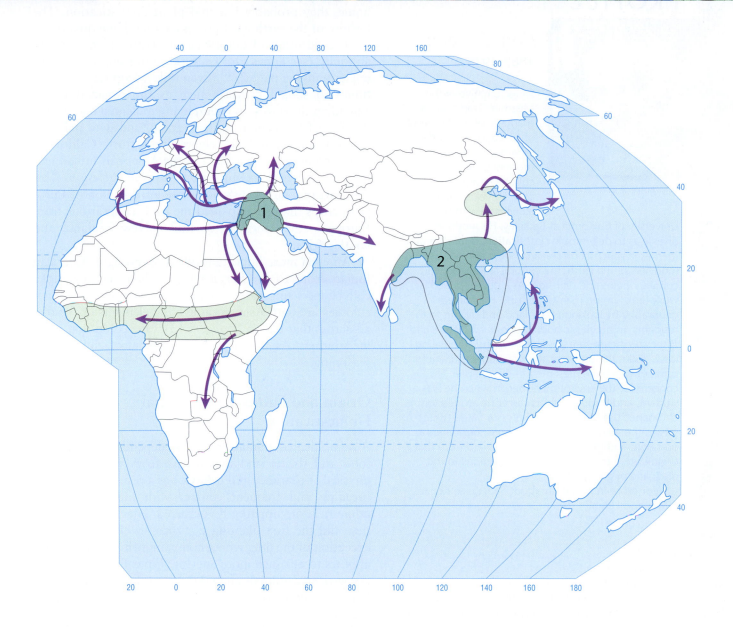

center of domestication developed through *stimulus diffusion*, adding crops such as sorghum, peanuts, yams, coffee, and okra.

The second great center of agricultural innovation developed in Southeast Asia, possibly including some lands now submerged by shallow seas. From it came rice, citrus, taro, bananas, and sugarcane, among other crops. There, too, stimulus diffusion apparently yielded a sec-

ondary center, in northeastern China, where millet was domesticated.

Later, about 5000 or more years ago, American Indians in Mesoamerica achieved the third great independent invention of agriculture, from which came crops such as maize, tomatoes, chili peppers, beans, and squash. Sauer was among the first scholars to argue that American Indians had independently invented agriculture, rather than

PROFILE

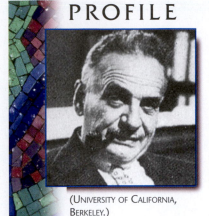

(UNIVERSITY OF CALIFORNIA, BERKELEY.)

Carl O. Sauer

1889–1975

Sauer, a native of the Missouri Ozarks and a graduate of the University of Chicago, was widely regarded as the most prominent American cultural geographer. For over 50 years, he was associated with the University of California at Berkeley. His works were so diverse as to defy simple classification, but important themes in much of his research were humans as modifiers of the Earth, the cultural landscape, and cultural origins and diffusion. As a geographer, his work took him on many field trips. He studied geography by looking at the land and talking to the residents. In his classic book, *Agricultural Origins and Dispersals,* he presented some new and stimulating ideas about the domestication of plants and animals, some of which are presented in this chapter. His concern for the environment began when he was a student, and throughout his career he argued for "humane" use of the Earth. Professor Sauer twice served the Association of American Geographers as president and in 1974 received an award from that organization for meritorious contributions to the discipline of geography.

For more information about Sauer, see Kenzer, 1987; and Leighly, 1987.

day-to-day contact with wild plants and stayed closer to home, they probably initiated plant domestication. The fertility of the earth itself possesses a feminine quality.

The diffusion of domesticated plants did not end in antiquity (see Focus On: Cultural Diffusion: The Potato in Germany on page 279). Even today, crop farming continues to spread in areas such as the Amazon Basin, extending the diffusion begun many millennia ago. Introduction of the lemon, orange, grape, and date palm by Spanish missionaries in eighteenth-century California, where no agriculture existed in the American Indian era, provides a recent example of *relocation diffusion.* This was part of a larger diffusion—the introduction of European crops that accompanied the mass emigrations from Europe to the Americas, Australia, New Zealand, and South Africa.

An even more important diffusion brought American Indian crops to the Eastern Hemisphere. For example, chili peppers and maize, carried by the Portuguese to their colonies in South Asia, became basic elements of the diet all across that region (Figure 8.13). One could not imagine southern Asian cuisine today devoid of chili pepper seasoning.

Origin and Diffusion of Animal Domestication

A **domesticated animal** is one that depends on people for food and shelter and that differs from wild species in physical appearance and behavior as a result of controlled breeding and frequent contact with humans. Animal domestication apparently occurred later in prehistory than did the first planting of crops—with the probable exception of the dog, whose companionship with humans appears to be much more ancient. Typically, people value domesticated animals and take care of them for some utilitarian purpose. Yet the original motive for domestication may not have been economic. People may have first domesticated cattle, as well as some kinds of birds, for religious reasons. Certain other domesticated animals, such as the pig and the dog, probably attached themselves voluntarily to human settlements to feast on garbage. At first, perhaps, humans merely tolerated these animals, later adopting them as pets and/or as sources of meat.

Farmers of the ancient crop hearth in southern Asia apparently did not excel as domesticators of animals. The taming of certain kinds of poultry may be attributed to them, but probably little else. Similarly, the American Indian, who made superior contributions to plant domestication, remained rather unsuccessful in taming animals, perhaps in part because suitable wild animals were less numerous. The llama, alpaca, guinea pig, Muscovy duck, and turkey were among the few American domesticates.

receiving stimulus diffusion from the Eastern Hemisphere. As the Mesoamerican crop complex spread southward, it too produced a secondary center of stimulus diffusion, in northwestern South America, from which came the white potato, sweet potato, and manioc.

Overall, the American Indians domesticated an array of crops far superior in nutritional value to those of the two Eastern Hemisphere centers combined. Try excluding all American Indian domesticates from your diet for just a single day. You will have to do without not only those foods just listed, but also pineapples, sunflower seeds and oil, vanilla, chocolate, pumpkins, papayas, various other foods, and tobacco.

The widespread association of female deities with agriculture suggests that it was women who first worked the land. Recall the almost universal division of labor in hunting-gathering-fishing societies. Because women had

Figure 8.13

Chili peppers in Nepal and Korea. A Tharu tribal woman of lowland Nepal prepares a condiment made of chili peppers from her garden, and in South Korea chili peppers dry under a plastic-roofed shed. This crop comes from the American Indians of Mexico. **How might it have diffused so far and become so important in Asia?** For the answer, see Andrews, 1993. (Courtesy of Terry G. Jordan-Bychkov.)

The early farmers of the Middle East in the Fertile Crescent deserve credit for the first great animal domestications, most notably herd animals. The wild ancestors of major herd animals—such as cattle, pigs, horses, sheep, and goats—lived primarily in a belt running from Syria and southeastern Turkey eastward across Iraq and Iran to central Asia. Most animal domestication seems to have taken place in that general region or in adjacent areas. In the Middle East, farmers first combined domesticated plants and animals into an integrated system, the antecedent of the peasant grain, root, and livestock farming described earlier. These people began using cattle to pull the plow, a revolutionary invention that greatly increased the acreage under cultivation.

As the grain-herd livestock farming system continued to expand, particularly in the Fertile Crescent area, tillers entered marginal lands, the *ecotone* of the bordering deserts, where crop cultivation proved difficult or impossible. Population pressures forced people into these districts. The herd animals became more important to the occupants of these dry lands, and they abandoned crop farming. They began to wander with their herds to avoid exhausting local forage. In this manner, nomadic herding probably developed on the ecotone of the Fertile Crescent.

Modern Innovations in Agriculture

Cultural diffusion did not end with the original spread of farming and herding. New ideas arose often during the succeeding millennia and spread through agricultural space as waves of innovation. The twentieth century, in particular, witnessed many such farming innovations and diffusions. The spread of hybrid maize through the United States in the twentieth century provides a good example of *expansion diffusion* (Figure 8.14 on the next page). Such innovations often gain initial acceptance by wealthier, large-scale farmers, providing a good example of *hierarchical diffusion*.

One of the major innovation diffusions in twentieth-century American agriculture involved the spread of pump irrigation through many parts of the western Great Plains. A detailed study of this irrigation innovation was made in the Colorado northern High Plains by geographer Leonard Bowden. Farmers there had to decide much more than whether to irrigate, because irrigation brought with it different crops, different markets, and different farming techniques. The Colorado High Plains farmers, in effect, decided whether they wanted an entirely different system of agriculture from the one they had traditionally practiced. The first irrigation well began operation by

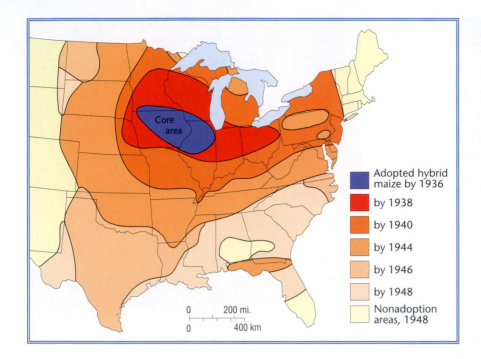

Figure 8.14
The diffusion of hybrid maize in the United States. Hybrid maize spread from a core area of initial acceptance in Iowa and Illinois through expansion diffusion, reaching most of the eastern United States in little over a decade. **What type of diffusion does the pattern suggest?** (AFTER GRILICHES, 1960: 277.)

Core area

Adopted hybrid maize by 1936

by 1938

by 1940

by 1944

by 1946

by 1948

Nonadoption areas, 1948

0   200 mi.
0   400 km

1935, but initial diffusion was retarded in part by a shortage of investment capital in the Great Depression years. Beginning in 1948, irrigation spread quite rapidly.

In studying the spread of pump irrigation, Bowden observed *contagious diffusion* from the core area of initial acceptance and *time-distance decay.* The closer a potential irrigation site lay to an existing irrigated farm, the more likely its owner was to accept the innovation—an example of the *neighborhood effect.* Some barriers to the diffusion of irrigation weakened over time. Banks and other moneylending institutions were initially reluctant to lend money to farmers for investment in irrigation. Once the technique proved to be economically successful, however, loans were easier to obtain and interest rates fell.

Not all innovations involve expansion diffusion and spread wavelike across the land, in the manner of pump irrigation and hybrid maize. A much less orderly pattern is more typical. The **green revolution** in Asia provides an example. The green revolution is a product of modern agronomy and has accompanied globalization. It involves the development of high-yielding hybrid varieties of crops, often genetically engineered, coupled with chemical fertilizers. The high-yield crops of the green revolution tend to be less insect- and disease-resistant, necessitating the widespread use of pesticides. The green revolution, then, promises larger harvests but ties the farmer to greatly increased expenditures on seed, fertilizer, and pesticides. It enmeshes the farmer in the global corporate economy.

In some countries, most notably India, the green revolution diffused rapidly in the latter half of the twentieth century. By contrast, countries such as Myanmar resisted the revolution, favoring traditional methods. A splotchy pattern of acceptance still characterizes the paddy rice areas today. In the lamentable jargon of Hägerstrandian diffusion studies (see the Profile on Hägerstrand in Chapter 1), nonaccepters are called "laggards" and the inevitability of acceptance of innovations is assumed.

Canadian geographer Aninda Chakravarti made a detailed study of the cultural diffusion of the green revolution in India. The new hybrid rice and wheat seeds first appeared there in 1966. Although requiring chemical fertilizers and protection by pesticides, the new hybrids allowed India's 1970 grain production to double in output from its 1950 level. However, poorer farmers—the great majority of agriculturists—could not afford the capital expenditures for chemical fertilizer and pesticides, and the gap between rich and poor farmers widened. Many of the poor became displaced from the land and flocked to the overcrowded cities of India, aggravating urban problems. To make matters worse, the use of chemicals and poisons on the land heightened environmental damage.

The adoption of hybrid seeds brought yet another problem: the loss of plant diversity, or genetic variety. Before hybrid seeds came into widespread use, each farm developed its own distinctive seed types, through the practice of setting aside seeds from the better plants annually at harvest time for the next season's sowing. Enormous *genetic diversity* vanished almost instantly when farmers began purchasing hybrids rather than saving seed from the

FOCUS ON

Cultural Diffusion: The Potato in Germany

How does a domestic plant spread into new areas and gain wider acceptance? The progress is often slow and not without resistance, as the following eyewitness account from the province of Pomerania, Kingdom of Prussia, shows.

> In 1743, through the goodness of King Frederick the Great, the people of Kolberg district received a present completely unknown to us. A large freight wagon full of potatoes arrived at the market square, and, by a beating of drums, the announcement was made that all farmers and gardeners were to assemble before the town hall. The town councilors then showed the new fruit to the assembled crowd. Detailed instructions were read aloud concerning the planting, cultivation, and cooking of the potato. However, few of the people paid attention to the oral instructions, choosing instead to take the highly-praised tubers in their hands, smelling, licking, and tasting them. Shaking their heads, they passed them around, eventually throwing them to the dogs, who also sniffed and rejected

them. "These things," they said, "have no smell or taste. What good are they to us?" Hardly anyone understood the instructions for planting. Quite general was the belief that potatoes would grow into trees from which you could gather like fruit in due time. Those who did not throw the potatoes on the rubbish heap, but instead planted them, did so incorrectly.

> The town councilors learned that some sceptics had not entrusted their tuberous treasures to the earth. For that reason they instituted a strict potato inspection during the summer months and levied a small monetary fine on those found to be obstinate.

> The next year the king renewed his benevolent gift, but this time the authorities sent along a man familiar with raising potatoes, and he helped the people plant and cultivate. In this manner, the new product first came to my district, and ever since has spread rapidly. Now a general famine can never again devastate the province.

Translated and condensed from Nettelbeck, 1910: 8–10.

---

last harvest. "Gene banks" have belatedly been set up to preserve what remains of domesticated plant variety, not just in the areas affected by the green revolution but also in the American Corn Belt and many other agricultural regions where hybrids are now dominant. In sum, the green revolution proved at best to be a mixed blessing. Perhaps the "laggards" were correct—in the long run, this globalization-financed Western innovation may have caused more harm than good in India and elsewhere.

Agro-Ecology

How are agriculture and habitat interrelated? Can the theme of cultural ecology help us understand types of agriculture? Agriculture is related to the physical environment at the most basic level, for farming involves direct use of the land. Agricultural types are *adaptive strategies*, developed in different *ecoregions*. Because farmers and herders work and live on the land, a very close relationship exists between agriculture and the physical environment. In many ways, the map of agricultural regions reflects adaptation to environmental influences. At the same time, thousands of years of agricultural use of the land have led to massive alterations in our natural environment.

Cultural Adaptation

Weather and climate exert perhaps the greatest influence on the different forms of agriculture. For example, the cultivation of many crops that are sensitive to frost becomes prohibitively expensive outside tropical and subtropical areas. This fact helps to explain why plantation agriculture has thrived. Plantation farmers in warm climates can produce cash crops desired by peoples in the middle latitudes, where such crops cannot be grown. Much market gardening in the southern and southwestern United States depends on a similar climatic advantage to produce citrus fruits, winter vegetables, sugarcane, and other crops that will not grow in areas closer to the large urban markets of the Northeast.

Similarly, the need for abundant irrigation water to flood the fields confines paddy rice farming to its present limits within Asia. Soils also play an influential role in agricultural decisions. In part, shifting cultivation reflects an adaptation to poor tropical soils, which rapidly lose their fertility when farmed. Groups that practice peasant grain, root, and livestock agriculture often owe their superior farming status to the fertility of local volcanic soils, which are not so quickly exhausted.

Terrain also influences agriculture. As a general rule, farmers tend to practice crop farming in areas of level

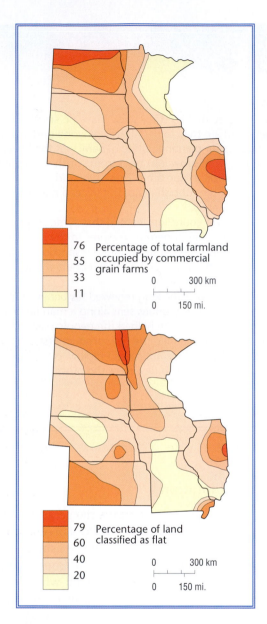

Figure 8.15

The influence of terrain on agriculture. The spatial relationship of commercial grain farming and flat terrain appears in the American Midwest, about 1960. "Flat" terrain is defined as any land with a slope of 3 degrees or less. Commercial grain farming is completely mechanized, and flat land permits more efficient machine operation. The result is this striking correlation between a type of agriculture and a type of terrain. **What other factors might attract mechanized grain farming to level land?** (AFTER HIDORE, 1963: 86, 87.)

terrain, leaving the adjacent hills and mountains forested. In the United States, commercial wheat, rice, and corn farming is concentrated in the flattest areas, partly because such farmers depend on heavy machines—and, in the case of rice, on large-scale irrigation (Figure 8.15).

Often environmental influence is more subtle. For example, in paddy areas near the margins of the Asian wet-rice region, where the unreliability of rainfall causes harvests to vary greatly from one year to the next, farmers developed complex cultivation strategies to avert periodic famine, including the use of many varieties of rice. Such farmers, including those in parts of Thailand, almost universally rejected the green revolution. The simplistic advice given them by agricultural experts working for the Thai government and speaking for globalization was not appropriate for their marginal lands. In their folk wisdom, the local farmers knew that the traditional diversified adaptive strategy was superior. A similarly subtle environmental influence can be observed in West Africa, where peasant grain, root, and livestock farmers raise a multiplicity of crops in the more humid lands near the coast. These crops fall away one by one toward the drier interior of the continent, where the careful observer finds instead numerous drought-resistant varieties of only a few basic crops.

Many geographers now believe that we must cease imposing globalizing Western technological innovations on farmers in the underdeveloped world. "The methods of traditional agriculture and resource management merit serious consideration," argues geographer Gene Wilken, and we should stop assuming that our scientifically based innovations are superior to the old ways. For too long, we have behaved arrogantly toward traditional farmers and have caused the irretrievable loss of millennia-old farming knowledge.

Agriculturists as Modifiers of the Environment

After the domestication of plants and animals, humankind began to alter the environment, especially natural vegetation, in a major way (Figure 8.16). To the preagricultural hunter and gatherer, the forest harbored valuable wild plants and animals. To the agriculturist, however, the woodland became less valuable as a source of food and had to be cleared to make fields. Over the millennia, as dependence on agriculture grew and as population increased, humans made ever larger demands on the forests. Farmers expanded small patches of cleared land until these areas merged with other clearings. They used ax and fire in their assault on the woodlands, with devastating effect.

In many parts of China, India, and the Mediterranean lands, forests virtually vanished. In transalpine Europe, the United States, and some other areas, they were greatly reduced (Figure 8.17). Aside from the loss of woodland, the burning of dead vegetation pollutes the air. Shifting cultivators in Africa's rain forest produce *acid rain* levels

Figure 8.16

Denuded land near the Aegean coast of Turkey. Thousands of years of overgrazing by goats and sheep have severely damaged this pasture. In its native condition, it was covered with an open forest of live oaks, interspersed with tall grasses. (COURTESY OF TERRY G. JORDAN-BYCHKOV.)

(see Chapter 9) comparable to those of industrial areas through their slash-and-burn practices.

Desertification

Grasslands suffered similar modifications. Prairies gave way to the plow or experienced severe damage through overgrazing. Farmers occasionally plow up grasslands too dry for sustainable crop production, and herders often allow their herds to overgraze semiarid pastures. The result could be **desertification,** a process first studied a half-century ago by geographer Rhoads Murphey. He as-

sembled convincing evidence that farmers caused substantial parts of North Africa to be added to the margins of the Sahara Desert (Figure 8.18 on the next page). He noted the catastrophic decline of countries such as Libya and Tunisia in the 1500 years since the time of Roman rule, when North Africa served as the "granary of the Empire," yielding huge wheat harvests. Many districts had substantially larger populations than they do at present, and agricultural production declined dramatically.

More recent research on desertification has centered on the *Sahel,* a region just south of the Sahara Desert in Africa (see Figure 8.18). In the Sahel, the destruction of

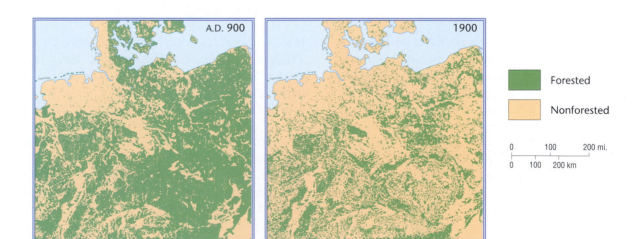

Forested

Nonforested

Figure 8.17

The agricultural impact on the forest cover of central Europe from A.D. 900 to 1900. Extensive clearing of the forests, mostly before 1350, was tied largely to expansion of farmland. The distribution of forests in 1900 closely resembles that of hills and mountain ranges. **Why might this pattern have developed?** (REDRAWN FROM DARBY, 1956: 202–203.)

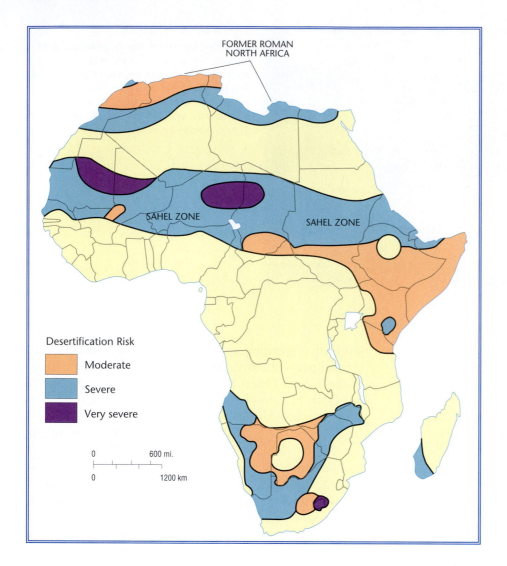

FORMER ROMAN NORTH AFRICA

SAHEL ZONE

SAHEL ZONE

Desertification Risk

Moderate

Severe

Very severe

0   600 mi.

0   1200 km

Figure 8.18

Risk of desertification in Africa. Are the deserts of the world expanding because of agricultural land use? Geographer Rhoads Murphey began this debate a half-century ago, and it still rages. Africa has been the center of the debate. (MURPHEY, 1951; AND THOMAS, 1993: 320.)

vegetation could pass a critical threshold at some point, beyond which the plant life cannot regenerate, leading to denudation. This, in turn, would have the effect of reducing rainfall and increasing temperatures. Soon lands that had been covered with pastures and fields could become permanently joined to the dunes of the adjacent Sahara. Africa confronts the greatest such problems, but Asia, Australia, the Americas, and even Europe may also have endangered districts (see Focus On: The Dust Bowl). Desertification could significantly reduce the land area devoted to food production in the decades ahead, with possible dire demographic consequences. Overpopulation leads to overuse of the land, which, in turn, may produce desertification, reduction of food supplies, and mass famine.

Certain other scholars, including David Thomas, challenge the notion that the world's deserts are on the march. Satellite imagery suggests to them that the semiarid lands possess more resiliency than was once thought. Since 1960, they claim, the Sahara-Sahel boundary has not migrated steadily south but instead fluctuated as it always has, responding to wetter and drier years. We need to distinguish these natural fluctuations from actual soil degradation, and if we do so, says Thomas, the actual areal extent of desertification is reduced to a third of the more pessimistic claims.

Those geographers who accept the alarmist notions about desertification suggest some drastic solutions. In North America, for example, geographer Deborah Epstein Popper proposed that huge areas of the Great Plains be withdrawn from farming and ranching and replaced by a "buffalo commons," a vast expanse of restored natural grassland grazed by native animals.

You might think that irrigation would provide a solution for desertification. However, such artificial watering can have both intentional and unintentional impacts on

FOCUS ON

The Dust Bowl

The Dust Bowl of the 1930s devastated the American Great Plains, in large part because farmers had plowed up the grasses that originally protected the soil from wind erosion. A nonsustainable adaptive strategy had come to grief. Woody Guthrie, the great folk balladeer, captured the disaster in his song "The Great Dust Storm":

The storm took place at sundown
It lasted through the night.
When we looked out next morning
We saw a terrible sight.
We saw outside our window
Where wheatfields they had grown,
Was now a rippling ocean
Of dust the wind had blown.

It covered up our fences,
It covered up our barns,
It covered up our tractors
In this wild and dusty storm.
We loaded our jalopies
And piled our families in,
We rattled down that highway
To never come back again

"The Great Dust Storm" (Dust Storm Disaster), words and music by Woody Guthrie. TRO—Copyright © 1960 and 1963 by Ludlow Music, Inc., New York. Used by permission.

---

the land. Obviously, the intended effect is to circumvent deficiencies in precipitation by importing water from another area, using dams and canals, or from another era, using deep wells and pumps to exploit groundwater accumulated over decades and centuries. Unfortunately, the beneficial effect of irrigation is often offset by unintentional environmental destruction. Ditch and canal irrigation can cause the local subsurface water table to rise, waterlogging the soil, and the mineral content of the water often salinizes the ground. In Pakistan, for example, the water table rose 10 to 30 feet (3 to 10 meters), and 800 to 2000 pounds of salt were added per acre of land (900 to 2200 kilograms per hectare) as a result of dam-and-ditch irrigation. Conversely, the water table has been drastically lowered by well-and-pump irrigation in parts of the American Great Plains, particularly Texas, causing ancient springs to go dry and promising an early end to intensive agriculture there. Irrigation, in other words, had the effect of spreading rather than diminishing desertification.

Another area where desertification resulted from irrigation lies on the borderland between Kazakhstan and Uzbekistan in central Asia. The once-huge *Aral Sea* became so diminished by the diversion of irrigation water from the rivers flowing into it that large areas of dry lake bed now lie exposed. Not only was the local fishing industry destroyed, but noxious, chemical-laden dust storms blow from the desiccated lake bed onto nearby settlements, causing assorted health problems. Irrigation water diverted to huge cotton fields, then, destroyed an *ecosystem* and produced another desert.

> ## Reflecting on GEOGRAPHY
> What might be some ecological consequences of expanding cropland to meet the world's rising food needs?

Equally as serious as desertification is the increasing chemical contamination of the land through both fertilizers and pesticides, used mainly by commercial farmers in Western cultures. Chemicals first became important as agricultural fertilizers in Germany in the middle 1800s, and central Europeans remain some of the most chemical-dependent farmers to this day. The chemicals diffused widely, spreading in conjunction with the green revolution and neoplantation. Together with the use of large machines, chemicals allowed drastic reductions in the amount of labor needed in agriculture. However, the ecological consequences could well be devastating, and in some areas serious contamination problems have appeared. **Sustainability**—the survival of a land-use system for centuries or millennia without destruction of the environmental base—is the central agricultural ecological issue. Western technological adaptive strategies, promoted through the process of globalization, are not sustainable.

Environmental Perception by Agriculturists

People perceive the physical environment through lenses their culture fashions for them. Each person's agricultural heritage can be influential in shaping these perceptions. This is not surprising, because human survival depends on how successfully people can adjust their ways of making a living to environmental conditions.

The American Great Plains provides a good example of how an agricultural experience in one environment influenced farmers' environmental perceptions and subsequent behavior in another environment. Plains farmers came from the humid eastern United States, and they consistently underestimated the problem of drought in their new home. In the 1960s, geographer Thomas Saarinen revealed that although the oldest and most experienced Great Plains farmers had the most accurate perception of drought, almost every farmer still underestimated the actual frequency of such dry periods. By contrast, *culturally preadapted* German immigrants from the steppes of Russia and Ukraine, an area very much like the American Great Plains, accurately perceived the new land and experienced fewer problems.

Above all, farmers rely on climatic stability. A sudden rash of unusual weather events can change agriculturists' environmental perceptions. Geographer John Cross recently studied Wisconsin agriculture, following a series of floods, droughts, and other anomalies. He found that two-thirds of all Wisconsin dairy farmers now believe the climate is changing, for the worse, and fully one-third told him that continued climatic variability threatened their continued operation. Perhaps they perceive the environmental hazard to be greater than it really is, but they make decisions based on their perceptions.

Agro-Cultural Interaction

How does agriculture interact with other facets of culture? Let us next observe some of the ways other cultural forces influence agricultural activities. Religious taboos, politically based tariff restrictions, rural land-use zoning policies, population density, and many other human factors influence the type and distribution of agricultural activities. Among some peoples, the system of crop and livestock raising becomes so firmly enmeshed in the culture that both society and religion are greatly influenced (see Focus On: Cultural Integration: The Example of Cattle Among the Dasanetch).

Intensity of Land Use

A great spatial variation exists in the intensity of rural land use. **Intensive agriculture** means that a great deal of human labor or investment capital, or both, is put into each acre or hectare of land, with the goal of obtaining the greatest output of produce. One can calculate intensity either by counting energy inputs or by measuring the level of productivity. In much of the world, especially the paddy rice areas of Asia, high intensity is achieved through prodigious application of human labor, with the result that the local rice output per unit of land is the highest in the world. In Western countries, high intensity is instead achieved by the massive application of investment capital in machines, fertilizers, and pesticides, resulting in the highest agricultural productivity per capita found anywhere.

Geographers employing the social-scientific approach generally support the theory that increased land-use

FOCUS ON

Cultural Integration: The Example of Cattle Among the Dasanetch

The Dasanetch are a herding people living close to Lake Rudolf in East Africa, where the borders of Ethiopia, Kenya, and Sudan meet. For them, cattle are more than mere domestic animals from which they derive milk, meat, blood, and skins. Cattle occupy a central position in their society, serving religious and social roles in addition to their economic function. Dasanetch men identify closely with their cattle

and sometimes even assume the personal name of a favorite ox. Cattle themes appear often in the song, dance, myth, and ritual of the Dasanetch. Cattle are also an essential aspect of the unmarried woman's dowry and serve as a medium of exchange. "Cattle are therefore central in the organization and functioning of Dasanetch society," bearing utilitarian, subjective, and monetary values. In this way, agriculture, religion, and society are thoroughly integrated.

Derived from Carr, 1977: 99–100.

PROFILE

(CORBIS-BETTMANN.)

Johann Heinrich von Thünen
1783–1850

Von Thünen was not a professional scholar but rather the landlord of an estate in the German province of Mecklenburg. He did attend several universities in Germany. A contemporary of von Humboldt and Ritter, he apparently never met them, and yet his contribution to geography has been very great. He was concerned with maximizing the agricultural profit from his extensive landholdings. This financial focus and his own curiosity led him to create the isolated-state model of land use. Modern location theory in agricultural geography is based on von Thünen's model, and he is widely regarded as the originator of spatial models. A Thünen Society was founded in Germany in 1990, and it has branches in North America and elsewhere. He was also honored by having a street named for him in Schwerin, the capital city of his native province in Germany.

intensity results when population growth forces the need for additional food and reduces the amount of land each farmer can have. As demographic pressure mounts, farmers systematically discard the more extensive adaptive strategies to focus on those that provide greater yield per unit of land. In this manner, the population increase is accommodated. The resultant farming system may be riskier, because it offers fewer options and possesses greater potential for environmental modification, but it does yield more food—at least in the short run. Certain other geographers reject this theory, believing instead that population density increases following innovations that lead to greater land-use intensity—that necessity is not the mother of invention.

The von Thünen Model

Still other social-scientific geographers, *economic determinists,* look to market forces and transportation costs as keys to level of land-use intensity. They use the *core-periphery model* developed in the nineteenth century by the German scholar-farmer, Johann Heinrich von Thünen (see Profile). In his model, von Thünen proposed an "iso-

lated state" that had no trade connections with the outside world; possessed only one market, located centrally in the state; and had uniform soil, climate, and level terrain throughout. He further assumed that all farmers living the same distance from the market had equal access to it and that all farmers sought to maximize their profits and produced solely for market. Von Thünen created this model to study the influence of distance from market and transport costs on the type and intensity of agriculture.

Figure 8.19 on the next page presents a modified version of von Thünen's isolated-state model. Improvements in transportation since the 1820s, when he wrote his work, render obsolete certain of his conclusions, such as the finding that bulky products would be produced near the market. The resultant revised model, in common with the original, reveals a series of concentric zones, each occupied by a different type of agriculture, located at progressively greater distances from the central market.

> ## Reflecting on **GEOGRAPHY**
> Why should we study spatial models, such as von Thünen's, when they do not depict reality?

For any given crop, the intensity of cultivation declines with increasing distance from the market. Farmers near the market have minimal transport costs and can invest most of their resources in labor, equipment, and supplies to augment production. Indeed, they have to farm intensively to make a bigger profit, because their land is more valuable and subject to higher taxes. With increasing distance from the market, farmers invest progressively less in production per unit of land because they have to spend progressively more on transporting produce to market. Moreover, highly perishable products such as milk, fresh fruit, and garden vegetables need to be produced near the market, whereas peripheral farmers have to produce nonperishable products or convert perishable items into a more durable form, such as cheese or dried fruit.

This concentric-zone model describes a situation in which highly capital-intensive forms of commercial agriculture, such as market gardening and feedlots, lie nearest to market. The increasingly distant, successive concentric belts are occupied by progressively less intensive types of agriculture, represented by dairying, livestock fattening, grain farming, and ranching.

How well does this modified model describe reality? As we would expect, the real world is far more complicated. Models are not meant to depict reality but to simplify conditions for some specific explanatory purpose. Still, on a world scale, we can see that intensive commercial types of agriculture tend to occur most commonly

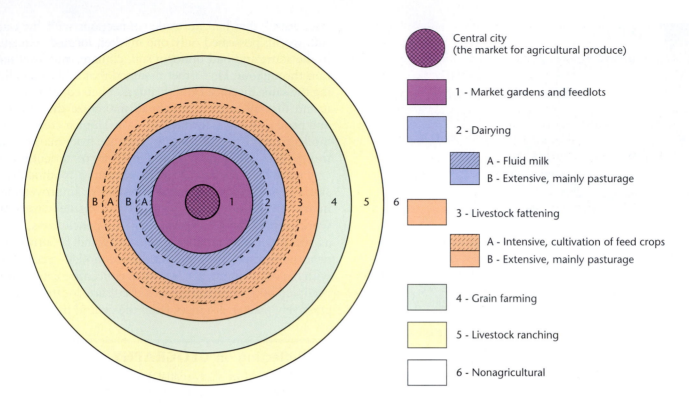

Central city
(the market for agricultural produce)

1 - Market gardens and feedlots

2 - Dairying

A - Fluid milk
B - Extensive, mainly pasturage

3 - Livestock fattening

A - Intensive, cultivation of feed crops
B - Extensive, mainly pasturage

4 - Grain farming

5 - Livestock ranching

6 - Nonagricultural

Figure 8.19

Von Thünen's isolated-state model. The model is modified to fit the modern world better, showing the hypothetical distribution of types of commercial agriculture. Other causal factors are held constant to illustrate the effect of transportation costs and differing distances from the market. The more intensive forms of agriculture, such as market gardening, are located nearest the market, whereas the least intensive form (livestock ranching) is most remote. **Why does the model have the configuration of concentric circles?** Compare this model to the real-world pattern of agricultural types in Uruguay, South America, shown in Figure 8.20.

near the huge urban markets of northwestern Europe and the eastern United States (see Figure 8.1). An even closer match can be observed in smaller areas, such as in the South American nation of Uruguay (Figure 8.20).

The value of von Thünen's model can also be seen in the underdeveloped countries of the world. Geographer Ronald Horvath made a detailed study of the African region centering on the Ethiopian capital city of Addis Ababa. Although noting disruptions caused by ethnic and environmental contrasts, Horvath found "remarkable parallels between von Thünen's crop theory and the agriculture around Addis Ababa." Similarly, German geographer Ursula Ewald applied the model to the farming patterns of colonial Mexico during the period of Spanish rule, and she concluded that even this culturally and environmentally diverse land provided "an excellent illustration of von Thünen's principles on spatial zonation in agriculture."

Can the World Be Fed?

Was Thomas Malthus correct? (See Chapter 7.) Are starvation and recurrent famine inevitable as the world's population grows and becomes increasingly concentrated in cities? Or can our agricultural systems successfully feed over 6 billion people?

In trying to answer these questions, we face a paradox. Today, some 850 million people are malnourished, some to the point of starvation. Almost every year we read of famines, usually in one African country or another. Yet—and this would astound Malthus—food production has grown more rapidly than population over the past 40 or 50 years. Per capita, more food is available today than in 1950, when only about half as many people lived on Earth as do today.

The explanation for this paradox surely lies in the theme of cultural interaction. If the world food supply is sufficient to feed everyone and yet hunger afflicts one of every six or seven persons, then some cultural or social factors must be responsible. The answer is that poverty and politics, not food shortage, cause hunger. Many Third World countries do not grow enough food to feed their populations, and they cannot afford to purchase enough imported food to make up the difference. As a result, famines can occur even when plenty of food is available. Irish starved by the millions in the 1840s while adjacent Britain possessed enough surplus food to have prevented this catastrophe. Bangladesh suffered a major famine in 1974, a year of record agricultural surpluses in the world.

Even when major efforts are made to send food from wealthy countries to famine-stricken areas, the poor transportation infrastructure of Third World countries often prevents effective distribution. Political instability can disrupt food shipments, and the donated food often falls into the hands of corrupt local officials. Famine, then, is mainly a cultural phenomenon. Its immediate causes could be environmental, but the failure to relieve hunger has a cultural explanation.

Globalization

Scattered through this chapter you have seen mention of the *globalization* process and its impact upon agriculture. The term **agribusiness** has accompanied globalization in a vaguely sinister way. Let's draw these references together now, here in the theme of cultural interaction.

Globalization, you will recall, involves the restructuring of the world economy by multinational corporations thriving in an era of unfettered capitalism, free-trade, rapid communications, improved transport, and computer-based

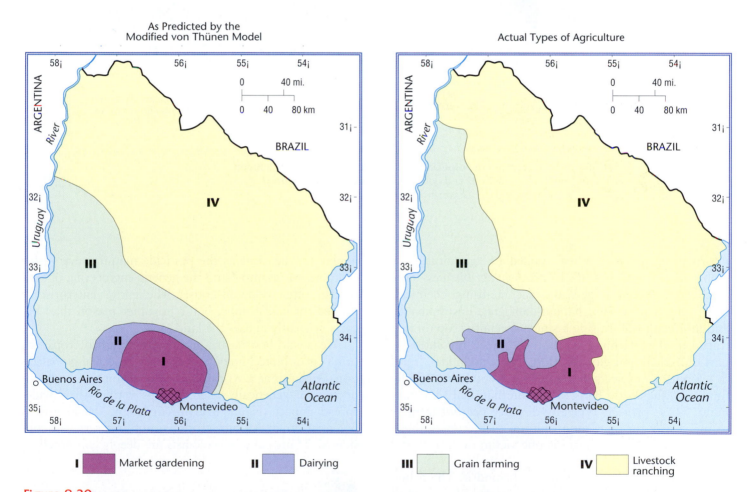

Figure 8.20

Ideal and actual distribution of types of agriculture in Uruguay. This South American country possesses some attributes of von Thünen's isolated state, in that it is largely a plains area dominated by one city. **In what ways does the spatial pattern of Uruguayan agriculture conform to von Thünen's model? How is it different? What might cause the anomalies?** (For the answers, see Griffin, 1973.)

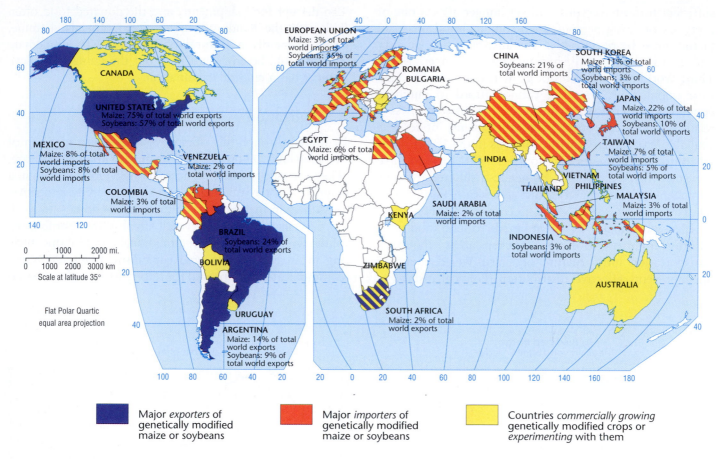

Major *exporters* of genetically modified maize or soybeans	Major *importers* of genetically modified maize or soybeans	Countries *commercially growing* genetically modified crops or *experimenting* with them

Figure 8.21

Worldwide use of genetically altered crop plants, especially maize and soybeans. This diffusion has occurred despite warnings from many ecologists and geneticists. **What could go wrong?** (SOURCES: NATIONAL CORN GROWERS ASSOCIATION; AND U.S. DEPARTMENT OF AGRICULTURE.)

information systems. When applied to agriculture, the globalization process tends to produce *agribusiness*—the totally commercial, large-scale, machine-using, chemical-dependent, hybrid-using, habitat-damaging, unsustainable, and **monocultural** (raising a single specialty crop on vast tracts) modern farming system. The green revolution is part of agricultural globalization, as are countless "rural development" projects in Third World countries, usually funded by the World Bank or the International Monetary Fund. These projects typically displace *peasant* farmers to make way for huge monocultural cash-crop agribusinesses. The family-run farm is one victim of agricultural globalization.

Multinational corporations are behind it. The 5 biggest hybrid vegetable seed suppliers control 75 percent of the global market, and the 10 largest agrochemical manufacturers command 85 percent of the world supply. Four corporations supply over two-thirds of the U.S. consumption of hybrid seed maize. Sometimes the seed companies are the same as the pesticide manufacturers—for example, Monsanto—and the genetic engineering of seed is also often done in-house. The entire enterprise is headed for catastrophe, if for no other reason than because it greatly abuses the land.

We would best regard genetically modified crops, the products of biotechnology, as another aspect of globalization. A glance at a world map of consumption and production of genetically altered crops verifies their widespread impact (Figure 8.21). Alarmingly, the long-term potential damage of such crops has not been seriously considered. Many cultural ecologists are deeply concerned.

Agricultural Landscapes

What is the agricultural component of the cultural landscape? What might we learn by using this fifth and final theme of cultural geography? A great part of the world's

PROFILE

August Meitzen
1822–1910

Geographers who study the agricultural landscape owe an enormous debt to the German scholar August Meitzen, widely acknowledged as the founder of rural settlement geography. Meitzen was the Prussian special commissioner for land consolidation, concerned with redrawing property lines to reduce farm fragmentation. In this capacity, he traveled over much of the German countryside, becoming intimately familiar with the agrarian landscape. Not content to study only the field and cadastral patterns, he also gave detailed consideration to village types and folk architecture.

Although Meitzen was not a professional geographer, he attended the first annual national meeting of German geographers in 1881 and read a paper on rural house types. Not an academician, Meitzen was nevertheless named honorary professor at the University of Berlin for many years.

His classic work, which provided a scholarly foundation for the study of agricultural landscapes, was published in four volumes in 1895. This work's English title is *Settlement and Agrarian Character of the West and East Germans, of the Celts, Romans, Finns, and Slavs.* Meitzen, more than any other scholar, was responsible for introducing the theme of cultural landscape into geography, and it was he who first proposed that landscape, particularly the relict forms, possesses diagnostic potential.

which deals with folk geography, we considered traditional rural architecture, another element in the agricultural landscape. In this chapter, we confine our attention to a third aspect of the rural landscape: the patterns of fields and properties created as people occupy land for the purpose of farming.

Survey, Cadastral, and Field Patterns

A **cadastral pattern** is one that describes property-ownership lines, whereas a *field pattern* reflects the way that a farmer subdivides land for agricultural use. Both can be much influenced by **survey patterns,** the lines laid out by surveyors prior to the settlement of an area. Major regional contrasts exist in survey, cadastral, and field patterns: for example, *unit-block* versus *fragmented landholding,* and regular, geometric survey versus irregular or unsurveyed property lines.

Fragmented farms are the rule rather than the exception in the Eastern Hemisphere. Under this system, farmers live in farm villages or smaller hamlets. Their landholdings lie splintered into many separate fields situated at varying distances and directions from the settlement. One farm can consist of a hundred or more separate, tiny parcels of land (Figure 8.22). The individual plots may be roughly rectangular in shape, as in Asia and southern Europe, or they may lie in narrow strips. The latter pattern is most common in Europe, where farmers traditionally

land area is cultivated or pastured. In this huge area, the visible imprint of humankind might best be called the **agricultural landscape** (see the Profile on August Meitzen). The agricultural imprint on the land often varies even over short distances, telling us much about local cultures and subcultures. This agricultural landscape also remains in many respects a window on the past. Archaic features abound. For this reason, the traditional rural landscape can teach us a great deal about the cultural heritage of its occupants.

In Chapter 7, we discussed some aspects of the agricultural landscape, in particular the rural settlement forms. We saw the different ways that farming people situate their dwellings in various cultures. In Chapter 2,

Buildings of the village

Holdings of one farmer

Figure 8.22

Fragmented landholdings surround a French farm village. The numerous fields and plots belonging to one individual farmer are shaded. Such fragmented farms remain common in many parts of Europe and Asia. **What are the advantages and disadvantages of this system?** (AFTER DEMANGEON, 1946.)

worked with a bulky plow that was difficult to turn. The origins of the fragmented farm system go back to an early period of peasant communalism. One of its initial justifications was a desire for peasant equality. Each farmer in the village needed land of varying soil composition and terrain. Distance of travel from the village was to be equalized. From the rice paddies of Japan and India to the fields of western Europe, the fragmented holding remains a prominent feature of the cultural landscape.

Unit-block farms, by contrast, in which all of the farmer's property is contained in a single, contiguous piece of land, are found mainly in the overseas area of European settlement, particularly the Americas, Australia, New Zealand, and South Africa. Most often, they reveal a regular, geometric land survey. The checkerboard of farms and fields in the rectangular survey areas of the United States provides a good example of this cadastral pattern (Figure 8.23).

The American *rectangular survey system* first appeared after the Revolutionary War as an orderly method for parceling out federally owned land for sale to pioneers. It imposed a rigid, square, graph-paper pattern on much of the American countryside, geometry triumphant over physical geography. All lines are oriented to the cardinal directions. The basic unit of the system is the *section,* a square of land 1 mile (1.6 kilometers) on each side and thus 640 acres (259 hectares) in area. Land was often bought and sold in half-sections or quarter-

sections. Larger squares called *townships,* measuring 6 miles (10 kilometers) on each side, or 36 square miles (93 square kilometers) of land, serve as political administrative subdistricts within counties. Roads follow section and township lines, adding to the checkerboard character of the American agricultural landscape. Canada adopted an almost identical rectangular survey system, which is particularly evident in the Prairie Provinces (Figure 8.24).

> ### Reflecting on GEOGRAPHY
>
> What advantages does the checkerboarded North American rural landscape offer? What disadvantages?

Equally striking in appearance are *long-lot* farms, where the landholding consists of a long, narrow unit-block stretching back from a road, river, or canal (Figure 8.25). Rather than occurring singly, long-lots lie grouped in rows, allowing this cadastral survey pattern to dominate entire districts. Long-lots occur widely in the hills and marshes of central and western Europe, in parts of Brazil and Argentina, along the rivers of French-settled Québec and southern Louisiana, and in parts of Texas and northern New Mexico. The reason for elongating these unit-block farms lay in the desire to provide each farmer with fertile valley land, water, and access to transportation facilities, either roads or rivers. In French America, long-lots appear in rows along streams, because waterways provided the chief means of transport in colonial times. In the hill lands of central Europe, a road along the valley floor provides the focus, and long-lots reach back from the road to the adjacent ridgecrests.

Some unit-block farms have irregular shapes rather than the rectangular or long-lot patterns. Most of these result from *metes and bounds* surveying, a type that makes much use of natural features such as trees, boulders, and streams. Parts of the eastern United States were surveyed under the metes and bounds system, with the result that farms there are much less regular in outline than those where rectangular survey was imposed. The juncture of the two survey systems is quite apparent from an airplane (Figure 8.26 on page 292).

The cultural geographer who seeks to "read" landscapes can learn much even from so apparently passive a feature as these survey and cadastral patterns. For example, in some parts of the Canadian Prairie Provinces, low, wet places called sloughs appear in the terrain, often filled with water to form small lakes. When the section lines of Canada's rectangular survey cross one of these sloughs, the roads are generally built right through the lakes, with no attempt to go around them. In some cases,

Figure 8.23
American rectangular survey creates a checkerboard in the Imperial Valley of California, a human mosaic indeed. (COURTESY OF TERRY G. JORDAN-BYCHKOV.)

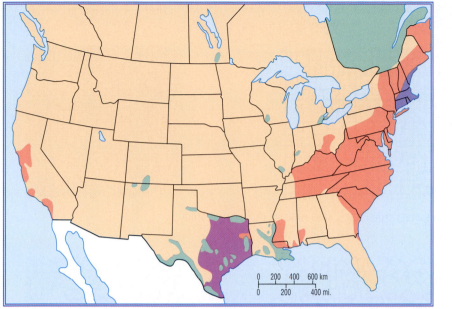

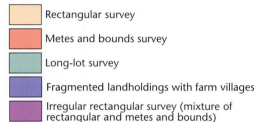

Figure 8.24

Original land survey patterns in the United States and southern Canada. The cadastral patterns still retain the imprint of the various original survey types. **What impact on rural life might the different patterns have?** The map is necessarily generalized, and many local exceptions exist.

Legend:
- Rectangular survey
- Metes and bounds survey
- Long-lot survey
- Fragmented landholdings with farm villages
- Irregular rectangular survey (mixture of rectangular and metes and bounds)

two roads intersect in the middle of a lake, built on causeways. What might the humanistic geographer make of this forceful application of the rigid geometric grid, in disregard of the natural habitat? He or she might conclude that North American culture seeks, through technology, to conquer and overwhelm nature rather than to live in harmony with it. A cultural determinist might go even further and ask whether people who spend their formative years in one of these checkerboard landscapes differ in any way from those raised in a more chaotic metes and bounds district. Are they less creative or more orderly in their daily lives? Do they tend more toward conservatism?

Fencing and Hedging

Property and field borders are often marked by fences or hedges, heightening the visibility of these lines in the agricultural landscape. Open-field areas, where the dominance of crop raising and the careful tending of livestock make fences unnecessary, still prevail in much of western Europe, India, Japan, and some other parts of the Eastern Hemisphere, but much of the remainder of the world's agricultural lands is enclosed.

Fences and hedges add a distinctive touch to the cultural landscape (Figure 8.27 on page 293). Different cultures have their own methods and ways of enclosing land,

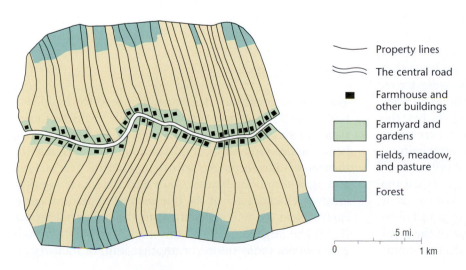

Legend:
- Property lines
- The central road
- Farmhouse and other buildings
- Farmyard and gardens
- Fields, meadow, and pasture
- Forest

Figure 8.25

A long-lot settlement in the hills of central Germany. Each property consists of an elongated unit-block of land stretching back from the road in the valley to an adjacent ridgecrest, part of which remains wooded.

Original Survey Lines

Property Lines, About 1955
(Those that follow original survey
lines are shown by thicker lines.)

Field and Woodlot Borders,
About 1955

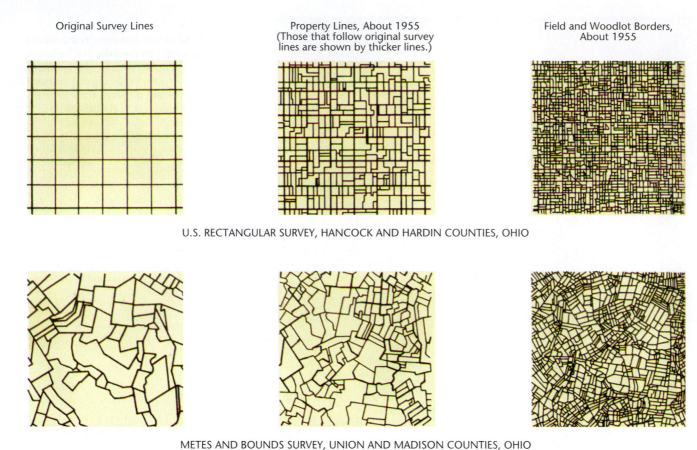

U.S. RECTANGULAR SURVEY, HANCOCK AND HARDIN COUNTIES, OHIO

METES AND BOUNDS SURVEY, UNION AND MADISON COUNTIES, OHIO

Figure 8.26

Two contrasting land survey patterns, rectangular and metes and bounds. Both types were used in an area of west-central Ohio. Note the impact these survey patterns had on modern cadastral and field patterns. **What other features of the cultural landscape might be influenced by these patterns?** (AFTER THROWER, 1966: 40, 63, 84.)

so that types of fences and hedges can be linked to particular groups. Fences in different parts of the world are made of substances as diverse as steel wire, logs, poles, split rails, brush, rock, and earth. Those who visit rural New England, western Ireland, or Yucatán may retain a visual memory of the mile upon mile of stone fence that typifies those landscapes. Barbed wire fences swept across the American countryside a century ago, but some remnants of older types can still be seen. In Appalachia, the traditional split-rail zigzag fence of pioneer times survives here and there. As do most visible features of culture, fence types can serve as indicators of cultural diffusion.

The hedge is a living fence. Few who have visited the mazelike hedgerow country of Brittany and Normandy in France or large areas of Great Britain and Ireland fail to perceive these living fences as a major aspect of the rural landscape. To walk or drive the roads of hedgerow country is to experience a unique feeling of confinement quite different from the openness of barbed wire or unenclosed landscapes.

Conclusion

We have seen that the ancient and honored form of livelihood called agriculture varies markedly from region to region, reflected in formal agro-regions, and that we can better understand this complicated pattern through the themes of agro-ecology, diffusion, cultural interaction, and agricultural landscape. Once again we have seen the interwoven character of the five themes of cultural geography. Next we will apply them to the industrial world. By far the large majority of the world's population finds employment today in one or another kind of industry.

Figure 8.27

Traditional fence in the mountains of Papua New Guinea. The fence is designed to keep pigs out of sweet potato gardens. The modern age has had an impact, as revealed in the use of tin cans to decorate and stabilize the fence. Each culture has its own fence types, adding another distinctive element to the agricultural landscape. (COURTESY OF TERRY G. JORDAN-BYCHKOV.)

 ## Agricultural Geography on the Internet

For more information about agriculture and feeding the world's population, check the following web sites:

International Food Policy Research Institute, Washington, D.C.
http://www.ifpri.cgiar.org
   Learn about strategies for more efficient planning for world food supplies and enhanced food production from a group concerned with hunger and malnutrition. Part of this site deals with domesticated plant biodiversity.

United Nations, Food and Agriculture Organization (FAO), Rome, Italy
http://www.fao.org/
   Discover an agency that focuses on expanding world food production and spreading new techniques for improving agriculture, as it strives to predict, avert, or minimize famines.

United States Department of Agriculture, Washington, D.C.
http://www.usda.gov/
   Look up a wealth of statistics about American farming from the principal federal regulatory and planning agency dealing with agriculture.

Urban Agriculture Notes
http://www.cityfarmer.org
   Canada's Office of Urban Agriculture site. Urban agriculture is a new and growing field that is not completely defined yet even by those closest to it. It concerns itself with all manner of subjects from rooftop gardens to composting toilets to air pollution and community development. It encompasses mental and physical health, entertainment, building codes, rats, fruit trees, herbs, recipes, and much more.

Worldwatch Institute
http://www.worldwatch.org/
   Learn about a privately financed organization focused on long-range trends, particularly food supply, population growth, and ecological deterioration.

World Bank Group, Washington, D.C.
http://www.worldbank.org
   Read about an agency that provides development funds to countries, particularly economically distressed regions. A driving force behind globalization and agribusiness.

Sources

Andrews, Jean. 1993. "Diffusion of Mesoamerican Food Complex to Southeastern Europe." *Geographical Review* 83: 194–204.

Binns, T. 1990. "Is Desertification a Myth?" *Geography* 75: 106–113.

Bowden, Leonard W. 1965. *Diffusion of the Decision to Irrigate.* Department of Geography, Research Paper No. 97. Chicago: University of Chicago.

Carr, Claudia J. 1977. *Pastoralism in Crisis: The Dasanetch and Their Ethiopian Lands.* Department of Geography, Research Paper No. 180. Chicago: University of Chicago.

SEEING GEOGRAPHY

Why does the "human mosaic" in this scene have curved lines?

A rural scene in southern Brazil.

Farmland in Brazil

This agricultural mosaic is displayed near Cascavel in the southern Brazilian state of Paraná. The crop is wheat. These odd patterns would reveal, even to a space alien on a flying saucer, the distinctive human imprint on the landscape, for this is clearly not natural but a *cultural* landscape.

What else might it reveal about the inhabitants of this land on the very border between the tropics and the middle latitudes? For one thing, they are concerned about ecology: the lazy contours follow the slope of the land and retard soil erosion, as do the remnant woodlands in the gullies.

The focus on one cash crop suggests the workings of cultural interaction. It also suggests that globalization has intruded and that these are modern commercial farmers and not traditional peasants. The absence of villages and houses implies a use of machines instead of hand labor, producing a sparse population. The focus on wheat labels it as a formal culture region devoted to that crop. Thus landscape, ecology, interaction, and region are all revealed here. When you wonder how wheat came to this land, so far removed from its Old World hearth, then cultural diffusion joins the other themes that are here overt or implicit.

Chakravarti, A. K. 1973. "Green Revolution in India." *Annals of the Association of American Geographers* 63: 319–330.

Chuan-jun, Wu (ed.). 1979. "China Land Utilization." Map. Beijing: Institute of Geography of the Academica Sinica.

Cowan, C. Wesley, and Patty J. Watson (eds.). 1992. *The Origins of Agriculture: An International Perspective*. Washington, D.C.: Smithsonian Institution Press.

Cross, John A. 1994. "Agroclimatic Hazards and Farming in Wisconsin." *Geographical Review* 84: 277–289.

Darby, H. Clifford. 1956. "The Clearing of the Woodland in Europe," in William L. Thomas, Jr. (ed.), *Man's Role in Changing the Face of the Earth*. Chicago: University of Chicago Press, 183–216.

Demangeon, Albert. 1946. *La France*. Paris: Armand Colin.

Ewald, Ursula. 1977. "The von Thünen Principle and Agricultural Zonation in Colonial Mexico." *Journal of Historical Geography* 3: 123–133.

Griffin, Ernst. 1973. "Testing the von Thünen Theory in Uruguay." *Geographical Review* 63: 500–516.

Grigg, David B. 1969. "The Agricultural Regions of the World: Review and Reflections." *Economic Geography* 45: 95–132.

Griliches, Zvi. 1960. "Hybrid Corn and the Economics of Innovation" *Science* 132 (July 26): 275–280.

Hardy, Thomas. 1891. *Tess of the d'Urbervilles*. New York: Harper & Brothers.

Hewes, Lewlie. 1973. The Suitcase Farming Frontier: A Study in the Historical Geography of the Central Great Plains. Lincoln: University of Nebraska Press.

Hidore, John J. 1963. "Relationship Between Cash Grain Farming and Landforms." *Economic Geography* 39: 84–89.

Horvath, Ronald J. 1969. "Von Thünen's Isolated State and the Area Around Addis Ababa, Ethiopia." *Annals of the Association of American Geographers* 59: 308–323.

Johannessen, Carl L. 1966. "The Domestication Processes in Trees Reproduced by Seed: The Pejibaye Palm in Costa Rica." *Geographical Review* 56: 363–376.

Kenzer, Martin S. (ed.). 1987. *Carl O. Sauer: A Tribute*. Corvallis: Oregon State University.

Leighly, John. 1987. "Ecology as Metaphor: Carl Sauer and Human Ecology." *Professional Geographer* 39: 405–412.

Meitzen, August. 1895. *Siedelung und Agrarwesen der Westgermanen und Ostgermanen, der Kelten, Römer, Finnen und*

Slawen. 3 volumes plus atlas. Berlin: Wilhelm Hertz.

Murphey, Rhoads. 1951. "The Decline of North Africa Since the Roman Occupation: Climatic or Human?" *Annals of the Association of American Geographers* 41: 116–131.

Nettelbeck, Joachim. 1910. *Ein Mann: Des Seefahrers und aufrechten Bürgers Joachim Nettelbeck Lebensgeschichte von ihm selbsterzählt.* Ebenhausen bei Munich: Wilhelm Langewiesche-Brandt.

Popper, Deborah E., and Frank Popper. 1987. "The Great Plains: From Dust to Dust." *Planning* 53(12): 12–18.

Saarinen, Thomas F. 1966. *Perception of Drought Hazard on the Great Plains.* Department of Geography, Research Paper No. 106. Chicago: University of Chicago.

Sauer, Carl O. 1952. *Agricultural Origins and Dispersals.* New York: American Geographical Society.

Sauer, Jonathan D. 1993. *Historical Geography of Crop Plants.* Boca Raton, Fla.: CRC Press.

Thomas, David S. G. 1993. "Sandstorm in a Teacup? Understanding Desertification." *Geographical Journal* 159(3): 318–331.

Thomas, David S. G., and Nicholas J. Middleton. 1994. *Desertification: Exploding the Myth.* New York: John Wiley.

Thrower, Norman J. W. 1966. *Original Survey and Land Subdivision.* Chicago: Rand McNally.

Thünen, Johann Heinrich, von. 1966. *Von Thünen's Isolated State: An English Edition of Der Isolierte Staat.* Carla M. Wartenberg (trans.). Elmsford, N.Y.: Pergamon Press.

Vogeler, Ingolf. 1981. *The Myth of the Family Farm: Agribusiness Dominance of United States Agriculture.* Boulder, Colo.: Westview Press.

Walsh, Richard J. (ed.). 1948. *The Adventures of Marco Polo, as Dictated in Prison to a Scribe in the Year 1298; What He Experienced and Heard during his Twenty-Four Years Spent in Travel through Asia and at the Court of Kublai-Khan.* New York: John Day.

Whittlesey, Derwent S. 1936. "Major Agricultural Regions of the Earth." *Annals of the Association of American Geographers* 26: 199–240.

Wilken, Gene C. 1987. *Good Farmers: Traditional Agricultural and Resource Management in Mexico and Central America.* Berkeley: University of California Press.

Ten Recommended Books on Agricultural Geography

(For additional suggested readings, see The Human Mosaic *web site:* www.whfreeman.com/jordan*)*

Galaty, John G., and Douglas L. Johnson (eds.). 1990. *The World of Pastoralism: Herding Systems in Comparative Perspective.* New York: Guilford Press. A multidisciplinary collection of essays spanning five continents that analyzes the productivity of different animal herding practices and their contributions to herding societies.

Grigg, David B. 1995. *An Introduction to Agricultural Geography,* 2nd ed. London: Routledge. A comprehensive introduction to the human and environmental factors that influence how agriculture and agricultural practices differ from place to place.

Hart, John Fraser. 1998. *The Rural Landscape.* Baltimore: Johns Hopkins University Press. A synthesis of Hart's work on America's rural landscape that illustrates and explains a wide array of rural landscape elements, including coal mines, fences, barns, and resort towns.

Ilbery, Brian, Quentin Chiotti, and Timothy Rickard (eds.). 1997. *Agricultural Restructuring and Sustainability: A Geographical Perspective.* Wallingford, U.K.: C. A. B. International. A selection of papers dealing with agricultural restructuring and sustainability delivered at a conference of rural geographers from Canada, the United Kingdom, the United States, and New Zealand.

Jordan, Bella Bychkova, and Terry G. Jordan-Bychkov. 2001. *Siberian Village: Land and Life in the Sakha Republic.* Minneapolis: University of Minnesota Press. An account of an agricultural way of life in the far north, on the very outermost limits of the farming world near the Arctic Circle, among a remarkable Turkic people.

Middleton, Nick, and David S. G. Thomas (eds.). 1997. *World Atlas of Desertification,* 2nd ed. London: Arnold. Look at the cartographic evidence and decide for yourself whether the deserts of the world are enlarging at the expense of agricultural lands.

Sachs, Carolyn E. 1996. *Gendered Fields: Rural Women, Agriculture, and Environment.* Boulder, Colo.: Westview Press. An exploration of the commonalities and differences in rural women's experiences and their strategies for dealing with the challenges and opportunities of rural living.

Sauer, Carl O. 1969. *Seeds, Spades, Hearths, and Herds.* Cambridge, Mass.: MIT Press. The greatest of all American cultural geographers presents his theories on the origins of plant and animal domestication—the beginnings of agriculture.

Thomas, Chris. 1997. *Rural Geography.* London: Routledge. Provides an introductory discussion of rural life at the end of the twentieth century and strategies to secure a sustainable future for the countryside.

Turner, B. L., II, and Stephen B. Brush (eds.). 1987. *Comparative Farming Systems.* New York: Guilford Press. An interdisciplinary collection of essays that integrates socioeconomic, political, environmental, and technical elements of farming systems in Latin America, Anglo-America, Africa, Asia, and Europe.

A Journal in Agricultural Geography

Journal of Rural Studies. An international interdisciplinary journal ranked as the best of its kind. Published by Pergamon, an imprint of Elsevier Science, Amsterdam, Netherlands. Volume 1 appeared in 1985. Visit the home page of the journal at http://www.elsevier.nl/locate/jrurstud.

Why do we find it difficult to guess where this scene might be?

An industrial landscape. (Wendell Metzen/Bruce Coleman, Inc.)
Turn to Seeing Geography *on page 330 for an in-depth analysis of the above question.*

INDUSTRIES
A Faustian Bargain

Faust was a sorcerer/scholar who lived some 500 years ago, and his life has been immortalized in numerous dramas, operas, legends, and biographies—most famously by the great German writer Goethe. Faust sought both an understanding of the universe and the pleasures of the flesh. Frustrated by his own limitations in these strivings, he made a pact with the devil, selling his soul for knowledge and pleasure.

We of the modern world long ago made our own Faustian bargain: to give up both the difficulties and the advantages of the ancient rural way of life to achieve, at what turned out to be a horrible cost, the comforts of the industrial age. In effect, we laid waste much of the Earth to live better. This Faustian bargain involved the second of two great economic revolutions that have occurred in the development of culture. The first of these, the domestication of plants and animals, occurred in our dim prehistory. This agricultural revolution, discussed in Chapter 8, ultimately resulted in a huge increase in human population, a greatly accelerated modification of the physical environment, and major cultural readjustments. The second of these upheavals, the **industrial revolution,** is still taking place, and it involves a series of interrelated inventions leading to the use of machines and inanimate power in the manufacturing process and transportation. We live today at a pivotal point in the destiny of our species, for we are witnesses to this second revolution, with its many attendant changes and dangers.

The industrial revolution, which began in the eighteenth century, released undreamed-of human productive powers. Suddenly, whole societies could engage in the seemingly limitless multiplication of goods and services. Rapid bursts of human inventiveness followed, as did gigantic population increases and a massive, often unsettling remodeling of the environment. Today, the industrial revolution, with its churning of whole populations and its restructuring of ancient cultural traditions into popular

Figure 9.1
Oil field at sunset. Primary industries extract natural resources from the Earth. (BILL ROSS/CORBIS.)

forms (see Chapter 2), is still running its course. Few lands remain untouched by its machines, factories, transportation devices, and communication techniques. Western nations, where this revolution has been under way the longest, feel most strongly its sometimes painful, sometimes invigorating effects.

On an individual level, no facet of Western life remains unaffected by the industrial revolution. On a Friday night out, you might drive in a car to a single outlet in a nationwide chain of restaurants, where you order fried chicken raised indoors several states away on special enriched grain, brought by refrigerated truck to a deep freeze, and cooked in an electric oven. Later, at a movie, you buy a candy bar manufactured halfway across the country. Then you enjoy a series of machine-produced pictures that flash in front of your eyes so fast that they seem to be moving. Just about every object and every event in your life is affected, if not actually created, by the industrial revolution.

This chapter concentrates on industry and the industrial revolution as the cultural geographer sees it. In Western culture, the majority of the population owes its livelihood either directly or indirectly to industry and its related products and services.

 ## Industrial Regions

How can the theme of culture region be applied to industrial activity? Five types of industrial activity can be distinguished, and each occupies a distinct culture region.

Primary industries involve extracting natural resources from the Earth. Fishing, hunting, lumbering, oil wells, and mining provide examples of primary industries (Figure 9.1). Agriculture, also a primary industry, was addressed in Chapter 8. **Secondary industry** is the processing stage, commonly called manufacturing. Secondary industries process the raw materials extracted by primary industries, transforming them into more usable form. Ore is converted into steel; logs are milled into lumber; fish are processed and canned. As a rule, several steps occur in manufacturing. Many factories turn out products that serve as raw materials for other secondary industries. Steel mills provide steel for automobile factories, and lumber mills make building materials for the construction industry, also a secondary industry. The other three types of industrial activity all involve *services* of some sort, rather than the extraction or production of commodities. So wide is the range of services that some geographers find it useful to distinguish three sectors. These three types of industries are referred to as *tertiary, quaternary,* and *quinary.*

Each of the five types of industrial activity displays unique spatial patterns. Applying the theme of culture region, geographers refer to these as industrial regions, and Figure 9.2 on pages 300–301 reveals some of these patterns on a worldwide scale.

Primary Industry

Primary industries extract both renewable and nonrenewable resources. **Renewable resources** are those that, with intelligent management, can be used without being permanently depleted, such as forests, water, fishing grounds, and agricultural land. Unfortunately, overexploitation of renewable resources causes depletion in all too many cases, as the demand for the products of primary industries increases. The 1990s, for example, witnessed the beginning of a worldwide crisis in the oceanic fishing industry, as a result of overfishing. **Nonrenewable resources** are those that are depleted when used—for example, minerals and petroleum. Most petroleum exports come from the Persian Gulf countries of southwestern Asia. Saudi Arabia and neighboring Persian Gulf states produce about 30 percent of the world's oil and possess an even larger share of the known petroleum reserves.

Secondary Industry

Most of the world's industrial activity has traditionally been found in the developed countries of the midlatitude Northern Hemisphere, especially in parts of Anglo-America, Europe, Russia, and Japan. This is particularly true of manufacturing. In the United States, secondary industries once clustered mainly in the northeastern part of the country, a region referred to as the American Manufacturing Belt (Figure 9.3 on page 302). On the opposite Atlantic shore, manufacturing occupies the central core of Europe, surrounded by a less industrialized periphery (Figure 9.4 on page 303). Japan's industrial complex lies around the shore of the Inland Sea and throughout the southern part of the country (Figure 9.5 on page 304).

Many different types of manufacturing exist within these major regions. Industrial regions usually consist of several zones, each dominated by a particular kind of industry. Iron and steel manufacture is concentrated in one of these zones, coal mining in another, and textiles in a third. This pronounced regional specialization arose with the industrial revolution in the 1700s, causing manufacturing to take on a heightened geographical character. Reflecting the heightened regionalism that accompanied the industrial revolution was the development of the economic core-periphery pattern. The evolving manufacturing core consisted of the developed countries, with their collective manufacturing regions, whereas the periphery had nonindustrial and weakly industrialized lands, including many colonies. Resources extracted from the increasingly impoverished peripheries flowed to the core. The resultant geographical pattern—one of the fundamental realities of our age—is often referred to as **uneven development,** or regional disparity. Uneven development has proved to be increasingly and unyieldingly present.

Although the manufacturing dominance of the developed countries of the core persists, a major global geographical shift is currently under way in secondary industry. In virtually every core country, much of the secondary sector is in marked decline, especially traditional mass-production industries such as steel making and other types of manufacturing that require a minimally skilled, blue-collar workforce. In such districts, factories are closing, blue-collar unemployment rates stand at the highest level since the Great Depression of the 1930s, and a "deskilling" of the workforce proceeds. In the United States, for example, where manufacturing employment began a relative decline about 1950, 9 out of every 10 new jobs in recent years have been unskilled, low-paying service positions. The manufacturing industries surviving and now booming in the core countries are mainly those requiring a highly skilled or artisanal workforce, such as high-tech firms and companies producing high-quality consumer goods. Because the blue-collar workforce has proved largely unable to acquire the new skills needed in such industries, many old manufacturing districts lapse into deep economic depression. Moreover, the high-tech manufacturers employ far fewer workers than the former heavy industries, and they tend to be geographically concentrated in very small districts, sometimes called **technopoles** (see Figures 9.2, 9.3, and 9.4).

The word **deindustrialization** describes the decline and fall of once-prosperous factory and mining areas, such as the American Manufacturing Belt, now often called the Rust Belt (see Figure 9.3). Geographer Shane Davies, who has studied deindustrialization in the coal and steel districts of Wales in Great Britain, speaks of "pauperized belts" and of "a dispirited people who reflect a growing passivity to their plight." Deindustrialization brings demoralization and erosion of the *spirit of place,* as Davies calls it—the vital energy and pride that makes places livable, viable, and renewable.

Manufacturing industries lost by the core countries relocate in newly industrializing lands of the periphery. South Korea, Taiwan, Singapore, Brazil, Mexico, coastal China, and parts of India, among others, have experienced a major expansion of manufacturing, a movement that continues and now involves many other peripheral countries. The ongoing locational shift in manufacturing regions is largely the work of **global corporations,** also called multinationals or transnationals. We can no longer think of decisions about market location, labor supply, or other aspects of industrial planning within the framework of a single plant controlled by a single owner. Instead, we now deal with a highly complex international corporate structure that plans on a gargantuan scale. Working through great corporations that straddle the Earth, people for the first time use world resources with an efficiency more completely dictated by the merciless logic of profit. It is all part of the process of *globalization,* to which we have alluded frequently.

Industry Types

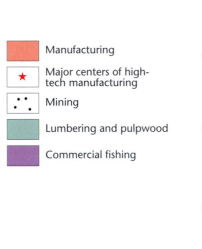

Manufacturing

★ Major centers of high-tech manufacturing

Mining

Lumbering and pulpwood

Commercial fishing

0   1000   2000 mi.

0   1000   2000   3000 km

Scale at latitude 35°

Flat Polar Quartic
equal area projection

Figure 9.2

Present regions of selected primary and secondary industries. Agriculture and hunting are not shown among the primary activities. (AFTER HUDSON AND ESPENSHADE, 2000: 50–60, WITH MODIFICATIONS AND SIMPLIFICATION.)

Tertiary Industry

The decline of primary and secondary industries in the older developed core, or *deindustrialization,* has ushered in an era widely referred to as the **postindustrial phase.** The three service sectors—tertiary, quaternary, and quinary—achieve dominance in the postindustrial phase. Both the United States and Canada can now be regarded as having entered the postindustrial era, as has most of Europe and Japan. **Tertiary industry,** part of both the industrial and postindustrial phases, includes transportation, communication, and utility services. Highways, rail-

roads, airlines, pipelines, telephones, radios, television, and the Internet all belong in the tertiary sector of industry. All facilitate the distribution of goods, services, and information. Modern industries require well-developed transport systems, and every industrial district is served by a network of such facilities. As one measure of the importance of transport, Figure 9.6 on pages 306–307 maps the number of persons per automobile by country.

Major regional differences exist in the relative importance of the various modes of transport. In Russia and Ukraine, for example, highways have less than average industrial significance; railroads, and to a lesser extent

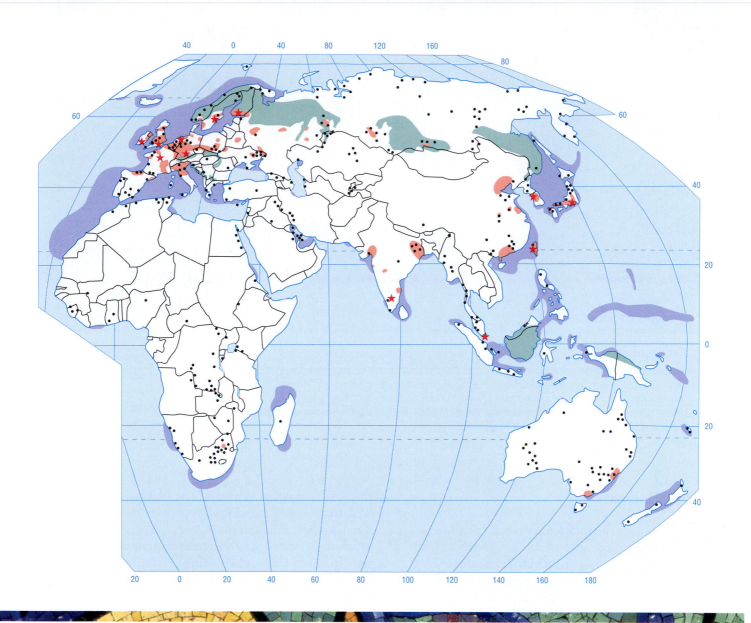

waterways, carry much of the transport load. Russia still lacks a transcontinental highway. In the United States, on the other hand, highways reign supreme, while the railroad system has declined. Western European nations rely heavily on a greater balance among rail, highway, and waterway transport. Beyond the industrialized regions, transport systems are much less developed. In most of Africa, interior Asia, and other weakly industrialized regions, drivable highways and railroads remain rare, but even there tertiary activity is increasing (Figure 9.7 on page 308). Meanwhile, in more developed countries, electronic transfers of funds and telecommunications between com-

puters continents apart add a new dimension and speed to the exchange of data and ideas. Utilities also belong in the tertiary sector, including the power plants that provide the energy to drive the entire industrial economy.

The transport division of tertiary industry, in particular automobiles, creates a special kind of functional culture region sometimes called *machine space*. As the number of automobiles increases, more and more space must be devoted to them, even in congested areas such as the central business districts of cities (Figure 9.8 on page 309). The result is often visual blight, another unaesthetic type of industrial culture region.

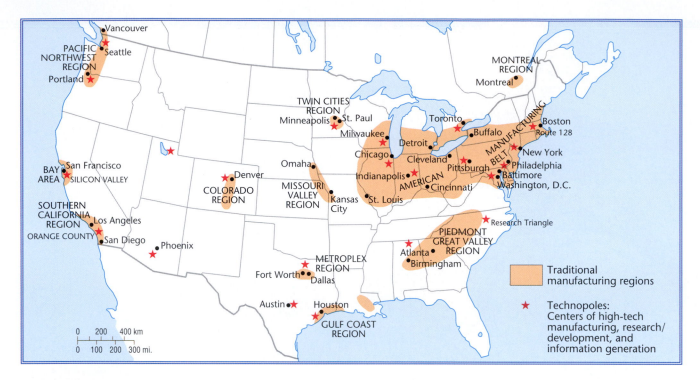

Figure 9.3

Major regions of industry in Anglo-America. The largest and most important region is still the American Manufacturing Belt, the traditional industrial core of the United States. Dispersal of manufacturing to other regions occurred after World War II and now involves mainly high-tech and information-based enterprises, or technopoles. **Why do high-tech industries have a distribution different from that of more traditional manufacturing?**

Quaternary Industry

Geographers include in **quaternary industry** those services mainly required by producers, such as trade, insurance, legal services, banking, advertising, wholesaling, retailing, consulting, information generation, and real estate transactions. Such activities represent one of the major growth sectors in postindustrial economies, and a geographical segregation seems to be developing, in which manufacturing is increasingly shunted to the peripheries while corporate headquarters, markets, and the producer-related service activities remain in the core. An inherent problem with this spatial arrangement is **multiplier leakage:** global corporations invest in secondary industry in the peripheries, but profits flow back to the core, where the corporate headquarters are located. As early as 1965, American-based corporations took, on the average, about four-fifths of their net profits out of Latin America in this way. As a result of multiplier leakage, the industrialization of less developed countries actually increases the power of the world's established industrial nations. In fact, although industrial technology has spread everywhere, today we face a world in which

the basic industrial power of the planet is more centralized than ever. The global corporations are headquartered mainly in quaternary areas where the industrial revolution took root earliest: the midlatitude countries of the Northern Hemisphere. Similarly, loans for industrial development come from banking institutions in Europe, Japan, and the United States, with the result that interest payments drain away from the poor to the rich countries.

Increasingly important in the quaternary sector is the collection, generation, storage, retrieval, and processing of computerized knowledge and information, including research, publishing, consulting, and forecasting. Postindustrial society is organized around knowledge and innovation, which are used to acquire profits and exert social control. The impact of computers is changing the world dramatically, a process that has accelerated since about 1970, with implications for the spatial organization of all human activities and each of the five industrial sectors. The proliferation of computers leads to new ways of doing things and to new products and services.

Many quaternary industries depend on a highly skilled, intelligent, creative, and imaginative labor force—and therefore are elitist. Although information-generating

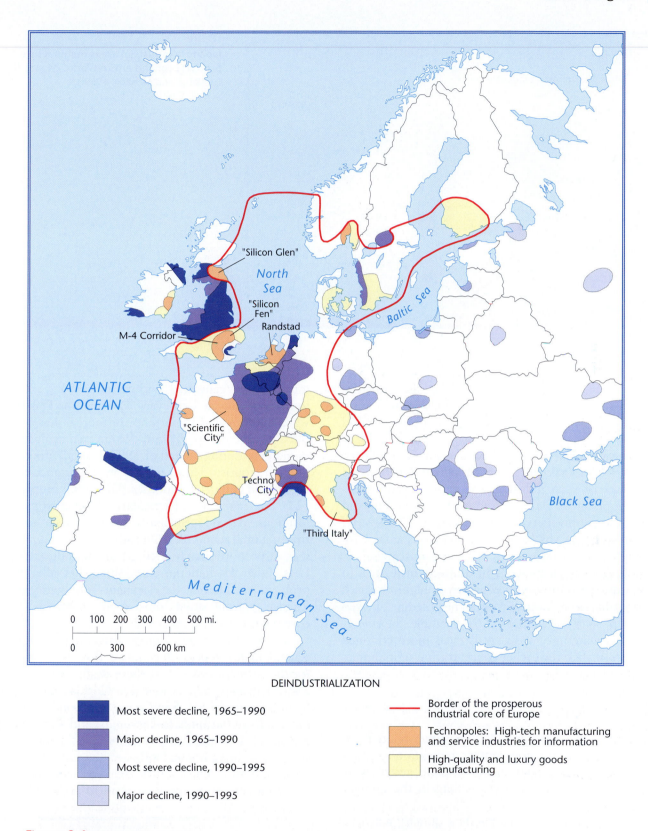

DEINDUSTRIALIZATION

◼ Most severe decline, 1965–1990

◼ Major decline, 1965–1990

◼ Most severe decline, 1990–1995

◼ Major decline, 1990–1995

▬ Border of the prosperous industrial core of Europe

◼ Technopoles: High-tech manufacturing and service industries for information

◼ High-quality and luxury goods manufacturing

Figure 9.4

Industrial regions and deindustrialization in Europe. New, prosperous centers of industry specializing in high-quality goods, luxury items, and high-tech manufacture have surpassed older centers of heavy industry—both primary and secondary. The regions in decline were earlier centers of the industrial revolution. **Why might the industrial districts in decline not have shared the new prosperity? Why did eastern Europe fall so far behind?** (SOURCE: JORDAN-BYCHKOV AND JORDAN, 2002: 300.)

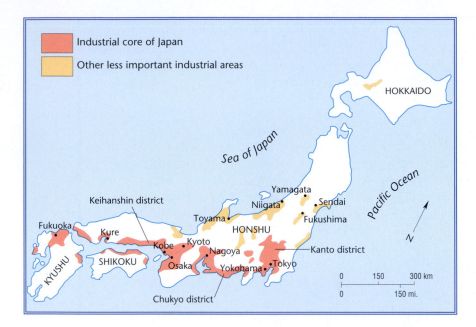

activity is focused geographically in the old industrial core, the distribution of this activity, if viewed on a more local scale, can be seen to coalesce in technopoles around major universities and research centers. The presence of Stanford and the University of California at Berkeley, for example, helped make the San Francisco Bay Area a major center of such industry, and similar technopoles have developed near Harvard and MIT in New England and near the triuniversity Raleigh–Durham–Chapel Hill "Research Triangle" of North Carolina (see Figure 9.3). These **high-tech corridors**—or "silicon landscapes," as some have dubbed them—occupy relatively little area. In other words, the information economy is highly focused geographically, contributing to and heightening uneven development spatially. In Europe, for example, the emerging core of quaternary industry is even more confined geographically than the earlier concentration of manufacturing (see Figure 9.4).

Quinary Industry

Quinary industry mainly involves consumer-related services, such as education, government, recreation/tourism, and health/medicine. Even such mundane activities as housecleaning and lawn services belong in the quinary sector.

One of the most rapidly expanding quinary activities is *tourism*. By 1990, this industry already accounted for 5.5 percent of the world's economy, generated $2.5 trillion in income, and employed 112 million workers—more than any other single industrial activity and amounting to 1 of every 15 workers in the world. Just a decade later, the

total income generated had risen to $4.5 trillion and tourism employed 1 of every 12 workers. This trend toward the increased importance of tourism has continued, often in spite of terrorist attacks directed against tourists, as in Egypt during the fall of 1997. Like all other forms of industry, tourism varies greatly in importance from one region and country to another (Figure 9.9 on pages 310–311). Some countries, particularly those in tropical island locations, depend principally upon tourism to support their national economies. One advantage of tourism is that it is disproportionately focused in the industrial peripheries rather in than the core, somewhat alleviating the problem of uneven development—although multiplier leakage typically drains most of the profits back to the core (Figure 9.10 on page 312).

Tourist movements can be categorized according to several major types. One major flow is from *interior locations-to-seacoasts,* and these destinations often bear alluring names, such as southern Florida's Gold Coast or Spain's Costa del Sol (Sun Coast). A second major movement is from *lowlands-to-highlands,* and many mountain ranges, such as the Alps, Rockies, and Himalayas, have tourism as their principal industrial base. Switzerland and Austria, both Alpine countries, each year receive twice as many foreign tourists as their resident population.

Reflecting on **GEOGRAPHY**

Give examples of the five types of industry—primary, secondary, tertiary, quaternary, and quinary—where you live.

The third major tourist flow, which overlaps to a degree with the first two, is *urban-to-rural,* as people seek vacations away from the crowded cities in which they live. Seasonal renting of farmhouses is increasingly common, as is the acquisition of vacation homes in isolated places. In rural Norway, about 40 percent of all farmers take in summer guests to supplement their income, and some farms, even in the United States, now cater exclusively to tourists. The "dude ranch" of the American and Canadian West provided a prototype of such rural-based tourism. More recently, **ecotourism** involving visits to very remote areas, particularly wilderness regions, has risen in importance, as has tourism based on fishing and hunting. We will discuss ecotourism in more detail later in the chapter.

A fourth tourist flow is directed to places of cultural and historical importance, such as archaeological sites (for example, Troy in Turkey), well-preserved medieval or colonial towns (such as Williamsburg in Virginia and Prague in Czechia), or museums of one kind or another. Less important nowadays is health-resort tourism, where people go to "take the waters," though most European spas still do a lively business. Amusement parks such as Disney World have enjoyed a meteoric rise in recent decades. Finally, *urban-to-urban* tourism takes large numbers of visitors to such places as Las Vegas, New York City, and Los Angeles, which have multiple attractions.

Perhaps most modern tourism involves multiple destinations—literally, "making a tour"—but cultural differences can be detected. Europeans, in general, prefer to go to a single destination and remain there for their entire vacation, whereas Americans generally seek multiple destinations. Increasingly, tourists travel in groups or on planned itineraries, rather than individually.

Industrial Diffusion

How do industrial regionalization, uneven development, and core-periphery patterns come to exist? The theme of cultural diffusion permits us to begin to answer such questions. Perhaps the most basic issue is the diffusion of the industrial revolution itself.

Origins of the Industrial Revolution

As a rule, people strongly resist substantial changes in their basic cultural patterns unless they perceive some great and immediate personal benefit. The enormous appeal and promise of the industrial revolution caused people in a great variety of cultures to discard tradition and adopt this new way of life. Until the industrial revolution, most people were concerned with the most basic of primary economic activities: acquiring the necessities of survival from the land. Society and culture remained overwhelmingly rural and agricultural. To be sure, industry already existed in this setting, because humans are by nature makers of things. For as long as our biological species has existed, we have fashioned tools, weapons, utensils, clothing, and other objects, but traditionally these items were made by hand, laboriously and slowly. Before about 1700, most such manufacture was carried on in two rather distinct systems: cottage industry and guild industry.

Cottage industry, by far the most common, was practiced in farm homes and rural villages, usually as a sideline to agriculture. Objects for family use were made in each household, and most villages had a cobbler, miller, weaver, and smith who worked part-time at these trades in their homes. Skills passed from parents to children with little formality.

By contrast, the **guild industry** consisted of professional organizations of highly skilled, specialized artisans engaged full-time in their trades and based in towns and cities. Membership in a guild came after a long apprenticeship, during which the apprentice learned the secrets of the profession from a skilled master. The guild was a fraternal organization of artisans skilled in a particular craft, so that guilds existed for weavers, glassblowers, silversmiths, steel makers, potters, and many other trades. Although the cottage and guild systems differed in many respects, both depended on hand labor and human power.

The industrial revolution arose among back-country English cottage craftspeople in the early 1700s and fundamentally restructured secondary industry. First, human hands were replaced by machines in the fashioning of finished products, rendering the word *manufacturing* ("made by hand") technically obsolete. No longer would the weaver sit at a hand loom and painstakingly produce each piece of cloth. Instead, large mechanical looms were invented to do the job faster and cheaper (though not necessarily better). Second, human power gave way to various forms of inanimate power. The machines were driven by water power, by the burning of fossil fuels, and later by hydroelectricity and the energy of the atom. Men and women, once the proud producers of fine handmade goods, became tenders of machines.

The initial breakthrough came in the secondary, or manufacturing, sector. More exactly, it occurred in the British *cotton textile cottage industry,* centered at that time in the district of Lancashire in northwestern England. At first the changes were modest and on a small scale. Mechanical spinners and looms were invented, and flowing water—long used as a source of power by local grain millers—was harnessed to drive the looms. During this stage, manufacturing industries remained largely

Cars per Population Unit

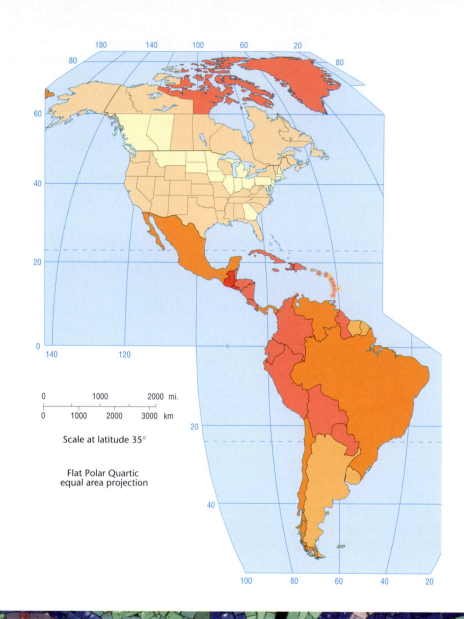

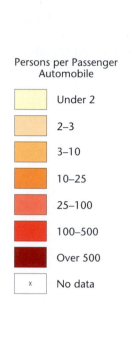

Persons per Passenger Automobile

- Under 2
- 2–3
- 3–10
- 10–25
- 25–100
- 100–500
- Over 500
- x   No data

0   1000   2000 mi.

0   1000   2000   3000 km

Scale at latitude 35°

Flat Polar Quartic
equal area projection

Figure 9.6

The number of persons per automobile today. The most highly industrialized nations have the largest numbers of cars per person. **Is this a valid measure of prosperity?** (UNITED NATIONS, 2000: 572–587).

rural, diffusing hierarchically to sites where rushing streams could be found, especially waterfalls and rapids. Later in the eighteenth century, the invention of the steam engine provided a better source of power, and a shift away from water-powered machines occurred. In the United States, too, the first factories were textile plants.

Traditionally, *metal industries* had been small-scale, rural enterprises, carried on in small forges situated near ore deposits. Forests provided charcoal for the smelting process. The chemical changes that occurred in the making of steel remained mysterious even to the craftspeople who used them, and much ritual, superstition, and cere-

mony were associated with steel making. Techniques had changed little since the beginning of the Iron Age, 2,500 years before.

The industrial revolution radically altered all this. In the eighteenth century, a series of inventions by iron makers living in Coalbrookdale in the English Midlands allowed the old traditions, techniques, and rituals of steel making to be swept away and replaced with a scientific, large-scale industry. *Coke,* nearly pure carbon derived from high-grade coal, was substituted for charcoal in the smelting process. Large blast furnaces replaced the forge, and efficient rolling mills took the place of hammer and

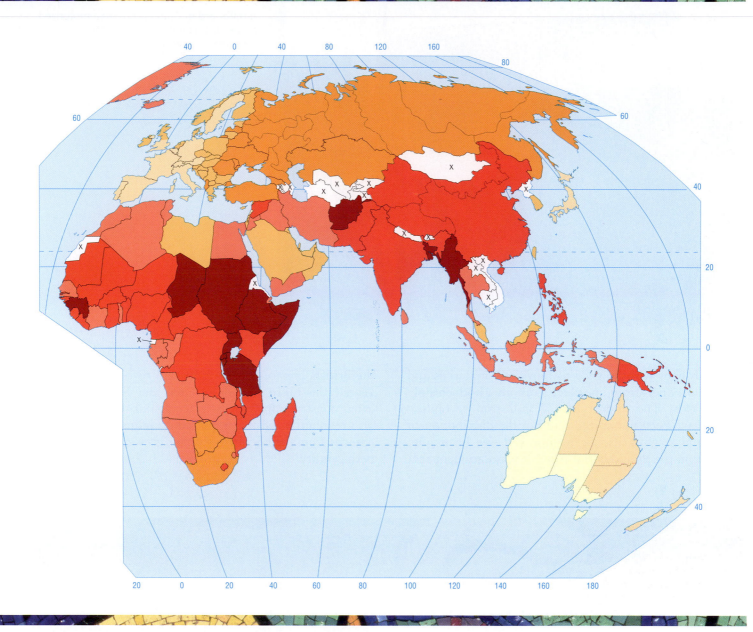

anvil. Mass production of steel resulted, and the new industrial order was built of steel. Other manufacturing industries made similar transitions, and entirely new types arose, such as machine making.

Primary industries were also revolutionized. The first to feel the effects of the new technology was coal mining. The adoption of the steam engine necessitated huge amounts of coal to fire the boilers, and the conversion to coke in the smelting process further increased the demand for coal. Fortunately, Great Britain had large coal deposits. New mining techniques and tools were invented, and coal mining became a large-scale, mechanized indus-

try. Coal, heavy and bulky, was difficult to transport. As a result, manufacturing industries began flocking to the coalfields to be near the supply, in a process of hierarchical diffusion. Similar modernization occurred in the mining of iron ore, copper, and other metals needed by rapidly growing industries.

The industrial revolution also affected the tertiary sector, most notably in the form of rapid bulk transportation. The traditional wooden sailing ships gave way to steel vessels driven by steam engines, canals were built, and the British-invented railroad came on the scene. The main stimulus that led to these transportation

Figure 9.7
A billboard in China promises a motorized future to a nation of bicycle riders.
(Courtesy of Terry G. Jordan-Bychkov.)

breakthroughs was the need to move raw materials and finished products from one place to another both cheaply and quickly. The impact of the industrial revolution would have been minimized had not the distribution of goods and services also been improved (see Focus On: Distance in the Preindustrial Age). It is no accident that the British, creators of the industrial revolution, also invented the railroad and initiated the first large-scale canal construction. Nor is it accidental that the British also revolutionized the shipbuilding industry and dominated it from their Scottish shipyards even into the twentieth century.

FOCUS ON

Distance in the Preindustrial Age

Our lives are a constant adventure in shrinking space. With a car, we're just minutes from a friend who lives miles away. The airplane has put us within jet-lag distance of Paris, Moscow, and Beijing. In such an age, we can hardly imagine what an obstacle distance often proved to be before the industrial revolution.

A record of 10,000 letters sent to Venice, Italy, in the early sixteenth century shows clearly how great a factor distance was in the preindustrial world. Letters from nearby Genoa took an average of 6 days to arrive; from London, 27 days; from Constantinople, 37 days; from Lisbon, 46 days; from Damascus, 80 days. But these average figures hardly tell the whole tale. Changing human and climatic conditions lent a striking elasticity to mail delivery. Deliveries from Paris ranged from a minimum of 7 days to a maximum of 34 days; from

Barcelona, 8 to 77 days; and from Florence, 1 to 13 days—to pick three places at random. Zara, which was separated from Venice by only a short stretch of the Adriatic Sea, held the record. Its letters, depending upon sailing conditions, took from 1 day to 25 days to arrive. Compared to other goods, however, letters moved briskly across the map. Sixteenth-century Italians knew that it took even their privileged goods 3 months to reach London.

In fact, before the eighteenth century, distance had been a relatively constant factor for centuries. In terms of travel, the Mediterranean was about the same "size" in the sixteenth century as it had been in Roman times over 1000 years earlier. Traveling times did not change much until the nineteenth century.

From Braudel, 1972, vol. I: 356.

Figure 9.8
Machine space in Atlanta, Georgia.
Tertiary industry, represented by the automobile, has created its own functional culture region in the heart of a great city. **Is this process unavoidable? Undesirable?**
(COURTESY OF TERRY G. JORDAN-BYCHKOV.)

The railroads and other innovative modes of transport associated with the industrial revolution, once in place, fostered additional cultural diffusion. Ideas could spread more rapidly and easily after the railroad network came into existence. In particular, the new industrial-age popular culture could easily penetrate previously untouched areas. Geographer Mark Jefferson, reflecting the cultural arrogance of this age, wrote in the 1920s of the "civilizing rails" as an agent of diffusion.

Nor has this process yet ended. As geographer Chris Airriess has noted, the transnational corporations linked by globalization created worldwide containerized shipping based in megaports such as Singapore, then further revolutionized the shipping industry by adopting new information technologies to speed the movement of goods even more.

Diffusion of the Industrial Revolution

For a century, Great Britain maintained a virtual monopoly on the industrial revolution. Indeed, the British government actively tried to prevent the diffusion of the various inventions and innovations that made up the industrial revolution, because they gave Britain an enormous economic advantage and contributed greatly to the growth and strength of the British Empire. Nevertheless, this technology finally diffused beyond the bounds of the British Isles (Figure 9.11 on page 313). Continental Europe was the first to receive its impact. In the last half of the nineteenth century, the industrial revolution took firm root hierarchically in the coalfields of Germany, Belgium, and other nations of northwestern and central Europe. The diffusion of railroads in Europe provides a good index to the spread of the industrial revolution there (Figure 9.12 on page 314). The United States began rapid adoption of this new technology about 1850, followed a half-century later by Japan, the first major non-Western nation to undergo full industrialization. In the first third of the twentieth century, the diffusion of industry and modern transport spilled over into Russia and Ukraine. More recently, countries such as Taiwan, South Korea, China, India, and Thailand joined the manufacturing age.

> ## Reflecting on **GEOGRAPHY**
>
> Industries continue to diffuse. Can you think of new industrial activities that have recently come to the area where you live?

 ## Industrial Ecology

How might the theme of cultural ecology best be applied to the geographical study of industries? The answer is clear: it is precisely industrial ecology that lies at the heart of our Faustian bargain. We have tacitly agreed to the ongoing destruction of the planet in exchange for living comfortably today. All five types of industrial activity create serious ecological problems. For example, primary

Tourism

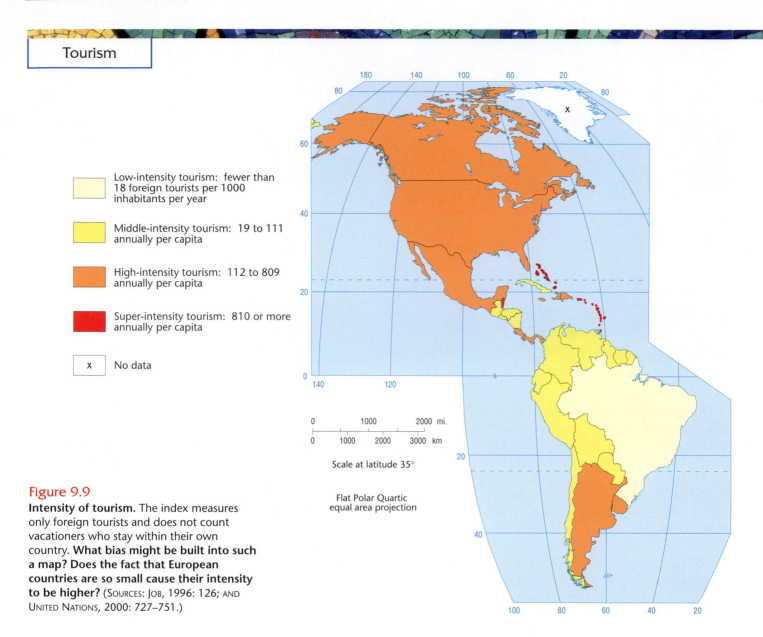

Low-intensity tourism: fewer than 18 foreign tourists per 1000 inhabitants per year

Middle-intensity tourism: 19 to 111 annually per capita

High-intensity tourism: 112 to 809 annually per capita

Super-intensity tourism: 810 or more annually per capita

x   No data

0   1000   2000 mi.
0   1000   2000   3000 km

Scale at latitude 35°

Flat Polar Quartic
equal area projection

Figure 9.9

Intensity of tourism. The index measures only foreign tourists and does not count vacationers who stay within their own country. **What bias might be built into such a map? Does the fact that European countries are so small cause their intensity to be higher?** (SOURCES: JOB, 1996: 126; AND UNITED NATIONS, 2000: 727–751.)

industries gouge huge scars on the Earth while extracting minerals, which has led Laurie Brown and her coauthors to speak of **terraforming,** the physical restructuring of the Earth's surface. Other examples follow.

Renewable Resource Crises

Even renewable resources such as forests and fisheries are endangered. *Deforestation* is an ongoing process that began at least 3000 years ago, but in just the last half-century, a third of the world's forest cover has been lost. Lumber use tripled between 1950 and 2000, and the demand for paper increased fivefold. Today, we witness the rapid destruction of one of the last surviving great woodland ecosystems: the tropical rain forest, in both the Eastern and Western Hemispheres (Figure 9.13 on page 314). The most intensive rain-forest clearing is occurring in the East Indies and Brazil, and commercial lumber interests are largely responsible (Figure 9.14 on page 315). Although trees represent a renewable resource when properly managed, too many countries are in effect mining their forests. Canadians and Americans can only hypocritically chastise countries such as Brazil and Indonesia for not protecting their tropical rain forests, because their own west coast midlatitude rain forests in the Pacific Northwest, British Columbia, and Alaska continue to

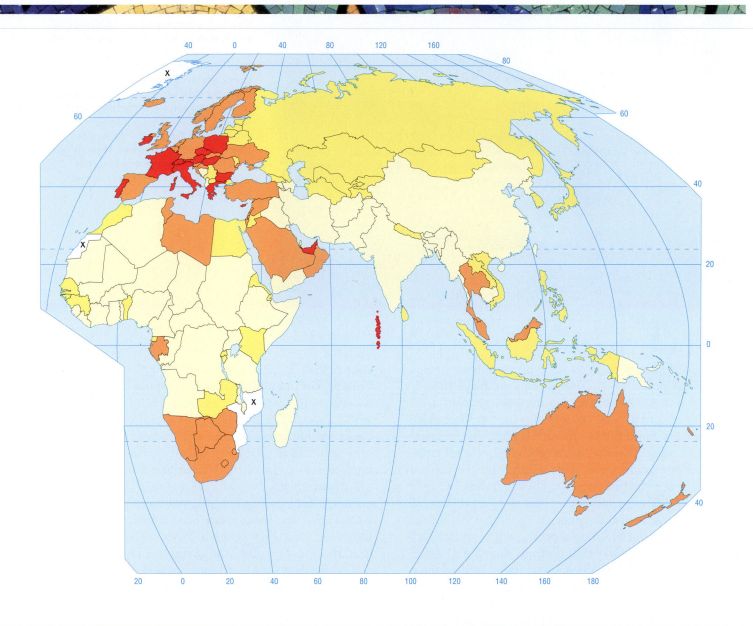

suffer severe damage as a result of unwise lumbering practices. In any case, *foreign* rather than Brazilian interests now hold logging rights to nearly 30 million acres (12 million hectares) of Amazonian rain forest. Even when forests are converted into scientifically managed "tree farms," as is true in most of the developed world, ecosystems are unavoidably destroyed. Natural ecosystems have plant and animal diversity that cannot be sustained under the monoculture of commercial forestry.

Similarly, *overfishing* has brought a crisis to many ocean fisheries, a problem compounded by pollution of many of the world's seas. The total fish catch of all countries combined rose from 84 million metric tons in 1984 to more than 122 million metric tons by the late 1990s, causing some species to decline. Salmon in Pacific coastal North America and cod in the Maritime Provinces of Canada can be said to have reached a "marine biological crisis." Overfishing caused a catastrophic recession in the Newfoundland cod industry, and some experts forecast a collapse of the world's fisheries in the near future.

Acid Rain

Secondary and tertiary industries pollute the air, water, and land with chemicals and other toxic substances. **Acid rain** is one example. Known to researchers for a century

Figure 9.10
Tourism, often on a primitive level, reaches even into remote areas. Small charter buses now deliver climbers to a thatched tourist hut, which lacks running water, at the foot of Mount Wilhelm in highland Papua New Guinea—an area totally unknown to the outside world as late as 1930. Increasing numbers of tourists from Europe, North America, and Japan seek out such places. **How might these places change as a result of tourism?** (Courtesy of Terry G. Jordan-Bychkov.)

and a half, acid rain received widespread publicity beginning in the early 1980s. The burning of fossil fuels by power plants, factories, and automobiles releases acidic sulfur oxides and nitrogen oxides into the air; these chemicals are then flushed from the atmosphere by precipitation. The resultant rainfall has a much higher acidity than normal. For example, a shower that fell on the town of Kane, in northern Pennsylvania, on September 19, 1978, had a pH reading equivalent to that of vinegar. Overall, 84 percent of the world's energy is generated by burning fossil fuels, making acid rain a prevalent phenomenon.

Acid rain can poison fish, damage plants, and diminish soil fertility. Such problems have been studied intensively in Germany, one of the most completely industrialized nations in the world. German scholars have been impressed by the dramatic suddenness with which the catastrophic effects of acid rain arrived. In 1982, only 8 percent of forests in western Germany showed damage, but by 1990 the proportion had risen to over half. Now only a crash program of pollution control and energy conservation can save the woodlands of Germany. In the words of geographer Wilfrid Bach, "The ongoing forest dieback demands that without any further delay, emission of these pollutants must be controlled at the source much more effectively," if the German forests are not to perish. Neighboring Czechia faces a comparable problem (Figure 9.15 on page 316).

In North America, the effects of acid rain accumulate, but not yet with the catastrophic speed seen in central Europe. More than 90 lakes in the seemingly pristine Adirondack Mountains of New York were "dead," de-

void of fish life, by 1980, and 50,000 lakes in eastern Canada face a similar fate. Since about 1990, the acid-rain problem has become less severe in many parts of the world, especially Europe, but the situation in the Adirondacks has not improved. Recent studies suggest that acid rain now causes mass killings of marine life along the northeastern coast of the United States and of forests in the Appalachians (Figure 9.16 on page 317). Oxides of nitrogen seem to be the principal culprit in the coastal waters, and the impact has been noted in Chesapeake, Delaware, and Narragansett bays, as well as in Long Island Sound. For years, the government of Canada urged U.S. officials to take stringent action to help alleviate acid-rain damage, because much of the problem on the Canadian side of the border derives from American pollution, but their pleas had little effect. Despite countermeasures, the acid-rain problem is not improving.

Global Warming

Most scientists now agree that we have entered a phase of **global warming** caused by industrial activity and, most particularly, by the greatly increased amount of carbon dioxide (CO_2) produced by burning fossil fuels. Geographer Greg O'Hare, among others, warns against unquestioned acceptance of this theory, but the circumstantial evidence seems overwhelming (Figure 9.17 on page 318). The eight hottest years on record all occurred in the period 1990–2001, based on records compiled at more than 14,000 locations. In 2002, a huge ice mass the size of Rhode Island broke off from Antarctica and frag-

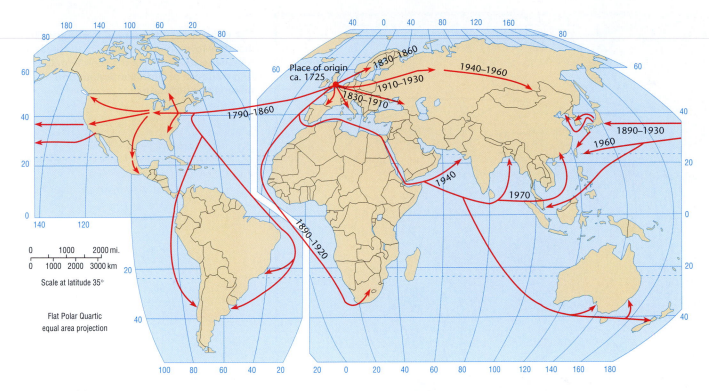

Figure 9.11

The diffusion of the industrial revolution. By diffusion from Great Britain, the industrial revolution has changed cultures in much of the world. **Why might the industrial revolution have originated in so small and peripheral a country?** See Figure 1.12, which would seem to make such an origin unlikely.

mented into icebergs in the ocean. This ice mass, before it shattered as a result of warming temperatures, measured 1260 square miles (3264 square kilometers) in area and 650 feet (226 meters) in thickness.

At issue is the so-called **greenhouse effect.** Every year billions of tons of CO_2 are produced worldwide by fossil-fuel burning, at a level 75 percent greater than in 1860. By some estimates, the atmospheric concentration of CO_2 has climbed to the highest level in 180,000 years (see Figure 9.17). In addition, the ongoing destruction of the world's rain forests adds huge additional amounts of CO_2 to the atmosphere. Although CO_2 is a natural component of the Earth's atmosphere, the freeing of this huge additional amount is altering the chemical composition of the air. Carbon dioxide, only one of the absorbing gases involved in the greenhouse effect, permits solar short-wave heat radiation to reach the Earth's surface but acts to block or trap long-wave outgoing radiation, causing a thermal imbalance and global heating.

The result could be, at worst, a runaway buildup of solar heat that would evaporate all water and make any

form of life impossible, causing planet Earth to resemble hostile Venus. Less catastrophically, the greenhouse effect could warm the global climate only enough to melt or partially melt the polar ice caps, causing the sea level to rise and inundate the world's coastlines. The long-term effects of even this lesser change could have disastrous results for humankind. The worst-case scenario for the year 2030 seems to include a climatic warming to the level known 4 million years ago, in the mid-Pliocene epoch.

An acceleration of the greenhouse effect could be sudden, as some critical, unknown threshold is reached in the concentration of atmospheric CO_2. This doomsday is possibly being delayed by another industrial-related environmental alteration: the addition of huge amounts of **particulate pollutants** to the atmosphere. Such pollution acts to block out solar radiation and cool the climate. In North America, particulate pollution is often produced by power plants, a problem that is most severe in the southeastern United States. The two atmospheric processes, greenhouse effect and particulate pollution, may

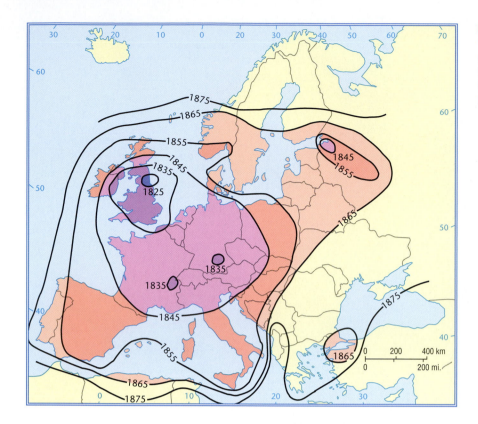

Figure 9.12
The diffusion of the railroad in Europe. The industrial revolution and the railroad spread together across much of the continent. **Can you find evidence of both contagious and hierarchical diffusion?**

have acted to neutralize each other, at least so far. If this is the case, the balance achieved is a precarious one.

So poorly understood is this phenomenon that some researchers deny that we are experiencing a global warming of climate. Part of the problem is that we lack good weather records for all but the recent past. Also, even if the climate is becoming warmer, the causes cannot conclusively be determined at this time.

Many experts believe that the greenhouse effect will be accompanied by major changes in precipitation patterns, with some regions becoming wetter and others drier (Figure 9.18 on pages 320–321). Some climatic

Figure 9.13
Destruction of tropical rain forest near Madang in Papua New Guinea by Japanese lumbering interests. The entire forest is leveled to extract a relatively small number of desired trees. **Why are overtly destructive policies employed?** (COURTESY OF TERRY G. JORDAN-BYCHKOV.)

Figure 9.14
The tropical rain forest of the Amazon Basin. In Brazil, the rain forest is under attack by settlers, ranchers, and commercial loggers. Its removal will intensify the impact of the "greenhouse gases," especially carbon dioxide, because the forest acts to convert those gases into benign forms. About 10,000 square miles (26,000 square kilometers) of Brazil's tropical rain forest is cleared each year. (SOURCE: WORLDWATCH INSTITUTE WEB SITE.)

models predict that global warming will make the tropics drier and the middle and higher latitudes wetter. Perhaps these changes are already upon us. Violent weather may also increase with global warming, and evidence suggests that this change, too, may already be occurring as we enter the twenty-first century.

Without question, sea level would rise with global warming. Some countries, such as the Maldives (in the Indian Ocean) and Kiribati (in the Pacific Ocean) would vanish completely beneath the waves. More catastrophically, a rise of sea level by 3 feet (1 meter) would submerge a fifth of densely populated Bangladesh and potentially force the relocation of as many as 100 million Chinese.

Ozone Depletion

Potentially even more serious is the depletion of the upper-atmosphere *ozone layer*, which acts to shield humans and all other forms of life from the most harmful types of solar radiation. Several manufactured chemicals are almost certainly the main culprits, including the freon used in refrigeration and air conditioning. Most of the industrialized countries of the world contribute large amounts of these chemicals, and they signed the Montreal Protocol in 1989 aimed at reducing the ozone-damaging substances.

> ## Reflecting on **GEOGRAPHY**
>
> If we cannot be certain that global warming and upper-level ozone depletion are caused by industrial activity rather than being natural fluctuations or cycles, should we take action or simply wait and see what happens?

Little progress has been made, however, and recent research suggests that the problem may be far worse than previously believed. In 2001, winter ozone levels in the Arctic high latitudes fell to 20–25 percent of normal. The ozone decrease in the Arctic was first noticed in the early 1990s and produced an ozone hole in that region comparable to the one first detected in the Antarctic during the 1980s. The problem continues today (Figure 9.19 on page 322). The activist organization Greenpeace, among others, warns that ozone depletion now threatens the

Figure 9.15
Forest death in Czechia caused by acid rain. Forest death, widespread in central Europe, is now beginning to appear in North America and certain other areas. (BAVARIA/ THE VIESTI COLLECTION.)

future of all forms of life on Earth. Perhaps in the end we will find that industrialization, which has become so integral a part of our culture in the past two centuries, is simply ecologically untenable and cannot be maintained. In short, our modern industrial way of life may prove a maladaptive strategy in terms of cultural ecology.

Radioactive Pollution

Like acid rain, *radioactive pollution* is invisible. It comes from nuclear power plants and waste storage facilities. The catastrophe at Chernobyl in Ukraine on April 26, 1986, clearly demonstrated the danger inherent in the Faustian bargain that has led Japan, much of Europe, and many other parts of the world to depend heavily on nuclear power.

When the Chernobyl nuclear reactor core melted down, causing two explosions, a sizable area around Chernobyl in Ukraine and Belarus became heavily contaminated with deadly radiation, and all land within an 18-mile (30-kilometer) radius of the destroyed reactor had to be evacuated. This area remains uninhabited today, save for a few elderly people who refused to leave. Beyond this zone, sizable swaths across Europe were bombarded with various radioactive isotopes, such as cesium-137, a long-term hazard because it has a *half-life* (the time required for its radioactivity to decrease by half) of 30 years and attacks the entire human body (Figure

9.20 on page 323). Another major component of the Chernobyl pollution was iodine-131, with a half-life of 8.1 days, which collects in the thyroid gland. Some estimates place the amount of cesium-137 released as equivalent to at least 750 Hiroshima atomic bombs. Ultimately, a sizable part of both Ukraine and Belarus may be declared unfit for human habitation, and additional tens of thousands of people could die from exposure to radiation caused by this single catastrophe. Strontium-90, another radioactive contaminant, continues to leak into the groundwater table at Chernobyl. The ominous term *national sacrifice area* is now heard in governmental circles in various countries as a potential euphemism for districts rendered permanently uninhabitable by radiation pollution, and some geographers speak of "hazardscapes" to describe such places.

Our experience with industrialization as an *adaptive strategy* has been too short and shallow to permit an adequate perspective on the problem. In the United States, we have lived with the industrial revolution for about 150 years. What would the ecological impact of this system be after 3 centuries, 10 centuries, 20 centuries? We can only guess, but many experts are not optimistic. What we do know is that the technology of the industrial revolution has demanded that we modify our habitat on a previously undreamed-of scale, and at the same time it has provided us with the tools and techniques to carry out that massive modification.

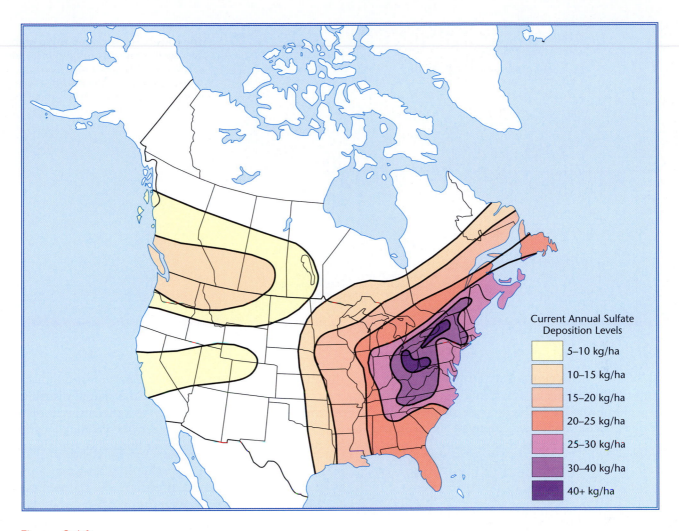

Figure 9.16

Distribution of acid rain in North America. Measurements are taken from the annual sulfate deposition, derived from airborne sulfur oxides (SO_2). Deposition levels of 18 pounds per acre (20 kilograms per hectare) are generally regarded as threatening to some aquatic and terrestrial ecosystems. Nitrate components of acid rain are not shown. Might this distribution cause Canada and the United States to engage in a dispute? (SOURCE: WORLDWATCH INSTITUTE WEB SITE.)

Current Annual Sulfate Deposition Levels

- 5–10 kg/ha
- 10–15 kg/ha
- 15–20 kg/ha
- 20–25 kg/ha
- 25–30 kg/ha
- 30–40 kg/ha
- 40+ kg/ha

The Environmental Sustainability Index

The key issue in all these industrial-related ecological problems is sustainability. Can our present industrial-based way of life continue without causing ecological collapse?

The Environmental Sustainability Index (ESI) has been devised to measure, country by country, the level of progress toward sustainability. The highest possible score on the ESI is 100, the lowest 0. No fewer than 22 "core indicators" involving 67 different variables are considered (Figure 9.21 on pages 324–325). These include air and water quality, biodiversity, population pressures, private business sector responsiveness, level of governmental in-

tervention, and so on. In 2001, the highest-ranked country was Finland, at 80.5; the lowest Haiti, at 24.7. Although far from being a perfect measure, the ESI clearly points to the regions of the world where ecosystems are most highly stressed. These lie mainly in the tropics and subtropics.

Some Good News

After all this depressing news, you are probably in need of a morale boost. And there is good news as well as bad.

For example, genuine progress is being made in the use of wind power to generate electricity. In the United States alone, wind power produced over 5000 megawatts of electricity by the end of 2001, and the United States

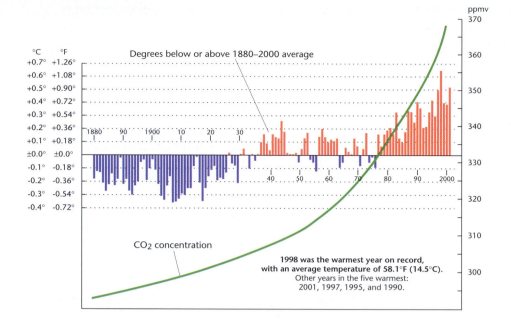

Figure 9.17

The correlation between rising globally averaged temperatures and increasing carbon dioxide emissions. Correlations prove nothing, but the evidence seems compelling. (SOURCES: O'HARE, 2000: 358; AND WORLDWATCH INSTITUTE WEB SITE.)

lags far behind such countries as Denmark, Spain, and Germany. California, Texas, Iowa, and Minnesota are the leading wind-power states (Figure 9.22 on page 326).

Another encouraging development is **ecotourism,** defined as responsible travel that does not harm ecosystems or the well-being of local people. Ecotourism arose when it was recognized that even seemingly benign quinary industries such as tourism can create ecological problems. Ecotourists tend to visit out-of-the-way places with exotic, healthy ecosystems. They disdain the comforts of large hotels and resorts, preferring more spartan conditions. Revenues from ecotourism helped rescue Uganda's mountain gorillas from extinction, especially when the government realized the wildlife served as a valuable tourist attraction.

We can also be encouraged by the rise of the **Greens,** political activists who advocate intelligent use of the Earth. Many countries now have Green political parties. Also active in helping save the environment are groups such as the Sierra Club, Greenpeace, and the Nature Conservancy.

 ## Industrial Cultural Interaction

Can our understanding of the industrialized world be aided by the theme of cultural interaction? Yes, but in a very different way from cultural ecology. Cultural interaction mainly allows us to understand the location of industries. The causal factors influencing *industrial location* include various economic features, and geographers seeking to explain industrial location have more than

once succumbed to *economic determinism*. Industrial location theory seeks to explain the spatial distribution of industry by referring mainly to other aspects of society. From the time of Alfred Weber (see Profile), location theorists have placed enormous importance on labor supply as a locational factor.

Labor Supply

Labor-intensive industries are those for which labor costs form a large part of total production costs. Examples include industries that depend on skilled workers producing small objects of high value, such as computers, cameras, and watches. Manufacturers consider several characteristics of labor in deciding where to locate factories: availability of workers, average wages, necessary skills, and worker productivity. Workers with certain skills tend to live and work in a small number of places, partly as a result of the need for higher education or for person-to-person training in handing down such skills. Consequently, manufacturers often seek locations where these skilled workers live.

In recent decades, the increasing mobility of labor throughout the Western world has lessened the locational influence of labor. Migration of labor accelerated after 1950, especially in Europe and the United States. Large numbers of workers in Europe migrated from south to north, leaving their homes in Spain, Italy, Greece, Turkey, and the Balkan States to find employment in the main European manufacturing belt. Today, labor migration is at an all-time high, lessening labor's influence on industrial location and reflecting the process of *globalization*.

PROFILE

Alfred Weber

1868–1958

Weber was the most influential pioneer theorist of industrial location. In 1909, he published his seminal work, later translated as *Theory of the Location of Industries.* Most subsequent research in industrial location theory represents attempts by others to refine or refute his model. Many aspects of Weber's theory remain viable today and are presented in this chapter.

Weber's wide-ranging intellect defies academic disciplinary boundaries. He dealt at one time or another with sociology, cultural history, economic geography, philosophy, political science, art, poetry, law, and economics—his writings are far too diverse to classify. Born in Erfurt, Germany, Weber earned a doctorate at Berlin in 1897. A decade later, he assumed the chair of social science and political economy at Heidelberg University in southwestern Germany, a position he occupied for the remainder of his long career. The Alfred Weber Institute for Social and Political Sciences at Heidelberg commemorates his achievements. He represents yet another of the German founding fathers of modern geography.

Indeed, a new global division of labor seems to be in the works. Behind these changes in the international labor market lies the strategic thinking by directors of the global corporations. According to a U.S. Department of Commerce study, as early as the mid-1970s, 298 American-based global corporations employed as many as 25 percent of their workers outside the United States. Since then, the practice has become even more common. Such factories, despite relocation costs, quickly drive up corporate profit margins. In addition, the ability of these corporations to plan on an international scale and to shift the production of a given product to faraway lands has a weakening effect on organized labor inside the United States.

Markets

A **market,** geographically, includes the area in which a product may be sold in volume and at a price profitable to the manufacturer. The size and distribution of markets are generally the most important factors in determining the spatial distribution of industries. Many experts consider the market attraction so great that they regard locating an industry near its market as the norm, revealing in the process their own economic determinism.

Certain industries, they say, should locate at the market. That is, some manufacturers have to situate their factories among their customers to minimize costs and maximize profits. Such industries include those that manufacture a *weight-gaining finished product,* such as bottled beverages, or a *bulk-gaining finished product,* such as metal containers or bottles. In other words, if weight or bulk is added to the raw materials in the manufacturing process, location near the market is economically desirable because of the transport cost factor. Similarly, if the finished product is more perishable than the raw materials, as with bakery goods and local newspapers, a location near market is also required. In addition, if the product is more fragile than the raw materials that go into its manufacture, as in the making of glass, the industry will be attracted to its market. In each of these cases—gain in weight or bulk, perishability, or fragility—transportation costs of the finished product are much higher than those of the raw materials.

Obviously, the degree of importance of the market as an attractive force increases with the degree of clustering of population. If population is relatively evenly distributed across a country, no single location can be said to be nearest to the market, but the clustering in cities so typical of modern industrial societies pulls manufacturers to the urban centers. Similarly, the type of market being served can affect the location of industries. Some manufacturers supply highly clustered urban markets; others, such as the makers of farm machinery, cater to a more dispersed body of consumers. Industries that sell goods to dispersed markets have greater freedom in their choice of locations. Small-scale service industries that deal in information, as well as specialized high-tech manufacturers, often have one or two principal customers, such as defense contractors, and their tendency is to locate near this market.

As a rule, though, we can say that in Western industrial cultures, the greatest market potential exists where the largest numbers of people live. Once an industry locates in a particular place, it provides additional jobs, attracting laborers into the area. This additional population in turn enlarges the local market, thereby attracting other industries. In the same way, the industries arriving later attract still more people and still more industries, creating an **agglomeration.** Industrial districts develop in this manner, through a snowballing increase in people, infrastructure, and industries. Agglomeration is very difficult to control in free-enterprise systems, and if allowed to run its course, it will produce serious overcrowding

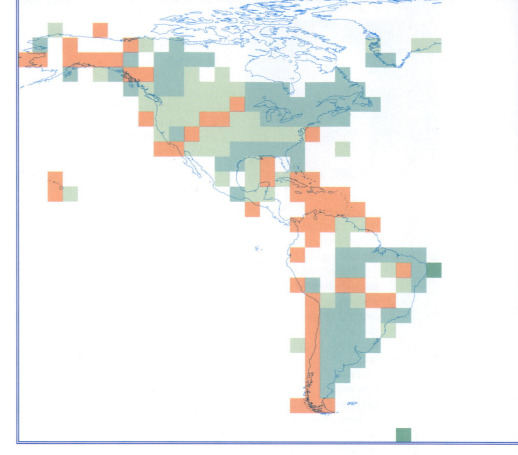

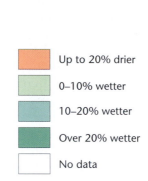

Up to 20% drier

0–10% wetter

10–20% wetter

Over 20% wetter

No data

Figure 9.18

Precipitation change during the century 1895–1995. More precipitation is being received at higher latitudes and less in the tropics. Some global warming models indicate that this trend would be expected if the greenhouse effect is indeed at work. **What consequences might this change, accompanied by warmer temperatures, bring?** (SOURCE: WORLDWATCH INSTITUTE WEB SITE.)

and an excessively clustered population. This intense concentration of industries and population is characteristic of most industrialized nations. Consequently, many such countries suffer from associated problems such as congestion, inadequate housing and recreational facilities, and extreme local pollution of the environment.

The Political Element

Political influence on the spatial distribution of industry is common. Governments often intervene directly in decisions about industrial location. Such intervention typically results from a desire to establish strategic, militarily important industries that would otherwise not develop; to decrease vulnerability to attack by scattering industry to many parts of the country; to place vital strategic industries in remote locations, far removed from possible war zones; to create national self-sufficiency by diversifying industries; to bring industrial development and a higher standard of living to poverty-stricken provinces; or to halt agglomeration in existing industrial areas. Such governmental influence becomes most pronounced in highly planned economic systems, particularly in certain social-

ist countries such as China, but it works to some extent in almost every industrial nation.

The scattering of industry in Russia, motivated partly by a desire to lessen the catastrophic effect of a military attack, provides an example. A major industrial complex in the Ural Mountains, deep in the interior of Russia, was developed partly in response to the German military advance in 1941. For similar strategic reasons, the U.S. government during World War II encouraged the development of an iron and steel industry in Utah, an economically inefficient location that would not have attracted such industry without government intervention. The American aircraft industry similarly became dispersed as a result of government policy. The Italian government has deliberately caused industries to be established in the impoverished southern part of that country in an effort to improve the standard of living. Similarly, the American government encouraged new industrial development in economically depressed Appalachia. The United Kingdom, with some limited success, has attempted to retard further industrial development in existing population centers, causing many new factories to be situated in rural areas or small towns.

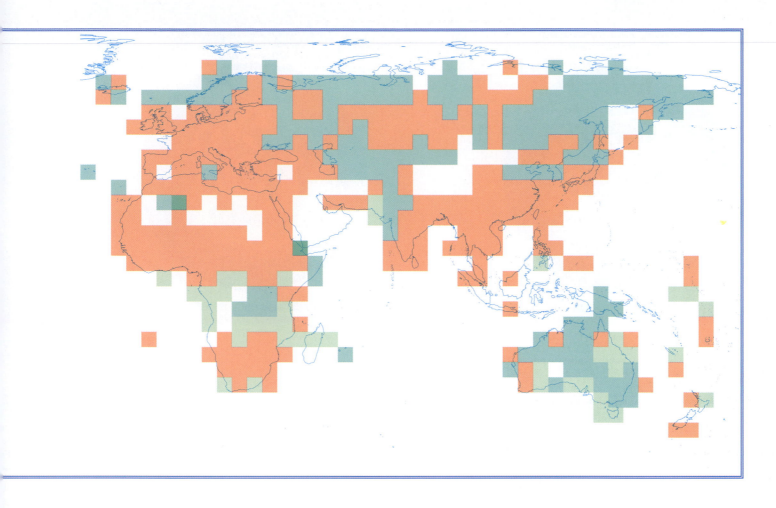

Local and state governments often directly influence industrial locations. Action by such governments sometimes takes the form of tax concessions, such as those granted by a number of states, counties, and cities in the United States. These concessions commonly last for a specified period of time, often 10 years or less, and are designed to persuade industries to locate in areas under the local or state jurisdiction. Conversely, governments can act to prevent the establishment of industries viewed as undesirable. A brewery, for example, could be kept out of an area where influential local church leaders hold prohibitionist views and bring their influence to bear on government officials. Some American municipalities have refused to allow development of particularly pollution-prone industries such as copper smelters, waste disposal, and paper mills.

Another type of government influence comes in the form of tariffs, import-export quotas, political obstacles to the free movement of labor and capital, and various types of hindrance to transportation across borders. Tariffs, in effect, reduce the size of a market area proportional to the amount of tariff imposed, a concept easily illustrated by building a model (Figure 9.23 on page 326).

A similar effect is produced when the number of border crossing points is restricted. In some parts of the world, especially Europe, the impact of tariffs and borders on industrial location has been greatly reduced by the establishment of free-trade blocs, groups of nations that have banded together economically and abolished most tariffs. Of these associations, the European Union (EU) is perhaps the most famous. Composed of 15 nations, the EU has succeeded in abolishing tariffs within its area. The North American Free Trade Agreement (NAFTA) among the United States, Canada, and Mexico—with future expansion to include other countries—is a similar achievement in the Western Hemisphere.

Global corporations, which scatter their holdings across international borders, would seem to diminish the political factor in industrial location. In reality, however, even the multinational enterprises must pay heed to boundaries. Various countries act differently to encourage or discourage foreign investment, creating major spatial discontinuities in opportunities for the global corporations. Even in an era of globalization, when industrial decisions have worldwide impact, the political locational factor continues to operate.

Total Ozone Analysis (Dobson Units)
Climate Prediction Center
October 7, 1995

180 210 240 270 300 330 360 390 420 450

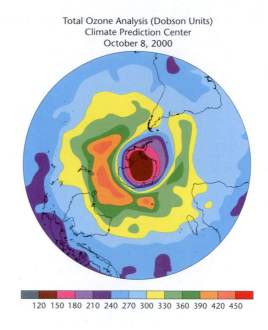

Total Ozone Analysis (Dobson Units)
Climate Prediction Center
October 8, 2000

120 150 180 210 240 270 300 330 360 390 420 450

Figure 9.19

Ozone depletion zone over the southern hemisphere, centered on Antarctica. After rapid growth for decades, the size of the ozone "hole" has begun to stabilize, though some deterioration is evident. The atmospheric concentrations of chlorofluorocarbons, which cause the problem, have declined in recent years, but it will require decades for the ozone hole to be "mended." (SOURCE: U.S. NATIONAL OCEANIC AND ATMOSPHERIC ADMINISTRATION.)

Industrialization and Cultural Change

In these various ways, different aspects of culture are integrated with industrial location, but equally pronounced are the effects of industry on culture. Indeed, industrialization is the most potent and effective agent of cultural change in modern times. Entire cultures have been reshaped as a consequence of the industrial revolution. Traditions thousands of years old have been discarded almost overnight. Much of the replacement of folk culture by popular culture can be attributed at least indirectly to the industrial revolution.

Perhaps the principal cultural change introduced by the industrial revolution, and a subsequent cornerstone of Western civilization, was the concept of technology-based *progress*, a by-product of continual invention and change. By accepting a faith in progress, people looked to a future that would be better than the present. Many discarded the notions of heaven and the afterlife to accept the belief in a better future on Earth, as industrial society became more secularized. In time, says Yi-fu Tuan, belief in progress led to a Western "arrogance based on the presumed availability of almost unlimited technological power." The optimism bred of faith in progress also allowed industrial cultures to discard, perhaps unwisely, "the age-less fear of the greater power and potency of nature."

Reflecting on GEOGRAPHY

Does a belief in technology-based progress survive at the beginning of the twenty-first century?

On a more prosaic level, the changes wrought by industrialization include increased interregional trade and intercultural contact, basic alterations in employment patterns, a shift from rural to urban residence for vast numbers of people, the release of women from the home, the ultimate disappearance of child labor, an initial increase in the rate of population growth followed by a drop to unprecedented low birthrates, greatly increased individual mobility and mass migrations of people, the dispersal of the multigeneration family, greatly increased educational opportunities for the nonwealthy, and an increase in government influence and functions. Perhaps the most basic change is the way in which people make their living.

 ## Industrial Landscapes

In what ways has industrialization altered the cultural landscape? The change has been profound, and we can properly speak of an **industrial landscape.** It forms part of daily life, a prominent and often disturbing visible feature of our surroundings. Industry creates a landscape not normally designed for beauty, charm, or aesthetic appeal but rather for profit and utility. Often, by almost anyone's standards, ugly, industrial landscapes are poor places for humans to spend their lives.

Each level of industrial activity produces its own distinctive landscape. Primary industries exert perhaps the most drastic impact on the land. The resulting landscapes contain slag heaps, clear-cut commercial forests, massive strip-mining scars, gaping open-pit mines, and "forests" of oil derricks. Some industrial landscapes take on a bizarre, otherworldly character, at once horrible and fascinating (Figure 9.24 on page 327). In geographer Richard Francaviglia's words, many "mining communities huddle amid barren piles of waste rock, and mountains of tailings and slag are left in the wake of milling and smelting activity." He calls these "hard places" and feels that they accurately reflect much of what we in the Western world value: competition, risk taking, and dominion over nature. Similarly, Robert Gordon speaks of "a landscape transformed" in a Connecticut iron-making district.

Certain other primary industrial landscapes, in contrast, please the eye and complement the beauty of nature. The fishing villages of Portugal or Newfoundland even attract tourists (Figure 9.25 on page 328). In still other cases, efforts are made to restore the preindustrial landscape. Examples include the establishment of artificial grasslands in old strip-mine areas of the American Midwest and the creation of recreational ponds in old mine pits along interstate highways in the same region. A study by geographer Timothy Brothers found the artificial grasslands to be inexpensive for mining companies to establish, poor and potentially toxic for cattle grazing, dominated by exotic Eurasian grasses, and concentrated in areas that bore a forest cover rather than prairie before strip mining.

The most obvious features of the landscapes of secondary industry, or manufacturing, are factory buildings. Some of these are imaginatively designed and well landscaped, others are less appealing and surrounded by gray seas of parking lots. They range from the futuristic, harsh, solid geometry of chemical refineries and the formless starkness of "brick-pile" factories to award-winning structures designed by famous architects (Figure 9.26 on page 328).

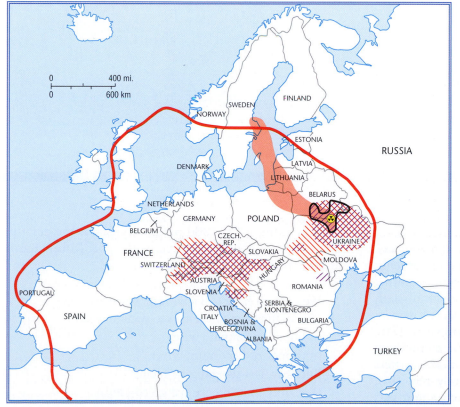

Figure 9.20

The most severe radioactive contamination from the Chernobyl catastrophe came from two isotopes, cesium-137 and iodine-131. The map is somewhat speculative because of inadequate data. The future of human habitation in the area most catastrophically affected remains uncertain, but some tracts there have been completely depopulated. **What impact has this catastrophe had on North America's nuclear power industry?** (ADAPTED FROM PARK, 1989: 66, 74, 79, 92.)

Environmental Sustainability

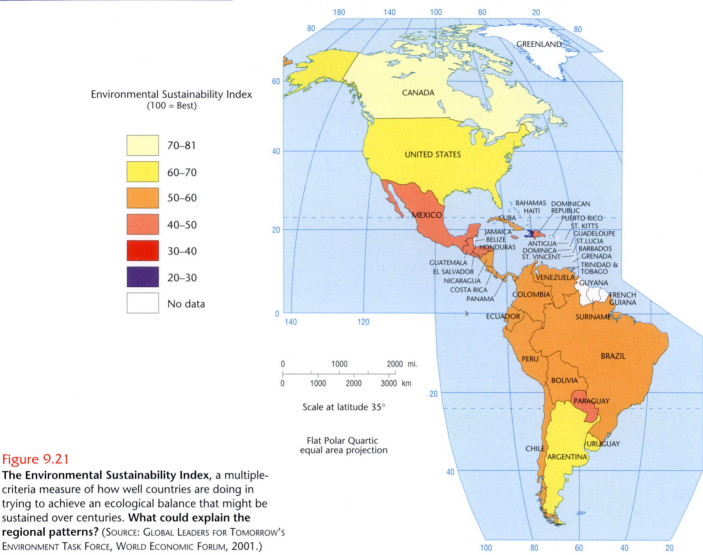

Environmental Sustainability Index
(100 = Best)

- 70–81
- 60–70
- 50–60
- 40–50
- 30–40
- 20–30
- No data

0   1000   2000 mi.

0   1000   2000   3000 km

Scale at latitude 35°

Flat Polar Quartic
equal area projection

Figure 9.21

The Environmental Sustainability Index, a multiple-criteria measure of how well countries are doing in trying to achieve an ecological balance that might be sustained over centuries. **What could explain the regional patterns?** (SOURCE: GLOBAL LEADERS FOR TOMORROW'S ENVIRONMENT TASK FORCE, WORLD ECONOMIC FORUM, 2001.)

Manufacturing landscapes initially appeared in Great Britain, the area first touched by the industrial revolution. British poets and artists of the eighteenth and nineteenth centuries reacted strongly to the emerging manufacturing landscape. Because poets and artists are aesthetically sensitive and are more perceptive than the average person, their reactions should interest us. Geographers Gary Peters and Burton Anderson, employing the methods of humanistic geography, studied the works of such writers and painters. They found that after an early period of optimism about industrialization, some poets and artists quickly sensed something amiss in the landscape. Their warnings, in the form of paintings and poems, began ap-

pearing in the 1775–1800 period. Typical is the description of an iron foundry written by the poet Robert Burns in his native Scottish dialect:

We cam na here to view your warks,
(We didn't come here to see your works)
In hopes to be mair wise,
(In hopes of becoming wiser,)
But only, lest we gang to Hell,
(But only that in case we go to Hell,)
It may be nae surprise.
(It will be no surprise.)

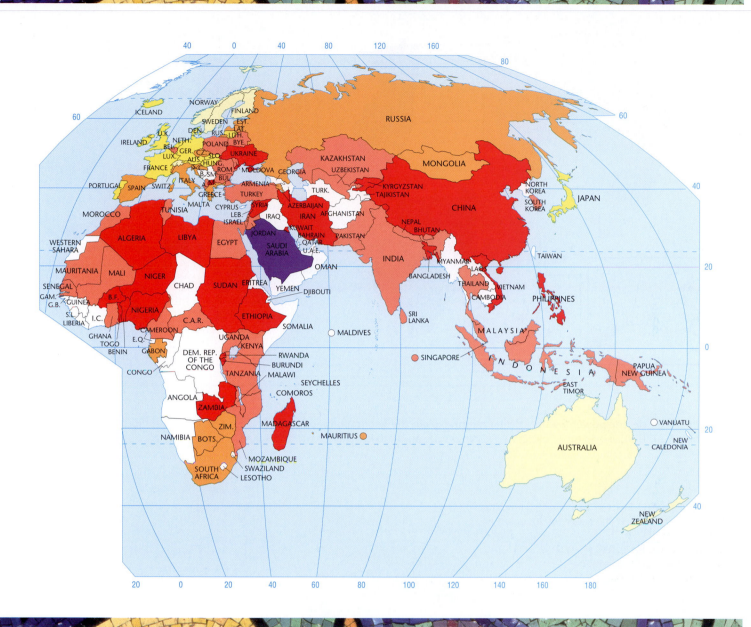

Some artists of the period left paintings that convey a sinister, forbidding, unpleasant landscape. By the time ordinary people began to see with the eyes of poets and artists, the manufacturing landscape seemed out of control, and much of the British industrial region was already known, appropriately, as the "Black Country" (see Focus On: "How Green Was My Valley" on page 329). Thomas Power, similarly, refers to decayed extractive industrial remains as "lost landscapes."

Other humanistic geographers have also addressed the issue of industrial landscapes. Douglas Porteous, writing about the impact of industrialization on his hometown in Yorkshire, England, coined the word **topocide,** meaning

the deliberate, planned killing of a place for the benefits of industry. Robert Burns would have understood.

Reflecting on **GEOGRAPHY**

Can you think of examples of topocide in your home area?

Another British geographer, Shane Davies, a son of the Welsh coalfields, offered a different, even nostalgic view of the industrial landscape. Noting the decline of the coal mining industry in South Wales and the accompanying

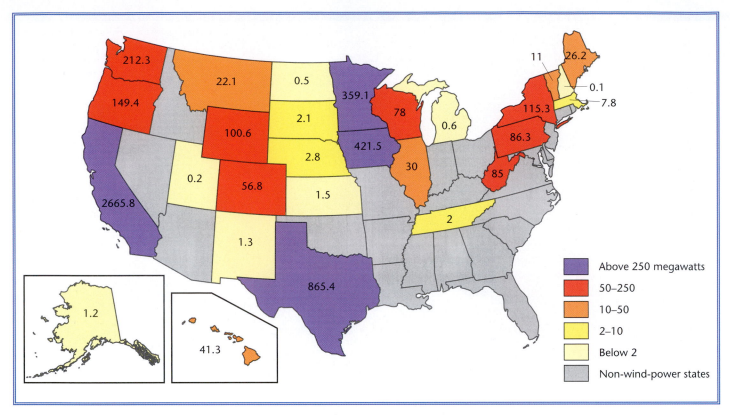

Figure 9.22
Wind-generated electric power, by state. What might explain the geographical pattern? (SOURCES: "WIND POWER," 2001: 31; AND STATELINE WIND POWER PROJECT, HTTP://WWW.STATELINEWIND.COM/PDFS/PPMPMAP.PDF.)

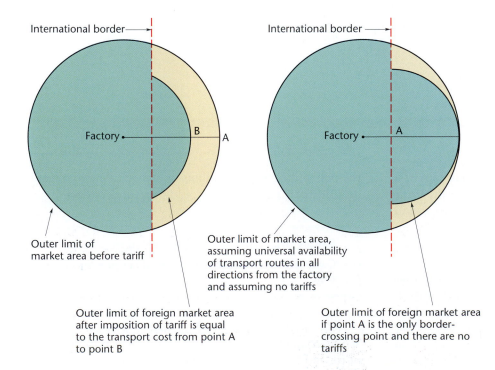

Figure 9.23
Model showing the impact of political borders on market area. The presence of a political border reduces the market area of a factory if a tariff is imposed or if the number of border-crossing points is restricted. As a result, factories tend not to be located in border zones. (AFTER GIERSCH, 1949–1950.)

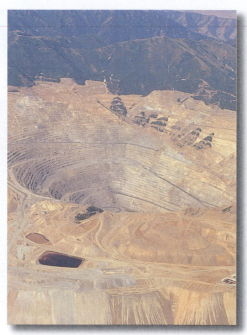

Figure 9.24
Three primary industrial landscapes. *Upper left:* This bizarrely colored "industrial mosaic" is on the margins of the Great Salt Lake in Utah, where chemicals and minerals such as metallic magnesium, potassium, and sodium chloride are derived from the water by solar evaporation. *Upper right:* This open-pit mine is Bingham Canyon in Utah, the second largest in the world. *Bottom:* This mind-boggling, artificial "Alp" is the result of potash mining near Kassel in Germany. (COURTESY OF TERRY G. JORDAN-BYCHKOV.)

deindustrialization since 1930, he lamented the deliberate, government-supported obliteration of the defunct mining landscape, a removal prompted, he believed, by the British preference for agrarian scenes. Wales, "its spirit and wealth now broken," is losing its coal-mining landscape. "So rapid," he wrote, "is the ongoing erasure of the mining scene—the dark, inner landscape of the pit and the more familiar surface features of pithead gear, slag heaps and grey streaked villages—that soon, there will be no palpable evidence of how thousands of ordinary people . . . worked and lived." In this manner, Great Britain seeks "to sanitize landscapes pillaged while forging an industrial empire."

Service industries, too, produce a cultural landscape. Its visual content includes elements as diverse as high-rise bank buildings, hamburger stands, "silicon landscapes," gasoline stations, and the concrete and steel webs of highways and railroads. Geographers John Jakle and Keith Sculle have written a book called *The Gas Station in America* about such an industrial landscape. Some highway interchanges can only be described as a modern art form, but perhaps the aesthetic high point of the tertiary landscape is found in bridges, often graceful and beautiful structures (see Figure 9.26). Few sights of the industrial age can match a well-designed railroad or highway bridge.

Figure 9.25
A fishing village in Newfoundland.
Primary industrial landscapes can be pleasing to the eye. **What problems might such a landscape also suggest?**
(Courtesy of Terry G. Jordan-Bychkov.)

Industrialization has even changed the way we view the landscape. As geographer Yi-fu Tuan commented, "In the early decades of the twentieth century vehicles began to displace walking as the prevalent form of locomotion, and street scenes were perceived increasingly from the interior of automobiles moving staccato-fashion through regularly spaced traffic lights." Los Angeles, the ultimate automobile city, provides perhaps the best example of the new viewpoints provided by the industrial age. Its freeway system allows individual motorists to observe their surroundings at nonstop speeds. It also allows the driver to look *down* on the world. The pedestrian, on the other hand, is slighted. The view from the street is not encouraged. In some areas of Los Angeles, streets actually have no sidewalks at all, so that the pedestrian viewpoint is functionally impossible. In other areas, the layout of the main avenues has been planned with the car in mind, and the pedestrian feels ill at ease amid the nonhuman surroundings—noise, traffic jams, drive-in banks, and parking lots. The shopping street is no longer scaled to the pedestrian—Los Angeles's Ventura Boulevard extends for 15 miles (24 kilometers).

Figure 9.26
The manufacturing and tertiary landscape of Detroit. Other than a graceful suspension bridge, the scene offers little to lift the human spirit and calls to mind the early warnings of the Scottish poet Robert Burns. (Farrell Greshan/Photo Researchers.)

FOCUS ON

"How Green Was My Valley"

Richard Llewellyn, a Welshman, wrote a beautiful novel about growing up in the coal-mining district of Wales in the late nineteenth century. He saw the industrial landscape expand across his native valley, and he lamented it:

> Bright shone the sun, but brighter shone the Valley's green, for each blade of grass gave back the light and made the meadows full of gold and greens, and yellows and pinks and blues were poking from the hedges where the flowers were hard at work for the bees. May and almond were coming, and further down, early apple was doing splendid in four tidy rows behind Meirddyn Jones' farm. His herd of black cows were all down in the river up to their bellies in the cool quiet water, with their tails making white splashes as they dropped after slapping flies, and up nearer to us, sheep were busy with their noses at the sweet green. When the wind took breath you could hear the crunching of their jaws.
>
> Beautiful was the Valley this afternoon, until you turned your head to the right. Then you saw the two slag heaps. . . .
>
> Below us, the river ran sweet as ever, happy in the sun, but as soon as it met the darkness between the sloping walls of slag it seemed to take fright and go spiritless, smooth, black,

> without movement. And on the other side it came forth grey, and began to hurry again, as though anxious to get away. But its banks were stained, and the reeds and grasses that dressed it were hanging, and black, and sickly, ashamed of their dirtiness, ready to die of shame, they seemed, and of sorrow for their dear friend, the river. . . .
>
> Big it had grown, and long, and black, without life or sign, lying along the bottom of the Valley on both sides of the river. The green grass, and the reeds and the flowers, all had gone, crushed beneath it. And every minute the burden grew, as cage after cage screeched along the cables from the pit, bumped to a stop at the tipping pier, and emptied dusty loads on to the ridged, black, dirty back.
>
> On our side of the Valley the heap reached to the front garden walls to the bottom row of houses, and children from them were playing up and down the black slopes, screaming and shouting, laughing in fun. On the other side of the river the chimney pots of the first row of houses could only just be seen above the sharp curving back of the far heap, and all the time I was watching, the cable screeched and the cages tipped. . . .

From Llewellyn, 1940: 103, 104, 116.

Conclusion

As we have seen, then, one of the most significant events of our age is the diffusion of industrialization, which has brought a host of far-reaching cultural changes. Already the industrial revolution has modified the regions, habitats, cultures, and landscapes of some lands so greatly that people who lived there in the past would be bewildered by the modern setting. As it turns out, much of the process of industrialization has been carried out in cities. Indeed, industrialization is the principal cause of urbanization. It is time, in the following two chapters, for us to turn our attention to the *city* as a cultural phenomenon.

Industrial Geography on the Internet

You can learn more about industrial geography on the Internet at the following web sites:

Recreation, Tourism, and Sport Geography Specialty Group of the American Association of Geographers, Washington, D.C.

http://www.for.nau.edu/geography/rts

Tourism is the fastest-growing quinary industry in the world. This web site lets you know about the activities of geographers who study tourism.

Greenpeace
http://www.greenpeace.org

The site for information about an activist group that uses both orthodox and illegal methods in its attempts to bring attention to environmental crisis.

Sierra Club
http://www.sierraclub.org

See this site for information about an established, mainstream organization of environmental activists.

United Nations Industrial Development Organization
http://www.unido.org

This specialist agency of the United Nations is devoted to promoting sustainable industrial development in countries with developing and/or transition economies. The site contains industrial statistics and information on women in industrial development, and it allows you to access data and maps of the least developed countries in the world.

SEEING GEOGRAPHY

Why do we find it difficult to guess where this scene might be?

An industrial landscape.

A River Runs Through It

What does this image of an industrial landscape tell us? Could it be that such pragmatic, utilitarian places can be beautiful? Even the river, its banks now dominated by industry, seems not to mind, creating in the rippled reflection an abstract or impressionist image that might hang in an art museum. Even the unreflected picture glows with a rosy beauty lent by the setting sun. Yes, one sees air pollution, but even the billowing artificial clouds offer a multicolored appeal to the eye.

Should we believe what we see? Is something sinister concealed here? Do cultural landscapes sometimes tell lies as we seek to "read" them? Frankly, yes. What could be hidden from view? Possibly, thermal and chemical pollution of the river, which could be lifeless beneath the reflection. Possibly, harmful air pollutants that poison both people and the land. Almost certainly heat pollution is present, and perhaps radioactive contamination.

What else can we learn? For one thing, industrial landscapes are similar all around the world. Where might this scene lie? North America? China? Europe? The image contains no locational clue, so effective was cultural diffusion. Industrial landscapes possess a sterile, globalized quality. And despite the paradoxical beauty, would you choose to live in this place? Why not?

And so landscape, ecology, region, and diffusion are all explicit or implicit here.

Worldwatch Institute, Washington, D.C.

http://www.worldwatch.org

This nongovernmental watchdog and research institute compiles and analyzes the latest information about such ecological problems as global warming, industrial pollution, and deforestation, and it seeks sustainable alternatives.

Sources

Airriess, Christopher A. 2001. "Regional Production, Information-Communication Technology, and the Developmental State: The Rise of Singapore as a Global Container Hub." *Geoforum* 32: 235–254.

Alfrey, Judith, and Catherine Clark. 1993. *The Landscape of Industry*. London: Routledge.

Aspinall, Richard, and Stan Openshaw. 1988. "Geographical Aspects of Radiation Monitoring in Britain." *Area* 20: 53–59.

Bach, Wilfrid. 1985. "The Acid Rain/Carbon Dioxide Threat—Control Strategies." *GeoJournal* 10: 339–352.

Braudel, Fernand. 1972. *The Mediterranean and the Mediterranean World in the Age of Phillip II*. New York: Harper & Row.

Brothers, Timothy S. 1990. "Surface-Mine Grasslands." *Geographical Review*, 80: 209–225.

Brown, Laurie, Martha Ronk, and Charles E. Little. 2000. *Recent Terrains: Terraforming the American West*. Baltimore: Johns Hopkins University Press.

Davies, C. Shane. 1983. "Wales: Industrial Fallibility and Spirit of Place." *Journal of Cultural Geography* 4(1): 72–86.

Davies, C. Shane. 1984. "Dark Inner Landscapes: The South Wales Coalfield." *Landscape Journal* 3: 36–44.

Francaviglia, Richard V. 1991. *Hard Places: Reading the Landscape of America's Historic Mining Districts*. Iowa City: University of Iowa Press.

Giersch, Herbert. 1949–1950. "Economic Union Between Nations and the Location of Industries." *Review of Economic Studies* 17: 87–97.

Global Leaders for Tomorrow's Environment Task Force, World Economic Forum. 2001. *Environmental Sustainability Index*. New Haven, Conn.: Yale University Center for Environmental Law and Policy; New York: Columbia University Center for International Earth Science Information Network; and Geneva: The World Economic Forum. Available online at http://www.ciesin.columbia.edu/indicators/ESI

Goethe, Johann W. von. 1957. *Faust*. George M. Priest (trans. and ed.). New York: Alfred A. Knopf.

Gordon, Robert B. 2000. *A Landscape Transformed: The Ironmaking District of Salisbury, Connecticut*. New York: Oxford University Press.

Holden, Andrew. 2000. *Environment and Tourism*. New York: Routledge.

Hudson, John C., and Edward B. Espenshade, Jr. (eds.). 2000. *Goode's World Atlas*, 20th ed. Chicago: Rand McNally.

Jakle, John A., and Keith A. Sculle. 1994. *The Gas Station in America*. Baltimore: Johns Hopkins University Press.

Jefferson, Mark. 1928. "The Civilizing Rails." *Economic Geography* 4: 217–231.

Job, Hubert. 1996. "Modell zur Evaluation der Nachhaltigkeit Tourismus." *Erdkunde* 50: 112–132.

Jordan-Bychkov, Terry G., and Bella Bychkova Jordan. 2002. *The European Culture Area*, 4th ed. Lanham, Md.: Rowman & Littlefield.

Llewellyn, Richard. 1940. *How Green Was My Valley*. New York: Curtis Brown.

O'Hare, Greg. 2000. "Reviewing the Uncertainties in Climate Change Science." *Area* 32: 357–368.

Park, Chris C. 1989. *Chernobyl: the Long Shadow*. London: Routledge.

Peters, Gary L., and Burton L. Anderson. 1976. "Industrial Landscapes: Past Views and Stages of Recognition." *Professional Geographer* 28: 341–348.

Porteous, J. Douglas. 1989. *Planned to Death: The Annihilation of a Place Called Howdendyke*. Toronto: University of Toronto Press.

Power, Thomas M. 1996. *Lost Landscapes and Failed Economies: The Search for the Value of Place*. Washington, D.C.: Island Press.

Thompson, John H., and Michihiro Miyazaki. 1959. "A Map of Japan's Manufacturing." *Geographical Review* 49: 1–17.

Trinder, Barrie. 1982. *The Making of the Industrial Landscape*. London: J. M. Dent & Sons.

Tuan, Yi-fu. 1989. "Cultural Pluralism and Technology." *Geographical Review* 79: 269–279.

United Nations. 2000. *Statistical Yearbook*. New York: United Nations.

Warrick, Richard, and Graham Farmer. 1990. "The Greenhouse Effect, Climatic Change and Rising Sea Level: Implications for Development." *Transactions of the Institute of British Geographers* 15: 5–20.

Weber, Alfred. 1929. *Theory of the Location of Industries*. Carl J. Friedrich (trans. and ed.). Chicago: University of Chicago Press.

"Wind Power: Maybe This Time." 2001. *Economist* (March 10): 30–31.

Ten Recommended Books on Industrial Geography

(*For additional suggested readings, see* The Human Mosaic *web site:* www.whfreeman.com/jordan)

Castells, Manuel, and Peter Hall. 1994. *Technopoles of the World: The Making of 21st Century Industrial Complexes*. London: Routledge. A geographical analysis of the secondary and quaternary industries worldwide that deal with high-tech manufacture, research, development, and information processing.

Cater, Erlet, and Gwen Lowman (eds.). 1994. *Ecotourism: A Sustainable Option?* Chichester, U.K.: John Wiley and the Royal Geographical Society. An excellent analysis of ecotourism, assessing whether it is as ecologically benign as the name suggests.

Chapman, Keith, and David F. Walker. 1991. *Industrial Location: Principles and Policies*, 2nd ed. Oxford: Basil Blackwell. A good basic primer on industrial location.

Cutter, Susan L. 1993. *Living with Risk: The Geography of Technological Hazards*. New York: John Wiley. The industrial age has created countless technological hazards, and this pathbreaking study by a leading American geographer presents them with the unique perspective of our discipline.

Drake, Frances. 2000. *Global Warming: The Science of Climate Change*. London: Arnold. A British geographer presents the complicated issue of global warming in terms intelligible to the undergraduate student, stripping away the jargon of science while retaining the essential message of climate change.

Hall, Colin M., and Stephen J. Page. 1999. *The Geography of Tourism and Recreation: Environment, Place and Space*. New York: Routledge. An excellent comprehensive introduction to the topic, containing case studies from North America, Europe, China, Australia, and the Pacific islands.

Harrington, James W., and Barney Warf. 1995. *Industrial Location: Principles and Practice*. New York: Routledge. Another useful basic primer on industrial location written for nonexperts.

Seager, Joni. 1995. *The State of the Earth Atlas*, 2nd ed. New York: Simon & Schuster. A basic source for anyone concerned about environmental problems. A collection of truly sobering maps.

Taaffe, Edward J., Howard L. Gauthier, Jr., and Morton E. O'Kelly. 1996. *Geography of Transportation*, 2nd ed. Upper Saddle River, N.J.: Prentice-Hall. A textbook devoted to this crucial element of tertiary industry; the best in the field.

Vance, James E., Jr. 1986. *Capturing the Horizon: The Historical Geography of Transportation*. New York: Harper & Row. An excellent companion volume to Taaffe et al., showing the development through time of the manufacturing-driven transport system.

A Journal in Industrial Geography

Journal of Transport Geography, published by Butterworth-Heinemann in association with the Transport Geography Study Group of the Institute of British Geographers. Volume 1 appeared in 1993.

View of Rio de Janeiro from Sugarloaf Mountain. (BLAINE HARRINGTON III/THE STOCK MARKET.)
Turn to Seeing Geography *on page 379 for an in-depth analysis of the above question.*

10

URBANIZATION
The City in Time and Space

Imagine the 2 million years that humankind has spent on Earth as a 24-hour day. In this framework, settlements of more than a hundred people came about only in the last half-hour. Towns and cities emerged only a few minutes ago, and large-scale urbanization began less than 60 seconds ago. Yet during these "minutes" we see the rise of civilization. *Civitas,* the Latin root word for *civilization,* was first applied to settled areas of the Roman Empire. Later it came to mean a specific town or city within an area. "To civilize" meant literally "to citify."

Urbanization over the past 200 years has strengthened the links among culture, society, and the city. An urban explosion has gone hand in hand with the industrial revolution. According to United Nations estimates, the world's urban population has more than tripled since 1950 (750 million in 1950 versus 2.85 billion in 2000) and will reach 4.89 billion by the year 2030. By then, over 60 percent of the Earth's population will live in cities. The cultural geography of the world will change dramatically as we become a predominantly urban people and the ways of the countryside are increasingly replaced by urban lifestyles.

In this chapter, we consider the overall patterns of urbanization, learn how urbanization began and developed, and discuss the differing forms of cities in the developing and developed worlds. In addition, we examine some of the external factors influencing city location. In Chapter 11, we look at the internal aspects of the city, seen through the five themes of cultural geography.

Culture Region

How are urban areas and urban populations spatially arranged? A quick look at Figure 10.1 reveals differing patterns of **urbanized population**—

Urbanized Population

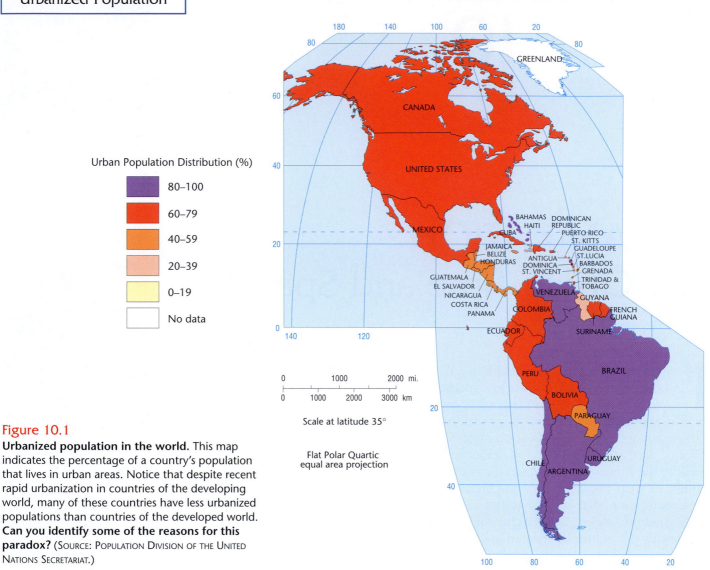

Urban Population Distribution (%)

- ▮ 80–100
- ▮ 60–79
- ▮ 40–59
- ▮ 20–39
- ▮ 0–19
- ▯ No data

Figure 10.1

Urbanized population in the world. This map indicates the percentage of a country's population that lives in urban areas. Notice that despite recent rapid urbanization in countries of the developing world, many of these countries have less urbanized populations than countries of the developed world. **Can you identify some of the reasons for this paradox?** (Source: Population Division of the United Nations Secretariat.)

0   1000   2000 mi.
0 1000 2000 3000 km

Scale at latitude 35°

Flat Polar Quartic
equal area projection

the percentage of a nation's population living in towns and cities—around the world. For example, the countries of Europe, North America, Latin America, and the Caribbean have relatively high levels of urbanization, with approximately 75 percent of each country's population living in urban areas; whereas the nations of Africa and Asia have relatively less urbanization, with approximately 38 percent of each country's population living in urban areas. What one cannot detect from this map is the spatial arrangement of urban areas within countries. Some countries—Mexico, for example—have their urban pop-

ulations concentrated in a few small sections; others, such as France, have a fairly even distribution of urban and rural areas. How do geographers explain these varying regional patterns of urbanization?

Patterns and Processes of Urbanization

According to United Nations estimates, virtually all the worldwide population growth in the next 30 years will be concentrated in urban areas, and most of that increase will be in the cities of the less developed regions. The rea-

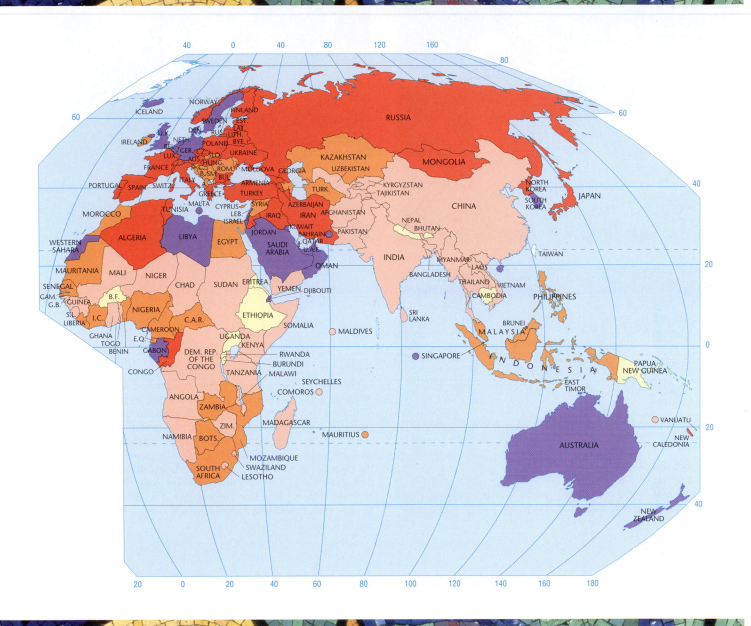

sons for this explosion in urban population growth and its uneven distribution around the world vary, as each country's unique history and society present a slightly different narrative of urban and economic development. To make matters even more complex, understanding these regional patterns of urbanization is often hampered by the lack of an agreed-upon international definition of what constitutes a city. The criteria used to calculate a country's urbanized population vary from nation to nation. Using data based on these varying criteria would reinforce a myth of comparability. We can learn more from examin-

ing how different countries define their urbanized population. To illustrate, the Indian government defines an urban center as 5000 inhabitants, with an adult male population employed predominantly in nonagricultural work. In contrast, the U.S. Census Bureau defines a city as a densely populated area of 2500 people or more, and South Africa counts as a city any settlement of 500 or more people. Furthermore, some countries revise their definitions of urban settlements to suit specific purposes. China-watchers were baffled in 1983 when that country's urban population swelled by 13 percent in one year, only

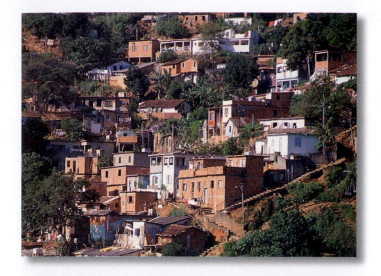

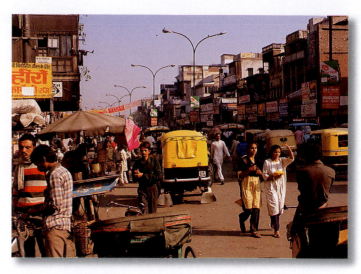

Figure 10.2

Urbanization. Shown here are scenes from a squatter settlement in Rio de Janeiro (*upper left*), the business district in Kolkata (Calcutta) (*upper right*), and a residential district of Manila (*bottom*). For more information about the growth of such cities, see the section "The Urban Landscapes of the Developing World." As is evident from this scene in Kolkata, the downtowns of cities in the developing world are often more vibrant than those of the developed world. **Can you think of some reasons for this?** (Top left: Najilah Feaney/Saba; Top right: Earl Young/Tony Stone Images; Bottom: Bruno Zehnder/Peter Arnold, Inc.)

to learn that China had simply revised its census definitions for urban settlements, with criteria that vary from province to province. In conclusion, an international comparison of urbanized population data can be made only by taking into account the varying definitions of what a city is.

Nonetheless, several generalizations can be made about the differences in the world's urbanized population. First, there is a close link between urbanized population and the more developed world. Put differently, highly industrialized countries have higher rates of urbanized population than do less developed countries. The second generalization, closely tied to the first, is that developing countries are urbanizing rapidly and their ratio of urban to rural population is increasing dramatically. An urban explosion is taking place in the developing world, caused by massive migration away from the country as people flock to cities in search of a better life (Figure 10.2). This

urban migration, however, should not be compared with the farm-to-city relocation that occurred during Europe's or America's industrializing period. Migration to cities in the less developed countries is often driven by desperation, as rural supply systems collapse; and urban migrants today cannot always find employment in the city.

Urban growth in these countries comes from two sources: first, the migration of people to the cities, and second, the higher natural population growth rates of these recent migrants. People move to the cities for a variety of reasons, most of which relate to the effects of uneven economic development within their country. Cities are often the centers of economic growth, whereas opportunities for land ownership and/or farming-based jobs are, in many countries, in decline. Because urban employment is unreliable, many migrants continue to have large numbers of children to construct a more extensive family support system. Having a larger family increases the chances of someone getting work. The demographic transition to smaller families seems to come only later, when a certain degree of security is ensured. Often, this transition occurs when women enter the workforce (see Chapter 7).

Impacts of Urbanization

Although rural-to-urban migration affects nearly all cities in the developing world, the most visible cases are the extraordinarily large settlements we call **world cities**—those having populations of over 10 million. Table 10.1 displays the world's 20 largest cities, over half of which are in the developing world. This is a major change from 30 years ago, when the list would have been dominated by Western, industrialized cities. Projections for future growth, however, must be qualified by two considerations. First, cities of the developing world will continue to explode in size only if economic development expands. If it stagnates because of political or resource problems, city growth will probably slow (although urban migration

might increase if rural economies deteriorate). For example, Mexico City's growth is linked to that country's economic growth and, more specifically, to Mexico's oil industry, which fluctuates according to the world market for oil. Second, because these world cities are plagued by transportation, housing, employment, and ecological problems—such as an inadequate water supply, in the case of Mexico City—some countries are trying to control urban migration. The success or failure of these policies will influence city size in the next 10 to 20 years. Accurate population projections, then, are difficult to obtain because they depend on variables that range from international economics to national and local policies.

The target for much urban migration is the **primate city**. This is a settlement that dominates the economic, political, and cultural life of a country and, as a result of rapid growth, expands its primacy or dominance. Once again, Mexico City is an excellent example of a primate city because it far exceeds Guadalajara, the second largest city in Mexico, in size and importance. Although many

TABLE 10.1 The World's 20 Largest Metropolitan Areas*

Rank	Metropolitan Area	Country	Population (millions)	Average Annual Change (percent)
1	Tokyo/Yokohama	Japan	31.8	0.48
2	Seoul	South Korea	20.7	1.76
3	Jakarta	Indonesia	19.9	2.99
4	Mexico City	Mexico	19.5	1.73
5	New York	United States	19.5	0.80
6	São Paulo	Brazil	18.1	1.80
7	Mumbai	India	17.4	2.43
8	Osaka/Kobe/Kyoto	Japan	17.4	0.27
9	Delhi/New Delhi	India	16.7	3.97
10	Kolkata	India	15.1	1.60
11	Manila	Philippines	15.0	3.42
12	Los Angeles	United States	14.5	0.97
13	Moscow	Russia	14.2	0.33
14	Buenos Aires	Argentina	13.7	1.18
15	Cairo	Egypt	13.7	1.84
16	London	United Kingdom	12.7	0.68
17	Shanghai	China	12.5	1.26
18	Rio de Janeiro	Brazil	11.3	1.42
19	Paris	France	11.3	0.33
20	Istanbul	Turkey	11.1	3.68

*Estimated as of January 1, 2001.

(Source: Prepared by Richard L. Forstall. Used by permission.)

developing countries are dominated by a primate city, often a former center of colonial power, urban primacy is not unique to these countries: think of the way London and Paris dominate their respective countries.

Nevertheless, the urban population in the developing world is growing at astounding rates. Even though the developed regions of the world are more urbanized overall than the less developed regions, the sheer scale and rate of growth in absolute numbers reveals a reversal in this pattern. According to geographer David Drakakis-Smith, there are now twice as many urban dwellers in the developing world as there are in developed countries. For example, the population of urbanites in the countries of Europe, North America, Latin America, and the Caribbean (according to the United Nations, that number is 1.2 billion) is lower than the population of urbanites in Asia (1.4 billion). And with this incredible increase in sheer numbers of urban dwellers in the less developed regions of the world comes a large list of problems. Unemployment rates in cities of the developing world are often over 50 percent for newcomers to the city; housing and infrastructure often cannot be built fast enough to keep pace with growth rates; water and sewage systems can rarely handle the influx of people (for more about this, see the section on "The Emerging City" later in this chapter). Consequently, one of the world's ongoing crises will be this radical restructuring of population and culture as people in developing countries move into the cities.

We are fast becoming a predominantly urban world, and our cultural geography is increasingly dominated by urban landscapes. Next we investigate the rise and evolution of the earliest settlements to understand the phenomenon of urbanization better.

Origin and Diffusion of the City

Where did urban life begin, and how did it spread throughout the world? As we seek explanations for the origin of cities, we find a relationship among areas of early agriculture, permanent village settlements, the development of new social forms, and urban life. The first cities resulted from a complicated transition that took thousands of years.

Early people were nomadic hunters and gatherers, constantly moving in their search for sustenance. As these hunters and gatherers became increasingly efficient in gathering resources, their campsites became semipermanent, often being occupied for months, seasons, or years at a time. As the quantities of domesticated plants and animals increased (see Chapter 8), settlements became even more permanent. In the Middle East, where the first cities appeared, a network of permanent agricultural villages developed about 10,000 years ago. These farming villages were modest in size, rarely with more than 200 people, and were probably organized on a kinship basis. Jarmo, one of the earliest villages, located in present-day Iraq, had 25 permanent dwellings clustered together near grain storage facilities. Although they lacked plows, the inhabitants of Jarmo cultivated local grains, probably wheat and barley. Domesticated dogs, goats, and sheep may have been used for meat, and food supplies were augmented by hunting and gathering.

Although small farming villages like Jarmo predate cities, it is wrong to assume that a simple quantitative change took place whereby villages slowly grew first into towns, then into cities. True cities differed qualitatively from agricultural villages. In agricultural villages, all the inhabitants were involved in some way in food procurement, tending the agricultural fields, or harvesting and preparing the crops. We can think of the city, however, as more removed, both physically and psychologically, from everyday agricultural activities. Food was supplied to the city, but not all city dwellers were involved in the actual farming. Instead, city dwellers supplied other services, such as technical skills or religious interpretations considered important in a particular society. Cities, unlike agricultural villages, contained a class of people who were not directly involved in agricultural activities.

Two elements were crucial to this dramatic social change: the creation of an **agricultural surplus** and the development of a stratified social system. Surplus food, which is a food supply larger than the everyday needs of the agricultural labor force, is a prerequisite for supporting nonfarmers—people who work at administrative, military, or handicraft tasks. Social stratification, the existence of distinct elite and lower classes, facilitates the collection, storage, and distribution of resources through well-defined channels of authority that can exercise control over goods and people. Without such a hierarchy, the communal surplus could not support city dwellers. A society with these two elements—surplus food and a means of storing and distributing it—was set for urbanization.

Models for the Rise of Cities

Some scholars who seek to understand the transition from village to city life prefer to construct models for the development of urban life based on one single factor as the "trigger" behind the change. These scholars ask what activity could be so important to an agricultural society that its people would be willing to give some of their surplus to support a social class that would specialize in that activity. Three answers to this question are discussed next. In addition, we will look at the multiple-factor explanation of the rise of cities.

Technical   The **hydraulic civilization** model, developed by Karl Wittfogel, sees the development of large-scale irrigation systems as the prime mover behind urbanization and a class of technical specialists as the first urban dwellers. Higher crop yields resulted from irrigated agriculture, and this food surplus supported the development of a large nonfarming population. A strong, centralized government, backed by an urban-based military, expanded power into the surrounding areas. Those farmers who resisted the new authority were denied water. Continued reinforcement of the power elite came from the need for organizational coordination to ensure continued operation of the irrigation system.

Class distinctions were reinforced by power differences, and labor specialization developed. Some people farmed; others worked on the irrigation system. Still others became artisans, creating the implements needed to maintain the system, or administrative workers in the direct employ of the power elite's court.

Although the hydraulic model fits several areas where cities first arose—China, Egypt, and Mesopotamia (present-day Iraq)—it cannot be applied to all urban hearths. In parts of Mesoamerica, for example, an urban civilization blossomed without widespread irrigated agriculture, and therefore without a class of technical experts. The hydraulic model also begs the question of how or why a culture might develop an irrigation system in the first place.

Religious   Geographer Paul Wheatley suggests that religion was the motivating factor behind urbanization. In early agricultural societies, knowledge of such matters as meteorology and climate was considered to fall within the domain of religion. These societies depended on their religious leaders to interpret the heavenly bodies before deciding when and how to plant their crops. The propagation of this type of knowledge led to more successful harvests, which in turn allowed for the support of more members of this emerging priestly class, as well as the support of people engaged in ancillary activities. The priestly class exercised political and social control that held the city together.

In this scenario, cities are religious spaces, functioning as ceremonial centers for the emerging civilization. The first urban clusters and fortifications are seen as defenses not against human invaders but against spiritual ones: demons or the souls of the dead. This religious explanation is applicable in some ways to all the early centers of urbanization, although it seems particularly apt in describing Chinese urbanization (see pages 340–341).

Political   Other scholars suggest that the centralizing authority in urbanization emanated not from the religious order but from the political order. Urban historian Lewis Mumford described the agent of change in emerging urban centers as the institution of kingship, which involves the centralizing of religious, social, and economic aspects of a civilization around a powerful figure who becomes known as the king. This figure of authority, who in the preurban world is accorded respect for his or her human abilities, ascends to almost superhuman status in early urbanizing societies. By exercising power, the king is able to marshal the labor of others. The resultant social hierarchy enables the society to diversify its endeavors, with different groups specializing in crafts, farming, trading, or religious activity. The institution of kingship provides essential leadership and organization to this emerging complex society, which becomes the city.

Multiple Factors   At the beginning of urbanization, and even much later in some places, sharp distinctions among economic, religious, and political functions were not always made. The king may have also functioned as priest, healer, astronomer, and scribe, thus in some ways fusing secular and spiritual power. Critics of the kingship theory, therefore, point out that this explanation of urbanization may not be different from the religion-based model. In other words, attempting to isolate one trigger of urbanization is difficult, if not impossible. A wiser course is to accept the role of multiple factors behind the changes leading to urban life. Technical, religious, and political forces were often interlinked, with a change in one leading to changes in another. Instead of oversimplifying by focusing on one possible development schema, we must appreciate the complexities of the transition period from agricultural village to true city.

Urban Hearth Areas

The first cities appeared in distinct regions, such as Mesopotamia, the Nile Valley, Pakistan's Indus River valley, the Yellow River (or Huang Ho) valley of China, and

Mesoamerica. These are called the **urban hearth areas** (see Focus On: Cahokia: An Early Urban Center on the Mississippi on page 342). Figure 10.3 gives the general dates for the emergence of urban life in each region.

Reflecting on GEOGRAPHY

Scholars are continually altering the dates for the emergence of urban life, as well as the location of the hearth areas. Why? Can you outline some of the reasons that it is so difficult to pinpoint the places and dates for the emergence of urban life?

It is generally agreed that the first cities arose in Mesopotamia, the river valley of the Tigris and Euphrates in what is now Iraq. Mesopotamian cities, small by current standards, covered 0.5 to 2 square miles (1.3 to 5 square kilometers) and embraced populations that rarely exceeded 30,000. Nevertheless, with such a population concentrated in such a small area, the densities within these cities could easily reach 10,000 people per square mile (4000 per square kilometer). This is comparable to many contemporary cities.

The spatial layouts of the cities of the urban hearth areas were similar. In particular, these early cities—which we can call **cosmomagical cities**—exhibited three spatial characteristics (Figure 10.4). The first is that great importance was accorded to the city's symbolic center, which was thought to be the center not only of the city but also of the known world. It was therefore the most sacred spot, and it was often demarcated by a vertical structure of monumental scale that represented the point on Earth closest to the heavens. This symbolic center, or **axis mundi,** took the form of the ziggurat in Mesopotamia, the palace or temple in China, and the pyramid in Mesoamerica.

Often this elevated structure, which usually served a religious purpose, was close to the palace or seat of political power and to the granary. The structure was walled off from the rest of the city, forming a symbolic center that dominated the city physically and spiritually. This walled inner city reflected the particular significance of certain societal functions. The food surplus was certainly of major importance, and its storage within the inner city suggests that it was often guarded from the general population. The presence of a temple or palace building within this inner city also tells us that power was held by

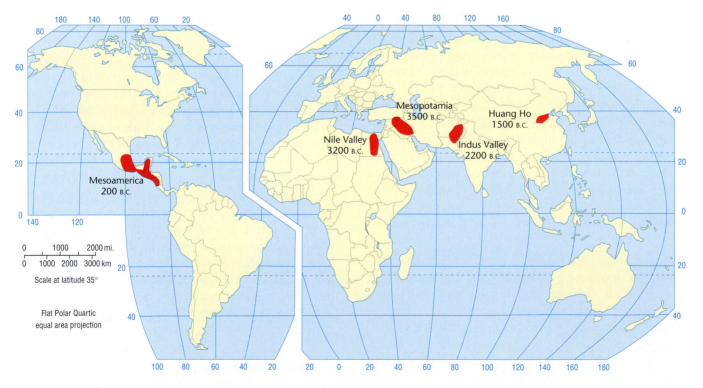

Figure 10.3

The world's first cities arose in five urban hearth areas. The dates shown are conservative figures for the rise of urban life in each area. For example, some scholars would suggest that urban life in Mesopotamia existed by 5000 B.C. Ongoing discoveries suggest that urban life appeared earlier in each of the hearth areas and that there are probably other hearth areas—in West Africa, for example.

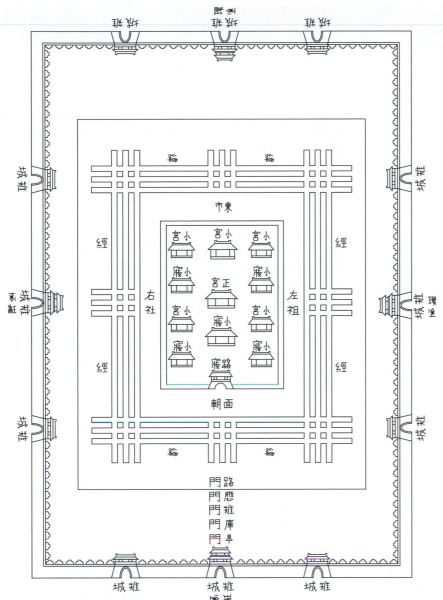

Figure 10.4
Plan of the city of Wang-Ch'eng in China. The city as built did not follow this exact design, but the plan itself is of interest because it suggests the symbolic importance of the three spatial characteristics of the Chinese cosmomagical city. The four walls are aligned to the cardinal directions, and the axis mundi is represented by the walled-off center city containing ceremonial buildings. The physical space of the city (microcosmos) replicates the larger world of the heavens (macrocosmos). For example, each of the four walls represents one of the four seasons. **What do you think the gates to the city represent?** (SOURCE: WHEATLEY, 1971.)

a class of people who were thought of as inhabiting a more sacred world than the city's other inhabitants. The Forbidden City in Beijing remains one of the best examples of this guarded, fortresslike "city within the city."

In Mesopotamia, this area was known as the citadel, and the elite who lived there inhabited a world of relative luxury (Figure 10.5 on page 343). Before 2000 B.C., the streets within the citadels were paved, drains and running water were provided, private sleeping quarters were built, bathtubs and water closets were installed, and spacious villas were constructed. But the privileges of the ruling class did not extend to the city as a whole.

The second spatial characteristic common to the cosmomagical world is that the city was oriented toward the four cardinal directions. By aligning the city in the north-south and east-west directions, the geometric form of the city would reflect the order of the universe. This alignment, it was thought, would ensure harmony and order over the known world. The walls that surrounded these cities delimited the known, and therefore ordered, world from the outside chaos, suggesting that these early rectangular fortifications served symbolic as well as functional purposes. In China, for example, when an emperor conquered a city or constructed a new city, he would walk ceremoniously around the square perimeter of the walls, symbolizing his control of, and his ability to bring order to, this new world.

In all these early cities, one sees evidence of a third spatial characteristic: an attempt to shape the form of the city according to the form of the universe. The ordering of the space of the city was thought to be essential to maintaining harmony between the human and spiritual worlds. In this way, the world of humans would

FOCUS ON

Cahokia: An Early Urban Center on the Mississippi

Cahokia, a pre-Columbian urban center on the Mississippi, shows that not all early cities were found in the five urban hearth areas mentioned in the text. Instead, Cahokia illustrates the process of independent city origin and can be taken as an example of events duplicated in hundreds of areas around the world.

The Cahokia settlement is an aggregation of mounds and living structures dating from about A.D. 100, located in the American Bottoms region of the Mississippi River valley, close to St. Louis. It is the largest of 10 large population centers and some 50 smaller farming villages that flourished between A.D. 900 and 1500.

How did this city arise? Archaeologists maintain that the city resulted from a complicated feedback process that involved population growth and an increase in agricultural productivity. In the late eighth century, the hoe replaced a less effective digging stick, and a new variety of maize—one that was better suited to the environmental conditions of the warm river valley—diffused into the American Bottoms region.

Peak population came centuries later, probably between 1150 and 1250, when Cahokia may have approached a population of 40,000. Archaeological evidence suggests that houses were mainly of pole-and-thatch construction and varied in size according to the status of the occupants. The settlement also contained many ceremonial structures, most notably large earthen mounds similar to the pyramids of Mesoamerican cities. Close to the largest mound was an enclosed area of large public structures that reminds one of the citadel areas of Mesopotamian cities.

Cahokia flourished because it was an ideally located central place, situated on fertile agricultural lands, with access to local and long-distance trade moving through the network of sloughs and rivers. Scholars who have investigated the site believe that Cahokia declined in importance around 1250. Perhaps this decline resulted from exhaustion of local resources, or perhaps Cahokia's trade hinterland was eclipsed by the growing strength of other Mississippi River cultures. Whatever the reason, further investigation is bound to shed light on the complicated processes that led to the rise and fall of cities.

Adapted from Fowler, 1975.

---

symbolically replicate the world of the gods. This characteristic may have taken a literal form—a city laid out, for example, in a pattern of a major star constellation. Far more common, however, were cities that symbolically approximated mythical conceptions of the universe. Angkor Thom was an early city in Cambodia that presents one of the best examples of this parallelism. An urban cluster that spread over 6 square miles (15.5 square kilometers), Angkor Thom was a representation in stone of a series of religious beliefs about the nature of the universe. Thus, the city was a microcosmos, a re-creation on Earth of an image of the larger universe.

Yet regional variations of this basic form certainly existed. For example, the early cities of the Nile were not walled, which suggests that a regional power structure kept individual cities from warring with one another. In the Indus Valley, the great city of Mohenjo-daro was laid out in a grid that consisted of 16 large blocks, and the citadel was located within the block that was central but situated toward the extreme western edge.

The most important variations in living conditions within the urban hearth areas occurred in Mesoamerica (see Focus On: City Planning in the New World: Teotihuacán on page 344). Here, cities were less dense and covered large areas (Figure 10.6 on page 344). Furthermore, these cities arose without benefit of the technolog-ical advances found in the other hearth areas, most notably the wheel, the plow, metallurgy, and draft animals. However, the domestication of maize compensated for these shortcomings. Maize is a grain that yields several crops a year without irrigation in the tropical climate, and it can be cultivated without heavy plows or pack animals.

The Diffusion of the City from Hearth Areas

Although urban life originated at several specific places in the world, cities are now found everywhere: North America, Southeast Asia, Latin America, Australia. How did city life come to these regions? Although many of these cities resulted from European colonialism in the last two centuries, let's first discuss the diffusion of cities before this period. There are two possibilities:

1. Cities evolved spontaneously as native peoples created new technologies and social institutions.

2. The preconditions for urban life are too specific for most cultures to have invented without contact with other urban areas; therefore, they must have learned these traits through contact with city dwellers. This scenario emphasizes the diffusion of ideas and techniques necessary for city life.

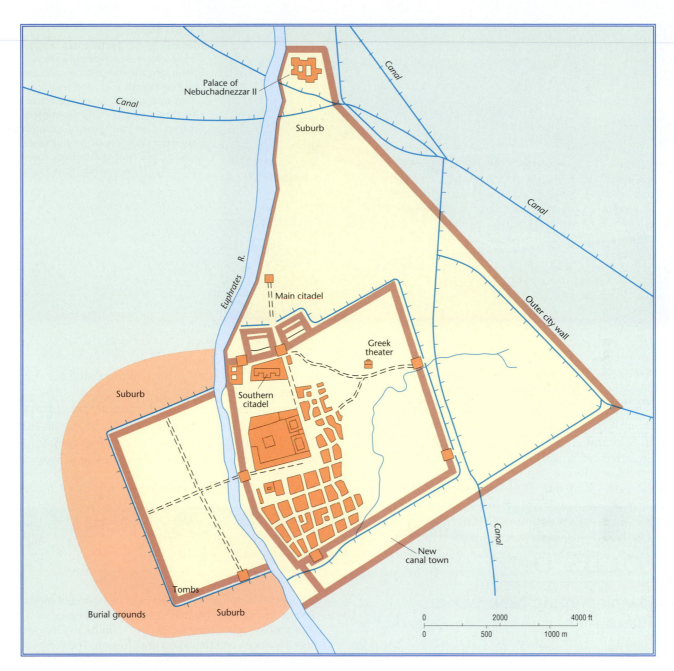

Figure 10.5

Map of Babylon, illustrating the urban morphology of early Mesopotamian cities. The citadel in the inner city is characterized by the ziggurat, main temple, palace, and granary. Beyond the citadel lay the residential areas; we can assume they extended out to the inner walls and occupied both sides of the river. Suburbs grew outside the major gates and were occupied by people not allowed to spend the night in the city, such as traders and noncitizens. (AFTER MAP IN ENCYCLOPAEDIA BRITANNICA, 1984: 555.)

Diffusionists argue that the complicated array of ideas and techniques that gave rise to the first cities in Mesopotamia was shared with other people, in both the Nile and the Indus river valleys, who were on the verge of the urban transformation. Indeed, these three civilizations had contact with one another. Archaeological evidence documents trade ties among them. Soapstone objects manufactured in Tepe Yahya, 500 miles (800 kilometers) to the east of Mesopotamia, have been uncovered in the ruins of both Mesopotamian and Indus river valley cities, which are separated by thousands of miles. Writings of the Indus civilization have also been found in Mesopotamian urban sites. Although diffusionists use this artifactual evidence to argue that the idea of the city was

Figure 10.6

Mayan city of Chichén Itzá. Monumental and ceremonial architecture often dominated the morphology and landscape of urban hearth areas and reinforced ruling-class power. **In what part of the city would you say this monument is located? Can you think of examples from your own daily life of monumental architecture that symbolizes some ruling authority?** (Malcolm Kirk/Peter Arnold, Inc.)

spread from hearth to hearth, an alternative view is that trading took place only after these cities were well established. There is also evidence of contacts across the oceans between early urban dwellers of the New World and those of Asia and Africa, although it is unclear whether this means that urbanization was diffused to Mesoamerica or simply that some trade routes existed between these peoples.

Nonetheless, there is little doubt that diffusion has been responsible for the dispersal of the city in historical times (Figure 10.7), because the city has commonly been used as the vehicle for imperial expansion. The sociologist

FOCUS ON

City Planning in the New World: Teotihuacán

Teotihuacán was a Mesoamerican city created by a society that had no metal tools, had not invented the wheel, and had no pack animals. At its height, Teotihuacán covered 8 square miles (20 square kilometers), which made it larger than imperial Rome. Its central religious monument, the Temple of the Sun, was as broad at its base as the Great Pyramid of Cheops in Egypt. Its population may have reached 100,000 by A.D. 600.

Strategically located astride a valley that was the gateway to the lowlands of Mexico, Teotihuacán flourished as a great urban commercial center. Yet it was more than that. It was the Mecca of the New World, a religious and cultural capital that probably housed pilgrims from as far away as Guatemala. Not a trace of fortification has ever been unearthed. Perhaps most startling, Teotihuacán was a totally planned city. Its two great pyramids, its citadel, its 100 lesser religious structures, and its 4000 other dwellings were laid out according to a cosmomagical design. Its streets (and many of its buildings) were organized on an exact grid aligned with the city center. Even the shape of the river that divided the city was changed to fit the grid pattern.

Planning for the construction of Teotihuacán's major temples must have been an astounding undertaking. The Temple of the Sun, for instance, rises to a height of 215 feet (65 meters) and has a base of 725 square feet (67 square meters). These dimensions mean that it took about 1 million tons of sun-baked mud bricks to build the temple. When the Spaniards conquered Mexico in the sixteenth century, they were amazed to find Teotihuacán's ruined temples. Local inhabitants claimed that the temples had been built by giants. They showed the Spaniards the bones of giant elephants (which had lived there in prehistoric times) to prove their point.

The small as well as the large was cleverly conceived in Teotihuacán. Houses were apparently planned for maximum space and privacy. Apartments were constructed around central patios, and each patio was designed to give dwellers light and air, as well as an efficient drainage system. In a Teotihuacán housing complex, a person could indeed have lived in relative comfort.

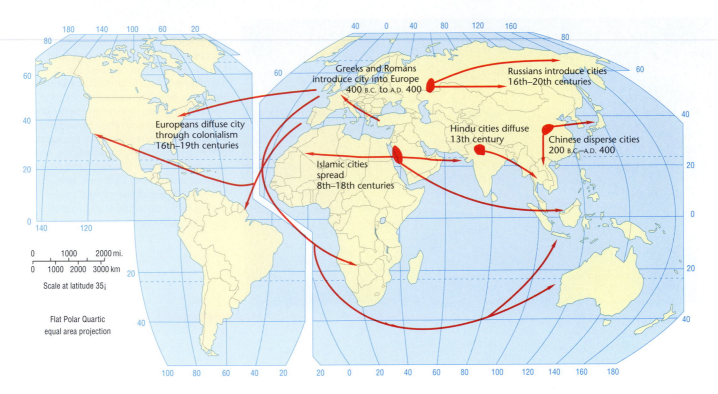

Figure 10.7

The diffusion of urban life with the expansion of certain empires. What does this map tell us about the importance of urban life to military conquest?

Gideon Sjoberg, in *The Preindustrial City,* states: "The extension of the power group's domain, notably through empire-building, is the primary mechanism for introducing city life into generally non-urbanized territories." Typically, urban life is carried outward in waves of conquest as the borders of an empire expand. Initially, the military controls newly won lands and sets up collection points for local resources, which are then shipped back into the heart of the empire and used for its economy. As the surrounding countryside is increasingly pacified, the new collection points lose some of their military atmosphere and begin to show the social diversity of a city. Artisans, merchants, and bureaucrats increase in number. Families appear. The native people are slowly assimilated into the settlement as workers and may eventually control the city. Finally, the process repeats itself as the empire pushes farther outward: first a military camp, then a collection point for resources, then a full-fledged city expressing true division of labor and social diversity.

This process, however, did not always proceed without opposition. The imposition of a foreign civilization on native peoples was often met with resistance, both physical and symbolic. Expanding urban centers relied on the surrounding countryside for support. Their food was sup-plied by farmers living fairly close to the city walls, and tribute was exacted from the agricultural peoples living on the edges of the urban world. The increasing needs of the city required more and more land from which to draw resources. However, the peasants farming that land may not have wanted to change their way of life to accommodate the city. The fierce resistance of many Indian American groups to the spread of Western urbanization is testimony to the potential power of folk society to defy urbanization, although the destructive long-term effects of such resistance suggest that the organized military efforts of urban society were difficult to overcome.

The Evolution of Urban Landscapes

What do cities look like? Understanding urban landscapes necessitates an appreciation of urban processes both past and present. The patterns we see today in the city, such as building forms, architecture, street plans, and land use, are a composite of past and present cultures. They reflect the needs, ideas, technology, and institutions of human occupancy. This section examines major stages

in the evolution of urban landscapes in both the developed and developing worlds.

Two concepts underlie our examination of urban landscapes. The first is **urban morphology,** or the physical form of the city, which consists of street patterns, building sizes and shapes, architecture, and density. The second concept is **functional zonation,** which refers to the pattern of land uses within a city, or the existence of areas with differing functions, such as residential, commercial, and governmental. Functional zonation also includes social patterns—whether an area is occupied by the power elite or by people of low status, by Jews or by Christians, by the wealthy or by the poor. Both concepts are central to understanding the cultural landscape of cities, because both make statements about how cultures occupy and shape space (Figure 10.8).

We begin our study of urban landscapes by examining the history of cities from Greek times to the postindustrial present.

The Greek City

Western civilization and the Western city both trace their immediate roots back to ancient Greece. City life diffused to Greece from Mesopotamia. By 600 B.C., there were over 500 towns and cities on the Greek mainland and surrounding islands. As Greek civilization expanded, cities spread with it throughout the Mediterranean: to the north shore of Africa, to Spain, to southern France, and to Italy. These cities were of modest size, rarely containing more than 5000 inhabitants. Athens, however, may have reached a population of 300,000 in the fifth century

B.C. (This figure includes perhaps 100,000 slaves, the labor power behind Greek society.)

Greek cities had two distinctive functional zones: the acropolis and the agora. In many ways, the acropolis was similar to the citadel of Mesopotamian cities. Here were the temples of worship, the storehouse of valuables, and the seat of power. The acropolis also served as a place of retreat in time of siege (Figure 10.9). If the acropolis was the domain of power, the agora was the province of the citizens. As originally conceived, the agora was a place for public meetings, education, social interaction, and judicial matters. In other words, it was the civic center, the hub of democratic life for Greek men (women were excluded from political life).

This physical separation of religious from secular functions, which distinguishes the Greek city from the cosmomagical city, implies that in Greek culture the religious domain was no longer the only source of authority. The agora represented, in some senses, a challenge to the acropolis. The location and architecture of the acropolis suggest that the power of the gods and the supernatural was tempered by human aesthetics and reason. Greek temples were located on sacred sites chosen to please the gods, but they were also sited and designed to please the human eye and to harmonize with the natural landscape. This tension between the religious and the secular created what many people consider to be one of the greatest achievements of Western architecture.

The earlier Greek cities probably were not planned but rather grew spontaneously, without benefit of formal guidelines. However, some scholars think that many ceremonial areas within these cities were designed to be seen

Figure 10.9
The Acropolis in Athens. The Acropolis dominates the contemporary city and reminds us that many cities throughout the world have been centered on fortified places that eventually became more symbolic than functional. **How does this landscape compare with other defensive acropolis sites?** (James Hanley/Photo Researchers.)

according to prescribed lines of vision, and that those lines of vision included not only the buildings but the natural landscape that surrounded it. Again, the human aesthetic sense was given a degree of authority that it did not have in the cosmomagical city.

More formalized city design and plan are apparent in later Greek cities that were built in areas of colonial expansion. One of the best examples of such planned cities is Miletus, on the eastern shore of the Mediterranean, in Ionia (present-day Turkey). The city was laid out in a rigid grid pattern, imposing its geometry onto the physical site conditions (Figure 10.10). Although the source of such a plan is debatable, clearly this orderly and coherent layout indicates an abstract and highly rational notion of urban life and seems to fit well with the functional needs of a colonial city. The grid system is a creation of the human mind, and its imposition on a highly irregular physical site shows that religious and aesthetic needs had taken a secondary role to the more pressing demands of controlling an empire.

Roman Cities

By 200 B.C., the focus for the Western city had shifted from Greece to Rome. The Romans adopted many urban traits from the Greeks, as well as from the Etruscans, a civilization of central Italy that the Romans had conquered. As the Roman Empire expanded, city life diffused into France, Germany, England, interior Spain, the Alpine countries, and parts of eastern Europe—areas that had not previously experienced urbanization. Most of these cities were military and trading outposts of the Roman

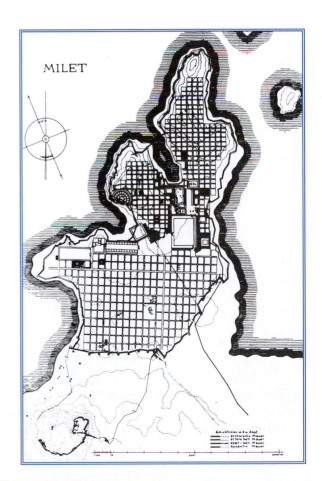

Figure 10.10
The plan of the city of Miletus by Hippodamus, ca. 450 B.C. Notice how the strict grid is imposed on the irregular coastline. The central agora is also regularized, characteristic of this colonial phase of the Greek city. (Source: Vance, 1990.)

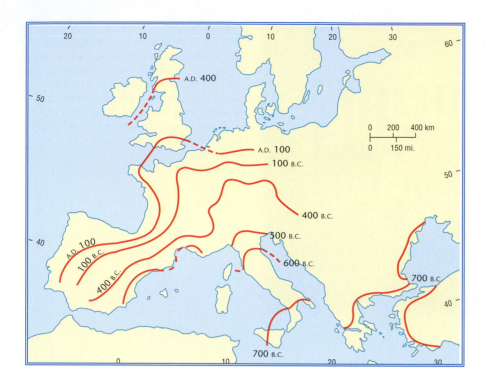

Figure 10.11

The diffusion of urbanization in Europe. The early spread of urban development moved in waves across Europe. The nucleus of city life was well established in the Greek lands by 700 B.C. In the following centuries, urbanization diffused westward and northward until it reached the British Isles. **What do you think were some of the effects of this imposition of urban life on agricultural peoples?** (Reproduced by permission from Pounds, 1969.)

Empire. They served as focal points for the collection of products from the agricultural countryside, as supply centers for the military, and as service centers for the long-distance trading network that was controlled from Rome. The military camp, or *castra*, was the basis for many of these new settlements. In England, the Roman trail of city building can be found by looking for the suffixes *-caster* and *-chester*—as in Lancaster or Winchester, cities origi-

nally founded as Roman camps. Figure 10.11 shows the diffusion of urban life into Europe as the Greek and Roman frontiers advanced.

The landscape of these Roman cities shared several traits with that of their Greek predecessors. The gridiron street pattern, used in later Greek cities, was fundamental to Roman cities. This pattern can still be seen in the heart of such Italian cities as Pavia (Figure 10.12). The straight

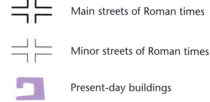

Main streets of Roman times

Minor streets of Roman times

Present-day buildings

Figure 10.12

The Roman grid street pattern in Pavia, Italy. Many of the straight streets from Roman times remain in use 20 centuries after they were first built. The dotted lines indicate the Roman streets that do not exist today. Beyond the Roman core, the streets developed in irregular patterns. **Why do the present-day buildings not necessarily follow the Roman grid?**

Figure 10.13

The Colosseum in Rome. Crowds of 60,000 were entertained in the Colosseum by mock battles, circuses, gladiators, and sports events. Most large Roman cities had similar structures. Today, most cities have stadiums and coliseums that continue the tradition of public spectacles started by the Romans.

streets and right-angle intersections make a striking contrast to the curved, wandering lanes of the later medieval quarters or the streets of Rome itself. At the intersection of a city's two major thoroughfares was the *forum,* a zone combining elements of the Greek acropolis and agora. Here were not only the temples of worship, administrative buildings, and warehouses, but also the libraries, schools, and marketplaces that served the common people.

Clustered around the forum were the palaces of the power elite. These palaces were sanitary, well heated in winter, and spacious—marvels of domestic architecture and engineering. However, despite the architectural accomplishments of the Roman engineers, most urban dwellers of the Roman Empire lived in squalor. Whereas the homes of the rich spread horizontally across the landscape, the homes of the poor rose vertically. They lived in shoddy apartment houses, often four or five stories high, called *insulae.*

Rome's most important legacy probably was not its architectural and engineering feats, although they remain landmarks in European cities to this day (Figure 10.13), but rather the Roman method for choosing the site of a city, which remains applicable today. The Romans consistently chose sites with transportation in mind. The Roman Empire was held together by a complicated system of roads and highways linking towns and cities. In choosing a site for a new settlement, the Romans made access to transport a major consideration. Other cultures, in contrast, placed primary emphasis on defensive locations;

hence, their settlements might have been located in inaccessible places such as marshes or islands or on hilltops. The significance of Roman location was that even though urban life declined dramatically with the collapse of the empire, many cities—such as Paris, London, and Vienna—were established centuries later on the same old Roman sites because they offered advantages of access to the surrounding countryside.

With the decline of the Roman Empire by A.D. 400, urban life also declined. Historians attribute the fall of Rome to internal decay, the invasion of the Germanic peoples, and other factors. Cities were sapped of their vitality. The highway system that linked them fell into disrepair, so that cities could no longer exchange goods and ideas. When Roman cities were invaded, they could no longer count on outside military support as the administrative structure of the empire collapsed. Isolated from one another, they lost vital functions. As symbols of a conquering empire, Roman outposts were either actively destroyed or, devoid of purpose, simply left to decay. Within 200 years, many of the cities founded by the Romans withered away.

Yet there were exceptions. Some cities of the Mediterranean survived because they established trade with the Eastern Roman Empire centered in Constantinople. After the eighth century, some cities—particularly those in Spain—were infused with new vigor by the Moorish Empire, which spread across the Mediterranean from northern Africa. The cities of northern regions were unable to survive, however. Cities became small villages. Where thousands had formerly thrived, a few hundred eked out a subsistence living from agriculture.

Urban decline occurred only in the areas that had been under Roman rule. Other civilizations continued to thrive throughout this period. The achievements of Chinese civilization and the great cities of the Mayan Empire remind us that urban decline occurred only in a particular area of Europe.

The Medieval City

The medieval period, lasting roughly from A.D. 1000 to 1500, was a time of renewed urban expansion in Europe and a period that deeply influenced the future of urban life. Urban life spread beyond the borders of the former Roman Empire, into the north and east of Europe, as the Germanic and Slavic peoples expanded their empires. In only four centuries, 2500 new German cities were founded. Most cities of present-day Europe were established during this period. Although many were on old Roman sites, others were new.

Scholars have debated why urban life began to regain vigor in the eleventh century. In essence, the revival of both local and long-distance trade was the result of a combination of factors, including population increase, political stability and unification, and agricultural expansion through new land reclamations and the development of new agricultural technologies. Sustained trading networks required protected markets and supply centers, functions that re-

newed life in cities. In addition, trading—particularly over long distances—led to the development of a new social class: the merchant class. Members of the merchant class breathed new life into early medieval cities, providing the impetus and the wealth for sustained city building.

The medieval city can be characterized by the presence of five features: the fortress, the charter, the wall, the marketplace, and the cathedral. The *fortress* expresses the importance of defense. Usually the cities were clustered around a fortified place. The importance of this role is reflected in many place names. The suffixes of many names of European cities—in Germanic lands ending with *-burg*, such as Salzburg and Würzburg; in France with *-bourg*, as in Strasbourg; and in English with *-burgh*, as in Edinburgh—all have the same meaning: a fortified castle. The terms *burgher* and *bourgeoisie*, which now refer to the middle class, originally referred to a citizen of the medieval city.

The *charter* was a governmental decree from a regional power, usually a feudal lord, granting political autonomy to the town. This act had important implications. It freed the population from feudal restrictions, made the city responsible for its own defense and government, and often allowed it to coin money. Thus city life became freer than life on rural feudal estates. These rights and responsibilities contributed to the development of urban social, economic, and intellectual life.

The *wall* served a defensive purpose, but it was also a symbol of the sharp distinction between country and city (Figure 10.14). Within the wall, most inhabitants were,

Figure 10.14

The medieval hill town of Carcassonne in southern France. Notice the double set of fortified walls that surround this medieval town. (Jonathan Blair/Corbis.)

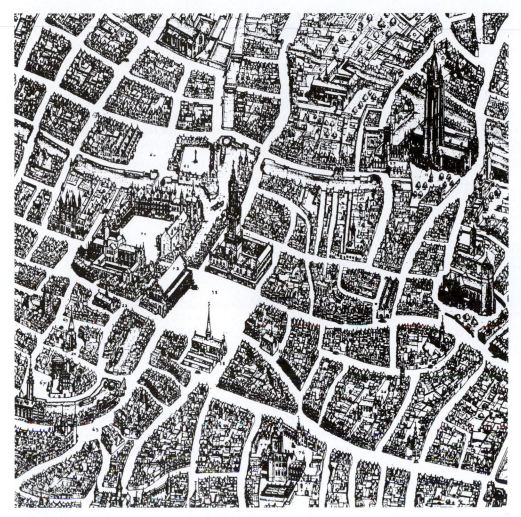

Figure 10.15
A 1562 panoramic map of the city of Brugge, Belgium, showing the central area. Directly in the center of the image is the great Halle building, the economic heart of the city. Just in front of it and to the left is the waterhall, so named because it straddled the canal, allowing goods to be delivered directly into the building. To the left is the old castle surrounded by guildhalls and the town hall. To the extreme right is the cathedral building. **How do the reasons for this organic urban plan compare and contrast with the reasons for the grid plan of Roman cities?** (See Figure 10.12.) (SOURCE: BENEVOLO, 1980.)

11. Cathedral of Notre Dame.
12. Church of St Sauveur.
18. Chapel of St Christopher.
20. Chapel of St John.
21. Chapel of St Amanda.
22. Chapel of St Peter.
26. Chapel of the Painters.

58. Fish market.
60. Grain market.
62. Leather market.
63. Bourse.
70. Castle, with the Town Hall and Chancellery.
71. Halle.

72. Waterhalle.
75. Prison.
76. Prince's Hall.
77. Mint.
88. So-called 'Castle of the Seven Turrets'.

by charter, free; outside, most were serfs. "City air sets a man free" went the medieval proverb. Indeed, even though the medieval city had feudal characteristics, it generally was a community of citizens able to move about with little restriction, free to buy and sell property and goods. A city of free citizens, not based on a vast pool of slave labor, was a first in the history of the Western world.

Another key zone was the *marketplace*. It symbolized the important role of economic activities in the medieval city. The city depended on the countryside for its food and produce, which were traded in the market. The market also was a center for long-distance trade, which linked city to city. Textiles, salt, ore, and other raw materials were bought and sold in the marketplace.

At one end of the marketplace stood the town hall, a fairly tall structure that provided meeting space for the city's political leaders. The town hall often served as a market hall, with many of its rooms used to store and display the finer goods that could not be exposed to the natural elements outside on the market square. Yet, in many of the larger commercial cities, civic and economic functions were located in separate buildings. Brugge, Belgium, an important trading center for northern Europe, had two distinct complexes of buildings at its center (Figure 10.15). Together, the town hall and castle formed an enclosed square. Next to this, forming the edges of a large, open marketplace, was the *wasserhalle*, or waterhall, so named because the building straddled a canal (goods were brought directly into the hall from the barges

Figure 10.16

Heidelberg, Germany, showing the typical narrow, winding street pattern of the medieval period. Besides the pedestrian-scale inner city, we see other typical medieval features, such as churches and residences located above street-level shops. **Can you identify any other characteristic features of a medieval city?** (ULRIKE WELSCH/PHOTO RESEARCHERS.)

underneath). On an adjacent edge of the marketplace was the great hall that served as the meeting place for the merchant class. The tower of the great hall rivaled that of the cathedral, an indication that the great hall was a symbol of a world where commerce was beginning to command more attention.

The medieval town's crowning glory was usually the *cathedral,* a dominating architectural symbol of the important role of the church. Often the cathedral, the marketplace, and the town hall were close together, indicating close ties among religion, commerce, and politics. However, the church was often the prevailing political force in medieval towns.

The functional zonation of the medieval city differed markedly from that of our modern cities. The city was divided into small quarters, or districts, each containing its own center that served as its focal point. Within each of these districts lived people who were engaged in similar occupations. Coopers (people who made and repaired wooden barrels), for example, lived in one particular district, attended the same local church, and belonged to the same guild. Their church and guildhall were located in the small center area of their district. Along the narrow, winding streets surrounding this center area were the houses and workplaces of the coopers (Figure 10.16). Many worked in the first story of their houses. Their families lived above the shop, and their apprentices lived above them. The more prestigious groups lived in occupa-

tional districts close to the center of the city, whereas those that were involved in noxious activities, such as butchers and leather workers, lived closer to the city walls.

Some of these districts, however, were defined not by occupation but by ethnicity, and these areas have been referred to as ghettos. The origin of the term *ghetto is* somewhat unclear, although one plausible explanation suggests that the word dates from the early sixteenth century when Venetians decided to restrict Jewish settlement in the city to an area already known as Ghetto Nuovo, or the "new foundry." This area was physically separated from the rest of the city and had a single entrance that could be guarded. The practice of spatially segregating the Jewish population was not limited to Venice. In most medieval cities, Jews were forced to live in their own districts. In Frankfurt am Main, Jews lived on the *Judengasse,* a street that was formed from the dried-up moat that had run along the old wall to the city. The *Judengasse* was enclosed by walls with only one guarded gate for entrance and exit. Because the area was not allowed to expand beyond those walls, a growing population led to denser living conditions. In 1462, the population of the *Judengasse* was only 110 inhabitants; but by 1610, 3000 people lived in the Jewish ghetto, creating one of the densest districts in the city.

In summary, there are three important points about the role of the medieval period in the evolution of the Western city: (1) Most European cities were founded during this period; (2) many of the traditions of Western urban life began then; and (3) the medieval landscape is still with us, providing a visible history of the city and a distinctive form into which twenty-first-century activities are placed.

The Renaissance and Baroque Periods

During the Renaissance (approximately 1500–1600) and Baroque (1600–1800) periods, the form and function of the European city changed significantly. Absolute monarchs arose to preside over a unified country. The burghers, or rising middle class, of the cities slowly gave up their freedoms to join with the king in pursuit of economic gain. City size increased rapidly because the bureaucracies of regional power structures came to dominate cities and because trade patterns expanded with the beginnings of European imperial conquest.

Cities and the surrounding countryside began to merge into countries ruled by all-powerful monarchs. One city, the national capital, rose to prominence in most countries. Provincial cities were subjected to its tastes, and

power was centralized in its precincts. Most important, the capital city was restructured to reflect the power of the central government and to ensure its control over the urban masses.

Hand in hand with these developments went a new concern with city planning. This interest grew from a revival of the classical period, including Greek and Roman urban planning; from a new philosophical emphasis on humankind's earthly home; and from new aesthetic concepts that gave urban planners a foundation from which to work (see Focus On: Planning the Ideal City: Humanism and Renaissance Urban Design). Most planning measures were meant to benefit the privileged classes. Rulers considered the city a stage on which to act out their destinies, and as a stage, the city could be rearranged at will. Typical of the time was the infatuation with wide, grandiose boulevards. The rich could ride along them in carriages, and the army could march along them in an impressive display of power. Other features of the Baroque city were large, open squares; palaces; and public buildings. Statues were everywhere.

FOCUS ON

Planning the Ideal City: Humanism and Renaissance Urban Design

Fifteenth-century humanism, with its emphasis on the individual as a microcosm of a universe constructed according to fixed mathematical relationships, provided a philosophical framework within which techniques for unitary perspectives could be developed. Many Italian architects and artists combined painting, architecture, and social theory to create imaginative plans for ideal cities, all constructed in accordance with humanist principles. By stressing supposedly universal values of reason and natural order, these ideal-city plans served to mediate between an aristocratic vision of the world—in which rank and status are regarded as natural and ensured by birth—and a bourgeois world view, in which rank and status are economically determined.

All of these plans for ideal cities had certain properties in common. The ideal city is conceived as a unitary space, an architectural totality, a changeless and perfect form. It is delineated by a fortified wall, circular or polygonal in shape. At the center is a large open space surrounded by key administrative buildings: the prince's palace; the justice building; the main church, generally referred to in classical terms as a temple; and often a prison, treasury, and military

garrison. Significantly, the market square is rarely discussed in detail and is often relegated to a subsidiary open space away from the center. The dimensions of the central piazza and its architecture are rigorously controlled and strictly proportioned. Road patterns are designed to provide visual corridors that give prospects on key urban buildings or monuments. The entire perception is visual, imaged either from above as a unity of plan or on the ground as a series of integrated perspectives to and from principal buildings. Individual structures are designed according to the rules of the classical orders; thus each is rendered a microcosm of the same geometric principles that govern the harmony of the whole city and that are displayed in the physical and intellectual properties of its citizens. The ideal city is designed for the exercise of administration and justice, for the civic life, rather than for production or exchange. It is purely ideological.

Ideal cities are social as well as architectural utopias, designed to regulate and determine relationships between classes in an environment where neither merchant nor landed aristocrat dominates. Instead, a class of noble administrators rules by virtue of its members' superior reason rather than their exercise of economic power or inherited privilege.

Adapted and abridged from Cosgrove, 1984.

Figure 10.17
A view of Paris, showing boulevards designed by Baron Haussmann. The boulevard was a favorite of Baroque planners. It was a ceremonial street that often led to public buildings and monuments, was lined with trees and upper-income housing, and offered public space for the wealthy. Boulevards were often created at the expense of thousands of poorer citizens, who were displaced as older housing was destroyed by the boulevard builders. **Has this happened in your city or one near you as freeways have been built?** (JEFF GREENBERG/PHOTO RESEARCHERS.)

This environment was strikingly different from the dark, closed world of the medieval quarters, where the middle classes still resided. The spacious, new aristocratic sections often were created at the expense of the middle class, whose homes were demolished to make way for a new palace or boulevard.

Although the height of Baroque planning was between 1600 and 1800, this autocratic spirit also carried into the nineteenth century, as is illustrated in Paris (Figure 10.17). There, Napoléon III had Baron Haussmann build a system of boulevards designed, among other things, to control the populace. Cobblestone streets were carefully paved so that no loose ammunition was available for rioting Parisians. Streets were straightened and widened, and cul-de-sacs were broken down to give the army—should the people arise—space to maneuver, with ordered sight lines for its artillery. Whole neighborhoods were torn down to build wide avenues. Thousands of residents were displaced as their apartment buildings were demolished. They had to seek new shelter on their own, and many ended up in the congested working-class sections of east and north Paris. These areas are still overcrowded today, and much of the blame can be assigned to the Baroque planners.

Renaissance and Baroque planning also influenced many American cities. For example, Washington, D.C., was originally designed by a French planner at the end of the Baroque period. Although the original plan has been compromised somewhat, its intent is still visible in the wide boulevards, open spaces, public buildings, and monuments of the city.

The Capitalist City

Underlying many of the changes in Renaissance and Baroque city planning was a sweeping socioeconomic transformation that reshaped western Europe. The transition from a feudal order to a capitalist one involved drastic changes in class structure, economic systems, political allegiances, cultural patterns, and human geographies. These changes occurred over a period that stretched from the mid-sixteenth century to the mid-eighteenth century. The countryside was reordered with the introduction of commercialized and specialized agriculture and with the enclosure of individual land units. The city was also reshaped, as the value of two-dimensional location and three-dimensional form in the city acquired economic significance.

Perhaps of greatest significance is how the capitalist mindset introduced a notion of urban land as a source of income. Proximity to the center of the city, and therefore to the most pedestrian traffic, added economic value to land. Other specialized locations, such as areas close to the river or harbor or along the major thoroughfares in and out of the city, also increased land value. This fundamental change in the value accorded to urban land led to the gradual disintegration of the medieval urban pattern.

In the emerging capitalist city, the ability to pay determined where one would live. The city's residential areas thus became segregated by economic class. The wealthy lived in the desirable neighborhoods; those without much money were forced to live in the more disagreeable parts of the city. In addition, places of work were separated from home, so that a merchant, for example, lived in one part of the city and traveled to another to conduct his business. This spatial separation of work from home, of public space from private space, both reflected and helped to shape the changing social worlds of men and women. In general, men generated economic income from work outside the home and therefore came to be associated with the public space of the city. Women, who were primarily engaged in domestic work, were considered the keepers of the private world of the home. This association of women with private domestic space and men with public work space deepened and became more complex throughout the next few hundred years.

Reflecting on GEOGRAPHY

How did (and does) the association of private domestic space with women and of public work space with men affect the daily lives of men and women? Can you think of counterexamples, that is, instances of the merging of private and public spaces?

The center of the capitalist city was not the cathedral and guildhalls, but instead the buildings devoted to business enterprises. A downtown defined by economic activity emerged that, with the coming of industrialization, eventually expanded and subdivided into specialized districts. The new upper classes of the city, whose status was based on their accumulation of economic wealth, not only made money from buying and selling urban land but also used urban land as a basis for expressing their wealth. With the downtown devoted to mercantile and emerging industrial uses, the upper classes sought newer land on the edge of the city for their residential enclaves. These new areas often acted as three-dimensional symbols of relatively recent wealth, conferring on their residents the legitimacy of upper-class membership.

One of the first and finest of these new enclaves for the wealthy was London's Covent Garden Piazza, a residential square designed by Inigo Jones in the early 1630s. The square was lined with townhouses that were edged in arcades, with one end of the square dedicated to a church. The inhabitants of Covent Garden included some of London's nobility and wealthier bourgeoisie. The presence of nobility lent an aristocratic aura to the area and provided social legitimacy to the new bourgeoisie who lived there. The economic success of this speculative real estate venture led to many imitations, and similar residential squares cropped up throughout the West End of London (Figure 10.18). These upper-class squares were transplanted to

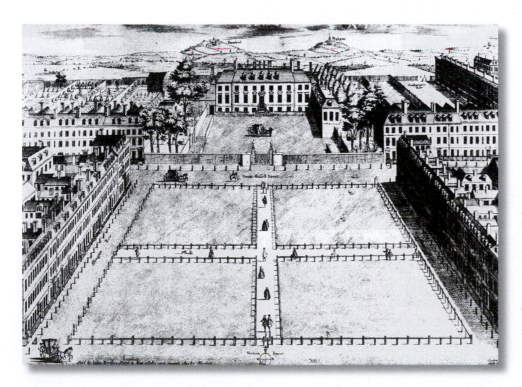

Figure 10.18

A 1730 view of Bloomsbury Square, laid out in 1661 by the earl of Southampton. Southampton House occupies the far end of the square, lending an aristocratic air to this speculative, mercantile development. Notice the men and women parading in their finery, suggesting the wealthy and leisurely life of the inhabitants. **What other signs of wealth are evident in this image?** (SOURCE: HAYES, 1969.)

Figure 10.19
New York City, looking southwest from the Bronx. The rows and rows of working-class housing in the foreground and the factories visible to the left indicate the horizontal spatial expansion of industrial urban form; the massive skyline indicates the degree of vertical expansion. (Courtesy of Mona Domosh.)

America throughout the seventeenth and eighteenth centuries, arising in such cities as Boston, New York, Philadelphia, and Savannah.

Class, "Race," and Gender in the Industrial City

The function, structure, and landscape of the Western city have changed dramatically since the industrial revolution (Figure 10.19). In turn, the industrial city has profoundly altered the fabric of society itself.

Until the industrial period, the rate of urbanization in Western countries was relatively low. For example, in 1600, urban dwellers made up only 2 percent of the German, French, and English populations; in the Netherlands and Italy, 13 percent of the population were urban dwellers. However, as millions of people migrated to the cities over the next 200 years, the rate of urbanization skyrocketed. By 1800, England was 20 percent urbanized, and around 1870 it became the world's first urban society. By the 1890 census, 60 percent of its people lived in cities. The United States was 3 percent urbanized in 1800, 40 percent in 1900, and 51 percent in 1920 (when it became an urban country), and now about 75 percent of its population live in towns and cities.

The industrial revolution and the triumph of capitalism turned the city from a public institution into private property—spoils to be divided with an eye to maximum profits. A new philosophy emerged: **laissez-faire utilitarianism.** Lewis Mumford, in *The City in History,* defined this philosophy as a belief that divine providence ruled over economic activity and ensured the maximum public good through the unregulated efforts of every private, self-seeking individual. One expression of this new philosophy was a changed attitude toward land and the buildings on that land. Once raw materials such as coal and iron ore could be brought to the city by rail, factories began to cluster together to share the benefits of **agglomeration**—that is, to share labor, transportation costs, and utility costs—and to take advantage of financial institutions found in the city. Industry concentrated in the city itself, around labor, the commercial marketplace, and capital. Land use intensified drastically. With the increased competition for land in the industrial period, land transactions and speculation became an everyday part of city life. Land parcels became the property of the owner, who had no obligations to society in deciding how to use them. The historical urban core was often destroyed, the older city replaced. The result was a mosaic of mixed land uses: factories directly next to housing; slum tenements next to public buildings; open spaces and parks violated by railroad tracks. A planned attempt to bring order to the city came only in the twentieth century with the concept of zoning (see Focus On: The Origins of Zoning in America: Race and Wealth). Yet even this idea was rooted in some of the same forces—profit, bigotry, and individualism—that had already made the industrial city unresponsive to the needs of most of its inhabitants.

FOCUS ON

The Origins of Zoning in America: Race and Wealth

The standard zoning ordinance of American cities was originally conceived from a union of two fears—fear of the Chinese and fear of skyscrapers. In California, a wave of racial prejudice had swept over the state after Chinese settlers were imported to build the railroads and work in the mines [in the mid-nineteenth century]. Ingenious lawyers in San Francisco found that the old common law of nuisance could be applied for indirect discrimination against the Chinese in situations where the constitution of the state forbade direct discrimination. Chinese laundries of the 1880s had become social centers for Chinese servants who lived outside the Chinatown ghetto. To whites they represented only clusters of "undesirables" in the residential areas where Chinese were living singly among them as house servants. By declaring the laundries nuisances and fire hazards, San Francisco hoped to exclude Chinese from most sections of the city. . . . Such nuisance-zone statutes spread down the Pacific coast. . . .

[Meanwhile,] in New York [City,] the Fifth Avenue Association, a group composed of men who owned or leased the city's most expensive retail land, demanded that the city protect their luxury blocks from encroachment by the new tall buildings of the garment district. . . . The Fifth Avenue Association feared that the ensuing decades would see the [skyscraper] lofts invading their best properties, bringing with them [lower-class] lunch-hour crowds and a blockade of wagons, trucks, and carts. In short, they feared that skyscraper lofts, low-paid help, and traffic congestion would drive their middle-class and wealthy customers from the Avenue.

The combination of West Coast racism plus the fears of wealthy New York merchants resulted in the New York Zoning Law of 1916, a prototype zoning statute for the nation. These were the roots of the first American attempts to deal coherently with urban growth. Not surprisingly, the zoning law was no sooner passed than it was seized on in the South and elsewhere as a way to extend [the] laws and practices of racial segregation. . . . A land or structure limitation . . . became a financial, racial, and ethnic limitation by pricing certain groups out of particular suburbs. Italians were held at bay in Boston, Poles in Detroit, Blacks in Chicago and St. Louis, Jews in New York.

Abridged from Warner, 1972: 28–32, 117–118. Copyright © 1972 by Sam Bass Warner, Jr.

Class Laissez-faire industrialism did surprisingly little for the working classes that labored in its shops and plants. In their slum dwellings, direct sunlight was seldom available, and open spaces were nonexistent (Figure 10.20 on the next page). In Liverpool, England, for instance, one-sixth of the population reportedly lived in "underground cellars." A study from the middle of the nineteenth century in Manchester, England, showed that there was but one toilet for every 212 people. Running water was usually available only on the ground floors of apartment buildings. Disease was pervasive, and mortality rates ran high. In 1893, the life expectancy of a male worker in Manchester was 28 years; his country cousin might live to 52. The death rate in New York City in 1880 was 25 per 1000, whereas it was half that in the rural counties of the state. The infant mortality rate per thousand live births rose from 180 in 1850 to 240 in 1870. Legislation correcting such ills came only in the latter part of the nineteenth century.

"Race" With all its faults, industrialization created some of the most vibrant centers of urban activity in modern times. American industrial cities, for example, relied on a diverse labor force, and each social group fought for its place in the urban land market. Despite the harsh living conditions, various groups of laborers carved out identities in the urban landscape.

Industrialization in the United States drew its workforce not only from European immigrants but also from African-Americans. After the Civil War, many former slaves in the South migrated to northern cities to work in a diverse array of skilled and semiskilled jobs, while industrialization in many southern cities led African-Americans to migrate from the countryside to the cities. In both northern and southern cities, the African-American population lived in segregated neighborhoods, forced by discrimination and often by law to keep its distance from Anglo-American residential districts.

Although the services provided to these neighborhoods were usually minimal, many people did find opportunities for cultural expression in the new urban mosaic. A recent study of African-Americans in Richmond, Virginia, after the Civil War found that residents effectively used public rituals in the streets and buildings of the city to carve out their own civic representations, as well as to

Figure 10.20

Lower Manhattan, looking north from the Produce Exchange. This view of mid-nineteenth-century New York depicts the very crowded living and working conditions as the city's population greatly expanded during industrialization. **Are any open spaces visible in this image?** (CORBIS/BETTMANN.)

challenge the dominant Anglo-American order. For example, African-American militias were formed that marched through the streets of Richmond on holidays certified by the African-American community as their own political calendar: January 1, George Washington's birthday, April 3 (Emancipation Day), and July 4. As urban historians Elsa Barkley Brown and Gregg Kimball state: "White Richmonders watched in horror as former slaves claimed civic holidays white residents believed to be their own historic possession, and as black residents occupied spaces, like Capitol Square, that formerly had been reserved for white citizens." Other spaces, such as churches, schools, and beauty shops, served as community centers and public statements of an African-American identity. In this way, the urban landscape acted as one arena for the struggle to control the meanings and uses of an environment often thought to be totally dominated by Anglo-American culture (Figure 10.21).

Reflecting on GEOGRAPHY

Consider how important the appropriation of space is to forming and maintaining cultural identity in the city. Why might such appropriation be more important for groups that are not dominant in a society? What do examples from your city tell you about struggles to control the meaning of its built environment?

Gender Industrialization, then, not only destroyed sections of cities to make way for railroads and factories but

also made possible the creation of new urban identities and neighborhoods. Throughout the nineteenth century, the industrial city became increasingly segregated by function; large areas of the city were dedicated to the production of goods and services, surrounded by working-class neighborhoods. At the same time, the center of the city was remade into an area of consumption and leisure, with large department stores, theaters, clubs, restaurants, and nightclubs. In New York City during the last half of the nineteenth century, one of the foremost displays of such a culture of consumption was located along Broadway and Sixth Avenue between Union and Madison squares. This area was called Ladies' Mile because, as the new class of consumers, middle-class women were the major patrons of the large department stores that architecturally dominated the streets.

Although industrialization led to the creation of separate spheres—the female sphere centered on the home and domestic duties, the male sphere dominating the public spaces and duties—it also created the need for mass consumption to keep the factories running profitably. With men as the class of producers, the duties of consumption fell to the women. Moreover, the locational logic of the urban land market meant that retailers were located in the most central parts of the city. This established what some scholars have referred to as a feminized downtown, meaning not only that the downtown was characterized by the presence of middle- and upper-class women but also that the retailers themselves created spaces considered appropriately "feminine." Interior spaces were well-

Figure 10.21

Sketch of an African-American congregation in Washington, D.C. African-American churches often served as centers of community organizations and as public statements of identity in the industrializing cities of the north.

arranged and orderly, external architectural design was heavily ornamented, and streets were paved and well-lit (Figure 10.22).

Although this type of ornate and "feminine" downtown retailing area is still evident in large cities such as New York and San Francisco, the decentralizing forces in the twentieth-century city led to the abandonment of many of these areas, which have been replaced by the sub-

urban shopping mall (Chapter 11). It would be interesting to speculate in what ways the shopping mall is also a "feminine" space.

Megalopolis

In the nineteenth century, cities grew at unprecedented rates because of the concentration of people and commerce.

Figure 10.22

Stewart's department store. One of the most ornate department stores along Ladies' Mile in New York City was Stewart's, located on Broadway at 10th Street. Because the store catered to the needs of Victorian women, it can be considered an example of "feminine" space. **Can you think of other examples of such "feminine" spaces in your city, or in a city with which you are familiar?**

Movement away from the central city quickened in the last decades of the century. The inner city became increasingly dominated by commerce and the working class. In the twentieth century, particularly after World War II, new forms of transportation and communication led to the **decentralization** of many urban functions. One metropolitan area blends into another, until supercities are created that stretch for hundreds of miles.

The prototype of this new form is found on the eastern seaboard of the United States, stretching from Boston in the north to Washington, D.C., in the south. Some call it the supercity of "Boswash." The geographer Jean Gottmann coined the term **megalopolis** to describe it. This term is now used worldwide in reference to giant metropolitan regions such as Tokyo-Yokohama in Japan. These urban regions are characterized by high population densities extending over hundreds of square miles or kilometers; concentrations of numerous older cities; transportation links formed by freeway, railroad, air routes, and rapid transit; and an extremely high proportion of the nation's wealth, commerce, and political power.

The problems of the megalopolis come on a giant scale with such an immense concentration of people and activities. Common problems in these supercities are congestion, high land prices, overcrowding, financial insolvency, deteriorating inner cores, a poor and disenfranchised population in contrast to the affluent in the suburbs, and air and water pollution. Unfortunately, solutions to these problems will not be found soon, for another characteristic of megalopolitan areas is political fragmentation. Because most of the problems are region-wide, they go beyond the legal jurisdiction of the smaller towns and counties. Often they cross state borders. Solutions will come only with increased cooperation among all political units and the formation of regional agencies. Until then, the megalopolis will continue to grow, and its problems will increase.

Edge Cities

The past 20 years have witnessed an explosion in metropolitan growth in areas that had once been peripheral to the central city. Many of the so-called bedroom communities of the post–World War II era have been transformed into urban centers, with their own retail, financial, and entertainment districts (Figure 10.23). Author Joel Garreau refers to these new centers of urban activity as **edge cities,** although many other terms have been used in the past, including "suburban downtowns," "galactic cities," and "urban villages" (see Focus On: Cities on the Edge, Cities of the Future?). Most Americans now live, work, play, worship, and study in this type of settlement. What differentiates an edge city from the suburbs is that it is a

Figure 10.23

Edge City. These new centers of economic activity are located on the "edges" of traditional downtowns. **How does this image compare with the one in Figure 10.20?** (Walter Jimenez/TexStock Photo Inc.)

place of work, of productive economic activity, and therefore is the destination of many commuters. In fact, the conventional work commute from the suburbs to the inner city has been replaced by commuting patterns that completely encircle the inner city. People live in one part of an edge city and commute to their workplace in another part of that city.

Many scholars are wary of referring to these new nodes of activity as cities because they do not resemble our nineteenth-century vision of a city. Edge cities contain all the functions of old downtowns, but they are spread out and less dense, with clusters along major freeways and off-ramps. This new form is attributable to changes in Americans' lifestyles and to the development of new transportation and communication technologies. The interstate highway system made possible an effective trucking system to transport consumer goods, thereby

FOCUS ON

Cities on the Edge, Cities of the Future?

Edge City is any place that:

1. *Has five million square feet or more of leasable office space—the workplace of the Information Age.* Five million square feet is more than downtown Memphis. The Edge City called the Galleria area west of downtown Houston—crowned by the sixty-four-story Transco Tower, the tallest building in the world outside an old downtown—is bigger than downtown Minneapolis.

2. *Has 600,000 square feet or more of leasable retail space.* That is the equivalent of a fair-sized mall. That mall, remember, probably has at least three nationally famous department stores, and eighty to a hundred shops and boutiques full of merchandise that used to be available only on the finest boulevards of Europe. Even in their heyday, there were not many downtowns with that boast.

3. *Has more jobs than bedrooms.* When the workday starts, people head toward this place, not away from it. Like all urban places, the population increases at 9 A.M.

4. *Is perceived by the population as one place.* It is a regional end destination for mixed use—not a starting point—that "has it all," from jobs, to shopping, to entertainment.

5. *Was nothing like "city" as recently as 30 years ago.* Then, it was just bedrooms, if not cow pastures. This incarnation is brand new.

An example of the authentic, California-like experience of encountering such an Edge City is peeling off a high thruway, like the Pennsylvania Turnpike, onto an arterial, like Route 202 at King of Prussia, northwest of downtown Philadelphia. Descending into traffic that is bumper to bumper in both directions, one swirls through mosaics of lawn and parking, punctuated by office slabs whose designers have taken the curious vow of never placing windows in anything other than horizontal reflective strips. Detours mark the yellow dust of heavy construction that seems a permanent feature of the landscape.

Tasteful signs mark corporations apparently named after Klingon warriors. Who put Captain Kirk in charge of calling companies Imtrex, Avantor, and Synovus? Before that question can settle, you encounter the spoor of—the mother ship. On King of Prussia's Route 202, the mark of that mind-boggling enormity reads MALL NEXT FOUR LEFTS.

For the stranger who is a connoisseur of such places, this Dante-esque vision brings a physical shiver to the spine and a not entirely ironic murmur of recognition to the lips: "Ah! Home!" For that is precisely the significance of Edge Cities. They are the culmination of a generation of individual American value decisions about the best ways to live, work, and play—about how to create "home." That stuff "out there" is where America is being built. That "stuff" is the delicate balance between unlimited opportunity and rippling chaos that works for us so well. We build more of it every chance we get.

If Edge Cities are still a little ragged at the fringes, well, that just places them in the finest traditions of Walt Whitman's "barbaric yawp over the rooftops of the world"—what the social critic Tom Wolfe calls, affectionately, the "hog-stomping Baroque exuberance of American civilization." Edge Cities, after all, are still works in progress.

They have already proven astoundingly efficient, though, by any urban standard that can be quantified. As places to make one's fame and fortune, their corporate offices generate unprecedentedly low unemployment. In fact, their emblem is the hand-lettered sign taped to plate glass begging people to come to work. As real estate markets, they have made an entire generation of homeowners and speculators rich. As bazaars, they are anchored by some of the most luxurious shopping in the world. Edge City acculturates immigrants, provides child care, and offers safety. It is, on average, an improvement in per capita fuel efficiency over the old suburbia-downtown arrangement, since it moves everything closer to the homes of the middle class.

That is why Edge City is the crucible of America's urban future. Having become the place in which the majority of Americans now live, learn, work, shop, play, pray, and die, Edge City will be the forge of the fabled American way of life well into the twenty-first century.

enabling new industries to locate outside the downtown. Breakthroughs in computer and communication technologies have allowed corporate executives to move company headquarters out of the downtowns and into slick new glass buildings with parking garages, jogging paths, and picnic tables under the trees. Real-estate speculation in emerging edge cities has fueled their development, resulting in an environment that many people feel is ugly and chaotic. As Garreau points out, however, even a place as revered by designers as Venice, Italy, began as an ad hoc mercantilist adventure; and the Piazza San Marco was the result not of great urban planning but of the

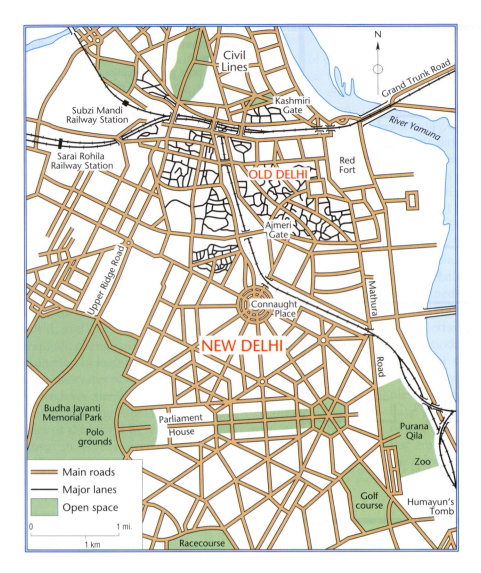

Figure 10.25
Map of Delhi and New Delhi, India. This map shows the contrast between the morphology and landscape of the indigenous city, Delhi, and the British colonial addition, New Delhi. Note the straight, symmetrical ceremonial boulevards and open space in the colonial city, expressions of Baroque planning in the colonial age. **How does it compare with the morphology of Old Delhi?** (After Drakakis-Smith, 1987: 20.)

few extreme cases, build a totally new city nearby. The British built New Delhi across from the original Delhi, and today the two still illustrate the contrast between colonial and indigenous cities. In old Delhi, gross density is 213 persons per acre (526 per hectare); in New Delhi, it is 13 persons per acre (32 per hectare). Old Delhi is medieval, with narrow, winding streets, little open space, and cramped residences (Figure 10.25). New Delhi, on the other hand, has wide streets; gardens surround the spacious houses of administrative staff; and parks and squares ring government buildings. All this reminds one of the Baroque period in Western urban development—and well it should. Much European colonialism was coincidental with the Baroque era, so it is not surprising that colonial cities express these planning ideas. As the Baroque style was used in Europe to express the power of the elite, so it was used in colonial cities. Grandiose boulevards were often cut through native residential quarters, large

monumental buildings demonstrated the presence of the new power structure, and the Europeans were housed in elaborate residences that constantly reminded locals of their new masters.

In his study of the city of Kandy, Sri Lanka, geographer James Duncan shows how British colonial rulers in the nineteenth century consciously manipulated the urban landscape to symbolize and reinforce their claims to legitimate rule. All the symbols of the former kingdom were either replaced by symbols of British rule or allowed to fall into disrepair (see Focus On: Colonial Rule Symbolized in the Urban Landscape of Kandy, Sri Lanka). For example, as Duncan states, the king's audience hall, located on hallowed ground between the Temple of the Relic and the palace, became the civic court during the week and the Anglican church on Sundays. In the alcove where the king of Kandy's throne once sat stood the pulpit, and behind it hung a picture of the English king. The palace of the king's relatives became the European hospital, and the queen's bath became a European library.

When new colonial cities were founded, they were often based on a standardized plan. For example, all Spanish cities in the New World were constructed according to the Laws of the Indies, drafted in 1573. The document explicitly outlined how colonial cities were to be constructed. According to the laws, a gridiron street plan was to be centered on a church and central plaza, and all individual lots were to be walled. Smaller plazas were to dot the neighborhoods, occupied by parish churches or monasteries, so that religious teaching would be evenly spread around the new city. In many ways, the formal guidelines for Spanish colonial cities duplicate the planning rules used by the Romans.

In some instances, the Spanish would superimpose their colonial cities on indigenous cities. For example, Mexico City was constructed on top of Tenochtitlán, the religious and political center of the Aztec culture (Figure 10.26 on the next page). As a type of cosmomagical city, Tenochtitlán had been laid out in a rectilinear pattern and could therefore fairly easily accommodate the Spanish colonial grid pattern.

Gendered Space and the Colonial City The goal of extending political control over foreign nations that characterized the policies of many western European nations in the nineteenth and early portions of the twentieth centuries is called **imperialism.** England, France, Germany, Spain, and the Netherlands scrambled to gain access to

FOCUS ON

Colonial Rule Symbolized in the Urban Landscape of Kandy, Sri Lanka

With the advent of British rule in Sri Lanka, the meaning of the urban landscape of Kandy was changed. A new cultural and political system had been ushered in, and the old landscape model that spoke of what had been important under the old system was being transformed or allowed to fall into ruination. Kandy was no longer the city of the god king, for he had been unceremoniously sent into exile. It was becoming a British colonial town and it had to look the part. The British realized that if they were to achieve legitimacy it would have to be largely on their terms. And while they never achieved the degree of legitimacy that they sought, they achieved a degree of cultural hegemony among the Sinhalese elites. This cultural hegemony was achieved in part through a conscious attempt to change the Sinhalese elites, but very largely it was achieved through an attempt to transform Kandy into an outlier of British culture. The assimilation was left to the Sinhalese themselves who were often all too ready to emulate the British. This creation of a bit of British culture in Kandy involved a transformation of the landscape of the place and the natural environment of the Kandyan area lent itself admirably to this task. Because of the elevation and topography of Kandy it was possible to create a facsimile of the landscape of home. One could see in residents' diaries and official plans the conscious attempt to transform Kandy into a hybrid that was part English and part Sinhalese. Their success in doing so was attested to in the journals and paintings of travelers who visited Kandy throughout the 19th century. Kandy was designed to resemble a romanticized image of a pre-industrial England. The landscape model of the English lake district was superimposed upon the mountains and the Kandy lake to recreate a place where English ladies and gentlemen could somehow escape the tropics and the native culture and symbolically return home.

And how exactly was this done? Promenades, such as Lady Horton's Walk, carriage drives such as Victoria Drive, and riding paths such as The Green Gallop, were created. The dense jungle around Kandy was pruned to reveal the best views of the town, the lake and the surrounding mountains. Travelers and residents alike often wrote about how one might "find enchanting views suddenly opening from the various points where the thick verdure of the trees has been judiciously cut away" (Dougherty 1890, p. 102) and that these openings, created an "exquisite framework through which . . . [to] see the distant landscape" (Cave 1912, p. 303). The term *sublime* was commonly used to describe the Kandyan landscape. English vegetables, fruits and trees were introduced and both formal and informal English gardens and parks were laid out. The Governor's Pavilion was laid out like an English country house situated in a parklike expanse of lawns and shrubbery overlooking the town, the lake and the mountains. Exclusive European residential quarters were located around the lake. English architect–designed bungalows, with their gardens full of roses and other English flowers climbed the hills from the lakeside. English style buildings predominated on the main thoroughfares such as Ward Street which contained the European stores like Cargills, Walker and Company, the Merchantile Bank, the Queen's Hotel, the Kandy Club, the Lawn Tennis Club, and the Planters Association of Ceylon.

Source: Agnew and Duncan, 1989: 192–193. Copyright © 1989 by John A. Agnew and James S. Duncan. Reprinted by permission of Routledge.

between economic growth and urbanization than there was in Europe. Cities increase in size not necessarily because there are jobs to lure workers, but rather because conditions in the countryside are so bad. People leave in hope that urban life will offer a slight improvement, and often it does. Given the new global economy, however, many of the jobs that are available in the cities of the Third World are low-skilled and low-paying manufacturing jobs, with harsh working conditions. The result is that rural-to-urban migrants often find themselves either unemployed or with jobs that barely provide them a living. In Europe during the nineteenth century, workers could migrate to the New World to find work or land. No such safety valve exists today in the emerging countries—the city is often the last hope. Recently, however, some scholars have noticed that in particular areas of the world where land rights have been maintained, some migrants return to their rural homelands when urban conditions deteriorate and leave open the possibility of migrating back to the city if economic trends reverse themselves, creating a sort of circular migration pattern.

Hance goes on to point out that emerging cities have weaker ties with their domestic **hinterlands** than did European cities. They are dependent on the outside world for raw materials. This means that the local countryside is excluded from the kind of development that could offer employment to rural populations. A vicious circle must be broken: people will leave the countryside for cities until jobs are available in the countryside, yet it will be difficult to develop rural employment as long as economic activities continue to cluster around cities.

Sociologist Alejandro Portes argues that the large internal migrations that bring impoverished agricultural people into the city are not a new phenomenon but one that can be traced back to colonial times. In colonial Latin America, for example, the city was essentially home to the Spanish elite, and when preconquest agricultural patterns were disrupted, peasants came to the city looking for economic livelihood. These people usually lived on the margins of the city and were completely disenfranchised, because only landowners had the right to hold office. The reaction by the elite to this ongoing pattern of movement of large masses of people into the city was a mixture of tolerance and indifference, with no one taking responsibility to integrate the migrants into the city. This pattern continues today in emerging cities.

The combination of large numbers of immigrants and widespread unemployment leads to overwhelming pressure for low-rent housing. Governments have rarely been able to meet these needs through housing projects, so one of the most common folk solutions has been construction of illegal housing: **squatter settlements,** or **barriadas.** In greater Cairo, for example, scholars estimate that 5.5 mil-

lion people live in squatter settlements (Figure 10.28). It is important to note, however, that such statistics often mislead, because what is considered unacceptable housing, or squatter settlements, varies by country and by household. As David Drakakis-Smith argues, "What is acceptable as adequate shelter to a poor household in São Paulo may be quite different from that of a similarly disadvantaged family in Singapore or Lagos."

Squatter settlements usually begin as collections of crude shacks constructed from scrap materials; gradually, they become increasingly elaborate and permanent. Paths and walkways link houses, vegetable gardens spring up, and often water and electricity are bootlegged into the area so that a common tap or outlet serves a number of houses. At later stages, such economic pursuits as handicrafts and small-scale artisan activities take place in the squatter settlements. In many instances, these supposedly temporary settlements become permanent parts of the city and function as many neighborhoods do—that is, as social, economic, and cultural centers. The story of one migrant named Sebastiano to the city of Arequipa, Peru, reveals how people negotiate their housing needs with the supply of legal and illegal housing available. It also shows the process by which barrios are actually built and often become "legal" (see Focus On: One Family's Tale on page 370).

Governments treat squatter settlements in various ways. Some bulldoze them periodically, not simply because they are illegal but also to discourage migration to the city. The reasoning is that if squatter settlements are destroyed, fewer migrants will come to the city, because they know that any housing solution they find will only be temporary. Some city governments turn their backs on the squatter settlements, viewing them as satisfactory solutions to the problem of low-cost urban housing. On the other hand, as Sebastiano's story reveals, some governments end up officially recognizing the de facto land rights of squatter settlers and provide civic services to these areas—creating, in effect, new urban neighborhoods with little outlay of resources.

Regardless of the official policy toward them, squatter settlements are an important part of the emerging city landscape. They occupy vacant land both on the outskirts and in the city center. Downtown parks are often covered by squatters' houses. More frequently, they spread over formerly unwanted land, such as steep slopes and riverbanks.

The outskirts of the growing cities manifest activities other than squatter settlement. This area is often where new economic activities are located, so a landscape of factories and warehouses is common. When government money is available, large high-rise apartment houses are built nearby for workers. Middle-class suburbs may also grow up, a function both of jobs in the outlying area for

Figure 10.28
Squatter settlements in Mexico City (*left*) and Kuala Lumpur (*right*). Migration to cities has been so rapid that often illegal squatter settlements have been the only solution to housing problems. (CAMERAMANN INTERNATIONAL, LTD.)

white-collar workers and of push factors driving the affluent out of the city center. Traffic noise, air pollution, and congestion make the central city less desirable than before, so those who can afford new housing often relocate. In some ways, this process is similar to the suburbanization of North American cities in the last decades, but because of the rapid growth of these emerging cities both in terms of sheer numbers of people and in expanse, scholars argue that this represents a different type of urban expansion. Some of these cities, such as Mexico City, Hanoi, and Manila, are expanding so rapidly out into the countryside that the city is encompassing or swallowing up smaller villages and rural areas. In this way, these new urban forms are blurring the distinction between the rural and the urban, creating what some scholars have called new types of regions: **extended metropolitan regions** (EMRs). These new urban regions are complex in both their landscape form and function because they developed rapidly, without any planning, and have in many cases incorporated preexisting places. These EMRs, therefore, include multiple nodes of economic activity, with few of those nodes any older than a decade. Scholars who write about Mexico City, for example, find it impossible to speak of the city as one place; rather, they suggest that it can now only be represented as a pastiche of different places, each with its own center and outlying neighborhoods.

Globalizing/Global Cities

The incredible population growth that characterizes these EMRs can best be explained with reference to the processes of *globalization*. Although globalization is dis-

cussed in more detail in Chapter 12, here it is important to understand the connection between globalizing economic and cultural processes and the development of new urban forms.

Global cities are cities that have become the control centers of the global economy—in other words, the places where major decisions about the world's corporations and financial markets are made. These cities house a concentration of multinational and transnational corporate headquarters, international financial services, media offices, and related economic and cultural services. As many industries and related economic activities have become global in the sense that their sites of production and consumption are spread throughout the world, the sites of decision-making have become centralized. According to sociologist Saskia Sassen, there are only three such cities operating at this level: New York City, London, and Tokyo. These cities have become, in many ways, the headquarters for a global economy.

Globalizing cities are those experiencing the major effects of the new global economy—whether that means transnational corporations establishing manufacturing plants in cities where there is a cheap labor force available; the global diffusion of American consumer culture, with McDonald's and Starbucks appearing in the center of Beijing; or the construction of high-rises to house the new managers and entrepreneurs of global business interests. In this sense, all cities can be referred to as globalizing. As geographer Brenda Yeoh indicates, cities have almost always been important hubs of activity beyond the national scale, and therefore it is not surprising that they figure prominently in discussions of the global economy.

FOCUS ON

One Family's Tale

Sebastiano and Maria used to live in a small village about 30 miles from Arequipa with Maria's parents. Work was difficult to obtain as the prices for the sugar that was grown in the area have been falling for years and only those with strong personal ties to the overseers were recruited. Sebastiano initially moved to Arequipa on his own in order to try to get work in the new factories in the city.

Sebastiano first moved into an inner city barrio with one of his distant cousins, but he only stayed there until he found out how the employment situation operated in Arequipa. Each day he would go to the western edge of the long-distance bus terminus where foremen from the building contractors would recruit their casual labor. Soon Sebastiano moved to his own rented room in a small house nearby. The accommodation was simple, even primitive, compared to his rural home. He had a bed, a cupboard and a recess for hanging his clothes. Washing was done at the tap in the yard.

All in all Sebastiano was reasonably happy with his rented room in the city center—he was near to his main source of work, to cheap services and he had an understanding landlord. The advertisements for the new low-cost housing schemes on the edge of the city held no appeal for him. He could not afford the regular rental demands, nor the transport costs to get into the city to find work.

However, Sebastiano did not want to live alone in the city. He missed his wife Maria and their young son Pedro. After a couple of years in the inner city he began to make inquiries about a plot in a new squatter barrio that was planned on some unused public land. His landlord knew someone who knew the local councilor and advised Sebastiano to go and talk to him. The councilor was impressed with Sebastiano's carpentry and building skills and recommended him to the informal committee that was organizing the 'invasion.' Sebastiano was accepted and with about ninety other families occupied the small piece of floodplain down by the river on the Ascension Day holiday when they knew the police would be busy elsewhere. Each family managed to put up basic walls and a roof on their allotted plot and, with the support of their councilor, were permitted to stay and improve their shelter as and when they could. They named the settlement St. Christopher as they were all travelers to the city. The municipal authorities knew better than to enforce the letter of the law. After all, these were determined, hard-working people who were housing themselves at no cost to the city government.

Eventually, sheer numbers forced the municipal authority to recognize the de facto rights of the settlement and to extend electricity, water, and sanitation services to the barrio. Access to regular water was a particularly important improvement, as residents had hitherto been forced to purchase from private water trucks at ten times the cost of the piped supply, but all of the upgraded services had resulted in a substantial improvement in the community's health and well-being. Sebastiano and Maria were now established members of the urban community.

Source: Drakakis-Smith, 2000: 158–159.

But some specific landscape forms are associated with these new globalizing cities, particularly those in the developing areas of the world. As we mentioned in our previous discussion of emerging cities, one such landscape form is the extended metropolitan region—a city that is expanding so rapidly into its surrounding countryside that there is a fusion of the urban and the rural. This form is particularly associated with primate cities in the developing world that are experiencing rapid population growth partly in response to the global economy. Multinational corporations often rely on the labor of new urban migrants, and so the city grows rapidly at the margins as factories are built in export processing zones (EPZ) (see Chapter 9) and squatter settlements emerge around them. At the same time, the downtowns of these cities often experience not dispersal but concentration: high-rises accommodate the regional offices of corporations and the services associated with them (media, advertising, personnel management, and so forth); and upper-class housing developments accommodate this new class of white-collar workers.

In addition, landscape forms associated with the global consumer, entertainment, and tourist economy are emerging: American-style shopping districts (with American stores) and new airports, hotels, restaurants, and entertainment facilities. Many of these landscape developments are funded by international investments. Entrepreneurs and governments in many parts of the world look to these new globalizing cities of the developing world as good places to make financial and real-estate investments. The extended metropolitan region of Hanoi, for example, is being built with funds from a range of countries (Figure 10.29): an export processing zone and a golf and entertainment facility are partly funded by Malaysia; South Korea is investing in a hotel, another golf course, and a

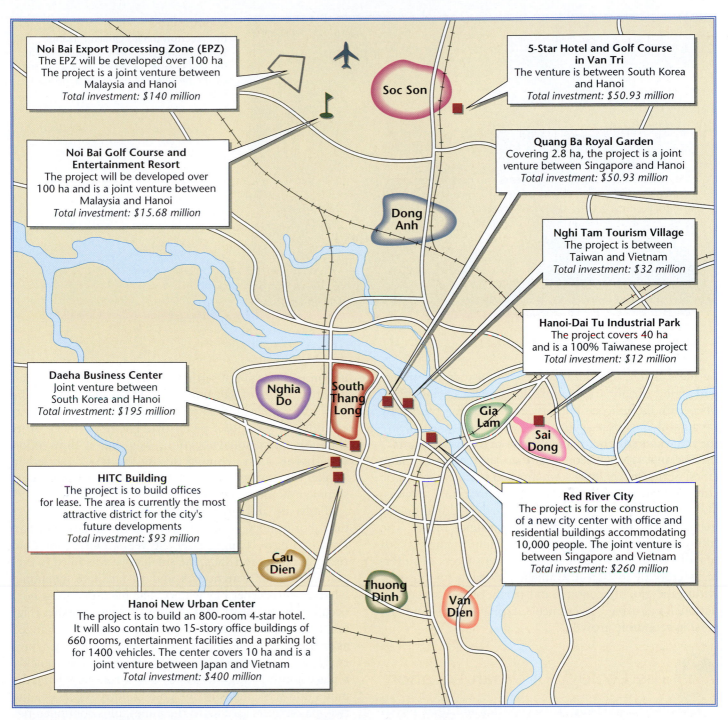

Noi Bai Export Processing Zone (EPZ)
The EPZ will be developed over 100 ha
The project is a joint venture between
Malaysia and Hanoi
Total investment: $140 million

**Noi Bai Golf Course and
Entertainment Resort**
The project will be developed over
100 ha and is a joint venture between
Malaysia and Hanoi
Total investment: $15.68 million

Daeha Business Center
Joint venture between
South Korea and Hanoi
Total investment: $195 million

HITC Building
The project is to build offices
for lease. The area is currently the most
attractive district for the city's
future developments
Total investment: $93 million

Hanoi New Urban Center
The project is to build an 800-room 4-star hotel.
It will also contain two 15-story office buildings of
660 rooms, entertainment facilities and a parking lot
for 1400 vehicles. The center covers 10 ha and is a
joint venture between Japan and Vietnam
Total investment: $400 million

**5-Star Hotel and Golf Course
in Van Tri**
The venture is between South Korea
and Hanoi
Total investment: $50.93 million

Quang Ba Royal Garden
Covering 2.8 ha, the project is a joint
venture between Singapore and Hanoi
Total investment: $50.93 million

Nghi Tam Tourism Village
The project is between
Taiwan and Vietnam
Total investment: $32 million

Hanoi-Dai Tu Industrial Park
The project covers 40 ha
and is a 100% Taiwanese project
Total investment: $12 million

Red River City
The project is for the construction
of a new city center with office and
residential buildings accommodating
10,000 people. The joint venture is
between Singapore and Vietnam
Total investment: $260 million

Soc Son   Dong Anh   Nghia Do   South Thang Long   Gia Lam   Sai Dong   Cau Dien   Thuong Dinh   Van Dien

Soc Son: Noi Bai International Airport is located in this area. Malaysia is investing in two projects there: a golf course and an EPZ.
Dong Anh: At the moment the area is one of the main vegetable-supplying sources for residents in Hanoi.
Nghia Do: Only five minutes from the West Lake, a property development area.
South Thang Long: Attracts a lot of foreign investment. The infrastructure is good, with the water supply system aided by the Finnish government.
Gia Lam Area: Called the "Daewoo area," it will soon become a satellite city of Hanoi.
Cau Dien: Recently approved project of traditional cultural tourism villages.
Thuong Dinh: Local industrial area.
Van Dien: An industrial park with infrastructure not yet developed. No foreign investment at present.

Figure 10.29

Diagram of Hanoi's extended metropolitan region. Foreign investment has been crucial to the spatial expansion of Hanoi, as you can see from the various projects under construction. **In what ways is this urban expansion different from edge cities?** (SOURCE: DRAKAKIS-SMITH, 2000: 24.)

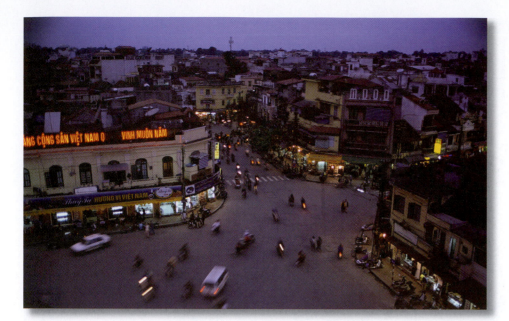

Figure 10.30
Intersection in Old Quarter, Hanoi.
Economic development is visible even in the Old Quarter of Hanoi, as you can see by the presence of neon lights. (MACDUFF EVERTON/CORBIS.)

business center; Taiwan is involved in a tourism project and an industrial park. Hanoi's downtown is being developed with more hotels and office construction funded by Japan and Singapore. Finland provided the infrastructure for the water supply to one of these new developments.

The new global economy, then, is reshaping many cities. Some, as we have seen, are becoming global cities: control centers for transnational corporations, services, and media. Others are heavily impacted by global investments in the manufacturing and consumer sector. The future of globalizing cities such as Hanoi (Figure 10.30) remains open, dependent partly on the success of differing sectors of foreign investment jockeying for position within the global economy and partly on the success of national and urban governments in planning for and dispersing economic growth.

The Ecology of Urban Location

What is the relationship between cities and their physical settings? Cultural ecology helps us understand how cultures have used and modified the physical environment during urban development. Interaction with the environment is a two-way street: humans may respond to different physical characteristics; at the same time, they may modify those characteristics to suit their needs.

Site and Situation

There are two components of urban location: site and situation. **Site** refers to the local setting of a city; the sit-

uation is the regional setting. As an example of site and situation, think of San Francisco. The original site of the Mexican settlement was on a shallow cove on the eastern (inland) shore of a peninsula. The importance of its situation, or regional location, was that it drew upon waterborne traffic coming across the bay from other, smaller settlements. Hence the town could act as a transshipment point.

Both site and situation are dynamic, changing over time. For example, both the site and the situation of San Francisco have changed over the years. During the gold rush period of the 1850s, the small cove was filled to create flatland for warehouses and to facilitate extending wharves into deeper bay waters. The filled-in cove is now occupied by the heart of the central business district (Figure 10.31). The geographical situation has also changed as patterns of trade and transportation technology have evolved. The original transbay situation was quickly replaced during the gold rush by a new role: supplying the mines and settlements of the gold country. Access to the two major rivers leading to the mines, plus continued ties to ocean trade routes, were the important components of the city's situation.

San Francisco's situation has changed dramatically in the last decade, for it is no longer the major port of the bay. The change in technology to containerized cargo was adopted more quickly by Oakland, the rival city on the opposite side of the bay, resulting in San Francisco's decline as a port city. One of the reasons that Oakland was able to adjust to containerized cargo was that it filled in huge tracts of shallow bay lands, creating a massive area for the loading, unloading, and storage of cargo containers.

Montgomery St

Shoreline,
1852 survey

Figure 10.31
This map shows how San Francisco's site has been changed by human activity. During the late 1850s, shallow coves were filled, providing easier access to deeper bay waters as well as flatland near the waterfront for warehouses and industry.

Certain attributes of the physical environment have been important in the location of cities. Those cities with distinct functions, such as defense or trade, have sought out specific physical characteristics in their original sitings. The locations of many contemporary cities can be partially explained by decisions made in the past that capitalized on the advantages of certain sites. The following classifications examine some of the different location possibilities.

Defensive Sites

There are many types of defensive sites for cities (some are diagrammed in Figure 10.32 on the next page). A **defensive site** is a location where a city can be easily defended. The *river-meander site*, with the city located inside a loop where the stream turns back on itself, leaves only a nar-

row neck of land unprotected by water. Cities such as Bern, Switzerland, and New Orleans are situated inside river meanders. Indeed, the nickname for New Orleans, Crescent City, refers to the curve of the Mississippi River.

Even more advantageous was the *river-island site*, which often combined a natural moat with an easy river crossing, because the stream was split into two parts. For example, Montreal is situated on a large island surrounded by the St. Lawrence River and other water channels. The *offshore-island site*—that is, islands lying off the seashore or in lakes—offered similar defensive advantages. Mexico City began as an Indian settlement on a lake island. Venice is the classic example of a city built on offshore islands in the sea. New York City began as a Dutch trading outpost on Manhattan Island.

Peninsula sites were almost as advantageous as island sites, because they offered natural water defenses on all

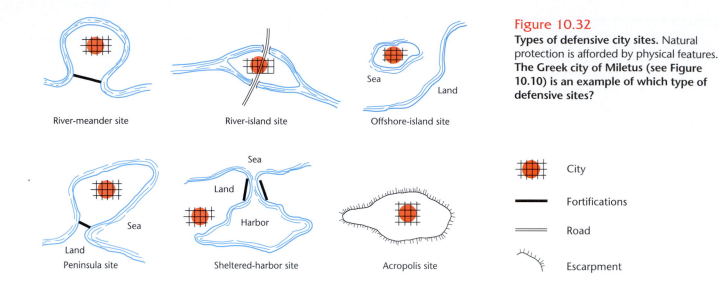

River-meander site

River-island site

Sea

Land

Offshore-island site

Peninsula site

Sea

Land

Sea

Harbor

Land

Sheltered-harbor site

Acropolis site

Figure 10.32

Types of defensive city sites. Natural protection is afforded by physical features. **The Greek city of Miletus (see Figure 10.10) is an example of which type of defensive sites?**

🟠 City

▬ Fortifications

═ Road

⌣⌣ Escarpment

but one side (Figure 10.33). Boston was founded on a peninsula for this reason, and a wooden palisade wall was built across the neck of the peninsula.

Danger of attack from the sea often prompted sheltered-harbor defensive sites, where a narrow entrance to the harbor could be defended easily. Examples of *sheltered-harbor sites* include cities such as Rio de Janeiro, Tokyo, and San Francisco.

High points also were sought out. These are often referred to as *acropolis sites;* the word *acropolis* means "high city." Originally the city developed around a fortification on the high ground and then spilled out over the surrounding lowland. Athens is the prototype of acropolis sites, but many other cities are similarly situated.

Trade-Route Sites

In many other instances, defense was not a primary consideration. Instead, urban centers were often built on **trade-route sites**—that is, at important points along trade routes. Here, too, the influence of the physical environment can be detected.

Especially common types of trade-route sites (Figure 10.34) are *bridge-point sites* and *river-ford sites,* places where major land routes could easily cross over rivers. Typically, these were sites where streams were narrow and shallow, with firm banks. Occasionally, such cities even bear in their names the evidence of their sites, as in Frankfurt ("ford of the Franks"), Germany, and Oxford,

Figure 10.33

The classic defensive site of Mont St. Michel, France. A small town clustered around a medieval abbey, which was originally separated from the mainland during high tides, Mont St. Michel now has a causeway that connects the island to shore, allowing armies of tourists to penetrate the town's defenses easily. (PHOTO RESEARCHERS.)

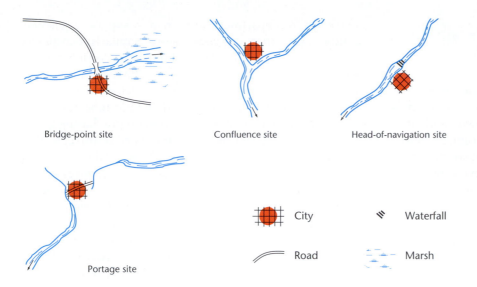

Figure 10.34
Trade-route city sites. These sites are at strategic positions along transportation arteries. **Is your city or one near you located on a trade-route site?**

Bridge-point site

Confluence site

Head-of-navigation site

Portage site

City   Waterfall

Road   Marsh

England. The site for London was chosen because it is the lowest point on the Thames River where a bridge—the famous London Bridge—could easily be built to serve a trade route running inland from Dover on the sea.

Confluence sites are also common. They allow cities to be situated at the point where two navigable streams flow together. Pittsburgh, at the confluence of the Allegheny and Monongahela rivers, is a fine example (Figure 10.35). *Head-of-navigation sites,* where navigable water routes begin, are even more common, because goods must be transshipped at such points. Minneapolis–St. Paul, at the falls of the Mississippi River, occupies a head-of-navigation site. Louisville, Kentucky, is located at the rapids of the Ohio

River. *Portage sites* are very similar. Here, goods were portaged from one river to another. Chicago is near a short portage between the Great Lakes and the Mississippi River drainage basin.

In these ways and others, an urban site can be influenced by the physical environment. Of course, many nonenvironmental factors can also influence the choice of site. Here, it is useful to distinguish between the specific urban site and the general location, or **spatial distribution,** of cities. Spacing implies a broader overall view of the pattern of urban centers. Site is often influenced by the environment, but the spacing of cities is less likely to be. The theme of cultural interaction will help us understand why cities are spaced as they are.

Figure 10.35
Pittsburgh's Golden Triangle. At the confluence of the Allegheny and Monongahela rivers, Pittsburgh is a classic example of how an early trade-route site has evolved into a commercial center. (HENRYK KAISER/LEO DE WYS, INC.)

Cultural Interaction in Urban Geography

How can we understand the location of cities as an integrated system? In recent decades, urban geographers have studied the spatial distribution of towns and cities to determine some of the economic and political factors that influence the pattern of cities. In doing so, they have created a number of models that collectively make up **central-place theory.** These models represent examples of cultural interaction.

Most urban centers are engaged mainly in the **tertiary industry** stage of production. Primary economic activities are extractive, such as agriculture, forestry, and mining. Construction and manufacturing are secondary activities, those that change the form of products. The tertiary activities of urban centers include transportation, communication, and utilities—services that facilitate the movement of goods and that provide the networks for the exchange of ideas about those goods (see Chapter 9 for a more detailed examination of these different industrial activities). Towns and cities that support such tertiary activities are called **central places.**

In the early 1930s, the German geographer Walter Christaller (see Profile on page 378) first formulated central-place theory, a series of models designed to explain the spatial distribution of tertiary urban centers. Crucial to his theory is the fact that different goods and services vary both in **threshold,** the size of the population required to make provision of the service economically feasible, and in **range,** the average maximum distance people will travel to purchase a good or service. For example, a larger number of people are required to support a hospital,

university, or department store than to support a gasoline station, post office, or grocery store. Similarly, consumers are willing to travel a greater distance to consult a heart specialist, record a land title, or purchase an automobile than to buy a loaf of bread, mail a letter, or visit a movie theater. People will usually spend as little time and effort as possible in making use of services and purchasing goods in a central place, but they will be obliged to travel farther to use those services that require a large market.

Because the range of central goods and services varies, urban centers are arranged in an orderly hierarchy. Some central places are small and offer a limited variety of services and goods; others are large and offer an abundance. At the top of this hierarchy are regional metropolises, huge urban centers that offer all services associated with central places and that have very large tributary trade areas, or hinterlands. At the opposite extreme are small market villages and roadside hamlets, which may contain nothing more than a post office, service station, or café. Between these two extremes are central places of various degrees of importance. Each higher rank of central place provides all the goods and services available at a lower-rank center, plus one or more additional goods and services. Central places of lower rank greatly outnumber the few at the higher levels of the hierarchy. One regional metropolis may contain thousands of smaller central places in its tributary market area (Figure 10.36). The size of the market area is determined by the distance range of the goods and services it offers.

With this hierarchy as a background, Christaller then tried to measure the influence of three forces in determining the spacing and distribution of tertiary centers. He accomplished this by creating models. His first model measured the influence of market and range of goods on

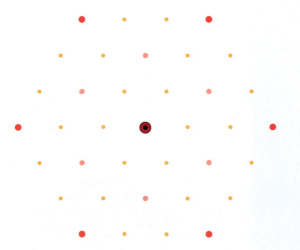

- ● First-order place (regional metropolis)
- ● Second-order place
- ● Third-order place
- ● Fourth-order place

Figure 10.36
Christaller's hierarchy of central places shows the orderly arrangement of towns of different sizes. This is an idealized presentation of places performing central functions. For each large central place, many smaller central places are located within the larger place's hinterland.

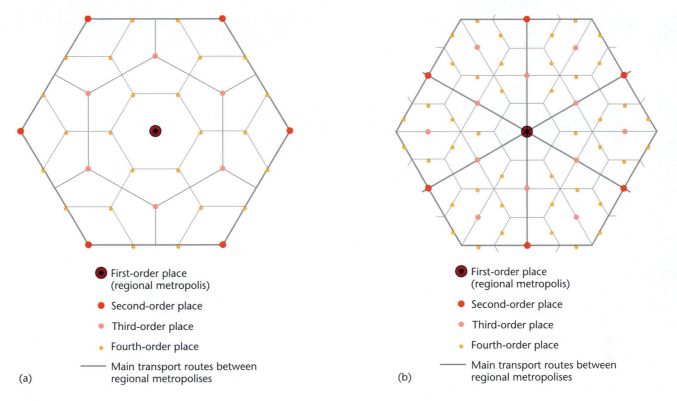

First-order place
(regional metropolis)

Second-order place

Third-order place

Fourth-order place

—— Main transport routes between
regional metropolises

(a)

First-order place
(regional metropolis)

Second-order place

Third-order place

Fourth-order place

—— Main transport routes between
regional metropolises

(b)

Figure 10.37

(a) The influence of market area on Christaller's arrangement of central places. If marketing were the only factor controlling the distribution of central places, this diagram would represent the arrangement of towns and cities. **Why, in this model, would hexagons be the shape to appear instead of a square, circle, or some other shape? (b) The distribution of central places according to Christaller's model.** If the availability of transportation is the determining factor in the location of central places, their distribution will be different from the distribution that would result if marketing were the determining factor. Note that the second-order central places are pulled away from the apexes of the hexagon and become located on the main transport routes between regional metropolises. (After Christaller, 1966. By permission of the publisher.)

the spacing of cities. To simplify the model, he assumed that the terrain, soils, and other environmental factors were uniform; that transportation was universally available; and that all regions would be supplied with goods and services from the minimum number of central places. In such a model, the shape of the market area was circular, encompassing the range of goods and services, with the city at the center of the circle. However, when central places of the same rank in the hierarchy were nearby, the circle became a hexagon (Figure 10.37a). If market and range of goods were the only causal forces, the distribution of tertiary towns and cities would produce a pattern of nested hexagons, each with a central place at its center.

Then Christaller created a second model. In this model, he tried to measure the influence of transportation on the spacing of central places. He no longer assumed that transportation was universally and equally available in

the hinterland. Instead, he assumed that as many demands for transport as possible would be met with the minimum expenditure for construction and maintenance of transportation facilities. Thus, as many high-ranking central places as possible would be on straight-line routes between important central places (Figure 10.37b). The transportation factor causes a rather different pattern of central places from the pattern caused by the market factor. This pattern results because direct routes between adjacent regional metropolises do not pass through central places of the next lowest rank. As a result, these second-rank central places are "pulled" from the points of the hexagonal market area to the midpoints to be on the straight-line routes between adjacent regional metropolises.

Christaller thought that the market factor would be the greater force in rural countries, where goods were seldom shipped throughout a region. He also thought that

PROFILE

(COURTESY GEOFFREY J. MARTIN.)

Walter Christaller

1893–1969

Although Christaller had a precocious beginning as a geographer, spending hours with an atlas as a youth, it was not until he was nearly 40 years old that he began his study of geography at a university. Christaller became a maverick among the geographers in Germany. His ideas about models were too radical for most of his fellow geographers in Nazi Germany to accept. As a result, he was never offered a professorship.

Christaller's classic work, *The Central Places of Southern Germany,* was written in the early 1930s as his doctoral dissertation in geography. In it, he proposed the central-place theory described in this chapter. Acceptance of central-place theory came belatedly, among American and Swedish geographers. Only in his later years did Christaller receive the honors due him.

the transportation factor would be stronger in densely settled industrialized countries, where there were greater numbers of central places and more demand for long-distance transportation.

Christaller devised a third model to measure a type of political influence: the effect of political borders on the distribution of central places. He recognized that political boundaries, especially within independent countries, would tend to follow the hexagonal market-area limits of each central place that was a political center. He also recognized that such borders tend to separate people and retard the movement of goods and services. Such borders necessarily cut through the market areas of many central places below the rank of regional metropolis. Central places in such border regions lose rank and size because their market areas are politically cut in two. Border towns are thus "stunted," and important central places are pushed away from the border, which distorts the hexagonal pattern.

Many other forces influence the spatial distribution of central places. Market area, transportation, and political borders are but three. For example, in all three of these models, it is assumed that the physical environment is uni-

form and that people are evenly distributed. Of course, neither of these is true, yet certain assumptions are necessary to construct a theoretical model that integrates different components of culture.

> ## Reflecting on **GEOGRAPHY**
>
> If these assumptions did not hold, in what ways would central-place theory need to be altered?

Conclusion

The first cities arose as new technologies, particularly the domestication of plants and animals, facilitated the concentration of people, wealth, and power in a few specific places. This transformation from village to city life was accompanied by new social organizations, a greater division of labor, and increased social stratification. These characteristics still distinguish rural and urban life. Although the first cities developed in specific hearths, urban life has now been diffused worldwide, and all indications are that our planet will become increasingly urban in the decades to come.

Many of the problems now plaguing our cities are expressions of uncorrected ills from the past. Traffic and housing problems in Europe, for example, may be understood in the context of the medieval urban landscape. Even though the landscape evolved 500 years ago, the narrow streets and cramped housing conditions of the medieval period still pervade the typical European central city.

Many problems of cities in the developing world are products of the twentieth century. Cities are bursting at the seams as thousands of new migrants crowd into urban places each day, seeking houses, jobs, and schooling. But jobs are scarce, so unemployment rates are often very high. Housing is also a problem. In some cities, over a third of the population lives in hastily constructed squatter settlements. Yet many of these same problems have historical roots, as an examination of the political and social history of colonial cities demonstrates. For example, massive rural-to-urban migration is not a new phenomenon. The disruptions of nineteenth-century colonial settlements deprived many people of their land and forced rural inhabitants into the city. This pattern continues today.

The future of the world's cities is uncertain. Strong governmental planning measures might alleviate many present-day ills, but the long-range hope lies with decreased population growth and increased economic opportunities. Whether this is possible under contemporary conditions remains to be seen.

SEEING GEOGRAPHY

Rio de Janeiro

Few cities boast such a spectacular site as Rio de Janeiro, located between the mountains and the Guanabara Bay along the Atlantic Ocean. This view looking southwest highlights the dramatic siting: the night lights of a bustling city, the colorful neon of the beaches, the outlines of rugged mountain peaks against the night sky. One can barely discern in this image the "other" side of Rio: the favelas, or squatter settlements, located on the mountainsides (although see Figure 10.2). Perched above the centers of economic activity and the middle- and upper-class residential areas located along the southern coastal areas of Rio, the favelas are an ever-present part of the urban landscape and are home to approximately one-fifth of the city's population.

The information in this chapter should help us to "read" this image of Rio de Janeiro. As a city of the developing world, Rio experienced rapid population growth in the twentieth century, and its metropolitan area now exceeds 11 million people. More striking is the dramatic increase in the urban population of Brazil. The percentage of the population living in metropolitan areas rose from approximately 31 percent in 1940 to about 78 percent in 1996. In Rio, that population growth is evident in the intensity of land use within the city, which is marked by the presence of skyscrapers; the metropolitan sprawl that extends well beyond the parameters of this image; and the presence of the favelas, home to many of the rural-to-urban migrants. Like other cities of the developing world, population growth has strained the city's infrastructure and its ability to provide services and has led to traffic congestion, pollution, and crime. It has also exacerbated ecological problems. When vegetation covered the hillslopes, the heavy summer rains Rio experiences were absorbed into the soil. Now the summer rains often flood the streets of the low-lying areas of the city and lead to landslides on the slopes that house the favelas. One such episode in 1996, for example, led to the death of 71 people, with approximately 2000 people left homeless. Yet Rio, like its larger neighbor 230 miles (370 km) to the south, São Paulo, is now experiencing much slower population growth (only 0.3 percent between 1991 and 1996) as a result of lower birthrates and less rural-to-urban migration.

Founded as a Portuguese colonial city in 1565, Rio grew quickly in the eighteenth century when it became the primary port for exporting the gold and diamonds discovered in the interior of the country. Later, in the first decades of the twentieth century, Rio underwent industrialization. The southern and coastal portions of the city that we see in this image became home to the elite, while the factories and working classes moved north and west of the downtown (out of the view of this image).

Today, Rio is part edge city (transit networks and economic nodes extend well beyond the frame of this image), part colonial city, and part global city. It is home to the regional headquarters of 10 multinational firms, marking it as a second- or third-level world city. Its beaches, particularly Ipanema and Copacabana, are icons for the global jet-setters. Yet its favelas, some of which have now been recognized by the government as legal communities, continue to grow, with little infrastructure and few public services. Like other globalizing cities, it experiences both the "bright lights" and the grimmer realities of the twenty-first century economic order.

What are some of the major environmental and social impacts of an increasingly urbanized world?

View of Rio de Janeiro from Sugarloaf Mountain.

The City on the Internet

To learn more about the city in time and space, check the following web sites:

City Beautiful: The 1901 Plan for Washington, D.C.

http://xroads.virginia.edu/~CAP/CITYBEAUTIFUL/dchome.html

An introduction to the City Beautiful movement, a late-nineteenth- and early-twentieth-century movement that attempted, through urban planning, to create more efficient and aesthetic cities.

Cyburbia: The Urban Planning Portal

http://www.cyburbia.org

A comprehensive directory of Internet resources about urbanism, planning, and architecture.

The Mega-City in Latin America

http://www.unu.edu/unupress/unupbooks/uu23me/uu23me00.htm#Contents

An online version of a book documenting urban growth in six Latin American cities.

United Nations Statistics Division

http://www.un.org/Depts/unsd/

The source for world population statistics, containing a comprehensive section on urbanization as a social indicator.

U.S. Department of Housing and Urban Development

http://www.hud.gov

Information about housing issues and urban economic development and about how to get involved personally in your own local community.

Sources

Agnew, John, John Mercer, and David Sopher. 1984. *The City in Cultural Context*. Boston: Allen & Unwin.

Agnew, John A., and James S. Duncan (eds.). 1989. *The Power of Place: Bringing Together Geographical and Sociological Imaginations*. Boston: Unwin Hyman.

Bell, Morag. 1995. "A Woman's Place in 'a White Man's Country'. Rights, Duties and Citizenship for the 'New' South Africa, c. 1902." *Ecumene* 2: 129–148.

Benevolo, Leonardo. 1980. *The History of the City*. Cambridge, Mass.: MIT Press.

Brown, Elsa Barkley, and Gregg D. Kimball. 1995. "Mapping the Terrain of Black Richmond." *Journal of Urban History* 21: 296–346.

Buswell, R. J., and M. Barke. 1980. "200 Years of Change in a 900-Year-Old City." *Geographical Magazine* 2: 81–83ff.

Carter, Harold. 1989. *An Introduction to Urban Historical Geography*. London: Edward Arnold.

Christaller, Walter. 1966. *The Central Places of Southern Germany*. C. W. Baskin (trans.). Englewood Cliffs, N.J.: Prentice-Hall.

Cosgrove, Denis. 1984. *Social Formation and Symbolic Landscape*. London: Croom Helm.

de Planhol, Xavier. 1959. *The World of Islam*. Ithaca, N.Y.: Cornell University Press.

Detwyler, Thomas, and Melvin Marcus (eds.). 1972. *Urbanization and Environment: The Physical Geography of the City*. Belmont, Calif.: Duxbury Press.

Domosh, Mona. 1995. "The Feminized Retail Landscape: Gender Ideology and Consumer Culture in Nineteenth-Century New York City," in Neil Wrigley and Michelle Lowe (eds.), *Retailing, Consumption and Capital*. Essex, U.K.: Longman.

Doxiades, C. A. 1972. *Architectural Space in Ancient Greece*. Cambridge, Mass.: MIT Press.

Drakakis-Smith, David. 1987. *The Third World City*. London: Methuen.

Drakakis-Smith, David. 2000. *Third World Cities*, 2nd ed. London: Routledge.

Duncan, James S. 1989. "The Power of Place in Kandy, Sri Lanka: 1780–1980," in John A. Agnew and James S. Duncan (eds.), *The Power of Place*. Boston: Unwin Hyman, 185–201.

Encyclopaedia Britannica. 1984. "Babylon." *New Encyclopaedia Britannica*, vol. 2. Chicago: Encyclopaedia Britannica.

Fowler, Melvin. 1975. "A Pre-Columbian Urban Center on the Mississippi." *Scientific American* (August): 93–102.

Garreau, Joel. 1991. *Edge City: Life on the New Frontier*. New York: Doubleday.

Gottmann, Jean. 1961. *Megalopolis*. Cambridge, Mass.: MIT Press.

Hance, William. 1970. *Population, Migration, and Urbanization in Africa*. New York: Columbia University Press.

Hayes, John. 1969. *London: A Pictorial History*. New York: Arco Publishing Company.

Hottes, Ruth. 1983. "Walter Christaller." *Annals of the Association of American Geographers* 73: 51–54.

Kenny, Judith T. 1995. "Climate, Race and Imperial Authority: The Symbolic Landscape of the British Hill Station in India." *Annals of the Association of American Geographers* 85: 694–714.

Mills, Sara. 1996. "Gender and Colonial Space." *Gender, Place and Culture* 3: 125–148.

Mumford, Lewis. 1961. *The City in History*. New York: Harcourt Brace Jovanovich.

Pirenne, Henri. 1996. *Medieval Cities*. Garden City, N.Y.: Doubleday (Anchor Books).

Portes, Alejandro. 1977. "Urban Latin America: The Political Condition from Above and Below," in Janet Abu-Lughod and Richard Hag, Jr. (eds.), *Third World Urbanization*. New York: Methuen, 59–70.

Pounds, Norman J. G. 1969. "The Urbanization of the Classical World." *Annals of the Association of American Geographers* 59: 135–157.

Samuels, Marwyn S., and Carmencita Samuels. 1989. "Beijing and the Power of Place in Modern China," in John A. Agnew and James S. Duncan (eds.), *The Power of Place*. Boston: Unwin Hyman, 202–227.

Sassen, Saskia. 1991. *The Global City: New York, London, Tokyo*. Princeton, N.J.: Princeton University Press.

Simon, D. 1984. "Third-World Colonial Cities in Context: Conceptual and Theoretical Approaches with Particular Interest to Africa." *Progress in Human Geography* 8: 493–514.

Sjoberg, Gideon. 1960. *The Preindustrial City*. New York: Free Press.

Spain, Daphne. 1992. *Gendered Spaces*. Chapel Hill: University of North Carolina Press.

Summerson, John. 1946. *Georgian London*. New York: Charles Scribner's Sons.

Vance, James E., Jr. 1971. "Land Assignment in the Pre-Capitalist, Capitalist and Post-Capitalist City." *Economic Geography* 47: 101–120.

Vance, James E., Jr. 1990. *The Continuing City: Urban Morphology in Western Civilization*. Baltimore: The Johns Hopkins University Press.

Ware, Vron. 1992. *Beyond the Pale: White Women, Racism and History*. London: Verso.

Warner, Sam Bass, Jr. 1972. *Urban Wilderness*. New York: Harper & Row.

Wheatley, Paul. 1971. *The Pivot of the Four Quarters*. Chicago: Aldine Publishing Company.

Yeoh, Brenda, S. A. 1999. "Global/Globalizing Cities." *Progress in Human Geography* 23: 607–616.

Ten Recommended Books on Urban Geography

(*For additional suggested readings, see* The Human Mosaic *web site:* www.whfreeman.com/jordan)

Boyer, M. Christine. 1996. *The City of Collective Memory: The Historical Imagery and Architectural Entertainments*. Cambridge, Mass.: MIT Press. A wide-ranging analysis of the role of history and memory in the shaping and function of contemporary Western cities.

Cravey, Altha. 1998. *Women and Work in Mexico's Maquiladoras*. Lanham, Md.: Rowman and Littlefield. A detailed analysis of the industrialization of Mexico and the role of women workers in maquiladoras.

Harvey, David. 1985. *The Urban Experience*. Baltimore: The Johns Hopkins University Press. A study of the relationship between capitalist economics and the cities it produces.

King, Anthony. 1990. *Urbanization, Colonialism and the World Economy*. Routledge: London. An examination of how colonialism shaped the geography of cities.

Knox, Paul, and Peter J. Taylor (eds.). 1995. *World Cities in a World System*. Cambridge: Cambridge University Press. An edited collection that examines the social and economic role of cities within the contemporary world system.

Legates, Richard T., and Frederic Stout (eds.). 1999. *The City Reader*, 2nd ed. New York: Routledge. An extensive edited collection of readings covering the evolution of cities and the contemporary forces that are restructuring them.

Marcuse, Peter, and Ronald Van Kempen (eds.). 2000. *Globalizing Cities: A New Spatial Order?* Oxford: Blackwell Publishers. A collection of studies of the impact of globalization on the spatial form of cities, from Singapore to Calcutta to New York.

Ogborn, Miles. 1998. *Spaces of Modernity: London's Geographies 1680–1780*. New York: Guilford Press. A historical study of the making of modernity within the spaces of eighteenth-century London.

Rose, Gillian, and Alison Blunt (eds.). 1994. *Writing Women and Space: Colonial and Postcolonial Geographies*. New York: Guilford Press. An edited collection that analyzes relationships between gender and colonial space, with several case studies focusing on urban space.

Stansell, Christine. 1987. *City of Women: Sex and Class in New York, 1789–1860*. Urbana: University of Illinois Press. An in-depth study of the contributions of working-class women to the making of modern New York.

Major Journals in Urban Geography

International Journal of Urban and Regional Research. Published by Edward Arnold, London. Volume 1 appeared in 1987.

Urban Geography. Published by Belwether Press, Lanham, Md. Volume 1 appeared in 1976.

How has globalization affected urban ethnic neighborhoods?

A street in Chinatown, New York City. (Bojan Brecelj/Corbis.)
Turn to Seeing Geography *on page 419 for an in-depth analysis of the above question.*

INSIDE THE CITY
A Cultural Mosaic

Finding patterns in a city can be a difficult matter. As you walk or drive through a city, its intricacy may dazzle you, and its form may seem chaotic. It is often hard to imagine why city functions are where they are, why people cluster where they do. Why does one block have high-income housing and another, slum tenements? Why are ethnic neighborhoods next to the central business district? Why does the highway run through one neighborhood and around another? Just when you think you are beginning to understand some patterns in your city, you note that those patterns are swiftly changing. The house you grew up in is now part of the business district. The central city that you roamed as a child looks dead. A suburban shopping center thrives on what was once farmland.

Chapter 10 focused on cities as points in geographical space. In this chapter, we try to orient ourselves within cities to gain some perspective on the patterns they hold. In other words, the two chapters differ in scale. In Chapter 10, we looked at cities from afar, as small dots diffusing across space and interacting with one another and with their environment. In this chapter, we study the city as if we were walking its streets.

Our tour guides in this close-up view of the city are the five familiar themes of cultural geography. Through culture region, we examine spatial differences within cities. Cultural diffusion shows how these internal and regional differences develop. Cultural ecology permits us to see the role of the physical environment within the structure of the city. Through cultural interaction, we see what a finely woven fabric the city really is. Of course, the visual impact of these elements is revealed in the urban landscape, a "townscape" perceived in different ways by different people.

Figure 11.1
The CBD of Boston. Notice the high density of land uses and the presence of skyscrapers that characteristically mark the CBD. (GEORG GERSTER/PHOTO RESEARCHERS, INC.)

 Urban Culture Regions

How are areas within a city spatially arranged? Much of the fascination of urban life comes from its diversity, from the excitement of different groups of people and different types of activities packaged in a fairly small area. Yet within this diversity, it is possible to discern regional patterns, because cities are composed of a series of districts, each of which is defined by a particular set of land uses.

Downtowns

For example, in the center of the typical U.S. city is the **central business district (CBD),** a dense cluster of offices and shops (Figure 11.1). The CBD is formed around the point within the city that attains maximum accessibility. In other words, businesses and services that are located in the CBD experience the most "action" as measured by the movement of people, money, and ideas and by the possibility for face-to-face communication. The competition for the most accessible space often leads to the construction of skyscrapers, creating a skyline that allows for the instant recognition of a city's CBD. These tall buildings tend to house financial services, corporate headquarters, and related services such as advertising and public relations firms. Just beyond the skyscrapers are often four- and five-story buildings that house the city's main shopping district, traditionally centered around several department stores. Also within the CBD are concentrations of smaller retail establishments, transportation hubs such as railroad sta-

tions, and often civic centers such as a city hall and main library. Surrounding the CBD is an area geographers call the zone in transition, because it is situated between the core commercial area and the outlying residential areas. It is a district of mixed land uses, characterized by older residential buildings, warehouses, small factories, and apartment buildings.

Residential Areas

Beyond the zone in transition are various types of residential communities, or regions. Geographers have studied these culture regions in depth, trying to discern patterns of diverse peoples living in a city. Some have focused on the idea of a **social culture region:** a residential area characterized by socioeconomic traits, such as income, education, age, and family structure. Other researchers who use the notion of **ethnic culture region** highlight traits of ethnicity, such as language and migration history. Obviously the two concepts overlap, because there can be social regions within ethnic regions and vice versa. Let's also remember that some researchers choose to look at both social and ethnic culture regions as functions of the political and economic forces underlying and reinforcing residential segregation and discrimination. (More information on ethnic areas is found in Chapter 5.)

One way to define social culture regions is to isolate one social trait and plot its distribution within the city. The U.S. census is a common source of such information because the districts used to count population, called **census tracts,** are small enough to allow the subtle texture of

Figure 11.2
An inner-city neighborhood near the Capitol in Washington, D.C. One of the most pressing problems facing the United States is reversing the continued decay of inner cities. **What factors have led to this decay of the inner city?** (For help, look at the section called "Suburbanization and Decentralization" in this chapter.)
(CAMERAMANN INTERNATIONAL, LTD.)

social regions to show. One of the more common social traits to be mapped is income. The patterns that result from a mapping of social regions determined by income form the basis of many urban land use models that are discussed later in the chapter (see "Cultural Interaction and Models of the City").

In addition to income, another important characteristic that often distinguishes one urban residential area from another is ethnicity. This is certainly not surprising, given the history of immigration to North America in the nineteenth and twentieth centuries and the propensity of immigrants to move to cities. During the middle to late nineteenth century, when waves of migrants left eastern and southern Europe, they arrived in North America at port cities and often took employment there as laborers in factories. With limited affordable housing available, most immigrants settled close to one another, forming ethnic communities or pockets within the mosaic of the city. Within these ethnic urban regions—with names such as Little Italy in New York and Chinatown in San Francisco—people were often able to maintain their native languages, holidays, foodways, and religions. Although the names of these urban enclaves still exist today, most of these regions have been transformed by new and different waves of immigrants who have arrived in North America in the past 20 years. Little Italy, for example, is now home to people from East and Southeast Asia, with Italian restaurants vying for space with noodle houses. We will discuss this new urban ethnicity later in the chapter. For now, what is important to note is that cities are composed of culture regions, some of which are defined by types of land use (the CBD), some by social indices (a middle-class district), some by ethnicity, and some by a combination of these and other social, economic, or cultural indicators (Figures 11.2 above and 11.3 on the next page).

> ## Reflecting on **GEOGRAPHY**
>
> As we look at these urban regions, various questions concern the cultural geographer: How do ethnic and social regions differ? Why do people of similar social traits cluster together? What subtle patterns might be found within these regions? How does one delimit different kinds of urban districts?

Social culture regions are not merely statistical definitions. They are also areas of shared values and attitudes, of interaction and communication. The concept of a **neighborhood** is often used to describe small social culture regions where people with shared values and concerns interact daily. For example, if we consider only census figures, we might find that parents between 30 and 45 years of age, with two or three children, and earning between $50,000 and $75,000 a year cover a fairly wide area in any given city. Yet, from our own observations, we know intuitively that this broad social area is probably composed of smaller units of social interaction where people link a sense of community with a specific locale.

A conventional sociological explanation for neighborhoods is that people of similar values cluster together to reduce social conflict. Where a social consensus exists about such mundane issues as home maintenance, child

Figure 11.3
Middle-income neighborhoods in Reston, Virginia. Social areas within the city can be delimited by certain traits taken from the census, such as income, education, or family size. **How would the social characteristics of this neighborhood differ from those in Figure 11.2?** (CAMERAMANN INTERNATIONAL, LTD.)

rearing, everyday behavior, and public order, there is little daily worry about these matters. People who deviate from this consensus will face social coercion that could force them to seek residence elsewhere, thus preserving the values of the neighborhood. Because this definition of neighborhood emphasizes people of like mind and background who choose to live together, it celebrates the social homogeneity or sameness of small spatial communities.

Increasingly, though, we find neighborhoods with more heterogeneity than this traditional definition would allow. Consequently, the current conceptualization of neighborhoods is more flexible and embraces traditional components of locality, such as geographical territoriality, political outlook, and shared economic characteristics. It also emphasizes the consensus that comes from both insiders and outsiders perceiving a certain area as a neighborhood. For example, a neighborhood might be ethnically and socially diverse, yet also think of itself as a social community sharing similar political concerns, hold neighborhood meetings to address these problems, and achieve recognition at city hall as a legitimate group with political standing. A recent article in the *New York Times* documenting the new ethnic composition of Woodside, Queens, is titled "From a Babel of Tongues, a Neighborhood" (Figure 11.4). For much of the late nineteenth century and into the late twentieth century, Woodside was predominantly an Irish-American community, but recent immigration has remade Woodside into a diverse neighborhood. In 1990, 55 percent of its residents were foreign-born: 29 percent from Europe, 37 percent from Asia, 23 percent from South and Central America, and 11 percent from other regions of the world. In struggling

for decent schools, housing, and jobs, many residents have united and forged a coalition of interests and a sense of communal identity—which are keystones of a neighborhood.

The concept of neighborhood usually implies that people have access to a permanent or semipermanent place of residence. In the cities of the United States, however, we increasingly find that many people are homeless and divorced from the ties of neighborhood. It is nearly impossible to determine the exact number of homeless people in the United States. Definitions of **homelessness** vary, depending on the criteria used and the cultural context of the particular situation. For example, does living in a friend's house for more than a month constitute a homeless condition? How permanent does a shelter have to be before it is considered a "home"? To some people, home connotes a suburban middle-class house; to others, it simply refers to a room in a city-owned shelter. Geographer April Veness has studied these various and often contested definitions of home and homelessness and has concluded that attempts to house the homeless are often bound up with middle-class, suburban definitions of home (see Focus On: Designer Homeless Shelters in the City on page 389).

Reflecting on GEOGRAPHY

Why is home such a difficult concept to define? How does it differ from the concept of a house?

In addition, homeless people are often not counted in the census or other population surveys. Our estimates of

Figure 11.4

Woodside, Queens, New York City. Once home to Irish immigrants, Woodside is now the destination of immigrants from a wide range of countries. **In what ways are these new ethnic neighborhoods different from those of the Irish-Americans? In what ways do you think they are similar?** (JAMES ESTRIN/NYT PICTURES.)

the number of homeless, therefore, are only rough approximations. Recent studies suggest that there are up to 3 million homeless persons in the United States, concentrated in the downtown areas of large cities, often in what we call the zone in transition (see the later section, "Cultural Interaction and Models of the City").

The causes of homelessness are varied and complex. Many homeless people suffer from some type of disorder or handicap that contributes to their inability to maintain a job and obtain adequate housing. Most have been marginalized in some way by the economic problems that have plagued the United States since the early 1980s, and therefore they have been left out of the housing market. Deprived of the social networks that a permanent neighborhood provides, the homeless are left to fend for themselves. Most cities have tried to provide temporary shelter, but many homeless people prefer to rely on their own social ties for support to maintain some sense of personal pride and privacy. In a study of the Los Angeles skid row district, Stacy Rowe and Jennifer Wolch explored how homeless women formed new types of social networks and established a sense of community to cope with the day-to-day needs of physical security and food (Figure 11.5 on the next page). This study points to the importance of social ties in maintaining personal identity and helps us understand the magnitude of a problem that deprives people of their home and neighborhood.

In summary, the neighborhood concept is central to the cultural geography of cities because it recognizes the sentiment people have for places and their attachment to them. It also recognizes how attachment becomes the basis for ongoing social and political action.

 Cultural Diffusion in the City

How can we understand the spatial movement of people and activities in the city? The patterns of activities we see in the city result from thousands of individual decisions about location. Where should we locate our store—in the central city or the suburbs? Where should we live—downtown or outside the city? The result of such decisions might be expansion at the city's edge or the relocation of activities from one part of the city to another. The cultural geographer looks at such decisions in terms of expansion and relocation diffusion (see Chapter 1).

To understand the role of diffusion, let us divide the city into two major areas, the inner city and the outer city. Those diffusion forces that result in residences, stores, and factories locating in the inner or central city are **centralizing forces.** Those that result in activities locating outside the central city are called **decentralizing forces,** or suburbanizing forces. The pattern of homes, neighborhoods, offices, shops, and factories in the city results from the constant interplay of these two forces.

Centralization

We can best examine centralization by breaking it into two categories: economic advantages and social advantages.

Economic Advantages An important economic advantage of central-city location has always been accessibility. For example, imagine that a department store seeks a new location. Its success depends on whether customers can

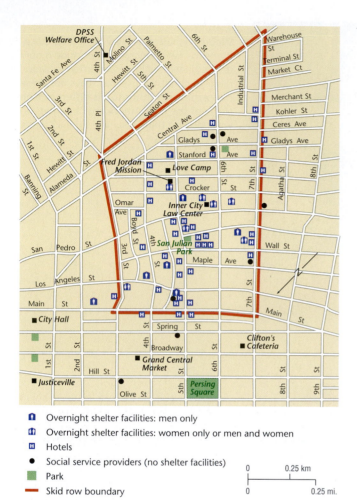

Overnight shelter facilities: men only

Overnight shelter facilities: women only or men and women

Hotels

Social service providers (no shelter facilities)

Park

Skid row boundary

0   0.25 km

0   0.25 mi.

Figure 11.5

The distribution of services for the homeless in the skid row district of Los Angeles. The population of the area is difficult to estimate, ranging from 6000 to 30,000. There are approximately 2000 shelter beds in the area, half of which are available to women. Single-room-occupancy hotels provide about 6700 units of longer-term housing. More than 50 social service programs are run through agencies, missions, and shelters. Love Camp and Justiceville are the sites of informal street encampments of homeless people. (AFTER ROWE AND WOLCH, 1990.)

Location near regional transportation facilities is another aspect of accessibility. Many a North American city grew up with the railroad at its center. Hence, any activity that needed access to the railroad had to locate in the central city. In many urban areas, giant wholesale and retail manufacturing districts grew up around railroad districts. Thus, they became "freight-yard and terminal cities" for the produce of the nation. Today, although many of these areas have been abandoned by their original occupants, a walk by the railroad tracks will give the most casual pedestrian a view of the modern "ruins" of the railroad city.

Another major economic advantage of the inner city is **agglomeration,** or clustering, which results in mutual benefits for businesses. For example, retail stores locate near one another to take advantage of the pedestrian traffic each generates. A large department store generates a good deal of foot traffic, so that any nearby store will also benefit.

Historically, offices clustered together in the central city because of their need for communication. Remember, the telephone was invented only in 1875. Before that, messengers hand-carried the work of banks, insurance firms, lawyers, and many other services. Clustering was essential for rapid communication. Even today, office buildings tend to cluster because face-to-face communication is still important for businesspeople. In addition, central offices take advantage of the complicated support system that grows up in a central city and aids everyday efficiency. Printers, bars, restaurants, travel agents, and office suppliers must be in easy reach.

Social Advantages Three social factors have traditionally reinforced central-city location. These are historical momentum, prestige, and the need to locate near work. The strength of historical momentum should not be underestimated. Many activities remain in the central city simply because they began there long ago. For example, the financial district in San Francisco is located mainly on Montgomery Street. This street originally lay along the waterfront, and San Francisco's first financial institutions were established there in the mid-nineteenth century because it was the center of commercial action. In later years, however, landfill extended the shoreline (see Figure 10.31). Today, the financial district is several blocks from the bay; consequently, the district that began at the wharf head remained at its original location, even though other activity moved with the changing shoreline.

The prestige associated with the downtown area is also a strong centralizing force. Some activities still necessitate a central-city address. Think how important it is for some advertising firms to be on New York's Madison

reach the store easily. If its potential market area is viewed as a full circle, then naturally the best location is in the center. There, customers from all parts of the city can gain access with equal ease. Before the automobile, a central-city location was particularly necessary because public transportation—such as the streetcar—was usually focused there. A central location is also important to those who must deliver their goods to customers. Bakeries and dairies usually were located as close as possible to the center of the city so that their daily deliveries would be most efficient.

FOCUS ON

Designer Homeless Shelters in the City

Transfer of government welfare responsibilities to local, often nonprofit, institutions, growing criticism by a public suspicious of the homeless in general, and local political decisions that increasingly monitor and manage the activities of those organizations that assist the homeless have led to the creation of a group of shelters whose outlook and roles differ from shelters established prior to the 1980s. These designer shelters have been given the role of remaking homeless people to fit a middle-class model of home. While this role, and the practices that must be reproduced in the shelter to make the role successful, is intended to help homeless/poor people, it may not live up to this goal. Under pressure to demonstrate that homeless people are home-worthy and home-ready, designer shelters must select among the homeless group those people whose attitudes and activities conform to normative expectations. People who cannot or will not conform are left to make do in whatever homes they can fashion for themselves. Meanwhile, people who do enter the designer shelter may find habits and attitudes that sustained them in a life of economic poverty questioned and devalued.

Personal observations of life in various shelters in Delaware demonstrate how service providers routinely identify residents' habits that do not conform with their ideals of appropriate home life. House rules, which are typed up and distributed to residents at the time they are admitted into the shelter, outline exactly which types of behavior are forbidden and favored. Embedded in these rules are some fairly obvious, and anachronistic, class-based assumptions about what constitutes a good home. Likewise there are many mixed messages and contradictions. In one shelter, for example, it is forbidden for residents to walk around the common rooms without shoes (although slippers in the evening are permissible). Nor are they allowed to lend or borrow items among themselves; to enter one another's rooms or child-sit for another; to do any personal grooming outside of bath or bedrooms; and to rearrange furniture in their rooms. Favored are "positive, constructive lifestyles," cleanliness and orderliness, and "disciplining children with love."

Women routinely complain that the traditional support systems upon which they rely are not approved of in the shelter. Sharing resources and responsibilities across rather fluid family and, by extension, friendship boundaries are common in lower-income black communities. This strategy of pooling and exchanging resources often enables poor families to seek and retain employment, to avoid evictions, to pay for emergency needs, and to instill in their children a sense of cooperation and confidence in the future. But this trait does not conform to middle-class definitions of the nuclear family and middle-class home life. Thus homeless women are given a model of home life in the shelter that supposedly is intended to enable them but that may in fact constrain them. For many of these women, marriage, a traditional nuclear family, and the ability to purchase the accouterments of middle-class home life all at one time are highly unlikely.

Another limitation is that while designer shelters hold open for poor people the expectation that they can enter the middle class, this expectation is by no means guaranteed. If we actively push a model of home on poor people that fulfills society's version of what home should be but may do little for the people it is intended to help, what are the consequences? Is it enough to press for shelter and measure our successes by the number of shelters that get sited or the numbers of people who leave the shelter for homes of their own?

Designer shelters in the city may well be relying on forms of oppression when they uphold a model of home that is socially constructed. These shelters emerged at a time and in a place when sponsors of the ideal felt that there was much to be gained for the homeless. Because many of the criteria upon which ideal homes, hence designer shelters, were built are arbitrary, elusive, and inherently exclusionary, it seems highly unlikely that the poor will be the benefactors of present-day efforts to rehome them. The designer shelter seems to be an old rehabilitative strategy packaged into a new institutional form. In our efforts to eliminate homelessness we need to take into account the various models of home that exist, as well as the limits of our compassionate responses and social justice strategies.

Avenue or for a stockbroker to be on Wall Street. This factor extends to many activities in cities of all sizes. The "downtown lawyer" and the "uptown banker" are examples. Residences have often been located in the central city because of the prestige associated with it. Most cities have remnants of high-income neighborhoods close to the downtown area. Although this trend has weakened in North America—downtown areas have become more congested and noisy, and transportation has encouraged suburban residences—it is still important elsewhere. London

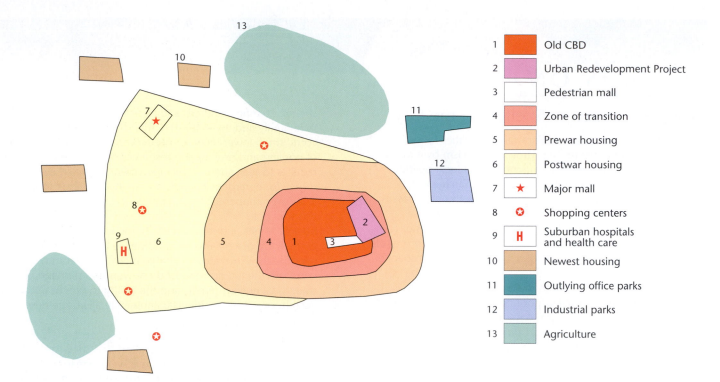

1		Old CBD
2		Urban Redevelopment Project
3		Pedestrian mall
4		Zone of transition
5		Prewar housing
6		Postwar housing
7	★	Major mall
8	✪	Shopping centers
9	H	Suburban hospitals and health care
10		Newest housing
11		Outlying office parks
12		Industrial parks
13		Agriculture

Figure 11.6

A hypothetical decentralized city. While the old central business district (CBD) struggles (vacant stores and upper floors), newer activities locate either in the Urban Redevelopment Project (offices, convention center, hotel) or in outlying office parks, malls, or shopping centers. However, some new specialty shops might be found around the new downtown pedestrian mall. New industry locates in suburban industrial parks that, along with outlying office areas, form major destinations for daily lateral commuting. **In what ways does your city follow this hypothetical pattern? In what ways does it differ?**

and Paris have very prestigious neighborhoods directly in the downtown area.

Probably the strongest social force for centralization has been the desire to live near one's employment. Until the development of the electric trolley in the 1880s, most urban dwellers had little alternative but to walk to work. Most people had to live near the central city because most employment was there. Upper-income people had their carriages and cabs, but others had nothing. Even after the introduction of electric streetcar lines in the 1880s, which made possible the exodus of some middle-class residents, many people continued to walk to work, particularly those who could not afford the new housing being constructed in what Sam Bass Warner, Jr., has called "streetcar suburbs."

Suburbanization and Decentralization

The past 40 years have witnessed massive changes in the form and function of most Western cities (Figure 11.6). In the United States in particular, the suburbanization of res-

idences and the decentralization of workplaces have emptied many downtowns of economic vitality. How and why has this happened? Geographer Neil Smith argues that the processes of suburbanization and decline of the inner city are fundamentally linked, because capital investment in the suburbs is often made possible by disinvestment, or the removal of money, from the central city. In post–World War II America, investors found greater returns on their money in the new suburbs than they did in the inner city, and therefore much of the economic boom of this time period took place in the suburbs at the expense of the city. Smith refers to these processes as **uneven development** (Figure 11.7). This type of explanation gives us a broad picture of the economic reasons that many cities are now decentralized. We will now look more locally, as we examine specific socioeconomic and public policy causes for the decentralization of our cities and for the problems that have resulted.

Socioeconomic Factors Changes in accessibility have been a major reason for decentralization. The department

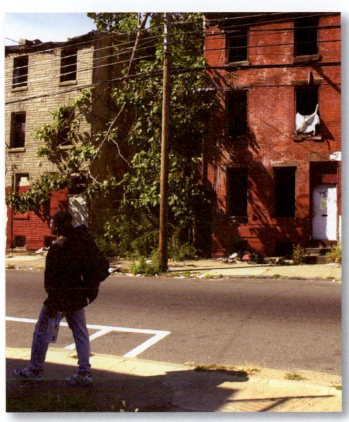

Figure 11.7

Abandoned row houses in North Philadelphia. Often the economic neglect of these areas is directly linked to economic investment in the suburbs. (ASSOCIATED PRESS.)

store that originally located in the central city may now find that its customers have moved to the suburbs. They no longer shop downtown. As a result, the department store may move to a suburban shopping mall. The same process also occurs among industries such as food-processing plants. They must move away to minimize transportation costs. The activities that were located downtown because of the railroad may now find trucking more effective. They relocate closer to a freeway system that skirts the downtown area. And many offices now locate near airports so that their executives and salespeople can fly in and out more easily.

Although agglomeration once served as a centralizing force, its former benefits have now become liabilities in many downtown areas. These disadvantages include increased rents as a result of the high demand for space; congestion in the support system, which causes delays in getting supplies or means standing in endless lines for lunches; and traffic congestion, which makes delivery to market time-consuming and costly. Some downtown areas are so congested that traffic moves more slowly today

than it did at the turn of the century. Traffic studies of midtown New York City show that the average automobile moves at a snail's pace of 6 miles (9.7 kilometers) per hour. According to a 1907 study, horse-drawn vehicles moved through the same area at an average speed of 11.5 miles (18.5 kilometers) per hour, almost twice as fast.

Often dissatisfied with the inconveniences of central-city living, employees may demand higher wages as compensation. This adds to the cost of doing business in the central city, and many firms choose to leave rather than bear the additional costs. For example, many firms have left New York City for the suburbs. They claim that it costs less to locate there and that their employees are happier and more productive because they do not have to put up with the turmoil of city life.

Clustering in new suburban locations can also have benefits, such as industrial parks, where the costs of utilities and transportation links are shared by all the occupants. Similar benefits can come from residential agglomeration. Suburban real estate developments take advantage of clustering by sharing the costs of schools, parks, road improvements, and utilities. New residents much prefer moving into a new development when they know that a full range of services is available nearby. Then they will not have to drive miles to find, say, the nearest hardware store. It is to the developer's advantage to encourage construction of nearby shopping centers.

The need to be near one's workplace has historically been a great centralizing force, but it can also be a very strong decentralizing force. At first the suburbs were "bedroom communities" from which people commuted to their jobs in the downtown area. This is no longer the case. In most metropolitan areas, most jobs are not in the central city but in outlying districts. Now people work in suburban industrial parks, manufacturing plants, office buildings, and shopping centers. Thus, a typical journey to work involves **lateral commuting:** travel from one suburb to another. As a result, most people who live away from the city center actually live closer to their workplaces. A testimony to this fact is a freeway system at rush hour; traffic is usually heavy in all directions, not just to and from the city center (see the discussion of edge cities in Chapter 10).

The downtown area might once have lured people and businesses into the central city because it was a prestigious location. But once it begins to decay, once shops close and office space goes begging, a certain stigma develops that may drive away residents and commercial activities. Investors will not sink money into a downtown area that they think has no chance of recovery, and shoppers will not venture downtown when streets are filled with vacant stores, transients, pawnshops, and secondhand stores. One of the persistent problems faced by cities is how to reverse this image of the downtown area so that people once again consider it the focus of the city.

Reflecting on GEOGRAPHY

Identify some of the efforts that your city has undertaken to create a better image of itself. Have these efforts been successful? Does this reimagining of the city actually help residents of the inner city?

Public Policy Many public policy decisions, particularly at the national level, have contributed greatly to the decentralization and abandonment of our cities. Both the Federal Road Act of 1916 and the Interstate Highway Act of 1956 directed government spending on transportation to the automobile and the truck. Urban expressways, in combination with the emerging trucking industry, led to massive decentralization of industry and housing. In addition, the ability to deduct mortgage interest from income for tax purposes favors individual home ownership, which has tended to support a move to the suburbs.

The federal government in the United States has also intervened more directly in the housing market. In *Crabgrass Frontier*, Kenneth Jackson outlines the implications of two federal housing policies for the spatial patterning of our metropolitan areas. The first involves the New Deal enactment of the Federal Housing Administration (FHA, established in 1934), and its supplement known as the GI Bill, enacted in 1944. These federal acts, which insured long-term mortgage loans for home construction, were meant to put people back to work in the building trades and to help house the returning soldiers after World War II. Although the FHA legislation contained no explicit antiurban bias, most of the houses it insured were located in new residential developments in the suburbs, thereby neglecting the inner city.

Jackson identifies three reasons that this happened. First, by setting particular terms for its insurance, the FHA favored the development of single-family over multifamily projects. Second, FHA-insured loans for repairs were of short duration and were generally small. Most families, therefore, were better off buying a new house that was probably in the suburbs than updating an older home in the city.

Jackson regards the third factor as the most important in favoring suburban locations for FHA loans. To receive an FHA-insured loan, the applicant and the neighborhood of the property were to be rated by an "unbiased professional." This requirement was intended to guarantee that the property value of the house would be greater than the debt. This policy, however, encouraged bias against any neighborhood that was considered a poten-

tial risk in terms of property values. The FHA explicitly warned against neighborhoods with a racial mix, assuming that such a social climate would bring property values down, and encouraged the enactment of **restrictive covenants** written in property deeds, which prohibited certain "undesirable" groups from buying property. The agency also prepared extensive maps of metropolitan areas, depicting the locations of African-American families and predicting the spread of that population. These maps often served as the basis for **redlining,** a practice in which banks and mortgage companies demarcated areas (often by drawing a red line around them on these maps) considered to be at high risk for loans.

These policies had two primary effects. First, they encouraged construction of single-family homes in suburban areas while discouraging center-city locations. Second, they intensified the segregation of residential areas and actively promoted homogeneity in the new suburbs.

The second federal housing policy that had a major impact on the patterning of metropolitan areas, the United States Housing Act, was intended to provide public housing for those who could not afford private housing. Originally enacted in 1937, the legislation did encourage the construction of many low-income housing units. Yet most of those units were built in the inner city, thereby contributing to the view of the suburbs as the refuge of the white middle class. This growing pattern of racial and economic segregation arose in part because public housing decisions were left up to local municipalities. Many municipalities did not need federal dollars and therefore did not want public housing. In addition, the legislation required that for every unit of public housing erected, one inferior housing unit had to be eliminated. Thus, only areas with inadequate housing units could receive federal dollars, again ensuring that public housing projects would be constructed in the older, downtown areas, not the newer suburbs. As Jackson claims, "The result, if not the intent, of the public housing program of the United States was to segregate the races, to concentrate the disadvantaged in inner cities, and to reinforce the image of suburbia as a place of refuge for the problems of race, crime, and poverty."

The Costs of Decentralization Unfortunately, decentralization has taken its toll. Many of the urban problems now burdening North American cities are direct results of the rapid decentralization that has taken place in the last 40 years. Those people who cannot afford to live in the suburbs are forced to live in inadequate and run-down housing in the inner city, areas that currently do not provide good jobs. Vacant storefronts, empty offices, and deserted factories testify to the movement of commercial functions from central cities to suburbs. Retail stores in

Figure 11.8

Suburban sprawl. Suburbanization gives us a familiar landscape of look-alike houses and yards; automobile-efficient street and transportation patterns; and, in the background, remnants of agriculture, awaiting the day that they are converted into housing tracts. (CAMERAMANN INTERNATIONAL, LTD.)

North American central cities have steadily lost sales to suburban shopping centers. Even offices are finding advantages to suburban location. Like industry, offices capitalize on lower costs and easier access to new transportation networks.

Decentralization has also cost society millions of dollars in problems brought to the suburbs. Where rapid suburbanization has occurred, sprawl has usually resulted. A common pattern is leapfrog or **checkerboard development,** where housing tracts jump over parcels of farmland, resulting in a mixture of open lands with built-up areas. This pattern occurs because developers buy cheaper land farther away from built-up areas, thereby cutting their costs. Furthermore, home buyers often pay premium prices for homes in subdivisions surrounded by farmlands (Figure 11.8).

This form of development is costly because it is more expensive to provide city services—such as police, fire protection, sewers, and electrical lines—to those areas that lie beyond open parcels that are not built up. Obviously, the most cost-efficient form of development is the addition of new housing directly adjacent to built-up areas so that way the costs of providing new services are minimal.

Sprawl also extracts high costs because of the increased use of cars. Public transportation is extremely costly and inefficient when it must serve a low-density checkerboard development pattern—so costly that many cities and transit firms cannot extend lines into these areas. This means that the automobile is the only form of transportation. More energy is consumed for fuel, more air pollution is created by exhaust, and more time is spent in commuting and everyday activities in a sprawling urban area than in a centralized city.

We should not overlook the costs of losing valuable agricultural land to urban development. Farmers cultivating the remaining checkerboard parcels have a hard time making ends meet. They are usually taxed at extremely high rates because their land has high potential for development, and few can make a profit when taxes eat up all their resources. Often the only recourse is to sell out to subdividers. So the cycle of leapfrog development goes on.

Many cities are now taking strong measures to curb this kind of sprawling growth. San Jose, California, for example, one of the fastest-growing cities of the 1960s, is now focusing new development on empty parcels of the checkerboard pattern. This is called **in-filling.** New growth takes place not by extending the sprawling outer edge of the city but by developing the existing urban area, where services are already available and can be provided at lower costs.

Other cities are tying the number of building permits granted each year to the availability of urban services. If schools are already crowded, water supplies inadequate, and sewer plants overburdened, the number of new dwelling units approved for an area will reflect this lower carrying capacity (see Focus On: Controlling Suburban Growth).

FOCUS ON

Controlling Suburban Growth

Although the first measures to control suburban growth were written more than three decades ago, the controversy over the desirability of such measures continues today. The issue is enmeshed in drawn-out legal battles and bureaucratic red tape.

One of the earliest, precedent-setting growth control plans came from Petaluma, California, a small suburb of 50,000 people within the commuter zone north of San Francisco. Once a sleepy service center for chicken ranches, the town began to sprawl with rapid growth in the late 1960s, and a few years later, the city council took strong measures to limit growth by adopting a plan whereby only 500 building permits would be issued yearly. This was roughly half the number granted in the previous years, so the intention was to slow growth by 50 percent. Five hundred permits would be awarded after careful review of all proposed building plans, with the coveted permits going to those builders that met rigorous criteria established by the city council.

Adverse reaction and opposition to this plan were immediate. Not only did the building industry object because the plan would limit construction and jobs, but they were joined by civil rights groups that saw control of suburban growth as a possible vehicle for racial discrimination. Because some types of suburban zoning, such as large-lot minimums and bans against apartment houses, tend to push up housing prices and discriminate against lower-income people, civil rights organizations saw the Petaluma plan as a threat to minority groups.

Consequently, the Petaluma plan was challenged in court as violating the constitutional "right to travel," a legal right traced to the Magna Carta and the legal basis for prohibiting housing with restrictive racial covenants. While a coalition of building industries, trade unions, and civil liberties groups supported a challenge to the Petaluma plan, the city—with financial backing and moral support from other cities interested in establishing a legal precedent for growth control—stood by its plan. Lower court decisions went both for and against the plan until the Supreme Court made a final decision in 1978 substantiating the legal basis for this approach to growth control.

Even if the legal foundation for growth control was established, numerous other complexities must be faced by cities and neighborhoods battling unrestricted expansion. First, there is the question of whether growth control restrictions increase housing prices. A recent California study shows that housing prices in areas with growth control are 5 to 8 percent higher than in areas without controls, because of market demand for a scarce supply and because developers tack on additional costs to compensate for the paperwork and delays from a more complicated permit-approval process. A second issue is whether growth control restrictions discourage developers from building low- and moderate-priced homes. If only a limited number of permits are available for building (as in the Petaluma plan), developers tend to maximize their investment by building higher-priced homes instead of a larger number of middle-income houses. Many cities have addressed this problem by granting incentives to developers who build for lower-income groups. Third, there are problems with how to limit the number of building permits. Some cities use a lottery system to grant permits; others use a complicated point system that rewards plans with the desired attributes. Another common approach is to limit construction to those areas of the city where services (such as water and sewers) are already available, thereby restricting leapfrog sprawl.

Finally, some cities link the number of building permits to the carrying capacity of public services, declaring building moratoriums when schools, water systems, sewer plants, or roads become overloaded. Because cities prefer to plan their future and control growth in an orderly manner, building moratoriums are the least desirable vehicle for growth control from a city's viewpoint, yet they are often forced on a municipality by citizen movements that place a moratorium on a local ballot by petition and then vote it into effect.

Working out an effective yet equitable way to limit and control suburban growth remains one of the challenges that cities and towns face in the twenty-first century.

Gentrification

Beginning in the 1970s, urban scholars began to observe what seemed to be a trend opposite to suburbanization. This trend, called **gentrification,** refers to the movement of middle-class people into deteriorated areas of city centers. Gentrification often begins in an inner-city residential district, with gentrifiers moving into an area that had been run down and is therefore more affordable than suburban housing. The infusion of new capital into the housing market usually results in higher property values, and

this, in turn, often displaces residents who cannot afford to stay in the area. Displacement opens up more housing for gentrification, and the gentrified district continues its spatial expansion.

Commercial gentrification usually follows residential, as new patterns of consumption are introduced into the inner city by the middle-class gentrifiers (Figure 11.9). Urban shopping malls and pedestrian shopping corridors bring the conveniences of the suburbs into the city, and bars and restaurants catering to this new urban middle class provide entertainment and nightlife for the gentrifiers.

The speed with which gentrification has proceeded in many of our downtowns, and the scale of landscape changes that it brings with it, are causing dramatic shifts in the urban mosaic. What factors have led to this reshaping of our cities?

Economic Factors Some urban scholars look to broad economic trends in the United States to explain gentrification. Throughout the post–World War II era, most investments in metropolitan land were made in the suburbs; as a result, land in the inner city was devalued. By the 1970s, many home buyers and commercial investors found land in the city much more affordable, and a better economic investment, than the higher-priced suburbs. This situation brought capital into areas that had been undervalued and accelerated the gentrifying process.

In addition, most Western countries have been experiencing **deindustrialization,** a process whereby the economy is shifting from one based on industrialization to one based on the service sector. This shift has led to the abandonment of older industrial districts in the inner city, including waterfront areas. Many of these areas are prime targets of gentrifiers who convert the waterfront from a noisy, commercial port area into an aesthetic asset. The shift to an economy based on the service sector also means that the new productive areas of the city will be dedicated to white-collar activities. These activities often take place in relatively clean and quiet office buildings, contributing to a view of the city as a more livable environment.

Social Factors Other scholars look to changes in social structure to explain gentrification. The maturing of the baby-boom generation has led to significant modifications of our traditional family structure and lifestyle. With a majority of women in the paid labor force, and many young couples choosing not to have children or to delay that decision, a suburban residential location looks less appealing. A gentrified location in the inner city attracts this new class because it is close to their managerial or professional jobs downtown, is usually easier to maintain, and is considered more interesting than the bland suburban areas where they grew up.

Living in a newly gentrified area is also a way to display social status. Many suburbs have become less exclusive, while older neighborhoods in the inner city frequently exploit their historical associations as a status symbol. Members of the middle class, often employed in service-sector industries, exhibit their new economic status by living in a gentrified neighborhood.

Political Factors Many metropolitan governments in the United States, faced with the abandonment of the central city by the middle class and therefore with the erosion of

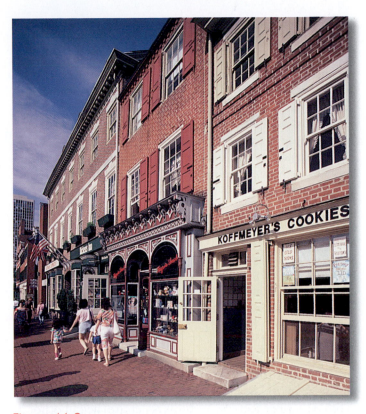

Figure 11.9
Commercial gentrification in the center of Society Hill, Philadelphia. This area caters as much to tourists as to local residents. Notice the attempts to appear historical, with brick streets and nineteenth-century storefronts. **Why do you think historical appearance is important for gentrification?** (CAMERAMANN INTERNATIONAL, LTD.)

their tax base, have enacted policies to encourage commercial and residential development in downtown areas. Some policies provide tax breaks for companies willing to locate downtown; others furnish local and state funding to redevelop center-city residential and commercial buildings.

At a more comprehensive level, some larger metropolitan areas have devised long-term planning agendas that target certain neighborhoods for revitalization. Often this is accomplished by first condemning the targeted area, thereby transferring control of the land to an urban-development authority or other planning agency. This area is often an older residential neighborhood that was built originally to house people who worked in nearby factories. To reshape the neighborhood for gentrification, the factories are usually torn down or transformed into lofts or office space. The redevelopment authority might locate a new civic or arts center in the neighborhood. Public-sector initiatives often lead to private investment, thereby increasing property values. These higher property values, in turn, lead to more investment and the eventual transformation of the neighborhood into a middle- to upper-class gentrified district.

Sexuality and Gentrification Gentrified residential districts are often correlated with the presence of a significant gay and lesbian population. It is fairly easy to understand this correlation. First, the typical suburban life tends not to appeal to people whose lifestyle is often regarded as different and whose community needs are often different from those of people living in the suburbs. Second, gentrified, inner-city neighborhoods provide access to the diversity of city life and amenities that often include gay cultural institutions. In fact, the association of urban neighborhoods with gays and lesbians is long-lived. For example, urban historian George Chauncey has documented gay culture in New York City between 1890 and the Second World War, showing that a gay world occupied and shaped distinctive spaces in the city, such as neighborhood enclaves, gay commercial areas, and public parks and streets.

Yet, unlike this earlier period, when gay cultures were often forced to remain hidden, the gentrification of the postwar period has provided gay and lesbian populations with the opportunity to reshape entire neighborhoods actively and openly. Urban scholar Manuel Castells argues that in cities such as San Francisco, the presence of gay men in institutions directly linked to gentrification, such as the real estate industry, significantly influenced that city's gentrification processes in the 1970s.

Geographers Larry Knopp and Mickey Lauria emphasize the community-building aspect of gay men's involvement in gentrification, recognizing that gays have seized an opportunity to combat oppression by creating neighborhoods over which they have maximum control and that meet long-neglected needs. Similarly, geographer Gill Valentine argues that the limited numbers and types of lesbian spaces in cities also serve as community-building centers for lesbian social networks.

According to geographer Tamar Rothenberg, the gentrified neighborhood of Park Slope in Brooklyn is home to the heaviest concentration of lesbians in the United States. Its extensive social networks are marking the neighborhood as a center of lesbian identity and a visible lesbian social space.

The Costs of Gentrification Gentrification often results in the displacement of lower-income people, who are forced to leave their homes because of rising property values. This displacement can have serious consequences for the city's social fabric. Because many of the displaced people come from disadvantaged groups, gentrification frequently contributes to racial and ethnic tensions. Dis-

placed people are often forced into neighborhoods more peripheral to the city, a trend that serves to disadvantage these people even more. In addition, gentrified neighborhoods usually stand in stark contrast to surrounding neighborhoods where investment has not taken place, thus creating a very visible reminder of the uneven distribution of wealth within our cities.

The success of a gentrification project is usually measured by its appeal to an upper-middle-class clientele. This suggests that gentrified neighborhoods are completely homogeneous in their use of land. Residential areas are consciously planned to be separate from commercial districts and are themselves sorted by cost and tenure type (home ownership versus rental). Thus, gentrification often draws on the suburban notion of residential homogeneity and eliminates what many people consider to be a great asset of urban life—its diversity and heterogeneity.

A study of the gentrification process in Society Hill, Philadelphia, highlights these social costs (see Focus On: The Social Costs of Gentrification).

The Cultural Ecology of the City

How can we understand the relationships between the urban mosaic and the physical environment? The physical environment affects cities, just as urbanization profoundly alters natural environmental processes. The theme of cultural ecology helps us to organize information about these city-nature relationships. Although we discuss these topics in general terms in the next pages, we should not lose sight of how the differing cultural fabric within and between cities affects the relationship between city and nature. Urban cultural ecology differs greatly from place to place because of different physical environments and, equally important, because of varying cultural patterns.

Urban Topography

In the Chapter 10 discussion of site and situation, we saw that cities both affect the physical environment and are affected by it. Let's explore further the relationship between urbanization and topography.

Topography can influence urban development in three ways: the direction of city growth, the patterning of social regions, and the routing of transportation. These potential effects, however, depend on a number of cultural variables. The most important variables are a society's technological level, the amount of energy and capital available for modification of the physical environment, and the stage in a city's development. Thus, topography

FOCUS ON

The Social Costs of Gentrification: The Case of Society Hill, Philadelphia

Society Hill, an old residential area in Philadelphia that dates from the colonial era, represents one of the earliest gentrification projects and is considered one of the more successful. The following account, however, points out that this first phase (Unit One) of Philadelphia's redevelopment brought many social costs with it.

The physical appearance itself of the redeveloped Society Hill manifests the special difficulty of marketing this inner-city neighborhood in the midst of the suburban age. Advertisements highlighted stereotypically nonurban attributes of the neighborhood, such as marinas and green pathways. The conscious re-sorting of heterogeneous into homogeneous land-use patterns unlike any of the other older neighborhoods of the city, is, we claim, drawn from a prominent motif in suburban design. The anthropologist Constance Perin, in *Everything in Its Place* (1977), an exploration of cultural and social symbolism in metropolitan land-use patterns, argues that one of the keys to the successful marketing of American suburbia has been the appeal of clearly ordered and discrete land-use units. Prospective homebuyers, who were not only purchasing shelter, but also deeply committing themselves financially, were reassured by the evident presence of neighbors "just like themselves." Thus in the design of Society Hill, residential tracts were separated from most other uses and also were internally sorted by cost and tenure type. In addition, building design was such as to maximize both privacy and physical security. The inward-facing plans of several new housing clusters, for example, with parking and entrance on the interior of blocks, exemplify one of the earliest applications of "defended space" principles.

Having ensured that "everything was in its place," so too the Society Hill concept carefully saw to it that everybody was in their place; social homogeneity, equally a stereotypically suburban attribute, was relentlessly pursued. Part of the appeal of homogeneity was to snobbery: the advertisements invited one to come live with Philadelphia's top people: a 1957 advertisement (early in Society Hill's redevelopment) insinuates, "The mayor is, why can't you?" (*Philadelphia Inquirer*, May 19, 1957). Just as important was the need to assuage fears about stereotypical in-city sub-cultures. ("See, you have to understand [that] the fundamental feeling in suburbia is fear [of the impingement of the city], let's face it," a realtor had informed Perin [1977:87].) So, in a suburban age, the advertisements felt they had to stress "nice people . . . coming to live in Society Hill."

It is a commonplace that the Society Hill renewal, so evidently "top-down" in conception and execution, imposed social costs upon preexisting residents of lower socioeconomic status. The prior residents of Unit One could remain only if the Redevelopment Authority was disposed to resell their property back to them with inevitably expensive contractual stipulations: a timetable for any of a number of specific repairs, mandatory upkeep requirements, plus remodeling to exacting and detailed "historically authentic" standards for facades. Unbending application of these criteria expelled all but a few of the original lower-income residents. Thus, at the public meeting held in conjunction with the unveiling of the Unit One plan (April 28, 1958), the complaint was heard from one resident that it was "a plan for an area of wealthy poodled people," and it was reported that "many [residents] . . . didn't like what they saw, or thought they saw, looming in the future." John P. Robin, president of the Old Philadelphia Development Corporation (the body that had contracted to implement the renewal) responded that "residents would have to compromise their desires with those of others and the city" (*Evening Bulletin*, April 29, 1958). This captures the general tone; in many cases the record documents a degree of insensitivity to or lack of concern with the special needs and claims of pre-existing Society Hill residents.

It was high-income people who were required in Unit One; any possibility of income mix was intendedly minimized.

Abridged from Cybriwsky et al., 1986. Copyright © 1986 Neil Smith, Peter Williams, and contributors. Reprinted by permission of Allen & Unwin.

---

may have a great effect on cities in their early stages of growth, when there is space to expand rather than expending energy and money on modifying terrain, or when technology is lacking for bulldozing, landfills, or high-stress building construction. At later stages of growth, in a rich, highly industrialized culture, there will be far more examples of humans modifying the physical environment (Figure 11.10 on the next page).

Topography often influences the early stages of city growth. Cities usually expand first in those areas where building costs are lowest: on flat, well-drained lands that are close to transportation and existing urban activities. As the topography becomes more rugged, building costs increase. Hills, marshes, and floodplains may be built on only at later stages of a city's growth when fewer alternatives are available.

Figure 11.10
Suburban homes built on landfills, Treasure Island, Florida. When land values are high and pressure for housing intense, terrain rarely stands in the way of the developer. In fact, particular physical site characteristics can actually increase land values. **What site characteristics evident in this photo tell you that Treasure Island is a very expensive place to live?** (CAMERAMANN INTERNATIONAL, LTD.)

Topography can also affect urban transportation systems. Urban patterns may express the close link between transportation and urban development. The first urban transportation system was the horse-drawn streetcar, which was obviously restricted to level parts of the city because horses could not pull a car and passengers up and down hills. Beginning in the 1890s, electric trolley systems profoundly altered the pattern of urban development. Electric trolleys also had limited hill-climbing abilities: only slight gradients could be negotiated. As a result, trolley lines ascended slopes only when it was possible to follow hillside contours. In the end, it was the automobile that led to widespread building on steep urban slopes. Even this form of development has been influenced by such factors as frequency of heavy snowfalls and ice storms.

Urban Weather and Climate

Cities alter virtually all aspects of local weather and climate. Temperatures are higher in cities, rainfall increases, the incidence of fog and cloudiness is greater, and atmospheric pollution is much higher.

The causes of these changes are no mystery. Because cities pave over large areas of land with streets, buildings, parking lots, and rooftops, about 50 percent of the urban area is a hard surface. Rainfall is quickly carried into gutters and sewers, so that little standing water is available for evaporation. Because evaporation removes heat from the air, when moisture is reduced, evaporation is lessened and air temperatures are higher.

Moreover, cities generate enormous amounts of heat. This heat comes not just from the heating systems of buildings but also from automobiles, industry, and even human bodies. One study showed that on a winter day in Manhattan, the amount of heat produced in the city is two and a half times the amount that reaches the ground from the sun. The result of this heat generation is to produce a large mass of warmer air sitting over the city. This is called the urban **heat island** (Figure 11.11). The heat island causes yearly temperatures in cities to average 3.5°F (2°C) higher than in the countryside; during the winter, when there is more city-produced heat, the temperature difference can easily be 7°F to 10°F (4°C to 5.6°C).

Urbanization also affects precipitation (rain and snowfall). Because of higher temperatures within the urban area, snowfall will be about 5 percent less than in the surrounding countryside. However, rainfall can be 5 to 10 percent higher. The increased rainfall results from two factors: the large number of dust particles in urban air and the higher city temperatures. Dust particles are a necessary precondition for condensation, offering a nucleus around which moisture can adhere. If the air has a greater number of dust particles, condensation will take place more easily. That is why fog and clouds (**dust domes**) are usually more frequent around cities (Figure 11.12 on page 400)

City-generated air pollution is one of the most serious problems of our times. No longer are **particulate pollutants**—bits of matter spewed into the air as a result of urban activity—simply a nuisance; they can cause serious

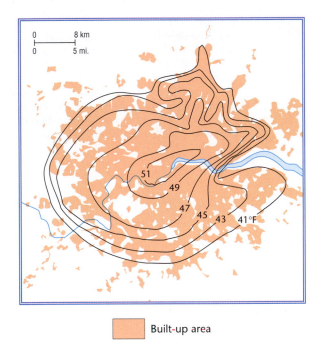

Built-up area

Figure 11.11
The London heat island forms a dome over the city. Notice the marked contrast in temperature between the built-up central part of the city and the surrounding "Green Belt" in the outer three rings. (AFTER CHANDLER, 1961.)

illness and even death. Pollution damages agriculture near cities; and it extracts a high cost from every urban dweller. Unless pollution can be halted, it may actually be the primary factor limiting urban growth. Some observers suggest that fresh air—not water—will determine the ultimate carrying capacity of the Los Angeles Basin. Federal and local air quality agencies are experimenting with regulations to limit further growth and development in those areas suffering from persistent air pollution.

Urban Hydrology

Not only is the city a great consumer of water, but it also alters runoff patterns in a way that increases the frequency and magnitude of flooding. Within the city, residential areas are usually the greatest consumers of water. Water consumption can vary depending on the kind of industry found in a city, but generally, each person in the United States uses about 60 gallons (264 liters) per day in a residence.

Of course, residential demand varies. It is greater in drier climates, where lots are larger, and in middle- and high-income neighborhoods. Higher-income groups usually have a larger number of water-using appliances, such as washing machines, dishwashers, and swimming pools.

The cost of water influences demand: people use less water when it costs more. Periods of drought in the West have demonstrated that residents can use considerably less water and find alternatives to freshwater consumption when the cost of water increases. Many of the rationing plans adopted during the California drought of the late 1980s restricted per capita daily use to around 40 gallons (176 liters).

We noted earlier that urbanization seems to increase both the frequency and the magnitude of flooding. Why might this be? Cities create large impervious areas where water cannot soak into the earth. Instead, precipitation is converted into immediate runoff. It is forced into gutters, sewers, and stream channels that have been straightened and stripped of vegetation, resulting in more frequent high-water levels than are found in a comparable area of rural land. Furthermore, the time between rainfall and peak runoff is reduced in cities; there is less lag than in the countryside, where water runs across soil and vegetation into stream channels and then into rivers. So, because of hard surfaces and artificial collection channels, runoff in cities is concentrated and immediate.

Urban Vegetation

Until a decade ago, it was commonly thought that the city was made up mostly of artificial materials: asphalt, concrete, glass, and steel. Studies, however, show that about two-thirds of a typical North American city is composed of trees and herbaceous plants (mostly weeds in vacant lots and cultivated grasses for lawns). This urban vegetation is usually a mix of natural and introduced species and is a critical component of the urban ecosystem because it affects the city's topography, hydrology, and meteorology.

More specifically, urban vegetation influences the quantity and quality of surface water and groundwater; reduces wind velocity and turbulence and temperature extremes; affects the pattern of snow accumulation and melting; absorbs thousands of tons of airborne particulates and atmospheric gases; and offers habitat for mammals, birds, reptiles, and insects, all of which play some useful role in the urban ecosystem. Furthermore, urban vegetation influences the propagation of sound waves by masking out much of the city's noise; affects the distribution of natural and artificial light; and, finally, is an extremely important component in the development of soil profiles—which, in turn, control hillside stability.

Our urban settlements are still closely tied to the physical environment. Cities change these natural processes in profound ways, and we must understand these disturbances to make better decisions about adjustments and control.

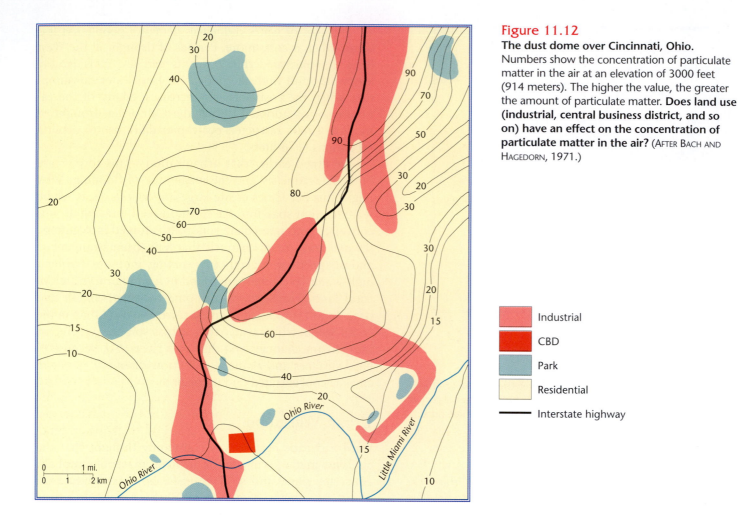

Figure 11.12
The dust dome over Cincinnati, Ohio. Numbers show the concentration of particulate matter in the air at an elevation of 3000 feet (914 meters). The higher the value, the greater the amount of particulate matter. **Does land use (industrial, central business district, and so on) have an effect on the concentration of particulate matter in the air?** (AFTER BACH AND HAGEDORN, 1971.)

Industrial

CBD

Park

Residential

Interstate highway

Cultural Interaction and Models of the City

Are there generalizable spatial patterns or models that describe types of cities? Geographers are interested in understanding both the uniqueness of each city's urban pattern and the similarities that a particular city may have with others. For example, most cities have central business districts and socioeconomic neighborhoods that are similar in form, function, and spatial organization. The positioning of the CBD in relationship to high-income, middle-income, and low-income neighborhoods produces similar spatial patterns in cities as diverse as Chicago, Frankfurt, and Sydney. Yet this type of urban pattern, or model, differs significantly from the spatial arrangement of such cities as Mexico City and Buenos Aires, which have been shaped by economic, cultural, and political circumstances quite dissimilar from those that shaped Chicago or Sydney. To provide insights

about the diverse urban mosaic, geographers have tried to describe some spatial models of land use within cities, each of which helps us understand a particular type of city.

Concentric Zone Model

The **concentric zone model** was developed in 1925 by Ernest W. Burgess, a sociologist at the University of Chicago. Although his model closely resembles Chicago (if the east side were not cut off by Lake Michigan), his intent was simply to construct a theoretical model of urban growth.

Figure 11.13 shows the concentric zone model with its five zones. At first glance, you can see the effects of residential decentralization. There is a distinct pattern of income levels from zone 1, the CBD, out to the commuter residential zone. This pattern shows that even at the beginning of the automobile age, American cities expressed a clear separation of social groups. The extension of trol-

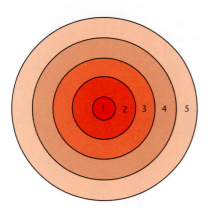

Figure 11.13

The concentric zone model. Each zone represents a different type of land use in the city. **Can you identify examples of each zone in your community?**

1 CBD (central business district)
2 Transition zone
3 Blue-collar residential
4 Middle-income residential
5 Commuter residential

ley lines into the surrounding countryside had a lot to do with this pattern.

Zone 2, a transitional area between the CBD and residential zone 3, is characterized by a mixed pattern of industrial and residential land use. Rooming houses, small apartments, and tenements attract the lowest-income segment of the urban population. Often this zone includes slums and skid rows. Here, also, many ethnic ghettos began. Landowners, while waiting for the CBD to reach their land, erected shoddy tenements to house a massive

influx of foreign workers. An aura of uncertainty is characteristic of life in zone 2, because commercial activities rapidly displaced residents as the CBD expanded. Today, this area is often characterized by physical deterioration (Figure 11.14).

Zone 3, the "workingmen's quarters," is a solid blue-collar arc, located close to the factories of zones 1 and 2. Yet zone 3 is more stable than the zone of transition around the CBD. It is often characterized by ethnic neighborhoods: blocks of immigrants who broke free from the ghettos in zone 2 and moved outward into flats or single-family dwellings. Burgess suggested that this working-class area, like the CBD, was spreading outward because of pressure from the zone of transition and because blue-collar workers demanded better housing.

Zone 4 is a middle-class area of better housing. From here, established city dwellers—many of whom moved out of the central city with the first streetcar network—commute to work in the CBD.

Zone 5, the commuters' zone, consists of higher-income families clustered together in suburbs, either on the farthest extension of the trolley or on commuter railroad lines. This zone of spacious lots and large houses is the growing edge of the city. From here, the rich press outward to avoid the increasing congestion and social heterogeneity brought to their area by an expansion of zone 4.

Burgess's concentric zone theory represented the American city in a new stage of development. Before the 1870s, an American metropolis, such as New York, was

Figure 11.14

An abandoned building in the uptown area of Chicago. The transitional zone in the city contains vacant and deteriorated buildings. **Why has this area become a likely target for gentrifiers?** (See the section on "Gentrification" in this chapter.) (Cameramann International, Ltd.)

a city of mixed neighborhoods where merchants' stores and sweatshop factories were intermingled with mansions and hovels. Rich and poor, immigrant and native-born rubbed shoulders in the same neighborhoods. However, in Chicago, Burgess's hometown, something else occurred. In 1871, the Great Chicago Fire burned out the core of the city, leveling almost one-third of its buildings. As the city was rebuilt, it was influenced by late-nineteenth-century market forces: real estate speculation in the suburbs, inner-city industrial development, new streetcar systems, and the need for low-cost working-class housing. The result was a more explicit social patterning than existed in other large cities. Chicago became a segregated city with a concentric pattern working its way out from the downtown in what one scholar called "rings of rising affluence." It was this rebuilt city that Burgess used as the basis for his concentric zone model.

However, as you can see from Figure 11.15, the actual residential map of Chicago does not exactly match the simplicity of Burgess's concentric zones. For instance, it is evident that the wealthy continue to monopolize certain high-value sites within the other rings, especially Chicago's "Gold Coast" along Lake Michigan on the north side. According to the concentric zone theory, this area should have been part of the zone of transition. Burgess accounted for certain of these exceptions by noting how the rich tended to monopolize hills, lakes, and shorelines, whether they were close to or far from the CBD. Critics of Burgess's model also were quick to point out that even though portions of each zone did exist in most cities, rarely were they linked in such a way as to totally surround the city. Burgess countered that there were distinct barriers, such as old industrial centers, that prevented the completion of the arc. Still other critics felt that Burgess, as a sociologist, overemphasized residential patterns and did not give proper credit to other land uses—such as industry, manufacturing, and warehouses—in describing the urban mosaic.

Sector Model

Homer Hoyt, an economist who studied housing data for 142 American cities, presented his **sector model** of urban land use in 1939. He maintained that high-rent residential districts ("rent" meaning capital outlay for the occupancy of space, including purchase, lease, or rent in the popular sense) were instrumental in shaping the land-use structure of the city. Because these areas were reinforced by transportation routes, the pattern of their development was one of sectors or wedges (Figure 11.16) rather than concentric zones.

Hoyt suggested that the high-rent sector would expand according to four factors. First, a high-rent sector

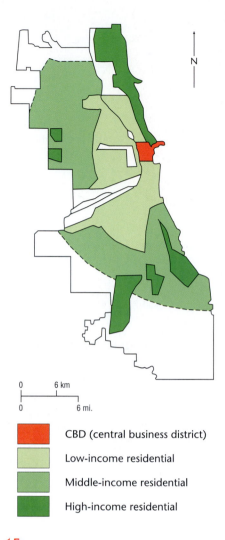

Figure 11.15

Residential areas of Chicago in 1920 were used as the basis for many studies and models of the city. Compare this pattern with the concentric zone and sector models.

0 6 km

0 6 mi.

- ■ CBD (central business district)
- ■ Low-income residential
- ■ Middle-income residential
- ■ High-income residential

moves from its point of origin near the CBD, along established routes of travel, toward another nucleus of high-rent buildings. That is, a high-rent area directly next to the CBD will naturally head in the direction of a high-rent suburb, eventually linking the two in a wedge-shaped sector. Second, a high-rent sector will progress toward high ground or along waterfronts, when these areas are not used for industry. The rich have always preferred such environments for their residences. Third, a high-rent sector will move along the route of fastest transportation. Fourth, a high-rent sector will move toward open space. A high-income community rarely moves into an occupied lower-income neighborhood. Instead, the wealthy prefer to build new structures on vacant land where they can control the social environment.

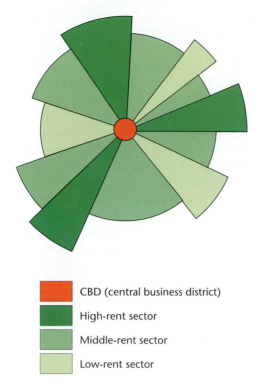

CBD (central business district)

High-rent sector

Middle-rent sector

Low-rent sector

Figure 11.16
The sector model. In this model, zones are pie-shaped wedges radiating along main transportation routes.

on cities. However, when we look at today's major transportation arteries, which are generally freeways, we see that the areas surrounding them are often low-rent districts. According to Hoyt's theory, they should be high-rent districts. Freeways are rather recent additions to the city, coming only after World War II. They were imposed on an existing urban pattern. To minimize the economic and political costs of construction, they were often built through low-rent areas, where the costs of land purchase for the rights of way were less and where political opposition was kept to a minimum, because most people living in these low-rent areas had little political clout. This is why so many freeways rip through ethnic ghettos and low-income areas. Economically speaking, this is the least expensive route. This problem will persist until low-income neighborhoods organize effective political resistance against such disturbances.

Multiple Nuclei Model

Both Burgess and Hoyt assumed that a strong central city affected patterns throughout the urban area. However, as the city increasingly decentralized, districts developed that were not directly linked to the CBD. In 1945, two geographers, Chauncey Harris and Edward Ullman, suggested a new model: the **multiple nuclei model.** They maintained that a city developed with equal intensity around various points, or multiple nuclei (Figure 11.17). In their eyes, the CBD was not the sole generator of change. Equal weight must be given to an old community on the city outskirts around which new suburban developments clustered; to an industrial district that grew from an original waterfront location; or to a low-income area that developed because of some social stigma attached to the site.

Harris and Ullman rooted their model in four geographical principles. First, certain activities require highly specialized facilities, such as accessible transportation for a factory or large areas of open land for a housing tract.

As high-rent sectors develop, the areas between them are filled in. Middle-rent areas move directly next to them, drawing on their prestige. Low-rent areas fill in the remaining areas. Thus, moving away from major routes of travel, rents go from high to low.

There are distinct patterns in today's cities that echo Hoyt's model. He had the advantage over Burgess in that he wrote later in the automobile age and could see the tremendous impact that major thoroughfares were having

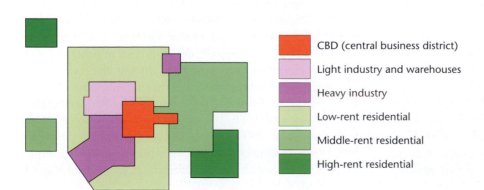

CBD (central business district)

Light industry and warehouses

Heavy industry

Low-rent residential

Middle-rent residential

High-rent residential

Figure 11.17
The multiple nuclei model. This model was devised to show that the CBD is not the sole force in creating land-use patterns within the city. Rather, land-use districts may evolve for specific reasons at specific points elsewhere in the city—hence the name *multiple nuclei.*
Compare this model to Figure 11.15. How and why are they different?

Second, certain activities cluster together because they profit from mutual association. For example, car dealers are commonly located near one another because automobiles are very expensive, and people will engage in comparative shopping—moving from one dealer to another until their decisions are made. Third, certain activities repel each other and will not be found in the same area. Examples would be high-rent residences and industrial areas, or slums and expensive retail stores. Fourth, certain activities could not make a profit if they paid the high rent of the most desirable locations. Therefore, they seek lower-rent areas. For example, car dealers may like to locate where pedestrian traffic is greatest to lure the most people into their showrooms. However, they need great amounts of space for showrooms, storage, service facilities, and used-car lots. Therefore, they cannot afford the high rents that the most accessible locations demand. They compromise by finding an area of lower rent that is still relatively accessible.

The multiple nuclei model, more than the other models, seems to take into account the varied factors of decentralization in the structure of the North American city. Many geographers criticize the concentric zone and sector theories as being rather deterministic, for they emphasize one single factor (residential differentiation in the concentric zone theory and rent in the sector theory) to explain the pattern of the city. But the multiple nuclei theory encompasses a larger spectrum of economic and social possibilities. Harris and Ullman could probably appreciate the variety of forces working on the city because they did not confine themselves to seeking simply a social or an economic explanation. As geographers, they tried to integrate the disparate elements of culture into a workable model. Most urban scholars agree that they succeeded.

Feminist Critiques

Most of the criticisms of the models just discussed focus on their simplification of reality or their inability to account for all the complexities of urban forms. More recently, feminist geographers have noticed some flaws in the models and in how they were constructed that call into question their descriptive power.

All three models assume that urban patterns are shaped by an economic tradeoff between the desire to live in a suburban neighborhood appropriate to one's economic status and the need to live relatively close to the center city for employment opportunities. These models assume that only one person in the family is a wage worker—the male head of the family. They ignore dual-income families and households headed by single women, who contend with a larger array of factors in making locational decisions, including distances to child care and school facilities and other services important for other members of a family. For many of these households, the traditional urban models that assume a spatial separation of workplace and home are no longer appropriate.

For example, a study of the activity patterns of working parents shows that women living in a city have access to a wider array of employment opportunities and are better able to combine domestic and wage labor than are women who live in the suburbs. Many of these middle-class women will choose to live in a gentrified inner-city location, hoping that this type of area will offer the amenities of the suburbs (good schools and safety), while also accommodating their activity patterns. Other research has shown that some businesses will locate their offices in the suburbs because they rely on the labor of highly educated, middle-class women who are spatially constrained by their domestic work. As geographers Susan Hanson (see Profile) and Geraldine Pratt found in their study of employment practices and gender in Worcester, Massachusetts, most women seek employment locations closer to their homes than do men, and this applies to almost all women, not just those with small children.

When we consider these factors, it becomes apparent that the urban structure described by the traditional models is becoming problematic for most families that now require two wage earners to keep pace with the cost of living. The Women and Geography Study Group, a specialty group of the Institute of British Geographers, suggests that these models tend to reflect an urban structure that results in the isolation of women who do not participate in the urban labor market, and that raises problems of timing and organization for those who combine wage and domestic labor. Feminist geographers are currently rethinking these long-held assumptions about the separation of home from work and are assessing the implications of such assumptions for urban structure and design.

The traditional models are also criticized for being created by men who shared certain assumptions about how cities operate and therefore presented a very partial view of urban life. The concentric zone and sector models were developed by sociologists and economists working in Chicago in the early twentieth century. Geographers David Sibley and Emily Gilbert, however, have brought to our attention the development of other theories about urban form and structure during the same time. These theories incorporated the alternative perspectives of female scholars. Drawing on the urban reform work done by Jane Addams at Hull House in Chicago, scholars in the first decades of the twentieth century examined the causes and possible solutions of urban problems. For example, Edith Abbott, Sophonisba Breckinridge, and Helen Rankin

PROFILE

(CLARK UNIVERSITY, WORCESTER, MASSACHUSETTS.)

Susan Hanson

1943–

A personal commitment to social justice is apparent both in the published works and the professional service of Susan Hanson. Before completing her Ph.D. in geography at Northwestern in 1973, she was a Peace Corps volunteer in Kenya. Her interest in understanding and explaining urban transportation patterns and problems, which began at Northwestern, led her to a sustained examination of how women's lives are impacted by those patterns. She published some of the very first articles that considered gender as an important component of geographical analysis and, together with geographer Janice Monk, published in 1982 the extremely influential article, "On Not Excluding Half of the Human in Human Geography" in the *Professional Geographer.* Her work throughout the 1980s and early 1990s continued to merge her interests in urban transportation, urban labor markets, and gender issues, culminating in the publication (with geographer Geraldine Pratt) of the highly regarded book, *Gender, Work, and Space.* She is considered one of the leaders of the emerging field of feminist geography and serves as a role model for other women in geography, particularly because she has held the highest positions in the discipline: President of the Association of American Geographers, 1990–1991, and editor of the *Annals of the Association of American Geographers,* 1981–1987 (coeditor 1981–1984). Susan Hanson is a professor of geography at Clark University.

Jeter, faculty at the School of Social Service Administration at the University of Chicago, worked with their mostly female students to produce a number of studies about "race," ethnicity, class, and housing in Chicago. These studies differed in several ways from those of such theorists as Burgess and Hoyt. For instance, they emphasized the role of landlords in shaping the housing market and included an awareness of how racism is related to the allocation of housing and a sensitivity to the different urban experiences of ethnic groups.

The following quote from an essay by Edith Abbott and Mary Zahrobsky (1936) highlights their insight into the role of racial discrimination in the housing market:

The prejudice among the white people of having Negros living on what they regard jealously as their residence streets and their unwillingness to have Negro children attending schools with white children confines the opportunities for residence open to Negros of all positions of life to relatively small and well-defined areas. Consequently, the demand for houses and apartments within these areas is comparatively steady and, since the landlord is reasonably certain that the house or apartment can be filled at any time, as long as it is in any way tenantable, he takes advantage of his opportunity to raise rents and postpone repairs.

This summary of why African-American communities are faced with limited and often poorly maintained housing is remarkable not only for its intelligent commentary about urban life in the 1920s and 1930s but also for its applicability to most urban areas today. For example, a study by urban historian Raymond Mohl chronicles the making of black ghettos in Miami between 1940 and 1960. His research reveals the role of public policy decisions, landlordism, and discrimination in that process—forces identified by Abbott and others that continue to operate today.

Reflecting on **GEOGRAPHY**

Consider why the insights gained from the studies done by these women have been ignored until recently. How do you think our knowledge of urban life would have been different if these studies had become part of our accepted urban curriculum?

The Apartheid and Postapartheid City

As we have seen, racism and the residential segregation that often results from it can have profound effects on urban patterns. In South Africa, the state-sanctioned policy of segregating "races," known as **apartheid,** significantly altered the urban patterns that we outlined earlier. Racial segregation was not the only force shaping the apartheid city, but it certainly was a dominant one. The intended effects of this policy on urban form are delineated in Figure 11.18 on the next page. To understand this illustration, we need to outline some of the important components of the apartheid state.

The policies of economic and political discrimination against non-European groups in South Africa were formalized and sharpened under National Party rule after 1948. To segregate the "races," the government passed two major pieces of legislation in 1950. The first was the

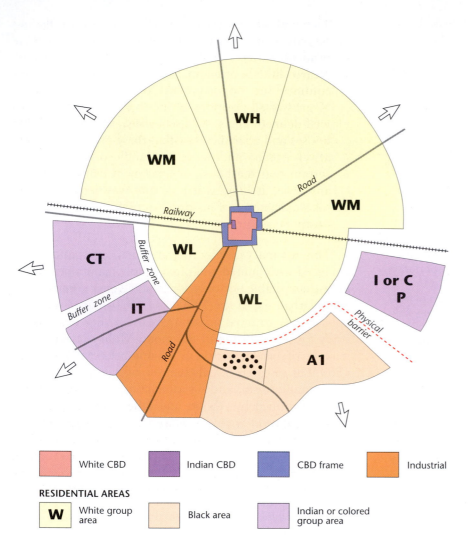

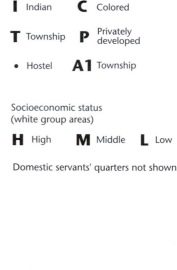

Figure 11.18

The model apartheid city. Townships were areas set aside by the government for members of nonwhite groups to live in, often located close to industrial areas of the city. Hostels were built to house black men from the rural areas who were needed to work in particular industries. **Why are nonwhite groups located close to industry?** (FROM CHRISTOPHER, 1994: 107. COPYRIGHT © 1994 BY A. J. CHRISTOPHER. REPRINTED BY PERMISSION OF ROUTLEDGE.)

I Indian **C** Colored

T Township **P** Privately developed

• Hostel **A1** Township

Socioeconomic status (white group areas)

H High **M** Middle **L** Low

Domestic servants' quarters not shown

White CBD | Indian CBD | CBD frame | Industrial

RESIDENTIAL AREAS

W White group area | Black area | Indian or colored group area

---

Population Registration Act, which mandated the classification of the population into discrete racial groups. The three major groups were white, black, and colored, although those groups were further subdivided into smaller categories. The second piece of major legislation was called the Group Areas Act; its goal was, in the words of geographer A. J. Christopher, "to effect the total urban segregation of the various population groups defined under the Population Registration Act." Cities, therefore, were divided into sections that were to be inhabited only by members of one population group.

Although the effects of these acts on the form of South African cities did not happen overnight, they were massive nonetheless. Members of nonwhite groups were by far the ones most adversely affected. Almost without exception, the downtowns of cities were restricted to whites, whereas those areas set aside for nonwhites were peripheral and restricted, often lacking any urban services, such

as transportation and shopping. Large numbers of nonwhite families were displaced with little or no compensation (estimates suggest that only 2 percent of the displaced families were white), as the state attempted to create homogeneous residential areas. Buffer zones were established between residential areas to curtail contact between groups, further hindering access to the central city for those groups pushed into the periphery.

The model apartheid city most closely resembles the sector model, but with significant changes: the residential areas are racially segregated, the CBD is racially divided, and buffers are established between racial groups. Although no cities in South Africa followed exactly the pattern suggested in Figure 11.18, all of them were artificially divided into discrete areas, and their nonwhite populations suffered the consequences. One of the most notorious examples was the total destruction of Sophiatown in Johannesburg, an inner-city black freehold neighborhood that was completely taken over by the government and the population resettled on the periphery of the city.

It remains to be seen how these patterns can be altered in South Africa today, under its new, nonapartheid, multiracial state. The consequences of apartheid will take a long time to erode, especially those that affected the built environment. The form the postapartheid city will take is certainly an important and interesting question for urban geographers and planners today, as they attempt to counter the devastating consequences of apartheid policies and create a more socially just built environment.

The Soviet and Post-Soviet City

The effects of centralized state policies on urban land use patterns are also evident in the cities of the countries that formed the Soviet Union. With the Bolshevik Revolution of 1917 came attempts by the state to confront and solve the urban problems attendant upon industrialization (see Chapter 10). Socialist principles called for the nationalization of all resources, including land, and the substitution of centralized planning as the means for allocating those resources, instead of relying on the needs of the market. In the words of geographer James Bater, "With the nationalization of land one of the principal historic forces shaping urban land use was removed. Economics would no longer dictate land-use allocation, planners would." (1980)

These ideals had profound effects on the form of Soviet cities. The principles that underlie the three models outlined earlier—that land is held privately and that the economic market dictates urban land use—were no longer the prime influences on urban form. Instead, Soviet policies attempted to create a more equitable arrangement of land uses in the city. The results of those policies included (1) a relative absence of residential segregation according to socioeconomic status; (2) equitable housing facilities for most citizens; (3) relatively equal accessibility to sites for the distribution of consumer items; (4) cultural amenities (theater, opera, and so on) located and priced to be accessible to as many people as possible; and (5) adequate and accessible public transportation. Although these results created better living and working conditions for many people, the situation was far from ideal. By the 1970s and 1980s, many Soviets realized that their standards of living were well below those in the West and that the centralized planning system was not successful. National policies of economic restructuring introduced in the late 1980s, referred to as *perestroika*, led to mandates to privatize resources and the land market.

In the post-Soviet city, market forces are once again dominant in shaping urban land uses, and the pace and scale of urban change are unprecedented (Figure 11.19). One of the most significant of those changes is the privatization of the housing market. In Moscow, for example, the percentage of the housing stock that is in private hands grew from 9.3 percent in 1990 to 49.6 percent in 1994.

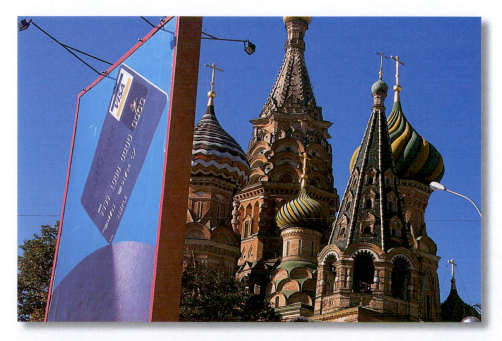

Figure 11.19

Downtown Moscow. The post-Soviet city, rekindled by market forces, demonstrates unprecedented urban change. (SEAN SPRAGUE/IMPACT VISUALS.)

However, this privatization does not necessarily mean better housing. In the new housing market, flats and homes are allocated according to market forces, and many people cannot afford the high prices. In the center of Moscow, apartments are particularly expensive, and most people have no choice but to continue to live in the communal apartments assigned to them under the Soviet system.

Post-Soviet cities are also taking on the look of Western cities. The downtowns, now the most expensive urban land, are increasingly dominated by retailing outlets of familiar Western companies, such as Nike and McDonald's. Tall office buildings that house financial activities are replacing industrial buildings. Processes akin to gentrification (see the earlier section in this chapter) are taking place in the center of cities such as Moscow, displacing residents to the peripheral portions of the city while housing others in Western-style elegance.

It is not yet clear whether Moscow will begin to follow the previously described three models of land-use forms or whether the combination of state policies and market forces will create new models of urban land use. Future research by geographers will undoubtedly yield insights into the effects on urban form of these massive socioeconomic and spatial transformations in post-Soviet cities.

Latin American Model

To illustrate cultural interaction in cities of the developing world, we draw upon a model specific to one region, Latin America—while keeping in mind that several other models can be applied to other parts of the developing world.

The model of the Latin American city is shown in Figure 1.16. Refer to the illustration as you read this section. This model is a generalized scheme that is sensitive to local cultures in Central and South America and also articulates the pervasive influence of international forces, both Western and non-Western, on urban structure. This dimension comes through in the description and explanation of each element of the model.

In contrast to contemporary cities in the United States, the CBDs of Latin American cities are vibrant, dynamic, and increasingly specialized. The dominance of the CBD is explained partly by a reliance on public transit that serves the central city and partly on the existence of a large and relatively affluent population close to the CBD. Outside the CBD, the dominant component is a commercial spine surrounded by an elite residential sector. Because these two zones are interrelated, they are referred to as the *spine/sector*. This combination is an extension of the CBD down a major boulevard, along which are the city's important amenities, such as parks, theaters, restau-

rants, and even golf courses. Strict zoning and land controls ensure continuation of these activities and protect the elite from incursions by low-income squatters.

Somewhat less prestigious is the inner-city *zone of maturity*, a collection of homes occupied by people unable to participate in the spine/sector. This is an area of upward mobility. The *zone of accretion* is a diverse collection of housing types, sizes, and quality, which can be thought of as a transition between the zone of maturity and the next zone. It is an area of ongoing construction and change, emblematic of the explosive population growth that characterizes the Latin American city. Although some neighborhoods within this zone have city-provided utilities, other blocks must rely on water and butane delivery trucks for essential services.

The most recent migrants to the Latin American city are found in the *zone of peripheral squatter settlements*. This fringe of poor people and inadequate housing contrasts dramatically with the affluent and comfortable suburbs that ring North American cities. Squatter houses are often built from scavenged materials, and these areas look like refugee camps, surrounded by a landscape bare of vegetation, which has been cut for fuel and building materials. Streets are unpaved, open trenches carry wastes; residents carry water from distant locations, and electricity is often pirated by attaching illegal wires to the closest utility pole. If residents have work, their commute is a long one that consumes much of the day. Although this zone's quality of life seems marginal, many residents transform these squatter settlements over time into permanent neighborhoods with minimal amenities (see Chapter 10).

 ## Urban Landscapes

What do these urban patterns look like? How can we recognize different types of cities from their three-dimensional forms, and how are these forms changing? Cities, like all places humans inhabit, demonstrate an intriguing array of cultural landscapes that give varied insights into the complicated interactions between people and their surroundings. By reading these **cityscapes,** we gain access to the past, open doors on the future, and better understand the various social forces shaping our settlements. Grady Clay, in his enchanting book on reading American cityscapes, says: "No true secrets are lurking in the landscape, but only undisclosed evidence, waiting for us. No true chaos is in the urban scene, but only patterns and clues waiting to be organized."

We agree. In this section, we offer some thoughts about how to view North American urban landscapes.

We begin by discussing some themes—geographical reference points, one might say—for investigating cityscapes. We follow with a brief discussion of the new components in urban landscapes. Much of what we say will strike a familiar chord, because our urban scene is the basis of so much of our life. You will find that you have great depths of intuitive knowledge about cityscapes.

Themes in Cityscape Study

Cultural geographers look to cityscapes for many different kinds of information. Here we discuss four interconnected themes that are commonly used as organizational frameworks for landscape research (Figure 11.20).

Landscape Dynamics Because North Americans are a restless people with little reluctance to reshape our environments incessantly, our settlements are cauldrons of change. Think of some familiar indicators in the cityscape: downtown activities creeping into residential areas; deteriorated farmland on the city's outskirts; older buildings demolished for the new. These are all signs of specific processes that create urban change; the landscape faithfully reflects this dynamic.

When these visual clues are systematically mapped and analyzed, they offer evidence for the currents of change expressed in our cities. Of equal interest is where change is *not* occurring—those parts of the city that, for various reasons, remain relatively static. An unchanging landscape also conveys an important message. Perhaps that part of the city is stagnant because it is removed from the forces that produce change in other parts. Or perhaps there is a conscious attempt by local residents to inhibit change—to preserve open space by resisting suburban development, for example, or to preserve a historic landmark.

Look to the landscape to understand how our cities are changing. Documenting landscape changes over time gives valuable insight into the paths of settlement development.

The City as Palimpsest Because cityscapes change, they offer a rich field for uncovering remnants of the past. A **palimpsest** is an old parchment used over and over for written messages. Before a new missive could be written, the old was erased, yet rarely were all the previous characters and words completely obliterated, so remnants of earlier messages showed through. This mosaic of old and new is called a palimpsest, a word geographers use fondly to describe the visual mixture of old and new in cultural landscapes.

The city is full of palimpsestic offerings, scattered across the contemporary landscape. How often have you noticed an old Victorian farmhouse surrounded by new tract homes, or a historic street pattern obscured by a re-

Figure 11.20

Boston's central city. There are various ways of looking at cityscapes: as indicators of change, as palimpsests, as expressions of visual biases, and as manifestations of symbolic traditions. This photo offers evidence of all approaches. **Which clues would you select to illustrate each cityscape theme?** (STEVE DUNWELL/THE IMAGE BANK.)

cent urban redevelopment project, or a brick factory shadowed by new high-rise office buildings? All of these give clues to past settlement patterns, and all are mute testimony to the processes of change in the city.

Our interest in this historical mosaic is more than romantic nostalgia. A systematic collection of these urban remnants provides us with glimpses of the past that might otherwise be hidden. All societies pick and choose what they wish to preserve for future generations, and, in this process, a filtering takes place that often excludes and distorts information. But the landscape does not lie.

The urban palimpsest, then, offers a way to find the past in the contemporary landscape. We can evaluate these remnants to glean a better understanding of historical settlement.

Symbolic Cityscapes Landscapes contain much more than literal messages about economic function. They are

Figure 11.21

Main Street, Ferndale, California. The symbolism of Main Street, USA, is a powerful force in shaping communities today, particularly because an ersatz Main Street is the central element of Disney World. **Think of the ways this symbol is used in art, literature, film, and television and of the messages and emotions conveyed by this landscape.** (CHROMOSOHM/SOHM/PHOTO RESEARCHERS, INC.)

also loaded with figurative or metaphorical meaning and can elicit emotions and memories. To some people, skyscrapers are more than high-rise office buildings: they are symbols of progress, economic vitality, downtown renewal, or corporate identities. Similarly, historical landscapes—those parts of the city where the past has been preserved—help people to define themselves in time; establish social continuity with the past; and codify a forgotten, yet sometimes idealized, past.

D. W. Meinig, a geographer who has given much thought to urban landscapes, maintains that there are three highly symbolic townscapes in the United States. They are the New England village, with its white church, commons, and tree-lined neighborhoods; Main Street of Middle America, the string street of a small Midwestern town, with storefronts, bandstand, and park (Figure 11.21); and what Meinig calls California Suburbia, suburbs of quarter-acre lots, effusive garden landscaping, swimming pools, and ranch-style houses. As Meinig explains: "Each is based upon an actual landscape of a particular region. Each is an image derived from our national experience . . . simplified . . . and widely advertised so as to become a commonly understood symbol. Each has . . . influenced the shaping of the American scene over broader areas."

More politically and problematically, the cultural landscape is an important vehicle for constructing and maintaining social and ethnic distinctions. This is often done in subtle and implicit ways that are intertwined with landscape symbols. To illustrate, geographers Jim and Nancy Duncan found that because conspicuous consumption is

a major way of conveying social identity in our culture, elite landscapes are created through large-lot zoning, imitation country estates, and the preservation of undeveloped land. They see the residential landscapes in upper-income areas as controlled and managed to reinforce class and status categories. Their study of elite suburbs near Vancouver and New York sensitizes us to how the cultural landscape can be thought of as a repository of symbols used by our society to differentiate itself and protect vested interests.

Cultural geographers are interested in how townscapes and landmarks take on symbolic significance and in whether these idealizations are based on reality or, instead, are fabricated from diverse predilections. In addition, they are interested in how to assess the impact of these symbolic landscapes. After all, the hidden and shared messages inherent in landscapes usually determine how we treat our environment—how it is managed, changed, or protected.

Perception of the City During the last 20 years, social scientists have been concerned with measuring people's perceptions of the urban landscape. They assume that if we really know what people see and react to in the city, we can ask architects and urban planners to design and create a more humane urban environment.

Kevin Lynch, an urban designer, pioneered a method for recording people's images of the city. He assumed that all people have a mental map. After all, they must find their way about their cities in the course of daily life. Lynch then figured out ways that people could convey their mental maps to others. With this information, he could discover which parts of the urban landscape are being used as visual clues by which people. What do people react to favorably or negatively? What do they block out?

On the basis of interviews conducted in Boston; Jersey City, New Jersey; and Los Angeles, Lynch suggested five important elements in mental maps of cities:

1. *Pathways* are the routes of frequent travel, such as streets, freeways, and transit corridors. We experience the city from the pathways. Therefore, they become the threads that hold our maps together.

2. *Edges* are boundaries between areas or the outer limits of our image. Mountains, rivers, shorelines, and even major streets and freeways are commonly used as edges. They tend to define the extremes of our urban vision. Then we fill in the details.

3. *Nodes* are strategic junction points, such as breaks in transportation, traffic circles, or any place where important pathways come together.

4. *Districts* are small areas with a common identity, such as ethnic areas and functional zones (for instance, the CBD or a row of car dealers).

5. *Landmarks* are reference points that stand out because of shape, height, color, or historical importance. The city hall in Los Angeles; the Washington Monument in Washington, D.C.; and the golden arches of a McDonald's are all landmarks.

Using these concepts, Lynch saw that some parts of the cities were more **legible,** or easier to decipher, than others. Lynch discovered that, in general, legibility increases when the urban landscape offers clear pathways, nodes, districts, edges, and landmarks. The less legible parts of the city do not offer such a precise landscape. Thus it is more difficult for a person to form a mental map of those areas. Further, some cities are more legible than others. For example, Lynch found that Jersey City is not very legible. Wedged between New York City and Newark, Jersey City is fragmented by railroads and highways. Residents' mental maps of Jersey City have large blank areas in them. When questioned, they can think of few local landmarks. Instead, they tend to point to the New York City skyline just across the river.

There are also distinct ethnic, gender, and age variables in mental maps of cities. These differences often influence everyday behavior. For example, both men and women perceive a risk of crime that alters their behavior. Women, however, are particularly vulnerable to rape, and studies have documented how this vulnerability leads women to engage in more precautionary behavior than men.

Women tend to avoid certain areas of a city at night, and many will even forgo activities that require them to be out alone at night in their own neighborhoods. Although recent studies have shown that many of the reported cases of violence against women, including rape, occur within the home, the perception that particular areas of the city are dangerous continues to alter women's experiences of the urban environment.

The New Urban Landscape

Within the past 25 to 30 years, our cityscapes have undergone massive transformations. The impact of suburbanization and decentralization has led to an emerging new urban form that we have called the edge city (see Chapter 10). In the older downtown areas, we have seen that gentrification, redevelopment, and immigration have also created novel urban forms. What we see emerging in our cityscapes, then, is a new urban landscape, composed of distinctive elements that we have not yet discussed.

New Ethnic Neighborhoods As many middle- and upper-class families continue to move out of traditional neighborhoods near urban centers, they are being replaced by new immigrants. According to the Population Reference Bureau, more than 8 million people immigrated to the United States between 1990 and 1997: 52 percent came from Latin America, 30 percent from Asia, 13 percent from Europe, and 5 percent from other regions. The vast majority of these immigrants found job opportunities and cultural connections that drew them to major metropolitan regions in six states (California, New York, Texas, Florida, New Jersey, and Illinois). Figure 11.22 on the next page reveals the places of origin for immigrants living in six metropolitan areas. Together, these cities housed over 43 percent of the migrants to the United States in 1993.

This spatial concentration of America's new immigrants has created diverse communities with distinctive landscapes, both within the downtown areas of these cities and in the suburban regions. Miami's Little Havana, for example, is easily recognized by the commercial signs in Spanish, Spanish street names, and the colors and styles of buildings. Parts of what were once run-down neighborhoods of the city have been remade into vibrant commercial and residential communities. Eighty years ago, a Saturday morning stroll through the CBD of Los Angeles would lead through streets lined with department stores, movie theaters, and offices. Now it is filled with the sounds of Latin music and vendors selling everything from electronics to mango ice cream.

But these new ethnic landscapes are not limited to the central city. Portions of America's suburbs have also become diverse. The decentralization of the downtown has

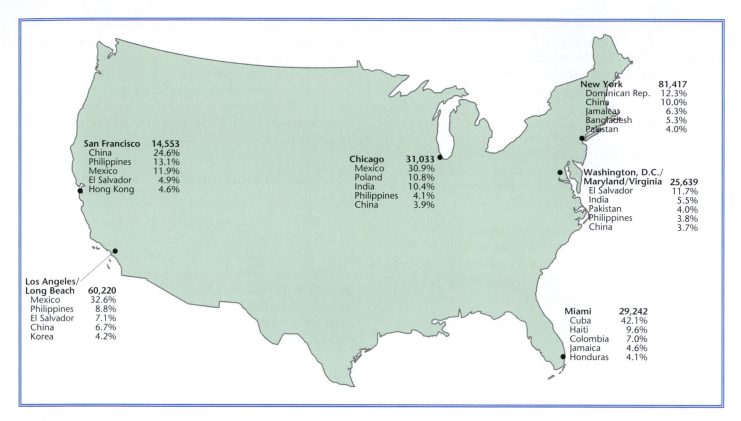

San Francisco 14,553
China 24.6%
Philippines 13.1%
Mexico 11.9%
El Salvador 4.9%
Hong Kong 4.6%

Los Angeles/
Long Beach 60,220
Mexico 32.6%
Philippines 8.8%
El Salvador 7.1%
China 6.7%
Korea 4.2%

Chicago 31,033
Mexico 30.9%
Poland 10.8%
India 10.4%
Philippines 4.1%
China 3.9%

New York 81,417
Dominican Rep. 12.3%
China 10.0%
Jamaica 6.3%
Bangladesh 5.3%
Pakistan 4.0%

Washington, D.C./
Maryland/Virginia 25,639
El Salvador 11.7%
India 5.5%
Pakistan 4.0%
Philippines 3.8%
China 3.7%

Miami 29,242
Cuba 42.1%
Haiti 9.6%
Colombia 7.0%
Jamaica 4.6%
Honduras 4.1%

Figure 11.22
Map indicating place of origin of legally admitted immigrants to six metropolitan areas in the United States. Why is immigration focused on these six cities? (Source: U.S. Immigration and Naturalization Service, 1998.)

created new economic centers in suburban regions, and immigrants are drawn to these centers. In Montgomery County, Maryland, a suburban community outside of Washington, D.C., almost a quarter of all households are headed by a person who is foreign-born. Instead of the dense residential and commercial districts that characterize downtown ethnic enclaves, the new suburban ethnicity is proclaimed within shopping centers, suburban cemeteries, and dispersed churches and temples. For example, most of the 50,000 Vietnamese-Americans who migrated to the Washington, D.C., area from the 1970s through the 1990s settled in suburbs in northern Virginia. According to geographer Joe Wood, their presence in the landscape is often not visible to observers precisely because it is suburban. Stereotypically, immigrant enclaves are located in the inner city and are characterized by residential density centered around commercial areas easily identified as belonging to a particular ethnic group. But as new economic nodes have dispersed out of the city centers, so too have ethnic neighborhoods. In northern Virginia, the focal point of the Vietnamese community is the Eden Center, a typical L-shaped shopping center that has been

transformed into a Vietnamese-American economic and social center (Figure 11.23). It serves a population that is widely dispersed throughout the surrounding suburban residential areas. This pattern of shopping plazas serving as ethnic community markers for a dispersed immigrant population is not peculiar to northern Virginia but is commonplace in the metropolitan areas of most major North American cities.

Shopping Malls Many people consider the image of the shopping mall, surrounded by mass-produced suburbs, to be one of the most distinctive landscape symbols of post–World War II life in North America. Yet, oddly, most malls are not designed to be seen from the outside. As a matter of fact, without appropriate signs, a passerby could proceed past a mall without noticing any visual display. Unlike the retail districts of nineteenth- and early-twentieth-century cities, where grand architectural displays along the major boulevards were the norm, shopping malls are enclosed, private worlds that are meant to be seen from the inside. Often located near an off-ramp of a major freeway or beltway of a metropolitan area, and

Figure 11.23
Eden Shopping Center in Fairfax, Virginia. This shopping plaza serves as a social and cultural center for the Vietnamese community of northern Virginia. (COURTESY OF JOSEPH WOOD.)

close to the middle- and upper-class residential neighborhoods, shopping malls can be distinguished more by their extensive parking lots than by their architectural design.

Yet shopping malls do have a characteristic form. The early malls of the 1960s tended to be a simple, linear form, with 2 department stores at each end that functioned as "anchors" and 20 to 30 smaller shops connecting the two ends. In the 1970s and 1980s, much larger malls were built, and their form became more complex.

Malls today are often several stories high and may contain 5 or 6 anchor stores and up to 400 smaller shops. In addition, many malls now serve more than a retail function—they often contain food courts and restaurants, professional offices, movie complexes, hotels, chapels, and amusement arcades and centers (Figure 11.24). The Mall of America in Bloomington, Minnesota, said to be the largest mall in the world, contains 14 movie screens, 6 supper clubs, and a 7-acre amusement park, in addition

Figure 11.24
Food court at the Fashion Mall in Plantation, Florida. A large percentage of the third story of this mall is devoted to fast-food outlets. The fountain and natural lighting are meant to create a gardenlike setting for mall dining. **Why do you think these fast-food outlets are all clustered together within the mall?** (COURTESY OF MONA DOMOSH.)

FOCUS ON

The Shopping Mall as Social Center: "Mallingering" and Consuming at the West Edmonton Mall (WEM)

The role of WEM as a social center cannot be divorced from the popularity of shopping centers in our consumer society. The popularity of "mallingering"—the act of lingering about a mall for economic and non-economic social purposes—can be partly attributed to the rapid proliferation of shopping centers during the economic and demographic booms of the post-World War II era and the ensuing rise in consumerism as a way of life. In an age in which consumerism is the dominant lifestyle and material consumption is a popular life objective, shopping malls—the dominant forum for commerce— become the principal forum for consumption and, thus, a popular place to spend money as well as time.

A more tempered explanation of mallingering considers the secondary social and recreational roles associated with retailing. The marketplace has traditionally played the role of communal meeting place. Given the latent social function of the marketplace in general and the congregative and community role of shopping malls in particular, WEM is not merely a mega-shopping mall, nor a mega-recreation center, but a mega-social center, which is claimed to bring together as many as 60,000 people per day from Edmonton and around the world. When placed in the context of the tradi- tional role of the marketplace and the cultural context of consumerism and mallingering, WEM's popularity as a social center is not surprising. The formal introduction of social activities (e.g., leisure and entertainment facilities) into a shopping center is more a confirmation of the social role of the marketplace than it is a novel marketing ploy. The socially congregative pull—"the sociopetal" factors—exerted by WEM's size, scale, and leisure factors, however, renders the mega- mall functionally and socially unique relative to other shop- ping malls. The fact that social interaction is under the control of a single corporation, like most indoor urban space, makes understanding the freedoms and constraints—the socially divisive or "sociofugal" factors—imposed upon patrons by WEM's physical design and operation all the more pertinent.

Theatres of Consumption

To suggest that shopping malls are manipulating wizards able to induce unsuspecting patrons into money-spending frenzies or irrational purchases not only insults the public's intelligence but also pays unwarranted homage to mall designers and management. There is growing recognition, nonetheless, that physical design and atmosphere are important factors influencing customer behavior. Shopping malls in this latter sense are literally theatres of consumption staged within a carefully contrived set designed to promote retail drama. Enclosure, protection, and control are the basic design formula, and organized happenings assist in promoting an exciting friendly atmosphere. Herein lie factors that may promote and retard social interaction at WEM.

The mega-mall (indeed most shopping malls and indoor space) offers a pleasant alternative to some of the discomforts of the world outside. Enclosure provides freedom from climatic extremes, clear signage, ease of mobility, and access to hundreds of stores and services. Pay telephones, plants, statues, fountains, washroom facilities, and benches further contribute to the value of WEM as a social centre. The many and varied sights and objects in the corridors promote "triangulation," whereby external stimuli may provide links between people and prompt strangers to talk to one another. A combination of sophisticated electronic security systems and uniformed and plain-clothes personnel ensures, accord- ing to the management, "a safe and secure atmosphere for [the] entire family" (WEM security brochure). No city street can as yet match the 24-hour protection provided by "480 computer monitored security points,1600 fire detectors, 42 strategically placed 'help phones' and hidden cameras that keep an eye on 38 locations throughout WEM at the same time" (WEM security brochure). Control is, therefore, a key ingredient in the success of WEM; its environment can more easily conform to the tastes, needs, and preferences of patrons, as perceived by mall management, than, say a city street of independent shop-owners.

From Hopkins, 1991. Reprinted by permission of the Canadian Association of Geographers.

---

to retailers. Many scholars consider these megamalls to be America's new main streets (see Focus On: The Shopping Mall as Social Center, and Chapter 2) because they seem to be the major sites for social interaction. After work- place, home, and school, the shopping mall is where most Americans spend their time.

However, unlike the open-air marketplaces of an ear- lier era, shopping malls are private spaces, not public spaces. The use of the shopping mall as a place for social

interaction, therefore, is always of secondary importance to its private, commercial function. If a certain group of people were considered a nuisance to shoppers, the mall owners could prevent them from what Jeffrey Hopkins calls "'mallingering'—the act of lingering about a mall for economic and noneconomic social purposes."

Office Parks With major interstate highways connecting our metropolitan areas, and the development of new communication technologies, office buildings no longer need to be located in the center city. Cheaper rent in suburban locations, combined with the convenience of easy-access parking and the privacy of a separate location, has led to the construction of **office parks** throughout suburban America. Figure 11.25 shows the location of office parks in metropolitan Atlanta in relation to the freeway network. Many of these office parks are occupied by the regional or national headquarters of large corporations or by local sales and professional offices. To take advantage of economies of scale, many of these offices will locate together and rent or buy space from a land development company.

The use of the word *park* to identify this new landscape element points to the conscious antiurban imagery of these complexes. In contrast to downtown skyscrapers, office parks tend to be horizontal in shape, usually three to six stories tall. Many of these developments are surrounded by a well-landscaped outdoor space, often incorporating artificial lakes and waterfalls (Figure 11.26). Jogging paths, fitness trails, and picnic tables all cater to the new lifestyle of professional and managerial employees.

Although providing many conveniences for employees, office parks do remove workers from the social diversity of an urban location. Lunchtime choices are usually limited to the corporate cafeteria, and the inclusion in the office complex of such nonessential functions as fitness centers indicates the often-intrusive role of the corporation in workers' social lives. Many office parks are located along what have been called **high-tech corridors:** areas along limited-access highways that contain offices

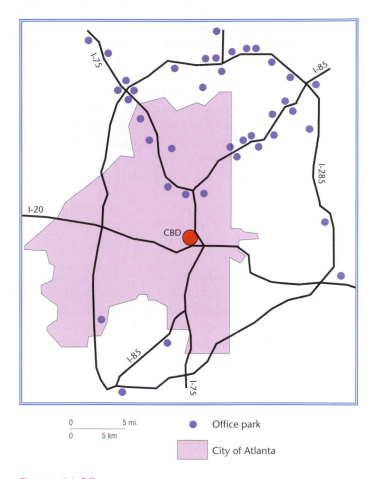

Figure 11.25

Office park locations in Atlanta, Georgia. This map clearly shows their locational ties to major freeways. (AFTER HARTSHORN AND MULLER, 1989.)

Figure 11.26

Compare this suburban office building in Yonkers, New York, with your image of downtown skyscrapers. Notice the green space around the building and its horizontal rather than vertical appearance. **Why do you rarely find very tall office buildings in the suburbs?** (MICHAEL MELFORD/ THE IMAGE BANK.)

and other services associated with new high-tech industries. Geographer Paul Knox suggests that these corridors differ from the small-scale in-filling that has taken place on many commercial strips. According to Knox, high-tech corridors "are set on a framework of large lots, usually several acres, and include large-scale structures, extensive on-site parking, generous amounts of landscaped parkland (including waterfalls, lagoons, terraces, gazebos, and sculptures), and a variety of services and amenities such as fitness centers, cycling trails, coffee shops, flower shops and day care facilities." As our discussion of edge cities suggests (see Chapter 10), this new type of commercial landscape is gradually replacing our downtowns as the workplace for most Americans.

Master-Planned Communities   Many newer residential developments on the suburban fringe are planned and built as complete neighborhoods by private development companies. These **master-planned communities** include not only architecturally compatible housing units but also recreational facilities (such as tennis courts, fitness centers, bike paths, and swimming pools) and security measures (gated or guarded entrances). Paul Knox points out that most of these communities exploit various land-use restrictions and zoning regulations to maintain control over land values, and that homes in these communities maintain their value better than homes elsewhere.

In Weston, a master-planned community that covers approximately 10,000 acres (4000 hectares) in southern Florida, land use is completely regulated not only within the gated residential complexes but also along the road system that connects Weston to the interstate (Figure 11.27). Shrubbery is planted strategically to shield residents from views of the roadway, and the road signs are uniform in style and encased in stylish, weathered-gray wood frames. This massive community—Weston developers estimate that it will be home to 60,000 people when it is completed in 2005—contains various complexes catering to particular lifestyles, ranging from smaller patio homes to equestrian estates. For example, in the mid-1990s, homes in Tequesta Point cost between $250,000 and $300,000, and they came with gated entranceways, split-level floor plans, and Roman bathtubs. Those in Bermuda Springs, on the other hand, cost $115,000 to $120,000, were significantly smaller, and did not offer the same interior features. Typical of master-planned communities, the name of the development itself was chosen to convey a hometown feeling. In this instance, developers carried out an extensive marketing survey before they settled on the name Weston.

Festival Settings   In many cities, gentrification efforts focus on a multiuse redevelopment scheme that is built

Figure 11.27
The master-planned community of Weston, Florida. These automated gates keep "undesirables" out of many subdivisions in master-planned communities. The more expensive areas have guardhouses at their entrances, whereas less expensive ones may have privately installed security systems. (COURTESY OF DONNA FARANDA.)

around a particular setting, often one with a historical association. Waterfronts are commonly chosen as focal points for these large-scale projects, which Knox has referred to as **festival settings.** These complexes integrate retailing, office, and entertainment activities and incorporate trendy shops, restaurants, bars and nightclubs, and hotels. Knox suggests that these developments are "distinctive as new landscape elements merely because of their scale and their consequent ability to stage—or merely to be—the spectacular." Such festival settings as Faneuil Hall in Boston, Bayside in Miami, and Riverwalk in San Antonio serve as sites for concerts, ethnic festivals, and street performances; they also serve as focal points for the more informal human interactions that we usually associate with urban life (Figure 11.28). In this sense, festival settings do perform a vital function in the attempt to revitalize our downtowns. Yet, like many other gentrification efforts, these massive displays of wealth and consumption often stand in direct contrast to neighboring areas of the inner city that have received little, if any, monetary or other social benefit from these projects.

"Militarized" Space   Considered together, these new elements in the urban landscape suggest some trends that many scholars find disturbing. Urbanist Mike Davis has called one such trend the "militarization" of urban space, meaning the increasing use of space to set up defenses against people the city considers undesirable. This includes landscape developments that range from the lack of street furniture to guard against the homeless living

on the streets, to gated and guarded residential communities, to the complete segregation of classes and "races" within the city. Particularly in downtown redevelopment schemes, the goal of city planners and others is usually to provide safe and homogeneous environments, segregated from the diversity of cultures and lifestyles that often characterizes the central area of most cities. As Davis says, "Cities of all sizes are rushing to apply and profit from a formula that links together clustered development, social homogeneity, and a perception of security." Although this "militarization" is not completely new, it has taken on epic proportions as whole sections of such cities as Los Angeles, Atlanta, Dallas, Houston, and Miami have become "militarized" spaces (Figure 11.29).

Reflecting on GEOGRAPHY

Some scholars might argue that the increasing "militarization" of our urban spaces will lead to situations little different from what happened to South African cities under apartheid (see Figure 11.18). Identify similarities and differences between these two urban situations.

Decline of Public Space Related to the increase in "militarized" space is the decline of public spaces in most of our cities. For example, the change in shopping patterns from the downtown retailing area to the suburbs indicates a change of emphasis from the public space of city streets to the privately controlled and operated shopping malls. Similarly, many city governments, often joined by private developers, have built enclosed walkways either above or below the city streets. These walkways serve partly to provide climate-controlled conditions and partly to provide pedestrians with a "safe" environment that avoids possible confrontations on the street. Again, the public space of the street is being replaced by controlled spaces that do not provide the same access to all members of the urban community. It remains to be seen whether this trend will continue or new public spaces will be formed that allow for the expression of all groups of people within the urban landscape.

Some scholars have suggested that the Internet is a new forum for social and political interaction and as such constitutes a new type of public space. Yet, like most technologies, access to the Internet is limited to those who have adequate resources and training, and it is not clear to what degree "virtual" encounters can replace face-to-face communication.

Conclusion

We have examined various components of the intricate urban mosaic. Culture regions are found at a smaller scale than we've previously explored; in the city, neighborhoods and census units can be thought of as social regions and culture regions.

We also see two major forces at work in the city that can be considered diffusion processes. One works to centralize activities within the city, the other to decentralize activities into the suburbs. The latter is the dominant force currently at work in North American cities. However, the costs of decentralization run high, not just to the suburbs, where unplanned growth takes its toll, but also to the inner cities, which are left with decayed and stagnant cores.

The cultural ecology of the city is a complicated issue because urbanization has modified natural ecosystems profoundly. The results of these changes—floods and air pollution, for example—cause significant problems for urban dwellers everywhere. Solutions to these problems will require long-term commitments of energy and resources.

Models of the internal structure of cities describe how social and economic activities sort themselves out in space. The simplification of these models calls into question their usefulness for describing the contemporary American city, as well as cities of the former Soviet Union and South Africa.

As dense collections of human artifacts, cities offer a fascinating array of cultural landscapes that tell us much about ourselves and our interaction with the environment. These cityscapes reveal contemporary change, the past, our scenic values, and our storehouse of symbols. New elements in the urban landscape relay information about our current social, economic, and political reality, and they indicate trends for the future that many scholars find disturbing.

 ## The Urban Mosaic on the Internet

To learn more about cities and suburbs, check the following web sites:

Burbs, Blockbusting, and Blacks
http://www.rut.com/mjalbert/burbs/index.html

A fascinating look at the relationships among racism, blockbusting, and the formation of American suburbs.

Levittown: Documents of an Ideal American Suburb
http://www.uic.edu/~pbhales/Levittown

A history of Levittown, New York, the first mass-produced suburb, with interesting historical and contemporary photographs.

The State of the Nation's Cities: A Comprehensive Database on American Cities and Suburbs
http://www.policy.rutgers.edu/cupr/sonc.htm

A comprehensive database on 77 American cities and suburbs that you can download onto your computer and display in graphic form.

Literature on Race, Ethnicity, and Multiculturalism
http://ethics.acusd.edu/race.html

An annotated list of Internet resources on issues pertaining to race, ethnicity, and human rights.

SEEING GEOGRAPHY

Chinatown, New York City

"Reading" this urban landscape is relatively simple: the signs of the stores and restaurants leave no doubt that this place is marked as a "Chinatown." Interpreting this scene is easy for most Americans because Chinatown has become a symbolic landscape: a place that connotes America's history and geography of immigration; the idea of the melting pot; and, now, a commitment to cultural pluralism. But there are other ways to understand this landscape as well, ways that rely on a keen eye and an urban geographical analysis. That some of the writing is in English and some in Chinese tells us that this streetscape is located in a place where both languages are spoken; the style of architecture, the types of cars, the street signs, and the American flag indicate a location in the United States. This Chinatown happens to be in New York City, but one could have guessed San Francisco, Boston, or Philadelphia.

Based on our understanding of the models of urban land use, we could surmise that Chinatown is located in a transitional zone, just outside the CBD. This certainly was the case in the late nineteenth and early twentieth centuries, when most of the brick buildings in this photograph were built. In this part of New York City, land values were relatively low. The financial center of Wall Street was to the south, and the retail areas along Broadway and Fifth Avenue were farther north, as were the middle- and upper-class residences. With few choices available, Chinese immigrants (and many others, including Italians and eastern European Jews) settled into this area and found jobs in the small industries and businesses nearby. The result was a series of neighborhoods of mixed land uses, on the edge of both the financial CBD and the retail CBD, in the zone of transition. Each of these neighborhoods came to be defined by the dominant Anglo culture as an ethnic region—in this case, Chinatown.

Today, Chinatown is still home to new migrants, but many of them come from other East Asian countries: Vietnam, Korea, the Philippines. In the United States between 1980 and 1997, the Vietnamese population grew 327 percent, the Korean population 175 percent, and the Filipino population 155 percent. Although we know that an increasing proportion of new immigrants to the United States move to suburban areas, Chinatown in New York City still attracts many immigrants because of its accessibility to a fairly diverse job market and to the services available for migrants who may not speak English and do not drive automobiles.

The Häagen-Dazs sign reminds us of the presence of globalizing forces and also indicates that Chinatown has become a tourist destination for visitors to the city. After a trip to the top of the Empire State Building or to the Metropolitan Museum of Art, tourists might go downtown for "authentic" Chinese food, stopping off for ice cream afterward. If they really wanted to sample the avant-garde club scene of the city, they might find themselves in a trendy bar on the edge of Chinatown. Much of the Lower East Side is already gentrified, and Chinatown is a likely next target. If that happens, the Mandarin Court sign might soon read Starbucks Coffee.

How has globalization affected urban ethnic neighborhoods?

A street in Chinatown, New York City.

Sources

Abbott, Edith, and Mary Zahrobsky. 1936. "The Tenement Areas and the People of the Tenements," in E. Abbott (ed.), *The Tenements of Chicago*. Chicago: University of Chicago Press, 72–169.

Agnew, John, John Mercer, and David Sopher (eds.). 1984. *The City in Cultural Context*. Boston: Allen & Unwin.

Anderson, Kay. 1987. "The Idea of Chinatown: The Power of Place and Institutional Practice in the Making of a Racial Category." *Annals of the Association of American Geographers* 77: 580–598.

Bach, Wilfred, and Thomas Hagedorn. 1971. "Atmospheric Pollution: Its Spatial Distribution over an Urban Area." *Proceedings of the Association of American Geographers* 3: 22.

Bater, James H. 1980. *The Soviet City: Ideal and Reality*. Beverly Hills, Calif.: Sage Publications.

Bater, James H. 1996. *Russia and the Post-Soviet Scene*. New York: John Wiley.

Bell, David, and Gill Valentine (eds.). 1995. *Mapping Desire: Geographies of Sexualities*. London: Routledge.

Burgess, E. W. 1925. "The Growth of the City: An Introduction to a Research Project," in Robert E. Park, Ernest W. Burgess, and Roderick D. Mckenzie, (eds.), *The City*. Chicago: University of Chicago Press, 47–62.

Castells, Manuel. 1983. *The City and Grassroots: A Cross-Cultural Theory of Urban Social Movements*. Berkeley: University of California Press.

Chandler, T. J. 1961. "The Changing Form of London's Heat Island." *Geography* 46: 295–307.

Chauncey, George. 1994. *Gay New York: Gender, Urban Culture, and the Making of the Gay Male World, 1890–1940*. New York: Basic Books.

Christopher, A. J. 1994. *The Atlas of Apartheid*. London: Routledge.

Clay, Grady. 1973. *Close-Up: How to Read the American City*. New York: Praeger.

Cybriwsky, Roman A., David Ley, and John Western. 1986. "The Political and Social Construction of Revitalized Neighborhoods: Society Hill, Philadelphia, and False Creek, Vancouver," in Neil Smith and Peter Williams (eds.), *Gentrification of the City*. Boston: Allen & Unwin, 92–120.

Daniell, Jennifer, and Raymond Struyk. 1997. "The Evolving Housing Market in Moscow: Indicators of Housing Reform." *Urban Studies* 34: 235–254.

Davis, Mike. 1992. "Fortress Los Angeles: The Militarization of Urban Space," in Michael Sorkin (ed.), *Variations on a Theme Park: The New American City and the End of Public Space*. New York: Hill & Wang, 154–180.

Detwyler, Thomas, and Melvin Marcus (eds.). 1972. *Urbanization and Environment: The Physical Geography of the City*. Belmont, Calif.: Duxbury Press.

Drakakis-Smith, David. 2000. *Third World Cities*, 2nd ed. London: Routledge.

Duncan, James, and Nancy Duncan. 1984. "A Cultural Analysis of Urban Residential Landscapes in North America: The Cause of the Anglophile Elite," in John Agnew, John Mercer, and David Sopher (eds.), *The City in Cultural Context*. Boston: Allen & Unwin, 255–276.

Gilbert, Emily. 1994. "Naturalist Metaphors in the Literatures of Chicago, 1893–1925." *Journal of Historical Geography* 20: 283–304.

Gordon, Margaret T., et al. 1981. "Crime, Women, and the Quality of Urban Life," in Catherine R. Stimpson, Elsa Dixler, Martha J. Nelson, and Kathryn B. Yatrakis (eds.), *Women and the American City*. Chicago: University of Chicago Press, 141–157.

Griffin, Ernst, and Larry Ford. 1983. "Cities of Latin America," in Stanley Brunn and Jack Williams (eds.), *Cities of the World: World Regional Urban Development*. New York: Harper & Row, 199–240.

Hanson, Susan. 1992. "Geography and Feminism: Worlds in Collision?" *Annals of the Association of American Geographers* 82: 569–586.

Hanson, Susan, and Geraldine Pratt. 1995. *Gender, Work, and Space*. New York: Routledge.

Harris, C. D., and E. L. Ullman. 1945. "The Nature of Cities." *Annals of the Association of American Academy of Political and Social Science* 242: 7–17.

Hartshorn, Truman A., and Peter O. Muller. 1989. "Suburban Downtowns and the Transformation of Metropolitan Atlanta's Business Landscape." *Urban Geography* 10: 375–395.

Hopkins, Jeffrey S. P. 1991. "West Edmonton Mall as a Centre for Social Interaction." *The Canadian Geographer* 35: 268–279.

Hoyt, Homer (ed.). 1939. *Structure and Growth of Residential Neighborhoods in American Cities*. Washington, D.C.: Federal Housing Administration.

Jackson, Kenneth T. 1985. *Crabgrass Frontier*. New York: Oxford University Press.

Knopp, Lawrence. 1995. "Sexuality and Urban Space: A Framework for Analysis," in David Bell and Gill Valentine (eds.), *Mapping Desire*. London: Routledge, 149–161.

Knox, Paul L. 1991. "The Restless Urban Landscape: Economic and Sociocultural Change and the Transformation of Metropolitan Washington, D.C." *Annals of the Association of American Geographers* 81: 181–209.

Lauria, Mickey, and Lawrence Knopp. 1985. "Toward an Analysis of the Role of Gay Communities in the Urban Renaissance." *Urban Geography* 6: 152–169.

Lynch, Kevin. 1960. *The Image of the City*. Cambridge, Mass.: MIT Press.

Martin, Philip, and Elizabeth Midgley. 1999. "Immigration to the United States." *Population Bulletin* 54: 1–44.

McDowell, Linda. 1983. "Towards an Understanding of the Gender Division of Urban Space." *Environment and Planning D: Society and Space* 1: 59–72.

Meinig, D. W. (ed.). 1979. *The Interpretation of Ordinary Landscapes: Geographical Essays*. New York: Oxford University Press.

Mitchell, William J. 1996. *City of Bits: Space, Place and the Infobahn*. Cambridge, Mass.: MIT Press.

Mohl, Raymond A. 1995. "Making the Second Ghetto in Metropolitan Miami, 1940–1960." *Journal of Urban History* 21: 395–427.

Portes, Alejandro, and Ruben G. Rumbaut. 1996. *Immigrant America: A Portrait,* 2nd ed. Berkeley: University of California Press.

Pratt, Geraldine. 1990. "Feminist Analyses of the Restructuring of Urban Life." *Urban Geography* 11: 594–605.

Robinson, Jennifer. 1997. "The Geopolitics of South African Cities: States, Citizens, Territory." *Political Geography* 16: 365–386.

Rothenberg, Tamar. 1995. "'And She Told Two Friends': Lesbians Creating Urban Social Space," in David Bell and Gill Valentine (eds.), *Mapping Desire.* London: Routledge, 165–181.

Rowe, Stacy, and Jennifer Wolch. 1990. "Social Networks in Time and Space: Homeless Women in Skid Row, Los Angeles." *Annals of the Association of American Geographers* 80: 184–204.

Sibley, David. 1995. "Gender, Science, Politics and Geographies of the City." *Gender, Place and Culture: A Journal of Feminist Geography* 2: 37–49.

Smith, Neil. 1984. *Uneven Development.* New York: Basil Blackwell.

Smith, Neil. 1996. *The New Urban Frontier: Gentrification and the Revanchist City.* New York: Routledge.

Sorkin, Michael (ed.). 1992. *Variations on a Theme Park: The New American City and the End of Public Space.* New York: Hill and Wang.

Stimpson, Catherine R., Elsa Dixler, Martha J. Nelson, and Kathryn B. Yatrakis (eds.). 1981. *Women and the American City.* Chicago: University of Chicago Press.

Suro, Roberto. 1999. "Crossing the High-Tech Divide." *American Demographics* (July): 55–60.

U.S. Immigration and Naturalization Service. 1998. *1998 Statistical Yearbook.* Washington, D.C.: U.S. Government Printing Office.

Valentine, Gill. 1993. "Desperately Seeking Susan: A Geography of Lesbian Friendships." *Area* 25: 109–116.

Veness, April. 1994. "Designer Shelters as Models and Makers of Home: New Responses to Homelessness in Urban America." *Urban Geography* 15(2): 150–167.

Ward, David. 1971. *Cities and Immigrants.* New York: Oxford University Press.

Warner, Sam Bass. 1962. *Streetcar Suburbs: The Process of Growth in Boston, 1870–1900.* Cambridge: Harvard University Press.

Warr, Mark. 1985. "Fear of Rape Among Urban Women." *Social Problems* 32: 238–250.

Watson, Sophie, with Helen Austerberry. 1986. *Housing and Homelessness: A Feminist Perspective.* London: Routledge & Kegan Paul.

Women and Geography Study Group of the Institute of British Geographers. 1984. *Geography and Gender: An Introduction to Feminist Geography.* London: Hutchinson.

Wood, Joseph. 1997. "Vietnamese-American Place Making in Northern Virginia." *The Geographical Review* 87: 58–72.

Ten Recommended Books on the Urban Mosaic

(*For additional suggested readings, see* The Human Mosaic *web site:* www.whfreeman.com/jordan)

Allen, James P., and Eugene Turner. 1997. *The Ethnic Quilt: Population Diversity in Southern California.* Northridge, Calif.: Center for Geographical Studies. A fascinating visual exploration of Southern California's diverse population.

Beauregard, Robert A. 1993. *Voices of Decline: The Postwar Fate of U.S. Cities.* Cambridge, Mass.: Blackwell. An examination of how the discourse on decline became the primary way of understanding postwar American cities.

Davis, Mike. 1990. *City of Quartz: Excavating the Future in Los Angeles.* New York: Verso. A rough-and-tumble historical guide through the past, present, and possible future of the landscape of Los Angeles.

Fincher, Ruth, and Jane M. Jacobs. 1998. *Cities of Difference.* New York: Guilford Press. A series of cases studies that examine the relationships between urban space and social identities and differences.

Ford, Larry. 1994. *Cities and Buildings.* Baltimore: Johns Hopkins University Press. A detailed landscape analysis of contemporary metropolitan areas.

Harvey, David. 1990. *The Condition of Postmodernity.* Cambridge, Mass.: Blackwell Publishers. An investigation into the social and economic basis of postmodernity and its impacts upon cities.

Jacobs, Jane M. 1996. *Edge of Empire: Postcolonialism and the City.* London: Routledge. An examination of how imperialism has shaped and continues to shape cities in the developed world.

McDowell, Linda. 1997. *Capital Culture: Gender at Work in the City.* Oxford: Blackwell. An exploration of how masculinities and femininities are created within the contemporary urban workplace.

Ruddick, Susan. 1996. *Young and Homeless in Hollywood: Mapping Social Identities.* New York: Routledge. A study of the causes and implications of homeless youth in Los Angeles.

Soja, Edward W. 2000. *Postmetropolis: Critical Studies of Cities and Regions.* Oxford: Blackwell. A wide-ranging examination of the restructured form of Western megacities.

How might a comparable "inner landscape" have differed 30 or 40 years ago?

A typical office in the age of globalization. (PICTOR INTERNATIONAL, LTD./PICTUREQUEST.)
Turn to Seeing Geography on page 437 for an in-depth analysis of the above question.

CHAPTER

12

ONE WORLD OR MANY?
The Cultural Geography of the Future

This final chapter is about the future, the world in which you will spend most of your life. Here we pose perhaps the most essential cultural geographical question of all: Will your future contain one world or many? Will it be a human mosaic or a human monochrome?

The new millennium offers at once an exhilarating, confusing, and troubling time in which to live, an age of continual, mindless, often purposeless change. Some people say geography is dead, the world dying of *topocide* and surrendered to *placelessness*. Others retain faith that the ancient diversity of human lifeways will endure. Both sides agree that change will remain pervasive and that the twenty-first century is not for sissies.

What, then, does the dawning new age mean in terms of geographical values and identities? Predicting the future is a risky business, given all the uncertainties, and geographers are usually not so foolish as to try. In fact, we will alleviate this problem by presenting several possible futures, though it will become obvious what we two geographers anticipate. As a result, this chapter will be full of voices shouting in vigorous disagreement.

Globalization, Again!

The debate over one-world-or-many hinges on the concept of *globalization*, which we have toyed with in almost every chapter. We need to begin with a fuller, more concise definition of globalization, because it seems to lie at the center of the debate. Although some scholars trace the origins of globalization to the great age of exploration and discovery, or to the *industrial revolution*, the process began in earnest in the 1960s, when a

Figure 12.1
Headquarters of Electronic Data Systems near Dallas, Texas, a typical multinational corporation. (ASSOCIATED PRESS.)

capitalist, free-market economy increasingly dominated by huge multinational corporations and high technology produced a new, efficiently integrated system of production, marketing, transportation, communications, and data processing. The world under globalization functions increasingly as a single fluid, highly organized system. As Michael Hardt and Antonio Negri suggest, globalism has no single seat of power, and no single country can control it. In that sense, globalism represents something radically new.

Among the more obvious symptoms of globalization are a weakened status of independent countries (including the United States); open borders; international mass migration of labor; the spread of democracy; urbanization; the rise of popular culture; the demise of socialism; accelerated resource exploitation and habitat damage; the growth of corporate power; an increased interconnectedness of places and regions; rampant consumerism with all its icons—Coke, McDonald's, Levi's, Starbucks, Marlboro; the computer and the entire "cybernetic revolution"; and the overall ascendancy of high technology (Figure 12.1). And—note this well—globalization means the spread of *Western* popular culture and values at the expense of alternative ways of life. Globalism wasn't planned as some sort of conspiracy to reshape the world. It just happened. Both good and bad elements exist within globalism.

Geographers have long been observing the globalization process, because it bears so profoundly upon the central geographical issue of human diversity. At the 2001 annual meeting of the Association of American Geographers in New York City, for example, close to 25 different sessions of scholarly papers were held under one or another title that included the word *globalization*.

One-World Geographers

Many geographers think that globalization does possess the power to produce one world, to destroy human variety. As long ago as 1951, before *globalization* had even entered our vocabulary, geographer George Kimble peered into the future and concluded that the new age would allow "no independent, discrete units . . . no worlds within worlds." A half-century later, a special issue of *National Geographic*, edited by Joel Swerdlow, was devoted to "global culture," confirming Kimble's prediction of one world. It was filled with such phrases as "vanishing cultures," "a world together," and "we are all in each other's backyard." Similarly, James Kunstler speaks of the "geography of nowhere" and Edward Relph of "placelessness," both in reference to the impact of globalization on place identity. Linda McDowell wonders whether we are "undoing place." William Greider warns of "one world, ready or not," and Pico Iyer notes that "everywhere is so made up of everywhere else."

Indeed, within these very covers of *The Human Mosaic*, we have witnessed the decline of folk cultures, the spread of a few great religions at the expense of many small ones, the rise of a handful of languages and the demise of countless others, the erosion of ethnicity through acculturation and assimilation, the decline of the power of independent states, the urbanization of the world, the rise of corporate agribusiness, the spread of the *green revolution*, and other homogenizing trends that reflect globalization and undermine diversity.

Pick up a newspaper almost any day and you can read about globalization, though the word may not always be used. Ecuador and Panama adopt the U.S. dollar as their official currencies; wine consumption and winemaking spread rapidly in Turkey, a country whose religion forbids alcoholic drink; the English lament that joining the European Union and the forces of globalization have made them more like other peoples; commercial loggers deforest Rendova Island in Malaysia and in the process destroy the culture and lifestyle of the native Haporai people; and so on—endlessly, it seems.

Resist, Resist!

Perhaps not surprisingly, many people see globalization, corporate power, habitat damage, and cultural homogenization as inherently evil. The increased democracy that accompanies globalization makes protest against these evils easier. No single seat of power and no single country or person can control the process. As a result, diverse groups can resist the new global economic order that seeks to decide what people produce, what they will be paid for their labor, how they will live, and when they will die. Protestors advocate resistance—both peaceful and, if need be, violent. The previously mentioned paper sessions at the 2001 meeting of the Association of American Geographers included six devoted to "globalism and activism." Ecoterrorists such as those working in the Earth Liberation Front (ELF) undertake a campaign of violent harassment of diverse corporations involved in resource exploitation and other environmentally destructive practices, such as the manufacture of sports utility vehicles (SUVs) and the building of houses in zones of suburban sprawl; cyberterrorist hackers attempt to sabotage the interlocked computer-based information and decision-making system that underlies globalization; street demonstrators (Figure 12.2) turn the 1999 Seattle meeting of the World Trade Organization—one of the mainsprings of the new free market—into riot and disorder (having, ironically, used the Internet and E-mail to spread advance information about the uprising); American Indian tribes in Québec halt dam and hydroelectric power development on their lands, using publicity gimmicks and the Canadian legal system; a well-financed Muslim terrorist organization roams the world attacking embassies, ships, airplanes, the World Trade Center, and other symbols of Western culture; and some entire countries—"rogue states" such as Libya, Iraq, North Korea, and Myanmar—stand fast against globalism.

Not infrequently, those who overtly oppose globalization acquire the status of protectors and defenders. The computer hacker, say geographers Paul Adams and Barney Warf, has become "a kind of subcultural hero."

Above all, globalization requires order and peace to advance. If enough resistance and protest is marshaled, the whole structure could come tumbling down. There are a

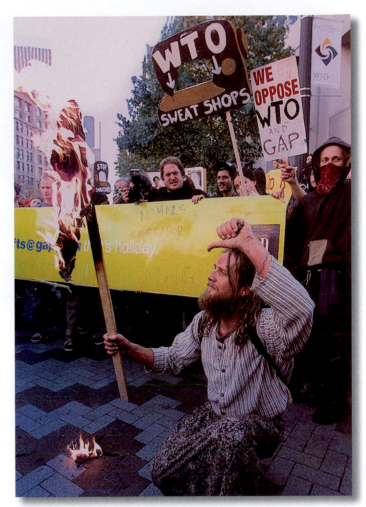

Figure 12.2

Burning a pair of Gap pants, part of a protest against the World Trade Organization (WTO) meeting in Seattle in 1999. (Itsu Inouye/Associated Press.)

lot of angry people out there, especially among the young and in the Islamic world. Indeed, as Harold James suggests, we may be approaching "the end of globalization."

Many Worlds

But from the perspective of geography, do the big corporations and the new systems of production, communication, marketing, and transportation really possess the power to produce one world? Does globalization truly have the ability to render cultural differences irrelevant? Cannot peoples take what they want from the new age and reject the rest, as the Amish do (Figure 12.3 on the next page)? Indeed, does globalization act to homogenize the world or, instead, to widen the differences between haves and have-nots? In fact, much of the resistance to globalization is based in the belief that it enriches and

Figure 12.3
An Amish horse-drawn buggy, Ohio.
Globalization seems irrelevant to the Amish and many other peoples who cling to traditional ways of life. (JIM STEINBERG/PHOTO RESEARCHERS, INC.)

empowers the few at the expense of the many, heightening class differences.

Many—perhaps most—geographers believe in a future that will continue to contain many worlds. They speak of profound and irreducible cultural contrasts and of the capacity of native peoples to "indigenize" Western popular culture. Globalization, they feel, produces different results in different lands. The global need not and cannot abolish the regional or the local. A yin and yang of opposed forces operate simultaneously, maintaining many worlds.

So who is right? Will it be one world or many? Maybe we can gain some insight by going back to the five themes of cultural geography: region, diffusion, ecology, interaction, and landscape. What do these themes tell us about the age of globalization?

 ## Culture Regions

Are culture regions weakening and fading? Do the diverse hues of the human mosaic as revealed in maps gleam less brightly than before? Has the Internet "made geography obsolete?" asks *The Economist*, a leading British news magazine, in its August 2001 special report "Geography and the Internet." Can we detect any such trends, using the theme of culture region? Some geographers look at the maps and do indeed see fading colors. Dave Nemeth, for example, suggests that regions are "being crushed and recycled into a bland, ambiguous amalgam," producing "something akin to a vast parking lot of global scale." And without question, people in all parts of the world must seek a new form of self-identity, torn as they are between their traditional attachment to place and local culture on the

one hand and their inevitable attraction to globalization-driven cosmopolitanism on the other. They feel the opposite tugs of hearth (region) and cosmos (world).

Core Versus Periphery

Most cultural geographers viewing the new age, by contrast, detect an ongoing vitality and vividness of culture regions. In particular, our old friend *core-versus-periphery* seems hale and hearty. Globalization, it seems, is not a geographically even process. Some regions—forming the core—are moving ahead and prospering, while many others—the peripheries—fall further and further behind. Global interdependence decidedly does not level out advantages and disadvantages. Increasingly, a First World core consisting of Anglo-America, the European Union, the coastal lands of East Asia, and Australia–New Zealand moves ahead of the remaining Third World peripheral lands. (If there ever was a Second World, it is today missing in action!)

Little pieces of the Third World periphery that lie adjacent to the core, such as Tunisia and Mexico, scramble to join the privileged part of the world, to be "fast" rather than "slow." Most peripheral countries function to some extent within the new world economic system, but their role at best is to provide raw materials and migrants. They lack power and prosperity. From such marginal regions can come resistance and struggle against globalization.

British geographer Rob Shields, in his book *Places on the Margin*, concentrates on an array of places and regions, at different geographical scales, that have been "left behind in the modern race for progress." He finds peripheries even within the core. Often these places and

Figure 12.4
Gamblers try their luck at the Oneida Casino in Green Bay, Wisconsin. Like many American casinos, it is owned and operated by American Indians on tribal lands. (Mike Roemer/Associated Press.)

regions become sites of illicit or stigmatized activities (Figure 12.4). Says Shields, such "margins become signifiers of everything centers deny or repress." Legalized prostitution in the state of Nevada and gambling casinos in Atlantic City, New Jersey, provide examples. Shields examined in detail the south-coast English resort town of Brighton, which has long had a reputation as a place on the margin where those proper Londoners who are so inclined can spend a "dirty weekend." He also focuses on the Canadian North—the arctic and subarctic regions of that country where native folk cultures survive at least in vestige and the North American popular culture intrudes more weakly. Southern Canadians mythologized the North as "a counter-balance to the civilized world" of the urbanized South and the seat of the "real" Canada.

One Europe or Many?

Viewing just one small part of the world, geographer Ray Hudson echoes our question: "One Europe or many?" He opts decidedly for "many," concluding that power and wealth will not be evenly distributed geographically within Europe and that one main role of the European Union should be to promote "complex geographies of identities." A similar outlook leads geographer Michael Keating to speak of a "new regionalism" in Europe, and David Hooson goes so far as to suggest that globalization actually *strengthens* people's bond between place and identity. This strengthening is suggested by the rise of ethnic separatism in countries as diverse as Spain, the United Kingdom, and Serbia & Montenegro. Increasingly, membership in the European Union connotes prosperity, whereas exclusion is equated with economic deprivation.

Glocalization

The theme of culture region, then, seems to be telling us that a new human mosaic is forming in the age of globalization. Change is pervasive, but its direction differs from one land to another. The future will not be like the past, but it will also not be monochromatic.

As geographer Jessie Poon says, "Opposed forces are operating simultaneously," producing new constellations of places and regions. These forces pit local against global, and the important thing is that the outcome seems to differ from one region to another. And, best of all, the results appear to be unpredictable—the new age will be invulnerable to the excesses of social-science theory.

The interaction between global and local prompted geographer Erik Swyngedouw to promote the term **glocalization** to describe the result (see Focus On: Glocalization Comes to Nunavut on the next page). In brief, he argues that the outcome of this interaction involves change both in the regional way of life *and* in the globalizing force. Put differently, glocalization is a process that ensures the survival of culture regions and places in the new age. The culture region theme leads us to conclude, then, that a planetary culture is almost certainly illusory and that potent forces are at work to prevent homogenization.

The Internet, Cyberspace, and Geography

Has the Internet rendered geography or culture regions obsolete? The Net is widely perceived "as being everywhere, yet nowhere in particular," says *The Economist* in its special report on the subject. It can cross borders,

FOCUS ON

Glocalization Comes To Nunavut

Zacharias Kunuk, 44, is an Inuit living at the village of Igloolik, well north of the Arctic Circle in Canada's Nunavut Territory (see Chapter 5). He knows and practices many of the traditional folkways. Kunuk prefers to live in the tundra, among his people. He believes in shamans and their powers.

But Kunuk also makes movies. His film, *Atanarjuat* (The Fast Runner), uses Inuit actors speaking only Inuktitut and tells a traditional folktale. It is also about identity and cultural survival. The film won several prizes, including one at the Cannes Film Festival in France, and in 2002 it was being shown in Europe, Canada, Australia, and the United States.

Kunuk daily uses E-mail and the Internet and makes long-distance telephone calls. He has access to a bank automatic teller machine. But he is just as likely to go out on his snowmobile and hunt seals. Kunuk finds no difficulty in "picking and choosing from distinct cultures as if they were platters on a buffet." This interaction between global and local culture epitomizes glocalization and demonstrates that globalization is a figment of the economic determinist's imagination.

Source: Kraus, 2002

---

both political and cultural; it breaks down barriers; it destroys distance.

The reality is far more complex and leaves culture regions intact. In truth, the Internet is much "constrained by the realities of geography." It can now be screened, censored, regulated, and blocked by governments, and *geolocation* technology allows a web site the same power. The fiber optic cables of the Internet have a location, and in fact the whole enterprise remains largely city-bound. A high-speed digital subscriber line requires proximity to a telephone exchange. The special report concludes that "the tyranny of geography" has not been ended by the Internet and cyberspace.

Moreover, the very computer systems that drive and power globalization have produced culture regions of their own, perhaps even entirely new kinds of places. One recent issue of the *Geographical Review*, edited by Paul Adams and Barney Warf, was devoted to "cyberspace and geographical space."

Many of the words and phrases we use to describe the Internet imply that it possesses a geography: *cyberspace, the virtual community, Net surfing, cyberhood, cyberbia,* and even *virtual geography,* to mention a few. The Internet connects not just two points but *all* points, creating a new sort of place in the process.

But, in fact, "is there a *there* in cyberspace?" John Barlow asks. Does the Internet contain a geography at all? Certainly, *places*—at least as understood by cultural geographers—cannot be created on the Internet. What is missing, geographically, in cyberspace? For starters, these "virtual places" lack a cultural landscape and a cultural ecology. In the broader context, on a worldwide scale, human diversity

is poorly portrayed in cyberspace. "Old people, poor people, the illiterate, and the continent of Africa" seem not to be "there," as Barlow notes (Figure 12.5 on pages 430–431). Users usually end up "meeting" others pretty much like themselves on the Internet. More important, the breath and spirit of place cannot exist in cyberspace. Barlow, resorting to a Hindu term, calls this missing essence *prana*. These are not real places, nor can they ever be.

 ## Cultural Diffusion

Is the theme of cultural diffusion relevant to the debate over "one world or many"? Almost certainly. After all, the computer and the Internet greatly facilitate access to and diffusion of data and speed its spread. At the same time, the spread of new ideas and innovations often produces disruptions that change the world in unpredicted, unintended ways. The globalization process is vulnerable to such disruptions and could be destroyed by them. At the very least, the theme of cultural diffusion cautions us against trying to predict the future.

The Information Superhighway

Terms such as *information superhighway* and *infobahn* imply the enhanced ability to achieve cultural diffusion. Moreover, the use of more efficient transportation systems, such as containerized cargo units, have greatly increased "the spatial dispersion of the production and consumption of economic goods," in the words of geographer Chris Airriess.

As geographer John O'Loughlin notes, the spread of democracy has accompanied the more rapid diffusion of information, goods, and services in the age of globalization. Dictatorships thrive by controlling and manipulating information—an increasingly difficult task when the infobahn is operating. And the Internet is certainly not the only means by which information spreads rapidly in our new age. Cellular telephones, satellite-beamed cable television, and news channels such as CNN all contribute to the diffusion of information, as does the increased volume of international travelers.

Diffusion of the Internet

The theme of cultural diffusion applies to the spread of the Internet itself. If the new age is to bring the universal diffusion of cultural elements, then surely this new homogenizing tendency ought to be revealed in the spread of this most essential element of globalization (Figure 12.6 on pages 432–433). The diffusion has now reached virtually the entire world, obeying the models set down in Chapter 1.

But although the Internet now reaches into almost every land, its use varies profoundly (compare Figures 12.5 and 12.6). Just because an innovation is available does not mean it will be accepted by most or even many people. Globalization, it seems, is more about the *possibility* of diffusion than about actual acceptance of the innovations diffused. In much of the world, use of the Internet remains arrested at a very early phase of *hierarchical diffusion,* and we should not necessarily expect it to diffuse much further. Barriers of wealth, education, and governmental opposition prove formidable.

So, "build it and they will not necessarily come" seems to be the verdict on cultural diffusion in the age of globalization. Increased linkages to other cultures do not necessarily disrupt regional cultures and institutions. Overwhelmingly, the Internet remains confined to North America and Europe, even after three decades of diffusion. It may be correct, in the words of Frances Cairncross, to refer to "the death of distance" caused by the revolution in communications, but it clearly does not follow that everything will diffuse everywhere. Indeed, as geographers Anne Gilbert and Paul Villeneuve ask, will diffusion in the age of globalization instead "amplify disparities between regions"?

 ## Cultural Ecology

How is the theme of cultural ecology related to the question of one world or many? The central issue is the impact of the globalization process upon the habitat.

Sustainability

Ecological limits will almost certainly bring globalization to a halt. The Westernized popular culture at the very root of globalization consumes enormous amounts of natural resources and produces prodigious quantities of pollutants. Americans alone consume one-fourth of the world's petroleum output and generate one-fourth of the carbon dioxide that is the main cause of global warming. Put simply, there is no conceivable way that the entire world population could be elevated to the American and European standard of living without destroying the planet (Figure 12.7 on page 434). Global culture is an ecological impossibility. The Western way of life is not environmentally sustainable, even if it never spreads beyond its present core region. Virtually every time trade and the environment come into conflict, the environment loses, and the World Trade Organization—dominated by global corporations—intimidates governments from passing environmentally beneficial legislation.

Think Globally

At the same time, the increased interconnectedness brought by the globalization process has led to a rising awareness that the world's environment constitutes a single ecosystem, that everything is tied together ecologically in basic ways. The last three or four decades, during which globalization advanced, coincided with this growing awareness that all of the Earth's ecological problems are interconnected.

Global environmental issues first came into focus in 1972, with the Stockholm Conference. This conference was followed in 1980 by the World Strategy for Conservation and in 1984 by the World Commission on the Environment and Development, which was concerned with "our common future." The 1990s witnessed a series of grand international conferences on the habitat. And we should not forget that James Lovelock's proposal of the *Gaia hypothesis*—the notion that the Earth is a single, self-regulating system—also occurred in the era of globalization. All of this led Luc Ferry to speak of a "new ecological order."

Act Locally

Still, the Gaia hypothesis remains merely an idea and the many international conferences on habitat damage usually lead to very little progress of any sort. Most such meetings involve politicians sitting and talking and accomplishing next to nothing.

Those activists who truly wish to save the planet place little faith in the politicians. They have moved independently to propose solutions, most of which the

Internet Connections

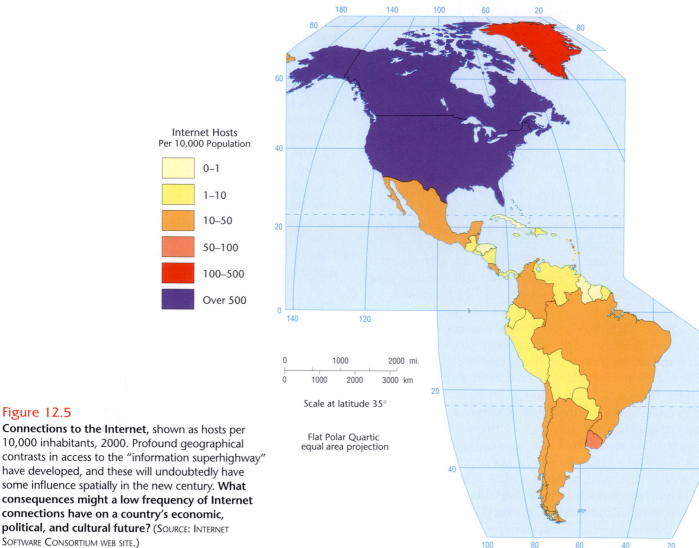

Internet Hosts
Per 10,000 Population

	0–1
	1–10
	10–50
	50–100
	100–500
	Over 500

Scale at latitude 35°

Flat Polar Quartic
equal area projection

Figure 12.5

Connections to the Internet, shown as hosts per 10,000 inhabitants, 2000. Profound geographical contrasts in access to the "information superhighway" have developed, and these will undoubtedly have some influence spatially in the new century. **What consequences might a low frequency of Internet connections have on a country's economic, political, and cultural future?** (SOURCE: INTERNET SOFTWARE CONSORTIUM WEB SITE.)

politicians oppose. One such proposal is *deep ecology,* a plan to exclude all human presence from sizable tracts of land, allowing nature to heal. Not even brief visits would be permitted. Meanwhile, *radical ecologists* seeking environmental justice struggle against multinational corporations that ravage the habitat, and defend native peoples who find their traditional adaptive strategies endangered.

In sum, the theme of cultural ecology leads us to reject a one-world future. Its message echoes what we have learned from culture region and cultural diffusion.

 ## Cultural Interaction

Can we learn something about the one-world-or-many debate from the theme of cultural interaction? If not, then we have been lying to you in the preceding 11 chapters.

Culture, Culture, Culture!

Perhaps the most relevant advice to be derived from the cultural interaction theme is that we should reject *eco-*

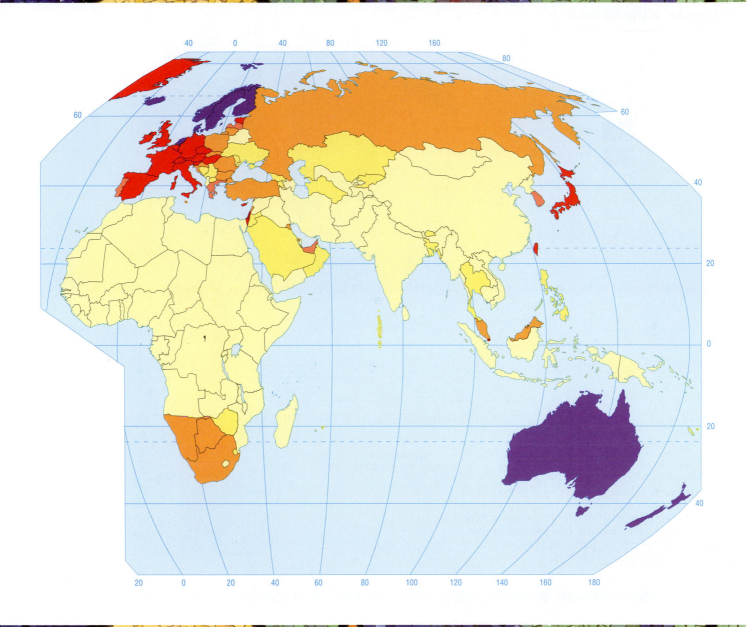

nomic determinism (see Chapter 1)—the notion that economic forces shape all aspects of the human condition. Frankly, economists believe that everything obeys the dictates of economics. They even think they can predict the future of the world using economic data, whereas in truth they have a rather poor record predicting merely the *financial* aspects of what is to come.

If you have learned anything in *The Human Mosaic,* it should be that the Earth and its peoples are far too complex to be understood in terms of a doctrine as simplistic and naive as economic determinism. We quoted geogra-

pher Anne Buttimer in Chapter 1. She declared that people were more than "materially motivated robots." Culture matters. Cultural differences do not evaporate in the presence of a pair of Nike tennis shoes or a cup of Starbucks coffee. Economic determinists who proclaim a one-world future never even consider culture. They should. They should know, for example, that some religions forbid the consumption of Starbucks or any other kind of coffee.

There is an unfortunate side to the importance of culture that can be summed up in the word *xenophobia:* the

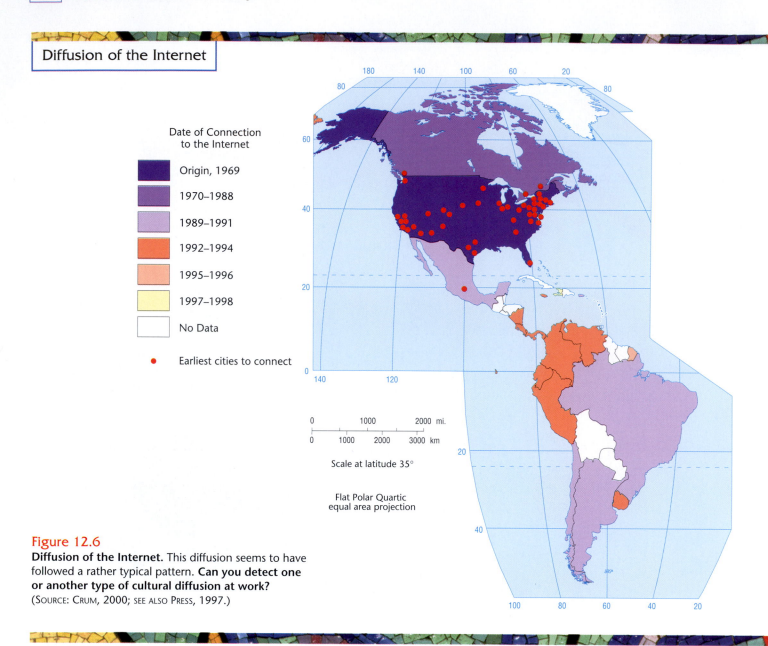

Diffusion of the Internet

Date of Connection to the Internet

- Origin, 1969
- 1970–1988
- 1989–1991
- 1992–1994
- 1995–1996
- 1997–1998
- No Data

● Earliest cities to connect

0   1000   2000 mi.

0   1000   2000   3000 km

Scale at latitude 35°

Flat Polar Quartic
equal area projection

Figure 12.6

Diffusion of the Internet. This diffusion seems to have followed a rather typical pattern. **Can you detect one or another type of cultural diffusion at work?** (SOURCE: CRUM, 2000; SEE ALSO PRESS, 1997.)

fear and rejection of anything foreign. The most sinister companions of xenophobia are nationalism, racism, bigotry, war, ethnic cleansing, and genocide (Figure 12.8 on page 434). These all work against globalization and will probably be a part of your future, just as they have shared our past. But there are also more benign reflections of xenophobia. One of these has been dubbed neolocalism.

Neolocalism

Neolocalism is the desire evident in many local communities to reembrace the uniqueness and authenticity of *place*. Governments and electorates at all levels—from local to national—have a far bigger say about globalization than you might imagine. A backlash against chain stores and conformity can find strength in local ordinances. A community can actually prevent McDonald's or Wal-Mart from establishing outlets. Neolocalism pits the cultural power of place against the economic power of globalization, and do not put all your money on the triumph of the latter.

Gimme a Beer, Please

Geographer Wes Flack applied the concept of neolocalism to one of the world's favorite beverages, beer. As

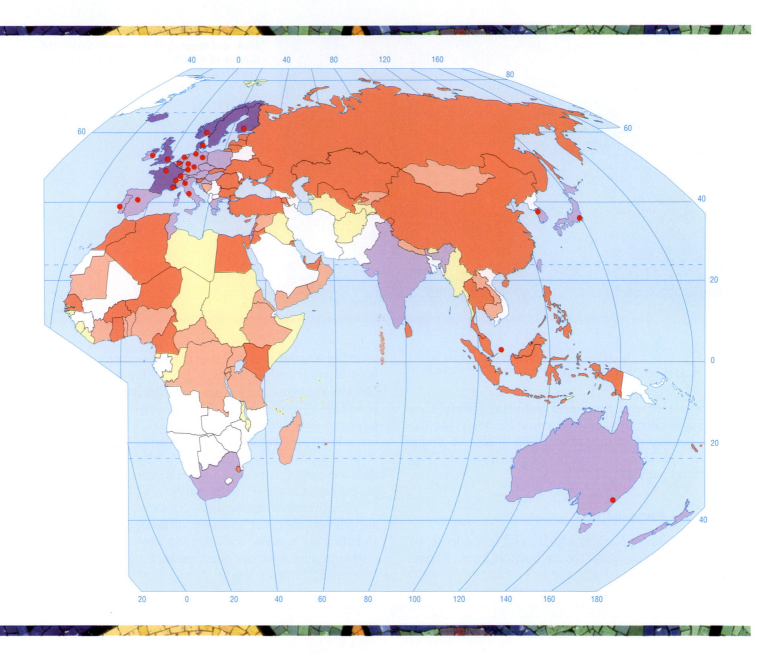

background, you need to know that around 1980, some misguided economist predicted that by the end of the twentieth century only two or three beer brewing companies would be left in the United States. The winners would be those that best played the globalization game, enhancing their production, distribution, and advertising functions.

No sooner had that prediction been made than the *microbrewery* phenomenon arose. The big brewers found, suddenly, that many consumers preferred to drink beer from local, small-scale breweries, often housed in old converted stores on Main Street. Within a decade, microbreweries proliferated mightily, spreading from an early base in Northern California and the Pacific Coast states (Figure 12.9 on page 435). The big companies fought back, marketing hundreds of fake brands with quaint, local-sounding names, but the ploy did not work. Microbreweries continued to sprout like mushrooms after a rain, and neolocal consumers were not fooled. Chalk one up for place. People refuse to surrender their sense of belonging to place and region. They refuse to be docile conformists. Both neolocalism and glocalization appear at every hand, at home and abroad. Cultural interaction has ruled that globalization (or even nationalization) of culture is not going to happen.

Figure 12.7
Clear-cut logging in the Queen Charlotte Islands of British Columbia, Canada. This practice is ecologically harmful, prompting both erosion and a decrease in biodiversity. (DEWITT JONES/CORBIS.)

 ## Cultural Landscape

Is the contest between one world and many visible? Can we get some clue about the outcome by observing the cultural landscape of the new age? Of course! Philip Kelly even speaks of "landscapes of globalization" (Figure 12.10 on page 436).

Globalized Landscapes

Geographer David Keeling sought visible evidence of globalization in the landscape of Buenos Aires, Argen-

tina—the capital of a country that desperately wants to become enmeshed in the world economy but struggles, perhaps in vain, against a peripheral location. He found abundant evidence of "a homogenized landscape" of glass-and-steel corporate office towers, of luxury hotels and conference centers for the economic power brokers, of megamalls and supermarkets. Global capitalism further announced its presence in neon signs projecting corporate brand names into the southern night.

Clearly, urban landscapes—cityscapes—can serve as an index to the level and type of engagement with the globalization process. Still, Keeling notes, the process is neither omnipresent nor omnipotent. Certain other Latin

Figure 12.8
Refugees in a camp in Congo (Kinshasa), who fled ethnic cleansing and genocide in Rwanda. (WESLEY BOCXE/PHOTO RESEARCHERS, INC.)

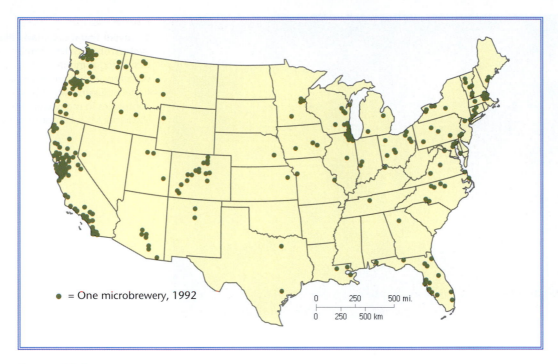

Figure 12.9

Distribution of microbreweries in the contiguous United States, 1992. This remarkable distribution was attained in just one decade, revealing the potent nature of neolocalism. **Why might the innovation have begun on the West Coast?** (SOURCES: FLACK, 1997: 48; AND BREWER'S DIGEST BUYERS' GUIDE AND DIRECTORY, 1992.)

American capitals, such as Quito, La Paz, and Havana, reveal minimal global influences in their cityscapes. Given the improbability of a global culture, these visible differences among cities seem likely to persist.

Striving for the Unique

Urban landscapes in the age of globalization reveal another element: the enduring spirit of place. One city after another has preserved or erected some building or monument so unique as to be a symbol or icon of that particular city. When you see a photograph of this structure, you know at once where it is (Figure 12.11 on the next page). Television journalists often stand in front of such visible icons to convince viewers that they are actually reporting on site. Examples would include the opera house in Sydney, Australia; the arch linking east and west in St. Louis; the Space Needle in Seattle; and the Eiffel Tower in Paris. True, many or most of these icons predate the era of globalization, but that is not the issue. Rather, their retention and protection offers the relevant message. The Kremlin walls in Moscow may retain few if any of

their original red bricks, as they fall victim to weathering and are replaced, but the structure is renewed and endures as the city's symbol.

Indeed, modern urban architecture is perhaps best defined by the creativity and uniqueness allowed to the architects. Once again—in this case visibly—the power of place thrives in the age of globalization. Uniqueness prevails over conformity.

Depart the cities and enter the rural countryside, and you will find far less visible evidence of globalization, even in the most highly developed countries. Rural cultural landscapes remain vividly different, and we should not expect that to change. Our eyes should tell us that global culture is illusory, a mirage seen only by those deluded by economic determinism.

Conclusion

One by one, the five themes of cultural geography have rendered their verdict. Many worlds will prevail. Placelessness will not be achieved. Cultural homogenization is

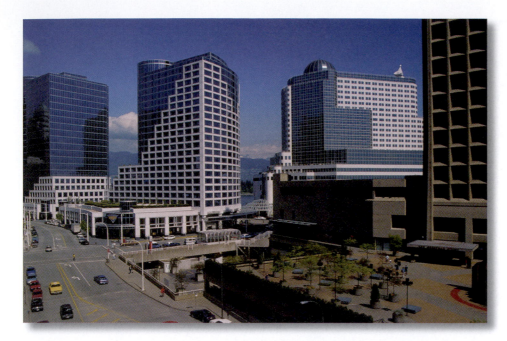

Figure 12.10
Granville Square, Canada Place, and the Waterfront Centre Hotel, a luxury complex designed for international business conferences, in Vancouver, British Columbia, Canada. Globalization has produced such complexes in many cities and countries. (© Gunter Marx Photography/Corbis.)

impossible. The future, geographically, will resemble the past in diverse, fundamentally important ways.

And so, our journey is over. We are, to borrow and paraphrase the words of Aldous Huxley, "poorer by exploded convictions" and "perished certainties" but richer by what we have seen on our vicarious world travels. Perhaps we, like Huxley, set out on the journey knowing how people should best "live, be governed, and believe." When one travels, as we have—even if just through the pages of a geography book—such convictions often get mislaid, as easily as eyeglasses. Unlike glasses, though, certainties are not easily replaced. The main message of *The Human Mosaic* is that you should inhabit the new millennium without needing certainties, without professing to have the answers, without telling other people how to live. They won't listen to you, in any case. Culture matters. And that is why cultural geography will endure.

Figure 12.11
The opera house at Sydney, Australia, has become a symbol for the city. Its unique design helps establish Sydney's identity as a city different from others. Uniqueness of design, a feature of much modern architecture, stands in opposition to cultural homogenization. (Courtesy of Terry G. Jordan-Bychkov.)

SEEING GEOGRAPHY

An Office Scene in the Age of Globalization

Globalization depends upon the constant use of the computer to provide data as well as to organize, project, innovate, plan, and coordinate the communications and information systems that allow the new international capitalist system to function. The photograph could be from almost anywhere in Europe, North America, or other lands that have so far benefited from and helped direct the globalization process.

What else is revealed? The workers are young rather than middle-aged, belonging to the same generation that so often protests in the streets when international meetings devoted to globalization assemble. Females and racial minorities are included, perhaps at a level never before achieved under capitalism, though we must understand that these workers are not the suit-wearing bosses.

A global cultural landscape—or one facet of it—is revealed. But what innovations and diffusions were required to produce this scene? What impact on the habitat might be wrought by such excessive use of electricity? What cultural interactions underlie the entire enterprise?

Are all regions of the United States equally involved in the undertaking, or do core-periphery contrasts exist? Again, a photograph can evoke all five themes of cultural geography.

How might a comparable "inner landscape" have differed 30 or 40 years ago?

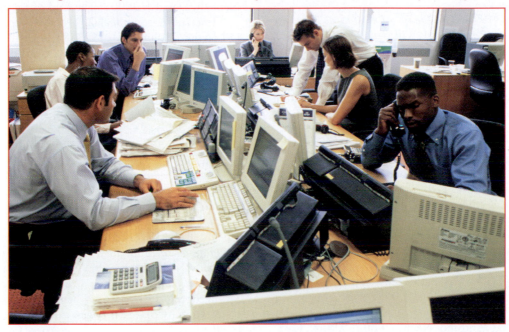

A typical office in the age of globalization.

 ## Globalization on the Internet

An Atlas of Cyberspaces, Martin Dodge
http://www.cybergeography.org/atlas/atlas.html

Cyberspaces made visible: graphic representations of the geography of the electronic territories of the Internet, the World Wide Web, and other new cyberspaces help you to visualize and comprehend the digital "landscapes" beyond your computer screen in the age of popular culture.

Guthrie Foundation
http://www.guthriecenter.org

The foundation seeks to protect indigenous cultures from globalization and to promote understanding among different religions.

Internet Software Consortium
http://www.isc.org/ds/new-survey.html

Offers the Internet Domain Survey, an index to use of the Internet by country.

AlphaWorld Maps
http://www.activeworlds.com/community/maps.asp
Two fascinating, time-lapse maps of a virtual space.

Sources

Adams, Paul C., and Warf, Barney (eds). 1997. "Cyberspace and Geographical Space." Special issue of *Geographical Review* 87: 139–307.

Airriess, Christopher A. 2001. "Regional Production, Information-Communication Technology, and the Developmental State: The Rise of Singapore as a Global Container Hub." *Geoforum* 32: 235–254.

Barber, Benjamin. 1995. *Jihad vs. McWorld: How Globalism and Tribalism are Reshaping the World.* New York: Ballantine.

Barlow, John P. 1995. "Cyberhood versus Neighborhood." Special issue of *Utne Reader* 68(3): 52–64.

Brewer's Digest Buyers' Guide and Directory. 1992. Chicago: Siebel Publishing Co.

Cairncross, Frances. 1997. *The Death of Distance: How the Communications Revolution Will Change Our Lives.* Cambridge, Mass.: Harvard Business School Press.

Crum, Shannon L. 2000. "The Spatial Diffusion of the Internet." Ph.D. diss., University of Texas at Austin.

Drummond, Ian, and Terry Marsden. 1999. *The Condition of Stability: Global Environment Change.* New York: Routledge.

Ferry, Luc. 1995. *The New Ecological Order.* Carol Volk (trans.). Chicago: University of Chicago Press.

Flack, Wes. 1997. "American Microbreweries and Neolocalism." *Journal of Cultural Geography* 16(2): 37–53.

"Geography and the Internet." 2001. Special report. *The Economist* (August 11): 18–20.

Gilbert, Anne, and Paul Villeneuve. 1999. "Social Space, Regional Development, and the Infobahn." *Canadian Geographer* 43: 114–117.

Greider, William. 1997. *One World, Ready or Not: The Manic Logic of Global Capitalism.* New York: Touchstone Books.

Hardt, Michael, and Antonio Negri. 2000. *Empire.* Cambridge, Mass.: Harvard University Press.

Homer-Dixon, Thomas, and Jessica Blitt (eds). 1998. *Ecoviolence: Links among Environment, Population, and Security.* Lanham, Md.: Rowman & Littlefield.

Hooson, David (ed.). 1994. *Geography and National Identity.* Oxford: Blackwell.

Hudson, Ray. 2000. "One Europe or Many? Reflections on Becoming European." *Transactions of the Institute of British Geographers* 25: 409–426.

Huxley, Aldous. 1926. *Jesting Pilate: An Intellectual Holiday.* New York: George H. Doran.

Iyer, Pico. 2000. *The Global Soul: Jet Lag, Shopping Malls, and the Search for Home.* New York: Alfred A. Knopf.

James, Harold. 2001. *The End of Globalization.* Cambridge, Mass.: Harvard University Press.

Keating, Michael. 1998. *The New Regionalism in Western Europe.* Northampton, Mass.: Edward Elgar.

Keeling, David J. 1999. "Neoliberal Reform and Landscape Change in Buenos Aires." *Yearbook, Conference of Latin Americanist Geographers* 25: 15–32.

Kelly, Philip F. 2000. *Landscapes of Globalization.* London: Routledge.

Kimble, George H. T. 1951. "The Inadequacy of the Regional Concept," in L. Dudley Stamp and Sidney W. Wooldridge (eds.), *London Essays in Geography: Rodwell Jones Memorial Volume.* Cambridge, Mass.: Harvard University Press, 151–174.

Kraus, Clifford. 2002. "Returning Tundra's Rhythm to the Inuit, in Film." *New York Times* (March 30): A4.

Kunstler, James H. 1993. *The Geography of Nowhere: The Rise and Decline of America's Man-Made Landscape.* New York: Simon & Schuster.

Lovelock, James E. 1979. *Gaia: A New Look at Life on Earth.* New York: Oxford University Press.

McDowell, Linda (ed.). 1997. *Undoing Place? A Geographical Reader.* London: Arnold.

Nemeth, David J. 2000. "The End of the Re(li)gion?" *North American Geographer* 2: 1–8.

O'Loughlin, John, et al. 1998. "The Diffusion of Democracy, 1946–1994." *Annals of the Association of American Geographers* 88: 545–574.

Poon, Jessie P. H., Edmund R. Thompson, and Philip F. Kelly. 2000. "Myth of the Triad? The Geography of Trade and Investment Blocs." *Transactions of the Institute of British Geographers* 25: 427–444.

Press, Larry. 1997. "Tracking the Global Diffusion of the Internet." *Communications of the Association of Computing Machinery* 40 (11): 11–17.

Relph, Edward. 1976. *Place and Placelessness.* London: Pion.

Sessions, George (ed.). 1995. *Deep Ecology for the 21st Century.* Boulder, Colo.: Shambala Press.

Shields, Rob. 1991. *Places on the Margin: Alternative Geographies of Modernity.* London: Routledge.

Swerdlow, Joel L. (ed.). 1999. "Global Culture." Special issue of *National Geographic* 196(2): 2–132.

Swyngedouw, Erik. 1997. "Neither Global nor Local," in Kevin R. Cox (ed.), *Spaces of Globalization: Reasserting the Power of the Local.* New York: Guilford, 137–166.

Wood, William B. 2001. "Geographic Aspects of Genocide: A Comparison of Bosnia and Rwanda." *Transactions of the Institute of British Geographers* 26: 57–75.

Zimmerman, Michael. 1994. *Contesting Earth's Future: Radical Ecology and Postmodernity.* Berkeley: University of California Press.

Ten Recommended Books on Globalization

(*For additional suggested readings, see* The Human Mosaic *web site:* www.whfreeman.com/jordan)

Bird, Jon, Barry Curtis, Tim Putnam, and George Robertson. 1993. *Mapping the Futures: Local Cultures, Global*

Change. London: Routledge. Will help you understand the diverse ways in which cultural groups are reacting to political, economic, and technological change.

Crang, Mike, Phil Crang, and Jon May (eds.). *Virtual Geographies: Bodies, Space and Relations*. London: Routledge. Explores how new communications technologies produce new types of space and even new geographies.

Goudie, Andrew S., et al. (eds.). 2001. *Encyclopedia of Global Change*. 2 vols. New York: Oxford University Press. A standard reference on the ecological changes accompanying globalization, written mainly by geographers.

Harrison, Lawrence E., and Samuel P. Huntington (eds.). 2000. *Culture Matters: How Values Shape Human Progress*. New York: Basic Books. A vigorous rejection of economic determinism, and much needed, though the authors come too close to cultural determinism in their explanation of why globalization will not lead to a homogenized world.

Johnston, Ron J., Peter J. Taylor, and Michael J. Watts (eds.). 1995. *Geographies of Global Change: Remapping the World*. London: Blackwell. Considers such issues as the collapse of socialism, global environmental change, international migration, the rise of nationalistic violence, the power of electronic media, and the changing character of capitalism.

Jussila, Heikki, Roser Majoral, and Fernanda Delgado-Cravidao. 2001. *Globalization and Marginality in Geographical Space*. Aldershot, U.K.: Ashgate. Case studies from Europe, the Americas, Africa, and Australia illustrate how geographical research aids our understanding of the way in which the policies and politics of globalization affect the more marginalized areas of the world.

Kotkin, Joel. 2000. *The New Geography: How the Digital Revolution Is Reshaping the American Landscape*. New York: Random House. Argues that computer and telecommunication technology has freed people and businesses to locate wherever they wish, thereby weakening venerable core-periphery patterns but strengthening place distinctiveness.

Norwine, Jim, and Jonathan M. Smith (eds). 2000. *Worldview Flux: Perplexed Values Among Postmodern Peoples*. Lanham, Md.: Lexington Books. An irreverent, occasionally funny look at how groups as diverse as Cajuns, South African whites, and Pacific Coast Indians are coping with the new age of globalization and the need to restructure their self-identities and place attachments.

Schaeffer, Robert K. 1997. *Understanding Globalization: The Social Consequences of Political, Economic, and Environmental Change*. Lanham, Md.: Rowman & Littlefield. Studies the complicated interplay of factors as diverse as agribusiness, climate change, the illegal drug trade, and economic fluctuations.

Skelton, Tracey, and Tim Allen (eds.). 1999. *Culture and Global Change*. London: Routledge. No fewer than 27 authors consider the interaction of culture and globalization, rejecting in the process both cultural and economic determinism.

GLOSSARY

absorbing barrier A barrier that completely halts diffusion of innovations and blocks the spread of cultural elements. (Chapter 1)

acculturation The adoption by an ethnic group of enough of the ways of the host society to be able to function economically and socially. (Chapter 5)

acid rain Rainfall with much higher acidity than normal, caused by sulfur and nitrogen oxides derived from the burning of fossil fuels being flushed from the atmosphere by precipitation, with lethal effects for many plants and animals. (Chapter 9)

adaptive strategy The unique way in which each culture uses its particular physical environment; those aspects of culture that serve to provide the necessities of life: food, clothing, shelter, and defense. (Chapter 1 and throughout)

agglomeration A snowballing geographical process by which secondary through quinary industrial activities become clustered in cities and compact industrial regions in order to share infrastructure and markets. (Chapters 9, 10, 11)

agribusiness Highly mechanized, large-scale farming usually under corporate ownership. (Chapter 8)

agricultural landscape The cultural landscape of agricultural areas. (Chapter 8)

agricultural surplus The amount of food grown by a society that exceeds the demands of its population. (Chapter 10)

agriculture The cultivation of domesticated crops and the raising of domesticated animals. (Chapter 8)

agro-region A culture region based on characteristics of agriculture, within which a given type of agriculture occurs. (Chapter 8)

America letter A letter written by early immigrants to friends and relatives in their former homes, describing the immigrants' new land in glowing terms and thereby inducing others to follow them. (Chapter 5)

animism The belief that inanimate objects, such as trees, rocks, and rivers, possess souls. (Chapter 3)

apartheid In South Africa, a policy of racial segregation and discrimination against non-European groups. (Chapter 11)

assimilation The complete blending of an ethnic group into the host society, resulting in the loss of all distinctive ethnic traits. (Chapter 5)

axis mundi The symbolic center of cosmomagical cities, often demarcated by a large, vertical structure. (Chapter 10)

barriadas Illegal housing settlements, usually made up of temporary shelters, that surround large cities; often referred to as squatter settlements. (Chapter 10)

bilingualism The ability to speak two languages fluently. (Chapter 4)

birthrate The annual number of births per thousand population. (Chapter 7)

buffer state An independent but small and weak country lying between two powerful countries. (Chapter 6)

cadastral pattern The shapes formed by property borders; the pattern of land ownership. (Chapter 8)

census tracts Small districts used by the U.S. Census Bureau to survey the population. (Chapter 11)

central business district (CBD) The central portion of a city characterized by high-density land uses. (Chapter 11)

centralizing forces Diffusion forces that encourage people or businesses to locate in the central city. (Chapter 11)

central place A town or city engaged primarily in the service stages of production; a regional center. (Chapter 10)

central-place theory A set of models designed to explain the spatial distribution of urban service centers. (Chapter 10)

centrifugal force Any factor that disrupts the internal order of a country. (Chapter 6)

centripetal force Any factor that supports the internal unity of a country. (Chapter 6)

chain migration The tendency of people to migrate along channels, over a period of time, from specific source areas to specific destinations. (Chapter 5)

checkerboard development A mixture of farmlands and housing tracts. (Chapter 11)

cityscape An urban landscape. (Chapter 11)

cleavage model A political-geographical model suggesting that persistent regional patterns in voting behavior, sometimes leading to separatism, can usually be explained in terms of tensions pitting urban against rural, core against periphery, capitalists against workers, and power group against minority culture. (Chapter 6)

colonial city A city founded by colonialism, or an indigenous city whose structure was deeply influenced by Western colonialism. (Chapter 10)

concentric zone model A social model that depicts a city as five areas bounded by concentric rings. (Chapter 11)

contact conversion The spread of religious beliefs by personal contact. (Chapter 3)

contagious diffusion A type of expansion diffusion in which cultural innovation spreads by person-to-person contact, moving wavelike through an area and population without regard to social status. (Chapter 1)

convergence hypothesis A hypothesis holding that cultural differences among places are being reduced by improved transportation and communications systems, leading to a homogenization of popular culture. (Chapter 2)

core area The territorial nucleus from which a country grows in area and over time, often containing the national capital and the main center of commerce, culture, and industry. (Chapter 6)

core-periphery A concept based on the tendency of both formal and functional culture regions to consist of a core or node, in which defining traits are purest or functions are headquartered, and a periphery that is tributary and displays fewer of the defining traits. (Chapters 1 and others)

cosmomagical city A type of city that is laid out in accordance with religious principles, characteristic of very early cities, particularly in China. (Chapter 10)

cottage industry A traditional type of manufacturing in the pre–industrial revolution era, practiced on a small scale in individual rural households as a part-time occupation and designed to produce handmade goods for local consumption. (Chapter 9)

cultural adaptation The concept, central to cultural ecology, that culture is the uniquely human method of meeting physical environmental challenges—that culture is an adaptive system. (Chapters 1 and others)

cultural determinism The viewpoint that the immediate causes of all cultural phenomena are other cultural phenomena. (Chapter 1)

cultural diffusion The spread of elements of culture from the point of origin over an area. (Chapter 1)

cultural ecology Broadly defined, the study of the relationships between the physical environment and culture; narrowly (and more commonly) defined, the study of culture as an adaptive system that facilitates human adaptation to nature and environmental change. (Chapter 1)

cultural geography The description and explanation of spatial patterns and ecological relationships in human culture. (Chapter 1)

cultural integration The relationship of various elements within a culture. (Chapter 1)

cultural landscape The artificial landscape; the visible human imprint on the land. (Chapter 1)

cultural simplification The process by which immigrant ethnic groups lose certain aspects of their traditional culture in the process of settling overseas, creating a new culture that is less complex than the old. (Chapter 5)

culture A total way of life held in common by a group of people, including such learned features as speech, ideology, behavior, livelihood, technology, and government; or the local, customary way of doing things—a way of life; an ever-changing process in which a group is actively engaged; a dynamic mix of symbols, beliefs, speech, and practices. (Chapter 1)

culture region   An area occupied by people who have something in common culturally; or a spatial unit that functions politically, socially, or economically as a distinct entity. (Chapter 1)

cyberspace   The figurative space of the online world. (Chapter 11)

death rate   The annual number of deaths per 1000 persons in the population. (Chapter 7)

decentralization   The tendency of people or businesses and industry to locate outside the central city. (Chapters 10, 11)

defensive site   A location where a city can be easily defended. (Chapter 10)

deindustrialization   The decline of primary and secondary industry, accompanied by a rise of the service sectors of the industrial economy. (Chapters 9, 11)

demographic region   A culture region based on characteristics of demography. (Chapter 7)

demographic transformation   A change in population growth that occurs when a nation moves from a rural, agricultural society with high birth and death rates to an urban, industrial society in which death rates decline first and birthrates decline later. (Chapter 7)

demography   The statistical study of population size, composition, distribution, and change. (Chapter 7)

desertification   A process whereby human actions unintentionally turn productive lands into deserts through agricultural and pastoral misuse, destroying vegetation and soil to the point where they cannot regenerate. (Chapter 8)

dialect   A distinctive local or regional variant of a language that remains mutually intelligible to speakers of other dialects of that language; a subtype of a language. (Chapter 4)

domesticated animal   An animal kept for some utilitarian purpose whose breeding is controlled by humans and whose survival is dependent on humans; domesticated

animals differ genetically and behaviorally from wild animals. (Chapter 8)

domesticated plant   A plant deliberately planted and tended by humans that is genetically distinct from its wild ancestors as a result of selective breeding. (Chapter 8)

double-cropping   Harvesting twice a year from the same parcel of land. (Chapter 8)

dust dome   A pollution layer over a city that is thickest at the center of the city. (Chapter 11)

ecofeminism   A new doctrine proposing that women are inherently better environmental preservationists than men, because the traditional roles of women involved creating and nurturing life, whereas the traditional roles of men too often necessitated death and destruction. (Chapter 1)

ecology   The study of the two-way relationship between an organism and its physical environment. (Chapter 1)

economic determinism   The social-scientific belief that human behavior, including spatial or geographical attributes, is largely or wholly dictated by economic factors and motivations. (Chapter 1)

ecoregion   A natural region, as opposed to a culture region; based upon the multiple defining traits of terrain, climate, flora, fauna, soils, and water; the area covered by a particular ecosystem. (Chapter 1)

ecosystem   The functional ecological system in which biological and cultural *Homo sapiens* lives and interacts with the physical environment. (Chapter 1)

ecoterrorism   The violent sabotage by activists of ecologically destructive practices pursued by governments or corporations. (Chapter 12)

ecotheology   The study of the influence of religious belief upon habitat modification. (Chapter 3)

ecotone   The border between ecoregions; for example, between forests and grasslands or plains and mountains. (Chapter 5)

ecotourism   Responsible travel that does not harm ecosystems or the well-being of local people. (Chapter 9)

edge city A new urban cluster of economic activity that surrounds our nineteenth-century downtowns. (Chapter 10)

emerging city A city of a currently developing or emerging country. (Chapter 10)

enclave A piece of territory surrounded by, but not part of, a country. (Chapter 6)

environmental determinism The belief that cultures are directly or indirectly shaped by the physical environment. (Chapter 1)

environmental perception The belief that culture depends more on what people perceive the environment to be than on the actual character of the environment; perception, in turn, is colored by the teachings of culture. (Chapter 1)

ethnic cleansing The removal by force of an ethnic minority from a region, usually by eviction and migration, sometimes by genocide. (Chapter 6)

ethnic culture region An area occupied by people of similar ethnic background, who share traits of ethnicity, such as language and migration history. (Chapter 11)

ethnic geography The study of the spatial and ecological aspects of ethnicity. (Chapter 5)

ethnic group A group of people who share a common ancestry and cultural tradition and who live as a minority in a larger society. (Chapter 5)

ethnic homeland A sizable area inhabited by an ethnic minority that exhibits a strong sense of attachment to the region and often exercises some measure of political and social control over it. (Chapter 5)

ethnic island A small ethnic area in the rural countryside; sometimes called a "folk island." (Chapter 5)

ethnic neighborhood A voluntary community where people of like origin reside by choice. (Chapter 5)

ethnic religion A religion identified with a particular ethnic or tribal group; does not seek converts. (Chapter 3)

ethnic substrate Regional cultural distinctiveness that remains following the assimilation of an ethnic homeland. (Chapter 5)

ethnogenesis The process by which ethnic groups, and in fact *all* cultural groups, originate, a process influenced in many cases by both the physical habitat and contacts with other peoples. (Chapter 5)

ethnographic boundary A political boundary that follows some cultural border, such as a linguistic or religious border. (Chapter 6)

exclave A piece of national territory separated from the main body of a country by the territory of another country. (Chapter 6)

expansion diffusion The spread of innovations within an area in a snowballing process, so that the total number of knowers becomes greater and the area of occurrence grows. (Chapter 1)

extended metropolitan region (EMR) A new type of urban region, complex in both landscape form and function, created by the rapid spatial expansion of cities in the developing world. (Chapter 10)

farmstead The center of farm operations, containing the house, barn, sheds, and livestock pens. (Chapter 7)

farm village A clustered rural settlement of moderate size, inhabited by people who are engaged in farming. (Chapter 7)

federal state An independent country that gives considerable powers and even autonomy to its constituent parts. (Chapter 6)

feedlot A factorylike farm devoted to either livestock fattening or dairying; all feed is imported and no crops are grown on the farm. (Chapter 8)

festival setting A multiuse redevelopment project that is built around a particular setting, often one with a historical association. (Chapter 11)

folk Traditional, rural; the opposite of popular. (Chapter 2)

folk architecture Structures built by members of a folk society or culture in a traditional manner and style, without the assistance of professional architects or blueprints, using locally available raw materials. (Chapter 2)

folk culture A small, cohesive, stable, isolated, nearly self-sufficient group that is homogeneous in custom and race; characterized by a strong family or clan structure, order maintained through sanctions based in the religion or family, little division of labor other than between the sexes, frequent and strong interpersonal relationships, and a material culture consisting mainly of handmade goods. (Chapter 2)

folk fortress A stronghold area with natural defensive qualities, useful in the defense of a country against invaders. (Chapter 6)

folk geography The study of the spatial patterns and ecology of traditional groups; a branch of cultural geography. (Chapter 2)

folklife All aspects of folk culture, including both material and nonmaterial (folkloric) elements. (Chapter 2)

folklore Nonmaterial folk culture; the teaching and wisdom of a folk group; the traditional tales, sayings, beliefs, and superstitions that are transmitted orally. (Chapter 2)

formal culture region A region inhabited by people who have one or more cultural traits in common. (Chapter 1)

functional culture region An area that functions as a unit politically, socially, or economically. (Chapter 1)

functional zonation The pattern of land uses within a city; the existence of areas with differing functions, such as residential, commercial, and governmental. (Chapter 10)

Gaia hypothesis The theory that there is one interacting planetary ecosystem, Gaia, that includes all living things and the land, waters, and atmosphere in which they live; further, that Gaia functions almost as a living organism, acting to control deviations in climate and to correct chemical imbalances, so as to preserve Earth as a living planet. (Chapter 1)

generic toponym The descriptive part of many place-names, often repeated throughout a culture area. (Chapter 4)

gentrification The displacement of lower-income residents by higher-income residents as buildings in deteriorated areas of city centers are restored. (Chapter 11)

geodemography Population geography; the study of the spatial and ecological aspects of population, including distribution, density per unit of land area, fertility, gender, health, age, mortality, and migration. (Chapter 7)

geography The study of spatial patterns and of differences and similarities from one place to another in environment and culture. (Chapter 1)

geolinguistics The cultural geographical study of languages and dialects. (Chapter 4)

geomancy A traditional East Asian form of environmental perception, also called feng shui, by which particular configurations of terrain, compass directions, soil textures, and watercourse patterns become more auspicious than others, influencing the siting of houses, villages, cities, temples, and graves. (Chapters 1, 3)

geometric boundary A political border drawn in a regular, geometric manner, often a straight line, without regard for environmental or cultural patterns. (Chapter 6)

geopolitics The influence of the habitat on political entities. (Chapter 6)

gerrymandering The drawing of electoral district boundaries in an awkward pattern to enhance the voting impact of one constituency at the expense of another. (Chapter 6)

ghetto A segregated ethnic area within a city forced on the residents by discrimination; an involuntary community. (Chapter 5)

global city A city that is a control center of the global economy. (Chapter 10)

globalizing city A city experiencing significant economic and social changes related to the global economy. (Chapter 10)

global corporation A giant company that operates in more than one country, dispersing its factories, headquarters, marketing, and service functions across international boundaries; also called a multinational or transnational corporation. (Chapter 9)

globalization The binding together of all the lands and peoples of the world into an integrated system driven by capitalistic free markets, in which cultural diffusion is rapid, independent states are weakened, and cultural homogenization is encouraged. (Chapters 1 and 12 especially, but throughout)

global warming The pronounced climatic warming of the Earth that has occurred since about 1920 and particularly since the 1970s. (Chapter 9)

glocalization The process by which global forces of change interact with local cultures, altering both in the process. (Chapter 12)

greenhouse effect A process in which the increased release of carbon dioxide and other gases into the atmosphere, caused by industrial activity and deforestation, permits solar short-wave heat radiation to reach the Earth's surface but blocks long-wave outgoing radiation, causing a thermal imbalance and global heating. (Chapter 9)

green revolution The recent introduction of high-yield hybrid crops and chemical fertilizers and pesticides into traditional Asian agricultural systems, most notably paddy rice farming, with attendant increases in production and ecological damage. (Chapter 8)

Greens Activists and organizations, including political parties, whose central concern is addressing environmental deterioration. (Chapter 9)

guild industry A traditional type of manufacturing in the pre–industrial revolution era, involving handmade goods of high quality manufactured by highly skilled artisans who resided in towns and cities. (Chapter 9)

hamlet A small rural settlement, smaller than a village. (Chapter 8)

heartland The interior of a sizable landmass, removed from maritime connections; in particular, the interior of the Eurasian continent. (Chapter 6)

heartland theory A 1904 proposal by Mackinder that the key to world conquest lay in control of the interior of Eurasia. (Chapter 6)

heat island An area of warmer temperatures at the center of a city, caused by the urban concentration of heat-retaining concrete, brick, and asphalt. (Chapter 11)

hierarchical diffusion A type of expansion diffusion in which innovations spread from one important person to another or from one urban center to another, temporarily bypassing other persons or rural areas. (Chapter 1)

high-tech corridor An area along a limited-access highway that houses offices and other services associated with high-tech industries. (Chapters 9, 11)

hinterland The area surrounding a city and influenced by it. (Chapter 10)

homelessness A temporary or permanent condition of not having a legal home address. (Chapter 11)

host culture The dominant, majority cultural group within a country or society, which usually occupies a dominant social-economic position. (Chapter 2)

humanistic geography A subfield of geography that stresses the subjectivity and individuality of humans as essential to analysis of spatial variations, deals with the uniqueness of each region and place, and rejects the notion that geography is a social science. (Chapter 1)

hunting and gathering The killing of wild game and the harvesting of wild plants to provide food in traditional cultures. (Chapter 8)

hydraulic civilization A civilization based on large-scale irrigation. (Chapter 10)

imperialism The extension of political control by one country over foreign nations often through military means. (Chapter 10)

independent invention A cultural innovation that is developed in two or more locations by individuals or groups working independently. (Chapter 1)

indigenous city A city formed by local forces. (Chapter 10)

industrial inertia The tendency of industries to remain in their initial locations, even after the forces that originally attracted them there have disappeared. (Chapter 9)

industrial revolution A series of inventions and innovations, arising in England in the 1700s, that led to the use of machines and inanimate power in the manufacturing process. (Chapter 9)

infant mortality rate The number of infants per 1000 live births that die before reaching one year of age. (Chapter 7)

in-filling New building on empty parcels of land within a checkerboard pattern of development. (Chapter 11)

intensive agriculture The expenditure of much labor and capital on a piece of land to increase its productivity. In contrast, *extensive agriculture* involves less labor and capital. (Chapter 8)

intertillage The raising of different crops mixed together in the same field, particularly common in shifting cultivation. (Chapter 8)

isogloss The border of usage of an individual word or pronunciation. (Chapter 4)

labor-intensive industry An industry for which labor costs represent a large proportion of total production costs. (Chapter 9)

laissez-faire utilitarianism The belief that economic competition without government interference produces the most public good. (Chapter 10)

language A tongue that is not mutually intelligible to the speakers of other tongues. (Chapter 4)

language family A group of related languages derived from a common ancestor. (Chapter 4)

lateral commuting Traveling from one suburb to another in going from home to work. (Chapter 11)

legible city A city that is easy to decipher, with clear pathways, edges, nodes, districts, and landmarks. (Chapter 11)

lingua franca An existing, well-established language of communication and commerce used widely where it is not a mother tongue. (Chapter 4)

linguistic refuge area An area protected by isolation or inhospitable environmental conditions in which a language or dialect has survived. (Chapter 4)

livestock fattening A commercial type of agriculture that produces fattened cattle and hogs for meat. (Chapter 8)

maladaptation Poor or inadequate adaptation that occurs when a group pursues an adaptive strategy that, in the short run, fails to provide the necessities of life or, in the long run, destroys the environment that nourishes it. (Chapter 5)

marchland A strip of territory, traditionally one day's march for infantry, that served as a boundary zone for independent countries in premodern times. (Chapter 6)

market The geographical area in which a product may be sold in a volume and at a price profitable to the manufacturer. (Chapter 9)

market gardening Farming devoted to specialized fruit, vegetable, or vine crops for sale rather than consumption. (Chapter 8)

master-planned communities Large-scale residential developments that include, in addition to architecturally compatible housing units, planned recreational facilities, schools, and security measures. (Chapter 11)

material culture All physical, tangible objects made and used by members of a cultural group, such as clothing, buildings, tools and utensils, instruments, furniture, and artwork; the visible aspect of culture. (Chapter 2)

mechanistic view of nature The view that humans are separate from nature and hold dominion over it and that the habitat is an integrated mechanism governed by external forces that the human mind can understand and manipulate. (Chapter 3)

megalopolis A large urban region formed as several urban areas spread and merge, such as Boswash, the region including Boston, New York, and Washington, D.C. (Chapter 10)

model An abstraction, an imaginary situation, proposed by geographers to simulate laboratory conditions so that they may isolate certain causal forces for detailed study. (Chapter 1)

monoculture The raising of only one crop on a huge tract of land in agribusiness. (Chapter 8)

monotheism The worship of only one god. (Chapter 3)

multiple nuclei model A model that depicts a city growing from several separate focal points. (Chapter 11)

multiplier leakage The process by which industrial profits flow back to major industrial districts from factories established in outlying provinces or countries. (Chapter 9)

nation-state An independent country dominated by a relatively homogeneous culture group. (Chapter 6)

natural boundary A political border that follows some feature of the natural environment, such as a river or mountain ridge. (Chapter 6)

natural hazard An inherent danger present in a given habitat, such as flooding, hurricane, volcanic eruption, or earthquake; often perceived differently by different peoples. (Chapter 1)

neighborhood A small social area within a city where residents share values and concerns and interact with one another on a daily basis. (Chapter 11)

neighborhood effect The rapid acceptance of an innovation in a small area or cluster around an initial adopter. (Chapter 1)

neolocalism The desire to reembrace the uniqueness and authenticity of place, in response to globalization. (Chapter 12)

node A central point in a functional culture region where functions are coordinated and directed. (Chapter 1)

nomadic livestock herder A member of a group that continually moves with its livestock in search of forage for its animals. (Chapter 8)

nonmaterial culture The wide range of tales, songs, lore, beliefs, superstitions, and customs that passes from generation to generation as part of an oral or written tradition. (Chapter 2)

nonrenewable resource A resource that must be depleted to be used, such as petroleum. (Chapter 9)

office park A cluster of office buildings usually located along an interstate, often forming the nucleus of an edge city. (Chapter 11)

organic view of nature The view that humans are part of, not separate from, nature and that the habitat possesses a soul and is filled with nature spirits. (Chapter 3)

paddy rice farming The cultivation of rice on a paddy, or small flooded field enclosed by mud dikes, practiced in the humid areas of the Far East. (Chapter 8)

palimpsest A term used to describe cultural landscapes with various layers and historical "messages." Geogra-

phers use this term to reinforce the notion of the landscape as a text that can be read; a landscape palimpsest has elements of both modern and past periods. (Chapter 11)

particulate pollutants Bits of matter spewed into the air by urban activity, such as incinerators, car exhausts, tire wear, and industrial combustion. (Chapters 9, 11)

peasant A farmer belonging to a folk culture and practicing a traditional system of agriculture. (Chapter 8)

permeable barrier A barrier that permits some aspects of an innovation to diffuse through but weakens and retards continued spread; an innovation can be modified in passing through a permeable barrier. (Chapter 1)

personal space The amount of space that individuals feel "belongs" to them as they move about their everyday business. (Chapter 7)

physical environment All aspects of the natural physical surroundings, such as climate, terrain, soils, vegetation, and wildlife. (Chapter 1)

pidgin A composite language consisting of a small vocabulary borrowed from the linguistic groups involved in international commerce. (Chapter 4)

pilgrimage A journey to a place of religious importance. (Chapter 3)

place A term used to connote the subjective, idiographic, humanistic, culturally oriented type of geography that seeks to understand the unique character of individual regions and places, rejecting the principles of science as flawed and unknowingly biased. (Chapter 1)

placelessness A spatial standardization that diminishes regional variety; may result from the spread of popular culture, which can diminish or destroy the uniqueness of place through cultural standardization on a national or even worldwide scale. (Chapters 2, 12)

plantation A large landholding devoted to specialized production of a tropical cash crop. (Chapter 8)

political geography The study of the spatial and ecological aspects of political behavior, from nationalism and the independent country to voting patterns, sectionalism, and regional separatism. Sometimes called *geopolitics*. (Chapter 6)

polyglot A mixture of different languages. (Chapter 4)

polytheism The worship of many gods. (Chapter 3)

popular culture A dynamic culture based in large, heterogeneous societies permitting considerable individualism, innovation, and change; having a money-based economy, division of labor into professions, secular institutions of control, and weak interpersonal ties; producing and consuming machine-made goods. (Chapter 2)

population density The number of people in an area of land, usually expressed as people per square mile or people per square kilometer. (Chapter 7)

population explosion The rapid, accelerating increase in world population since about 1650 and especially since 1900. (Chapter 7)

population geography Geodemography; the study of the spatial and ecological aspects of population, including distribution, density per unit of land area, fertility, gender, health, age, mortality, and migration. (Chapter 7)

population pyramid A graph used to show the age and sex composition of a population. (Chapter 7)

possibilism A school of thought based on the belief that humans, rather than the physical environment, are the primary active force; that any environment offers a number of different possible ways for a culture to develop; and that the choices among these possibilities are guided by cultural heritage. (Chapter 1)

postindustrial phase The way of life produced by dominance of the tertiary, quaternary, and quinary sectors of economic activity. (Chapter 9)

postmodernism In geography, the ideology that rejects theory, science, and the search for universal principles; denies the attainability of absolute truth, definitions, and classifications; challenges all academic authority; and tolerates conflicting or contradictory ideas. (Chapter 1)

preadaptation A complex of adaptive traits and skills possessed in advance of migration by a group, giving them survival ability and competitive advantage in occupying the new environment. (Chapters 5, 7)

primary industry An industry engaged in the extraction of natural resources, such as agriculture, lumbering, and mining. (Chapter 9)

primate city A city of large size and dominant power within a country. (Chapter 10)

proselytic religion A religion that actively seeks converts and has the goal of converting all humankind. (Chapter 3)

push-and-pull factors Unfavorable, repelling conditions and favorable, attractive conditions that interact to affect migration and other elements of diffusion. (Chapter 7)

quaternary industry The producer-oriented service sector of industry; includes business services such as trade, insurance, banking, advertising, research, retailing, and wholesaling. (Chapter 9)

quinary industry The consumer-oriented service sector of industry; includes services such as health, education, government, tourism, and recreational facilities. (Chapter 9)

raison d'être In French, literally "reason for being"; the main unifying force within a country, the principal basis of nationalism. (Chapter 6)

ranching The commercial raising of herd livestock on a large landholding. (Chapter 8)

range In central-place theory, the average maximum distance people will travel to purchase a good or service. (Chapter 10)

redlining A practice by banks and mortgage companies of demarcating areas considered to be high risk for housing loans. (Chapter 11)

refuge area A region in which the physical habitat has provided natural protection for a minority cultural group. (Chapter 4)

region A grouping of like places or the functional union of places to form a spatial unit; see also *culture region*. (Chapter 1)

relic boundary A former political border that no longer functions as a boundary. (Chapter 6)

religion A social system involving a set of beliefs and practices through which people seek harmony with the universe and attempt to influence the forces of nature, life, and death. (Chapter 3)

relocation diffusion The spread of an innovation or other element of culture that occurs with the bodily relocation (migration) of an individual or group that has the idea. (Chapter 1)

renewable resource A resource that is not depleted if wisely used, such as forests, water, fishing grounds, and agricultural land. (Chapter 9)

restrictive covenant A statement written into a property deed that restricts the use of the land in some way; often used to prohibit certain groups of people from buying property. (Chapter 11)

return migration A type of ethnic diffusion that involves the voluntary movement of a group of migrants back to its ancestral or native country or homeland. (Chapter 5)

rimland The maritime fringe of a country or continent; in particular, the western, southern, and eastern edges of the Eurasian continent. (Chapter 6)

sacred space An area recognized by a religious group as worthy of devotion, loyalty, esteem, or fear, to the extent that it becomes sought out, avoided, inaccessible to the nonbeliever, and/or removed from economic use. (Chapter 3)

satellite state A small, weak country dominated by one powerful neighbor to the extent that some or much of its independence is lost. (Chapter 6)

secondary industry An industry engaged in processing raw materials into finished products; manufacturing. (Chapter 9)

sector model An economic model that depicts a city as a series of pie-shaped wedges. (Chapter 11)

sedentary cultivation Farming in fixed and permanent fields. (Chapter 8)

sex ratio The numerical ratio of males to females in a population. (Chapter 7)

shatter belt A zone of great cultural complexity containing many small cultural groups. (Chapter 4)

shifting cultivation A type of agriculture characterized by land rotation, in which temporary clearings are used for several years and then abandoned to be replaced by new clearings; also known as slash-and-burn agriculture. (Chapter 8)

site The local setting of a city. (Chapter 10)

situation The regional setting of a city. (Chapter 10)

social culture region An area in a city where many of the residents share social traits such as income, education, and stage of life. (Chapter 11)

social science The branch of learning that seeks to apply the scientific method to the study of humankind, seeking universal principles, theories, and laws of behavior, often through the use of mathematics. (Chapter 1)

space A term used to connote the objective, quantitative, theoretical, model-based, economics-oriented type of geography that seeks to understand spatial systems and networks through application of the principles of social science. (Chapter 1)

spatial distribution The arrangement of a particular landscape feature or features throughout a unit of space. (Chapter 10)

squatter settlement An illegal housing settlement, usually made up of temporary shelters, that surrounds a large city. (Chapter 10)

state church A church designated by the government as the official, legal faith in a country, usually receiving financial support from the government. (Chapter 3)

stimulus diffusion A type of expansion diffusion in which a specific trait fails to spread but the underlying idea or concept is accepted. (Chapter 1)

subsistence agriculture Farming to supply the minimum food and materials necessary to survive. (Chapter 8)

suitcase farm In American commercial grain agriculture, a farm on which no one lives; planting and harvesting is done by hired migratory crews. (Chapter 8)

supranational organization A group of independent countries joined together for purposes of mutual interest. (Chapter 6)

survey pattern A pattern of original land survey in an area. (Chapter 8)

sustainability The survival of a land-use system for centuries or millennia without destruction of the environmental base, allowing generation after generation to continue to live there. (Chapters 8, 9, and others)

technopole A center of high-tech manufacturing and information-based quaternary industry. (Chapter 9)

teleology A philosophy proposing that the Earth was created specifically as the abode for humans, that the Earth belongs to humans by divine intention. (Chapter 3)

terraforming The massive, large-scale restructuring of terrain caused by industrial activity. (Chapter 9)

territoriality The tendency of humans, perhaps instinctual, to seek control of portions of the Earth's surface. (Chapter 6)

tertiary industry A service sector of industry that includes transportation, communications, and utilities. (Chapters 9, 10)

theocracy A government guided by a religion. (Chapter 3)

threshold In central-place theory, the size of the population required to make provision of services economically feasible. (Chapter 10)

time-distance decay The decrease in acceptance of a cultural innovation with increasing time and distance from its origin. (Chapter 1)

topical geography The division of geographical subject matter into topics, such as agricultural geography, rather than into regions. (Chapter 1)

topocide The deliberate killing of a place through industrial expansion and change, so that its earlier landscape and character are destroyed. (Chapter 9)

toponym A place-name, usually consisting of two parts, the generic and the specific. (Chapter 4)

total fertility rate (TFR) The number of children the average woman will bear during her lifetime. A TFR of less than 2.1, if maintained, will cause a natural decline of population. (Chapter 7)

trade-route site A place for a city that is at a significant point on transportation routes. (Chapter 10)

uneven development The tendency for industry to develop in a core-periphery pattern, enriching the industrialized countries of the core and impoverishing the less industrialized periphery. This term is also used to describe urban patterns in which suburban areas are enriched while the inner city is impoverished. (Chapters 9, 11, 12)

unitary state An independent state that concentrates power in the central government and grants little authority to the provinces. (Chapter 6)

urban agriculture The raising of food, including fruit, vegetables, meat, and milk, inside cities, especially common in the Third World. (Chapter 8)

urban hearth area One of the five regions—Mesopotamia, the Nile Valley, Pakistan's Indus Valley, China's Yellow River area, and Mesoamerica—where the world's first cities evolved. (Chapter 10)

urbanized population The proportion of a country's population living in cities. (Chapter 10)

urban morphology The form and structure of cities, including street patterns and the size and shape of buildings. (Chapter 10)

vernacular culture region A region perceived to exist by its inhabitants; based in the collective spatial perception of the population at large; bearing a generally accepted name or nickname (such as "Dixie"). (Chapters 1, 2)

world city One of the largest cities in the world, generally with a population of over 10 million. (Chapter 10)

zero population growth A stabilized population created when an average of only two children per couple survive to adulthood, so that, eventually, the number of deaths equals the number of births. (Chapter 7)

INDEX

The Major Linguistic Culture Regions

Indo-European Family

- Slavic
- Germanic
- R Romance
- Iranic
- Indic
- Other Indo-European

Afro-Asiatic Family

- Semitic
- Hamitic
- Altaic family
- Niger-Congo family
- Austronesian family
- Uralic family
- Sino-Tibetan family
- Austro-Asiatic family
- Japanese and Korean
- Other families

I = Inuktitut
A = Amerindian (several language families)
C = Caucasic
N-S = Nilo-Saharan
K = Khoisan

Ps = Paleosiberian
D = Dravidian
P = Papuan
Ab = Aborigine

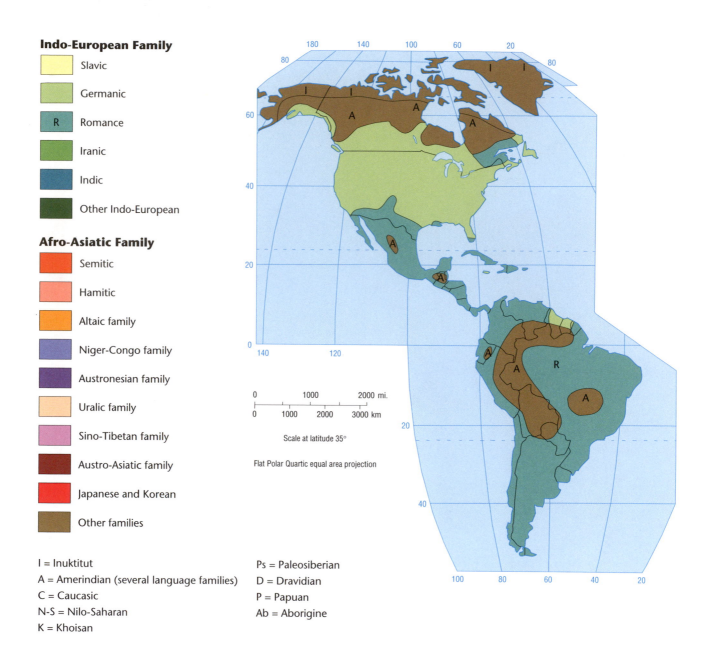

0   1000   2000 mi.

0   1000   2000   3000 km

Scale at latitude 35°

Flat Polar Quartic equal area projection